RHETORIC, RELIGION, AND THE CIVIL RIGHTS MOVEMENT, 1954–1965

Volume 2

Davis W. Houck
David E. Dixon

Editors

BAYLOR UNIVERSITY PRESS

Studies in Rhetoric and Religion 15

Editorial Board

To Ingrid Houck, author and archivist of the most important "book,"
and
Lawrence Guyot (1939–2012), who fulfilled his president's call for
A More Perfect Union and whose memory burns bright in the students he
educated

In memoriam, Arthur F. Holmes, Guillermo O'Donnell,
and Georgean Nygaard Brink

Cover design by Andrew Brozyna, AJB Design, Inc.
Cover photograph by Warren K. Leffler, August 28, 1963, courtesy of the
          Library of Congress

The ISBN for volume 2 (paperback) is 978-1-60258-965-0. Volume 2 is the 15th title in Baylor University Press' Studies in Rhetoric & Religion series.

The Library of Congress has catalogued volume 1 as follows:

Rhetoric, religion, and the civil rights movement, 1954–1965 / Davis W. Houck, David E. Dixon, editors.
     p. cm. ~ (Studies in rhetoric and religion ; 1)
   Includes index.
   ISBN-13: 978-1-932792-54-6 (pbk. : alk. paper)
   1. African Americans—Civil rights—History—20th century—Sources. 2. Civil rights movements—United States—History—20th century—Sources. 3. United States—Race relations—History—20th century—Sources. 4. Civil rights—Religious aspects—Christianity—History—20th century—Sources. 5. Race relations—Religious aspects—Christianity—History—20th century—Sources. 6. Rhetoric—Political aspects—United States—History—20th century—Sources. 7. Speeches, addresses, etc., American. 8. Sermons, American. I. Houck, Davis W. II. Dixon, David E.

   E185.61.R48 2006
   323.1196'073~dc22
                              2006021173

Printed in the United States of America on acid-free paper with a minimum of 30% post-consumer waste recycled content.

CONTENTS

1963

1964

1965

Acknowledgments

We have incurred a number of debts in taking on a project of this magnitude, and while we doubt that we can ever fully repay them, we do want to acknowledge the help of so many students, colleagues, archivists, and activists. For their work transcribing speeches and working on headnotes we thank our students: Pablo Correa, Britten Finlen, Briana Frazier, Jen Funt, Alexis Garber, Emily Gervais, Logan Henderson, Jonathan Henry, Emily King, James Lawrence, Erin Lockett, Tracee Mason, Justin Maynard, Lucy Morton-Hicks, Derik Mosrie, Ray Murat, Krystin Olinski, Megan Oliver, Lindsay Opsahl-McKinney, Kristi Powers, Allison Shuffield, Shari Smith, Jenna Stolfi, Laura Stoltzfus, and Sarah Timberlake. Special thanks is due to Nic Arete, Marc Periou, and Maureen Minielli for their yeoman's work in searching the archives at Wake Forest University, the University of Minnesota, and the New York Public Library. Gerald Ensley of the *Tallahassee Democrat* was very helpful in helping track down information on C. A. Roberts Jr. and his time at First Baptist Church in Tallahassee, Florida. Maggie Hambrick generously shared a copy of a William Sloane Coffin speech that appears in this volume. And Chevene King, with whom Mary Sterner Lawson graciously put us in touch, helped acquire an important family consent at a late hour.

Without the generous help of so many archivists from around the country, this project would still be just an idea. In a time of pared budgets and shrinking personnel their timely assistance to two strangers is greatly appreciated. Thanks to Mattie Abraham, Benjamin Alexander, Burt Altman, Elizabeth Chase, Elizabeth Clemons, Joellen El Bashir, Jennifer Ford, Jason

Fowler, Ed Frank, Shawna Gandy, Taffey Hall, John Hanley, Sara Harwell, Dorothy Hazelrigg, Sally Jacobs, Andrew Donald Johnston, Nancy Kaiser, Margaret Kimball, William LeFevre, Steve Lucht, Debra McIntosh, Bob McInnes, Maggie McNeely, Leigh McWhite, Eileen Meyer Sklar, Charles Nolan, Amanda Paige, Eileen Parris, Gwen Patton, Jordan Patty, Susan Pevar, Elaine Philpott, Leila Potts-Campbell, Clyde Putman, Edie Riehm, Sarah Roberts, Kathy Shoemaker, Jane Stoeffler, Ruth Tonkiss Cameron, Annie Tummino, Eric White, Anne Woodrum, and Gary Zola. Thanks also to Bridwell Library at the Perkins School of Theology, Southern Methodist University, for extending a residential fellowship to advance this project. The Edwin G. Kaiser Fellowship at Saint Joseph's College, as well, allowed the editors rare face-to-face collaborations.

We also had the good fortune to work with a number of civil rights movement veterans, whose activism has gone undimmed five decades on. We thank John Chatfield, Joseph Ellin, Ralph Engelman, Lawrence Guyot, Margaret Kibbee, Reverend Edwin King, and Charles McLaurin. We especially want to thank Queen's College alumnus and movement veteran Mark Levy for his painstaking research on an Andrew Goodman query. As always, our projects allow us brief moments to collaborate with establishment mass media professionals. Thanks to Joseph Lelyveld, David Lelyveld, and Sam Sifton for their support.

In selecting "only" fifty speeches for this project, many deserving addresses simply could not be included. Even so, two people in particular were exceedingly gracious with their time and memories though their speeches are not included. Joby Stafford Robinson's father, Reverend Jack Stafford, was run out of the First Baptist Church of Batesburg, South Carolina, in 1956 for daring to support the Supreme Court's 1954 *Brown* decision. He never returned to the pulpit—in the North or South. Thanks, Joby, for sharing this painful part of your family's past with us. We also had the great privilege of meeting Methodist Bishop Clay Lee, whose unflinching bravery in Philadelphia, Mississippi, following the murders of Goodman, Schwerner, and Chaney has been poignantly documented by Florence Mars. One day soon we hope you track down that important sermon-turned-state paper, "Herod Is in Christmas." Perhaps it deserves its own book.

Our friends at Baylor University Press have been supportive from beginning to end—remarkably patient, too. To Jenny Hunt and Diane Smith, thank you doesn't quite seem good enough. And to Carey Newman, BUP's intrepid leader, thank you for believing that a second volume was warranted.

Our friend and colleague Marty Medhurst, whose entrepreneurial spirit is directly responsible for a generation of rhetorical scholarship, championed this project from the beginning. Thanks, MJM.

DWH
Tallahassee

DED
Mishawaka

INTRODUCTION

Regrets, Recovery, Prospects

When Baylor University Press approached us back in the spring of 2004 about the possibility of a book project on religion and the civil rights movement, we were flattered, and just a bit flummoxed. Flattered because being trusted with the inaugural volume in its Rhetoric and Religion series reflected an editorial belief that we had something to say and we could deliver it in a timely manner. Flummoxed because, well, to put the matter bluntly, we were not exactly experts in the field; in fact, we were very much novices. Our expertise was in presidential rhetoric and Latin American religion and politics—not the American civil rights movement and its Judeo-Christian underpinnings. But when Martin J. Medhurst puts his substantial arm across your shoulders and beseeches with the persuasive powers that even a Lyndon Baines Johnson might admire, let's just say that we were inspired to believe—however fleetingly—that we had something important to offer. And we could complete it in a looming two-year window.

Informed by our own experiences, as well as by scholarly publishing traditions, we had initial visions of an anthology comprised of twenty to thirty speech texts and accompanying headnotes. We also figured that such texts would largely represent major movement figures; after all, where were we going to find "minor" players in this drama so dominated by Dr. Martin Luther King and his largely Baptist lieutenants in the Southern Christian Leadership Conference (SCLC)? But we also did not want to simply reissue the same texts that scholars have been publishing for the past forty-plus years, either. Before we made any final decisions, we did what any novices might do: we jumped into the literature; it was a literature, we learned rather quickly, that had once been dominated by Dr. King, but in recent years had

found room for more regional and local voices and histories. We also consulted small-circulation but important periodicals from the movement years
such as *The New South*, *The Christian Century*, *Katallagete*, *Freedomways*, and
The Pulpit. This led us to black newspapers and the not uncommon tradition of printing full speech texts. Departments of special collections quickly
became our home away from home, however virtual. Slowly, names, places,
and dates began to accumulate. So, too, did our enthusiasm.

And then we had something of an epiphany. While working through
yet another fairly obscure article, we did our due diligence with yet another
works cited page. But this author's evidences were coming from an entirely
new and intriguing archival source: the Moses Moon Audio Archive at the
Smithsonian Museum of American History in Washington, D.C. Better follow up with them; there might be something more than a single recorded
or transcribed speech. Not long after discovering this new lead, we were on
the phone with the Smithsonian's head archivist, Wendy Shay. She had
promising news for us: the collection consisted of more than eighty hours of
high-quality audio that had been transferred to cassettes; speeches and meetings had been recorded in non–SCLC movement outposts like Greenwood,
Jackson; Hattiesburg, Mississippi; Selma, Alabama; and Danville, Virginia;
yes, she would be happy to set up listening stations for us in the Smithsonian's reading room; and, perhaps most importantly for our particular
project, we could rerecord and take home just as much of the original audio
material as we wanted! We had never known of an archive or archivist more
generous with such a unique collection.

That seemingly insignificant endnote in Janice Hamlet's obscure journal article on Fannie Lou Hamer opened a new world to us.[1] For the
first time we could actually hear what a civil rights meeting sounded like.
We could begin to understand how the spirit moved local blacks to risk
everything—including their lives—to attempt to register to vote. We could
begin to understand on what scriptural sources preachers and laypersons
relied to convince audiences that God was indeed moving in present-day
history—their history. We returned home with twenty-three hours of movement eloquence and an entirely new outlook on what civil rights and religion actually might mean. We were also blessed with an offer to transcribe
the Moon recordings by Furman University's Sean O'Rourke and his
intrepid group of communication undergraduates.

---

[1] Janice D. Hamlet, "Fannie Lou Hamer: The Unquenchable Spirit of the Civil
Rights Movement," *Journal of Black Studies* 26 (1996): 560–76.

But even as we celebrated these remarkable recordings and their exceptional status as primary source materials, a corresponding and sobering thought came rather quickly: imagine how much movement eloquence vanished upon utterance. The Moon archive represents, perhaps above all else, a rather stunning exception. These precious few hours are about all we have left from a movement that moved based largely on its embodied sounds. Moreover, because tradition in the black church often militated against a carefully prepared script, or any script for that matter, unless a recording device was running, speeches, songs, prayers, and the movement's many rhythms simply weren't preserved. To listen to and experience the Moon recordings is to simultaneously understand the profundity of that silence.[2]

Our good fortune at the Smithsonian engendered an archive fever that led us around the nation. We visited locations in Georgia, Florida, Tennessee, Louisiana, Virginia, North Carolina, and Mississippi. Generous archivists from California to Maine offered invaluable assistance in our efforts to get stories and texts far less familiar than the relatively common ones of Montgomery, Birmingham, Selma, Jackson, Nashville, Greensboro, and Oxford. We discovered new stories in places such as Covington, Virginia; Lincoln, Pennsylvania; Belzoni, Mississippi; Danville, Virginia; Madeira Beach, Florida; and Denver, Colorado. In addition to more well-known civil rights speakers such as King, Evers, Wilkins, Farmer, Stokely, Malcolm, JFK, and LBJ, we recovered the voices of Ed King, Robbins Ralph, Sarah Patton Boyle, Bruce Klunder, James Hudson, and Will D. Campbell. But such fevered recovery and discovery work posed its own very vexing problem: what to do with all of it? In a fairly short period of time we had accumulated nearly two hundred germane addresses. How could we winnow such inspiring eloquence from a lot to a little? Further, who would be interested in a concise book of Ed Kings?

What happened next still brings a smile to our faces. Faced with the perennial problem of manuscript length, we emailed the director of the press, Carey Newman, and asked very tongue-in-cheek, "What would you do if we sent you a manuscript of 1,500+ pages?" We knew there was not

---

[2] Archival recordings of the movement's sounds are very rare. Two collections that hold great promise but remain largely untapped because of both recording quality and a lack of indexing are the Guy and Candie Carawan collection in the Southern Folklife Collection at the University of North Carolina and the Highlander Folk School Audio Collection at the Tennessee State Library and Archives in Nashville. The Pacifica Radio Archives also features important movement voices.

a snowball's chance of even sniffing such *War and Peace* dimensions—even if we discovered the lost addresses of a major deity; university press books approaching even four hundred pages were (are) rare. But within five minutes we had a very earnest answer: we would welcome it; send it; we are going to go big with this. Such generosity, bordering on profligacy, we could hardly believe. But rather quickly did that old maxim "Be careful what you ask for," rear its head.

As much as we wished to declare sweepingly that every speech we wanted to include should be published under provisions of "fair use" law, as much as we had seen others do it without apparent legal consequence, we knew we had to do it the right way, the thorough way, the just way. And so we set out to find the copyright holders of more than one hundred speeches; and, if we could find the legal owners, would they allow us to publish their loved ones' cherished intellectual property as a gift to well-meaning strangers? Frankly, minus the Internet and search engines Google and Zabasearch, we would have never completed this phase of the project. But with a lot of hard work, a little bit of luck, and some timely help from the Press, we eventually found widows, sons, daughters, brothers, sisters, and friends. We even happily found a few speakers still alive and active in their eighties. And though arduous and often trying—we spoke with many wrong strangers with the right names—the permissions phase turned out to be the most rewarding part of the project, more rewarding than even the archival sleuthing. Two brief stories illustrate why.

One of the speeches we were particularly enamored of was delivered by the famed educator Horace Mann Bond in March of 1956. In "A Cigarette for Johnnie Birchfield," delivered in Montgomery, Alabama, during the then three-month-old bus boycott, Bond eloquently narrates a death-row interracial encounter—and his regrets.[3] It is a masterful speech, delivered with striking attention to detail and unadorned by stylistic extravagances. We discovered the speech by happenstance when combing through the Bond papers on microfilm. Though barely legible from a poor facsimile and deteriorating film, we faithfully transcribed it. We also learned that Horace Mann Bond's son is Julian Bond, former Georgia congressman, publicity director for the Student Nonviolent Coordinating Committee (SNCC) and narrator of the sui generis documentary *Eyes on the Prize*. We tracked down an email address

---

[3] For the full text of the address, see Davis W. Houck and David E. Dixon, eds., *Rhetoric, Religion, and the Civil Rights Movement, 1954-1965* (Waco, Tex.: Baylor University Press, 2006), 178-87.

from a SNCC listserv, sent off a note to Mr. Bond, and crossed our fingers. Eleven long days later we had a reply: "Thanks and thanks again. This is wonderful. . . . I'm sending it [to] my brother, sister and 97-year-old mother—and my children. When will the book be published—what will it be called?"[4] To our surprise, this civil rights legend did not even know the speech existed; more importantly, ours was a most consequential and personal gift that he could share and cherish with his entire family. But for nearly fifty years it awaited discovery. We shared in his joy, even if virtually.

Unlike Horace Mann Bond, Will D. Campbell is alive and well and still actively writing at his home in Mt. Juliet, Tennessee. We had discovered the papers of the Southern Baptist preacher and former Ole Miss director of religious life at the University of Southern Mississippi. Campbell was well aware of the speeches we wished to reprint, but he was not in a hurry to get off the phone with us. Instead, this gifted raconteur and son of the Old South told us the story about how word of his civil rights activism played back home in Amite County, Mississippi, the same area that would experience some of the most sustained and deadly violence during the early 1960s. Specifically, his "best friends" promised to kidnap and murder him in the Homochitto Bottoms if he continued his civil rights activism and showed his face in the area. In relating the story, Campbell was still incredulous: these were his closest boyhood friends, the young men with whom he had literally grown up. More than fifty years after the searing incident, a mix of wonder, amusement, and fear could still be heard in his voice. He shared that story and that pain without prompting. He wanted us to know something of the depth of his commitment and how that commitment meant literally life and death in his hometown.

Campbell and Bond, though, were not alone in sharing with us. Many families, especially families of white clergymen who made a stand for civil rights in their southern congregations, spoke with a great sense of betrayal and shock over community ostracism, of forced moves (usually north), of loved ones whose lives were devastated by a single speech, a single sermon, an unwillingness to retract or apologize. Time and again we heard these stories of hate and hurt; and yet we also heard a message of thanks from these same families: thank you for sharing our father's words with the larger world; thank you for helping tell our stories; thank you for seeking out our family and for finding us. In the deep pathos of their stories they helped

[4] Email correspondence with Julian Bond, August 11, 2005. In editors' possession.

two novices understand that civil rights was a far more complicated story than a heroic tale of a nation's brief suffering and ultimate redemption. These strangers taught us that the popular version of American civil rights history—"Rosa sat down, Martin stood up, and the white kids came down and saved the day"—mocked their families' many and painful sacrifices.

Books, when published, usually bring a sense of closure, completion, a subject thoroughly explored and examined. Not ours. Even as Ambassador Andrew Young, one of King's most important ministers in SCLC, gave his seal of approval to the project to a standing-room-only crowd at the 2006 National Communication Association annual meeting in San Antonio, Texas, even as we were kidded by colleagues that at 1,002 pages, in a bind the book could do double duty as a weapon, we recognized that we had only scratched a significant surface. We did not let on, at least publicly, but our findings told us we were still novices. Maybe not rookies anymore, but beginners all the same. We somewhat sheepishly asked Carey on the way to lunch with Mr. Young for another crack at it, a volume 2. Not only did he not say no, but he affirmed that yes, we should do volume 2. As we look back at our first volume in this introduction, we note several of the mistakes we made—and how those mistakes inform what is here in volume 2. We also highlight the extent to which civil rights was contested on biblical grounds. In the many years we have devoted to the project of civil rights and the Judeo-Christian tradition, we are only just now beginning to understand the extent of the hermeneutic battle that was waged in pulpits and congregations around the country—and how that battle was animated by a most quotidian and secular issue.

For starters, even a casual reader of *Rhetoric, Religion, and the Civil Rights Movement, 1954–1965* (RRCRM) will notice that many speakers get more than one speech; in fact, Unitarian minister Duncan Howlett and Birmingham legend Fred Shuttlesworth each get five addresses; Sarah Patton Boyle has two addresses delivered on the same day in 1955. The discerning reader might plausibly ask: these three speakers/speeches are fine, but where in your tome is William Sloane Coffin, the firebrand chaplain from Yale who was instrumental in the movement generally and the 1963 Mississippi Freedom Vote more specifically? Why have you omitted T. B. Maston, the influential seminarian who helped bring the Southern Baptist Convention around to the view that integration was biblically warranted? In brief, the math is rather revealing—and damning: five Shuttlesworths and no Mastons? Five Howletts and no Coffins? Really? Surely you are aware that the exuberance of your inclusions editorializes on just how important/influential/eloquent you think Coffin et al. are—not very! Indeed, novices make such mistakes: excesses of commission rather quickly become errors of omission. And so it was with RRCRM. Here in volume 2, we have opted for a far less exuberant approach: nobody featured in the first volume appears in these pages (with one exception; see ahead). Additionally, of the fifty speeches we include in volume 2, each speaker gets only one speech; by doing so we acknowledge, albeit belatedly, that we still have not, nearly ten years later, exhausted the possibilities of recovery and discovery. We doubt that we ever will.

Speaking of those possibilities, what of the women of civil rights and religion? In our own research and in the work of others, it is fairly clear that in many (most?) locales, women led local movements. Just a casual reading of the papers of SNCC and the Congress of Racial Equality (CORE) reveals that women's names and addresses appear on organizing sheets far more frequently than men's; in fact, Charles Payne argues that black women in the state of Mississippi between the ages of thirty and fifty were three and four times more likely to be involved in the movement than similarly aged black men.[5] Organizing stalwart and rhetorical firebrand Stokely Carmichael noted that "the ones who came out first for the movement were the women. If you follow the mass meetings, not the stuff on TV, you'd find women out there giving all the direction. As a matter of fact, we used to say, 'Once you've got the women, the men got to come.'"[6] Payne's and Carmichael's observations beg the obvious question: why were black women relatively overrepresented in the movement? The question was in fact posed to Fannie Lou Hamer, who only at the age of forty-four became involved in the movement when it came to her community in Ruleville, Mississippi, in the summer of 1962. Said the sharecropper-turned-SNCC fieldworker, "Well, you would understand it [the question of black women's participation] if you had lived in Mississippi as a Negro. . . . As much as Negro women are precious, men could be in much more danger. If my husband had gone through or attempted one-third of what I've gone through, he would have already been dead. So we understand why it's more women involved. And until it's where that men can actually speak out, there will be more women

[5] Charles Payne, "Men Led, but Women Organized: Movement Participation of Women in the Mississippi Delta," in *Women in the Civil Rights Movement: Trailblazers and Torchbearers, 1941–1965*, ed. Vicki L. Crawford, Jacqueline Anne Rouse, and Barbara Woods (Brooklyn, N.Y.: Carlson, 1990), 2.

[6] Cited in Lynn Olson, *Freedom's Daughters: The Unsung Heroines of the Civil Rights Movement from 1830 to 1970* (New York: Scribner, 2001), 15.

until they can speak out, but it's so dangerous. . . . You have to live in Mississippi as a Negro to understand why it's not more men involved than there is."[7] Hamer gives voice to what several other black women activists suggested, labeled by Payne as the "differential reprisal hypothesis": namely, that white violence was far more likely to be carried out on black men than black women.[8] Whether the cause was a white and misanthropic southern chivalry or something else, both the scholars and the activists agree: black women were relatively safer doing the daily work of the movement: organizing, speaking, and canvassing.[9]

And yet in a book featuring more than 130 speeches across a twelve-year period, we included only seven speeches by women! Surely given the demographics of movement participation we could do much better. Surely. So consuming and vexing was the question that we addressed an entire book to proving that we were not sexist, sloppy, or both. That book, *Women and the Civil Rights Movement, 1954–1965* (WCRM), contains thirty-nine addresses by thirty-nine different women.[10] But several of those speeches were plucked directly from RRCRM. Many did not address the movement's aims in terms of the Judeo-Christian tradition. Many were delivered by educated and highly literate white women. And so we kept looking with anticipation toward volume 2. At the Schlesinger Library at Harvard; at the National Council of Negro Women's archive in Washington, D.C.; at the Rosa and Raymond Parks Institute in Detroit; in the microfilm collections of the NAACP, SNCC, CORE, SCLC; in the *Congressional Record*—and we have all of one speech to show for our efforts in this volume. And, just to rub a bit more salt into the wound, that one speaker, Lillian Smith, was already featured in our first volume.

---

[7] Fannie Lou Hamer Oral History, Stanford University Project South Oral History, sponsored by radio station KZSU, Summer 1965, 0491, 1–18. The complete transcripts of this important but vastly underutilized collection are available through the Microfilming Corporation of America, Glenrock, New Jersey. Stanford University possesses the original audio recordings.

[8] Charles M. Payne, *I've Got the Light of Freedom: The Organizing Tradition and the Mississippi Freedom Struggle* (Berkeley: University of California Press, 1995), 267–71.

[9] Davis W. Houck and David E. Dixon, "Introduction: Recovering Women's Voices from the Civil Rights Movement," in *Women and the Civil Rights Movement, 1954–1965*, ed. Davis W. Houck and David E. Dixon (Jackson: University Press of Mississippi, 2009), xiii–xviii.

[10] Houck and Dixon, eds., *Women and the Civil Rights Movement, 1954–1965*.

All of which returns us to Moses Moon. Had the Chicago nightclub owner (then known as Alan Ribback) not traveled south at the invitation of SNCC's executive secretary, James Forman, we simply would not have any traces of these remarkable meetings held throughout the Deep South. As best as we can judge, there was no written record, no carefully typed up speeches, nothing for posterity or historians, nor even their families. No, these meetings were largely impromptu affairs in which people spoke and participated as the spirit led. Dr. King had typists and stenographers—and almost always television cameras; Fannie Lou Hamer and Annie Devine did not. They did possess advanced and sustained training in the black oral tradition, passed down by church and family, but writing, duplication, and preservation were largely strangers to them. As we documented in WCRM, we are simply still missing the voices of a generation of women who made the movement move. We would, though, underscore the temporal qualifier "still" because our experience leads us to believe that those voices exist; we just haven't found them yet.

Spearheaded by Maegan Parker Brooks, we recently completed a collection of Fannie Lou Hamer's speeches—nearly all of which survived because someone had a tape recorder going. They were in random places—in a private attic in Madison, Wisconsin, in an obscure collection of documents at the Avery Institute in Charleston, South Carolina, in a collection recently deeded to the Oral History Center at the University of Southern Mississippi, and in government documents.[11] If two people with fairly limited resources, tracking different leads in different states, and in just a few years' time, can find nearly twenty addresses that heretofore did not exist, one can see that our optimism about such recovery and discovery efforts is not misplaced. In fact, having recently witnessed firsthand the extent to which significant resources can be brought to bear on a missing document turned federal evidence, we are confident that the speech texts of Septima Clark, Rosa Parks, Gloria Richardson, Ella Baker, Annell Ponder, Ruby Hurley, Prathia Hall, and Daisy Bates, among many others, exist.[12]

---

[11] Maegan Parker Brooks and Davis W. Houck, eds., *The Speeches of Fannie Lou Hamer: To Tell It Like It Is* (Jackson: University Press of Mississippi, 2011).

[12] The missing document in question is the official court transcript from the Emmett Till murder trial held in Sumner, Mississippi, during September 19-23, 1955. Historians of the case had long acknowledged that the last known surviving transcript was in the hands of Hugh Stephen Whitaker, who had written an M.A. thesis on the murder and trial at Florida State University in 1962. Whitaker's copy,

While RRCRM suffered from a decided lack of women's voices—how did they mobilize differently than their male counterparts? Did they employ the same scriptural appeals? Did they, like Mamie Till and Hamer, invoke motherhood as an inventional resource?—there is also a decided bias in favor of the individual over the institutional. That is, many of the "stars" of the movement are represented in the collection, as opposed to the far less glamorous and less well-known denominational speakers. Dr. King, in other words, speaks as the leading spokesman of the movement, not as a member of the National Baptist Convention. College chaplain and ordained Methodist minister Edwin King speaks as a candidate for lieutenant governor on the Freedom Party ticket as opposed to a member of the United Methodist Church. Roy Wilkins speaks as a leader of the NAACP, not as a member of a specific church. Until we began visiting libraries that featured major archival denominational holdings, including Southern Baptists, Episcopalians, Disciples of Christ, Reformed Judaism, Roman Catholics, Mennonites, and Methodists, we had no idea the extent to which "religion and race" or "religion and human rights" conferences and committees proliferated among ecclesiastical bodies.[13] More importantly, we did not know the extent to which different denominations tried to adjudicate "the race question" nor how individual members translated their theology as Baptists or Jews or Methodists into a contemporary and theologically fitting response to vexing questions such as segregation, civil rights legislation, racial violence, and civil disobedience. Unlike RRCRM, this volume takes up these questions directly as we were able to recover unpublished conference proceedings, workshops, denominational keynote addresses, and other texts that bear on theologically doctrinal matters.

---

though, was later destroyed in a flood. When the Till case was reopened in 2004 by the federal government, a key part of the investigation involved finding the missing transcript. We know because they called us, inquiring if we possessed a copy. The FBI eventually located a faded copy, in the hands of a local Mississippi Delta man; later, it put the entire 300+-page trial transcript as well as its summary of evidence online at www.fbi.gov. For a much consolidated version of his original thesis, see Hugh Stephen Whitaker, "A Case Study in Southern Justice: The Murder and Trial of Emmett Till," *Rhetoric & Public Affairs* 8 (2005): 189–224.

[13] Hadden notes that "hundreds of commissions and committees on religion and race" proliferated in the 1950s and 1960s; see Jeffrey K. Hadden, "Clergy Involvement in Civil Rights," *Annals of the American Academy of Political and Social Science* 387 (1970): 119.

Not surprisingly, denominations did not often speak with one voice on civil rights matters. And while more hierarchical church structures such as Roman Catholicism engendered a far more outspoken and integrationist rhetoric since church leaders were often progressive on the race question, more independent denominations such as Southern Baptists were often in diametrically opposed camps—even within the same church. The story of Rev. G. Jackson Stafford is illustrative.[14] After graduating from Louisville's Southern Baptist Theological Seminary in 1951, Stafford was called to the Batesburg Baptist Church (today, the First Baptist Church of Batesburg), a community thirty miles south and west of Columbia, South Carolina. There the young minister and World War II marine quickly added to the church membership and its annual budget. By nearly all accounts, Stafford enjoyed the widespread and enthusiastic support of his board of deacons and his congregants.

Things began to unravel, though, not long after the minister returned from the Southern Baptist Convention's annual conference in June 1954. Meeting in St. Louis just weeks after the tectonic *Brown* school integration decision, the denomination's Christian Life Commission issued a report that included a weak, if supportive, commendation for the Supreme Court's verdict. That report was voted on by convention attendees and accepted by a nearly unanimous margin—including by Rev. Stafford. His vote quickly followed him home to Batesburg, and to his board of deacons, including a most interested member, seventy-three-year-old federal district judge George Bell Timmerman Sr. As part of a three-judge federal panel adjudicating the *Briggs v. Elliott* school integration case of 1951 (one of the five school integration cases later rolled into *Brown*), Timmerman had voted against integrating the Clarendon County, South Carolina, schools. Later during the summer of 1954, the judge privately queried the young minister how he had voted in St. Louis. Stafford did not lie, nor did he shirk the question. On Stafford's account, Timmerman was furious, saying, "that God had created a race of servants, had turned them black as a mark of their servitude, and intended for them to remain servants forever. He had said that his biblical support

---

[14] We are grateful to Ms. Joby Robinson for sending us her father's papers on the controversy at Batesburg Baptist Church. Rev. Stafford kept detailed records on the fight with Timmerman, later depositing them with the South Carolina Council of Human Relations at the University of South Carolina, and at the Southern Baptist Convention archives in Nashville, Tennessee, where we first learned of the controversy.

was found in the ninth and tenth chapters of Genesis." To the estimable board of deacons chair, federal judge, father to the sitting governor of South Carolina, and unanimously rebuffed appellant, Stafford parried with loving your neighbor as yourself, per Christ's teaching in the New Testament. Not capitulating to Timmerman cost Stafford his ministry in Batesburg. "I have definitely come to the conclusion—based on thoughts I have had for quite some time—that you and I do not belong in the same church," thundered Timmerman. "I am unwilling to support any movement in or out of church that has as an objective the abasement or mongrelization of my race." And though he still had the support of many congregants, Rev. Stafford resigned on October 23, 1955, having never preached on the subject of race relations, nor having offered public support, beyond an anonymous vote, of the Supreme Court's *Brown* decision. He left Batesburg never to return to a Baptist pulpit, hurt and angry that power politics and racial custom and not scriptural precept had prevailed.

G. Jackson Stafford's story is not terribly unusual; we encountered many similar stories of public humiliation and private threats, some of which are in this volume.[15] We highlight Stafford's story less for Southern Baptist racial intrigue and more for what it reveals about the dialogic nature of so many of the speeches we included in RRCRM. That is, though we did not know it at the time, so many of the speeches and sermons are refutative in nature; in other words, speakers were often making a case for racial integration and racial justice precisely because someone else was claiming just the opposite—and that someone was more times than not a fellow clergyman or congregant, often in the same community or congregation. Our initial ignorance on the subject was informed by a very consequential historiographical fact: so little of that religiously grounded and proracial segregation literature circulates. As Charles W. Eagles argues in his important essay, "Toward New Histories of the Civil Rights Movements," there is an overwhelming and consequential bias when it comes to the vast literature on the black freedom movement. On his account, scholars "have tended to emphasize one side of the struggle, the movement side, and to neglect their professional obligation to understand the other side, the segregationist opposition." Such an "asymmetrical" result simply means that "important parts of the

---

[15] For other accounts, see Jason Sokol, *There Goes My Everything: White Southerners in the Age of Civil Rights* (New York: Knopf, 2006), 50-52.

story remain untold."[16] To reduce Eagles' argument to the more colloquial: why research and write about a bowdlerizing racist like Judge Timmerman when Rev. Stafford's heroic story (and his papers) beckon? Why spend precious research time with racists when such beguiling saints and their stories remain to be told?

We confess to being guilty: our work on the civil rights movement has also been rather asymmetrical. Even lukewarm speeches (by so-called "moderates") we have rejected in favor of a more robust and full-throated declaration for interracial freedom—here and in RRCRM. So, too, has nearly everybody else.[17] And while we will not apologize for that choice, Eagles' admonition is most apt for our project: Jack Stafford's defense of an integrated church is not going to make a lot of sense without George Bell Timmerman's offense justifying an eternally accursed servile and black class—who have no business sitting in the pews of "his" church. Surely there's a book or two waiting to be published on the segregationist church's defense of what it called the Southern Way of Life. Already the books, dissertations, documentaries, and articles are beginning to appear on the so-called "bad guys" of the movement.[18] And with Eagles we agree that a more symmetrical

[16] Charles M. Eagles, "Toward New Histories of the Civil Rights Movement," *Journal of Southern History* 66 (2000): 816.

[17] A notable and recent exception includes W. Stuart Towns, ed., *"We Want Our Freedom": Rhetoric of the Civil Rights Movement* (New York: Praeger, 2002). A more typical selection of movement greats is Josh Gottheimer's *Ripples of Hope: Great American Civil Rights Speeches* (New York: Basic, 2003).

[18] Stephanie Renee Rolph's 2009 Mississippi State University dissertation, "Displacing Race: White Resistance and Conservative Politics in the Civil Rights Era," is exemplary in this regard. Rolph did scholars a great service by transcribing the entire collection of the Citizens' Council Forum, a radio and television program sponsored by the Citizens' Council of America. That collection is housed in Special Collections at Mississippi State University and is available electronically. For recent books, see Joseph Crespino, *In Search of Another Country: Mississippi and the Conservative Counterrevolution* (Princeton, N.J.: Princeton University Press, 2007); Paul Hendrickson, *Sons of Mississippi: A Story of Race and Its Legacy* (New York: Knopf, 2003). We can expect scholarship on Mississippi's staunchly racist senator James O. Eastland in the coming years as his papers have recently been made available at the University of Mississippi. For a beginning on Eastland, see Chris Myers Asch, *The Senator and the Sharecropper: The Freedom Struggles of James O. Eastland and Fannie Lou Hamer* (New York: New Press, 2008). Several rhetoricians have been relatively early to this topic; see in particular Eugene E. White, "Mississippi's Great White Chief:

treatment is in fact a historiographical necessity. But we have chosen not to enact that symmetry here; instead we have noted in our headnotes, where germane, the opposition to the movement's aims, whether in the bombing of a synagogue or the vote of a congregation not to integrate.

Before we leave this subject of the movement and the church's other side, we would like to return to a term used by Judge Timmerman, a term we do not much see in circulation these days: mongrelization. In so doing, we would like to highlight something of the defining secular and sacred matter in religious rhetoric about race. In contemporary parlance a "mongrel" might attach itself to a stray canine, but certainly not a human. But back when the term was in frequent circulation, especially in civil rights debates, the term and its synonyms—abasement, amalgamation, mingling—were not-so-high-frequency dog whistling for interracial sex. Specifically, black-male-on-white-female-sex. One can simply not read the history of the post-Civil War South without encountering the dread specter of the black beast rapist pillaging at will magnolia-scented blonde and blue-eyed belles.[19] "Whatever its origin and character, whether the product of violence and exploitation or of mutual consent and affection, sex between the races was Jim Crow's

The Speaking of James K. Vardaman in the Mississippi Gubernatorial Campaign of 1903," *Quarterly Journal of Speech* 32 (1946): 442–46; Waldo W. Braden, *The Oral Tradition in the South* (Baton Rouge: Louisiana State University Press, 1999); Dallas C. Dickey, "Southern Oratory: A Field for Research," *Quarterly Journal of Speech* 33 (1947): 458–63; Waldo W. Braden, ed., *Oratory in the New South* (Baton Rouge: Louisiana State University Press, 1979); Howard Dorgan and Cal M. Logue, *Oratory of Southern Demagogues* (Baton Rouge: Louisiana State University Press, 1982); and Cal M. Logue and Howard Dorgan, eds., *A New Diversity in Contemporary Southern Rhetoric* (Baton Rouge: Louisiana State University Press, 1987). More recently, see E. Culpepper Clark, *The Schoolhouse Door: Segregation's Last Stand at the University of Alabama* (New York: Oxford University Press, 1995). Many documentaries examine segregationists as well as Klansmen, but Henry Hampton's multivolume *Eyes on the Prize* remains without peer in examining the Southern resistance; see *Eyes on the Prize*, directed by Henry Hampton (1986; Washington, DC: PBS Home Video, 2010), DVD.

[19] Brookhaven, Mississippi judge and Yale University law graduate Tom P. Brady wrote memorably, "The loveliest and purest of God's creatures, the nearest thing to an angelic being that treads this terrestrial ball is a well-bred southern white woman, or her blue-eyed, golden-haired little girl." Brady, *Black Monday* (Winona, Miss.: Association of Citizens' Councils, 1955), 46.

most vexatious problem," claims Neil McMillen. Moreover, and borrowing from Mississippi writer David Cohn, McMillen argues that "Whites 'instinctively' understood that 'sex is at the core of life,' . . . and in their 'conscious or unconscious minds' they knew that the 'negro question' was 'at bottom a blood or sexual question.' "[20] McMillen and Cohn both implicitly mention The Big Question: in rather cloyingly alluding to "origins," "instincts," and the "unconscious," both men raise—but do not try to answer here—the question of why: why did the prospect of interracial sex between black men and white women come to have such an overwhelming influence on all matters of black-white relations in the South? Two anthropologists writing in the 1930s suggest answers.

One of the more remarkable coincidences in the history of academic publishing occurred in a three-year period during the Great Depression: in 1937 John Dollard published his book *Caste and Class in a Southern Town* with Yale University Press; in 1939 Hortense Powdermaker published her book *After Freedom: A Cultural Study in the Deep South* with Viking Press. The fact that two prominent and northern cultural anthropologists would publish soon-to-be canonical books about race relations in southern communities just a few years apart might not raise too many eyebrows. But readers of both books will quickly realize that Dollard's "Southerntown" and Powdermaker's "Cottonville" are the same small community—Indianola, Mississippi! That Powdermaker's research was sponsored by Yale University adds an additional anomalous layer. Remarkable coincidences notwithstanding, both Dollard and Powdermaker address the question of interracial sex rather directly; in fact, Dollard spends an entire chapter on the subject. Both arrive at similar conclusions: white male projection is the primary culprit; that is, as Powdermaker notes, "It is a commonplace beyond dispute that the two groups have had sexual relations ever since they have been in contact; and that the relations have been almost exclusively between white men and Negro women."[21] In other words, white Southern men had simply projected their collective sexual guilt onto black men. But in order for that guilt to be transferred effectively and held at bay, the black male needed to be transformed into something insidious. Notes Dollard, "If Negro women are represented as sexually desirable in the folk imagination of the whites, Negro

[20] Neil R. McMillen, *Dark Journey: Black Mississippians in the Age of Jim Crow* (Urbana: University of Illinois Press, 1990), 14.

[21] Hortense Powdermaker, *After Victory: A Cultural Study in the Deep South* (New York: Viking, 1939), 181.

men are viewed as especially virile and capable in this sphere." Dollard specifies further, "The idea seems to be that they are more like savages, nearer to
animals, and that their sexual appetites are more vigorous and ungoverned."
Materially speaking, "There is a widespread belief that the genitalia of Negro
males are larger than those of whites; this was repeatedly stated by white infor-
mants."[22] John Howard Griffin, in his remarkable story *Black Like Me*, found
out just how widespread that belief was as he hitchhiked through rural Alabama in 1959 and as random white southern men actually demanded to see
his supposedly outsized genitalia. Still other white men randomly inquired
as to whether his wife had "had it from a white man."[23] From a different gendered lens, Endesha Ida Mae Holland tells unflinchingly, and in tragically
quotidian terms, of her childhood rape at the hands of an elderly white man
in Greenwood, Mississippi.[24] As to whether a white southern woman could
ever have a mutual romantic relationship with a black man, that was simply
out of the question for white southern men: "Sexual congress between black
men and white women, of course, was all but unthinkable. As the savage
tradition of unpunished lynchings suggests, it was the presumption of both
[the] white public and white law that intercourse between white women and
black men could result only from rape."[25] In sum, and on Powdermaker's
and Dollard's separate anthropological accounts, the sexual demonization
of black men was so total, so rhetorically complete, that reciprocal affection
was simply beyond the pale; rape was the only "logical" conclusion from the
premises of an animalistic black male sexual appetite unshackled by slavery
and stoked by southern white beauty.

[22] John Dollard, *Caste and Class in a Southern Town*, 3rd ed. (New York: Anchor,
1957), 160.

[23] John Howard Griffin, *Black Like Me* (New York: Signet, 1961), 85–92. Griffin
notes, "Some [who picked him up while hitchhiking] were shamelessly open, some
shamelessly subtle. All showed morbid curiosity about the sexual life of the Negro,
and all had, at base, the same stereotyped image of the Negro as an inexhaust-
ible sex-machine with oversized genitals and a vast store of experiences, immensely
varied" (85).

[24] Endesha Ida Mae Holland, *From the Mississippi Delta: A Memoir* (New York:
Simon & Schuster, 1997). For an excellent historical account of the sexual realities
and rhetorical politics of white-on-black rape, see Danielle McGuire, *At the Dark
End of the Street: Black Women, Rape and Resistance—A New History of the Civil Rights
Movement from Rosa Parks to the Rise of Black Power* (New York: Vintage, 2010).

[25] McMillen, *Dark Journey*, 15.

Into this world of racial and gendered psycho-sexual complexity was added the combustible *Brown* decision of 1954—a decision, lest we forget, that would put black boys into daily and close proximity with white girls.[26] Young adults, too. This smacked of the very "social equality" sure to (re)ignite black male carnal desires, leading eventually to intermarriage and the ruination of the white race. But well before *Brown* Dollard already had specified the racial-sexual calculus: "It seems clear that any move toward social equality is seen on its deepest level as really a move toward sexual equality, that is, toward full sexual reciprocity between the castes." This meant that "the white men would have to abandon their exclusive claims to women of the white caste and to admit reciprocal rights to Negro men." Perhaps only the psychologically fraught might interpret "the innocent-seeming intimacies of everyday social life" as a warrant for "always-greater intimacies of sexual contact."[27] Especially in the South might a shared drink of water or a dip in the community pool reveal a not-so-covert desire to intermarry and/or "amalgamate."

As the foregoing suggests, sex qua sex was only part of the "problem" for southern and typically "religious" white men. Interracial sex needed to be part of something bigger; it needed a telos that was just as insidious as the sexual act itself—if only to offer more psychological comfort. Segregationists found their answer, at least in the 1930s when Dollard and Powdermaker were conducting their research, in the argument that black-male-on-white-female-sex would cause the white race to become "mongrelized," an outcome that would lead directly to the collapse of American civilization. Importantly, black men were not engaged in this diminution of the gene pool on purpose; it was simply part of their bestial nature, something they could not help. By the time of the *Brown* decision, though, and thanks largely to World War II, the natural black bestial rapist argument had diminished in public discourse; only the most extreme racists like Mississippians Senator Theodore Bilbo and Judge Tom Brady might invoke it. But in the postwar world of 1950s America, segregationists needed a new set of public arguments to make the case against "social equality." Interracial sex had to have a new deadly aim, and segregationists found it in the Cold War.[28]

[26] For the best one-volume treatment of the *Brown* case, see Richard Kluger's remarkable book, *Simple Justice: The History of* Brown v. Board of Education *and Black America's Struggle for Equality* (New York: Vintage, 1977).

[27] Dollard, *Caste and Class in a Southern Town*, 170.

[28] For a recent review of the literature on Communism and civil rights, see

In other words, segregationists latched onto the rather kairotic argument that social equality was a most lethal weapon in the Soviet Union's arsenal. Sex and intermarriage between black men and white women would precipitate the worldwide Communist revolution by decimating the superior American (and white) gene pool. Nuclear weaponry would not win the Cold War; rather, interracial sex and its concomitant offspring of dumbed-down, mixed-breed, and post-*Brown* children would vouchsafe the Communists' ultimate and worldwide victory. This argument was not available during Dollard's and Powdermaker's fieldwork. But in the McCarthy-dominated 1950s, southern segregationists had found a new and potentially potent rhetorical ally. That it looks to us in the twenty-first century as the veriest nonsense—a conspiratorial Communist eugenics leavened by NAACP Jews—is beside the point. It was an argument equally at home in Congress as it was in the pulpit.[29]

Matthew A. Grindy, "Civil Rights and the Red Scare," *Rocky Mountain Communication Review* 4 (2008): 3–15.

[29] In 1956 and 1957 senators and congressmen inserted into the *Congressional Record* six sermons/articles that attempted to legitimize segregation on biblical grounds. These six included a "talk" by editor Lawrence W. Neff delivered in January 1956, and inserted by Georgia representative James C. Davis; a sermon by Dr. James A. Chandler delivered in May 1956; a sermon by Dr. Roy O. McClain preached on June 24, 1956, in Atlanta, Ga., and inserted by Georgia representative John J. Flynt Jr.; a sermon by Rev. George O. King delivered on September 9, 1956, and inserted by Georgia senator Richard B. Russell; an article by Rev. G. T. Gillespie, president emeritus of Brookhaven College, published on June 5, 1957, and inserted by Mississippi representative John Bell Williams; and an address by Walter B. Jones, presiding judge of the Fifteenth Judicial Circuit of Alabama, delivered on July 11, 1957, and inserted by Alabama representative George M. Grant. While each of the speakers/writers is not necessarily an ordained minister, each speech/article is addressed to a religious body—from a Sunday school class to a gathering of Baptist laymen. The texts bear titles such as "Religion and Race," "Race Relations," "Is Racial Integration the Answer?" "The Race Question," "A Southern Christian Looks at the Race Problem," and "Is It Un-Christian to Believe in Segregation?" Houck uses these texts to argue that they were leveraged rhetorically to attempt to preempt debate on civil rights bills that would culminate in the 1957 Civil Rights Act; see Davis W. Houck, "Sex, God, and Country: The Racial Rhetoric of Preemption and the 1957 Civil Rights Act" (paper presented at the National Communication Association Annual Convention, New Orleans, La., November 2011).

Grafted onto the white southern racial logic was, perhaps not surprisingly, biblical authority. In an effort to legitimize its thoroughly secular and increasingly imperiled defense of segregation, the Bible was retrofitted by many white southern clergymen to justify racial separateness.[30] From southern pulpits white congregants were reassured that the God who they worshipped "was the original segregationist." After all, had not God created his own Chosen People who were to be set apart from racial, ethnic, and spiritual others? More to the point, did not God want Jews marrying other Jews, not their heathen—and decidedly unchosen—neighbors?

Across several years and many archival collections, we have discovered a modest cache of documents that offer biblically grounded justifications for segregation. But perhaps none is more revelatory than an unattributed article we happened upon in the Mississippi Department of Archives and History (MDAH). In its vast microfilm collection, the MDAH contains back issues of a small-circulation weekly newspaper, the *Ruleville Record*. Located in the heart of the Mississippi Delta in Sunflower County, home to the then powerful Senator James O. Eastland, Ruleville was the adopted home of Fannie Lou Hamer; it was also one of the organizing hubs for civil rights workers who had volunteered for what became known as Freedom Summer.[31] Just weeks into that 1964 campaign, and as white northern clergy "invaded" its state, the *Record* ran what amounted to an extended list on its front-page, middle column. Titled "Is Segregation Unchristian?" the lengthy article offers without comment thirty-six separate Bible verses with accompanying text—thirty-one from the Old Testament and five from the New Testament—each of which functions rhetorically as a defense of racial segregation.[32] Not surprisingly, the animating principle behind the list is the threat of interreligious (thus interracial) marriage. That threat has its origins, per Judge Timmerman, in the "curse upon Canaan," as narrated in the ninth and tenth chapters of Genesis. In this well-known account, an unsuspecting Ham finds his father Noah unconscious and naked from too much of the family grape. The rather sullen and hungover father later

---

[30] See, e.g., Numan V. Bartley, *The Rise of Massive Resistance: Race and Politics in the South during the 1950s* (Baton Rouge: Louisiana State University Press, 1999), 293–305.

[31] For the best recent treatment of Freedom Summer, see Bruce Watson, *Freedom Summer: The Savage Season of 1964 That Made Mississippi Burn and Made America a Democracy* (New York: Penguin, 2011).

[32] "Is Segregation Unchristian?" *Ruleville Record*, July 16, 1964, 1.

rebukes and curses the son who was destined to be the father of Canaan. "And he [Noah] said, cursed be Canaan; a servant of servants shall be unto his brethren. And he [Noah] said, blessed be the Lord God of Shem; and Canaan shall be his servant. God shall enlarge Japheth, and he shall dwell in the tents of Shem; and Canaan shall be his servant."

Never mind that the 601-year-old Noah could have prevented this entire family imbroglio by not getting liquored up and going pre-serpent Adam exhibitionist on his vineyard. Never mind, too, that Ham's intrafamilial offense pales in comparison to Cain's. And never mind that the curse comes from a bellicose Noah, not Yahweh, whose beneficent same-chapter covenant is promised to Noah's entire male brood. Read, however, within the hermeneutic lens of racial segregation, Ham is the ur-Ethiopian, the black-marked man destined to live with his ancestors in eternal bondage as a slave/servant. That curse, as sequenced artfully by the *Ruleville Record*, leads narratively and logically to Genesis 24:3, "And I will make thee swear by the Lord, the God of heaven and the God of the earth, that thou shalt not take a wife unto my son of the daughters of the Canaanites, among whom I dwell." Such was Abraham's wish for his son, Isaac, as dictated to a favored servant—not God's command to his people. In this and several other verses, readers of the *Ruleville Record* are instructed in a manner reminiscent of Burke's repetitive form that not only is segregation Christian but also God commands it based largely on the consequences of interracial marriage.[33] How could the different "nations" of the earth remain separate, after all, if intermarriage were to occur? And to extend the terms just a bit closer to Freedom Summer, how could America maintain its chosen status as a blessed "city upon a hill" if the nation did not hue to the Pentateuch's provisions? Thus does the Soviet Union function as a Canaanite proxy in this unfolding and increasingly vertiginous millennial drama.

Jack Stafford lost his job over Genesis chapters 9 and 10; George Timmerman made sure of it. But the great irony of the South's defense of segregation, whether scriptural, secular, or otherwise, is that white southern men were more typically doing the "integrating at night," as movement activists liked to remind their audiences; proof was embodied visually in a spectrum of brown complexions. This vestige of chattel slavery in which white men had ready access to black women's bodies is fraught with an emotion not

---

[33] Burke describes repetitive form as "the constant maintaining of a principle under new guises. It is the restatement of the same thing in different ways." Kenneth Burke, *Counter Statement* (Berkeley: University of California Press, 1968), 125.

unfamiliar to the Judeo-Christian tradition: guilt. And what better method of alleviating oneself of racial-sexual guilt than projecting it onto a despised other?[34] Only in the haunted white imagination might the docile, agreeable (and lest we forget, Christian) smiling black "boy" of slavery become the rampaging ravisher of white womanhood within the attenuated voting cycle of the thirteenth, fourteenth, and fifteenth constitutional amendments. Thus was the Bible retrofitted for southern political—and thus personal— ends. Ham came to his racial awareness, in sum, rather late in the hermeneutic tradition.

Readers of this volume and RRCRM will note that many speakers base their claims for racial justice and integration on the New Testament, specifically the parable of the Good Samaritan, Christ's encounter with the woman at the well, the second greatest commandment, to love your neighbor as yourself, and most often, it seems, the apostle Paul's teachings in the seventeenth chapter of the book of Acts. Before his Athenian interlocutors convened in the Council of the Areopagus, Paul preached on the universality of humankind. "And hath made of one blood all nations of men for to dwell on all the face of the earth, and hath determined the times before appointed, and the bounds of their habitation." If the civil rights movement shared a common Bible verse, it was Acts 17:26. So frequently did we encounter it in the pro–civil rights religious literature that we assumed the verse shared something of a universal interpretation. And then we discovered the same verse printed as one of five New Testament justifications for segregation in *The Ruleville Record*! How could each side offer as scriptural evidence the same chapter and verse for segregation and integration? We are a long way in Acts from besotted and naked castaways making intrafamilial curses. The Council of the Areopagus is not an outpost valley winery near Mt. Ararat. Or is it?

Pro-integration speakers typically emphasized the first part of the verse, translated by the *Oxford Study Bible* as "He created from one stock every nation of men to inhabit the whole earth's surface." Every nation, white, black, and otherwise, springs from a common ancestry. The "brotherhood

---

[34] One is reminded here of Burke's admonition, "Whenever you find a doctrine of 'nonpolitical' esthetics affirmed with fervor, look for its politics." Kenneth Burke, *A Rhetoric of Motives* (Berkeley: University of California Press, 1969), 28. We might restate the germane principle here as, whenever you find a white southern politician affirming with fervor the black man's sexual longing for white women, look for his black mistress(es)—across the railroad tracks.

of man" and the "fatherhood of God" so frequently invoked by promovement clergy never lacked for a clearer scriptural articulation. Southern clergy defending the racial status quo emphasized the second half of Paul's declaration: "He determined their eras in history and the limits of their territory."[35] In other words, God, not man, decided who got what and when; God, not man, divided nation into nation; and God, not man, saw fit to divide said nations into white and black. In brief, it seems we're back to Ham and a divvying up of people and geography not unlike Noah's curse.

As two novices set out to put together with dispatch a collection of addresses giving weight to the not-uncommon claim that the Judeo-Christian tradition really made the movement move, we did not know the extent to which a countermovement had its own powerful and persuasive Judeo-Christian rhetorical traditions. The "asymmetry" of the extant literature did not suggest as much. And so for every G. Jackson Stafford represented here in the pages of RRCRM volume 2, we would encourage our readers to aid in recovering the multisided and messy story, the hermeneutic battles that shaped lives and split congregations and denominations. As Karlyn Kohrs Campbell reminds us, recovering texts is vital, but so too is recuperating them through careful and historically informed interpretation.[36] Not to engage the heated (and very symmetrical) debate over civil rights diminishes the movement's remarkable achievements, as well as the personal and professional sacrifices made by its foot soldiers. Even as our nation engages in a new battle of theological interpretation in the area of gay, lesbian, and transgendered rights, we would do well to remember that our rhetorical tradition is nourished in the soil of debate, disagreement, and, yes, defeat. Victory, too. But in here publishing for the very first time some of the texts vital to that larger victory, nothing about it was necessarily inevitable or, per Paul, "determined." As a contingent art, rhetoric functions to change hearts, minds, and, yes, spirits, too. Even in the argot of the church, hard-hearted ones.

---

[35] J. Jack Suggs, Katharine Doob Sakenfeld, and James R. Mueller, eds., *The Oxford Study Bible* (New York: Oxford University Press, 1992).

[36] Karlyn Kohrs Campbell, "Consciousness-Raising: Linking Theory, Criticism, and Practice," *Rhetoric Society Quarterly* 32 (2002): 45, 46.

1954

1954

§1 Simcha Kling

Rabbi Simcha Kling was born in 1922 in Fort Thomas, Kentucky. He earned a bachelor's degree at the University of Cincinnati, a master's degree from Columbia University, and a master's and doctorate from Jewish Theological Seminary in New York City. He was ordained in 1948. He and his wife, Edith (née Leeman), raised three daughters. He served as rabbi to congregations in Greensboro, North Carolina, and St. Louis, Missouri. Rabbi Kling was also an active scholar, authoring a book on conversion titled *Embracing Judaism* and also staying current on Zionist theorists such as Ahad Ha'am and Nahum Sokolow. He was heavily involved in the Rabbinical Assembly from 1956 to 1984. Rabbi Kling died February 26, 1991, at the age of sixty-nine. His papers are housed at the Jewish Theological Seminary.

In this May 21, 1954, sermon to his congregation in Greensboro titled "Proclaim Liberty," Rabbi Kling tells congregants of his recent meeting with conservative rabbis. The most notable occurrence at the meeting, he says, was the U.S. Supreme Court's *Brown v. Board of Education* decision to abolish segregation in public schools. Lest the Greensboro faithful disagree in principle with mixing religious services and politics, he insists several times that the *Brown* decision is so monumental and far-reaching that it demands the attention of religious leaders and their communities. Judaism and Christianity insist that all humans are of the same origin and of equal value to the God who made them in His own image. The secular ideals of the U.S. founders side with the Judeo-Christian ethic in this regard, as can be seen in such artifacts as the Liberty Bell inscription. Racism, in these traditions, is irreligious, and little by little, even secular institutions are progressing toward a more complete version of these ideals. Though he suspects his congregation is less racist than most, he assumes there are still vestiges of prejudice such as stereotyping. He offers a positive vision that integration will allow us finally to see that all races can be equal in intellect, and casts aside the specter of racial intermarriage. Such an assumption, he argues, is the same as saying that Christians and Jews will intermarry if they attend schools together. His solution to that possibility is to assert the value of all traditions and guarantee their continuity by making their ways of life attractive to new generations.

ॐ

Proclaim Liberty
May 21, 1954
Greensboro, North Carolina

This past week, I have told several interesting experiences which I hope to relate to you shortly. Not only did I meet with other Conservative rabbis and have the privilege of listening to our revered teachers, Professor Mordecai Kaplan and the chancellor of the Jewish Theological Seminary, Professor Louis Finkelstein, but saw the Conservative movement take several forward steps. However, one event this week so surpassed anything and everything else that I feel duty bound, precisely because we are a southern community, to address myself to it. The decision of the Supreme Court to abolish segregation in the public schools was of such historic and religious significance that I feel I must speak of it from the pulpit at a *religious* service. And I am glad that our children are present. Whether they understand me or not, they will come to realize, as they grow up, that the discussion of this historic decision on Shabbat is evidence of the *religious* teachings about man.

Indeed, the court's decision was not a mere judicial decision; it was an overwhelming act of faith. Dr. Finkelstein told us that he was in Washington just last week and spoke with one of the Supreme Court justices who told him that the outcome of this case would be difficult to predict. Just last week, no one could foresee that the decision would be a unanimous one! The fact that it was is not only a tribute to our highest tribunal: it is a tribute to the strength and power of American democracy. And, in these days, it is wonderful and exhilarating to know that democracy is still strong and courageous, that it is not merely an abstract ideal but a concrete reality. Indeed, at a time when many of us are depressed at the turn of world affairs—at a time when most of us are sorely distressed at the Senate of our United States degenerating and disgracing us—at a time when we are seriously worried about liberty and freedom—precisely at such a time, the highest court of the United States reaffirmed the essential democracy of this land. It proclaimed officially and fearlessly that discrimination is evil and therefore can no longer be permitted. It acted in keeping with the religious teaching of our Torah and of our rabbis, the religious teaching accepted by our daughter-religion, Christianity, the faith that all men are brothers, that we are all children of one God. It has helped make a reality of the biblical injunction "Thou shalt love thy neighbor as thyself," of the teaching "Justice, justice shall ye pursue." The first man and woman in the Garden of Eden were not depicted as white or black or red or yellow. The parents of all mankind were simply human beings, and the color of skin never had a place in asserting human values. The world, however, did not readily accept the teachings of our faith. Every group felt that it was superior, innately superior, born superior. There is a Chinese legend which tells that man came from clay. God first baked some clay, but it burned and came out black. He therefore rejected it. Then, he prepared the next brick of clay out of which he would create man. But he took it out of the fire too soon and it was a pale color. That was not good either. The third attempt was successful—the clay brick was neither burnt nor underdone, neither black nor white. It was yellow or tan, a medium color—just right. Similar legends can be found among other peoples, each trying to show that its particular group is the best, is chosen by God because of group superiority. Do we not know, in our own day, the pagan myth of the superiority of all blond hair and blue eyes, the "Aryan" race? The Torah is therefore all the more amazing in insisting that every race and every nation is created in the same image as the Jew and therefore must be treated with the dignity befitting God's creatures. Rabbinic literature reflects the same lack of chauvinism, the same demand for respect and equal treatment for all. Whereas other religions may have condemned to perdition all who did not accept its teachings, the rabbis taught the righteous of every nation have a share in salvation and that we should encourage non-Jews to be faithful to their own traditions and highest beliefs.

The founding fathers of America were quite familiar with the Bible and were deeply influenced by our religious teachings. On the Liberty Bell, they inscribed a verse from last week's sidra: "And ye shall proclaim liberty throughout the land, to all the inhabitants thereof." No one could say that we have actually carried out democratic principles throughout all of

American life, but we have continually spread those principles throughout more and more of life. At one time, we had slavery, but a great president and a determined people put an end to that. At one time, Jews were not permitted to enter certain areas of American life. These areas have now been narrowed down, limited, virtually eradicated. And soon we shall be able to say that at one time people happened to be born of a different color used to be subjected to inferior education, to the insult of segregation, to the disgrace of not being able to contribute the best of an individual's abilities and capabilities; but, on May 17, 1954, the Supreme Court of the United States rendered a decision that advanced liberty and spelled triumph for our religious and democratic convictions.

I fully recognize that implementation and transition may be slow and difficult. It is very hard to eradicate prejudice, even though it be irrational and completely unfounded. Some of the rabbis at the convention asked me if I, occupying a pulpit in the South, would preach on the Supreme Court decision this Friday night, and I told them that I most assuredly would do so. It so happens, I said, that my congregation, fortunately, does not need such a talk as much as other, more prejudiced ones would. But even we must have brought before us the great *spiritual* accomplishments of this week. I am sure that even though no one has actually expressed their bias to me, personally, there no doubt must be some anti-Negro prejudice, even among our people. If there is such, I can only say unhesitatingly that such prejudice is *absolutely* unfounded and is *unequivocally* irreligious. One cannot be prejudiced and be true to God! One cannot be biased and believe in the Jewish or Christian religion! Negroes are not born more or less intelligent than whites, are not born slower or quicker than whites, are not born with any different brain capacity from other peoples. If we find some who are poor and apparently unintelligent, we find whites who are the same. If we find some who are slow, we find whites the same. If you believe the charge that Negroes exude a peculiar odor, you must know that every human being does. I can but repeat the statement of Marshall Wingfield: "Prejudice is not held against people because they have evil qualities. Evil qualities are imputed to people because prejudices are held against them." We can rest assured that once Negroes are given the same opportunities as other people, given the same kind of education and the same social and economic opportunities, we will find that they think, act, react, produce, and create the same as other citizens. Perhaps the South has not had much chance to find this out until now; now, it will have the opportunity.

And it *is* a great opportunity. Now, many more boys and girls will grow up to contribute to the welfare of our communities and of our country. Until now, we have foolishly withheld from ourselves a great source of better citizenry. Once the insult of segregation is removed and our schools are opened up to the children of every member of our community, we shall produce a more educated and more tolerant population. Remember that all children attending the same school is democracy in action. It is more than removing a stigma from colored children, and it is more than giving all children equal educational opportunities. It also means a lessening of all prejudice. We are afraid of or dislike that which we do not know or are unfamiliar with. Once all children begin going to school together and playing together, they will grow up to be friendly with one another, to understand one another, to cooperate, and to live in harmony.

And let me point out that the charge that Negroes and whites will come to intermarry is as false as the statement that intergroup marriage of Jews and Christians will ensue because they attend the same school and play together. We do not wish *any* group to disappear! *All* groups are valuable and have something important to contribute to the welfare of society. But it is the duty of the home to teach particular values and to make the group way of life so attractive and so wonderful that its young people will seek to preserve it, marrying only within the group. The role of the public schools in a democracy, on the other hand, is to teach children how—while maintaining their own group identity—at the very same time, to live together harmoniously, to know one another and cooperate with each other, to live as friends and brothers.

This goal, thanks to the Supreme Court decision, is now in the realm of reality. We no longer pay lip service to the ideal of democracy; now, we can *live* it. God grant that the verse from Leviticus engraved on the Liberty Bell will be deeply engraved on the hearts and minds of each one of us: "And ye shall proclaim liberty throughout the land, to all the inhabitants thereof."

1955

1955

§2 Thomas Buford Maston

Thomas Buford Maston, born on November 26, 1897, was the youngest of four sons born to Samuel and Sarah Maston. The Mastons lived in Jefferson County, Tennessee, during Thomas' youth. He received his bachelor's degree from Carson-Newman Baptist College in 1920. He then moved to Fort Worth, Texas, to attend Southwestern Baptist Seminary. While at Southwestern, Maston married fellow seminary student Essie Mae McDonald, and both Thomas and Essie began teaching at the school. After Southwestern, Maston enrolled at Texas Christian University, graduating with a master's in sociology. Over time he became concerned with ethics and the everyday application of Christian teachings. No program existed within the Southern Baptist seminaries specifically focused on ethics, so in hopes of forming such a program, Maston first went to Yale to earn a Ph.D. While there, Maston worked under H. Richard Niebuhr, one of the most prominent social ethicists of his generation. During his schooling, Maston's first son, Tom, was born. An injury caused cerebral palsy, and so Essie quit teaching to take care of their incapacitated son. T. B. Maston returned to Texas after Yale and started a program in Christian ethics. Maston taught at Southwestern Seminary from 1922 to 1963. During his time as a professor, he also devoted considerable energy to the civil rights movement. Maston wrote twenty-seven books and numerous articles on Christian approaches to global issues such as racism. Maston passed away on May 1, 1988, at the age of ninety. His papers are housed at the Southern Baptist Historical Society.

This address before the Southern Baptist's Christian Life Commission offers a near ideal example of Aristotelian organizational principles; it cleaves neatly into three general points: What is the origin of racism? What does the Bible say about racism? What should we do about racism? Each of these broader categories is further divided into subpoints. Concerning the origin of racism he notes: it is a universal problem—we are in the midst of a world crisis where the majority of humans are dark-complected and losing patience; it has economic and political aspects, but it is most importantly a spiritual and moral problem. Concerning the Bible's treatment of racism, he offers a barrage of memorized scriptural passages while patiently telling his audience that there is no need to open the book and try to flip through all of them. Familiar themes here are unity of origin, the image of God, and universal salvation. Perhaps his most unusual inclusion is the antimaterialist vein. If we had a cotton scale, and put any single human on one side, and tried to balance it with all the material things in existence, the one human would outweigh the totality of material reality. Concerning our proper response to racism, his answers are blunt: recognize the problem; stay calm; do not let fear of intermarriage make you do the wrong thing; apply Christian ideals as best you can; side with those who wish for education to exist for all; obey the law; and face up to the realities of what the U.S. Supreme Court and Christianity require.

❧❧

I Have Not a Demon

August 18, 1955
Christian Life Conference

This morning the discussion is on the teachings of the Bible concerning race and relations. I want to say three things introductory as we begin.

First of all is that race feelings or race prejudices are universal, or at least practically so seemingly universal—at least so far as I have been able to find out. I find folks every once in a while who claim that they have no racial prejudice. I do not make that kind of a claim. I think practically all of us have some racial prejudice. There are many factors that contributed to that racial prejudice—I do not believe that racial prejudice is innate. I do not believe that we are born with it. I think there is at least one psychological basis for it, but I do think we have naturally an aversion for those who are drastically different from the norm—from the generally accepted—and if the norm for our group is to be white then we may have an aversion for those who differ very noticeably from it—that norm. I think we see that a little bit in our attitude toward those who are deformed—toward those who are peculiar—who are eccentric—if extreme, we tend to have an aversion for them; we tend to withdraw from them—and if there is any psychological basis for racial prejudice, I think that's about all there is to it. But I do not think that it is inborn, that it is innate—I do think that our racial prejudices in the main are caught like we catch the measles—we're exposed. The environment in which we live is highly charged with racial prejudice. It would be a miracle if we did not become prejudiced. It is a part of our social heritage in being exposed to the prejudice that we ourselves become prejudiced to some degree. You see that in children. In the main at least you have noticed small children in communities where there are those of different racial groups they do not have any aversion for playing one with the other, from a free association with one another. But as they get older, and their associates, and sometimes their parents, and shame on us, sometimes even Sunday school teachers and church workers tend to build these prejudices in too.

You remember what the Quaker said—I've heard it quoted one time since I've been here—that all the world is peculiar except me and thee—and sometimes I think thee is a little peculiar. And we do have some tendency to withdraw from those that are a little peculiar. And incidentally, I do not know that there is anything that will come nearer testing how much we've caught of the Spirit of Christ than our attitude toward those who are different—and I mean different along [word missing] lines—I'm talking about the handicapped—I'm talking about the crippled—I'm talking about the infirmed—I'm talking about the one who is mentally handicapped even—and shame on us for the attitudes in the main that we have toward them.

The second thing introductory that I want to say is just a little bit about the scope of the race problem. It is worldwide—it is a major factor in the world crisis of our day. It is found in the Orient, in Africa, among the colored peoples in general around the world. There is a color consciousness at the present time that we have not had. At least it is more vocal than it has been anytime in the past so far as I know. Pearl Buck says something like this somewhere—I'm not real sure, but Pearl Buck has said this—that the deep patience of the colored people is at an end—that colored people around the world—and we need to remember that about three-fourths of the people of the world are colored to some degree—that their deep patience is at an end.

Many of you are well acquainted with Frank Laubach's little book *Wake Up or Slow Up*, and Frank Laubach there deals with the march of the masses.

Now all of those masses are not colored, but many of those masses are colored, and it is Frank Laubach who says that that march of the masses is inevitable and irresistible. That those marching masses will run over any people who get in their way—the masses are on the move and many of those masses are colored people. A missionary of ours from Nigeria some time ago—about two or three years ago—told me that she did not believe that we had as missionaries and as missionary people more than ten years in Nigeria because of the growing national consciousness and the growing color consciousness of the people. Now more recently I have talked to other missionaries from Nigeria, and they're not quite as pessimistic. They say that about 50 percent of the missionaries will be permitted to remain—those who have identified themselves to a considerable degree with the people—they will be allowed to remain—but the others will not—they will be forced out. That movement is on everywhere. We see it not only in Africa, but we see it in other places as well. Now the statement is made that that period has been moved up to five years and that has been true by some.

I heard a Negro some time ago who made this statement—that we're not going to settle the problems of the world without doing something about Africa—that we must settle the problem of Africa. The same thing could be said not just of Africa but of the Orient and elsewhere.

Now what about in our own country—there are many racial problems—not just the Negro problem of the South, but we have had at least a very acute Japanese problem on the West Coast—not as acute now as it was a few years ago, but it was in there. There are some areas in the Southwest where we still have the Spanish-American problem. Some of you have probably found some communities or know of some communities where there is a very acute prejudice against our Mexican friends or our Spaniard friends. There are other problems, but the most acute problems that we have at the present time is the Negro problems, or the white-Negro problems that we have in the South. It's closer to home to most of us and we're touched more vitally by it than any of these others—at least that's true of most of us. And there's been an increase in pressure and tension due to the Supreme Court decision of last May—May 1954. And then of course we've had this more recent decision, implementing largely the action of May 1954 leaving it up to the local communities, to the states—to the federal court in those areas.

Now isn't it correct that the implications, at least of the Supreme Court decision, created for us a lot of trouble. It's going to be the most serious revolution that the South has had since the days of Reconstruction, and we'd better be realistic about it.

Now one other thing introductory that I want to say and that's the nature of the race problem. The problem or problems that we face in regard to race relations are economic and political to a degree, but they're primarily moral and spiritual. Do not let anybody, as one of our denominational editors in the South attempted to do at the Southern Baptist Convention, brush this problem aside by saying that it is a political problem. It is not a political problem primarily—it is basically a moral and a spiritual problem. Now that's the reason why we feel justified, at least I do and I hope you do in discussing this kind of thing—in a week like this where we are dealing with the teachings of the Bible. Someone has described it as American Christianity's test case. American Christianity's test case is what are we going to do about our great problems. Many of you are acquainted with Myrdal's two big volumes that he wrote a [few] years ago, a Swedish sociologist brought over here for the special purpose of making a study of our race problems—an objective study by somebody from the outside—and you remember that when he completed that study, he gave that study the title "An American Dilemma." And by the American Dilemma he suggested that he meant this: that in America we have a dilemma between our ideals on the one hand and our very imperfect application of those ideals on the other hand to the Negro problems and that itself has created for the American a dilemma within his own soul—within his own conscience. There's a conscience in them—and that is particularly true of the southern white Christian. There is a conflict within—the conscience—within the thinking, of the southern white man, and particularly is that true of the southern white who is a Christian. Because certainly all of us—it doesn't make any difference what may be our final conclusions—of what we ought to do—certainly all of us will agree that our practice has fallen far short of our theory. That is true in the practice of our democratic ideals—it is true of our Christian ideals.

Now let's turn to the Bible—what about the Bible? What does the Bible have to say? Will the Bible give us any guidance, give us any help in regard to this race issue or these race issues that we face?

Now let me say again as I said the other day that there are some things on which we can find very specific guidance from the Bible—chapter and verse—and I do not belittle—I know a good many preachers do—but I do not belittle the use of proof texts where you can find a good proof text and not take it out of its context. No, I think it's perfectly all right to use them. But when we come to the study of the teaching of the Scriptures concerning race and race relations, we're going to have to depend largely upon some fundamental principles that we find there and make the application to those principles to the problem. Because so far as we can find in the Old Testament or New Testament they did not have anything exactly parallel to the problem that we have in our country in the relationship of white and Negro. So we find some fundamental principles, however, that are very important. And I'm inclined to believe that many times those fundamental principles are more important than any specific Scriptures that we can find. Now what do we find in the Scripture? Very little that is directly on race but some tremendously significant principles that can be applied to the race problem and should be applied to the race problem. Now again, I'm assuming that all of us as Christians believe in the authority of the Scriptures—that where the Scripture speaks that that is final. I'm going to state these as propositions and I think state them distinctly enough and clear enough and I hope slowly enough that if you care to you can take them—that's entirely up to you.

The first of those propositions that we find—certainly in the Bible—that is, that all people and races come from one family stock. We do not have several sources for the races of the world; we have only one source for a human race, from one family stock. We find that certainly in the record of the creation of man and woman. Then we find it over and over again in the Scriptures certainly implied and stated: Acts 17:26, "And he made from one every nation and man that live on all the face of the earth having determined allotted periods and boundaries of their habitation." He made from one or made of one. That statement was in Paul's address or sermon at Athens. And the context if you will read it will show that Paul was stressing that there was one God and that this God was the Creator of the world. He was the Lord of heaven and earth. The Cambridge Bible in its comments on this particular verse suggests that they are made of one—that is that all are created by God; that he is a Creator of all. The Athenians were a proud people. They made a sharp distinction between the Greeks and the barbarians, and everybody who wasn't a Greek was a barbarian. But Paul says that all are creations of God—he puts a Jew on the same plane as a Greek. Now if Paul were speaking in Athens or Birmingham or Dallas or Jackson, Mississippi, what application would he be making? See what I mean. God is the creator of all. That puts all on the same plane certainly, in the presence of God. He also stresses that nations are dependent upon God. He determines their status—the time when they will arrive and when they will fall. God is the final arbitrator—the verses following this twenty-sixth verse of the seventeenth chapter—those verses reveal the one purpose of God and all the blessings that he gives to men—that they might seek God and find him.

Seek him—feel after him, and the picture there is like a blind man groping in the dark—feeling—seeking—groping but what does Paul add—you remember what he adds, "Yet he is not far from every one of us." From every one? Yes. From the Athenians? Yes. From the Jews? Yes. Now this last statement there—and that is that science agrees with the Bible. Science generally speaking agrees with the Bible that all men sprang from the common stock. Just one quote from Ruth Benedict, "The Bible story of Adam and Eve, the father and mother of the whole human race, told centuries ago is the same truth that science has shown today that all people of the earth are a single family and have a common origin." Well, that's personal, the first one—I do not suppose there is any question on the part of any one about that—that if we go back far enough we all come from one family stock.

Now the second statement is this—or the second proposition—that is that man was created in the image of God. We might vary a little bit—and there [have] certainly been various interpretations of what that image may mean—but certainly one thing it means was that he was created a spiritual being. Man was created in the image of God; he was made for communion with God; he was made for fellowship with God. And if this is true of all men—men of all nations of all races—of all colors—they are created in the image of God. Pretty hard for us to realize that sometimes, isn't it? And pretty hard sometimes for us to feel that it is really true when we come in contact with some people. But God has created man for fellowship with himself. A spiritual being. All men.

A third proposition—and we'll come back to one or two of these in just a moment—the third proposition is that Christ died for all men. And one reason that he died for all men was to restore the image of God that had been marred or damaged by the fall. Now my viewpoint is—not entirely lost—no—there's a point of contact there, at least enough left there that there's a point of contact for the gospel. But one purpose of Christ's dying was that he might restore to completeness—to fullness—his image that had been marred through sin. And how grateful all of us are, and certainly every one of us, I am sure, [is] grateful for the whosoevers of the gospel. Whosoever. No restriction here.

Now the fourth proposition and that is that the human person as such is of infinite worth and dignity—worth more than all things material. Now, what does that mean? Does that mean any human person? Yes. Any human person—anywhere—is worth more than all things material. Some of you can remember because I am sure some of you have picked cotton—and you know the old kind of scales that they used to weigh cotton—at least I think they use them in the main even yet—you have balances over here. Now I like to think of those scales demonstrating to some degree the thing we are talking about here. If you could take the whole material universe and put it over here on the one side of that scale, and put one human soul over here, that human soul weighs more than all the things material—all things. Now is that true of the blackest little pickaninny in our community—yes, it is. Just as true as it is of one of us—just as true as it is of our own in our own home. The human person is of infinite worth and dignity.

Here's where we're going back a little bit—what is it that gives him his worth and dignity—the two things that we've just suggested, and that is created in the image of God, and that Christ came and died for him. Christ came and died for him—the fact that he's created in the image of God and Christ came and died for him—to restore that image—that makes him of infinite worth and value. Now you folks, I do not believe that there's anything—I cannot think of anything, any truth in the gospel that will do really more for us than for that truth to really grip our soul—I mean not just be a theory—but to really grip our souls that any individual—anywhere under God's shining sun—is of infinite worth and dignity simply because he is a person created in the image of God—a person for who Christ died. I say to young people quite often in talking with them about their going to the foreign mission field—that if you do not love people just because they are people—you'd better not go to the foreign field. But I would say the same thing about those of us who work here in the homeland: "We're not going to work and work very effectively with the people unless we love people just because they are people—not because of the color of their skin—no. Not because of where they live—not because of conditions surrounding them nor because of what they have but because they have been created in the image of God, and Christ died for them.

I made a trip to Latin America last summer—when I woke up this morning I was thinking that one year ago I was in South America, visiting our mission field. Before I went to the mission fields in South America to visit our work there, I had heard of course a lot about a lot of folks, but there's one particular missionary that I had heard a great deal about and folks had told me, "There isn't a better missionary in South America than so and so," I'll not call his name. About a year ago I went with him and a small group of young women to a slum section in Rio, for a Thursday afternoon service that they had every Thursday afternoon. Up on one of those hills overlooking the main part of the city—that's interesting, isn't it, their slums are up on the hills and the mountains—where we have our better residential sections. But up on one of these hills they'd had a service inside—some of those children had come clean that day—it was a terrible slum condition and under which they would live—some of the children would come clean—a lot of them would come dirty—filthy, filthy. After these young women had had the service we had a group of them outside and took their pictures—and I noticed this missionary that I had heard so much about hunker down—you understand what "hunker down" means—put his arm around one of these little Negro boys and talked to him—I don't know what he was saying to him but put his arm around him and as he got up patted him on the head—and I think that day I saw something of his secret of the greatness of the missionary. Here's a dirty little black boy—and what does he do? Cultured, refined university, seminary graduate—doctor's degree—and earned at that, and he gets down and puts his arm around a little Negro boy and talks to him and pets that dirty, filthy head of his, and I imagine it had vermin in it at the time—pats that head with his hand. I bet about half of you know who I'm talking about—the cause—Edgar Halleck. Edgar Halleck knew that that little old pickaninny in the slums of Rio was one who was created in the image of God and Christ died for him. How the effectiveness of what we do is going to be determined to a considerable degree by how much of that spirit we have—is that right? Well, okay.

Now, a fifth proposition is this—that we as children of God are in the family of God. Now I'm not talking about universal fatherhood of God and the universal brotherhood of man. I do think, though, as Baptists that we are a little too scared of it sometimes. I do think we need to remember this other thing—certainly one is not a child of God until he has become a child of God by accepting Christ. How that's so—we can put a peg down there—but we do need to remember this other thing—and that is that God has the fatherly attitude even to those who have not become his children because they are his potential children. But anyway, if we are children of God then we are in the family of God—and what does that make us? That makes us brothers and sisters in Christ. Now I know that sisters don't like to be called sisters—but they're sisters whether they like it or not. We're brothers and sisters in Christ. I never will forget a few years ago when it gripped me for the first time the tremendous implication of the first two words in that model prayer, "Our Father." "Our Father." Now what does it mean? It means this to me—that the blackest man in the heart of Africa—that the most isolated individual in the world—anywhere, that the most deprived — well, it doesn't make any difference, you can just put anything you want to in that—if that individual knows Christ as his personal Savior, he has as much right to pray that prayer as I have or anyone else. "Our Father." "Our Father." And when I pray "Our Father" I'm praying with every other man and woman, boy and girl, in the world who knows Christ as Savior. "Our Father, who art in heaven." Now brother, again, and sister, if that will really grip us that will do something to us too. "Our Father." We're in a family. Now you may have, I hope you do not have, but you may have a brother or sister and they may do some things that you don't like—and maybe you'd just kind of like to disown them—but nevertheless it doesn't change the relationship in the family—we're in a family. And incidentally, and some of you won't like this I guess—I incidentally, I never have thought that in a family that because there was one child in the family that maybe we didn't like and maybe his table manners were not good and such as that—that we'd push him off in the kitchen—better be careful—pushing him off in the kitchen.

Okay—another proposition—here we're going to stop a little longer—and that is that God is no respecter of persons. You remember the background for the first statement of that we find in the New Testament—we find in Simon Peter and the house of Cornelius—the truth of the business is, it's the very first words they spoke. Acts 10:34, truly I perceive that God shows no partiality—that's the Revised Standard Version or that God is no respecter of persons. What had brought Peter to that conclusion? Well, you reconstruct it—let me just mention some of it. What had happened? Cornelius over here had been praying. Cornelius who was a good man—who gave alms—and he prayed and God heard him pray. God heard his prayers and God said to Cornelius, you remember, "Well, now you send some messengers over to Joppa over there, there is a fellow by the name of Peter and you invite him to come over." Now while Cornelius was praying over here, what about Brother Peter. Peter was up on a housetop and he was doing a little praying. He was up there I think waiting for dinner—well, we know that he was hungry, he said he was hungry—and as he prayed—did you ever go to sleep when you prayed—I don't know that Peter did, but it said he went up on a housetop to pray and it also said he had a trance up there—I don't know whether he went to sleep and had a dream or not—but nevertheless that trance of his revealed something very appropriate for a hungry man. You remember the story. You remember that Brother Peter said to the Lord, "No, I can't eat anything unclean—no, can't do it." And the Lord said, "Now don't you call anything unclean that I've made." That was repeated twice—three times. Peter waked up and he was wondering, "Well, what in the world does all this dream mean, what does all this trance mean? And then the word was sent to him there are some folks downstairs who want to see you. He went down and he invited them in—that's a violation of his social position. He invited them in. And he housed them that night—he went with them—went back to Cornelius' house. You remember what he said when he entered Cornelius' house. You know now, you know that it's against the traditions and customs of a Jew for me to do this kind of thing. Because a Jew is not supposed to go in the house and eat with those who are not Jews. Then Brother Cornelius told him the experience that he had had. Then Peter starts his sermon and he says, "I perceive that God is no respecter of persons"—"that God shows no partiality." You know what I wish—and I don't mean to be catty about this at all—I wish that a lot of Southern Baptists, including a lot of Southern Baptist preachers, could have a vision on a housetop if it would do for them what it did for Peter.

He came to the conclusion that God is no respecter of persons—now a little later he kind of reneged on that a little and Brother Paul had to get him straightened out. You remember when Peter went to Jerusalem and reported about this experience that he had had in Cornelius' house, you remember that some of the circumcision party criticized him, asking him, why did you go to uncircumcised men? This shows that the result of that vision was social as well as spiritual. We have lots of folks saying, "God is no respecter of persons"—that just means salvation. All men are under condemnation—he has provided one method of salvation—now let's hope that that's not all it means. This idea that God was no respecter of persons or was impartial must have been very simple in the thinking of the New Testament writer. We find the idea specifically mentioned in four or five places and implied over and over again. If you have your Bibles there I want us to open to two or three of those places—I think maybe three if we have plenty of time. Romans—second chapter—we begin reading I believe at the sixth verse—it breaks right into a sentence, but you know of course that some of Paul's sentences were very long. "For he will render to every man"—that is, God will render to every man according to his works to them that by patience in well-doing seek for glory and honor and incorruption, eternal life, but unto them that are factious and obey not the truth, but obey unrighteousness shall be wrath and indignation, tribulation and anguish upon every soul of man that worketh evil of the Jew first and also of the Greek—but glory and honor and peace to every man who worketh good to the Jew first and also to the Greek for there is no respect of persons with God. God does not look on the outer countenance. God is not partial; he is no respecter of persons.

Then Ephesians—Ephesians 6:9, where he is talking to the master. I think we'll start with the fifth verse. "Servants be obedient to them that according to the flesh are your masters with fear and trembling in singleness of your heart as unto Christ—not in the way of eye service or men-pleasers but as servants of Christ doing the will of God from the heart—with good-will doing service as unto the Lord and not unto man—knowing that whatsoever good thing each one doeth the same shall be received again from the Lord whether he be bond or free. And ye masters do the same thing unto them and forbear threatening, knowing that he who is both their master and yours is in heaven and this one who is in heaven is no respecter of persons." There is no respecter of persons with him. They're on the same basis.

Now we'll not take time to turn to Colossians 3:25, but we'll find similar emphasis in Colossians 3:25 and we find similar emphasis in 1 Peter 1:17. But I do want us to turn to James, second chapter—now I know that James is talking about a different type of partiality or respect, but I think the principle would apply. He is talking about in the church; and he's talking about a respect for the well-to-do in contrast to the poor, to the common people. "Now brethren hold not the faith of our Lord Jesus Christ the Lord of Lords with respect of persons." James 2. Go to eighth and ninth verses. "How be it if ye fulfill the royal law according to the scriptures to love thy neighbor as thyself, ye do well; but if you pay respect of persons ye commit sin—being convicted by the law as transgressors." Are we respecters of persons even in our churches? I'm afraid we are. He says that we're not to be—that we're not to be.

Okay—another proposition is this: that Jesus reveal the Father's attitude toward all men. We've just suggested that God was no respecter of persons—showed no partiality. Jesus revealed that attitude. We see his attitude revealed in his general relationship to men—but in particular in the area that we're interested in here is his relationship to an attitude toward the Samaritan. They were the ones most hated by the Jew—you know of course that the Jews in going from Galilee to Jerusalem for festival occasionally—most of them at least would not go through Samaria at all. They hated the Samaritans very much—would not go through Samaria. It was the woman at the well who stated the general attitude when she said to Jesus, "The Jews have no dealings with the Samaritans." Now so far as we know Jesus did not have any opportunity—any contact with the black man—with the Negro—but he did with a Samaritan. I think that his attitude toward the Samaritan and his relationship to the Samaritan—we will find what would be his attitude toward any of the outcasts of society—or racial group. Now what do we find—on one occasion when the Jews were thoroughly provoked with Jesus and did not know how to answer him, they blurted out, do you remember?

They blurted out, "Thou art a Samaritan and have a demon." That's in John 8:48. We'll not take time to turn to it. What was Jesus' answer? His answer was, "I have not a demon, I honor my Father and you dishonor me." Now, do you notice his reply—he doesn't say anything about the charge that he was a Samaritan. Thou art a Samaritan—and you have a demon. Well, he says, I don't have a demon—didn't say anything about the charge that he was a Samaritan. What would be the closest thing to that today in the average southern community? I really think now about the closest thing to it would be for somebody to charge that you are a Negro—that would be about the closest thing to it. You're a Negro. Jesus didn't think there was anything bad about being accused of being a Samaritan, he didn't pay any attention to that charge at all. You know what they did that day is one of our favorite ways of answering people—of trying to answer people—that we really cannot answer. He had stumped them. They could not answer him. For they do what? They put a label on him—yes, they put a label on him. He's a Communist or he's a socialist. And a lot of that has been done in recent weeks concerning the Supreme Court decision and concerning some other things. You remember on another occasion he healed ten lepers. There was only one of the ten who returned to express his gratitude, and Jesus called special attention to the fact that that one was what? A Samaritan—they hated Samaritans—and Jesus' attention of that to his disciples who were Jews. In no instance does Jesus reveal more fully his skill in dealing with the spiritual problems of individuals than with the woman at the well—the Samaritan woman. Here Jesus crossed over the highest possible barriers to reach her. The barrier of sex—he's a man, talking to a woman. He crosses over the barrier of moral condition. She's an immoral woman; she's living in adultery—but Jesus crossed over that barrier to reach her. But he also crossed the racial or national barrier—she was a Samaritan. And she it was, as suggested a while ago, who said to him, "Jews don't have any dealings with Samaritans." But Jesus was not a typical Jew. You remember the rest of that story, and we'll not take time to try to refresh your minds on it at all, but you'll also remember that the first really great revival outside of Jerusalem was in Samaria. And I wonder if the explanation is not the fact that Jesus had stopped there—that he had talked to the Samaritan woman, that she had believed, that many others had believed—some because of her testimony and others because they had heard Jesus personally because he remained there a couple of days and there was a great revival. One of the greatest of his parables and some think the greatest was the parable of the Good Samaritan. Now did Jesus pick out the Samaritan deliberately? Certainly. Jesus didn't do anything by accident.

Here is a man who fell among thieves. The implication is of course that that man was a Jew. He fell among thieves—they beat him up, they robbed him, they left him beside the road half dead. Who comes along? The priest comes along, but he wraps his righteous robes around him and goes by on the other side. The Levite—or, I started to say the deacon—but I'm a deacon myself and I'd better not put that label on him—the Levite comes along—and he likewise goes by on the other side. But the Samaritan comes along and he stops. He anoints his wounds, he takes him in to the inn, he pays the bill, and he said, "Now if there is anything left—anything over—I'll pay it when I come back." And you remember the question that Jesus asked the lawyer at the end of that, he asked him this, "Who was neighbor unto him that fell among thieves?" And that old Jewish lawyer could not bring himself to use the naughty word "Samaritan." He said, "He that showed mercy unto him that fell among thieves." He that showed mercy. Jesus used this Samaritan very deliberately I think in this illustration.

And then one other thing about his attitude toward the Samaritan. You remember as we found it recorded in Acts 1:8, Luke's record of the Great Commission, after power has come upon you etc., then what? "Then ye shall be my witnesses, in Jerusalem, Judea, and Samaria, and the uttermost parts of the earth." Now again, Jesus doesn't do anything accidentally. And I do not believe it is any mere accident that Jesus added, "And Samaria." Why not "And Perea"? Why not "and somewhere else"? "And Samaria." Those were the people these Jews hated more than anybody else. He puts in "And Samaria."

Now I do not want to get aside from the thing that we're discussing, but I suspect most of us have got some place in our lives—some source of prejudice in our lives that we need an "And Samaria." And Samaria might be for us down there somewhere on the other side of the railroad tracks. Or it might be the big house up on the hill, you see. The people against whom we are prejudiced. And Jesus would say to us "Be sure that you . . . on Samaria," in the commission.

Two other things just briefly as propositions without necessity of discussing. We are to love our neighbor as ourselves. And remember now that Jesus never set a limit on neighbor. The Jew did, yes. The Jew would say according to Jesus' statement himself, "Thou shalt love thy neighbor and hate thine enemy. But I say unto you love your enemies." There was a lawyer in the story of the good Samaritan who wanted Jesus to build a fence for his "Who is my neighbor." Jesus didn't answer that question at all. He just answered a far more important question: "How can I be your neighbor?"

Last of those propositions is this: "To whom much is given, much will be required." That's a fundamental spiritual fact, that to whom much is given, much will be required. Now how does that apply to this race issue? As I see it, it applies in this way. We white people are the privileged—in the South at least. We're the majority. We have a primary responsibility to work out the problem or problems that we have in this area of work. It is basically our problem. Now certainly we need the cooperation of the minority group—but it is fundamentally our problem. And I am persuaded that God is going to hold us accountable for working it out. And for working it out on a Christian basis.

Now, what should Christians do concerning the race question in general and the segregation issue that we have right now in particular and I want to outline about five or six or seven different things that I think we ought to do.

One that I do not include in my outline here but one I believe I will state negatively and that is that as Christians we will not become identified with those who have set aside our Constitution. Who would set aside the ordinary procedure of government and say that the Supreme Court is all wrong—there's a bunch of Communists, etc. Now that means to me that we will not identify ourselves with these citizens' councils that are being organized everywhere. We'll encourage our people not to either.

These are things that I think we can do that we should do. First of all, recognize the seriousness of the problem created for the South. This is not going to be any easy thing. It is going to be extremely difficult. It's going to take years to do it. And there are going to be lots and lots of problems.

A second thing is to keep calm. Keep calm. Try to approach every phase of the problem coolly and objectively. Permit no superficial emotionalism. That means for me that we will not permit ourselves to be stirred up by political or religious demagogues. And don't forget we've got some religious demagogues as well as political. We'll keep calm. We'll be objective about this thing.

A third thing is this: that we will not let any scarecrow or bogeyman keep us from maintaining the attitudes that we should as Christians. Now the main boogerboo is intermarriage—you know that as well as I do. And we're not going to let that scare us away from doing what we ought to do as Christians. A lot of folks think that this whole thing is dangerous. Yes, it is dangerous—but I'll tell you it is dangerous to be Christian anyway. It's dangerous to be Christian. We ought to be Christian about it.

A [fourth] thing is this, that we'll apply the best we can the Christian spirit of this and every other phase of the race problem—I'm talking about the integration issue. That we'll apply the best we can the Christian spirit to this and every other phase of the race problem.

Fifth, that we will be on the side of those who defend our public schools. That we will not be a party to any program to eliminate them. I didn't hear an amen there and I thought I ought to. I'm terribly concerned—maybe you are not—but I am very much concerned that a lot of our Baptist people including some of our Baptist preachers are going to be on the wrong side on this whole issue.

All right—a sixth general statement is this—that we're going to be law-abiding citizens. And let us never forget this, that it is a part of our government set up that the Constitution of the United States means what the Supreme Court says it means. Now the Supreme Court may change sometimes and it does—but nevertheless—that's fundamental to our whole way of life. That our Constitution means what the Supreme Court says it does. The truth of the business is I don't see how they could have said anything else, do you?

All right, finally, my brethren, in our churches we must face up to the implications for us of the Supreme Court decision. And that isn't very easy. But what is far more important in our churches and in our church-related institutions is we need to face up to what the gospel means to us—not just the implications—but the specific teachings of the message we proclaim and the message that we claim to follow. What would it mean? It's not going to be easy to be really Christian. But at least we ought to make an honest attempt to be.

§3 Leo A. Bergman

Rabbi Leo A. Bergman was born on November 23, 1913, in Cleveland, Ohio. His parents, a barber and a housewife, had emigrated to Cleveland from Germany and Hungary on account of the growing Nazi menace. After graduating from Western Reserve University with a degree in chemistry, Bergman attended Hebrew Union College and graduated in 1940. Bergman served congregations in Boston, where he met his wife, Adelaide Hubbard, and in Rockford, Illinois, before coming to New Orleans' Touro Synagogue, one of the oldest synagogues in the United States, in 1946. Though a thoroughly committed "Yankee," Bergman's love for New Orleans was bound up with the cuisine and the culture. For nearly thirty years, Bergman moved his conservatively inclined Touro congregants toward an acceptance of desegregation and full civil rights for black Americans in the Crescent City.

Segregationists and White Citizens' Council members made life difficult for the Bergman family, so much so that many nights were spent away from the family home for fear of it being bombed. Unlike his fellow New Orleans rabbi Julian Feibelman at Temple Sinai, Bergman spoke out forcefully and often on civil rights—so much so that he often advertised sermon topics in local newspapers and on the synagogue's marquee. Not infrequently would the press attend and report on his sermons, leading often to friction with Touro's more conservative members. He and his wife, a concert cellist with the New Orleans Symphony Orchestra, had two sons, Lee and William. After retiring from Touro in 1976, Bergman taught religion at Loyola University. Bergman died on February 6, 1981. Several of his speeches are housed at the American Jewish Archives at Hebrew Union College in Cincinnati, Ohio.

In the days and weeks after his shocking murder, Emmett Till's name was heard in pulpits around the country. Typically those pulpits were in black churches. And typically those sermons were delivered shortly after Till's horrifically battered body had been discovered on August 31 or after the not-guilty verdict was returned by an all-white, all-male jury on September 23. At first blush, that Rabbi Bergman waited until November 18 to address the case appears curious, but in hindsight it's clear that he was still holding out hope for justice. That is, the accused killers, half-brothers J. W. Milam and Roy Bryant, while acquitted of murder in September, still faced the prospect of kidnapping charges in November—a kidnapping that they'd already confessed to two different police officers during their murder trial. But on November 8, a Leflore County grand jury refused to indict the men. Not long thereafter they confessed to both the kidnapping and the murder to journalist William Bradford Huie in *Look* magazine. In this address filled with righteous anger, Bergman invokes the example of Old Testament prophets and the ministry of Jesus as warrants to speak out against the absurdity and injustice of the verdict. In so doing Bergman commits some factual errors—Till was certainly not a "man" at fourteen, and he had not had anything to drink on the evening of August 24, when he whistled at Carolyn Bryant—but his outrage at Mississippi's behavior is tempered by several nonreligious signs—the most important of which he specifies as the white southerner's deep shame at the murder and the trial's outcome. Bergman is also acutely aware of the role of the press, and how the massive coverage of the case had fundamentally changed racial dynamics. No longer could white men "do anything to a nigger"—even in Mississippi.

❧

God Looks on Mississippi and Emmett Till
November 18, 1955
New Orleans, Louisiana

To the newspaper reporters and visitors to the congregation this evening I want to bid a warm and most cordial welcome. Then I want to hasten to add that whatever is written or spoken about my remarks this evening must make clear that I am speaking only for myself as an individual, *as I do every Friday evening.* I am NOT speaking for my congregation. I am NOT speaking for the Jews of New Orleans or Jews anywhere else. But most definitely I am speaking for myself and as a rabbi of the Reform Jewish faith who has been trained in a faith founded upon the prophetic message of the Bible.

This is a sermon I must preach, for myself and the sake of my soul if for no one else. For one whose calling is speaking there are many times in his lifetime when he would give much to recall the words that left his lips, on certain occasions. But I have discovered, too, that there are times when to be silent is never to forgive yourself. There are times when one who hears the responsibility of speaking the truth must speak, come what may, else he perverts his pulpit, himself, and his calling. For silence is also vocal. Too vividly I remember the meaning of silence when six million Jews were being slaughtered by the Nazis and the Christian Church and the Western democracies remained vocally silent.

To me the pulpit is the voice that must be made articulate when justice and righteousness and mercy are silenced. Mine is not the safe religion that says nothing, means nothing, and is nothing. My brand of religion stems back to Moses fighting the injustice of slavery imposed upon his people, to Amos, Isaiah, Jeremiah, who spoke forth against political, economic, and social injustice whenever and wherever they beheld it.

Was Jesus silent to injustice? To the defilers of the Temple he took a whip, and the self-righteous hypocrites who asked him to condemn a fallen woman—he whipped with the admonition: let him who is without sin cast the first stone. When the pulpit becomes safe, silent, and harmless then religion is dead in that pulpit. If you do not believe me read your own Bible.

If you have come to wallow in an orgy of emotion tonight, you had better leave now, for you will be disappointed. If any came to witness an impassioned outburst of melodramatic self-righteousness, you will be disappointed. I have little to share with you but my *tears,* my *pity,* and my *heartbreak.*

My tears are for the victim of violence, Emmett Till, and his mother. My pity is for America's ideal of justice that has been ravaged and shamed not once but twice. My heartbreak is for a great state that I know and admire and for a section of our nation that had at long last eradicated from its vocabulary and its records the stain of *lynch*. And now with one fell swoop has smashed the national goodwill it has carefully built over a quarter of a century. For no man, white or black, is safe where violence is rampant. For as long as the face is bashed in and a body beaten until unrecognizable, any man may escape the charge of murder. How could this happen in America? How could it be that there should be two kinds of justice—one for the man whose skin is white and one for the man whose skin is black? This is a travesty of American justice, if anything is.

At this moment in world history our nation is standing at the bar of history. The showdown is here and now. The people of the world, the majority of whom are colored, must take their cue either from America or Russia. Dare we proclaim ours is the way of Freedom, Equality, and Opportunity with the ghost of an Emmett Till to haunt our words? How the Communists must rejoice. Sumner, Mississippi, has handed them one of the greatest victories of the Cold War.

Anyone of intelligence who lives here and understands and loves the South knows full well the race problem is going to take time and intelligence, patience and goodwill on both sides before it will be solved. But it will not be solved by our hiding our heads in the sand—ostrich-style. Neither will it be solved by unyielding, unmoving, unthinking resort to prejudice, and jingoist slogans that scream about keeping the southern way of life. Greater than the southern or eastern or western way of life is the *American way of life*. And greater still is the Judeo-Christian way of life.

The gauntlet was long ago flung down. Not the Supreme Court and not the federal court and not the state court are going to solve the racial problem here in the South. It is a religious problem. Either the churchgoers and their ministers believe in the Fatherhood of One God and the Brotherhood of All Men—or they do not. God has no stepchildren. Either religion will prevail or fail. Catholics, Protestants, and Jews are on trial here in the South more so than anywhere else in the nation. A moral issue of faith confronts them, their emotions and their innate inborn reactions. Only a fool or a fanatic will deny the trying inner struggles they face. May God help them. I for one do not envy them the task of overcoming barriers of the ages.

One day, standing at one of the corners where my older son attends school was a man passing out handbills to the children to be taken home. I read it carefully. It told me that equality and brotherhood were terms typical of those used by Communists and Communist propaganda. I pray not! I pray not because if equality and brotherhood and justice are truly communistic then the Communists have stolen the most precious teachings of Christianity and Judaism; then the Communists have stolen the very foundations of America. If we no longer believe in these ideals and they are communistic—then cease now. The battle is lost before we begin.

Neither I nor the majority of fair-minded people in America may, I will emphasize—neither I nor the majority of thinking southerners—will be duped and deceived by red herrings no matter how crudely they be dragged across the trail.

We have been told that Emmett Till, a Chicago Negro visiting in Mississippi, while inebriated, insulted a white woman. For that he deserved the punishment as does any man who insults any woman. But you do not murder a man for words. When a white man insults a white woman when he has had one too many drinks, is he beaten to an unrecognizable pulp? Whoever said a drunken, insulting white man is one whit better than a drunk be he black, brown, or yellow?

And to take the law in one's hands is violence and to murder is lynching, no matter be it in Maine or Mississippi.

But when the culprits are brought to justice and not a Negro is on the jury because Negroes are not permitted to vote in that county, the mockery of justice is manifest.

When the identification of a body is disputed even when mother and uncle identify it, when a dead father's ring is found on it, then justice is betrayed. But when law officers claim the body has been planted by Communists, then justice is ravaged. The jury's verdict was not even necessary to complete the travesty.

Is Mississippi now safe for any murderer who bashes in the face of his victim? Is there anything hopeful about any aspect of the entire matter? I answer a most emphatic yes! Remember, if I am a damned Yankee, I am a northerner looking north from New Orleans, not a Northerner looking south. I have seen and known the South and come to appreciate and love it. Mine is a better perspective in many respects than that of either northerner or southerner. Last January in St. Louis a dignified, gracious lady, when she learned I was from New Orleans, informed me she too was from the South, from Corinth, Mississippi. Praying she had a sense of humor, I turned and answered her, saying, Compared to me she was a damn Yankee. Fortunately it struck her funny.

But what I am saying is that from down here I look up and see hope even in this tragic occurrence.

First: The full light of public information was shed on the case. Radio, press, American journalism covered it fully, exposing it to the nation and without any interference from the community or police. Justice is an American concern, a national issue.

Secondly: The case was brought to trial and the trial was held with dignity and fairness by the judge and prosecutor, who more than the police and the jury knew America, nay the world, was looking over the shoulder.

Thirdly: A Negro, Mose Wright, the uncle, dared testify with the protection of the court against white men whom he accused of murder.

Fourth: And this to me is most important, not once have I met a single solitary person who, in discussing the case, was not ashamed of it as a southerner, who was not aware of what the verdict would be, yet dared hope it would be otherwise, who as an American abhorred the vicious violence that was acquitted.

I understand the nerves of the people of Mississippi are stretched and strained to the breaking point about this case. I think I know why. The vast majority of the people of Mississippi are decent, upright, fine, wonderful people who are faithful to their state publicly, but privately ashamed of the disgrace and stain on their proud, noble escutcheon of honor.

I know the state of Mississippi fairly well. I have travelled through it often. Its people are gracious and hospitable and generous. Its roads are a motorist's dream—its police most polite. Its scenery is breathtaking. Its system of high school and junior colleges on the border of every two counties is an educator's dream. Its industry and agriculture are prosperous. In the last few years Mississippi has and will continue to surpass other southern states. Let the best of Mississippi prevail is my prayer.

Emmett Till is a martyr. He did not ask to be, he did not choose to be. Yet his death—pitiful, violent, and tragic—was not in vain. Mississippi will long remember Emmett Till. I doubt if there will ever be another Emmett Till lynching in the South. Never again will the spotlight of shame be permitted to focus on Mississippi.

God moves in slow, mysterious ways. Years ago I saw a horrible, shriveled little boy dancing for pennies on a street in a Delta town in Mississippi. When I asked how the child became so deformed, I was told a drunken white man soaked the boy with whiskey, then set him afire. In horror I asked how did they punish the white man. I was laughed at. "Are you kidding," I was told, "you can do anything to a 'nigger.'"

Today, a Negro can demand a trial in Mississippi. Someday he shall even receive justice—because of Emmett Till.

Amen.

§4 Clyde Gordon

Clyde Gordon was born on October 25, 1913, in Nicholson, Mississippi. At age three, he was pronounced dead of pneumonia, but began breathing again, to embark on what his son refers to as "the Borrowed Years" in the biography consulted for much of the information which follows. Six months earlier, his mother died of complications related to childbirth. The remainder of his childhood was spent with little schooling, much cotton picking, revolving homes, occasional homelessness, and a bout with smallpox. Though a white man, he experienced a caste system where people surrounding him knew of his immense misfortune and intended to exploit as well as perpetuate it. Though he originally intended to pursue a career in country music, he chose the ministry in the wake of his girlfriend's tragic death when a car hit her as she crossed the street while reading one of his love letters. Gordon attended New Orleans Baptist Bible Institute in 1931. He received room and board in the Baptist Rescue Mission in exchange for leading the singing during evening services and some cleaning. As the economy worsened this became untenable, and he left school to join the marines. On July 29, 1935, he married Mary Bloominger, who managed to raise four sons while furthering her education and career. She received her bachelor's degree and teaching certification from the University of Southern Mississippi in 1956 and her master's from Mississippi College in 1961. She was a teacher for thirty-eight years in Mississippi and Kentucky. Rev. Gordon was licensed and ordained in 1937. His early years as a minister required that he pastor four churches simultaneously while working full-time six days a week at a general store. Eventually he returned to seminary. He pastored churches in Mississippi from 1935 to 1963, and in Kentucky from 1963 to 1992, with the exception of 1967 to 1973, when he was a full-time evangelist.

The following sermon took place at First Baptist Church in Poplarville, Mississippi, in 1955. It is exceptional. Unlike other sermons featured with it, this sermon does not call the audience to immediate full integration. He reasons that full integration is too expensive, there would be bloodshed, crime would increase, and unprepared black students would slow down the progress of white students. But he does have an elaborate plan to begin integration immediately with graduate students first, then undergraduates, on the assumption that these people would be able to return to their communities to train African Americans on an equal basis so that meaningful integration will soon be possible. His vision is an invitation to all races to be educated with his wife, who was one year shy of earning her college degree, and soon to embark on graduate school. Another exceptional moment occurs when Rev. Gordon pleads to his congregation, "[D]on't have anything to do with the murder of anybody." He also addresses the issue of lynching and mob violence, specifically in the case of rape. For Rev. Gordon, vigilantism is a quotidian reality, even if Emmett Till had not been recently murdered elsewhere in the state. When he was barely a teen, a bystander with a big knife intervened when Gordon's guardian nearly beat him to death. As a young minister, when authorities refused to intervene, he led several dozen unarmed men to a mob-run brothel and speakeasy to tell them to leave town, and he would return armed if necessary. On another occasion, when rousting illegal taverns, he and another congregant disarmed the sheriff. In addition to his experience with lawless conflict, Rev. Gordon knows he speaks to the powers that be as well. Deacon and sheriff Osborne Moody is a member of the congregation, and four years later would be the authority charged with the duty of reporting to the FBI the abduction from jail and lynching of Mack Charles Parker, a young man accused of raping a white woman in Poplarville.

❧❦

A View of the Race Issue
1955
Poplarville, Mississippi

I call your special attention to that catching phrase in [Acts] verse 24: "God hath given thee all them that sail with thee." I can see in that verse a message for every Christian, everywhere, and in every era.

I want you to relax and open your hearts and minds this morning. I am completely conscious of the fact that the issue upon which I am speaking is controversial, and perhaps that is a good enough reason to speak on it. If it were all settled there would really be no need for this message. Also, if you listen with an open mind, you will be able to glean from it whatever truth it may contain. I am not going to speak passionately upon this message today, but reasonably and sanely. I'm not going to try to speak radically. This is a critical hour in our history, and we need our minds clear and free from radicalism and prejudice so that our actions may be guided by sanity and truth.

No issue ever arises that's too big for the church, and no minister should ever be afraid to speak on anything that concerns his people.

Why do I speak on this issue anyway? I remember a little story about a woman who didn't like the decision her husband made so she said, "If I were you I'd have more sense." He replied, "Indeed you would, dear, if you were me." So if you were me, maybe you would have more sense than to speak on this subject.

First and negatively: I do not speak on this subject to be sensational. If that were my purpose, I would have done it a year ago. I do not do so to stir up strife. I do not speak on this subject to please or displease anyone.

Positively: I speak on it because it is a major issue and the church should face foursquare and sanely any issue that is of such vital importance to the spirit and attitude of its people. Again, I speak because, as members of this church, you have a right to know what I, your pastor, think on this subject. So I'm giving you this morning what I think about it all.

History reveals that the problem of race relation is as old as the human race itself.

When Israel went down into Egypt, the Egyptians segregated the Jews by placing them in the land of Goshen, and there they lived and multiplied until centuries passed over their heads. They knew persecution and slavery and the merciless lash of the taskmaster until they were delivered by the mighty hand of God.

Then the Jews in Jesus' day segregated themselves from the Samaritans, giving as their reason that they were a generation of half-breeds, half-Jew and half almost anything else. So they had no dealings with the Samaritans. They wouldn't even so much as pass through their land. They would cross the Jordan River to the east and surround Samaria to go to Galilee.

I remember, also, that in the Second World War Hitler started race prejudice in Germany because he wanted to exploit the Jews, and that he did, killing thousands of them, and confiscating their wealth for his war machines. This he did, not because he hated them, but he used hatred and race superiority to make his dastardly deeds excusable. We all resented it very much when the Germans segregated themselves from the rest of the world, saying that they were the Aryans, the superiors. So the problem is not a new one at all. It is as old as civilization.

Just who is the Negro in our midst? I believe that a sane consideration of "who he is" will bring us to a better understanding of what our attitude should be toward him.

Biologists have divided the human group into three subdivisions called "races": the Mongoloid or "yellow race," the Negroid or "black race," and the Caucasoid or "white race." The major differences are skin color, eye form and color, texture and color of hair, nose shape, stature, and blood such as A, B, AB, O. Since this is a message on race relations and not the different aspects of the human race as a whole, let us consider the Negro.

He is a "Negro" and not a nigger.

That term "nigger" is a hangover from slavery. He is a "Negro," and the term is a dignified one. There is nothing wrong with it at all. The term "Negroid," referring to the black race of people, is just as dignified as the term "Caucasoid," referring to the white race.

Why is he black?

He is black for the same reason that I am white: because God, the all-wise Creator of the universe, made him so. God placed within every human body two chemicals that determine the color one shall be. They are carotene and melanin. Every human being has the two chemicals within him (except the albino), and his complexion is a function of the relative amounts of both elements present. Thus skin color is a quantitative rather than a qualitative matter. Where the carotene predominates, the skin is yellow, and the melanin in larger quantity makes the black man. The white man has a larger quantity of carotene than the yellow man; however, he still has the melanin within himself.

Where did the Negro come from?

There are some false impressions and conceptions that we need to fight bitterly today. Some of our writers try to take the Bible and prove by it that God is color-conscious and, in such an attempt, reveal a staggering ignorance of God and his word.

Some say that Noah placed a curse on Ham and he became black. That is not truth. It is not so stated in the Bible. Furthermore, Noah had nothing to brag about. After God so miraculously saved him and his loved ones from his judgment upon the world by water, the first thing Noah did was to spit in God's face by pitching a drunk. He looked like placing a curse on someone.

The Negro race, along with every one of us, had its beginning back there in Eden when God created Adam and Eve. They are the first parents and all of us had our beginnings in them.

Climatic conditions and geographical situations have had more to do with skin color than anything else. The chemicals in every human body were put there to take care of the race in specific localities to build up the outer body that it might withstand the heat of the sun and the attacks of nature.

Again: the Negro is a diamond in the rough.

He is a human being made in the image of God. The inexperienced eye would not realize the value of a diamond if he saw it in the rough, and would not offer you a dollar for one as large as a marble. And, yet, when that same diamond is properly cut and polished, it will bring a fortune. The same is true with minds and hearts, darkened by prejudice, they do not see the value of another race of human beings that live among us. They are as capable as any of us of reaching the highest.

Now how does he happen to be our problem?

He is our problem because our forefathers brought him to this country, and we have nothing to brag about on this point. We should be humbled by the fact that we brought the colored man to America. He is not an intruder. He did not migrate to America as others have done. Our forefathers went over to Africa and by every low method under heaven, including murder and kidnapping, brought him to these shores. Actually, whole tribes were completely wiped out by the white man. This stings a little but somehow history is merciless in its statements of facts.

The Negro is here but he is not the loser for it. The Negro race in America realizes it, and the following letter from a Negro proves what I stated: "We have gained from our experience and contact with you, and the American Negro is the best off of any other section of his group to be found anywhere on earth today. God be praised. We are not mad about being kidnapped and brought to America. And one of the characteristics of our group, of which we feel most proud, is that we can know of a certainty that we have been exploited and nurse no antipathies toward those who exploited us. So why should your group have hatred toward us."

Why is there a yellow race of Negro in America?

Before we pull our robes of self-righteousness too closely around us and look too smug, we had better consider this. It is not the fault of the Negro man, nor the Negro woman, nor the white woman, but the white man. One of our eminent Baptist preachers spoke to a large gathering of Negroes and just burned them up, verbally, for being so low morally. At the conclusion of his message the colored pastor arose and said, "We have just been told that we are a low race of people, and if you do not believe it is true, just look at the shade of this congregation." Our eminent minister stated that that was the sternest rebuke he had ever received and he would never forget it.

What shall be our attitude toward the Negro?

He is our responsibility. The Bible says, "God hath given thee all them that sail with thee." God has charged us with the responsibility of those who sail with us on the voyage of life. There is a principle as true as truth itself that I am my brother's keeper. God has also stated generally that "to whom much is given shall much be required." He who has what the world needs automatically becomes debtor to the world. Therefore, having what a race of people need, we are obligated to do everything within our power to lift them to a higher level. If we have an ugly spot on our lawn, it is up to us to elevate it and make it blend in with the rest of the yard. We feel that our neighbors might criticize if we do not. It is our duty to elevate the colored race that there may be no ugly spots of illiteracy and ignorance on the lawn of our citizenship.

Our first duty as Christians is to give him Christ. This is the greatest thing that one person can do for another.

To teach him. He is teachable. Some of the greatest minds America has ever produced have been the minds within a skull that was black. Booker T. Washington, George Washington Carver are two of America's greatest. They were looked up to by scientists and educators as leaders. We had just as well face it: we have never sincerely tried to teach them. If we had we would not be in this mess today.

We had better not exploit him.

Some make use of him basely for their own personal advantages and profit. Some say he has equal opportunities in our southland. That is not true. There are many places where he doesn't have [a] ghost of a chance. I know there are many people who would not do him wrong for anything, but there are others who will take what he has and build with it his own house, and feed and clothe his own children with what he takes from the humble Negro. Take from a man who does not have a ghost of a chance. Don't forget it, there is a just God on the throne and everybody who ever took a rotten penny from an illiterate Negro had better get ready to pay, for he will. There are people who have built their palaces on the bone of Negro tenants. Don't ever forget, there is a just God on the throne.

We must not hate him.

A few, thank God, very few, of the newspapers of this state have preached hatred until their hands are dripping red with murder now. They are largely responsible for some of the murders that have been committed. There are sections of our state where a Negro can be shot down like a mangy dog and the murderer set free. Also, a lot of half-baked politicians bleat like screaming idiots about the Negro. I heard one say, "We will eliminate them by taking every baby and making it sterile." Such ignorance! And that man was running for a state office. He took his hearers for fools. The following is a letter from an illiterate Negro woman. She said, "They talks about us on the radio and television like we was not as good as dogs. I could go on for weeks but my heart is too full."

I remember being present at the regular meeting of a Rotary Club where a politician spoke. His subject was about the Negro. He made a marvelous display of his ignorance about it all and then poured out a deluge of bitterness. The spirit was at such high pitch that if a Negro had walked down the street afterward, he would have been poked in the nose. This thing is sinful and wrong. They yell about the agitation caused by the NAACP. What is that except senseless agitation. This is a day when we need levelheaded statesmen rather than screaming politicians.

I realize that a lot of this hullabaloo has been stirred up by northern politicians to put the South in a bad light so that they can elect the next president. And they shout, "Why doesn't the church do something." They want the church to be the "quarterback" on the political football team. The church is not going to do it. I am not going to have any part of it.

Some groups say that Communists have infiltrated the NAACP. I don't know whether this is true or not. A person cannot tell whether what he reads is truth or someone's warped idea, but one thing I do know: there is agitation from both sides and the average citizen is caught in the middle. The result is that we have been set back fifty years in our relations.

For two years during my pastorate here at First Baptist Church, Poplarville, our young people from our church have conducted a Vacation Bible School for the Negroes. They carried Christ to them. They are the finest young people of our town, from the best families, and they are just as white as they were before. It would be difficult for them to do that now because of the strained relations. I say, we have been set back fifty years.

The Negro's crime should be punished by law and not by mob violence. Mob violence has no sanity to it. It is murderous. There must be no double standard in our courts of law. If a Negro man is to be put to death for rape, then the white man must be given the same penalty for the same crime. Miscarriages of justice in our courts are eating away at the foundations of our democracy like a cancer.

What about integration?

I do not believe that immediate integration would serve the best interests of either race at this time. I believe that it would create more problems than it would solve. I do not believe that conditions are right. Not because the white people are any better than the colored, but for the following reasons:

- We do not have the facilities, and it would bankrupt the state to build them overnight.
- If integration should be immediately forced upon the South there would be a lot of bloodshed, and a situation created that would be chaotic.
- It is altogether possible, if not probable, that criminal attacks would increase.
- It would retard the progress of white children because the colored people are not ready.

If, like many northern states, there were only a few Negro children in each school district, there would be no problems. I do not believe that southerners would object to their entering the white schools. Even in pre–Civil War days a few slaves were permitted to attend white schools down in the deep South. The average southerner does not hate the Negro but likes him and is his friend. A few radicals are causing the big trouble.

The problem is not a small one; it is tremendous in its proportions and therefore cannot be settled overnight. It is going to take years.

Northern agitators are responsible for a lot of the feeling of resentment that southerners have. They neither understand the southern white man nor the southern Negro, and so far as love goes, there is a lot more of it for the Negro in the South than in the North. We will all be better off when the northerners stop looking at the South out of slanted eyes, and down long noses, trying to tell us what to do about a situation that they themselves do not understand.

We should, even must, make a start toward settlement of this problem. I believe that senior colleges and universities should admit eligible Negroes to do graduate work. Then, in succeeding years, admit others to the junior, sophomore, and freshman classes.

Those being trained in the colleges and universities could go back and teach and train their own people. I believe that in time everyone would agree that integration was the best thing; then it would be a simple matter.

I believe this would make for peace and understanding and everybody would be satisfied, and no free-born American citizen would have to accept second-rate citizenship.

Oh, my people, I plead with you, don't have anything to do with bloodshed. Under God, don't mistreat a man of a neighbor race just because his skin is not the color of yours. It is so necessary for Christians to have the right attitude. Organizations that are springing up are dangerous unless they are led by levelheaded Christian men. My people, members of my church, I love you and I plead with you, don't have anything to do with the murder of anybody, under any circumstances. Don't listen to radicals. Don't listen to people who run off at the mouth and talk about colored people as though they were worse than dogs.

My brother, Raymond Gordon, said that when he was overseas, on the front line in the Signal Corps, that he ran right into a German machine gun nest. He thought to himself, "This is where I die." Suddenly, there was a burst of machine-gun fire from behind. He turned quickly and saw that an American Negro had saved his life by blasting the Germans. Then, from another direction, another volley rang out and cut the Negro down. He toppled backward into a ditch. My brother leaped into the ditch and took the Negro's head in his lap. The rich, red, American blood gushed out. He was dead, but my brother is still alive, and he said, "Every time I see the face of a black man, there is only love in my heart for him."

Once in a train wreck, a line burst and the coach was being filled with deadly steam. The Negro porter put his strong body against the door and closed it, cutting off the flow of steam, but in so doing, he was fatally burned. When the doctors came through giving first aid, they stopped by him. He said, "No, sir, not me, that little white girl." They had not seen the child. They gave first aid to her and turned to help the Negro, but he was dead.

Dr. George W. Truett said, "When I remember that it was a Negro who took the cross of my Savior upon his strong shoulders and bore it for Jesus, when from loss of blood he fell under the load, I will say, God's blessings on the black man forever."

I will never consider myself better than any other human being that God has created upon this earth.

§5 Herbert M. Baumgard

Rabbi Herbert M. Baumgard was born on August 3, 1920, in Norfolk, Virginia. After completing high school in Norfolk, Baumgard attended the

University of Virginia. Upon graduation he entered the U.S. Army and served as an information specialist during the war. He later recalled being assaulted by an officer in Hattiesburg, Mississippi, for his interfaith teaching on just black-white relations. Following the war Baumgard married Selma Geller and he continued his studies at the Jewish Institute of Religion at Hebrew Union College, where he was ordained in 1950. Later he received his Ph.D. from Columbia University in the field of Semitics. His first rabbinate was on Long Island, New York ,where he founded Temple B'nai Israel. Baumgard and his family moved south to Miami, Florida, in 1955 at the behest of the Union of American Hebrew Congregations (UAHC). He was charged with overseeing the daily operations of the UAHC and also starting a new temple, the latter task of which soon overwhelmed him. Baumgard resigned his administrative duties in 1956 and devoted all of his energies to Temple Beth Am, which he founded that same year, and which became one of the largest synagogues in Miami. Long an outspoken defender of equal rights and better race relations, Baumgard marched with fellow Miami clergy to integrate local restaurants. He also marched with the NAACP to protest discriminatory hiring practices in Washington, D.C. After thirty-one years leading Temple Beth Am, Baumgard retired in 1987, but his pace didn't slow as he was elected president of the Synagogue Council of America. He also served as chairman of the South Florida Interfaith Agency for Social Justice and the Dade County Community Relations Board. Baumgard and his wife have three children and continue to make their home in Miami.

This address before fellow Jews gathered to celebrate the High Holy Days in Miami aims to combat the silence of black equality. The problem, on Baumgard's account, is both uniquely Jewish and uniquely American. Regarding the former he rehearses some Old Testament history to underscore that Jews did not practice slavery—despite the prevalence and acceptability of that cultural practice. He invokes Amos to remind his listeners that the Ethiopian and the Egyptian are no different to Jews in the eyes of God. The problem of integration is also an American problem to the extent that it gives the lie to the U.S. Constitution. Baumgard relies on a personal story from World War II to convey just how simple is the act of integration. Throughout his address, Rabbi Baumgard reminds his audience that to "rehearse the future" is to bring God's justice in the present; furthermore, Jews have a godly mandate to usher in that future by being "in the vanguard of those who fight for freedom."

❧❧

Those Who Have Felt the Lash of the Taskmaster
September 1956
University of Miami, Coral Gables, Florida

Since I have come to Miami, I have heard stories about the existence of anti-Semitism in public schools. I have heard persistent reports about anti-Semitism in the Coral Gables High School. All of us here are agreed that something should be done about this, and I can assure you that I shall work with the established Jewish authorities in doing what I can about this matter.

No one discussed with me, however, the Negro problem in Miami. This might be caused by the attitude prevalent among many Jews that as a minority, we are unable to act in such a way as to do the Negro or ourselves any good.

As a native southerner, I am able to detect in most southern communities a conspiracy of silence about the Negro question. People sort of hope that, by ignoring the issue, it will evaporate. Then, there are those people who sincerely feel that integration in the public schools is an evil to be avoided. My mother is one of those people. There never was a more kind and gentle person than she, yet she feels that the Negro is an inferior being. When I was in high school in Norfolk, Virginia, a Mrs. Rorer taught me American history. Through her I gained a profound respect for the American democratic way. Recently she told me, "I am convinced that the Negro is an inferior being to the white person."

On Rosh Hashanah we discussed the spirit of the Jewish Sabbath. You might recall that we defined that spirit as the rehearsal of the future, or ideal world, in order that its coming might be hastened. My mother and Mrs. Rorer, two sweet and gentle souls, have practiced the Sabbath in reverse not because of their own evil, but because they lived in a society which rehearsed every minute of every day the inferiority of the Negro. While Mrs. Rorer taught in her classroom the constitutional principle that all men are created equal, she left the classroom to go home on a bus in which she rehearsed the inequality of the Negro. When you practice something constantly, you come to believe it. In fact, it becomes impossible to believe otherwise, for to believe other than what you see and do is to argue against all experience. My mother and Mrs. Rorer, born and reared in the South, practiced the superiority of the white race in the schools, in the buses, in the lavatories, and in the home. Today, therefore, each of them is faced with the necessity of admitting that her entire life has been a lie. This is a difficult thing to ask of any person.

Those of us, like myself, who favor desegregation, must bear in mind at all times the difficult task which the average southerner now faces. Even while we oppose that in which he believes, we must try to understand him. It is too easy to call the southerner intolerant and prejudiced. He is chained by something more complex than this. He is caught in the tentacles of habit.

Yet we take hope from previous triumphs by Americans in overcoming old habits. Our menfolk, North and South, used to think that women were actually second-class citizens, incapable of mastering the complexities of politics and, therefore, unworthy of the vote. Men repeated this fact to themselves until they believed it in perfect faith. It took a wild and ferocious campaign plus a constitutional amendment before women gained the right to vote. Today we think lightly upon this whole matter, but short years ago it was almost a life-and-death struggle. The success of women on the political front has demonstrated to the men that they were wrong in their previous notions about women. By fighting for their own rights, American women have proven that old habits and old thoughts can be dramatically changed for the better. It is to be hoped that these feminine victors over archaic prejudices will rally to the support of those who seek to overcome an equally unfounded notion.

During my army career, I spent six weeks at the School for Information and Education at Washington and Lee University. The army openly advocated the equality of the races, and at this school attempted to carry out that policy. Negroes were assigned to the same dormitories as white men. I recall that one of the white men taking the course with us was Sergeant Overton from Alabama. I will never forget Overton because he performed a terribly difficult task before my eyes. He had been taught all of his life that the Negro was dirt. Now he was being asked to believe the contrary. He observed that other white men entered the room of the Negroes and conversed with them as if they were ordinary human beings. Overton determined that he would try to do the same. He summoned all of his courage and, perspiring profusely and almost quivering from the conflict within himself, he entered the room with the Negroes and initiated a conversation. He returned a few minutes later, pale and shaken, but happy. He had taken the all-important first step in contradicting the total experience of his life. Overton was then and is now a hero to me. I am confident that today, he is one southerner who is trying to get others to rehearse the future and to deny the past. Other southerners must summon the same courage to face the inevitable as he did. It is terribly difficult to change one's habits, but in the end, it is more costly to live a lie.

People come to believe in the things they perform regularly. In most European countries racial segregation is not practiced. The Europeans are, therefore, unable to understand Americans who look upon the Negro as inferior. Since Europeans have always treated the Negro as their equal, the Negro has never been forced to assume a substandard position in European society. Europeans have observed that when the Negro is given the opportunity, he responds to a situation with as much ability as the white man. To believe that the Negro is inferior would be contrary to their experience and practice.

Which is the true relationship of the races? Today we have scientific data which points to their essential equality. But thousands of years ago, the problem was not a scientific one. In biblical days slavery was one of the pillars of national life of every group except the Hebrews. Even the advanced Greeks based their democratic society of Greeks upon a foundation of enslaved foreigners. The Hebrews solved the question by a leap of faith—they taught, "All men are in the *image of God*"; that is to say, in each of us there is divine potential. The Hebrews could not have come to this conclusion merely because some of their great men conceived the notion. In the hundreds of years during which the Hebrews were small wandering tribes, they had practiced constantly the free and equal stature of the members of each tribe. Raised in a free environment themselves, they then projected this notion to extend to other nations than themselves. The prophet Amos, speaking in God's name, proclaimed, "Are you not as the Ethiopians and the Egyptians to me, oh children of Israel?"

The chapters in Genesis and the Ten Commandments are like the constitution of ancient Israel. Yet, periodically throughout its history, Israel had to generate a new birth of freedom. It had to cast out the reactionary practices which developed in its midst. It had to remind itself of its glorious beginnings and make a new leap of faith. Americans today are in need of such a declaration of faith. WE HAVE TO BEGIN TO ACT AS IF OUR CONSTITUTION WERE TRUE, and then we will find that it is true. We must rehearse the equality of all men, and then we will discover that all men are indeed equal.

On the other hand, so long as we push the Negro to the back of the bus, bar him from jobs for which his skill is fitted, and deny him the education for which he thirsts; just so long do we prove that our Constitution is a lie.

A hypothesis, a rule for conduct, becomes truth only when it is woven into the fabric of life through constant rehearsal and experience.

When England faced its greatest challenge in the last war, Winston Churchill arose to say, "Let us thank God that it has given to us to make a decision which will change the course of history." The English could have surrendered to the Germans, as did the French, and no one would have blamed them, for the odds were overwhelming. Yet the English understood that what hung in the balance was not only their own lives, but the lives of generations to come.

The American people today are confronted by such an opportunity. If we act boldly and quickly, integration will be a "fait accompli" and our children will be free of the dilemma we now face. Otherwise, we will continue to rehearse the inequality of the races even while we quote our Constitution and our Bible to the contrary.

I do not suggest today we as Jews climb to the highest housetop to proclaim the urgency of integration. I suggest merely that the place of the Jew is in the vanguard of those who fight for freedom. We must join with those non-Jews who share our conviction to act as a united front. We need not act as an isolated battalion attacking an impregnable fortress. Tact and understanding are as important in this struggle as resolve and principle. We are not out to destroy ourselves al kidush ha-shem, but to live al kidush ha-shem, and to help others live.

On one matter, however, I must caution you. The Bible teaches, "lo tuchal l'hi talame, thou mayest not hide thyself." No Jew can put his hands over his eyes and say, "I don't see the suffering of the Negro." You see, all right, and "you cannot stand idly by the blood of your neighbor!" It is further written in our Bible, "He who harms the down-trodden, harms me, and he who raises up the fallen, honors me."

In this great opportunity which confronts us, not to act in favor of integration is to act against it; not to raise up the fallen is to tolerate and to participate in his oppression. Let us who have felt the lash of the taskmaster not be guilty of the enslavement of others.

1956

1956

§6 Charles Kenzie (C. K.) Steele

Reverend Charles Kenzie Steele was born on February 17, 1914, the only child of Henry and Lyde (née Bailor) Steele in Bluefield, West Virginia. As a child the Steele family moved to Gary, where his father worked as a brakeman in the coal mines. Because his father suffered from black lung, Charles often dropped out of school to help the family make ends meet. While he graduated high school three years behind his peer group, Steele found his calling as a young boy as he loved to preach; in fact his mother nicknamed him "preacher" even before he was baptized at the age of ten. Steele delivered his first sermon when he was only fifteen. As the Great Depression devastated West Virginia, Steele moved south to Atlanta to attend Morehouse College, and he earned his B.A. in 1938. His matriculation at Morehouse proved to be very consequential as he met the prominent King family, becoming quite close to Martin Luther King Sr., and his inspired oratory kept him in steady demand in area pulpits. Steele's first call took him to Toccoa Baptist Church in Toccoa, Georgia. Not long thereafter he moved to Montgomery, Alabama, to take the head pastor position at Hall Street Baptist Church. Lois Brock lived on Hall Street and Steele soon made her acquaintance; the two were married in 1941 and would have six children. After a brief stint at Augusta, Georgia's Springfield Baptist Church, Steele came back to Hall Street. In 1952 the thirty-eight-year-old minister made perhaps his most consequential vocational decision: with his three boys and wife, the family moved to Tallahassee, Florida, to take the job at the very prominent Bethel Missionary Baptist Church. It was the same year that Tampa's Robert W. Saunders became head of the Florida NAACP.

On May 26, 1956, two Florida A&M University students, Wilhelmina Jakes and Carrie Patterson, boarded a Tallahassee city bus and took their seat immediately behind the white bus driver. He ordered them to move. They refused. Thus began the Tallahassee Bus Boycott, which was modeled directly on the ongoing Montgomery Bus Boycott just four hours north and west. While some locals advocated for NAACP leadership of the boycott, others urged the creation of a local organization; this latter group eventually won out and thus was created the Inter-Civic Council, which was modeled directly on the Montgomery Improvement Association. C. K. Steele was elected president of the organization, which was made up of black clergy and businessmen who were not dependent economically on local whites. Steele's leadership throughout the boycott was so esteemed that in 1957 he was elected as the first vice president of the fledgling Southern Christian Leadership Conference, which elected Martin Luther King Jr. as its president. While not all parishioners of Bethel Baptist were fond of their minister's outspokenness on civil rights, C. K. Steele became something of a legend in Tallahassee. Today the city honors his memory with the C. K. Steele Plaza, a charter school, and academic scholarships. Rev. Steele died in 1980 from bone cancer; two sons and a daughter survive him.

Steele's address in Tampa, no doubt at the invitation of the NAACP's Saunders, tells the story of the Tallahassee Bus Boycott, with particular emphasis on the old and the new: Old Tallahassee and Old Uncle Toms have given way to a new militancy reflected in Christian nonviolent protest. Like many black activist preachers, Steele situates the kingdom of God in the context of temporal racial justice; waiting for God's will in the bye and bye is a cop-out on the part of both whites and blacks. Importantly Steele also calls upon his listeners to broaden the fight for civil rights to include voting and economic justice. Instead of debt-inducing spending at white-owned stores, Steele urges his audience to shop at black-owned stores—but to spend their money abstemiously. He also encourages them to register and to vote; this is what the white man fears most. "A vote-less people is a hopeless people," intones Steele. He closes his inspiring and confrontational message with a popular hymn, "I've Seen the Lightning Flashing."

୨୭⚭

The Tallahassee Bus Protest Story

October 26, 1956
St. Paul A.M.E. Church, Tampa, Florida

The Tallahassee Bus Protest story concerns a town that has for more than ninety years taken pride in being the only unconquered state capital of the Old Confederacy. Therefore, the customs, traditions, and prejudices that have grown up out of the seedbed of such racial pride and unfairness have caused our town to move forward with a snail's pace until within the last fifteen years.

Southeast Georgia is twenty miles northeast of us, southeast Alabama is less than ninety miles of us, but in spite of Tallahassee's fortunate or unfortunate location it has made some marked progress within the last fifteen years—progress that has been occasioned by the influx of new people and new ideas brought in to a large measure by the expansion of Florida State University, and Florida Agricultural and Mechanical University. Here was a progress of which many people of both races were totally unaware.

Therefore, it was to the horrible shock of some, and the pleasant surprise of many of us, that on May 26, 1956, an incident occurred that brought to focus the fact that *Old Tallahassee is not what she used to be.* For it was on this day that two young women students of Florida A&M University were asked to stand rather than occupy the only available seat on a city coach. They were ordered to stand on this crowded bus simply because a white woman was on the other end of the seat. The white lady did not object, but the bus driver insisted that it would be an unpardonable sin for these neatly clad college women of color to share a seat with a white woman. But it so happened that these young ladies from A&M had too much of this twentieth-century Negro blood in their veins to pay their fare for segregated service. The driver would not refund their money; instead he had them arrested and carried to police headquarters, where they were charged with placing themselves in a position of starting a riot. On Saturday night a cross was burned in front of their residence. This was purposed to frighten the young women and make them an example for the rest of the students as well as for all Tallahassee Negroes. But thank God! Instead, it had the opposite effect. It rang a bell that pealed forth the robust truth that *Old Tallahassee is not what she used to be.*

On a Monday following the cross burning, the entire student body of more than two thousand met in Lee Auditorium and voted unanimously that they would register their protest by staying off city buses. They came out of their meeting with passions running high and spirits that were so fiery and contagious that their protest captured the imagination of the entire Negro community. On Tuesday night citizens from all walks of life in our city met at the Bethel Baptist Church and heard the unfavorable report from the city manager, and the manager of the bus company. It was then that we voted in mass that until riding conditions on city coaches were amended, improved, and made democratic that Negroes would avoid them. Wednesday morning, the next day, found Tallahassee city buses empty, for fifteen thousand Negroes had decided that they had suffered and endured enough humiliation, injustice, and unfairness at the hands of a company kept in business primarily on money from Negro patrons. From this heart-felt conviction the Inter-Civic Council was born. By this time many of us knew that *Old Tallahassee is not what she used to be.*

Many and varied have been our experiences throughout the past *four* months of our protest. There have been mountains of laughter and joy, and there have been valleys of tears and sorrows. There have been long, weary nights of disappointments, and there have been sunshiny days of knowing ourselves to be in the great and unconquerable *will of God*—yes, thank God that on the darkest night we have been able to see the star of being right, the brilliance of which no cloud has been able to hide and no darkness has been able to put out.

Nearly every two weeks since the beginning of our movement we have faced a crisis of one kind or another—a crisis created by our prejudiced city officials or the "Uncle Toms" in our midst. There is quite a difference in the Uncle Toms that resulted from the period of Reconstruction and the Uncle Toms of the twentieth century and now. The old Uncle Toms stooped, bowed, and conducted themselves to the end of obtaining some favors for the race. He felt that his conduct was necessary in an age of fear for the people of color in America, but this Uncle Tom stoops, grins, and talks out of both sides of his mouth to feather his own nest and to sell his own people down the river. I really don't know which group has been the most alarmed by our movement in Tallahassee, the white city officials or the new Uncle Tom. They have both learned the hard way that *Negro Tallahassee is not what she used to be.*

There is power in oneness. It took the Negroes in Tallahassee thirty-three days to put the bus company out of business. Yes, it took us thirty-three days to demonstrate to the world that Tallahassee Negroes had been keeping alive a company and business that had no appreciation for our patronage—for it was only thirty-three days after the beginning of our protest that the bus company declared itself dead—killed by "rabble rousing suitcase newcomers" to the city, and *I happened to be one of them accused.*

With the pending collapse of the bus company in Tallahassee, the Inter-Civic Council was faced with the crisis of having to decide between the rising dignity of a downtrodden race and the perpetuation of a segregated transportation system. The officials of the city (city commissioners and others) sought to take advantage of the religious nature of our people by showing how evil, sinful, and awful it would really be to deprive a capital city of a transportation system. They further pointed out how we would suffer and how handicapped we would become without buses to ride. It was then that Tallahassee Negroes decided that it is far better "to walk in humble dignity, than to ride in shameful humiliation." Thus for some thirty-odd days there were no city buses running in Florida's capital city, simply because Negroes would not ride them.

If the collapse of the bus company was a crisis and a time of testing for the Inter-Civic Council, the resurrection and return of them to the streets was even more so. They returned with courtesy promised, with Negro drivers on routes predominately serving Negro communities, but with the sworn policy that never would a Negro and a white person share seats side by side. This, of course, meant that there would always be the possibility of someone having to stand while there were still vacant seats available. With this, the Inter-Civic Council could not and would not agree. The people themselves without the prodding of leadership turned all of these half measure proposals down—and in some cases in spite of the fact that there were some few leaders who advocated them.

Whereas the NAACP did not start our protest, they came to our help as soon as the news got out that we were having trouble in Tallahassee. They have been with us every step of the way. Even now they have supplied us with a lawyer to help us in our defense. I cannot exaggerate the meaning of this militant organization to us.

A—They have the lawyers equal to any in the country.

B—They don't have all the money they ought to have, but no organization makes better use of what they have than our own NAACP.

C—I would be a member of the NAACP for no other reason than they are feared by the southern white man. Why else would he try to outlaw it from the states?

D—Ladies and gentlemen, I am somewhat like the little boy was about being a Baptist. If I were not a member of the NAAP I would be ashamed of myself.

The southern white man has the police force, the city, state, and even the national representatives of legal powers; the one organization that Negroes have that is always out there in battle, and the southern politicians are so little, unfair, and afraid until now he wants to destroy the NAACP. The Inter-Civic Council is indeed thankful for what the National Association for the Advancement of Colored People has meant to Tallahassee.

Ladies and gentlemen, the time has now come when Negroes throughout America must stand up and be counted. Please don't misunderstand me—for whereas I am positive that love will win, I know that nowhere must we stoop, bow, or cry before the idle god of racial prejudice and exclusiveness of any kind and within anyone. We must push our fight of nonviolence and legal procedure, not only to the city halls, but to the governor's office, and to the White House if need be. To do this, we must be prepared with prayer, love, and faith in our hearts, the technique of nonviolence in our heads and the ballot in our hands.

The white man here in America has great respect for dollar bills, lead bullets, and paper ballots. We don't have the bullets, tanks, guns, and ammunition with which to fight our battles. If we did have them, I would not advocate the use of them; violence is unwise and immoral and carries upon its head the fading crown of death and hell. So violence is for us of all things both impractical and immoral. Moreover, we don't have the money with which to altogether wage our fight, but what little we have can go a long way toward helping us come to the place of first-class citizenship. Somewhere and at some time we must come to the maturity of knowing that sugar from a Negro store is as sweet as that from a white store, and that Negro insurance money will spend in the same places that the money that comes from a white company. Castor oil or aspirins prescribed and filled by Negro doctors and druggists will have the same effects as if given by white doctors and druggists. Ladies and gentlemen, I am trying to say that we must put our money together and when possible, use it to the advancement of our race. Economically, we must adopt the practice of early Christians. They *worked honestly*, *lived simply*, and *saved carefully*. By so doing, they soon became the most powerful force within all the confines of the Roman government. It is to this end that I have humbly asked that we would avoid getting in debt and to not loiter in town on Central and Scott Streets. We must, like the early Christians, make ourselves indispensable to the good and well-being of our city, state, and nation.

Guns are powerful, money is effective, but I know of nothing that the American white man is more afraid of than the ballot. The southern white man is afraid of the ballot. Do you know why Negroes are by the powers that be frightened always from the polls in Gadsden County? I'll tell you—it is because the white man is afraid that if the Negro votes he may take over the affairs of county and city governments. Do you know why all the registrars in Tuskegee, Alabama, resigned? Well, I'll tell you—it's because the white man in Macon County is afraid that the Negroes there will wake up and really make use of his united power at the place of voting. *All politicians know that a vote-less people is indeed a hopeless people.* So I am pleading that we will each and all register and vote in all elections. Remember every vote counts one. Your vote will carry the same weight as any white vote. Listen, even President Eisenhower's vote can count no more than yours. If we fail now to register and vote, we are of all people most pitiable. The test of one's worthiness to first-class citizenship is his appreciation of the *ballot.* Listen, in the voting booth, every man is a *king* and every woman is a *queen.*

Ladies and gentlemen, there is better day for this American Negro now rapping at the door of now. We must with love, faith, and prayer force that door open in the name of Christ. God has no brakes nor speed limit on the coming of freedom, fraternity, and the Kingdom of God. Our God has promised this world the Kingdom and it must come. It has not come yet but it's still a-coming.

Yes, it's still a-coming in spite of the Eastlands and the Tallmadges. Yes, it's still coming in spite the Ku Klux Klan and the White Citizens' Councils. Yes, thank God, the day of freedom is still a-coming in spite of hell and high water. There are some things that even God can't give us until we get ready and [are] worthy of them. Listen, God is waiting on the right spirit, interest, love, and appreciation in us, and then and not until then will the day of full freedom dawn for the black man of America. Until then we must work and fight, trusting our God for happy and heavenly results.

Now a word about the nature of our fight in Tallahassee. We are committed to waging our battle against evil principles and not against people; therefore, it must be nonviolent, and motivated by love. Whereas we hate segregation, racial prejudice, and injustice, we are committed to loving our white friends. We know that they are victims in need of rescue from the poisonous fangs of racial customs and traditions that have grown up out of the hotbed of ignorance and prejudice. Love is the most powerful force (agreements between ends and means) in the world. Protesting in love is not easy. It requires prayer and faith.

Another very important factor in our struggle has been the sense of worth and dignity that goes along with the conviction that you are right. All along we have been confident that we are economically right, socially right, politically right, and, above all, morally right and in line with divine teachings.

> Right cannot be destroyed:
>   –Crushed to the ground, it will rise.
>   –On a scaffold, it will sway the world.
>   –I watched them mishandle right in Jerusalem.
>   –If you are right God through Jesus has promised, "And lo I am
>   with you always even until the end of the world."

He has never left us alone:
I've seen the lightning flashing,
And heard the thunder roll,
I've felt sin's breakers dashing,
Trying to conquer my soul:
Telling me still to fight on,
He promised never to leave me,
Never to leave me alone.

No, never alone, No, never alone,
He promised never to leave me,
Never to leave me alone.

The world's fierce winds are blowing
Temptations sharp and keen,
I feel a peace in knowing
My Savior stands between;
He stands to shield us from danger.
When earthly friends are gone,
He promised never to leave me,
Never to leave me alone.

When in affliction's valley
I'm treading the road of care
My Savior helps me to carry
My feet entangled with briars,
Ready to cast me down,
My Savior whispers a promise:
"I never will leave thee alone."

He died for me on the mountain,
For me they pierced his side,
For me he opened that fountain,
The crimson, cleansing tide;
For me he's waiting in glory,
Seated upon his throne,
He promised never to leave me,
Never to leave me alone.

1957

1957

§7 Aubrey N. Brown

Dr. Aubrey Neblett Brown was born on May 6, 1908, in the west Texas town of Hillsboro. Raised in a progressive and politically engaged family, Brown began his writing career at Mineral Wells High School near Fort Worth. A scribe for the student paper and editor of the yearbook, Brown also served as class president. Brown left the state of Texas in 1925, eventually receiving his bachelor's degree from Davidson College in 1929 and a divinity degree from Union Theological Seminary in Richmond, Virginia, three years later. That same year, 1932, Brown married Sarah Dumond Hill; the couple would have eight children. Brown began his ministry in the Presbyterian church in West Virginia, first at a congregation in Ronceverte and six years later in Montgomery. Brown moved back to Richmond at the behest of a former faculty member in 1943 to serve as editor of the *Presbyterian Outlook*, a national weekly publication serving both the Presbyterian Church, U.S., and the United Presbyterian Church, USA. For the next thirty-five years Brown would serve as a progressive voice in the denomination as he advocated for equality in race and gender relations as well as interfaith dialogue. Brown's commitments, though, went well beyond the pages of the *Outlook*. He was elected as the first president of the Richmond area chapter of the Virginia Council on Human Relations. His three-year tenure coincided with the state of Virginia's campaign of "massive resistance" to the Supreme Court's *Brown* decision. Brown would later serve as president of the same organization at the state level. In 1966 he was named chairman of the Virginia Advisory Committee to the U.S. Commission on Civil Rights. For his work in advancing the cause of human rights Brown won several awards, including the Virginia B'nai B'rith's first Torch of Liberty Award; he also received several honorary degrees, including two from his alma mater, Davidson. He was a very active member and teacher at Ginter Park Presbyterian Church; the church established an annual lecture in his name beginning in 1987. Brown died on August 6, 1998, survived by his eight children and fifteen grandchildren. His papers are housed at the Virginia Historical Society in Richmond.

In this relatively upbeat survey of race relations delivered to his fellow Presbyterians, Brown argues that the Supreme Court's *Brown* decision has forced Christians to discuss race in ways heretofore unknown. Moreover, even the many silences engendered by the decision underscore the ubiquity of race-based discourse in the church. And while Brown sees a good bit of economic pressure leveraged against outspoken clergy, the work of desegregation goes forward. As a journalist, Brown keenly describes how rhetorical balance is often invoked in and out of the pulpit: the White Citizens' Council and the NAACP are both similarly excoriated for extremism—when in fact the latter group, he emphasizes, is a "law-abiding" organization. So-called "moderates" on the race issue would frequently use this ostensibly "balanced" rhetorical strategy to appear reasonable. Brown reveals that strategy to be nothing but a poorly thought-out conceit.

❧❧

The Church in Southern United States

March 13, 1957
Atlantic City, New Jersey

Few people would have dared predict three years ago that by today so many gains could, under any circumstances, have been made in modifying the rigid lines of racial segregation in the southern United States as we can see in many areas . . . in the areas of integrated schools, in employment, in transportation, in public services, and in some aspects of church life.

While there has been stubborn resistance in several states to the Supreme Court ruling on desegregation of the schools, there has been an unbelievably swift compliance with the ruling in many others.

To be sure, there are people who will insist that race relations in the South have not been so bad in a hundred years as they are today, but one cannot fail to recognize that the relations in question, now so highly praised, were always within well-defined boundaries, the limits of which were not to be transgressed.

No one will easily deny the strained relationships and a consequent lack of communication between different racial groups, and also between groups of white people. These create no pleasant social climate. In many situations it is as though friends who have lived their lives together suddenly awake to discover that a language barrier has come between them and they have no idea what the other is saying. This, they tell us, has been the case in Britain recently, where a hostess had first to discover the attitudes of her respective friends on the Suez crisis before she could plan a social gathering that would not end in a riot of bitter disagreement. Many people in the South who are still willing to accept each other simply avoid talk of segregation as they would the plague.

This has required a hard choice for ministers and churchmen, for they have had to decide whether to deal with the most relevant and pressing issue before their community or to act as if it did not exist and thereby suggest that Christian faith and practice are unreal and insignificant.

There have been plenty of people to charge that the churches are being led about by the Supreme Court—that the preachers never had anything to say about the issue until the May 17 decision of 1954.

As to the timing of pronouncements, it is only fair to point out that the Southern Presbyterian statement condemning segregation preceded the Supreme Court decision, though immediately after the decision the General Assembly supported it and urged compliance with it.

But in some respects it may be true that until the issue became so pointed and urgent in terms of personal involvement many people had never understood what the preacher had been trying to say during all those years in terms of simple justice and brotherhood and the Golden Rule and fair play and the obligations of Christian love. They had not understood why so many preachers had been at work in community race relations groups; why they had tried to arrange exchanges of individuals between racial groups in efforts to establish bonds of friendship and understanding; why they had talked about the practice at home of what we are trying to export to the mission fields. They had not recognized what many wise people had always understood—that advances must be made on the basis of mutual respect and understanding, and that these are only slowly and gradually developed through personal contacts.

Now, it is true that in some cases churchmen have blessed and in occasional situations led the movement to support segregation. Sometimes they have become virtual priests of the Ku Klux Klan and the White Citizens' Councils. They have accused their brethren of supporting atheism, socialism, Communism, and mongrelization of the race. In their church's judicatories they have been willing to drive a preacher from their midst if he antagonized the supporters of segregation, though such a move is, in almost every instance, allowed to become so involved that the execution is performed for some high purpose, or at least for the so-called peace of the church.

It is not easy for any of us to be sure that we are held by a consistently lofty motive or to demonstrate that we, too, are not susceptible to social or economic pressures. So, it may become us to tread softly if we are inclined to judgment. Still, it is instructive to review an episode like the famous debate of Virginia legislators in 1837 where the upholders of slavery feared that despite all their efforts that honorable institution would be overthrown and the slaves would be set free in Virginia. For two full weeks they debated the issue and the final vote was surprisingly, threateningly close. An analysis of the vote shows that, like some today, it followed almost in exact proportion the number of slaves held in the respective regions of the state. And it is obviously true today that the problem is solved most easily in areas where the economic and population factors are least acute.

But it is also instructive for us to note that following the 1837–1838 debate, when it was insisted that sheer bankruptcy of the state's finances would result if even token payments were made for the slaves, the theological forces and the biblical exponents fell readily in line and brought forth convincing arguments, based upon the Holy Writ, as to why slavery was not only expedient but a humane necessity for the benefit of the slave himself.

The South today is in a changed economy, and other economic pressures are at work to spell the doom of a system of economic or political slavery. So long as there are local economic pressures that can be exerted to maintain a crumbling structure they will be exerted and they are being exerted—else, it is difficult to explain the silence of many churchmen who in their hearts know the demands of Christian compassion and brotherhood, and must some day speak them as they know them.

Meanwhile the Koinonia interracial farm in Americus, Georgia, lives only by its faith in God; Dr. [David] Minter and Mr. [Eugene] Cox with their families make their way quietly from Mississippi to less dangerous ground, and a preacher who stood up in public meeting in defense of the democratic ideal finds himself another church. Another stands quietly and modestly for building some bridges across these chasms of misunderstanding until he finds his work at a standstill and he moves along. A Baptist pastor says nothing about the issue from the pulpit, but in private conversation he reveals his sympathies, and, because of the powerful political leaders in his congregation, he finds himself without a church.

In few churches is there even a symbolic step toward integration of members. For one reason, because housing is segregated and most churches serve neighborhoods, but where this is not true, there is little effort to change the requirements for membership so as to eliminate an unspoken but insuperable racial clause. There are a few congregations with one or two members of another race, but they are conspicuous exceptions.

At the level of church courts and conferences and training classes there are evidences of change, and it will doubtless be that these experiences of acquaintance and understanding will precede those on local or neighborhood levels. Many synods and some presbyteries have taken strong stands in support of the principle of desegregation and have set an example at their level. They have also called upon congregations and colleges to do likewise.

In the struggle with state legislative bodies some churchmen have made effective stands, not to the extent of halting the politically inspired measures, but at least they have raised a cry for simple justice and a reminder of elemental democracy.

Most of them appear to feel, however, that in order to prove that they are fair-minded they must castigate White Citizens' Councils on the one hand and on the other the NAACP, even though they must admit that the NAACP is law-abiding and seeks only what the law interprets as an individual's right. Not many have attempted to help their people understand that the same fury that is now directed at the NAACP would be visited upon any other organized group that sought desegregation.

Some institutions are moving ahead—like Maryville College in Tennessee, with a few Negro students and one part-time faculty member who is a Negro; the Southern Presbyterian seminaries, some of which have had Negro graduate students for many years, and almost all now have undergraduates in residence; and the General Assembly's Training School. The Duke Divinity School only last week, unfortunately, refused a student petition to admit qualified Negro students.

Something doubtless should be said about the inflow of "hate" publications into the South, almost all published in the North and West and heavy with a mixture of anti-Semitic and fascist appeals, mixed with segregation doctrine and inflammatory pictures. In an area very suspicious of outside influences this phenomenon is noteworthy.

This survey should not be completed without reference to the part the Negro leadership has played and of the contributions of able Negro ministers who serve as guides through dangerous waters. It is true that these men have much more to gain personally from advances in their own status, and they have a considerable body of support and financing which a white minister usually cannot count on receiving, and they are not going to be made unacceptable to a congregation because of their stand on this issue, but the disciplines learned through group action and the restraints which are accepted in patient but firm dealing have revealed possibilities hitherto unrecognized.

In many ways this is a great day for the church in the South. It is a day of trial and terror, of heartache and disappointment, of grief and heavy burdens, but it is also a day of triumph. Never, it would be safe to say, have more men and women in the South been driven more resolutely to discover the real meaning of the Christian gospel, never have they confronted more starkly the grim, forbidding, and corporate nature of sin, never have the claims of the Christian conscience been pressed more demandingly upon them, never have they been challenged more persistently to fulfill the mission of the church of Jesus Christ.

Trevor Huddleston, in his *Naught for Your Comfort*, reminds us that unless we seize the time that comes to us to make our witness as a Christian group, a day may dawn when that witness will be silenced and we cannot, for life itself, do what we recognize should have been said and done long before. Now, he says, in many ways, the day of opportunity in South Africa has passed, just as it did in Germany when the Nazis rose to power in the 1930s. It can pass for us in any area, if we are silent for too long.

We can be grateful, it seems to me, for those men in the midst of pressing situations who have learned to speak with courage and with compassion and whose daily lives are being lived in honest and unintimidated confidence. We can also be grateful for a growing body of enlightened and dedicated laymen and women who want their spiritual leadership to be true to the vision of greatness which this hour demands. They deserve our prayers and the knowledge of our trust.

§8 Merrimon Cuninggim

Dr. Merrimon Cuninggim was born May 11, 1911, in Nashville, Tennessee. He married Whitty Daniel on June 10, 1939, and together they had two daughters. Cuninggim earned an A.B. from Vanderbilt University in 1931, an M.A. from Duke University in 1933, a B.A. and M.A. from Merton College, Oxford, in 1935 and 1937 respectively, and a B.D. from Yale University in 1939, followed by a Ph.D. in 1941. He attended Oxford University as a Rhodes Scholar. Cuninggim taught at Emory and Henry College, Denison University, and Pomona College. An avid tennis player, he was a ranked competitor at Wimbledon, and coached tennis at Pomona. He was the director of religious studies at Duke University. In 1952 Cuninggim was named dean of the Perkins School of Theology at Southern Methodist University. Many consider Perkins the first integrated southern university. He began integrating Perkins immediately by recruiting five able students: John W. Elliott, James A. Hawkins, James V. Lyles, Negail R. Riley, and Cecil Williams. He also recruited three prominent integrationist theologians: Albert Outler (who also arrived in 1952, knowing that Cuninggim would be there), John Deschner, and Schubert Ogden. The three are still remembered reverently by former students as God the Father, God the Son, and God the Holy Spirit. After leaving Perkins he built a firm, Cuninggim Associates, which advised foundations, colleges, and universities. Cuninggim was the head of various foundations and on the board of several institutions, including Duke University and Vanderbilt University. He was named president of Salem Academy and College in 1976. Dr. Cuninggim died on November 1, 1995. Many of his important papers are housed in the Bridwell Library at the Perkins School of Theology, Southern Methodist University.

Dr. Cuninggim's address, "To Fashion as We Feel," delivered on April 25, 1957, targets inaction on the part of southern, white Christians as an element hindering the lack of progression in regards to race relations and equality. In reference to the stone blocking the entry to Jesus' tomb, Cuninggim states that "the path is not blocked except for those who think it is blocked." He is not admonishing southern, white Christians for their inaction, but rather relaying that he understands that a systematic approach toward bettering race relations is lacking. Although Cuninggim realizes that southern "ministers and laymen react as southerners first and Christians second," he realizes that a clear methodology is needed first in order for southern Christians to act. He then proposes a framework, consisting of seven concepts, on which to build a methodology. Cuninggim concludes his address by explaining that cohesiveness among whites and African Americans is possible if southern Christians are "faithful both to the Christian goal and to the Christian method."

✌

To Fashion as We Feel

April 25, 1957
Nashville, Tennessee

Margaret Halsey used these appropriate words of Shakespeare as the last line in her book of some ten years ago, *Color Blind*. Her point was that we in America face a magnificent task. She wrote, "The integration of the Negro into American society is one of the most exciting challenges to self-development and self-mastery that any nation of people ever faced." All of us these days see the nettle; she saw the flower.

It is a most useful reminder. We are accustomed to stating the problem, not the chance of solution. We hear all around us the threats of disaster, not the possibilities for overcoming prejudice and fear. As for the South, we give ear too easily to such defeatisms as "The decision of the Supreme Court has set us back twenty-five years," or, "The actions of the NAACP have postponed good relations for fifty years." We have emphasized too much the difficulty the South faces, and much too little the opportunity.

But you, I daresay, are not impressed. Your presence here, the very existence of this conference, indicates the conviction of Christians all across the South, as well as of course in other parts of the county, that there are affirmations that can be made and ways of advance that can be mapped, that our problem has an enabling as well as a disabling aspect. Neither Christianity nor democracy can show its real fiber in days of ease and clear sailing; on the other hand, neither Christianity nor democracy has any chance in a situation in which disciples of firm commitment are not present to make their testimony. Here in the South are days of stress; here in the South are also persons of faith ready to testify to it. Here, then, both conditions are fulfilled. The South today is the best laboratory I know anywhere for testing both Christianity and democracy.

In such a conviction this conference was called. To the effort to seize our opportunities this conference is dedicated. When the printed program first came to hand I was struck by the reference on the first page not only to the task but to the timing of these sessions. The explanatory comment read, "Conference on Christian Faith and Human Relations . . . toward the building of Christian community in a time of trouble—a post-Easter evaluation." It was that last phrase that caught my attention. In the Gospel of Mark the account of the first Easter morning includes an item that is omitted from all the other gospel records. We are told that "When the Sabbath was past, Mary Magdalene, and Mary the mother of James, and Salome, bought spices, so that they might go and anoint him. And very early on the first day of the week they went to the tomb when the sun had risen. And they were saying to one another, "Who will roll away the stone for us from the door of the tomb?" And looking up, they saw that the stone was rolled back."

Mark's addition is in the question that the other gospels skip over in order to get as quickly as possible to the telling of the empty tomb. But the question is important, for it is our question. The stone of racial discord sometimes seems to block our access to the presence of the living Christ. And because we of the South know the peculiar potency of the question "Who will roll away the stone?" we can perhaps understand more fully the promise in the answer, "Looking up, they saw that the stone was rolled back." The way is open! The path is not blocked except for those who think it is blocked. I for one am grateful for Mark's additional comment in the Easter account; and I am grateful that this conference is being held so close upon the Easter season.

And so we are met in this final session to take stock. Where do we as Christians stand? What can we say to ourselves and our fellows in this hour of turmoil? What ought we to do? This is a great hour, and we would be faithful to it. We approach it as a time of opportunity.

And as we pause to analyze the position at which we have arrived, two main categories take shape in our conclusions. A number of the items of our concern fall within the category of *what we know*; a number of others constitute the area of *what we don't know*. I propose, then, that we spend our attention upon each of these in turn. And if the larger share of our consideration should logically be spent upon what we don't know, we need to give at least introductory notice to what we do know, that our knowledge may be pinned down and that the extent and limitations of our uncertainties may be the better defined.

Let us begin, then, with *what we are fully aware of*. We know at least four things. *First, we know that we must have facts.* It is not my task, as I conceive it, to summarize the factual situation. This is being done by any number of individuals and institutions. It has been done in this conference. It will continue to be done well, by scholars and newspapermen, churches and foundations, universities and governmental agencies. The facts are available—facts on every angle of our problem; the progress and lack of it in the desegregation of the public schools, the thought of the Old and New Testaments, the advantage that Communism is trying to seize elsewhere in the world because of our southern strife, the status of restrictive and permissive legislation in the various states, the incidents of discord and of courage.

All this and much more is to be had for the searching, but the availability of the facts is not my point. My emphasis, rather, is on the wide awareness that we must have them, that we cannot safely tackle our task without them. The problem that we as Americans, and particularly that we as southerners, face is of such crucial dimensions that we must not talk off the top our head, or act at the irresponsible urging of our feet; and we know this. That we know it is one of the healthy factors in the present situation.

A second thing we know is the Christian ethic. Here, of course, is occasion for quibbling, if we had the taste or the time for it. Fortunately we seem to have a little of either, though it might well have been otherwise. We could have tried to manipulate the words of Scripture to fit our fancy. There is some of this, of course, but real scholarship has not succumbed to such temptations, and ministers and laymen generally have had little truck with it. We as Christians could have closed our eyes to our problem, or tried to, but we realize it wouldn't have worked. There is some of this, too, but aren't you surprised by how little rather than how much? We could have blamed God for our troubles: he is color-blind, and in his sympathies distressingly lacking in discrimination; but I have heard none of this at all. We could have debated, and we do, about particular elements in the Christian ethic, the derivative items of moral sensitivity as to how much, how far, when, and where. But we know, even as we discuss them, that they are secondary; and the remarkable thing in the picture is that on primary matters we are in substantial agreement.

As I wrote that sentence I had spread out before me on my desk official statements from a host of plenary church bodies in the South, representing various interchurch councils and the following denominations: Baptist, Catholic, Congregational, Disciples, Evangelical and Reformed, Episcopal, Methodist, and Presbyterian. All these statements were drawn up in the last three years or so, in consequence of the Supreme Court decision of May 17, 1954; and all but one of them expressed the approval of the sponsoring body for that earthshaking development. I am sorry to have to record that the sole dissenting voice was that of an annual conference of the church to which I belong. It is tempting to quote at length; but since they say much the same thing, and since you are already aware of their content, I shall read only one as an example. It is the statement of an interdenominational Council of Church Women; as we all know, the ladies go to the heart of such matters. They said:

1. Because of our high calling of God in Christ Jesus, we reaffirm our belief in human brotherhood and the inclusiveness of the Christian fellowship. Therefore, we feel we are impelled to promote a Christian society in which segregation is no longer a burden on the human spirit.
2. We accept with humility the Supreme Court decision as supporting the broad Christian principles of the dignity and worth of human personality and affording the opportunity of translating into reality Christian and democratic ideals.

We know what the Christian ethic compels us to say—the love of neighbor in the light of God's love, and the impartiality and universality of God's love. As a result of his meeting with Cornelius, "Peter suffered considerable stress of mind before he was forced to admit, "Truly I perceive that God shows no partiality." The brethren in Jerusalem were suspicious of Peter's reluctant mission until he finally persuaded them to conclude, "Then to the Gentiles also God has granted repentance unto life." And so it has been to this day: the insight comes slowly, but eventually it comes. It has come to the Christians of the South. One of the greatest assets in our present distress is our near-unanimity as to what the Christian position is.

The third thing we know is the shallowness of our defense. As white Christians of the South, we would gladly escape the cutting edge of these first two entries in the account of our knowledge. We would if we could! But the facts don't add up as we'd often like them to, and the Christian ethic simply refuses to go away and hide. And so the defenses of us who are white southerners and presumably Christians get pretty moth-eaten and decrepit. But again, that they do is not my point; rather, my point is that we know this. Others know it, the world knows it; but it is conceivable that the realization might not have dawned upon us. It is conceivable but not actual, for the actual circumstance is that we have become convinced of the absurdity of our own shibboleths.

Let us not spare ourselves. Let us pull our pat formulas out into the sunshine of both our data and our ethic, and see how they wither in that light. Since we know these defenses by heart I will take time only to list them; and since we know quite clearly that they are not conclusive, I will refer only in passing to their patent frailty. There are at least thirteen, unlucky number for us:

1. "The situation is easier elsewhere." So what? Does this mean there is *less* for us to do?

2. "Our people are not ready." Maybe not; but what are we doing to make them more so? Do we just wait? "Sit down, O men of God; have done with greater things."

3. "The Negroes are not ready." Again, maybe not; but when and where can we cut into this vicious circle? The Negroes aren't ready for first-class citizenship because we haven't given them the chance to be; and so we won't give them the chance to be because they aren't ready.

4. "The Negroes don't *want* desegregation." All right, then that's *their* argument, not ours. But isn't it strange how few of them are making it?

5. "The Negroes lack our standards in health, morality, and marital fidelity." Then if so, let's get to work on it. What do we do when the house catches fire? Even the back room? Take a walk?

6. "What will it lead to?" You will note, I hope, that I have not phrased this question in its Ku Klux form: "You don't want a nigger marrying your daughter, do you?" I haven't done so because I have respect both for your integrity and my daughter's judgment. "What will it lead to?" It might lead to a chance for the integrity of the Negro, too.

7. Here we begin to turn on our northern tormentor: "Leave us alone." We've been left alone a good long time, with nothing but our Christian consciences to guide us.

8. "You've got your problems, too." Right! There's not a Yankee in the land that doesn't share in our damnation, and we ought to dislike the condition as much as the company.

9. "We believe in states' rights." Oh, so *this* is the real reason; and if it weren't for states' rights we'd be glad to do the decent thing—is that it?

10. "We've got a state law." Yes, we've got one where I come from, too. And it hasn't kept us from doing a thing which our feeble courage persuaded us to try. We've got a federal law now; and all along we've had a Christian command.

11. "The Supreme Court was pressured." Right again! It *was*! But by what? By the mounting evidence of injustice and discrimination. Is that what we want to perpetuate?

12. "The NAACP is suspect, probably subversive." How awkward that the FBI can't prove it. Or maybe the Bureau is in on the conspiracy, too.

13. "*We love* the Negroes!" We do! And I love my dog!

There they are! In all their stark poverty, there are the pretexts we use for dragging our feet. But the truth is breaking upon us, and we begin to see these shibboleths for what they are. There is good news in this sorry pictures, I submit; and the good news is that most of us are getting tired of seeing ministers and laymen react as southerners first and Christians second. We know the shallowness of our defenses.

Fourth, and because of these first three, we know one final thing. *We know our own guilt.* Outside commentators all the way from Gunnar Myrdal to the editors of *Time* have pointed out that the most decisive opponent of the segregationist is his own conscience. Well and good; let them point! For they speak the truth. In a sensitive little article on "The Racial Crisis and the Prophet's Task," published in the *Duke Divinity School Bulletin*, Waldo Beach recently wrote, "The troubled conscience of the Southerner . . . may be deeply hidden beneath layers of custom and rationalization, but it is there. Even the fury of the fanatic racist (and there is usually one in every church), which seems so sure and unambiguous, is the more frenetic because it covers an anxious insecurity or hides a deep alienation from self."

Now the "fanatic racist" often succeeds in his cover-up, succeeds with himself, at any rate. But you and I don't. We know within our own hearts the conviction of sin and the need for repentance. Yes, and more: we often repent. It was a Presbyterian group in the South, though it might have been any group of Christians, that stated, "The action of the Supreme Court . . . points up the failure of the Church. . . ." Sense of guilt is our portion, and penitence is increasingly our response.

These, then, are the four insights of which we are fully aware: first, not only the facts but the need for them; second, the central emphases of the Christian ethic; third, the shallowness of our own defense; and fourth, our sin. Others may or may not possess these understandings in as large a measure. For example, one often suspects that our brothers in other parts of the country are so alert to our sin that they fail to see their own. But that is not our concern, except to help them toward their own self-enlightenment as they have helped us. No, our interest is in *our* self-understanding, the analysis of the self-knowledge of white, southern Christians; and at the midpoint of this task we find that we can safely take these four things for granted.

But the second part of our introspection is more difficult, for it has to do with *what we don't know.* The list is large, and the temptation to make it less exhaustive than it ought to be is even larger. Is it not true for all of us that we know much less than we like to think we know, whereas we fail really to know much more than we pretend? If we were to allow ourselves the luxury of exaggeration, we might have mentioned many more than four items in the listing of what we know; but fewer might suffice for what we don't know, if we were to give ourselves the benefit of the doubt. Yet symmetry must be preserved at all costs! Thus I shall again compress into four the items of ignorance, unawareness, and misunderstanding that beset us.

First, we are perplexed as to what to do. We know what the Christian ethic says, to be sure, in its broad directives of faith and practice, but we don't know how to use it. So we content ourselves with simply talking about it. In solemn assembly we speak the truth as God has given us to see it, but when we go home we quickly lose the courage and certitude we felt while still in conference session. Back in the corporate body—such a one as this, perhaps—we had a sense that the world was watching, and we painted a portrait of God's command on a broad canvas. But now each of us is alone in his own community, only the corner store or the courthouse square is watching, and we daub away at picturing man's desires in a limited frame. The courthouse square is speaking as well as watching; the citizens are counseling together, and some of them are donning their cowardly sheets. Too often we play dead before the drumbeats; or worse, we may even carry a drum. Not long ago I was cut to the quick by the plaintive comment of a Negro friend of mine, a sponsor, incidentally, of this conference. He said, "If only some local churches would act on what their denominations say . . ." and the rest of the sentence was tactfully unspoken.

But *how* shall we act? We really *are* puzzled as to what to do. Protestants among us are especially bewildered. We admire what has been accomplished by such Catholics as Bishop Vincent S. Waters in North Carolina and Archbishop Joseph F. Rummel and Bishop Jules B. Jeanmard in Louisiana, and yet we Protestants know that we must employ different tactics. This was recognized by Lee Nichols and Louis Cassels in an article in *Harper's* entitled "The Churches Repent." They said:

> While Protestant spokesmen acknowledge that the Catholics have moved farther and faster in race relations in the South, they also assert that the Roman Church faces a somewhat different problem, both because of the relatively small number of Negros involved and because of the much greater authority that Catholic priests and bishops exercise over church affairs. No Protestant bishop could successfully end segregation in a diocese by edict. A Protestant clergyman bent on breaking down racial barriers in his own church must have not only the personal courage and determination to do so, but also the leadership to carry with him the

laymen who, through vestries, presbyteries, boards of deacons or congregational meetings have the final word on church policy.

The position is sound, of course, but we need not make it a crutch to lean on. To the contrary, it can serve as incentive for us to do a better job, as well as one more fitted to our Protestant principles and polity. Since our church leaders cannot issue edicts, their leadership can assume the proper Protestant form of guidance rather than fiat. Since we must educate our laymen, then our program can be stronger because it must depend upon an understanding and sympathetic laity. Moreover, since one or another individual cannot speak or act for all of us, we can gain the strength that comes from cooperative endeavor. The difference between Protestants and Catholics represents a greater ease of movement for them, but may represent a larger opportunity for us, if we see it that way.

I keep skirting the central concern, don't I? For the question of the moment is "What can we do?" and all that I'm doing is to underline the question. And I think I know why—let the cynical point out that here comes another deferment of the answer! One of the major reasons that we don't know what to do is that the methodology of the Christian ethic has seldom been discussed by philosophers and theologians. Take a look, if you will, at any of the so-called standard works in Christian ethics that have spoken meaningfully to the life of our times. Take a look, as I have done, at the volumes that appear most often today on the reading lists in our seminaries. They deal with brilliance, though often with many a contradiction of emphasis, on the content of the Christian ethic, but almost never do they turn to the problem of its methodology. They are strong on theory; they are short on practice. Stray references in the books are helpful; numerous magazine articles give guidance on what has happened, or might be tried, in specific situations. But we still wait for a systematic examination of the general strategy which the Christian ethic calls for.

And while we wait, perhaps we ourselves can make an indirect beginning on the task simply by adding up what we have learned from our own experience. Every one of us has learned a lot, enough to keep us from speaking ex cathedra, yet also enough to point fingers of useful direction toward, hopefully, the eventual answering of our question as to what we can do. Let me be so presumptuous, therefore, as to try to pull together the major hints of a successful strategy that any one of us could call to mind. Since my reminiscences in illustrating them would be no more illuminating than your own, I'll spare you the stories I could tell, and leave you to furnish your own examples. I shall mention *seven suggestions* that grow out of our common experience—and perhaps this will be a lucky number for us:

1. We realize that in preparation for any particular action designed to lessen prejudice and foster the Christian spirit we must *consider all the factors* that have gone to create the situation we face, or as many of them as we can get our fist around. We ourselves can't know them all intimately; and thus part of this realization is the recognition that we must *call upon the experts* for those aspects of the situation that we do not fully understand. Some of these experts may not share our Christian inclinations, but that doesn't matter, for we can still learn from them. The problem in "human relations" to which the title of this conference refers is in the field of what we have come to call "social ethics"; and the juxtaposition of those two words suggests that we must understand society as well as ethics, before we can act intelligently and helpfully.

2. Yet even the mastery of all relevant information will not enable us to act alike in every circumstance. On the contrary it will lead us to realize that we can't and ought not to try to. We learn that each local situation is different from every other, and that *any contemplated action must be fitted to the local community.* Thus we *eschew sweeping conclusions and prescriptions*, and point whatever programs we have in mind to the particular place and problem it is designed to serve.

3. But to take a whole host of factors into consideration, to try to give each its proper weight, and to be guided by particular circumstances as well as by general premises means that we must make adjustments among the concerns we feel. Thus we realize that *compromise is inevitable*, but the corollary also occurs to us, that *rationalization is inviting*. To recognize that adjustments are always called for is to open the door for the play of extraneous considerations and for self-justification. Compromise and rationalization!—Let's have as little of both as possible, but let's distinguish between them. The former will be present whether we will or [not], and may not be altogether deplorable; the latter must be dispensed with as far as we are able.

4. But we cannot rid ourselves of rationalizations if each of us operates to himself alone. No more can we, on the positive side, attain the full measure of our effectiveness if every person works in isolation. We need the *sense of community* that such conferences as this provide; we need to *engage in* as much *cooperative endeavor* as possible; we need to

develop sinews of association, to the end that facts and tactics may be widely known. If we use the churches, the professional societies, and the other organizations to which we belong, then the Citizens' Councils and the Ku Klux Klans will not be the only agencies that know the meaning of fellowship in pursuit of a common cause.

This may be as good a point as any to bring the Negro into the circle of our concern. Thus far we have spent our attention on the role of the white Christians in the South, but the Negro must play his part, too, and we must be willing for him to do so. An important element in this fourth realization, therefore, is that lasting progress takes place when *Negro and white work together*, not when either tries to fight his battle for brotherhood alone.

5. It will be a battle! *Opposition is unavoidable*, whatever we attempt to do. Those who "mean to keep the Negro in his place" are angry, frightened men, and sweet reasonableness will not be enough to defeat them. But we who seek to respond to the Christian gospel are not thereby promised escape from strife. *We expect it. We have it. We are* engaged in it right now.

6. Yet in the ordering of our plan for battle we find the military metaphor breaking down. *Our efforts must be educative*, not punitive. If the Negro can't be moved back to Africa, no more can the bigot be annihilated. And to do our bit toward enabling the Negro to become a full citizen of our society means that we believe in full citizenship for all, the perpetrators as well as the victims of injustice. This takes education, and our opponents are in direr need of it than any other Americans I know.

7. *Our purpose muse be redemptive* as well as educative. Here we draw upon our Christian rather than merely American understandings. We have good news of God's love to share, and we are committed to sharing it. Those who hate need to be rescued from it, as from a treacherous sea. It is a better metaphor to guide our actions than that of the clash of arms. For it suggests a quality that is necessary, a temper we need to possess, an atmosphere we must seek to create. One who undertakes a rescue operation identifies himself with his human derelict, and bends every effort to save him, yes, even when he doesn't want to be saved. Some people enjoy their prejudices, even as some enjoy their idols; but Christianity still has a missionary impulse. Any person who stands athwart the development of decent human relations is the object of our missionary endeavor and the subject for redemption.

All these things we have learned through our experience. When we add them all up, and illumine them with the Christian ethic itself, do we not begin to see a general strategy taking shape? Let me repeat these realizations quickly; our experience has taught us that, one, we must consider all the factors and call upon the experts; two, any contemplated action must be fitted to the local community, for we must eschew sweeping conclusions and prescriptions; three, compromise is inevitable, and by that token rationalization is inviting; four, we need to build a sense of community and to develop sinews of association, and this means that Negro and white must work together; five, opposition is unavoidable—we expect it; thus, six, our efforts must be educative; and seven, our purpose must be redemptive. When we join to this totality the ethic of love that we already know, we discover, I believe, the outlines of a methodology. Is it not what has come to be called by that most inadequate term "gradualism"?

Our question is still with us: What can we do? What must we do? Gradualism at best is only a generalized answer; specifics are not available. But until the time when some wise theologian develops a dependable methodology for the Christian ethic, gradualism will have to serve, for it embraces the best that we have observed and experienced. We must move ahead, with courageous prudence. We must not move precipitately, for that way is to fail. On the other hand, not to move at all is apostasy. As to the temper in which we act, the Christian ethic calls us to be neither sentimental nor mean. It demands loving, gradual, stubborn advance toward enabling all men to realize their birthright as children of God. Even as we have already learned to speak affirmatively in the full freedom of the gospel, so each of us in his own limited area must learn to act affirmatively to the full limit of the particular possibilities we face. Nobody can tell us exactly what we ought to attempt; but *each of us must be prepared to take the step just beyond the one that caution says is all we can do.*

Which leaves us still with a large measure of perplexity. But that was my point, for the first item in the listing of the things we don't know was, we don't know what to do. *The second* follows close upon it. *We don't know the nature of the personal demand that the Christian ethic lays upon us.* The previous puzzlement had to do with the what; this has to do with the way. Why should we respond to the claim of the Christian ethic? In order to be virtuous? In order to achieve personal perfection, or as close to it as we can come? Or maybe our concern is still with the what after all, though now in a different sense. What is the Christian moral imperative? Be righteous? Be moral?

Conduct yourself so that, no matter the outcome of the cause in which you are engaged, you at least will emerge unspotted from the world?

Confronted with such direct questions we would probably reject their sanguine simplifications of man's moral predicament. We can't be virtuous, we would say; we can't achieve righteousness. All men are sinners, and we are the chief. That is the orthodox response to the overt challenge. Yet without such confrontation, and allowed to live out our normal days in the safety of our normal reflexes, we give unwitting, though continuous, evidence that the contrary is what we really believe. How many of you, for example, had a twinge of disappointment when it was suggested, a moment ago, that the Christian methodology is one of gradualism? How many of you caught the tone of apology with which I offered the suggestion? "That most inadequate term, 'gradualism,'" I said. What is actually inadequate about it? It fits all we know about the difficult task of making fruitful contact between the Christian ethic and the social situation. Yet many of us don't like it because it has, we think, the mark of expediency about it. And somehow, we have been trained by all the idealism imbibed from church and home and school, to believe that the man who is fully loyal to the Christian ethic is the one who mounts his great white charger and dashes off to glorious battle for the Lord. It doesn't matter if his strength is of ten, for, lo, his heart is pure.

Let me tell you a story. About twenty-five years ago at a southern college that sought to govern itself by Christian principles, the student body became concerned over the subject of better race relations. This college was way ahead of the procession, and at that early date was allowing Negroes to eat in its dining hall as guests of the regular students and faculty. But the students, in their idealism, were not satisfied. They went to the president with a petition that Negroes be allowed the full freedom of the institution, and asked that it be presented to the trustees, so that by their proclamation the position of the college could be made forthright, for all the world to see. The president agreed to present the petition, but added, "If you ask my opinion about it, I think it is unwise." "Why?" they said; and so he explained in words something like these:

"We are still living in a stratified society here in the South. The trustees, I can assure you, won't pass any such petition as this at the present time. They can't do so, and still maintain any sort of connection with their constituency. If they are faced with the issue, they will have to vote against you; and then they'll be on record, and it will be at least a full generation before your desire can be considered again. You'll have a good fight; you'll give yourselves a holy glow of righteousness; you'll take a stand—but you'll lose.

And what is more, far from advancing the cause, you will actually retard the whole problem of better race relations. For once the trustees are forced to go on record, you won't be able to do the things you now do. Leave them alone, and you can be sure they won't raise the question either. And thus you will be free to continue working on the problem as you are now doing, quietly, slowly, efficiently. What do you want to do? Have a fight, or help the cause?"

To the credit of that student body it should be added that they saw the point and dropped the petition. It should further be added that that college has continued through the years to be in the vanguard. Incidentally, it is no accident that this illustration should come to mind, for the college was the one on whose campus we are now meeting, and the president was my father. Quite simply, that is how I come to know the story. "Aha," one might say, "you've got gradualism in your blood"; and my only answer is to confess it gladly. And since this has turned into personal testimony, perhaps I'd better say that I am a gradualist simply because I am a bad loser. And I say, in the effort to bring the Christian witness to bear upon the ordeal of the South, we can't afford to lose.

But what I am and what I say don't make any difference. The point is, what does the Christian ethic ask of us? Remember the final comments in the story, for they give a clue, I believe, to the proper answering of our question. "What do you want to do?" the president asked the students. "Have a fight, or help the cause?" The alternative might have been phrased, be virtuous, or be effective? Be righteous, or be faithful to the task? You and I don't like to have the dilemma posed in that fashion; we would prefer to believe that that kind of choice isn't required of us. All right, it isn't, 90 percent of the time. But what about that tragic 10 percent? When that time comes we don't always know which option to exercise. Thus too many of us too easily take the answer, Be virtuous, in one of two possible and self-deceptive interpretations: either, I'll protect my virtue by staying away from the problem, or, I'll assert my virtue by self-righteous attack on the evils all around me. As long as either of these reactions is tempting to us we give evidence that we don't know the nature of the Christian demand upon our lives.

In pursuing the second half of our self-analysis, the part dealing with what we don't know, I have hinted at answers that are available to our quandaries and in the process suggested that we are loath to adopt them. First, we don't know what to do, and the available answer to the effect that we should follow the method of gradualism is not always the one we want to hear. Second, we don't know what should be our response to the Christian imperative, and the proffered suggestion that we be effective in the task rather than protective of our own virtue is often distasteful to us. The third thing that we don't know grows logically out of these first two, and of our reluctance to follow the little light we see. Here, however, we use the word "know" in a different sense, for *the third is "We don't 'know' the requisite will."* Thus far we have used the word to refer to cognitive understanding, but now we mean something more—namely, emotive possession. We simply don't have a sufficiently strong purpose, a determination, to get ahead with the job. This is my reluctant conclusion as to the third thing we don't "know."

In *Time* magazine's recent magnificent and deserved tribute to Martin Luther King Jr., the writer inserted an editorial comment to the effect that "the influential white clergy . . . could—if it would—help lead the South through a peaceful and orderly transitional period toward the integration that is inevitable." That little slur, "could—if it would," made me mad. But before I could take my protesting pen in hand, I had a second thought. "What's wrong?" I said. "It's true." The fault is not that we can't do anything; the fault is that we won't. On the one hand we have suffused the subject of better race relations with sentimentality—we have made sweet statements. On the other we have succumbed to caution and finally to fear. We don't know what to do, sometimes, and we don't know the freedom from righteous self-protection with which to do it. But we know more than enough to outweigh these uncertainties if we were willing. We know the facts of the present situation, or know where we can get them. We know the essence of the present situation, or know where we can get them. We know the essence of Christian ethic. We know that our defenses against its applicability are frail. And we know, in a measure, our guilt. But there may be the key: we don't know the *depth* of our guilt and our sin. For the depth of our guilt is that, knowing it, we are still satisfied to rest in it. *We are willing to be unfaithful. We are unwilling to be faithful.*

> We know the paths in which our feet should press,
> Across our hearts are written thy decrees,
> Yet now, O Lord, be merciful to bless
> With more than these.
> Grant us the will to fashion as we feel,
> Grant us the strength to labor as we know, . . .
> Knowledge we ask not; knowledge thou hast lent;
> But, Lord, the will, there lies our bitter need; . . .

There is a *fourth and final item* in our catalogue of what we don't know, and it can be briefly told. In the present distress that is upon us, and in our efforts, sometimes feeble, mayhap earnest, to seize upon the opportunities it presents, we have to admit that *we don't know what the future holds.* We don't need to know. All we need is to be faithful both to the Christian goal and to the Christian method.

§9 Thurgood Marshall

Thoroughgood Marshall was born on July 2, 1908, to Norma and William Marshall. Living in the relatively prosperous black Baltimore neighborhood of Druid Hill, Marshall's parents reared their two sons in a loving and safe environment—and with high expectations. As an esteemed elementary school teacher, Norma Marshall stayed home with her sons before they attended school. And, while she fretted over her youngest son, who was forced to memorize the U.S. Constitution as discipline for his frequent class disruptions, young Thoroughgood showed promise as a student. He also prevailed upon his parents to shorten his curious moniker—from Thoroughgood to Thurgood—when he was in elementary school. After graduating high school, Marshall followed in his older brother's footsteps and headed to Lincoln University, just thirty miles from Baltimore. The gregarious young man quickly found a niche in college debate and public speaking and parlayed his successes into an interest in law school. He married Vivien Burey in the fall of 1929. Because the University of Maryland law school was closed to him—it did not then admit black students—Marshall was compelled to attend Howard University Law School; it would prove to be a most serendipitous choice, however coerced. Early in his matriculation he came under the spell of Howard's dean, Charles Houston, who quickly sensed in Marshall a precocious legal talent. As the top student in his class, Marshall was awarded with the plum assignment of apprenticing with the estimable Houston, whose legal work with the NAACP was earning him national attention. Upon graduating in 1933 and hanging his shingle back in Baltimore, Marshall's first big break came the following year when he worked with Houston and the NAACP on what came to be known as *Murray v. Maryland*—a case that effectively integrated the University of Maryland law school in 1936. Thus began a nearly twenty-five-year odyssey to reshape the nation's civil rights laws, culminating in the historic 1954 *Brown v. Board of Education* decision, which effectively ended legal segregation in the nation's public schools, and for which Marshall was the chief legal architect. Marshall's wife Vivien died of cancer in February 1955 and he was later remarried, to Cecilia Suyat. In 1961 Marshall left his post as the executive director and chief legal counsel for the NAACP's Legal Defense and Education Fund, and entered public service. He was first appointed by President Kennedy to serve on the Second Circuit of the U.S. Court of Appeals in New York. Four years later in 1965, President Johnson appointed Marshall solicitor general of the United States. And in 1967, Johnson made legal history by appointing Marshall to the U.S. Supreme Court, the first African American ever to serve on the nation's highest court. His tenure would last for nearly twenty-four years, and he retired from the court in 1991. Hailed by some as the greatest lawyer of the twentieth century, and having won twenty-nine of the thirty-two cases he argued before the Supreme Court, Marshall died on January 24, 1993, survived by his second wife and two sons. His papers are housed at the Library of Congress.

In this very revealing extemporaneous address before a northern and Methodist audience, Marshall confesses something of his own civil rights problem: law can go only so far. That is, and as Marshall reminds his listeners throughout the wandering address, the fight against legal segregation in the public schools has been won; he has gone as far as he can go. It is now time for the nation's moral leaders to take a public stand against those preventing what the Supreme Court has mandated. As he rehearses recent racial skirmishes—from Emmett Till and Autherine Lucy to school integration in Clay County, Kentucky, and Clinton, Tennessee—Marshall highlights exceptional leaders, but the problem is precisely that they're exceptions. "Good men" in the North and the South need to "stand up" and negotiate around tables in their own communities. Until such rhetorical leadership is actively practiced, White Citizens' Councils, Klaverns, and obstreperous politicians will continue to bully good citizens into silence. Marshall calls on the church to get in the civil rights game and practice its moral calling; lawyers simply can no longer mitigate the nation's racial problems.

ço~

The Good People Sat Down
April 29, 1957
Detroit, Michigan

Friends, it is not too much I have to say now. And I am really serious about it, because in this so-called struggle for human rights, racial equality, or what-have-you, Dr. Crane was around when Detroit was nowhere near as good as it is now, and it is far from perfect. But he belongs to that group that were out there fighting when it was really tough. And I think that those of us today who have a chance to do something have to look at those who stood up under those terrific ordeals. That is why I am particularly grateful to Dr. Crane for what he said about our work. And I have at least as much ego as anybody else, and I am reasonably sure I have considerable more, but I have no trouble about such fine words you said about our work because Ace Carter, who is head of the White Citizens' Council of Northern Alabama said that I reminded him of a monkey who had been taught to roller-skate. So I put that in the scale; I put the fine things you said in the scale and I divide it by two. That is where I am.

Why talk about segregation or integration in Detroit or in the North, and what interest does a church group have in the North, the northern areas, and what is happening in Mississippi and Alabama and the other southern states?

Well, on the first point, the administration at last found out that the race problem was important. Vice President Nixon came back from Africa with the conclusion that the United States could not talk equality to the darker races of the world and practice inequality in this country. While Secretary of State Acheson found it out a long time ago, Secretary of State Dulles hasn't noticed it yet, but that is understandable. Secretary of State Byrnes found it out. Everybody in foreign affairs has found it out. So that is the interest that the country in general would have in the segregation problem. That is the interest that people in the North have about it.

But why would a church group have interest? Because, I think, as a government and as a group of people we would be less than equal to our governmental principles if we geared our attack on segregation and discrimination and racial prejudice to the fact that we lost prestige in the world because that is a selfish motive.

I think, rather, we should be against it, because, as two or three of our Southern State Conferences of the NAACP said ten years ago, that segregation is not only unlawful and unconstitutional, it is downright immoral. And I believe today we are moving out of that area of constitutionality and unconstitutionality.

The Supreme Court has spoken. There is no other court over it. That is the law. Why can't we have it obeyed and what interest does the North have in it? I get real tired of reading newspapers, magazines, and listening to people in the North who are so sorry about the poor South, that horrible problem they are dealing with. Everybody is against them. It is awful that they have to give up their customs. It is horrible to think of what they are going through.

Well, as good Christians, when did it become so horrible, so horrible, so unfortunate to be forced to abide by the law? When did it become horrible? Monday, two weeks ago? I think that was April 15, I did something that was peculiarly horrible to me. I paid my income tax and didn't a soul grunt and groan about it but me.

Do you know what the real problem is? The people in the North know today as they have known for seventy or eighty years that the reason that the purposes of the Civil War and the Fourteenth Amendment were never carried out was because the North demonstrated by its inaction and sympathy for the South that they were right in what they were doing to the Negroes, and today the southern newspapers and some of the northern newspapers and in many books that are being published, it is pointed out that the North isn't so good about the race problem, either. They are not doing such a good job, either. So, in the South and in the North, we have an awfully hard tug of war with our consciences.

This is where we get in trouble, and the only way out is through our moral teachings, because, you see, we don't want to admit we were wrong in all of the segregation business. We don't want to, in Detroit, blame Mississippi when we know what happened here a few years ago when we had a little housing difficulty resulting in several deaths and a real tough race riot. We don't want to remember that. We want to get away from our own conscience.

We are very much like the old gentleman, the old farmer down south that was on his knees praying one night, and he prayed on and on, very quietly. He prayed so long, his wife wondered what happened to him. She watched him carefully and saw he was breathing. She shook him and said, "What's going on there?"

He said, "You know, I'll tell you what's taking me so long. Every time I start explaining to the Lord how I came about that big hog I brought home this afternoon, I get in trouble explaining how I came to get it."

And, in this problem of race relations and segregation, we have reached the stage after the two-year period since those decisions came down when the soul searching [was] going on, and, that is why Dr. Crane said so many people say, "Let's throw it aside and not side with either side." There are people on both sides of this question who, deep down in their hearts, hope that one morning they will wake up and the problem will be gone.

There is one group that hopes one morning they will wake up and segregation will be gone. And the other group hopes they will wake up and the NAACP will be gone. They are both working on miracles.

As Rev. Martin Luther King said on May 17 of last year, it was, that the real trouble in the country was that after the school desegregation decisions came down, all the good people of the country, North and South—and the good people are so far in the majority that nobody will dispute it—here is what happened to the good people. The good church people, good citizens, stalwart Americans, one group said, "Segregation is gone; Glory, Hallelujah. There is nothing else for me that I need to do," and sat down. The other half said, "The decision is just a piece of paper. It will never be carried out. There is nothing I can do to bring it about." And they sat down.

On both hands, 100 percent of the good people sat down for two different reasons, but they sat down. And so they left the average good citizen, North as well as South, to the tender mercies of the people that preyed on innate prejudices which everybody has. Everybody has some form of prejudice. There are many of us that spend our whole life to make sure we control them and don't let them get out. But they are there. Everybody knows it.

And so they let these people move in, and so today, in the North, they say it will never happen. You can't desegregate the schools in Mississippi ever. You can't do it in South Carolina, and you can't do it here. And the reason the North says it is because they know if they keep the heat on the South, somebody will point to their own front yard—and I didn't say backyard—and, so there is this vicious circle going on, and let's see what brought it about.

We have the bright spots, the really heartening situation. We not only have Rev. Martin Luther King, but we also have that pastor down in Clinton, Tennessee, Rev. [Paul Turner], if I remember correctly, the pastor that on that last day went with the Negro children and was attacked by the mob. The reason I love him is not so much that he did that, took the consequences, but he said that when they backed him up against the car and he couldn't go any further on retreating, he did his best to defend himself and beat the daylights out of two of them at least. That is what I love him for. He at least got two of them.

You will find other pastors in the South like Rev. [Turner], but you won't find many, because too many of them have lost their pulpits as a result of speaking out. So there is a lot that the church can do.

But what I am talking about tonight is developed on one point only. This is that in the North unless a climate of public opinion is built up strong enough, loud enough to be heard once again, the South is going to be able to say with just pride that the North is at least not opposed to what they are doing. It is unbelievable that eight states can dictate to forty states. It is unbelievable that sixteen senators can control eighty. And it is unbelievable that a handful of voters in Mississippi can outmaneuver states like Michigan, Illinois, and New York.

And there is only one reason they can do it. The good people of the country have been sitting down waiting for miracles to happen. When the decisions came down May 17, two years ago, then May 31, the following year, everybody who was anybody felt good. For once we were proud to be Americans. I am not talking about those down behind the cotton curtain, so many who can't read, but those who can read don't pay any attention to it. I am talking about the good people South as well as North.

But, in two years' time, we found how much can be accomplished with not too much prodding. They say, "Let us work it out." We have let them work it out. Now, we have desegregation moving along in nine states, but eight won't move. And, so it is time now for us to say, North as well as South, that there must be some other means of getting this thing moving.

Slavery would have been in existence in this country until this day but for the fact that a group of [hard]headed Americans, bullheaded, if you please, put slavery on the level where it could be attacked—on the high moral plane. Every effort to attack it on the legal plane was lost. The *Dred Scott* case, for example. And it was not until it got on the high moral plane.

Well, this fight today has to be put on this same level. They say the NAACP is on one side and the White Citizens' Council is on the other side. Okay, for a moment, let's agree. Well, who is in the middle? Who is in the middle?

Here is an issue that is important to the South, to the nation, to the world, and they say there are two groups of extremists fighting each other over it. Certainly, we don't belong to either the White Citizens' Council or the NAACP.

It is that large group of inactive people that have allowed this situation to come almost to a head. And there has been no evidence of large-scale moral leadership. Sure, there has been some. In Texas, for example, they got an injunction and temporarily put the NAACP out of business, and we weren't allowed to operate. As a matter of fact, we can't operate now. The truth of the matter is the case is going on in Texas right now. I am playing hooky up here. Right after the injunction was granted over a hundred Negro preachers met in Dallas, Texas, from all over Texas as far west as El

Paso and as far south as Corpus Christi. They came to Dallas and organized and the radio and television people came in and said, "Big deal, what is this? Are you going to take over the NAACP?"

They said, "No. This meeting has no association with the NAACP."

"What is the purpose of this meeting?"

"We'll tell you when the meeting is over."

"It must have some connection."

They held their meeting.

"Have you organized?"

"Yes."

"What is the name of your organization?"

"The National Association for the Advancement of the Christian Principles."

They said, "That is the NAACP, isn't it?"

They said, "No."

"What is your program?"

"We haven't worked out a whole program. We have two points. Our first method of attack, our first project, rather, will be to raise money to defend the lawsuit you have against the NAACP. Our second project is to take over and handle the school segregation cases that the NAACP can't handle, but this is an entirely different organization."

There are bright spots like that. There are bright spots of leadership exemplified by Rev. King and Rev. [William Holmes] Borders in Atlanta; that they said they would settle for no less than jail. They would not move off the bus or anyplace else. They said, "We decided last night we are going to jail and we won't take anything less."

Well like Mrs. [Theresa] Gordon up in Clay, Kentucky; she had nobody on her side and carried her children to that school to get an education. She didn't even have her husband on her side, and her husband was right. He lost his job. And, in case you don't know, that family is now over in Ohio. We are going to build them a home. I think they are entitled to not be living in the street. There are other people like that. There is a fine member of our association in Charlottesville, Virginia, that I just talked to Saturday night; a nice lady. She was a housekeeper for a pretty wealthy family there, and when the petition was filed to desegregate schools in Charlottesville, Virginia, her madam called her in when it came out in the paper that morning.

She said, "These names in the paper, they related to you?"

She said, "They are my grandchildren."

She said, "I never knew you would do a thing like that. I didn't know you belonged to the NAACP."

She said, "Madam, I'm not like a whole lot of other people in my race. I don't make it my business to discuss with you my business. You haven't made it your business to discuss the clubs you belong to with me, and I don't discuss the clubs I belong to with you."

She said, "I don't put up with things like that."

She said, "You give me the key."

She said, "I thought you would take that position, so I brought the key."

She said, "I will take you home."

She said, "No, I don't need to have you take me home. I have my own car that I paid for. And I will get in the car that I paid for and go to the home that I paid for."

People have to realize that this thing is built around Negroes that were born fifty or sixty years ago. They are people that are not going to take less than their rights. So there is no possibility of waking up one morning and finding that this case has been decided the other way.

The NAACP could be run out of business in every state in the Union, and there will still be Negroes that will stand up and insist on their rights and won't now or any other time ask for any help in doing so, because that is what our government is built on.

They say that Negroes and their friends are too impatient. Negroes are no more impatient than the members of the Boston Tea Party were. They are no more impatient than other people that have been asked to wait for their rights. Separate but equal is not so long-standing as you would believe.

I want to go down, one by one, these arguments in favor of them. Separate but equal came about in 1890. There was no separate but equal in slavery. There was just nothing. And there was nothing until citizenship was granted by the Fourteenth Amendment. You see, the *Dred Scott* case was based on the fact that the Negro did not have federal citizenship, so the government had to give him federal citizenship. There, like everything else that happens to Negroes, somebody else goes along with him.

Prior to the Fourteenth Amendment, nobody had federal citizenship in this country; no white man had federal citizenship. The Fourteenth Amendment gave all persons born naturalized in the United States citizenship for the first time. So there is not a single individual in this country, regardless of race, creed, or color, whose ancestors had federal citizenship before the Negroes had it.

We started off equal on federal citizenship. In the law, we started off equal. It is awfully hard convincing people of that. At times, I have difficulty convincing myself. The record shows it.

Then, after the Reconstruction period that I mentioned, they left the Negroes to the tender mercies of the South. Then, we get separate but equal. The Supreme Court in 1896 said separate but equal is valid. Separate but equal became the law from one end of the South to the other and areas of the North. What is wrong with separate but equal? What is wrong with taking people in different places? It was ostracism. It was setting up everything in the mainstream and putting Negroes out of the mainstream. I think when we get on the high moral plane or level or standard, I don't see how a white person can tolerate separate but equal.

A friend of mine in New York, very prominent, who happens to be white—his wife happens to be white—she, today, I think, is the strongest opponent of segregating that I know of, and she has been that way for ten or fifteen years. The reason she is so violently opposed to segregation is that on a trip to Florida, they went across the Chesapeake Bay from the Eastern Shore of Maryland over to Norfolk. They had rigid segregation on those ferries; one-half of the boat for Negroes and one-half for whites. She didn't pay any attention to it. She sat on the sunny side of the boat, which any sensible person would do. They told her she couldn't sit there.

She said, "Why?"

They said, "Because it is reserved for Negroes. You are violating that."

From that day to this, she has been opposed to segregation, not because of the Negroes, but as she puts it, because she was free, white, and twenty-one, and couldn't sit where she wanted to sit.

And I say today that any southern white man that allows himself to be segregated under laws that are unconstitutional according to the Supreme Court is less than a man and certainly is less than a Christian. I could understand it when the law said he had to do it, because we are law-abiding people. But the real trouble in the South today is that the good people have lost the moral leadership in this fight against what is not a southern problem.

It is not whether a poor, little colored boy can be murdered in Mississippi and the murderer can go free. Don't worry about that little boy; he is dead. I can't worry too much about his parents, because there is nothing I can do to bring him back. But you must worry about those people who have set up an atmosphere in Mississippi where if you kill a dog, you have to at least go to trial for it. But, if you kill a black human being, a Christian, you can't be convicted for it. That is what worries me, because that is the type of hatred, that is the type of political shenanigans that made the Klan control the country back in the 1920s.

The newspapers now, at this late date, are getting very excited because the Klan has come back. Is there anybody in this audience that would like to tell me when the Klan left? Never left. They stopped wearing their bed sheets because they found out they were paying twenty-four dollars for it and the man was making twenty-four dollars out of each one they bought.

The eating sore, the cancer has been there waiting for an excuse to come out. And so men like John Kasper, and this man Carter, can go and stir them up. Don't worry about Kasper. They had an investigation of Kasper in Florida. The great, white supremist in Clinton, Tennessee; they put him on the witness stand; they made him admit when he was in New York during his leisure time he was in Greenwich Village going around with colored girls. So they kind of lost faith. The Klan put him out.

There will be others. Do I worry about Kasper? Not in the least. Kasper is a little pipsqueak that has never made a success of anything he tried until he tried preying on people's innate racial prejudices and was allowed to go unchecked by the good people in the community. Not [to] worry about Kasper. I am worried about the good people that let him take over. I don't say they should ride him out of town or run him out of town. By all means, give him his freedom of speech and listen to him. And, then, tell him politely, "No, thank you; I don't care for what you peddle."

But it was the lack of moral leadership in that town that allowed Kasper to get a hold so that it has taken them a year to bring about trying to break his hold, because he was preying on their innate prejudices, and on the other side, somebody wasn't doing enough of exciting people's Christian spirits that would, of course, push aside prejudices.

This thing is not sudden. They tell you that it was a shame how we forced Autherine Lucy into the University of Alabama so suddenly last year. You remember that statement. A lot of people think that. Some of my best friends, two of my best friends stopped speaking to me. Do you know how suddenly we put her in the University of Alabama? She applied and was accepted at the University of Alabama in 1952, and the case was in court for four years and it was four years later that they ran out of legal gimmicks and they had to admit her. Other girls who had applied at the same time she applied had graduated.

Now, what was so sudden about it? They said she drove up in a big Cadillac car. Remember that story? Well, it wasn't a Cadillac; it was a Pontiac.

And, when people say we were wrong in sending her to the University of Alabama, maybe we were wrong. I think it is wrong to send somebody to school where they don't know the difference between a Cadillac and Pontiac; it is wrong.

Could have been a big mistake.

Do you realize that you can remember the *Lucy* case; everybody can. And yet nobody remembers that in twelve other states in the South, Negroes have been going to those state universities for three and four years without one single incident or not one single campus has one student opposed to it. In twelve states. We don't remember the good things because they are not news. It is the bad things that are news.

They said we were wrong to put Virgil Hawkins in the law school in Florida last May; May of '56. His case was filed in February of '49, seven years ago. The case has been to the Supreme Court three times. And so they said suddenly we pushed him in. If we don't hurry up and get him in, we might have to make a place for his son.

How long can we wait on these things? They say that they admit that they have held the Negro back. They admit that they have denied him equal education and have given him inferior education. They admit that. And then they say, "However, on achievement tests, invariably the Negro on an average comes up below the white student; therefore, we can't put him in the same class as the white student."

You understand, the same people say that they are responsible for the Negroes getting the inferior education, but they, the same people, can't do anything about it because they can't let them now go to school because they are inferior. It is simple.

It is very much like a famous case that is told about in Texas, of the man who was on trial, charged with murdering his mother and father, and pleaded for mercy on the grounds that he was an orphan.

The real truth is that invariably in segregated school systems, Negroes will come up, on an average, below the average of the white students, but it is also true and admitted by scientists that individual Negroes will be found to not only be above the average of the whites, but up with the best white students, and vice versa.

And our government's Constitution and our whole principle of government is based on the equality of the individual; the individual's right not to be held down by any class or any group factor. I wonder if there is any blond in this audience that would be willing to have all of his rights determined by the average of all blonds in the country or with the redheads or brunettes.

Certainly, you would think it was silly. It is silly for everybody else. But it is always logical for Negroes.

Now, if you want to place children in classes according to an achievement test, without regard to race, but in regard to where they stand, nobody would object to it. Put the smart Negroes in with the other smart students in most of these school systems, they have three channels, three steps they call them in some area; but not because of race. So there is not one single argument in favor of maintaining segregation that will stand up on a scientific test left on the books today.

The only reason is that they have had it so long and it is a problem to change what you become used to. Yes, it is, I agree and nobody that would not agree would be crazy. But it is not an insoluble [problem]. The simple solution is to get the men of goodwill—I don't mean the politicians; I don't mean the school boards; I don't mean people of that type—I mean the good, substantial citizens of both races that have no axes to grind; men of goodwill. Put them around the table in each town and let them work, not on whether they should desegregate, because that has been decided by the Supreme Court, and there is nothing anybody can do about it, but when and how we shall desegregate. Let both sides give and take and the problem would be solved in town after town, but for the fact that they have organized these groups like the White Citizens' Councils that dare anybody to move. And they use economic boycotts against the Negroes and the white man as well.

There is a man I know in a town in Mississippi. He owns a medium-sized furniture store and his trade is about fifty white and fifty Negro. And the White Citizens' Council told him if he doesn't join up, they are going to boycott him. If he joins up, the Negroes will boycott him. All that man is trying to do is run his business and make a buck. That is all. He is not interested one way or the other. But I told him, unfortunately, that he was a fairer man than I am because all the other stores had joined the White Citizens' Council. So he wants to make a buck. What he should do is not join and tell all the Negroes that all the others did join, and he would get enough Negro business to take care of the other business.

But, my friends, I hope you can understand the reason I put these things this way, because in many respects, this fight has degenerated into the type of thing that is just that silly. And, over and over again, I have been able to use examples which we have understood, I think, to show how silly it is.

That is the second point. It is the conscience of having denied these people their rights all along and now the recognition that there is no basis for it—as a matter of fact, it is silly and laughable. But, in order to get rid of it, the man or woman has to admit that he has been wrong and that what he has been doing has actually been silly and so, today, you find starting with the governor of the state, the attorney general, and on down the line, they say we can't move a peg. It is not gradualism involved.

The Supreme Court provided for gradualism, if you want to use that word. Not one single instance has anybody demanded [integration] tomorrow. But, certainly, after two years, somebody should be thinking about it.

Finally let me just put this down. In the North today, the support has to come from the same people; it must come from the South. That is the group of people recognized as leaders of the community for other than selfish purposes. I, for one, believe that even in the separation of church and state, there are certain state matters that are of such high moral purpose as to demand and require support from the organized church.

Certainly the Fourteenth Amendment was brought about by, written by, and adopted in Congress in the interest of that old Judeo-Christian ethic based upon the equality of man. The Fourteenth Amendment either has high moral ground or it has no basis or foundation in fact.

I think we have waited as long as we can to get this along without the support of the church. The condemnation of the U.S. Supreme Court, the condemnation of the NAACP, the condemnation of anybody who even opens his mouth about integration must be met or there won't be any more desegregation.

If you can desegregate schools in West Virginia, you can do it in Virginia. If you can desegregate schools in the District of Columbia, you can go across the Potomac River and desegregate schools in Arlington, Virginia. But the powers that be in Virginia know when we desegregate schools in Arlington, the county next to it is going to do it, and the county next to that, and eventually the whole state is going to be desegregated.

And, as soon as Negroes and white children go to elementary school together in the South and understand each other, and the white students find out that there are some decent Negroes and some bums in the group and vice versa, when they go to school together, high school together and college, and serve in the Armed Forces together and come home, they are going to know that a man is measured by his worth and not his race. And, once that is done, all these politicians in the South are going to have to find something else to get elected on instead of running around and talking about Negroes, and also know they have brains and intelligence or common sense enough to find another program and they will be out of office.

They have a vested interest in maintaining segregation, and I think it is high time we recognized it. The normal American courage and will to abide by the law has effectively brought to the end that good Americans in the South and North as well permit them to tolerate the actions of White Citizens and Klans and groups.

First, there was this misunderstanding of the purpose and effect of the separate but equal doctrine. Secondly, there has been almost complete immobilization of trained community leadership otherwise dedicated to seeking obedience to the morality and law. There has been an intensive mobilization of action aimed at the Constitution and Supreme Court. It is time to reverse this trend. If a reversal is to come, it will not happen by silence and inaction and lack of courage. If it is to come, it must be spearheaded by organized community groups under the guidance of people trained in the field of social relations and those trained in the organized churches.

Deep in the minds of too many people is the feeling still that there is some rhyme or reason to the claim of inherent inferiority in Negroes. In many respects, separate but equal [doctrine] has been more devastating than slavery itself, because it has created this feeling in too many people's minds.

There is a wealth of publicity that the Supreme Court exceeded its authority in desegregation. These stories are all aimed at convincing Americans in high and low places that the Supreme Court need not be respected. Congressmen, senators, and attorney generals, and others have made derogatory statements about the Supreme Court. The arguments against the decisions themselves are facetious and can be dispelled. Everyone knows our Constitution is supreme; all state law to the contrary must yield.

That is what Article Six says. There is no middle ground as far as constitutional law is concerned. There is no longer any legal justification for any community not getting a program of cleaning up racial prejudice in its area. There is adequate legal protection from the federal government for any school board, North as well as South, wishing to desegregate its schools.

The one stumbling block is the lack of will to desegregate in many areas, or maybe it is the fear of action from the White Citizens' Councils or KKK or local politicians. Whatever the reason is, it is not a legal one; it is not a valid one; and it has no basis in our moral teaching. Individuals and communities under the guidance of organized religious groups, trained religious leaders, trained community workers, must take over from the lawless, and the timid as well.

As one great American said some years back, not too long ago, there is really nothing to fear but fear itself. There is no peace during slavery. There has been no peace through separate but equal. None of us can escape our democratic principles, our Constitution, our law, nor our own conscience. There will be no peace in the field of race relations until our country and all of us in it can enjoy the calm that can come only from knowing that we have done what is right.

§10 Charles C. Diggs Jr.

Charles C. Diggs Jr. was born on December 2, 1922, to Charles and Ethel Jones Diggs. As the only child of a prominent Detroit family, Diggs quickly assumed the mantel of achievement. After graduating from Miller High School as class president in 1940, Diggs entered the University of Michigan, where he won the school's oratory contest in 1941. After transferring to Fisk, Diggs somewhat reluctantly joined the U.S. Air Force in 1943; the Navy refused to enlist him because he was black. Diggs served with the famed Tuskegee Airmen in Alabama though his poor eyesight prevented him from becoming a pilot. While in the Deep South Diggs felt the sting of racism firsthand as he watched German prisoners of war receive far better treatment than black servicemen. After the war Diggs earned a degree in mortuary science from Wayne State University, and he continued the family business. He entered Michigan state politics in 1951 by winning a state senate seat. Three years later he won the race for Michigan's thirteenth congressional district; in so doing he became the state's first black person to serve in the House. Sworn into office in 1955, Diggs served with just two other black men: Adam Clayton Powell Jr. and Charles Dawson. That same year, in April, Diggs spoke at a huge gathering of black activists gathered at the estate of Mound Bayou, Mississippi, surgeon Dr. T. R. M. Howard. Diggs leveraged that relationship several months later when he showed up unannounced at a courthouse in Sumner, Mississippi, for the trial of Roy Bryant and J. W. Milam—the two men accused of murdering Chicago youth Emmett Till. He quickly became a hero to the small contingent of black journalists gathered in Sumner; to southern whites he was vilified as a northern intruder who had no business in a Mississippi courtroom. After the trial he spoke out frequently against the miscarriage of justice, along with Howard and Emmett's mother, Mamie Till.

During a lengthy career in the House, Diggs cofounded the Congressional Black Caucus and served as its first chairman in 1969. Later he became known as Mr. Africa for his unstinting lobbying for its emerging nations—and for his aggressive campaign against the apartheid regime. His twenty-five-year political career came to a swift end in 1980 when he was forced to resign his seat after being convicted of twenty-nine counts of mail fraud and taking kickbacks from his congressional staffers. After serving fourteen months in an Alabama federal prison, Diggs earned a political science degree at Howard University and opened a funeral home in Maryland. He died on August 24, 1998, of complications from a stroke. A wife and six children survived him. His papers are housed at the Moorland-Spingarn Library at Howard University.

Diggs was likely invited to this anniversary event in Jackson, Mississippi, by Medgar Evers, NAACP field secretary for the state, whose office bordered the Masonic Temple. No doubt many attendees remembered Diggs fondly for his outspokenness during and after the Till trial. As a trained mortician, Diggs' identification of "separate but equal" as a "rotting carcass" too long above ground creates a telling contrast with the rotten corpse of Emmett Till too long below ground. In the first half of his address, Diggs carefully autopsies that carcass: it bears the traces of the Klan, the White Citizens' Councils, bellicose state legislatures, and those hypocrites infatuated with interracial sex. He concludes that integration will eventually triumph—even in Mississippi. But in order for that to happen, Diggs calls on the church to continue to lead, and especially the black clergy, "our talented and trained people." Blacks also have a "definite responsibility in our initiative and our personal conduct" to be equal to the call of freedom and equality; further, blacks must patronize black-owned businesses. Diggs closes his eloquent address by calling on the young and the old to register and vote. Little did he perhaps realize that that particular battle would be fought in the state for the next eight years—a fight that the state would initially win, Governor Coleman's testimony notwithstanding.

The Star Beckons Again

May 19, 1957
Jackson, Mississippi

It is a genuine privilege to return once again to the home state of many of my ancestors and friends. The seed of the Diggs family, though planted originally in Africa, was transplanted to America and watered with the blood, sweat, and tears of this state. It pushed its small sapling up through Mississippi soil, grew and sprouted the branches of my great-grandfather, my grandfather, who was an esteemed Baptist minister and builder of churches here and there who in turn germinated other branches, which, of course, included my father, Charles C. Diggs Sr., of Issaquena County, now Michigan's beloved and respected benefactor, philanthropist, business executive, and public servant. That tree—rooted in Africa—transplanted in Mississippi—and now flowering in Michigan—gives me a genuine kinship with you and should dispel any notion that I am a "northern agitator" who does not understand your problems.

Despite whatever attainments I may have made, I have not missed the whiplash of second-class citizenship—in a segregated school—and in a thousand other ways that have touched every facet of my life. Notwithstanding all the humiliation and frustration of these experiences, however, I do not reject the principles of democracy as my ultimate savior.

The Negro people have been tenaciously loyal to America. From Crispus Attucks to the last black finger that pulled a trigger in Korea, we have made human sacrifices upon the altar of freedom. After each sacrifice, we have returned home and peacefully pressed to share the benefits of our nation's victory. Yet in our fervent and common need with all mankind for liberty, and equality, no group has suffered greater indignities. No group has been more patient, more considerate, more level-headed in the face of tyranny. From the May 1854 *Dred Scott* decision, a hundred years prior to the mandate we are presently commemorating, through the Emancipation Proclamation, through the executive decrees and judicial directives of our day, over the bodies of the Emmett Tills, and under the determination of the Martin Luther Kings, Negroes have peaceably pursued their quest for freedom down the legal pathways of the land. Go almost any day and in any direction outside this country and you will hear shouts and shots coming from people who have rebelled against their government for FAR less than the painful conditions to which the American Negro is subjected. Yet our adversaries all across this country, especially in the Deep South, demand even more moderation—demand that we continue to accept the inferior status implicit in legal segregation and discrimination—demand that we bow yet longer to the unrewarding gods of bigotry and oppression—despite such historic decisions as rendered by the highest judicial body in this land on May 17, 1954.

Is the justice of equality always to be for us just out of reach?—the mirage on the desert of our yearnings? Americans, Europeans, Asians, Africans—all have come to the time when they have stopped still to vow—"No! I shall never believe this good—so universally preferred to all others—without which all others are nothing is not meant for ME." This is today the protest and the vow of a uniting Negro people.

They call this date—May 17, 1954—"Black Monday" in Mississippi. Let us not deplore this derisive description mouthed by demagogues whose minds are shackled by fearful visions of the onrushing judgment day. In a sense, it was "Black Monday"—a burial day for the old "separate but equal" doctrine whose rotten carcass had been above ground for too many years—a diseased body which had infected our values because with only one-fourth as much money being spent on Negro education in the Deep South as was expended on whites, it created an average lag in achievement which completely distorted the potentialities of our people, intellectual and otherwise. Add to this the factor of sheer discrimination and its effect upon the Negro's general development and you have him caught in a vise so tight any of his attainments are wonders to behold. Of no less significance is the implication in a segregated society that certain symbols of disassociation between the races denote a superior and inferior status. Separate schools, separate water fountains, separate sections of a bus, theater, sports stadium, etc.—all of these overt discriminations gnaw at our self-respect. To compound the inconsistency of this crime against human dignity, we find Negroes in the South standing in line with white people at the bank, mingling with them at grocery and department stores, and yet Negroes cannot sit next to white people on any occasion. Perhaps we should give serious consideration to the observation of Harry Golden, the editor of the *Carolina Israelite*, who says, "No one in the South pays the slightest attention to their 12 million *vertical* Negroes who buy standing up each day. It is only when the Negro *sits down* that the fur begins to fly. So to solve the school segregation problem, why not provide only desks in all the public schools?; NO SEATS—like the old fashioned bookkeeping desks. If the present pattern of accepting Negroes in this position is followed, it should not make anybody mad."

There is little question that the Deep South has won the first round in the battle for compliance with the Supreme Court decision. After three years, we unfortunately cannot point to one instance of submission to this verdict by Mississippi, Georgia, South Carolina, or Alabama. On the contrary, not only have they erected a maze of legal entanglements through which the soldiers of freedom must march to their inevitable victory, they have outflanked our main position with several diabolically clever devices.

They have established such a resolute stand against integration that no elected official dares to support it publicly. They have created an atmosphere which had stifled expressions from reasonable white people who, at least, respect the mandates of the Supreme Court. They have discouraged the interracial cooperation, discussion, and informal desegregation which began to emerge after World War II. They have purposely misconstrued the intent of the Supreme Court decision to mean instant and complete school integration everywhere with no time to work out reasonable plans—which is the remotest thing from the truth. They have prepared to close down the public schools if necessary to prevent integration. The ignorant have taken the hooded robes of the Ku Klux Klan out of the mothballs and reminded us of their infamous activities in the 1920s. The more intelligent, but equally dedicated to white supremacy, have initiated Citizens' Councils, which principally use economic reprisals, but which are not above other forms of intimidation of nonconformists. They have made the NAACP the target of a multipronged attack—bitter denunciation, including charges of Communist infiltration—eight suits filed in six states against the organization and its officers—the enactment of legislative measures designed to make the NAACP impotent. They have popularized the sex angle tune until it has returned as number one in the Hate Parade, despite the Negro's plea that he wants to be the white man's brother, not his brother-in-law. They have stormed the bastions of the Mason-Dixon line and started the biggest barrage of race and religious hate literature in American history, flowing into the North in an effort to recruit additional support.

We are experiencing some trouble-filled times, but those of us who have actually lived with the problem of color prejudice had predicted that the transitory stage of desegregation would be fraught with flaming issues. The Supreme Court recognized this situation when it issued its edict. First of all, because of varied local school problems, local school authorities were given the primary responsibility for solving them. Secondly, because of their proximity to local conditions and the possible need for further hearings, the local courts which originally heard these cases were given the responsibility for determining whether the action of local school authorities constitutes good faith implementation of the governing constitutional principles. However, the court also said that while due weight may be given to the public interest and private considerations, it would require a prompt and reasonable start toward full compliance.

No rational person can read this decision and charge that the court is inflexible and inconsiderate in applying its mandate. If Mississippi,

Georgia, South Carolina, and Alabama had followed the lead of other affected states, they would not be in their present predicament. Instead, these four recalcitrant states have chosen to take the hands off the clock and ignore the admonition that—there is time but none to spare. This they have done despite reports from other previously segregated school districts that explode the myth of the amateur and professional hatemonger.

No rational person can deny the ultimate triumph of integration. It is inevitable as the rising sun, even in Mississippi. America cannot afford, in the interest of justice, to let hoodlums and race baiters crawl out from under the rocks and defy the law of the land. America cannot afford to have her international prestige, as leader of the Free World, diminished in the eyes of the African-Asian bloc of nations which comprise two-thirds of the earth's population. There is much more at stake than just the personal preference of some misguided people. To give you a local example I refer you to a Mississippi study made public recently which showed white residents to be departing at a faster rate than Negroes, upsetting a trend to the contrary that had prevailed for more than fifty years. From April 1950 to July 1956, according to an article in today's Memphis *Commercial Appeal*, Mississippi lost 51,335 whites, but only 28,842 Negroes, increasing the proportion of Negroes in this state from 45 to 46 percent. Losses of white persons represent a far greater economic depletion to any community than that of Negroes because they have a higher level of education, representing a greater investment. It takes no genius to see the implications of segregation entwined in those figures. The white people who are forced to leave Mississippi to seek their fortunes elsewhere are young in age and principally high school graduates who do not find enough outlets for their training or potentialities. They do not find it because many prudent northern industrialists hesitate to invest in a state so preoccupied with the immoral and illegal subjugation of 46 percent of its citizens. Mississippi will never realize its cherished dreams of a successful "Balance Agriculture with Industry" program until it balances the books on human equality. Oh!, what price segregation, white Mississippians! You exhort your governor and other state and local officials to economize on one hand and then endorse the establishment of a $250,000 commission to preserve a system of separate racial facilities which drives your whole economy to its knees. You exhort the president and Congress of the United States to cut the expenditures for foreign aid, and yet it is your discriminatory acts which challenge the sincerity of democracy and helps cause us to have to spend more money abroad to counteract the resulting anti-American propaganda.

The Negro wants so little that it is a constant source of amazement that he does not demand a higher price for his pain and suffering. He seeks an equal opportunity, to be judged on his merits alone, and to be treated with the same dignity and respect as any other human being. Could not such a treaty be signed in the interest of lasting peace? Would it not preclude the greater sacrifice inherent in the current war of racial conflict?

When England realized she could no longer keep her colonists in subjection she gave them membership in the British Commonwealth. A long and bitter fight was thus avoided which would have converted her colonials into enemies instead of partners and friends. This is what can be accomplished in the South if the decent people of the section would exercise courage and imagination.

Right methods inevitably produce right results. Our greatest reservoir of potential assistance lies in those who create an atmosphere of opinion—in their service clubs—in their coffee break talks—in business transactions—in grassroots political decisions—in church affairs—in parent-teacher associations—in the home—in a multitude of daily contracts. They elect the local officials who compete with each other in proposing spiteful methods to keep the Negro in "his place." They exert the pressures of ridicule and censorship against those who stray from the fold. They foster and support the white supremacy groups which kindle the basest passions of the community.

How then do we reach into their hearts and awaken the Christian spirit which lies dormant therein? Here is our answer: a black Alabama minister, Rev. Martin Luther King, a modern Moses sent to Montgomery to deliver his people into the Promised Land, has lifted his hand and quietly but effectively pointed the way to the cross. A white, southern-born and bred minister, the Reverend Robert B. McNeil, of Columbus, Georgia, a converted nonsegregationist, speaks the same language from the pages of the current edition of LOOK magazine and says, "With all our concentration upon making or altering our laws so that they are just, there must be some social organism that toils without ceasing at the task of making or altering men. Of all the institutions we know—economic, political and social—the church, whose prime function is the revealing of Christ, is the only one that possesses the seeds of its own regeneration. The church's weakness is caused by its human composition, but its permanence is because it is God's. Paradoxically, it toughens on persecution, reverts to strength when it becomes weakest, waxes greater when it becomes smaller, grows militant when it loves peace, profits as it sacrifices, wanes under the excesses of success, but lives again as it dies. It is as inevitable as change, enduring as sin, as everlasting as

God. There can be no destruction of it from within or without. The church will always be as strong as it self-critical."

There is evidence, despite the discouraging inventory in the Deep South, that the star which guided the Wise Men to the Christ child almost two thousand years ago beckons again to lead the wise men of today back to HIM so that HE can wash away their sins of inequality. There is a ground swell of church organizations going on record against the evil of segregation. We are cheered by this spiritual nourishment. It transforms our despair into hope—our fear into courage. It sustains our belief that majorities do not rule America or the world. Thought rules it, and it does not make any difference whether that thought is under a white—a red—a brown—yellow—or a black skin.

This was graphically demonstrated to me during my recent trip to Africa with the vice president of the United States. Time and time again—in Morocco, in Ghana, in Liberia, in Sudan, in Ethiopia, in Uganda, in Tunisia, in Libya—the voices of 200 million nonwhite people persistently taunted us with questions about the racial problem here in America. You can run, but in 1957 no one can HIDE! Even on my way back home through the European continent, I read of American racial incidents in the newspapers of London and Paris. As the world shrinks the brown man thinks. As the world shrinks, the yellow man thinks. As the world shrinks, the black man thinks. As the world shrinks the decent white man thinks. How long will it pass before some stubborn people heed the warning of our diplomats, our statesmen in Congress, our vice president, and our president, that isolationism and provincialism and hatesmanship result in the destruction of the Free World and everything we hold so dear?

The salvation of our people is bigger than the white man's ability to achieve it. Neither his proud history of attainments nor his inventive genius is sufficient to cope successfully with this problem alone. This is why it is always amuses me whenever I hear him say, "I've been around Negroes all my life; I know what is best for them." I've got news for him: We do not always know what is best for ourselves, but we do know that the solution to interracial harmony demands a policy of partnership. We Negroes have a definite responsibility in our initiative and our personal conduct, and we have to recognize it more and more. Everyone pities a beggar, but no one respects him. A dependent race is a poor race. A poor race is a despised race. Let us wake up to the advantages of economic cooperation and support amongst us and stop being the commercial footmat of other people. If the average Negro would patronize Negro-owned businesses as he does the

Negro undertaker, he could bury many of his problems including economic reprisals. If the Negro would be bold enough to try to venture onto new fields of endeavor and break the binds that tie him to traditionally Negro jobs and professions, he could open up many doors of opportunity that are not actually closed.

If the Negro would only recognize the power in unity of purpose, especially in a place like Mississippi where he resides in such preponderant numbers. Whether we are a cotton picker or a college president, a busboy or a bishop, a domestic or a doctor, each and every one of us must take a maximum contribution to the cause of equality. We must translate the yearning of our soul for liberty, freedom, and justice into positive action to achieve our goal. In my opinion, the number one target for the black people of Mississippi is to obtain the right to vote.

In February of this year, high-ranking elected officials from this state came to Washington and testified before the committee in Congress which was considering legislation to strengthen the protection of the right to vote. Permit me to read you an excerpt from that testimony. (On page 737 of the printed record) Congressman Miller, of New York, asked Governor Coleman of Mississippi the following question: "Do I understand, Governor, that anyone, colored or white, who wishes to vote in the State of Mississippi may just present himself to the registrar and give vital statistics and then answer a questionnaire?" Governor Coleman replied, "That is right, it is uniform for everybody . . . and prescribed from the state law to be sure there will be no discrimination." Congressman Miller further asked the governor: "So the same questions are asked of all white and colored?" Governor Coleman: "Exactly." Congressman Miller: "So in the State of Mississippi you ask the same question on the questionnaire to all and the same questionnaire is submitted to all and all pay the same poll tax proposed by the state; there is no discrimination between colored and white as the right to vote?" Governor Coleman: "These are not secret questions. The truth is when they get these questionnaires containing the questions they hold what they call voting classes where they teach people how to answer the question. No effort is made to stop them. If he is interested in voting and exercising the franchise and wants to learn what the questions are about, there is no effort made to stop him. He knows before he goes up to the courthouse what the questions are going to be. It is not something that is sprung on him when he is not prepared."

The governor went on further to explain on page 740 of the hearings that in Mississippi all those who become twenty-one years of age before the date of the general election in that year vote without payment of poll tax. And all those sixty years of age and over vote without payment of poll tax.

There you have it, my friends, in black and white—the sworn testimony of the governor of Mississippi before a committee of the Congress of the United States. Now I am not going to question the integrity of the governor of a sovereign state in this union. I am further not going to consider that a person has been gifted with the highest position which the people of this state can confer would be so naïve that he was not aware that the representations he made could not be substantiated. And so, on the basis of these facts, I want to urge with every fiber of my being that every black man and every black woman of twenty-one years of age or over pick out a convenient time on his or her next birthday and march to the appropriate place and endeavor to qualify for registration. Those of you who hide behind hearsay, rumors, or your own disinterest do not deserve the benefits of first-class citizenship. I urge also that you make Jackson, the largest city in the state, the testing ground of your initial effort. If you are not successful in Jackson, with all of the advantages usually found in a large metropolitan area, in addition to the fact that it is the capital, the prospects for further enfranchisement in the rest of the state will be indeed limited.

In the days of heartaches and headaches, our forebears spit the dust of the ages from their mouths and cry out for us to sustain the courage they bequeathed. It is this spirit of courage which nourished the black race through bondage, through disenfranchisement, through lynchings, through iniquitous Jim Crow laws, and through all the insults and indignities heaped upon us by the unreasonable prejudice of the American peoples. It is this spirit of courage which Rev. Martin Luther King says teaches us paradoxically to love our enemy even though we hate his misdeeds. It is this spirit of courage which motivates us to tell old Uncle Tom to move on out of our house—that he has overstayed his time. It is this spirit of courage, coupled with unselfishness, which should inspire to greater activity our talented and trained people who have had superior education because of the support of the masses who now so desperately need their leadership. This is especially true of our ministers. They generally have the ear of their congregation as no one else has. There should be a strong, nondenominational union of all our ministers in Jackson through whom plans of action can be transmitted to the people. This new, dynamic, inspired Christian leadership has been manifested in Montgomery, in New Orleans, in Tallahassee, in Birmingham, and in Atlanta, among other places, and can well be emulated here.

Lastly, it is this spirit of courage which forever reminds us to support the NAACP as first and foremost among the expanding number of other organizations motivated by righteous instincts.

Let us maintain faith in our fellow man, faith in God, and in faith in our fist, if necessary. Then one day that sign on the outskirts of Sumner, Mississippi, site of the Emmett Till trial, which proudly boasts that it's a "good place to raise a boy" will really mean something to every boy in America, whether he be black or white, and the muted calls for freedom coming from the graves of our ancestors which echo down the long corridor of time will be forever silent in the sweet repose of peaceful sleep.

§11 C. O. Inge

Rev. Clinton Owen Inge was born on February 25, 1909, in Geiger, Alabama. He attended a Presbyterian high school before receiving a bachelor's degree in religious education at American Baptist Theological Seminary in Nashville, Tennessee. On June 16, 1941, he married Laura Mae Holloway, who suggested that his high school training may have been the reason he did not resort to "whooping and hollering" in the pulpit. The Inges raised eight children together. Rev. Inge served as pastor in Laurel, Mississippi, from 1947 to 1959 and at New Hope Baptist church from 1959 to 1974. He died on May 10, 1993. His wife's and daughter's oral histories are available online at the University of Southern Mississippi's Civil Rights Documentation Project.

The following sermon is a keynote address at Pratt Memorial Methodist church before the Ministerial Improvement Association of Mississippi on October 1, 1957. Though the setting is tense—just days after the Little Rock Nine's dramatic integration of Central High School in neighboring Arkansas, the Inge family had not yet faced the most difficult moments of the era. Several years later in Meridian, Inge's son was forbidden to join Chaney, Goodman, and Schwerner on their fateful trip to Philadelphia. Rev. Inge would soon awake early mornings to clean up threatening graffiti before children could be intimidated, drive his daughter and four others to desegregate Mississipi's largest high school, sit evenings in the dining room with a rifle, and arrive to his miraculously preserved brick church after several attempts were made to burn it to the ground, and host Andrew Young, Medgar Evers, and others needing safe haven in the early to mid-1960s. Yet the context is tense. Inge lauds his audience for their courage to assemble, and uses biblical references to remind them that prophecy has always gone hand in hand with crisis and courage. He reminds them as well that those in power who sin will be called to justice, whether the sin be the "whoredom of Sodom and Gomorrah," the "water meter past due" of the three-and-half-year drought during Ahab and Jezebel's reign, the parole of Paul and Silas, or the sins of Nineveh. Likewise he reminds his audience of ministers that there is no one better than a preacher to be active in the most tumultuous events of the day, whether in Isaiah's, Martin Luther's, or the current day.

ৎ৯৫৶

No Time for Cowards
October 1, 1957
Jackson, Mississippi

Mr. President, Officers, Members, and Persons present:

I have been assigned the task of bringing the keynote address, and I would like to begin by saying WE ARE HERE. And when God's truly called and anointed ministers are somewhere somebody is there.

When Elijah stood on the palace porch of Ahab and Jezebel and told them of their sins, somebody was on the front porch that day. When Elijah read the water meter and sent in a past due bill, God cut the water off for three years and six months. When Elijah prayed on Mt. Carmel, God struck a match in heaven and set fire to the bullock and the water around the altar burned like kerosene.

When Paul and Silas prayed in the Philippian jail God sent an angel down with keys to fit every door in the jailhouse and paroled all of the prisoners.

When Jonah walked the streets of Nineveh for a day's journey and cried, "Yet forty days and Nineveh shall be overthrown," there was a man in town that day.

Nobody can stir the world like a preacher. Paul shook Asia, Europe, Greece, and Italy. Peter shook the world on the day of Pentecost. Martin Luther shook Germany. And I could go to name a catalog of ministers who have shaken the world. When God's man gets in town and gets right he stirs things.

To be here bespeaks courage. Who would date, in such a time as this, but men of courage? These times demand men of courage; this is no time for cowards. The words of the poet who long ago are up to date today when he said:

God, give us men. A time like this demands
Strong minds, great hearts, true faith and ready hands;
Men whom the lust of office does not kill;
Men whom the spoil of office cannot buy;
Men who possess opinions and will;
Men who have honor, men who will not lie;
Men who can stand before the demagogue
And damn his treacherous flatteries without winking;
Tall men, sun-crowned, who live above the fog,
In public duty and private thinking;
For while the rabble with their thumb worn creeds,
Their large professions and their little deeds,
Mingle in selfish strife . . . lo, freedom weeps
While wrong rules the land, and waiting justice sleeps.
God, give us men; men who serve not for booty.
But real men, courageous, men who flinch not a duty;
Men of dependable character; men of sterling worth;
Then wrongs will be redressed, and right will rule the earth.
GOD GIVE US MEN.

Yes, these times call for men of quality and width—men who are all wool and a yard wide. So to be here is an evidence of courage.

We are not here as a bunch of radicals trying to stir up something; there is a plenty already up. We are not here for publicity—to be seen, or to get on the front page, so to speak. We're here on business for the King. We are ambassadors of goodwill from earth, crying to his confused world, "Be reconciled to God." We are God's angels of the church—the seven stars standing amidst the seven candlesticks. We are God's flames of fire to purge the sinful lips of every twentieth-century sinner.

We are here to let hell know that heaven still rules; that God is still on the throne; we are here to tell the world that, just as sure as the whoredom of Sodom and Gomorrah went up before God, as definitely as Abel's blood cried from the ground, as sure as the wickedness of Nineveh went up before God, as truly as the groans of the children of Israel went up before God, so does the sins of America, and the groans of the oppressed minorities of our country going up before Him.

We are here to warn America not to fool herself, God is not to be ignored, for whatsoever a man soweth the same shall he also reap. We are here to tell the nations in the words of Isaiah, "Come near, ye nations, and hear; and harken, ye people; let the earth hear—for the indignation of the Lord is upon all nations, and his fury is upon all armies." We are here to tell America in the words of the prophet, "Woe to thee that spoils, and thou was not spoiled; and dealest treacherously, they shall deal treacherously with thee." We are here to tell America that "Righteousness exalts a nation, but sin is a reproach to any people."

We are here because the world needs our spiritual leadership. We face grave problems today—problems that cannot be solved by might nor power; problems that must be solved by the spirit of God alone. These problems demand our best thinking, our best understanding, our best tolerance, on the side of both groups, if they are to be solved in any degree of satisfaction. We cannot solve these problems by losing our heads; we cannot solve them through misunderstanding; we cannot solve them by running from them; we cannot solve them by letting them alone. We must face the facts, plan the course, and work the plan.

No one is as qualified as God's anointed minister to lead the way in bringing people and harmony among the people of the world. God used a minister to get the races together during the early Christian era. It was the preacher Peter, deeply seated in race prejudice, who said, "Of a truth I perceive that God is no respecter of persons." It was a preacher who said, "Out of one blood God made all men for to dwell on all the face of the earth." God first worked on his preacher. And God must first line us preachers up before he can do anything with the world. So we are here today because we realize that the world needs our spiritual leadership.

We are here to mobilize our spiritual strength and leadership in order to help prepare our people for the coming change. Our people need to be prepared that they may know how to use the privileges that are theirs; and thus we are here to organize ourselves for leadership in this direction.

We lament the way in which some of our southern leaders are conducting themselves in the midst of this great crisis. I believe that men of brain and culture (especially those who have been exposed to Christian culture) should conduct themselves sanely; they should redress themselves to plans instead of passions.

We have always had race problems, and we shall continue to have them until we find a definite solution by which they can be solved. Such solutions are found in God's eternal word, and the Constitution of the United States of America, which promises "liberty and justice for all."

The question that came to the prophet in the dark days of the ancient past is still ringing in our ears today: "Watchman, what of the night?" In other words, how does it look in the dark? God's minister must be able to see in the dark. In the darkness of the turmoil and strife we should be able to see a way out. God's man has always had a solution in the time of crisis. When there was no meal in the barrel God's man had a solution; he said every man hold to a plank. Every one of us has something to which we can hold. You remember Jesus told John to tell the church in Asia to hold to that which she had. When the lame man sat by the beautiful gate begging for alms, Peter and John had a solution—they said look on us. When there was no food and the disciples wanted to send the people away that they might buy food Jesus had a solution—he said bring me the lunch. God's man, and God's man only has the solution for a sin-cursed world.

Let us have faith; let us hope. Let us have faith in what God said; "My world shall not return unto me void. . . ." Therefore let us not forget in all our planning for world peace not to forget to put the preaching for the word on the list. The only remedy that Jesus left here for making a crooked world straight was the preaching of the gospel. Let us preach that

> In Christ there is no east nor west
> In him no north or south
> But one great fellowship of love
> Throughout the whole wide world.
>
> In him shall true hearts everywhere
> Their high communion find
> His service is the golden cord
> Uniting all mankind.
>
> Join hands then, brothers of the faith
> Whatever your race may be
> Who serves the Father as a son
> Is surely kin to me.

Preach Jesus, the chief cornerstone for a building of world fellowship; preach Jesus, the door to the fold of all right relationships; preach Jesus, who must walk the roads of all of our Sychars and meet the prejudiced water drawers; preach, Isaiah's wonderful counselor, John's lion from the tribe of Judah, Nicodemus teacher sent from God. Then shall races sing with the poet when he said, "In Christ now meet both east and west, in him meet south and north. All Christly souls are one in him, throughout the whole wide earth."

§12 Joseph A. De Laine

Reverend Joseph Armstrong (J. A.) De Laine was born near Manning, South Carolina, on July 2, 1898, the eighth of Tisbia De Laine's thirteen children. His father, Henry Charles De Laine—a man born into slavery four years before the Emancipation Proclamation—was a farmer, an entrepreneur, and a minister in the African Methodist Episcopal (AME) Church. J. A. De Laine's first recorded encounter with racial injustice occurred when he was fourteen years old. According to family history, a white boy touched De Laine's sister inappropriately, and the young J. A. retaliated. As punishment, he was sentenced to receive twenty-five lashes. Firm in the conviction that the white boy should also be punished, he fled to Atlanta rather than be the only one subjected to flogging. A few years later, he returned to South Carolina and, as a young adult, enrolled in high school classes at Allen University, a school operated by the AME Church in Columbia. In 1923 he followed in his father's footsteps and became a minister in the AME Church. De Laine supported himself and paid for his education by working as a carpenter, running a pressing club, teaching, and preaching. Upon completion of Normal School coursework in 1925, he received a teaching license. His first teaching position after graduating with a bachelor of arts degree in 1931 was in Jamison, South Carolina, where he was hired as principal and eighth grade teacher.

De Laine endured his first professional hardship soon after he married Mattie Belton, another teacher at the school; he was ordered to fire his wife because the young black couple made "too much money." He also resisted this challenge to what he believed was right. The newlyweds left Jamison and found employment at Macedonia Baptist Training School in Blackville, South Carolina. While serving as principal in that position, he also pastored a nearby AME church. The trustees of the school asked him to change denominations and become a Baptist. He refused and was dismissed from his position. He returned to Clarendon County and continued as an elementary school principal and pastor of AME churches for fifteen years.

De Laine's first foray into civil rights seems to have begun with his limited involvement in the early 1940s in efforts to gain voting rights and teacher salary equalization. In 1943 he started organizing Clarendon County's first NAACP chapter, but the effort came to a standstill when he fell ill.

The seed for De Laine's important contribution to civil rights was sown in June 1947 when James N. Hinton, leader of the South Carolina state NAACP, challenged a group of black teachers to find a parent who would sue for school bus transportation. This struck a chord with De Laine because Clarendon County operated thirty buses for white students and none for blacks. He immediately undertook a campaign for racial justice by finding someone to sue for school bus transportation. Although his effort would ultimately be highly successful, it would also force him to flee from the state eight years later. The bus transportation case was dismissed because of a contested property line. However, NAACP leaders realized they had a stalwart leader in J. A. De Laine, and that he, in turn, had a committed group of local supporters. Thus, in March 1949, Thurgood Marshall advised De Laine to find twenty petitioners who would sue for equalization of educational facilities—including not only buses but also teacher pay, school supplies, and school facilities. By November 1949, De Laine had succeeded in getting 107 signatures on a petition.

Soon after the recruitment of petitioners began, white retribution came swiftly—De Laine was fired from his teaching job in the small Clarendon County community of Silver. A year later, his wife and several family relatives also lost their teaching positions. And there was violence, with threats to kill him, which were followed by the burning to the ground of his home in Summerton. After De Laine had relocated his family to a Florence County town, the *Briggs et al. v. Board of Education et al.* petition for equalization of schools was withdrawn. At a preliminary hearing, the sympathetic—but judiciously fair—district court judge J. Waties Waring encouraged attorney Thurgood Marshall to argue more vociferously for school desegregation—and to drop the idea of suing for school equalization. A petition for school desegregation was drawn up, signed, and filed in district court in December 1950 as *Briggs et al. v. Elliott et al.* Harry Briggs was alphabetically first of the twenty plaintiffs (whose children attended Scott's Branch School and who were all residents of the same school district.) *Briggs* was eventually heard by the U.S. Supreme Court as one of five consecutively argued cases. The judicial opinion for the cases was famously delivered in a unanimous verdict on May 17, 1954, and has come to be known as *Brown v. Board of Education.* The Supreme Court's decision exacerbated white anger. On October 6, 1955, De Laine's church, St. James AME in Lake City, was burned to the ground. Four days later, a posse of eight cars opened fire on De Laine's parsonage. De Laine returned a volley of buckshot. In doing so, he crossed the final Rubicon. That very night, he fled out of harm's way, ultimately reaching New York state. South Carolina officials did not file the requisite paperwork to force his return, claiming relief to be rid of a troublemaker.

De Laine and his wife spent approximately two years in Buffalo, New York, where he founded the De Laine-Waring AME Church. Subsequently, the couple moved to Queens, New York, where they remained until they retired and moved to Charlotte, North Carolina. Rev. De Laine died on August 3, 1974, with a warrant still on the books for his arrest. (The warrant remained in effect until October 10, 2000.) He was survived by his wife and three children. Although he was never able to return to Summerton, his spirit continued as a symbol of the fight he had successfully waged on behalf of school children. De Laine's papers are housed at the University of South Carolina.

Despite his remarkable achievements in fighting the "separate but equal" doctrine, Rev. De Laine clearly didn't think of himself as being an important person. In the following address, prepared for a northern audience, De Laine did not use the first person in his account of the *Brown* decision; instead he noted that "A minister of the community" helped organize the local people. Furthermore, he refused to put himself in the company of the "first-class" men, despite embodying the very distinctions he drew. De Laine closed this relatively brief address by dwelling on the topic of freedom—and the concept of what makes a person truly free. He held that people who are free are people who practice what they know to be just and true—regardless of consequence; they are willing to take a gamble in their pursuit of that which is right even when law and custom are not on their side.

ॐ

God Himself Fights for You
1957

The *Dred Scott* case of 1857 is the most famous—or notorious—in all judicial history. It is the only one that every [black] schoolboy knows by name, but rarely by its full name, which was *Dred Scott v. Stanford*. It is the only one that helped to bring on a major war—the Civil War. It is one of three decisions that, in 168 years of U.S. Supreme Court annals, were eventually reversed. [It was not reversed] by the court itself, [nor] by war, but by amendments to the U.S. Constitution.

The *Dred Scott* case deserves to be memorialized after one hundred years because it was one decision of the Supreme Court that was reversed in less than ten years.

It supported slavery because the Supreme Court and the government were dominated by southerners at that time. [The] decision [was] so unpalatable that the whole country was willing to go to war to reverse it.

Sometimes the Supreme Court reverses itself. This was the case with *Plessy v. Ferguson* (1896). It had said that the Fourteenth Amendment [which] guaranteed colored people equality [actually] meant "separate but equal."

The vicious interpretation that began with the work of [the] southern-dominated Supreme Court [continued to] afflict this country until 1954 when Chief Justice Earl Warren said, "Separate educational facilities are inherently unequal. . . . We conclude that in the field of public education the doctrine of 'separate but equal' has no place."

A long story is behind the first of the five cases which caused the courts to reverse "separate but equal." This story takes its beginning in 1946 and continues until the present day. There on the banks of the Santee River where the Santee-Hydro-Electric Dam is built, colored children were not transported to and from school like other schoolchildren. Neither did they have comfortable buildings to warm their little bodies in when they arrived at school. In the Jordan section of Clarendon County, South Carolina, the backed-up waters flooded some of the bridges, and thus the colored children had to paddle a boat across the water and walk the rest of the way to their inferior school. A minister of the community tried every possible source to have this condition adjusted. Finally, by his request, the NAACP came to the rescue of those parents and children who were active in his movement. This oldest segregation case with twenty families suing jointly, [which came] from the Deep South, is legally known as *Harry Briggs v. Clarendon County, S.C.* By two judges holding jurisdiction [of the case] for six additional months, Topeka, Kansas, became the first [desegregation case that] the U.S. Supreme Court recognized. Through toil, sweat, blood, and tears, these cases won a reversal of the "separate but equal" doctrine.

Through this we see that life is a gamble. Since life is a gamble, I challenge you to gamble with truth rather than lies; to put your life on the side of justice rather than injustice, democracy rather than fascism, the Christian religion rather than Communism.

If you can do this, though in bondage, you are free; though proscribed and circumscribed, you will be free. "You may be in bondage but free."

The human family is roughly divided into two classes:

First, [there is] a small minority who believe that difficult jobs can be accomplished; that mountains, however high, can be climbed; that human nature, however depraved, can be redeemed and changed; and that the mores and folkways of our day, however deeply entrenched, can be uprooted. And when they are uprooted, as strange as it may seem, the sun will continue to shine; the moon will be as regular with its changes [as ever]; the stars will not fall any faster; and just as much outer space will be left for Sputnik and Jupiter as before.

Given the right method and attitude, the time is always ripe to do right, to tell the truth instead of lies. To do justly and correct injustices; and from the small minority [that do so], you get men like Charles Darwin, who expounded the doctrine of evolution; Galileo, who expounded the doctrine that the earth revolved around the sun; Roger Bacon, who originated the experimental method of science; Micah, Amos, and Moses, who crusaded for social justice; the apostle Paul, who smashed the bondage of the law; Jesus Christ, who taught that the life of every man is of intricate value and that when you hurt a man you hurt God.

The second group is the vast majority—the conservative class—who argue that difficult things cannot be done, that high mountains cannot be climbed, and that the mores and folkways and customs are sacred and you cannot change them.

These conservatives will argue with the fluency of a Cicero, the logic of a Socrates, the choice diction of a Shakespeare, and the piety of a St. Francis that "the time is not ripe" to do the right thing and to be just. They are the lazy, selfish, stingy, shiftless, short-sighted fifth-columnists of progress. They are the people who find conditions bad, and leave them worse. They oppose surgery on the ground that the body is the temple of the Holy Spirit and so you must not cut it. This class showed [its] ugly head with the twelve spies [who were] sent to [explore] the Promised Land. The ten reported that it could not be done. They told of great big giants, "too big for us to fight," and a land [that] was, after all, not so attractive; and they recommended returning to Egypt's fleshpots—and slavery.

Two of the spies constituted the minority. Joshua and Caleb were stout-hearted and said, "It can be done, with God's help." The conservatives turned coward and said, "We can't do it," or in the modern language, "The time is not ripe. We might be able to take the land, 'but not now.'" [Their opinion was,] "It is better to be a slave in Egypt than to be dead in the Promised Land. It is true that in Egypt you have to cringe and crawl, but it is better to cringe and crawl on your belly than to go up and to fight these giants."

"A slave doesn't have to carry responsibility. Pharaoh will run the government. In Egypt we just do what we are told to do, and at night we go to bed and sleep. Let's go back to the fleshpots."

Now these ten men had logic on their side. There were giants, there were walled cities, there was the Jordan [River] that rolled between them and the Promised Land. In World War II, the experts said, "You can't cross the English Channel without losing a million men." But Uncle Sam did it and didn't lose nearly that many. We should learn not to depend too largely on the experts. Nearly every sociologist and anthropologist who wrote a hundred years ago said the Negro could not absorb an education. George Washington Carver, W. E. B. Du Bois, Ralph Bunche, and a host of others have disproven the correctness of these experts.

Those ten men who formed that conservative majority were slaves; they were conditioned to slavery in their own minds. There were no chains around their ankles and Pharaoh was many miles away, but they were slaves.

It is possible for a man to be down [for] so long that he believes God Almighty sent him into this world to be trodden upon. If one's mind is [not] free, [he may believe that] social distinctions and Jim Crow are not so bad. No man is a slave until he accepts it in his mind. There are thousands of people who are so conditioned—who if all the proscriptions were removed would still stay as they are.

Paul was in prison, but not a slave. He wrote many letters to the churches from his prison walls. John Bunyan stayed in Bedford Jail twelve years, but while he was there he wrote nine books, among them was the immortal *Pilgrim's Progress*.

In Florida, there lived an ordinary carpenter [named Henry], who was not decorated with any degree and who went about shaking his head because of a nervous disease. But, when Jim Crow street cars came in, he started walking to and from work five, ten, and fifteen miles a day. Now I am not telling you what to do. I am just illustrating a point. Old man Henry was a free man.

You can't emancipate a people by adding an amendment to the Constitution or by giving them economic security. I have seen men with great wealth who were slaves. Neither can you make a man free by giving him a college education.

The ten spies magnified the difficulties. It is possible to magnify trouble until you can't do a job. It is possible for us to complain so much about the shortcomings of others that we will not be able to take the advantage of our opportunities. You can even make a mountain out of a molehill.

Finally, I want to speak for a moment on what can make you free. You can have fine houses and ride in Cadillacs and still be a slave. You can ride in an airplane and travel the world over but that won't make you free.

You can graduate from college and get a master's degree or a Ph.D. from Harvard or Yale and yet not be a free man. I want to suggest to you how to be free in a world which is fighting all kinds of totalitarianism, such as fascism, Communism, KKK [White] Citizens' Councils, state rights segregationism, and the like.

If America has not yet implemented her democracy, she is leaning in that direction since May 17, 1954. This is the best country on earth where free people can press for their freedom.

If you would be free, give your allegiance and loyalty to the best that is in you, and the highest that you know. If you know truth and choose falsehood, you are a slave. If you know virtue and choose vice, you are a slave. If you believe democracy is better than Communism and do not practice democracy, you are not free.

Since life is a gambling game and you must gamble, I challenge you to gamble with truth rather than with lies, with justice rather than with injustice.

I hear you retort, "Yes, but suppose I stand alone? Suppose I lift up my voice and stand alone in pleading for justice and human kindness between the races?" I say to you with all the power I have, "Nobody stands alone." There are thousands who have not bowed their knees to Baal. When a man steps out and takes a stand for right, thousands will rally behind him.

If you stand up for social justice, you will not stand alone; Amos, [Micah], and Moses will stand with you. If you stand for the Fatherhood of God and the brotherhood of man, Jesus will be by your side. If you believe in academic freedom, Socrates is with you. If you espouse racial equality, federal judge J. Waties Waring and Chief Justice Earl Warren, [as well as] the best there are in science, democracy, and religion, will be with you. No man stands alone.

But I hear you say, "Yes, but what if I lose?" I say to you with every ounce of my weight that it is better to stand alone and lose than to give allegiance to lies. But you can't lose. History and human experience testifies that every injustice must fall. Every corrupt government and economic order will crumble and fall. And every corrupt ecclesiastical order will die. The universe fights on your side. The everlasting God himself fights for you.

Gamble with right, justice, social righteousness, and truth because nothing else will live or ought to live. If you lose, go down smiling with the thought that you have been true. Go down with the poet, William Cullen Bryant, who said,

Truth, crushed to the earth, will rise again:
The eternal years of God are hers,
But Error, wounded, writhes in pain,
And dies among his worshippers.

1958

1958

§13 Ralph McGill

Ralph Emerson McGill was born on February 5, 1898, in a small farm community near Soddy-Daisy, Tennessee, to Benjamin Franklin McGill and Mary Lou Skillern. The oldest of four children, McGill began his writing career at the McCallie School in Chattanooga, where he wrote for a student publication. He continued writing for the student newspaper at Vanderbilt University from 1917 to 1922. McGill's studies were interrupted by World War I as he joined the U.S. Marine Corps from 1918 to 1919. During his senior year at Vanderbilt, McGill was suspended after writing a column which insinuated that the Vanderbilt administration had not complied with a professor's will. McGill was unable to graduate, but he quickly found a job as a sportswriter for the *Nashville Banner*. Connections at the *Banner* and writerly talents led McGill to the *Atlanta Constitution*, where he became assistant sports editor in 1929. That same year he married Mary Leonard, and the couple would have three children. His copy began to migrate from the sports pages to the editorial pages in the 1930s. After winning a Julius Rosenwald Fellowship in 1937, McGill traveled to Europe and was angered by the conditions of Nazi-occupied Austria. Upon his return to America, and after speaking out against what he'd witnessed, McGill was promoted to executive editor of the *Constitution*. Four years later, in 1942, McGill was named editor of the paper, and his progressive southern voice began to be heard around the nation. Along with Greenville's Hodding Carter Jr., McGill's stand on the burgeoning racial crisis angered many southern whites; in fact enemies began to refer to him as Rastus McGill.

His columns were syndicated throughout the nation in the 1950s, and in 1959 he was awarded a Pulitzer Prize for editorial writing. The Pulitzer Committee specifically singled out for comment his 1958 editorial "A Church, A School," which examined the racial terrorism in Clinton, Tennessee, and the Atlanta temple bombing. A year later in 1960, McGill became publisher of the *Constitution*. Though McGill seemed to lead a charmed existence, tragedy was not unknown in his family: a daughter died in infancy, and an adopted daughter passed away at the age of three because of leukemia. McGill also lost his wife to cancer in 1962. He would remarry—to Dr. Mary Lynn Morgan—in 1967. McGill was honored with the Presidential Medal of Freedom in 1964, but that same year suffered a heart attack, which would slow his frenetic pace. On February 3, 1969, and just two days shy of his seventy-first birthday, McGill passed away, survived by his second wife and a son. His papers are housed at Emory University. Although he never received a degree from Vanderbilt, he was given honorary degrees from Morehouse, Harvard, Columbia, Notre Dame, and many others. Ralph McGill was also recognized by Dr. Martin Luther King Jr. in his "Letter from Birmingham Jail." Dr. King wrote, "[S]ome of our white brothers in the South have grasped the meaning of this social revolution and committed themselves to it. They are still too few in quantity, but they are big in quality. Some such as Ralph McGill . . . have written about our struggle in eloquent and prophetic terms." In 2004 McGill was inducted into the Georgia Writers Hall of Fame.

McGill's short speech to parishioners at St. Paul's Episcopal Church in Richmond, Virginia, recalls the heated rhetoric of pre–Civil War America to draw a parallel: those voices "loud in the land" on both sides of the civil rights divide again threaten the nation—less its perpetuity of union, and more the godless and robotic Communism that, too, preaches brotherhood. The answer—to both the Soviet menace and the civil rights crisis—will be found when we export the second commandment: to love our neighbors as ourselves. That commandment will be kept only with God's grace as intermediary, and not man's will. The present crisis is compounded, according to McGill, because Christianity is getting leveraged in ways that don't resemble "our Lord." Only an authentic Christianity committed to national survival, not regional isolation, will see the country through its "battle for survival."

ॐॐ

Send Not to Know for Whom the Bell Tolls
January 22, 1958
St. Paul's Church, Richmond, Virginia

Memories came to me as I began to try, in trepidation, to put down words for this hour—an experience new to me.

I remembered the colored lithograph of our Lord on the wall of Mahatma Gandhi's small room in faraway India—and of his saying that if there were no religious writing anywhere in the world but the Sermon on the Mount it would be enough for man to live by. And only a few evenings ago a television program showed us the moving scene of Mrs. Marian Anderson, one of our great artists, standing by the Gandhi Memorial in New Delhi, with an immense throng before her, lifting up her voice to sing Gandhi's favorite hymn, "Lead, Kindly Light."

I remembered, too, tea with the then mayor of Haifa, Israel, who was a collector of antiques. I was preparing to go when he asked, "How good a Christian are you?"

"Not good enough," I answered, puzzled.

"Wait," he said.

He went into another room and returned with a small but heavy patina-encrusted silver cross, dug up in the ruins of an old Byzantine church, and authentically some nine hundred or more years old.

"This symbol," he said, "has meant much to this world." And then he put it in my hand. "Be a better Christian," he said. A Hindu saint in faraway Asia saying that our Lord's Sermon on the Mount contained the great rules of life—and giving ear to the words of "Lead, Kindly Light"—a devout Jew holding up an ancient cross and saying this symbol means much to the world—these and countless other incidents make us aware of the continual seeking and yearning in the hearts of mankind everywhere for faith and strength through that faith.

Like you, I do not know the answers to things. Like you, I am a seeker, trying always to hold and strengthen my faith. Like you, perhaps, I am almost daily frustrated by the problem of taking our faith and our creed into my daily job. I have had enough prayers answered to believe in prayer. I have studied and seen enough to make me believe, without question, that as man has evolved his spiritual life, the great secrets of the earth and life are opened to him. The power of the atom, its fission and fusion, is as old as the earth itself. Penicillin and others of the great disease-curbing antibiotics were first derived from the soil of earth itself. There are always problems given us by life, and always there are keys when man has earned them by bringing himself closer to his Creator's will and wisdom.

We have now before us the struggle with the corrosive power of Communism, which would, if it could, reduce man, made in God's image, to a human robot. The Western world, at present sorely tried, can, without question, win this struggle if we match our necessary military power with the power of our ideas. Last summer I saw much of Europe. Our blue jeans, our ponytail hairdos, our movies, our television kinescopes, our fashions, our soft drinks, our supermarkets, our style of gasoline filling stations, our system of installment credit—all these things and more are winning much of the world. We have somehow not yet been able to send enough of our own selves, our faith, our affirmation of the second great commandment which is so like the first.

It is not at all fantastic that the *New York Times* reporter Harrison Salisbury, in reporting from the Soviet satellite countries last summer, found a great yearning among the people to be able to go to America.

Whatever else we may have lost, the picture of America as the great land of freedom, of opportunity and promise, has not yet been eroded away.

And that is our greatest conservation problem—of the vision and the dream of America which exists more strongly than we believe when we hear, as we do, the criticisms and abuse whipped up by political claques in countries abroad.

One cannot be here in this great church without first, a feeling of reverence, and next, there presses in on one a great weight of history. One thinks inevitably of Robert E. Lee, perhaps the noblest character the nation has produced—certainly one of the noblest. I read in last Sunday's newspapers a dispatch from Gettysburg, Pennsylvania. A letter from General Lee, little noticed through the years, was made public by Gettysburg College, in whose library it had been kept. In the summer of 1869, David McConnaughy, a Gettysburg lawyer, wrote to General Lee at Washington College, asking him to join other officers whose troops had been engaged in battle there for the purpose of marking upon the ground, by enduring memorials of granite, the positions and movements of the armies.

"My engagements will not permit me to be present, and I believe if there I could not add anything material to the information existing on the subject. I think it wiser moreover not to keep open the sores of war, but to follow the examples of those nations who endeavored to obliterate the marks of civil strife and to commit to oblivion the feelings it engendered."

Those words of this noble man, who always was the moderate and temperate man, seem to have special meaning for our time.

These are the days when the fiery echoes of the Yanceys, the Barnwells, the Rhetts, and their counterparts on the other side, again are loud in the land. The people nowhere wanted that great tragedy of which they were so vocal a part. But the voice of reason and of moderation and compromise was drowned out, and even Christianity wore many faces other than that of our Lord. It is almost so today.

I am not naïve. I know this is something we must somehow live through. Here again there is no open sesame, no formula, no golden key. We are, as is plain to see, at one of those great pivots of history. It has been revealed to us, almost in a twinkling of an eye, that our educational system must be reexamined, that our military strength, too, requires reappraisal.

This nation of ours is deeply involved in a grave problem which is, we are told, without parallel in our history. A battle for survival has been forced upon us. It is not our choosing.

Arms and missiles are but a part of it.

It is a problem which will test all our institutions—our system of government, our educational and scientific systems and our economics.

These are no words of mine. Our president, our two ex-presidents, our leading military figures, active and retired, our economists, and our educators all have said as much.

It seems to me there can be but one answer. And if it be somewhat trite, I still cannot apologize for it. The answer, as I see it, is that without hesitancy we must put our country first. Our paramount loyalty must be to the nation and not to any state or region. I do not see how it can be otherwise if we have any wish to survive. There is, it seems to me, another inevitable testing—and that is of Christianity. Communism shrewdly is preaching the brotherhood of man. "We speak to you as brothers," Nikita Khrushchev said a few days ago in offering aid to Asians.

We all know—or should know—what the missionaries of all denominations are writing back to our churches.

I wish it were a time when we could afford to do the easy thing, the comfortable, the things we'd prefer to do. I'd like that. There is much of the "Let us alone" of the lotus-eater in me—but it is no longer possible.

Today, more than ever, an old line from John Donne seems fitting—"No man is an island entirely unto himself—therefore, send not to know for whom the bell tolls—it tolls for thee."

We paid a great price in the long years of want brought on by the cruelty and injustices of the Reconstruction, which was a final chapter of the tragedy produced by the inflexible, defiant men, North and South. The dogmatic men who were so sure they knew the answers. Shall we do so again? Shall we be concerned only about the tax debt we put on the backs of children and our children's children?

I know there is no way to avoid the problem. I do not know the answer. I know it must be lived through. But I cling to the hope that before disaster comes, and the nation is reduced to ruin, we somehow may find a way which is American and which will not destroy the dream of America as a land of decency, as a place where every family and every child is safe and has equal opportunity.

Last year I attended services at a small Episcopal church in Fernandina, Florida. A young rector, combat veteran of the great war, was preaching on the second great commandment.

"Man," he said, "cannot will to love his neighbor as himself—he cannot consciously make himself always to cross over the street and render necessary aid in the symbolic manner of the Samaritan—no man can of himself will to be such a person. It can be done only by the grace of God—only by the man who asks God's help."

As I said, I do not know the answers. I could be wrong. I often am. But this I believe—if we heed only the angry, dogmatic voices of violent men who profess to know all the answers—if we fail to seek God's help—we shall fail not only ourselves but man's last best hope on earth.

§14 William B. Silverman

Rabbi William Silverman was born in 1913 in Altoona, Pennsylvania. In 1941 he was ordained by Hebrew Union College in Cincinnati, Ohio. From 1941 to 1943 he served his congregation in Battle Creek, Michigan, while serving as chaplain at Fort Custer. From 1943 to 1946 he led his congregation in Gastonia, North Carolina, while interpreting Judaism for local Christians and serving as a spokesman for Zionism. In 1945 the Central Conference of American Rabbis called for civil rights involvement. From 1946 to 1950 he served as advisor to the Minnesota governor. In October 1950 his Vine Street Temple congregation in Nashville was thrust into the segregation issue when the local Jewish center and elementary school were bombed. Rabbi Silverman launched an aggressive media campaign to fight the White Citizens' Council and American Legion textbook elimination from libraries and schools. The Tennessee legislature took his lead concerning the textbooks, which they determined had no subversive content. In 1957 Silverman was attacked following a sermon at a Methodist church, and in March 1958 he received bomb threats and threats to shoot a local judge by phone. Members of the Confederate Underground made good on their threats, bombing the Nashville Jewish Community Center in 1958. His work for the Jewish and broader American community continued in many venues until his death in 2001.

The title of his sermon of March 28, 1958, is a remarkably efficient indicator of his life's work: "We Will Not Yield." And despite the blunt response to a recent bombing, the sermon is nuanced. The weekend in question was the last before Passover, and dedicated to Isaac Mayer Wise, a founding father of Reform Judaism. Rabbi Silverman begins the sermon saying many have told him to stick to religion, Judaism, and the Bible. He complies, referring to Leviticus, Jeremiah, Wise, and the Pittsburgh Platform of 1885. Leviticus, he says, informs us that the sacrificial fire is to be an eternal light of truth, morality, justice, and God. Jeremiah commands that we walk in obedience, justice, and morality. Isaac Mayer Wise urges us to do away with all obsolete forms to focus on social justice, the rights of the oppressed, universal courage, freedom, and righteousness. The eighth point of the Pittsburg Platform of 1885, a founding document of Reform Judaism, exhorts us to justice and righteousness against evil. After this introduction, Silverman narrows his focus: what do these authorities tell us about dynamiting a Jewish center? After a brief expression of pride in his family's and community's courage, he builds a two-faceted argument. One facet is a three-term variation of a disjunctive syllogism. He offers an ethical world of three choices, two of which are eliminated as unsound, leaving us with the one term remaining. The other facet is the Aristotelian golden mean, whereby the extremes are eliminated in favor of the moderate course of action. Specifically, the path of timidity, on the one hand, and of rejecting the totality of the broader community (golus—life in exile) are extremes. The moderate, and therefore, the good, is to side with secular officials, Christian integrationists, and all other decent, moral people to do the right thing, even if it is a frightening thing to do. He gives a brief outline of who the extremists are, including John Kasper, Israel Cohen, Conde McGinley, and M. B. Sherrill, outsiders intending to foment extremist behavior, before returning to his original theme that both Jewish and American values demand our allegiance to integration and tolerance.

❧❧

We Will Not Yield
March 28, 1958
Nashville, Tennessee

During the course of the past week, it has been said that the rabbi should *stick to religion, to Judaism, and the Bible!* On this Shabbos Hagodol, on this Great Sabbath before Passover, on this Sabbath when we memorialize Isaac Mayer Wise, the founder of Reform Judaism in America, on this Sabbath when we consider the implications of the dynamiting of the Nashville Jewish Community Center, the threats against the rabbi of this congregation, against our temple, our house of God—I propose to follow that advice, and to adhere by text and exposition to religion, to Judaism, and to the Bible, in order to determine, not my answer, not the answer of a rabbi, but the answer of prophetic Judaism to violence, threats, and dynamite.

Reference has been made *to the Bible.* Let us turn for a moment to the Torah portion, assigned for this Sabbath, parasha TZAV, beginning with the sixth chapter of the Book of Leviticus: "*And the Lord spoke unto Moses saying, 'Command Aaron and his sons: This is the law of the burnt offering: It is that which goeth up on its firewood upon the altar all night into the morning.'*" This refers to the Tamid, the burnt offering, the continual sacrifice brought every morning and evening in the name of the community. As the various sacrifices are enumerated, the meal offering, the guilt offering, the peace offering, it is commanded: "*A perpetual fire shall be kept burning upon the altar continually: it shall not go out.*"

Do those who so emphatically urge me to stick to the Bible mean that we should restore and reinstitute the sacrificial system and place animals upon this altar of God—or will they agree with the rabbis that we must keep a perpetual light, a ner Tamid, burning continually to remind us of Israel's identification with what? Sacrifices? Ritual? Forms? Or, the light of truth, the light of morality, the light of justice, and the light of God?

Reference has been made to *adherence to Judaism.* We say that Judaism achieved its noblest and most exalted expression through the teachings of the prophets. What do the prophets have to teach us about Judaism? We turn, then, to the Haftorah for this Sabbath, the seventh chapter of

Jeremiah, who, speaking in the name of God, declared, "*For I spoke not unto your fathers, not commanded them in the day that I brought them out of Egypt, concerning burnt offerings of sacrifices. But this thing I command them saying, Hearken unto my voice and I will be your God, and ye shall be my people: and walk ye in all the way that I command you.*"

What is the *way* that God has commanded us? The prophet clearly says that God does not want sacrifices, *God wants obedience of his moral commandments! God wants justice!* With passionate conviction, Jeremiah asserts that the moral laws have precedence over the ceremonial law—and to desert the way of justice, the way of decency, the way of morality is to betray our heritage and repudiate the covenant of Israel with God. What is prophetic Judaism if not a dedication to justice, and the implementation of the moral precepts of our faith?

"But that happened of 2,500 years ago," it may be said. "Let's be practical. Let's be realistic. Is this the attitude of modern Judaism?" If anyone doubts the identity of modern Judaism with social justice, then let him study the life and the teachings of Isaac Mayer Wise, the founder of Reform Judaism in America, who declared, "*All forms to which no meaning is attached any longer are an impediment to our religion, and must be done away with.*" With prophetic fervor, Wise insisted that *Judaism must devote itself to social justice, the rights of the oppressed, the cause of universal brotherhood and truth.* With singleness of purpose and prophetic courage, Isaac Mayer Wise brushed off the attacks, the calumny, the vilification of his opponents, and as a modern Jeremiah he taught that God does not delight in sacrifices or ceremonials, but in justice and righteousness and freedom.

"Stick to Reform Judaism, Rabbi!" Let me quote from the eighth point of the Pittsburgh Platform of 1885, the platform of classic Reform Judaism: "*We deem it our duty to participate in the great task of modern times, to solve, on the basis of justice and righteousness, the problems presented by the contrasts and evils of the present organization of society.*" Isn't this Judaism? Isn't this the teaching of Isaac Mayer Wise, who insisted that the disciples and devotees of Reform Judaism must be irrevocably committed to worship the God of freedom by serving the cause of freedom for men of every race and every faith?

With this as background—with the Torah, the prophets of Israel, the rabbis, and the founders of Reform Judaism demanding that Israel must be the eternal light aflame with divinity, dedicated to freedom and justice for all men and all nations, we turn now to a consideration of the implications of the dynamiting of the Nashville Jewish Community Center.

You know the essential facts, and there is no need for me to reiterate the sordid story, the repercussion of threats, poison-pen letters, and promise of further violence. Permit me to digress with these words of acknowledgment. I am proud of my wife and my sons, who met threats of violence with courage and dignity; I am proud of the leadership of our Jewish Community Center; I am proud of our board of trustees; proud of our congregation and the attitude of calm and confidence manifested during these troubled weeks.

Now that we have had the time and calm to view these events in sober perspective, what was revealed? There were three points of view expressed by our Jewish community. Two points of view were extreme to the extent of hysteria, the third, the calm, courageous, and dignified reaction of the majority.

What were the two extremes? The first insisted that what happened is undeniable proof that we are in golus, exile; that the community of Nashville is rampant with anti-Semitism; that America is no longer safe for those of the Jewish faith; that the Jews of America are doomed. I repudiate this extreme [view] with all the conviction of my heart. I refused to listen to those who would have me protest over radio and television—who urged me to protest through newspapers and magazines—who insisted that I, in my capacity as a rabbi, proclaim to the world that *Jews are in danger.* Quite to the contrary, when I was asked to appear on television it was my suggestion that the president of the Ministerial Association, the chancellor of Vanderbilt University, and the secretary of the Nashville Association of Churches speak and clearly demonstrate that this is *not* a Jewish problem, but a *community problem*—a problem of civil liberty, a problem of moral decency, a problem of law and order for the church as well as the synagogue, for Catholic and Protestant, as well as for those of the Jewish faith.

I also repudiate the other extreme of escapist, jittery Jews, representing the counsel of timidity and silence. There were those who said the word "Jewish" should never have been on that building—and if it had been called the *community center,* and not the *Jewish* Community Center, the dynamiting would never have occurred.

There were those who said that the center is responsible for what happened—and that the center brought all the trouble upon itself, just as the Jews of Germany brought all the trouble upon themselves—and if the center had maintained a segregationist point of view, refused to even consider the possibility of interracial meetings, the center would not have been dynamited. I abhor this point of view as shallow and despicable.

This same extremist group further stated that I was responsible for the dynamiting of the Jewish Community Center—and that because of my pulpit utterances during the Holy days and my pro-integration stand in the community, all the Jews of Nashville have been and will continue to be endangered.

I say this, not with pride, but with a profound sense of shame, that with the exception of my sermons during the High Holy days last September and one Parent Teachers Association address wherein I complied with a request to speak on the implications of the bombing of the Hattie Cotton School, I have not made a single public utterance or statement on this subject of integration, and have not been as active in behalf of social justice as my faith demands.

"Why then," it was asked, "was the center dynamited and the temple threatened and not the YMCA or a church? Doesn't this prove we are our own worst enemies?" How naïve can we be? Dr. John Rustin of the Belmont Methodist Church has spoken frequently on this subject and sponsored interracial meetings. Why wasn't his church dynamited? The Westminster Presbyterian Church and other churches have sponsored interracial meetings within the past month—why weren't these churches dynamited? Peabody Graduate School, Vanderbilt Divinity School, Scarritt College have Negro students—why weren't these schools bombed? The Catholic Church has integrated its parochial schools—why weren't these schools bombed?

While we do not believe that Nashville is anti-Semitic, can we possibly conclude that anti-Semitism is not being exploited by the racists and the segregationists in our community? Do we think that the hate groups throughout the nation have not concentrated upon Nashville—with the pattern and the line that the Communist Jew forced the Supreme Court decision in behalf of integration, that the Communist Jew controls the Nashville newspapers and the school board. On March 14, two days before the dynamiting of our Jewish Community Center, the Anti-Defamation League issued a report stating that "hate publications from across the country had been distributed in Nashville to agitate the smoldering fired started by local individuals." These included such well-known anti-Semitic sheets as Conde McGinley's *Common Sense* which stated that "Jewish Communist organizers from New York have been agitating and indoctrinating Negroes in the South." A letter sent to W. A. Bass, superintendent of schools of Nashville, signed by M. B. Sherill of Florida, "called for the establishment of groups of four to six to eight with bomb throwing and incendiary training." Letters have been mailed from England from Israel Cohen asking for mongrelization of races. There is no Israel Cohen. Do we think that we can have a John Kasper in a community without a pouring forth of verbal venom against the Jews? Notice the plan and the pattern—wherever John Kasper has incited against the Jews: Miami, Charlotte, North Carolina, Gastonia, North Carolina, and Nashville, there have been bombing and dynamiting of Jewish institutions. When will we learn with the authors of the book the *Authoritarian Personality* that when you scratch a Negro hater, you find an anti-Semite, and a bigot dedicated to the destruction of the Catholic Church, civil liberties, and the values of Christianity itself?

Whether we are silent, or whether we speak forth in behalf of decency, morality, law, and order, the Jew will be attacked, because this has been the historic stereotype of anti-Semitism—but is this to deter us from preserving the values and ideals that are sacred to Judaism? Does this mean that we must scuttle into caves of cowardice and pull the covers of silence over our conscience, because of bigots, goons, and men of violence? Does this mean that we must tremble and cower because we advocated not only the teachings of our Jewish faith but the basic principles of our American heritage?

I, for one, refuse to yield to threats. I refuse, as a rabbi and as an American citizen, to surrender to intimidation and violence—and I am not alone. I have referred to two extremes, but I feel and I am confident that the vast majority of this congregation and of the Jewish community of Nashville shares the conviction that we must stand for decency, law, morality, and social justice for those of every faith and every race—and not prostrate ourselves and crumble into whimpering, fear-ridden devotees of doom.

We are not alone, because there has been an outpouring of messages, letters, resolutions, from the clergy, from the Christian Church, from the decent, respected citizens of our community expressing shame, indignation, and a sense of outrage—but what is even more significant, the realization that this isn't a Jewish problem, but a Christian problem, a community problem, an attack upon Christian values as well as upon Jewish property. They know as well as we do that the purpose of this violence is not to take human life, but to deter and frighten the community to prevent the integration of our public schools and frighten respectable leadership from supporting the decision of the Supreme Court.

And now you have the right to ask: Where do we stand? and *Where do we go from here?*

Let me first speak for myself, as your rabbi, and I believe that any spiritual leader who does not speak forth and lead his congregation on moral issues is not worthy of being the rabbi of this or any other congregation—and I speak clearly and without equivocation that all may understand: together with the Central Conference of American Rabbis and the Union of American Hebrew Congregations, *I favor integration*—not only because I am a Jew, not only because my religious faith teaches that God is our universal Father, that all men are brothers, created in the divine image; that all men regardless of their faith or their race are endowed by God with equal rights. I favor integration—not only because of an Amos who asked in the name of God, "Are ye not as the children of the Ethiopians unto me, O children of Israel": not only because the Torah commands, "Justice, justice shall ye pursue"; not only because of the religious heritage of Judaism that insists upon social justice for white and black, for brown, yellow, and red—not only because I am a Jew, but because I am an American—and as an American I not only have the right, but the moral mandate to support the Constitution, the Bill of Rights, the decision of the Supreme Court, and the laws of our nation.

It has been said that I am a nigger-lover. That is true! I love and I want God to help me love even more, Negroes and Caucasians, those of every race, every faith, every nationality—because to love one's fellow man is a moral requirement of the Jewish faith, and to be a Jew is to despise prejudice and bigotry in every form.

Does this mean that I will embarrass my congregation? Does this mean that I urge you, my members, to undertake a rash, reckless, immoderate course of action in behalf of integration? No. I might yearn and hope with Moses when Eldad and Medad were reported prophesying in the camp, "Would that all the children of Israel were prophets of the Lord"—but as I stated in my letter to you, as a southern congregation we need not initiate or take an overly conspicuous role in advocating integration—but we are not only a southern congregation, we are a Jewish congregation, and as a religious congregation dedicated to the principles of prophetic Judaism, we are morally committed to join the law enforcement agencies, the federal judiciary, the Christian clergy and church, and the citizens of our community in supporting decency, religious values, and the democratic rights of all the citizens of our nation. We want to do something; we want action? I urge the members of our congregation to join and support the Nashville Community Relations Conference, a reputable, moderate organization that is concerned with much more than racial understanding, but with the immediate need to further harmonious and high-minded human relations. I urge my congregation to study Judaism and learn what Judaism has to teach about racial justice. As disciples of Isaac Mayer Wise, as proponents of prophetic

Judaism, committed to love righteousness and morality, I urge my congregation to identify itself with the eternal laws of God and not the transitory mores of a geographic area; I urge my congregation to believe that the Voice of Jacob is more powerful than the hands of modern Esaus who kindled the fuse, or the explosive potential of dynamite.

We will not set our sights by the bigoted scum, the potential murderers, who would degrade man to the gutters of depravity and reduce him, degrade him to the level of savages—but with abiding faith we lift our eyes to the psalmists and the prophets of Israel who would dignify, raise, and elevate man to a status but little lower than the angels.

We will not yield to evil. We will not capitulate to fear. We will not surrender to violence. We will not submit to intimidation but, as Reform Jews, we shall continue to speak for truth; we shall continue to dedicate ourselves to social justice and to the brotherhood of *all* men, knowing and believing that all men are created in the divine image, and this includes Negroes as well as Caucasians. And even as we stand at the threshold of Passover, our Festival of Freedom, the season of liberation, with resolution and reverence, our hearts touched, warmed, and ignited by the Eternal Flame of an eternal faith, we shall continue to consecrate ourselves to human rights, and civil liberties—we shall, with God's help, continue to dedicate ourselves to the cause of freedom and justice for all the children of man.

And so, in the words of the Haggadah, in the spirit of Passover, we pray, "May He who broke Pharaoh's yoke forever shatter all fetters of oppression. Soon may He cause the glad tidings of redemption to be heard in all lands so that mankind, freed from violence and from wrong, and united in an eternal covenant of brotherhood, may celebrate the universal Passover in the name of our God of Freedom." Amen.

§15 Harry Golden

Harry L. Golden was born Herschel Goldhirsch on May 6, 1902, in Milulintsy, Galicia, what is today eastern Ukraine. At the age of two he and his family settled in New York City's Lower East Side. He attended the City College of New York from 1919 until 1922. Golden married Genevieve Gallagher, an Irish Catholic, in 1926, and they had four sons. That same year Golden started his own securities trading company, or what was then known as a "bucket shop." In 1929, though, Golden was convicted of mail fraud and sentenced to five years in a federal prison in Atlanta, Georgia.

Following his release, Golden alternately worked at his brother's Hotel Markwell on Manhattan's West Side and wrote and sold advertising for the *New York Daily Mirror* and the *New York Post*. Golden's big move came in 1941 when he ventured south, first to Newport, Virginia, and later to Charlotte, North Carolina, where he would spend the rest of his life. Golden first joined the staff of the *Charlotte Labor Journal* and later sold advertising for the *Charlotte Observer*. Not long thereafter, Golden embarked on a quixotic adventure: he began the *Carolina Israelite*, a Jewish newspaper, a one-man shop that featured his progressive take on labor issues, foreign policy, and race relations. The novelty of a Jewish newspaper located geographically in the South did not go unnoticed; circulation swelled in major metropolitan areas even as Golden's views on race angered many southern whites. Golden's fame spread in 1958 with publication of his bestseller, *Only in America*. Later he became a featured writer for several major publications and was a frequent guest on television talk shows and the campus lecture circuit. He eventually closed the *Carolina Israelite* in 1968. He died on October 2, 1981. His papers are housed at the University of North Carolina, Charlotte.

When asked how he managed to get away with his progressive views on race in the South, Golden responded, "I get away with my ideas in the South because no southerner takes me—a Jew, a Yankee, and a radical—seriously. They mostly think of a Jew as a substitute Negro, anyway." Golden also employed humor to great rhetorical effect. He touted what he termed the "Golden Vertical Negro Plan," based on the idea that since whites and blacks mingled easily while standing, sitting needed to be abolished in schools and buses.

In this remarkable address delivered to Jewish trade unionists, Golden expertly crafts his goodwill for nearly a third of the address; even in the North among a group of liberal-minded auditors he understands the difficulty of discussing race relations. Once he turns to race relations in the South, Golden makes a brilliant psychological, sociological, and economic diagnosis of the problem and its solution. The problem is not interracial sex, he avers, but rather the danger and fear of social mobility. If poor whites did not have blacks as their social and economic inferiors, "social oblivion" will result. Despite daily humiliations, "degradation and death," blacks resisted Communism, and they cling to the same vision of democracy as did the nation's founding fathers. If only black and white southerners might communicate honestly with each other, claims Golden, the race problem would vanish—and with it, the nation's economy would prosper and its democratic ideals would flourish. In such a revitalized context, Jews, too, would find a new tolerance and a new security.

❧❧

The Struggle to End Racial Segregation in the South
May 31, 1958
Unity House, Forest Park, Pennsylvania

This could only happen in America. Here it is this morning, an old-time New Deal liberal who gets written up in the *New York Herald Tribune*. But, there's something more significant about this *Herald Tribune* article than the headline that "a southern Jew solves the integration problem." I think the more important thing is the part of the headline which refers to "*a southern Jew*." Twenty or twenty-five years ago they would have hesitated about using such a headline—and the word "Jew" in such big letters. And I like to think that I may have helped along the way; that I may have helped everybody become a little more relaxed about the whole thing; the Gentiles of America as well as the Jews themselves, of course.

I remember in the South how the Jewish merchants used to shake and shiver every time the word "Jew" appeared in the press, in a headline, God forbid; and now I find that many Jews in the South look upon the word without inhibitions or misgivings.

It is a terrible responsibility to come here and speak to you people. The trade unionists have been brought up on speeches. I know that from the first day that you entered your shop, and the union hall, you were listening to speeches, and I am sure you are now saying to yourself, "What can this guy tell us that we haven't heard before?"

But I'll not be coy about it. Actually—I make more speeches than George Jessel. The only difference is that I can't make the same speech every night as he does. During this past year I spoke to the student body of Davidson College, of about 1,500 boys who may be Presbyterian ministers someday; and I spoke before an Urban League, and an NAACP chapter, and the Christ Episcopal Church of Charlotte, and a dozen Rotary, Kiwanis, and Lions Clubs, and dozens of synagogues and temples, and now this Jewish Labor Committee.

Now, this is something. The Jewish Labor Committee—I was thinking about it this morning. I don't know whether any of you has ever thought of this idea before. You know, in the South, when we sing "Hatikvah," we don't just plain ordinary sing "Hatikvah," God forbid. First, we sing "My Country 'Tis of Thee," then we sing "Hatikvah," we sort of sandwich it in, and then this is followed by "The Star Spangled Banner." We protect ourselves at both ends. If someone sings "Hatikvah," a guy says, "Quick, 'The Star Spangled Banner.'" Well, I was thinking about that very thing, the Jewish Labor Committee. You know, you're the only one in America. Maybe I'm wrong—I haven't looked it up, but we have American Jewish Committee, American Jewish Congress, American Jewish Veterans, but you guys aren't afraid—just plain Jewish Labor Committee—and that's that, and that's wonderful, too. And paradoxically this is the highest point of the true American ideal—the completely relaxed liberalism which would have warmed the hearts of Benjamin Franklin and Thomas Jefferson. I congratulate you from the bottom of my heart.

Recently, in the South, I had a fire in my establishment; it destroyed all my papers and books, and luckily, it was an accident. But that's really not the point of my story. The big point is the overwhelming response I received. I was wondering why hundreds of Christian clergymen in the South sent me letters of such warmth and fellowship and friendship. Southerners. The world has turned upside down. But I think there's a clue to this fellowship I've had in the South. I speak in many basements of Protestant churches; Episcopal, Presbyterian, Baptist, and I always give them a little preamble to my speech. I say, "Folks, I've got something to tell you of great importance; you know if Jesus were to come to Atlanta (or to Birmingham, Montgomery, or Charlotte) I'd be the first man he'd look up. He'd contact me first." I tell my audience why this would happen. "In the first place, I'm a kinsman, a relative, and second he'd need an interpreter; you don't suppose he talks that 'you all' business; and then, he'd need a trained reporter; He'd want to be briefed; he'd want to know what are Christians, what are Methodists, what are Baptists, and so forth." Well, a lot of these people meet me on the street, and they greet me graciously, but I could see a gleam in their eyes as if to say, "Don't forget me, Harry, I'm your friend."

In the South they invite me to various Rotary and Kiwanis clubs in many small towns, and the southerner is very gracious, a gentleman. When I get there, the chairman comes over and says, "Mr. Golden, we have ham on the menu today and we know you don't eat ham, so we prepared a special dish of fried chicken for you, fried in pure country butter, too." And then, of course, the lady comes down the aisle with the shrimp cocktail. I suspect that the best-kept Jewish secret is shrimp. We made a wonderful deal with the Christians. We let them think of us in terms of ham, that's the big deal. The goyim say, "They don't eat ham," but they know nothing about shrimp and lobster, and we'd be fools to tell them.

But things have changed a little bit there. I've come into a town, and you know the goyim even at the intellectual level think that all the Jews meet in some cellar once a week—Baruch, Frankfurter, and I and every one of us. So when I come to the town to make a speech they automatically invite their Jewish merchant, like he needs a hole in the head. But the poor guy has to come. The first thing I say when I get up to speak is, "I'm going to talk to you about the Jews," and the Jewish merchant immediately begins to shake, ehr ziteritt. But he watches the goyim; he wants to see what the goyim will do, and when he sees the goyim laughing then he relaxes a little. After he wipes his brow he may even laugh a little, too. Eventually he invites me to his store and asks me what size shirt I wear.

We could take a lesson from this fellow in our study of human relations. I believe the best job in this world is that lone Jew in a small southern town. There is nothing like this in the entire world. This fellow is on top of the world, and for several reasons. In the first place, the Gentile community guards this fellow like they guard the Confederate monument in the square. This is our Jew. "We have a fine Jewish family in our town," they always say that—it is always "a fine Jewish family in our town," entirely different from those New York Jews. Of course. And once in a while they change the geography and say, "not like those Miami Jews."

But this happy Jew has trouble, too. The Baptist Sunday school teacher who knows the Five Books of Moses by heart may be puzzled over some involved biblical problem and automatically he says, "Let's go ask Goldstein," because he identifies Goldstein with Jeremiah, Amos, Moses, and Isaiah, but poor Goldstein hasn't the faintest idea what they are talking about.

A friend of mine teaches at Livingston College at Salisbury, North Carolina, a Negro ministerial seminary. So this friend is proud of the fact that he understands a bit of Hebrew. Recently he went into a Jewish store, in Salisbury, and he said, "Boker Tov," which I think means "Good morning," but this "Boker Tov" to the Jewish merchant sounded like "Booker T. Washington," and so he said to my friend, the seminary student, "All right, Mr. Boker, what can I do for you?"

Today we have a problem of our own—the racial problem. But this is not strictly a southern problem. You may sum it up in a bit of folklore which some of you may have heard. In the North the white man says, "Nigger, go as high as you can, but don't come close, and in the South, the white man says, "Nigger, come as close as you can, but don't go up." The problem, of course, is caste; it is a matter of caste more than anything else. Up at the Dan River mills, one of the largest in the world, about three years ago, there was a strike, an unauthorized strike. The spinners were white women. Then they have what is called the lap-haulers, Negro women. Now a lap hauler is one who hands the raw material to the spinner. They touch hands constantly. They work very closely together. The relationship has always been good. Then management wanted some new spinners, so they picked a few of these lap haulers who had been there twenty years and who knew more about the machines than anyone else, and they wanted to make spinners out of them, and the white spinners went out on strike. And now they used all the legends, such as body odor, and all of that business. As spinners, mind you, these Negro women would have been in a building a quarter of a mile away. The white spinners would have never seen them again, completely segregated, but they went out on strike. As lap haulers, working body-to-body, it was all right, but as spinners–equal status, it was evil. Caste is the most important part of the racial problem of the South. There was a speech recorded by the leader of the strikers, who stated the matter correctly: "I am a member of the Pythian auxiliary and I am a spinner, and here comes this big, fat Negro woman and she's a spinner too." An interesting thing is that they are always referred to as "big, fat Negro women." You'll find the same references among the southern white men. They always refer to "that big buck nigger." And of course we know what bothers them. A myth, of course, the sexual prowess of the Negro. Caste, of course, but sex also plays its part in this human drama.

The white man has slept with the Negro woman for two or three hundred years, and now he fears retaliation. This is a great tragedy, and it is also a great insult to the white women of the South. I can't understand why they stand for it, this idea of their men worrying about the matter.

But no one seems to get the point. No one seems to be insulted by this thing. If you let the Negro vote and give him equal job opportunity and equal educational facilities, why should the white women fall for him? Why should they? I believe this is nonsense and an insult of the first order. And here is the greatest tragedy of all. The South has produced some of the most creative minds of the American civilization, but right now all creativity has come to a halt. This great civilization is preoccupied with this thing in human relations—this nonsense about interracial sex, this resistance to a Supreme Court decision, this determination not to grant first-class citizenship to 26 percent of its population. This great civilization with many of its brilliant and warmhearted people are not thinking about foreign affairs.

They are not thinking of the expansion of their educational and health facilities. They're not thinking of the basic strategy of the free world against statism and totalitarianism. No, they are completely preoccupied with the project of trying to keep a fifteen-year-old Negro girl from going to a public school. All creativity has been postponed indefinitely. And this is the crux of the entire problem. It is not what racial segregation has done to the Negro, but what it has done to the white man, and this is a problem which he refuses to acknowledge. He has paid a bigger price for this segregation than the Negro. This is one of the most fantastic stories in the history of human relations.

First let us look at this phenomenon, the response of the Negro race to this American wrong. Over eleven million people, half of whom are illiterate, another third of whom are semiliterate, a civilization of sharecroppers, truck drivers, and janitors, and they haven't done a single thing wrong. This will be recorded eventually as one of the most noble stories of the human spirit. They bomb their houses, and they say, "Let's go to church and pray for the fellows who have bombed our houses." They burn a cross on their hills, and the Negroes roast marshmallows in the embers.

But this story goes way back, back to the 1930s when it became evident that the Negroes of the South—second-class citizens by law—offered the greatest resistance to the blandishments of the Communist propagandists. And this is all the more remarkable when we realize that the local Communist medicine men automatically promoted the Negro no matter how unfit for the job, to positions of greatest honor within their individual cells, a promotion that had nothing behind it but the color of a man's skin, and therefore was as dehumanizing as legal segregation itself. And the Negroes of the South who fell for this degradation through "honor" would not fill a respectable telephone booth.

It was as if the Negro race had suddenly seen the same vision that had inspired the founding fathers of America, and they became the greatest connoisseurs of the true American democracy, the process of going to the judge with a writ, and the judge says, "You haven't exhausted all your means of possible relief," and the Negro says, "Thank you, I'll start all over again in the morning," and a year later he's back again with the writ, and his children march up to the public school and they are stopped, and so they go home and the next morning they march again to the school, and Americans, all, of all races, creeds, and societies will one day rise up with pride and pay honor to this great phenomenon of the human story.

But what are they talking about when Senator Harry Byrd of Virginia and Governor Marvin Griffin of Georgia demand that racial segregation remain part of the culture? What do they mean by this? Is it a matter of whether a Negro child may or may not go to a free public school? That is only part of it, and a very small part of it. What are they talking about racial segregation? They are talking about human degradation and death; that's what they are talking about. Because of the entire system of racial segregation seven Negro women die in childbirth to one white woman. Because of the system of racial segregation tuberculosis, which is eighth as the cause of death among the white race, is second as a cause of death among the Negroes, and because of racial segregation you have that deadening sense of hopelessness among millions of young people who were born to share and contribute to the creativity and the glory of America. You are fifteen years old and you've never seen your father in anything but overalls, and you've never seen your mother in anything but a uniform on the way to another woman's home, and a car pulls up in your filth-littered yard and a man shouts to you, "Boy, tell Jim to come at seven o'clock tomorrow instead of eight," and Jim is your father, or the occupant of the car says, "Boy, tell Nettie not to come tomorrow," and Nettie is your mother, and so you take a carton of cigarettes off a truck or get behind the wheel of a car that is not yours, because of the degradation, the lack of self-esteem, the uselessness of trying to prove your individual worth, because you know by instinct that a record of even four arrests will not disqualify you from that job of janitor which is waiting for you.

But why the resistance? Why do the people in the state capitols of the South sit up nights trying to figure out a new plan to "beat" the Constitution? And what is happening to their own children in the process? Education takes place at many levels; in the school, in the home, in the church, on the street, in the newspaper accounts of the work of the state legislatures, and in the speeches of the governor. How can they tell the children on Monday that to obey the law is the highest point to which an American boy may aspire, and on Tuesday maneuver and connive to get around the law?

And what is this resistance all about? Why should an old aristocrat like Senator Byrd of Virginia talk like a barber of a mill village when he discusses the problem of one-third of the citizens of his state? Why? Why did the entire upper-middle class turn on the Negro after the Supreme Court decision? All of this relates to the statement of a woman recorded by a reporter for *Life* magazine outside the Central High School of Little Rock as the nine Negro children finally went through the door. This woman gasped, "My

God, the niggers are in." Why should this woman have felt that her world had suddenly come to an end? Actually this woman has been brought up in an atmosphere which tried to give her caste the easy way. While the Negroes were going to the back of the bus and to separate schools and filling the jobs of janitors, this woman had status without money, status without the necessity of voting, and without the need to join a labor union; and she felt secure with this caste because the Negro stood between her and complete social oblivion. You take the Negro away from her and she must seek self-esteem elsewhere, and where will she find it if not in the voting booth and in social legislation, and where will she find this if not in an accelerated attempt to catch up with all the benefits of our industrial age and with all its comforts, and she will now look to another kind of caste—the caste of economic and political security within the framework of the great American democracy.

What can we do? How will this come about? And in my opinion it revolves around the need for communication. There is no communication. Both races are talking about entirely different things. The white woman says, "The Negroes are very happy, they do not want to end racial segregation, my maid told me so." She calls in her maid and says, "Nettie, what do you think of this Supreme Court decision?" and the maid says, "Lordy, Miz Emily, we never sees the paper," and that night the maid goes home and says to her husband, "Jim, get a move on you with that supper, we'll be late for the NAACP meeting, and let's try to put some life into that integration committee of ours."

There is no communication. In my state we have a white high school which has had a linotype machine and other printing facilities to teach the children this highly skilled trade. There isn't a Negro school with any such facilities. And so when the white men get together they talk about how the Negroes want to go to bed with white women, and when the Negroes get together they talk about a linotype machine. I've heard about that linotype machine a thousand times in a hundred meetings. And I have yet to hear a Negro, even by the most remote innuendo, even during a thousand unguarded moments, express "desire" for a white woman. This is utter nonsense. In the first place the Negro has all the "white" women he needs. The white men of the South "gave" them to him. The white man can choose only a white woman; the Negro can pick from a dozen different shades among his own people all the way from redheads with freckles down to the very blackest of the black. Secondly, we have learned that as a race or ethnic group rises in self-esteem there is not only less crime but much less sex promiscuity. If she knows she can someday be a nurse, or a dental technician, or a stenographer, the day when you can take her to the haystack is over—gone forever; and self-esteem leads to pride of race, and pride in peoplehood, and as the Negro enters first-class citizenship in our country and takes his rightful place in the industrial society, this so-called "mongrelization" which has been part of the culture will finally come to a grinding halt. Exactly opposite to what the white men fears will take place.

Now what does this mean to us, to us as Jews, to you as trade unionists, to all of us as Americans? First of all, it means an expansion of incalculable wealth. You have in the South the greatest untapped consumer market on this continent. These same fellows who are opening factories in the South to escape from David Dubinsky are building better than they know. One day they'll find a new consumer's market right outside their door such as they hadn't thought of in their wildest imagination. There are some eleven million people who need everything from the skin out from the moment they begin to take their rightful places in the industrial age. Let me tell you this, my friends, that in this most prosperous era in our history in the two most progressive cities in the South, Atlanta and my own Charlotte, they still have 18,000 and 6,000 dwellings respectively without inside toilets. Just imagine what that does for the boy and for the girl and for the human spirit, and for ambition, and for hope.

That will mean for all of us, a tremendous burgeoning of the American ideal in terms of humanity and in terms of decency and honor.

But it means much more, and here I must confess my work in this area is purely selfish. I am thinking of my sons and my grandchildren. I am thinking of the kind of world I would like them to live in thirty years from now. You know we Jews work hard for our children, and our daily prayer is that our children survive us, and how happy that prayer can be if we know that the American idea is undergoing this tremendous expansion of democracy that will give our children and our grandchildren a better hope for security.

Yes, security, basic security. With the end of racial segregation in the South, it not only means that we will have eleven million new allies for democracy, but that we will have over thirty million new allies. Your next great liberal movement in America will have the Negro for its vital center. He will want things, things such as better housing, and better clothing, and the best for his children, and so will the white southerner. Once that artificial caste has been taken away from him, he will seek self-esteem and he will ask for social legislation. This is your next liberal movement in America, the white and the Negro of the South, and they will eventually take up where the Roosevelt New Deal left off. And these people will ask for social legislation in the name of Jesus, and this will be an entirely different kind of liberalism, and perhaps even the unanswerable liberalism. And as our allies it will make us a bit more tolerant too, and give us, as Jews, a new sense of security and a new dedication to what the founding fathers of America had intended all the time when they laid the foundations of this great civilization.

§16 Milton A. Galamison

Milton Arthur Galamison was born on March 25, 1923, to Dorothy Woods and Gladstone Galamison. Raised in segregated Philadelphia by his mother and her grandmother, Nellie Woods, Galamison later expressed no small bitterness that the family had been essentially abandoned by its father. The young boy's budding curiosity was nourished by Nellie as she encouraged him to read. The family attended St. Michael's Episcopal Church, and it was at the church that Galamison's theological fires were kindled by a young priest who mentored him. After graduating from Overbook High School in 1940, Galamison began his undergraduate studies at St. Augustine College in Raleigh, North Carolina. He left after only a year—a year in which he also led a successful strike directed against the school's cafeteria. Back home in Philadelphia, Galamison decided to enroll at nearby Lincoln University, and he eventually graduated with honors in 1945. While at Lincoln, he met Gladys Hunt, who was from a prominent Presbyterian family. The two married in 1945 and would have one son. Several of Galamison's professors convinced the budding scholar to stay on at Lincoln to enroll in its divinity school. To do so, though, Galamison had to change his denominational allegiances, from Episcopal to Presbyterian. His wife's influence did not harm his conversion. Galamison earned his bachelor's of divinity in 1947; later that same year he was ordained and began pastoring a church in Princeton, New Jersey. While at Princeton, Galamison enrolled in Princeton's seminary, and he earned his master's degree in 1949. Galamison's big break came in late 1948 when he was called to Siloam Presbyterian Church in Brooklyn, New York, one of the most prominent Presbyterian churches in the country. He would lead the large congregation for the next forty years.

Galamison quickly leveraged his newfound prominence for sociopolitical action, specifically the integration of New York City's public schools. An active member of the Brooklyn NAACP, Galamison served as chairman of its education committee from 1957 to 1959. He left this committee to form his own group, the Parents Workshop for Equality in New York City Schools. His efforts to meaningfully integrate the city's schools came to a head in 1964 when he led a broad coalition of civil rights groups in a one-day boycott of the schools. On that day, February 3, 1964, nearly 460,000 students stayed out of school, more than 40 percent of the student population. While that coalition eventually frayed, Galamison's commitment to quality education did not. In 1967 he organized a vocational school in Brooklyn which was an offshoot of Leon Sullivan's work back in his hometown of Philadelphia. In an interesting twist of history, Galamison was invited by Harlem's Malcolm X to be the featured speaker at a February 21, 1965, meeting of the Organization of Afro-American Unity. He was late for the 3:00 p.m. scheduled start, so Malcolm began the meeting without him. Moments later the charismatic civil rights leader was dead from a fusillade of bullets. Galamison died on March 9, 1988, from pancreatic cancer, survived by his wife and son. His papers are housed at the New York Public Library's Schomburg Center.

The occasion for Rev. Galamison's Sunday sermon at Siloam was the attempted assassination just the day prior by a mentally disturbed black woman, Izola Ware Curry, who plunged a letter opener into Dr. King's chest as he signed copies of his book *Stride Toward Freedom* in a Harlem store. While Galamison offers up a paean to King's leadership, he also has a generous amount of spleen to vent on his unsuspecting parishioners. Why is it that when Dr. King comes to town the publicity seekers find their way by his side—but when danger is present they are nowhere to be found? Galamison is one of the few ministers to praise a woman for her leadership—Little Rock's Daisy Bates—but he wonders where that leadership might come from in the future, especially when his congregants are willing to settle for a "milk-and-water Christianity." An easy and undemanding faith simply can't compete in an age of rabid ideologues. Galamison urges his listeners to the strenuous life, even the life of martyrdom since the next world—the world unseen—is precisely the source of our soul's nourishment; from that source we will get the strength to serve God and humanity.

Ties in Times of Tension

September 21, 1958
Siloam Presbyterian Church, Brooklyn, New York

It had been my hope to give my people a rest this morning from talk about race problems and race violence; a rest from discussions about integration and desegregation and disintegration. Everyone has his own idea about what my ministry should be like, how I should apportion my time and what I should be interested in. In fact, there are many people who feel that we all should live as they live; as if there were nothing wrong in this world; as if there were no debasing evils to turn a man's stomach; as if there were no towering problems to call out a man's wrath and loyalty. It was my intention to somewhat change the subject this morning. But when I left Harlem Hospital late last night, where Martin Luther King lay with a near-fatal stab wound in his chest, I have the feeling that the times will not let us rest. We cannot hide our heads in the sand of a milk-fed Christianity, like ostriches, while the world is moving so swiftly around us; while others are giving their life, and the last full measure of their devotion—even dying—that the dreams for which Jesus died might come true.

Thousands of people stood for hours outside the Theresa Hotel Friday night to hear Martin Luther King speak. The ovation they gave him was unbelievably thunderous. Hundreds of autograph seekers were in line at the Harlem department store on Saturday, to buy his book, when this woman appeared from nowhere and stabbed him in the chest. Governor Harriman stood in the corridor of Harlem Hospital for four hours yesterday as did many other outstanding leaders of the city, just waiting mostly because there wasn't much anybody could do.

But before Martin Luther King could get to the operating room, the southern press had begun to spout its venom. They described Harlem as a lawless community. They, along with every other news source, were certain to identify the assailant as a Negro woman. They implied that this Negro leader was safer in the South with the White Citizens' Council, than in New York with the NAACP. On the whole, this attack on Dr. King by a Negro was interpreted to mean that he does not speak for the masses of people, and that large numbers do not respect him and the things he stands for. Of course, the bigoted mentality of the South would have twisted this incident to its own purposes no matter how the knifing had occurred, no matter who had done it.

But we are faced with a much larger problem this morning: the problem of which this attack on Dr. King is but a symbol. And the larger problem is the national atmosphere in which this kind of thing could happen to be distorted and perverted by the southern press.

How could a Negro woman suppose that Dr. King, who preaches and lives love and nonviolence, is her enemy? I think these questions ought to be raised here. Why should this woman seek out a man who is a modern Moses to many, and unquestionably the strongest single voice to the conscience of this nation—why should Mrs. Curry single him out to kill?

Certainly the growing atmosphere of hatred and violence against Negro leaders, even by Negroes themselves who feel they have interests to protect—certainly this is a possible answer. But the more I talked with former police commissioner Billy Rowe and others who had heard this woman questioned yesterday, the more I felt that her motives were not satisfactorily explained. The police appear content to report that this woman appears demented, mentally ill, and possibly insane. Most people who murder are! But underneath their sickness are motivations which need to be uncovered. This woman rallied against the NAACP, against integration; she spoke of wanting the schools open; she sounded more like a member of the White Citizens' Council than a Negro. Nobody seemed interested in uncovering her connections in the South nor discovering why she left only a month ago. And after an attack on Rev. Abernathy a few weeks ago, by a Negro with a hatchet and a gun who accused him of relations with his wife, events seem to be taking on a peculiar pattern. These two people, who cannot coherently explain their actions, take on the appearance of assassins, brainwashed and sent to do a job. They are reminiscent of some slaves, so brainwashed and dedicated to their masters that they betrayed to whiplashings and to the death their fellow slaves. To say that this woman is mad explains nothing. If you wanted somebody killed who else could you get to do the killing except someone who is mad?

Martin King said on Friday night that some will have to sacrifice and even die before freedom is won. He said that he, himself, was ready for any eventuality, ready to pay any price. And certainly, having lived these years in the midst of bombings and threats and violence, he is ready for anything. But Martin King is a very lonely man. When he comes to New York he is beset and surrounded by opportunists and a lot of camera hogs who never expended an ounce of sweat for civil rights in their own community, and it appears that he has lots of company. But the day he was beaten and arrested in Montgomery, he said on the telephone that he was lonely. Lonely because all the adulation and praise and applause on all the platforms across the nation can't be heard when a man is carrying a cross everyday by himself. And all these phony big shots in the North, who like to be identified with him, who clutter up the platform and make bold speeches to the crowd—people who wouldn't risk a week's pay on any issue: these are poor company when a man is sitting in a prison cell; or in his home with a bomb under the front porch. These people who are always in the right place at the right time, where the only shot is the camera flash, but never on the battlefield—these are also poor company for Christ. And this morning is as good a time as any to refresh our memory on what Christianity is all about.

In these times of numbing tension, when some men are living up to the fullness of their manhood—and some women, like Daisy Bates, are living up to the fullness of their womanhood—we are blessed to live in an age with people who are beginning to master some of the deeper and overlooked principles of our Christian religion. People who in the face of ugliness and hate and brutal facts are being guided by the hopes and dreams and ideals of a world unseen.

The writer of Hebrews calls our attention to people like this. Here on one side is the actual world of tension where Abraham lived, Ur, but here on the other side is his possible world too, his promised land, made real by faith until it became real indeed. Here is the visible world of evil, like Egypt, where Moses lived, a world of suffering and slavery. But the writer says that *he endured as seeing him who is invisible.* He endured until the unseen world proved true. Here is the one world with its ever-changing problems which drive men to distraction. But here also is the eternal world where Jesus Christ is the same yesterday, today, and forever. Here is the horrid world of turmoil and inhumanity. But here also is the inviolable world of God *removing the things that are shaken in order that the things which cannot be shaken may remain.* It's the ties to the world unseen: to the hopes and dreams and ideals of the world unseen to which we must cling in these times of tension.

When the writer of Hebrews spoke of Moses enduring with his vision of the invisible, he was speaking to the struggling Christians of his own day. Everywhere there was catastrophe and trial and persecution. And these first Christians found their strength by not living in this world alone and being frightened into looking out for number one. They found their strength living in this world and keeping their ties in another: a world they described as unshaken and unshakable; an anchor of the soul, both sure and steadfast. This is how they managed to endure.

Many years ago in a commencement address, Douglas Freeman told the students how many people have managed to work for beauty and truth and goodness amid the ugliness and darkness of their time. When did Words-worth write some of his greatest poetry? When Napoleon was collecting his Armada for a planned assault of the English coast at Dover, England. When did Beethoven write his Fifth Symphony? During the first year of the Peninsular War when Napoleon was trampling all over Europe. When did Keats write his finest sonnet on Chapman's Homer? The summer that Waterloo was fought. And always, those who have given the most to the world have been those who, in spite of the actual facts, were able to work for potentials and possibilities. People who believed in a light that no darkness could put out. *He endured as seeing him who is invisible.*

Peter talks about this relationship to the world unseen and to its God, which is so hard to define, but by which men endure. It's a philosophy of life, but it's more than a philosophy of life. It's a moral code, but it's more than a moral code. It's a social creed, but it's more than a social creed. It's more than moral maxims and more than ethical ideals. And it's at this point that the Christian who endures parts company with all others. Ours must be a personal relationship, a personal attachment to Christ. Whom, Peter says, having not seen, yet love; in whom, though ye see him not, yet believing, ye rejoice with joy unspeakable and full of glory; receiving the end of your faith, even the salvation of your souls.

This is no pipe dream. It speaks to the deepest need of men and women in our time; to endure and to have something to endure with. After all, what are we witnessing all over the world today? We are witnessing a demand for two things: *a leader and a cause.* Because people seek a leader, they will flock to a Hitler or a Franco or a Faubus. And because people are looking for a cause they will serve the cause these men represent. Everywhere men are begging for something that will claim them absolutely, sacrificially, body, mind, and soul. And causes like nationalism and Communism are exploiting this need in men, demanding all they have to give.

But we religious people who have a great leader, who have a great cause: we want a milk-and-water Christianity. Other people are giving their all to lesser causes, and we don't even want to put a decent offering in the offering plate. We're insulted if everything doesn't go our way. We give the little that we give grudgingly, we dissipate our time and energy on things that are either unimportant or none of our business—then we expect to see significant victories for Christ in this world. It isn't going to happen. Nothing is going to happen so long as people support and live and die for things like nationalism and Communism and fascism, while we Christians excuse ourselves from going to church because it rains. A mild, undemanding religion is ineffective against these other militant, masterful movements. There is no use in our setting some poor, apologetic copy of Christ against the widely publicized demagogues of our age. But to see the real Christ, strong Son of God, stand committed to real Christian adventure, to serve God with every beat of the heart: this is the thrill that no other cause, no other leader, can generate in the soul of man. It's what Peter called the *joy unspeakable and full of glory.* It's the invisible source from which men find the power to endure.

This is just about the diluted brand of Christian dedication that we accept in the church today. And the truth is that if we can't even get Christians out of bed, we don't stand much chance getting them into the lion's den. It's because there are so few Martin Luther Kings and so many of this caliber of Christian that man's journey to the stars is so long delayed.

There is an amphitheater in Smyrna where Polycarp was martyred—Polycarp, the great Christian teacher who always endured like someone who had seen the unseen. It was during the reign of one Statius Quadratus that Polycarp was killed. And not long after the church at Smyrna dated Polycarp's death with an inscription like this: *Statius Quadratus being proconsul, but Jesus Christ being king forever.* They lived in the kind of world where Polycarp could be martyred. But they also lived in another world. You fill in the names any way you like: James Folsom being governor; Faubus being governor— *Statius Quadratus being proconsul but Jesus Christ being king forever.*

§17 Paul L. Stagg

Paul Leonard Stagg was born into a racially bigoted family in Eustis, Louisiana, on February 24, 1914. Growing up, Paul's father would often take the family to local Ku Klux Klan rallies. After graduating from Louisiana College and being ordained as a Baptist minister in 1934, Paul attended seminary at the Southern Baptist Theological Seminary in Louisville, Kentucky. Before earning his degree in 1939, Paul married Margaret Mathilde Persinger in Montgomery, West Virginia, where he also pastored a church. After serving as an Air Force chaplain during World War II, Paul came to Front Royal, Virginia's First Baptist Church in 1947 and began preaching the good news of racial justice to a less than hospitable audience. Not only were many Front Royal congregants opposed to their pastor, but community members harassed the family, bomb threats to the home were common, the Klan burned more than one cross on the family's lawn, and the couples' two daughters were often traumatized with shouts of "nigger lover." The Staggs left Front Royal in July 1959, as the pressure was simply too great, and the congregation was left reeling over the state's school integration crisis. Given his fearless racial bona fides, Rev. Stagg signed on as the program associate for evangelism with the American Baptist Convention's Home Mission Societies and traveled the country in support of the civil rights movement— landing in jail on more than one occasion. Later Stagg worked for the New

Jersey Council of Churches and continued his work with progressive political causes. Rev. Stagg passed away on January 3, 2007. His two daughters, Brenda Butler and Mickey York, survive him.

Along with several other Front Royal ministers, Rev. Stagg spoke out against local plans to avoid the federal government's mandate to integrate Warren County schools. Instead of integrating the public schools per a court order, local segregationists sought to use area churches as "private schools" and thus maintain racial separation, while ostensibly not disobeying the law. While First Baptist congregants eventually voted not to allow such a plan to take place, Rev. Stagg and his family endured an enormous strain during the school integration tempest. He resigned from First Baptist in June 1959, fearful for his own life and the life of his family. Recalling the gravity, and the language, of Martin Luther before the Diet of Worms, Reverend Stagg offers an eloquent dissent for the proposal of using First Baptist's facilities to make an end run around the court order to integrate Virginia's public schools. He offers his dissent on several grounds: separation of church and state, the violation of federal law, scriptural evidences, and the church's missionary function. By the close of the address, Stagg has elevated his dissent into something of a sacred church paper—invoking both the minor prophet Habakkuk and leaving to posterity, and also to his errant congregants, his prophetic "vision."

Here I Stand

October 5, 1958
Front Royal, Virginia

Our church has been approached with a request to offer its facilities for private school purposes. This matter is of great concern to all.

To many the issue is a simple one: namely, a compassionate concern to remove our youth from the street and to provide education for them during an emergency period. When put in this simple way, I have great sympathy for it. Having served this congregation for eleven years, I hardly need to say that I have been sympathetic with every move for the good of the community and that I have been active in many. Whether the building of Warren County Memorial Hospital, the formation of the Recreation Association, the beginning of the Teen Age Canteen, the Organization of the Community Chest, the bringing of the Salvation Army to Front Royal, or the beginning of the Mental Health Chapter, I have given active support. If our high school had burned down or had been destroyed by some natural calamity, I would be among the first to say, let us offer sanctuary to the public school.

The situation, however, is far from this simple. There are issues involved which jeopardize the gospel and which imperil the church as the revelation of God's truth to the world. While I have respect for those who may not see the matter as I see it, I feel bound by my oath of ordination to be true to the gospel, and in the discharge of this stewardship to register my dissent to the proposal that our church be made available for private schools and to state the issues as I see them. While solely responsible for what I say, I hope it will be clear that I am not expressing my personal opinion. I have consulted with my fellow ministers, who are on record as opposing the use of the church for the proposed private school. I have also consulted with eminent theologians in Christian ethics, and I have studied the statements of important bodies in Protestantism, including statements made by Baptists and the Christian Life Commission of the Southern Baptist Convention. Finally, I have studied the Bible as the record of God's revelation.

In the light of this respected body of informed opinion and the result of my own study of God's Word, I am prompted to make this statement of dissent. In making it I desire neither to curry favor nor to offend, but only to save the church from the embarrassment of being put in an untenable position.

Here are the grounds of my objection: to consent to the use of church facilities for the proposed private school would be to agree to a plan which in its effect is an evasion of federal law. I should like to save the church the embarrassment of consenting to an action which may well be declared in contempt of court. Personally I must dissociate myself from any such action.

To consent to the use of the church property for this purpose would be to sanction segregation in the name of God and to bless a pattern of life which the Church in its responsible statements regards as contrary to the Bible, the teaching of Christ, and the meaning of the Church. In the name of God who has made all men in His image and who is "no respecter of persons" (Acts 10:34), whose will is "to unite all things in Christ" (Ephesians 1:10), and whose church is a fellowship "where there is neither Jew nor Greek—neither slave nor free—neither male nor female; for you are all one in Christ Jesus" (Galatians 3:28), in the name of this God, I say, whose most characteristic invitation is "whosoever will, let him come," the church cannot bar its facilities to any group, class, or race. The proposal before us would exclude some whom the love of God includes.

Although bound by ties of love and friendship with all who think this action necessary, my understanding of the gospel and of the church as a fellowship rising above the accidents of race, class, and nationality leads me to dissent. As some of you have graciously expressed it, while you disagree with my position, you would not want me to renounce my conviction. I am grateful for this and for the kind of spirituality which prompts it. I cannot betray the gospel of which I am steward. As a minister, I have little in house or land; I have only my integrity as a minister to whom the gospel has been entrusted. Here I must stand.

To agree to the use of church facilities for a proposed private school may well open the way for the use of the church by worldly forces for the purposes alien to the teachings of the Church. I stand in a proud line of historic Baptist witness. As Baptists we have always believed in religious liberty and in separation of church and state. We have believed that the church has a message from God to the world and that its pulpit should be free to declare it. We have decried all attempts on the part of the state to use the church and to make it a tool of its purpose. We have believed in a free church, in a free society, a church free to declare the gospel whether or not the gospel is palatable to those who hear it in a given age or culture. The church cannot be an echo of its time or of prevailing opinions or else it loses its integrity and its right to exist. It must speak the accents of heaven or else earth will have no redeeming word.

While the intent among many people is surely not for this effect to come to pass, as a minister true to my high calling, I must warn that this is a grave danger. The church in America must remain strong and free if it is to discharge its God-given mission. If we make the church into a lackey of world powers, if we give our consent to its becoming messenger boy of "the world rulers of this present darkness" to run their errands, and if we allow the church to be made into the image of the society it was called to redeem, we will betray the church. If we love the church, let us rise up to defend it and keep its name unsullied and its fellowship unmarred by the rankings, the discriminations, and the caste system of our society.

Finally to agree to the proposal before us would embarrass the Missionary Commission of the church. Our Lord has commissioned us to go into the uttermost part of the earth and to preach the gospel. This is not an option for Christians. It is a mandate. If we are to fulfill this commission then we need to watch the example we set before the world.

The eyes of the world are upon us. In the last few weeks I have received letters from two continents. I have been heartened by letters commending the statement of the ministers of Warren County. I have been sobered by letters which look expectantly to the church here to proclaim the gospel in a way that will not embarrass the church before the world.

Let us be clear about it. If we identify the church with the cultural pattern of our society, we will alienate multiplied millions of persons in the world whom we desire to reach. The world is watching to see what witness the church will make here. If we fail to make plain that the gospel is a universal gospel whose temple is "a House of Prayer for all people" (Isaiah 56:7), we will weaken our witness and undercut our mission as a church.

In taking this stand, I do so with love for each of you. I have shared your joys in the arrival of a newborn and in the glad company of a wedding festival. I have held your infant children in my arms to dedicate them to God. I have kept vigil with you by the bedside of the sick, and I have stood with you when the shadows of death cast their gloom. Whether you agree or disagree, I pray that the bonds of Christian love will keep us together. In this we will witness to the world that we are a fellowship, not of coercion or of conformity, but of God's spirit where liberty of conscience and freedom of expression are encouraged. It is only in this context that we can solve the problem before us.

With the prophet of old, I must inscribe my witness in a book. The ultimate issue belongs to God, whose purpose none can make void. Like the prophet Habakkuk whom the Lord instructed, "Write the vision, and make it plain upon the tablets, that he may run that readeth it" (Habakkuk 2:2), I write my witness on the record of this church. "For the vision awaits its time; hastens to the end—it will not lie. If it seems slow, wait for it: it will surely come" (Habakkuk 2:3). Therefore, I make this statement a part of the record of the church, and I hereby file it with the clerk and request that a copy be sent to the Virginia Baptist Historical Society. In the spirit of Luther, "Here I stand. I can do no other. So God help me."

§18 Jacob M. Rothschild

Rabbi Jacob Mortimer Rothschild was born on August 4, 1911, to Lillian and Meyer Rothschild in Pittsburgh, Pennsylvania. Jacob eventually graduated high school in Pittsburgh and headed south and east for the University of Cincinnati in 1927. After graduating he attended Hebrew Union College and was ordained a rabbi in 1936. After serving congregations in Davenport, Iowa, and Pittsburgh, Rothschild entered military service as an American Division chaplain in the Pacific theater. After being discharged in

1946, Rothschild became senior rabbi at Atlanta's Hebrew Benevolent Congregation, a prominent Reform temple located on Peachtree Street. That same year he married Janice Oettinger, and the couple would have a boy and a girl. As a "Yankee," Rothschild was surprised by the extent of racial hostility in his new city, and he quickly set about to sermonize about it, to the chagrin of some of his congregants. He also wasn't bashful about organizing for civil rights, as Rothschild was involved with the Greater Atlanta Council on Human Relations, Atlanta's Community Relations Commission, the Human Relations Council of Georgia, the Southern Regional Council, and the National Conference of Christians and Jews. Because of his commitment to interfaith relations and civil rights, Rothschild also developed a close personal friendship with Martin Luther King Jr.; in fact, he helped organize an Atlanta banquet for King in honor of his Nobel Peace Prize, serving as the master of ceremonies.

Rothschild's outspoken activism was met with potentially deadly force in the fall of 1958. Following a string of bombings of southern Jewish centers in Miami, Nashville, and Jacksonville, and several failed attempts in other major cities, Hebrew Benevolent was attacked on the morning of October 12. The bombers used fifty sticks of dynamite to rip an eighteen-foot-square hole in the synagogue's outer wall, causing $200,000 worth of damage. Though no one was hurt in the huge blast, Atlanta was badly shaken and the story quickly went national. With the help of the Federal Bureau of Investigation, five men were arrested and indicted for the attack. But only one, George Bright, would stand trial. His first trial ended in a hung jury in December of 1958. He was acquitted in a retrial one month later. The bombing and its aftermath did nothing to quiet Rothschild, who continued in his frank critique of racial inequality from the pulpit at Hebrew Benevolent. Rothschild died on December 31, 1973, survived by his wife and children. His papers are housed at Emory University. Several people have written about the Atlanta bombing; it even gets referenced in the popular film *Driving Miss Daisy*.

Rothschild delivered this sermon at Friday services, just five days after the bombing. The critique he makes implicates the rhetorical at every turn. First, he notes that the explosion's sounds rocked not just Atlanta, but the entire United States; second, he inquires as to the "message" of the explosion and concludes that it unleashed "a new courage and a new hope"; third, he criticizes white southern leaders whose "words loose the uncontrolled passions of men"; fourth, blame also falls on the many "good" and "decent" citizens who allowed injustices to go without comment. Ironically, and fifth, the bombing has resulted in a prolixity of speech, a freeing of "tongues" all across the nation. Of course Rothschild's own speech enacts the very forms of speech he lauds.

⟡

And None Shall Make Them Afraid

October 17, 1958
Hebrew Benevolent Congregation (The Temple), Atlanta, Georgia

The night was clear and very quiet. A myriad of stars twinkled in the darkened heavens. A city slept—secure and unaware. In a few hours, streets would be busy with cars and sidewalks bustling with fathers, mothers, and their children—all hastening to fill countless pews in hundreds of houses of worship. For this was the early morning of another Sunday and the city was a city of churches; its citizens a deeply religious folk. But this was destined to be a Sunday morning different from all those that had gone before it. For the date was October 12, 1958—and the city was Atlanta, Georgia.

A shattering blast rent the silence of that quiet night. Walls crumbled. Pillars fell. The clear, high sound of tinkling glass added a note of shrillness to the symphony of destruction. A temple had been bombed. How loud was the sound of destruction? How far had it travelled? An investigation indicated that calls had come from miles around. But future events were to prove that its reverberation could not be measured by physical distance alone. Once the light of day revealed the awesome destruction, its raucous thunder was quickly heard by an entire nation and found its way inward to the deepest recesses of the souls of men everywhere.

What message was the explosion meant to deliver? What effect was it supposed to have? Its intent was clear enough. This was an act designed to strike terror into the hearts of men. It was intended to cause panic and confusion.

Never was a message so garbled in its transmission. Never did a band of violent men so misjudge the temper of the object of their act of intimidation. For this is what really happened: Out of the gaping hole that laid bare the havoc wrought within, out of the majestic columns that now lay crumbled and broken, out of the tiny bits of brilliantly colored glass that had once graced with beauty the sanctuary itself—indeed, out of the twisted and evil hearts of bestial men has come a new courage and a new hope. This single act of devastation has taught lessons which all words, all prayers, all pleas had been unable to teach. It is these truths of which I would speak to you today.

The first of them is that this must be a land ruled by law and not by men. To advocate the disregard of one law creates an atmosphere of lawlessness in which men feel that they can choose the rules by which they will live. One man decides that it is within his personal province to decide which laws he will obey and which he will ignore—then there is no law at all. And this is anarchy. Southern leaders made possible—unwittingly, I am sure—the creation of just such a society as this—a society without control by law, a government of anarchy. To be sure, they do not advocate violence. They, themselves, abhor it. But their words loose the uncontrolled passions of men who are quick to get their way by violence and who seize the opportunity in their march for personal power. Thus, it is clearer now than ever before that we must restore America to the rule of law.

And that law must be the moral law. This is the second lesson we have learned. It is not easy to live by the rigorous demands of our spiritual forbears. Yet it is more dangerous not to. For every time we stray from the paths they have set for us, we bring ourselves near to danger and destruction. The difficult way is still the safest way, after all. Once again we are confronted with and challenged by the prophetic ideal that teaches us that all men are brothers, that we must love our neighbors as ourselves and pursue with diligence the path of justice.

It is the moral law that undergirds the very foundations of democracy. Our country is founded upon the biblical ideals first taught by the prophets of Israel and later incorporated into the ideology of Christianity. When we fail to live by the spiritual truths of our religious faith, we weaken the principles of democracy. And conversely, when we fall short of the goals of freedom and equality set forth by the founders of our republic, we have demeaned our religious faith. Long ago, a biblical writer set forth the challenge in simple and stirring words: "Behold, I have set before thee this day life and good, the blessing and the curse; therefore, choose ye life." We have now determined to meet the challenge in our own day. We, too, shall choose the good so that we may live.

It is in the realm of choice that the third lesson lies. For who is to blame for the wave of violence that has swept across our land? The guilty ones are not alone the political leaders whose words fan the flames of hatred and incite to violence. Not even those who perpetrated the very acts themselves bear all the blame. Responsibility rests with those good and decent people who choose to remain silent in such a time. Too many of us, motivated by fear, led by the desire to be comfortable and safe, have failed to live by the ideals which we know to be right and good. Now we have discovered at long last what can happen when men are afraid to speak and when they allow the shadow of cowardice to creep into their souls. Thus, a strange phenomenon has taken place: where the fear of violence did serve to silence men, the act of violence has freed their tongues and loosed their hands for the work of righteousness. So men, now, say aloud what they have always known in their hearts to be true but could not bring themselves to utter. Editors, ministers, educators, men and women in every walk of life have demonstrated a new-found determination to affirm with courage the principles by which men must live. The curtain of fear has been lifted. Decent men are at least convinced that there can be no retreat from their ideals. Neither violence nor the threat of violence shall force us to abrogate the spiritual foundations of life itself. We do not make such an affirmation out of sheer bravado. We do not say it just to keep our spirits high. We affirm our spiritual heritage because we know that only when man—every man—lives by God's law, no matter how dangerous or difficult it may seem to be—that only then can he find personal security and help achieve peace and tranquility for all humanity.

Nor do we stand alone. On that certain knowledge rests the most heartening lesson we have learned. This dastardly and despicable act of desecration has roused the conscience of decent men and women everywhere. The countless messages of comfort and encouragement that came to us expressed the shock and revulsion of all America. They were addressed to us, but their words bring comfort and hope to all whose hearts have been gnawed by fear and whose souls were corroded by doubt. They assure us that the dynamiters—whoever they are—do not represent America. They are a cancer to be cut out of the body politic and left to die. Except for these few—our letters tell us—all Americans stand united and strong—a people dedicated to righteousness.

On that fateful morning in October, one building dedicated to the worship of our Heavenly Father stood in ruins—mute witness to the evil that lurks in the hearts of men, when men are ruled by hate. But our answer speaks to them, louder even than the monstrous blast that pierced the silence of a peaceful night. The symbols of that answer stand untouched and strong in every Jewish house of God—even as they still stand in our own sanctuary which bears even yet the scars of man's sad failure to become worthy of his status as a child of God. Here burns the Eternal Light with its shining message of reassurance and faith. God dwells in every human heart—if only we will seek to find Him there. Even as this light is everlasting, so God lives eternally. Even as this light never fades, so our faith in him cannot be extinguished by the wanton acts of witless men.

Here are the scrolls of the Mosaic law. Crowned with their silver ornaments, the scrolls bear proud witness to the word of God, to the ideals toward which men must ever strive. This law still lives in our hearts, still beckons our steps, still lifts us up to a vision of universal brotherhood and a world of peace. No—the lamp of our faith has not been dimmed, nor the word of God blurred. On the contrary, this despicable act has made brighter the flame of courage and renewed in splendor the fires of determination and dedication. It has reached the hearts of men everywhere and roused the conscience of a people united in righteousness. All of us, together, shall rear from the rubble of devastation a city and a land in which all men are truly brothers—and none shall make them afraid.

1960

1960

§19 Edward P. Morgan

Edward P. Morgan was born on June 23, 1910, in Walla Walla, Washington. After growing up in Idaho, he returned to Walla Walla to attend Whitman College. His career in broadcast journalism included work for CBS, ABC, UPI, and many other prestigious media outlets. He received numerous awards, including the George Foster Peabody Award and the Sidney Hillman Prize. Perhaps his earliest nationwide exposure as a journalist came in two instances. First, as a UPI reporter he scooped his competition in covering the assassination of Leon Trotsky in Mexico. Later, in 1956, he covered the maritime accident of the SS *Stockholm* and the SS *Andrea Doria*. His daughter, Linda Hardberger (née Morgan) was aboard, surviving the accident when flung from the *Andrea Doria* to a deck of the *Stockholm*. Morgan's radio program, *Edward P. Morgan and the News*, enjoyed AFL-CIO sponsorship until he left in 1967. During his broadcast days, he covered the 1960 election (including the Nixon/Kennedy debates) and the 1964 conventions, and he served with Howard K. Smith as the ABC co-anchor for the aftermath of the assassination of President John F. Kennedy. Morgan retired from media in 1975 and died on Wednesday, January 27, 1993.

The following speech of April 1960 is Morgan's acceptance speech for the Hillman Prize for his broadcast journalistic efforts of 1959. The prize is named for Sidney Hillman, a founding member of the U.S. labor movement, including the AFL-CIO, the largest federation of unions in the nation. The speech begins with an admonition that noble causes rather than material comforts are the pursuits Americans seek. He then observes that with so many global causes to embrace, we often lose track of domestic causes—namely, equal rights and decency in the United States. The remainder of the speech details the ideological sophistication of young, well-read student leaders such as Ezell Blair Jr., of the Greensboro sit-in movement staged just two months earlier. Morgan argues that Blair et al. have synthesized Gandhian and Christian principles to produce a new moral code for civilized acts of protest. Morgan uses several other events (Chapel Hill ministers, the Little Rock Nine, and the Montgomery bus boycott) to convince his audience that these ideals are mainstream, not extremist. He ends by pointing out how these new ideals return our attention to Sidney Hillman and his legacy.

❧❧

Gandhi in Greensboro

April 26, 1960
New York, New York

Somebody suggested over a drink in Washington recently that what Americans need today is not a good five-cent cigar but a cause. Most of us have, if not as much as we want, at least more than we require of worldly goods. But our comforts are making us uncomfortable. We are squirming and groping for something to live for beyond frozen television tray dinners and motel swimming pools.

Disarmament is a good cause. But it is difficult and in some respects undesirable to become personally engaged with a megaton bomb. The community chest is a worthy enterprise. We pay lip and passing pocketbook service to it and then deduct the payment from our income tax. Justice for Tibet! Self-determination for the Eastern European satellites! These are goals we readily identify ourselves with in principle and then lose interest in, defaulting, eventually, our support. What about a cause closer home? The cause of equal rights and human decency, the dignity of that inconsistent, inefficient, irreplaceable piece of machinery, the human individual, including you and me.

Why is it that we cringe a little at these terms, equal rights, decency, and dignity of the individual? Perhaps it is because we have been dignifying the wrong things lately. In a public discussion of morals the other day, Carl Sandburg said we now have an eleventh commandment: "Do whatever you want to do to be comfortable." So, blessed are the status seekers for theirs is the heavenly kingdom of payola and the fixed quiz show. In this atmosphere of the kickback and influence peddling, we have forgotten a central truth: people are more important than anything. The fabric of our social system was woven to protect the individual with equal justice, to clothe him with freedom and self-respect. But somehow we have threaded into the garment the fat, bulky strands of materialism, the tight dark thongs of selfishness, fear, prejudice, and outright hatred. The garment has been twisted into a degrading shape.

Our cause, I suggest, is to make it fit properly, so that it will once more ennoble the society that wears it. Do we have an inspiration for a pattern? Has anybody been ennobling the human species lately? Down in Greensboro, North Carolina, last February 1, a handsome eighteen-year-old freshman at the state Agriculture and Technical College, named Ezell Blair Jr., led three schoolmates to the lunch counter in Woolworth's store and asked for service. Thus inauspiciously began an auspicious movement, the Negro sit-ins against segregation which have spread to nearly every state in the South. More than 55,000 Negro students and a thousand white undergraduates have become directly involved in these demonstrations from 150 college campuses, and there have been repercussions by sympathetic picketing in some one hundred cities outside the South.

Ezell Blair and his mates didn't know quite what they were starting, but they knew where they got their inspiration. They got it from Mohandas K. Gandhi. "I've never forgotten a television show I saw last year called *Pictorial Story of India*," young Blair told a *New York Times* reporter. He was impressed with how the strength of Gandhi's passive resistance seemed to grow each time he was thrown into jail. Blair and his fellows like to think of themselves as part of a movement of "passive insistence."

Many of these current young followers of the Mahatma have already been put in jail. In Petersburg, Virginia, it was for seeking equal access to the public library. Hardly a day goes by in the town where I live, Washington, D.C., especially now that the election campaign season is open, without some aspiring statesman or doom-cracking pundit sounding a warning about the deterioration of the democratic system and the need to do something about it. But while we talk, a Negro teenager, not old enough to vote even if his election board would let him, is doing something about it. With quiet courage, he is daily braving tear gas, fire hoses, truncheons, prison, fines, taunts, spittle, threats, and the gravest bodily harm because he believes in something as other American revolutionaries did before him.

There is the key. This is a revolution. Here is a new generation of Negroes, well-dressed, college-educated, restrained, determined, asserting its constitutional rights to a freedom promised a century ago but never really fulfilled, North or South. We follow the news from Algiers, from Leopold-ville, Capetown, and Johannesburg with excited concern over the latest chapters in the unending history of men's struggle for independence. But to the convulsive developments in a liberation movement rising right under our noses in Miami, Atlanta, Charlotte, Orangeburg, and Baton Rouge, we react with about as much attention as we ordinarily give the National Safety Council's figures on Memorial Day traffic deaths.

And what an astonishing depth there is to the disciplined dedication of these passive insisters.

Acknowledging the teachings of Christ and Gandhi, and looking to the Reverend Martin Luther King for counsel, says one recent newspaper dispatch, "College students in Nashville, Tennessee, drew up the code below to govern student conduct in 'sit-in' protests at lunch counters discrimination against Negroes:

- Don't strike back or curse if abused.
- Don't laugh out.
- Don't hold conversations with floor workers.
- Don't block entrances to the stores and the aisles.
- Show yourself courteous and friendly at all times.
- Sit straight and always face the counter.
- Remember love and non-violence.
- May God Bless each of you."

In Chapel Hill, where the unsegregated University of North Carolina is located, the Negro demonstrators made the following declaration of purpose:

- "We do not picket just because we want to eat. We can eat at home.
- "We do not picket to express our anger or resentment at anyone.
- "We do not picket to humiliate anyone or put anyone out of business.
- "We do picket to help the businessman make changes that will bring us closer to the Christian and democratic practices. . . .
- "We do picket to protest the lack of dignity and respect shown us as human beings."

All twenty-seven ministers of Chapel Hill signed a statement endorsing that declaration. "We deplore the fact that any group of our citizens is placed in the position of having to ask to be treated with dignity and respect," the statement said in part. "We confess our own responsibility for the existence and toleration of such attitudes and practices as make this request necessary. . . . We commend the leaders of these . . . protests for their dedication to the principles of non-violence. We believe that the right to protest in this fashion is a right generally recognized in our society. . . ."

There is something far more dramatically moving, more deeply convincing to the quiet dignity of this passive offensive than the pathetic belligerence raised against it. This latter answer reflects an anachronistic leadership and the frustrated flatfoot mentality of a country cop, a mentality which the British, with a little more polish perhaps, applied against Gandhi to their everlasting sorrow. And supporting the jungle law of fear and hate is the rabble, the mob.

One of the voices of the Old Dominion, the *Richmond News-Leader*, sorrowfully described a battle scene of this new conflict recently in these words: "Many a Virginian must have felt a tinge of wry regret at the state of things as they are, in reading of Saturday's 'sit-downs' by Negro students in Richmond stores. Here were the colored students, in coats, white shirts, ties and one of them was reading Goethe and one was taking notes from a biology text. And here, on the sidewalk outside, was a gang of white boys come to heckle, a ragtail rabble, slack-jawed, black-jacketed, grinning fit to kill, and some of them, God save the mark, were waving the proud and honored flag of the southern states in the last war fought by gentlemen."

Let us not make the disastrous mistake of enshrining the Negroes as a population of paragons. There is evil, lethal delinquency and tragic corruption of leadership among them too, and you only have to step up the street to Harlem to find evidences of both. But on balance, Negro demagogues do not begin to match the number of viciousness of the bullies of white supremacy, and if erring Negro teenagers have often been brutally violent in their rebelliousness, the duck-tailed delinquents of the white rock-'n-roll set have no prouder record. Indeed with the legacy of repression and prejudice which our Negro citizens have inherited, it is a monumental wonder that they have been able to hold on to their patience and restraint so well.

Ironically, the steadiness of their deportment has inspired some emotional inclination to endow them with certain superhuman faculties, which, when you stop to think about it, involves a sin of racial prejudice in reverse. I have been guilty of this. Shortly after the explosion at Little Rock in the autumn of 1957 I found myself talking to Dr. Alfonso Elder, the Columbia-educated president of North Carolina College, a Negro school in Durham. I told him I had been deeply moved by the high courage of those nine Negro students as they went out utterly alone to run the gamut of hostility and danger and enter Central High. "I am not sure," I said, "that anybody else could have done that."

"You are wrong," Dr. Elder replied rather sharply. "Courage is a human trait, not restricted to any race. If the tables had been turned, white children would have behaved the same."

There, in a nutshell, was the whole lesson. The Negro is simply fighting for full and recognized membership in the human race, with all its inherent strengths and weaknesses. In struggling to break the bonds of his second-class citizenship he is demanding his constitutional rights, nothing more. Let this testimony stand against the absurd, fear-mongering charge of Police Commissioner Eugene "Bull" Connor of Birmingham, Alabama, that the Negro is trying to establish "black supremacy." Let Commissioner Connor look only to the record of the bus boycott in his sister city of Montgomery, to learn the essence of black hordes to impress a pagan supremacy on genteel citizens of lighter skin. It is not a swaggering ultimatum, bloodshot with passion as so many seem to fear, that a Negro shall marry your sister. It is the insistence of some of the gentlest souls God ever fashioned to choose their own seat on a municipal bus, to travel afoot or on horseback, in a Cadillac convertible or to stay at home. In reaching out for these simple rights for himself, the Negro is doing something else for everybody. He is refreshing the roots of the tree of freedom. He is, as Thurgood Marshall so truly said to a thousand students at Yale last month, fighting our battles for us.

There is the cause which I recommend. It is not a narrow cause. It is a cause which has been coursing like a great river through the terrain of history, carrying with it since the beginning of man his fragile but persistent hope for true freedom. We detach ourselves from this main stream at our own peril. And don't think that the world at large doesn't have the impression that we have already pulled away from it. At a time when the Soviet Union was announcing to the world at large that it would open in Moscow during this year a new university affording free education to thousands of African, Asian, and Latin American students, that great Jeffersonian Democrat, Mississippi's James Eastland, was on the floor of the Unites States Senate denouncing civil rights decisions of the Supreme Court as "crap." At a time when South African Negroes were being shot down outside

Johannesburg and Capetown, American Negroes were being deprived of their rights, intimidated, even terrorized in this country.

We are carelessly inclined to think of the struggle for fulfillment of civil rights as basically a racial problem. It is not. It is a human problem in which every citizen has a stake. As long as a bull-voiced police commissioner in Birmingham can be a law unto himself, conditions are not safe for democracy in Boise or the Bay of Boston. No American would be quicker to embrace this truth, none would be more tireless or brave in pushing the cause we all must identify ourselves with—the rights and dignity of man—than the man we have really come here to honor in memory today, Sidney Hillman.

§20 Thomas F. Pettigrew

Thomas F. Pettigrew was born in Richmond, Virginia, on March 14, 1931. His unique family experiences in the 1930s and 1940s sensitized him to race relations. His father's youth had been spent in the Appalachian Mountains (Eagle Rock, Virginia) with little experience in relating to African Americans. The mountains also formed the border between the formerly Union and Confederate Virginias, so nearby opinions on racial matters likely varied considerably. Pettigrew's mother and grandmother had migrated to Virginia from Scotland, harboring no anachronistic Southern attitudes toward race. On one occasion, Pettigrew's mother and grandmother defended him when school officials called him to account for identifying his teacher as a bigot. The Pettigrew family's housekeeper, Mildred Adams, gradually introduced Pettigrew to the quotidian limitations of career and community for African Americans. Many of his writings are dedicated to Ms. Adams. Pettigrew received his B.A. in psychology from the University of Virginia in 1952. Harvard awarded him an M.A. in social psychology in 1955. He took his Ph.D. from Harvard in 1956, the same year he married Ann Hallman, a medical doctor with a background in public health who collaborated in his research. The two raised a son, Mark Fraser Pettigrew, who also pursued an academic career. Pettigrew's academic affiliations, awards, political appointments, and writings are too numerous to list. The lion's share of his career took place on the faculties of Harvard University (1957–1980) and University of California at Santa Cruz (1980–1994). His contributions to his professions have focused on sociological and psychological aspects of race relations.

A similar speech was later delivered in July 1962 as one of three by Pettigrew as the keynote speaker in a Valparaiso University summer institute conference on "The Image of the Professional Church Worker." The conference was organized by Rev. Andrew Schulze, founder of the Lutheran Human Relations Association of America. The audience is primarily Lutheran ministers. While this and other similar events at Valparaiso do not generally command our attention when remembering the civil rights era, the summer institute conferences are a silent tsunami. In 1923, when the Indiana Ku Klux Klan was at its peak (with perhaps a quarter of a million members including important politicians), Valparaiso University faced bankruptcy. University officials reached an agreement to sell the college to the Klan. Klan officials at the national headquarters in Georgia abrogated the contract by not proffering the agreed-upon cash. In 1925 the Lutheran University Association bought the college and took it in a much different direction.

The speech begins with a provocative question: who in the white community will lead us in civil rights? He answers that organized liberals might help. There aren't many professors—the courageous ones have been dismissed. A few editors, such as Ralph McGill (who had spoken at Valparaiso University recently), might help. But clergy are socially the most important in this regard. The South makes up part of the Bible Belt, so religious leaders have some influence. Ministers are unique as moral authorities; they are also in a strategic position to end subtle appearances of Jim Crow unity. Pettigrew uses Asch's study on group conformity to illustrate how ministers can make a difference. So why haven't more ministers come forward to lead? Pettigrew again turns to social psychology to answer this question. Protestant individualism, economic concerns, and the myth of moderation undermine ministers' ability to lead. The focus on moderation echoes Pettigrew's reasoning in his 1961 article in *Christian Century*. Those who portray themselves as middle-of-the-road, passively lament extremism, but do not actively stand with the victims are the greatest part of the extremist problem. Pettigrew's fascinating case studies of Little Rock, Charlottesville, and other communities struggling with Jim Crow's death are a convincing cautionary tale for Lutheran ministers struggling with their similar commitments.

Religious Leadership and the Desegregation Process
June 27, 1960
Race Relations Institute, Fisk University, Nashville, Tennessee

I would like to put my discussion of "religious leadership" in a broad context to start with—that is, to ask the general question of where is southern white leadership for desegregation coming from. Leadership in the Negro community seems to be forthcoming from many sources we did not even anticipate. But what about the white community? Well, we can run down a few possibilities: organized liberals such as they are in the South. We can think of a few newspaper editors such as my own personal hero, Ralph McGill—but, then, there are not many Ralph McGills around. There are a very few professors, I am ashamed to add, and you would expect substantial intellectual leadership from this source; but it has not come. The University of Mississippi, in three years after the 1954 decision, lost 40 percent of its associate and full professors, almost none of whom it can replace. Many southern universities tend to lose the best men and not to be able to replace them at the same level. So we cannot expect much from the professors, I am afraid. So we come down to the subject of today's talk, the clergy, and this is what really makes the clergy so crucial. As a group they have provided more leadership within the white community for desegregation than all other groups combined. That is, I think, a safe statement and with room to spare.

Three further considerations make the role of the clergy even more important than seems apparent. First, the South is still relatively the nation's Bible Belt. It is certainly not the Bible Belt of a generation or two ago, but compared to the rest of the country, all of our social science data indicate that southern church attendance for both white and Negro Protestants is much higher than in the rest of the country. Also, in prestige ranking, the Protestant ministers in the South are rated much higher than in other sections of the country. All of our data, in other words, indicate that religious values are still much stronger in the South than in any other place. This puts the Protestant minister in a role of at least potentially greater influence than in other regions.

A second thing that makes us consider him as important is simply that the minister has been given a unique societal sanction—that is the sanction of the moral leadership. And many writers on race relations—Myrdal and Lillian Smith, among others, all agree that the real "Achilles heel" of segregation is guilt. The minister, in other words, more than any other person, by the very sign of his role, has a natural position, a strategic position, to get at the "Achilles heel" of segregation. I think the power of the "sit-in" movement has in large part been due to its strong religious implication.

The third reason is that the minister is in a strategic position to break the unanimity of sentiment and opinion favoring segregation. Now, one of the real troubles of getting leadership in the white community on desegregation is not that it does not potentially exist, but that it does not come forward simply because of what seems to be unanimity of opinion in the white community. It is easier to live in a small town in southern Georgia, for instance, and think that everybody in the white community is a segregation-ist. In fact, I even think they believe everyone in the Negro community is a segregationist, too. There is almost no data to the contrary. Of course, there is a rule of charity here and a rule of conformity that requires everyone to at least appear that he is in agreement. Now this makes any deviation on the part of the ministry important—makes any deviation on the part of anybody important—just because it breaks the unanimity.

I would like to give an analogy from an experiment in social psychology. Many of you are probably already familiar with the brilliant classic experiment done by Solomon Asch of Swarthmore College. Asch hired seven students as stooges in this experiment. He lined the seven up in a long row and instructed them what he wanted them to do. Then he had other students to come in and act as subjects. Now they were under the impression that the other seven were subjects also, like themselves, but the real subject was in seat 8. And then Asch showed them a series of lines, just pairs of lines. These were not hard to distinguish lines—one would be five inches, another four inches—and Asch would simply ask which of the two lines was *longer*. Then he would go down the lines of the eight people, to get their judgments. Well, all seven would say the one which was conspicuously shorter. Now they did not necessarily believe this, but they mostly said this, just to get along with the group. Asch then decided to change the situation, and had the man sitting in the fourth seat of the seven among the stooges start giving the right answer on some of the test lines. Then you would have the first three giving the wrong answer, the fourth giving the right, the fifth, sixth, and the seventh giving the wrong answer again. Even at Swarthmore, the percentage drops very drastically—rather than *one out of three* people conforming to the situation, only *one in ten* will conform. In other words, to reduce the strength of the buildup of all seven people, all it really takes is somebody, somewhere, to break the unanimity. The exception of one person seems to affect the behavior of many others.

Now to draw a rather broad analogy from that laboratory situation—five-inch lines are widely being described as four inches in our society. And when no one comes forward as, possibly, in Moultrie, Georgia, until recently, to say that the five-inch line is five inches, then everyone, at least publicly, has to say it is four inches. Now, if a minister comes forward and says it isn't, he might lose his job, but at least he breaks the unanimity. The effect of this action is probably much stronger than we can judge, at least at first.

Therefore, I would give as the third reason as to why the clergy is so crucial: we need desperately for white leadership in the South to break what otherwise appears to be the solid wall of segregationist unanimity.

Of course we know that with religion there is a great hiatus existing between the lofty-to-level pronouncements that every major denomination has made in favor of integration and the not so lofty, tightly segregated local parish. Underlying this tremendous gap, I think, there are at least three major causes. The first is that Protestantism, one of the great strengths of the church—namely, the dignity and responsibility conferred on the individual worshipper—is, ironically, a deterrent to effective social action. Second, there is the church's dilemma between principle and organization. Money and members are necessary to any social movement—and organized religion is, after all, a social movement, sensitive to money and members—and when a minister defends the principle of integration he loses both money and members. So there is naturally a built-in dilemma between principle and organization which deters effective social action on race. The third reason is what may be called "the myth of moderation." What makes the other structural reasons so important is this myth of moderation, this idea that, somehow, a God-fearing Christian should be moderate—a "middle-of-the-roader." I want to discuss this because I think the myth of moderation is deeply embedded not only in southern culture but within our major Protestant denominations generally.

Now let me discuss each of these in some detail. The first one, I think, is fairly obvious—the difficulty caused by the great strength of the church, the dignity and responsibility with the individual worshippers, the individual Protestants. This is a deterrent simply because the racially prejudiced Protestant is free to ignore the church's insistence on the unity of mankind. He can say, "Well, those pronouncements up in New York sound pretty good, of course. You know they are for the press up there and haven't got anything to do with us down here." He is free then to continue going, at eleven o'clock on Sunday morning, to his own white church; and with not even the slightest twinge of guilt unless the minister takes it upon himself to make sure there is some guilt.

The second major problem of religious leadership in the desegregation process, I think, requires considerably more discussion. This is the one that we centered on in our Little Rock study. It can be simply stated, and it involves all social movements—the conflict, mainly, between idealism and organization. On the one hand, a movement can hold so uncompromisingly to its principles that it alienates most of the potential and needed adherents.

In other words, the idealistic alternative may fail because it never achieves the broad base of support necessary to implement its principles. I think we have seen social movements that did precisely that: they were so high in principle they never got off the ground. On the other hand, the alternative, which Protestantism is much more in danger of becoming, is the other extreme of the organizational alternative in which a movement modifies its ideals so sharply that it attracts a very wide following but has sacrificed its distinctive aims in doing so. This organizational alternative fails, obviously, because it loses all of its purpose once it gains its influence. Milton Yinger has shown in his *Religion in the Struggle for Power* that religious movements have, historically, been most influential when an effective balance between these two things—between principle and organization—is achieved. Now in Protestantism the spark is burning and has not died completely, but it is certainly in danger of it.

What I am saying is that the church as employer, money-raiser, and investor has superseded largely the church as social reformer. The reason for this became more obvious as we studied Little Rock and what ministers *did* and *did not* do to support racial integration in our nation. However, let us get one fact straight before we start. Four out of five Protestant ministers in the major Protestant denominations in the southern United States—not including the sects—are integrationist. The problem is not that they are not integrationist; the problem is getting them to lead.

My parents' Episcopal church in Richmond, Virginia, has had sixty rectors in twelve years. I am very proud of this. They turn the rectors out pretty rapidly, and God seems to have a higher calling for them almost as soon as they arrive. Now what is happening, in my terms, is that each man coming has been a little better than the one before, and a little stronger on the subject of race relations, making it more and more obvious that he is an integrationist, believes in it, wants it for Richmond, and wants it for his church—which is the most unforgivable thing of all. Now the last man who has come by all odds, on my terms, is the finest yet. He has been there now for three years and they did not even move a foot to get rid of him; he is a northerner, too. I could not understand it, so I asked my father recently, "How come, Pop, there isn't even a move on foot to get rid of this man?" I said, "I think he is great but that is usually the sign they are not going to be around much longer." And my father said, "Well, I don't think much of him, as you have gathered, but, frankly, we are afraid to get rid of him." He said, "If we do, the next one might still be worse." I offer this at this time as evidence that Protestantism is not dead, though it is in danger of dying. If there comes a time when every church, every parish in the southern United States cannot find a conservative minister on these basic rights, then we will know that Protestantism has arrived completely and that religious leadership is what we might hope it to be.

In Little Rock, the ministers did not come forward—a few did. Only two of the men who came forward in Little Rock to publicly defend integration are still there. All the other five of them lost their jobs—the statistical southern pattern. Most did not come forward. Why? We think, because of the second movements between idealism and principle, on the one hand, and organization, money, and members, on the other.

One convenient way of looking at the minister is to look at his role and the pressures focusing upon him for action. He has really three sets of pressures. On one hand he has professional pressures—the conception of the ministerial role as held by the denominational officials, ministerial colleagues, his local ministerial association, and others. These people form a professional view of what he should be doing. The second conception is what he himself feels—like self-conception of what a minister should do and what he would like to see himself, as a minister, do. The third set of conceptions is a membership conception—namely, what the laity expects him to do as a minister. Now two of these pressures are clearly for him, publicly, to defend integration. As to self-conception, as I have already pointed out, four out of five Protestant ministers have no doubt about what they should be doing. They should be leading, and they know this and believe it. The professional conception is, on the whole, almost uniform with the self-conception. It is that a minister should, by the nature of his role, be defending integration.

The third set of conceptions, the membership conception, places pressures on the minister to stay out of the fight—saying, in effect, that it is none of the church's business. And I think this largely comes from the "myth of moderation" that I mentioned. Now you would think that numerically the chances are two out of three for getting ministerial action if professional conception is for integration and self-conception is for integration, particularly in a crisis. But, because of the dilemma between principle and organization, the first two sets of conception, professional and self, are split up, made weak and confused by the very uniform and unambiguous pressures from the membership and the laity.

How this happens, many of you know all too well. The members stop coming at eleven o'clock Sunday morning. They start telephone campaigns against the minister—not necessarily on race. They tell stories about him on anything, to drum up oppositional resistance to him in the church. They don't give money, and they urge other members not to give money. In other words, they try to put the "money and member" squeeze on the minister. One minister who was a very courageous defender of integration in Little Rock is still there because when a significant segment of his church did this to him he, in turn, had Quakers fill the pews and fill the coffers on Sunday morning. When he survived the crisis and some of the members started coming back, he attracted members of their own fellowships, having accomplished their purpose. Now not all integrationist ministers are so lucky as to have Unitarians and Quakers quickly come to their rescue. Most of them, in fact, are not. But this shows how membership pressures can be brought to bear upon the self and professional conceptions.

At the professional level a superintendent or bishop may judge a minister's performance only in terms of money and members. It is easy to keep records of money and members. It is easy to know when the minister has gained a 100 or a 150 members in the last year; and whether the contributions to the church are up 5 percent or 6 percent. But whether the man is doing a decent job of defending Christian principle, however, on race or any other thing, is very hard to check up. But what about the minister who defends, at the core, the idealism of his denomination? Well, he will not have bricks set aside for the new north wing; or, if he does, they are not paying off the debt on the building. Now, he has lost a hundred members in the last two months and money is down even more than that. This means that the pressures coming from the professional role system are very easily broken up. The laity says, "Well, the advice of the bishop was, 'Be as liberal as you can, boys, but don't stick your neck out.'" Now what he meant was, "Don't lose any money and members." He was asking them to do an impossible thing; he was asking them to defend integration and not to lose a single time. It cannot be done in Little Rock or in any other place in the southern states. As a matter of fact, I doubt if it can be done in the entire United States.

Now you say to yourself, "I can understand how it is ambiguous under professional pressures, but what about the man himself? Wasn't he terribly guilty?" Yes, some were—a few were. Some of the people we interviewed actually broke down and cried. Some were guilty, very guilty. Some were not, however. *Most* were not. Why? We think there were four reasons why most of them were not guilty for not defending integration, even in Little Rock; even in 1957 and 1958; even when they were integrationist. The first reason is that there are not criteria of success as a social reformer. The minister could say to himself, "Well, I did a lot in this field before September '57,

and this isn't the time to do it. I was successful in the past and I will be successful in the future, but, strategically, it is shrewd not to do anything right
now. I am still a social reformer."

Second, the denominational clergyman usually operates on a number
of not necessarily incorrect assumptions, but these assumptions help him
allay guilt in the time of a crisis like Little Rock. An example of what I
mean is an assumption typical of our present sophisticated, modern Protestant minister who does not believe in immediate conversion anymore. He
believes in the slow education process. Now you can see what this will do
for him in 1957 Little Rock. He says to himself, "You can't convert people
dramatically anymore, anyway. This is a long pull and the fall of 1957 just
isn't a part of this long pull. I've got to wait a little longer."

Another assumption that our sophisticated ministers operate on—not
necessarily incorrect either—is the necessity to maintain close communication with the congregation at all cost. Their words here are frequently something like this: "You cannot teach those you cannot reach." I defy you to
argue with that as an assumption; but look what it does for him on the guilt
level. He says now, "If I really told the people what I thought, they would all
leave and then I wouldn't have *anybody* to talk to." Well, that is possible. On
the other hand, he is not doing much although he still has communication.
You see, all these things help him with his guilt; and related to these assumptions in Protestantism is the idea of just the intrinsic value of a preserved
fellowship, in and of itself, regardless of what the fellowship involves.

A third way the Little Rock ministers handled their guilt, or managed
to allay it from becoming conscious, was to do what we called "speaking on
integration without being heard." Now what we mean by this, if we will just
be honest with ourselves, is "the deeper issues" technique. This name was
given us by a Methodist minister who put his feet up on his desk and said,
"I have never talked about integration of the races specifically, of course. I
believe in it. I haven't avoided the whole thing." He said he talked about
deeper issues, about Christian charity, and the brotherhood of mankind.
Now, he knows, I know, and you know that he can talk about brotherhood
of man and Christian charity from now until doomsday and that church
will never connect it with Central High School two blocks away.

The "God is watching" technique is another one. This reminds the laity
that God is watching their every step in the crisis, without directly linking just whatever he is watching and how he is judging. The most explicit
example of this was a Baptist minister in Little Rock who every Sunday
would warn his congregation, with a dreading finger, "Now, remember, you

know," he said, "God is watching your every step in this crisis." And he said, "I am perfectly willing and prepared to talk to you on this subject and tell you what you should be doing, but you are not ready to hear me." There is a reasonable argument that they were not ready to hear him; but you see how this operated to keep him from talking.

A third technique is "the discouragement of segregationist" technique. The Episcopal rector would hear that some member of his church—an Episcopalian, mind you—had joined the Citizens' Council. Imagine. So he would go to the man's home, and instead of telling the man that it was immoral and starting from there, he would start by saying, "John, I understand that you joined the Citizens' Council." Then the rector would go on and say, "John, these people, they don't even hold their forks and knives correctly—how can you associate with them?" Now I admit this is a successful technique for getting Episcopalians to drop out of the Citizens' Council, but I submit that it is the substitution of one form of prejudice for another, and has nothing to do with morality or the Christian church. It also relieved the minister of the necessity of talking about the morality of segregation—or the immorality.

Another technique which we have all seen is the "law and order" technique. We have seen this recently in Atlanta—particularly in their "Save the Schools" program. There is nothing wrong with law and order as a technique of some of us; there is nothing wrong with saving our schools, to be sure. But for ministers it has nothing to do with these moral wrongs. If he wishes, a minister can support law and order and "save our schools," but that is not fulfilling his obligation of defending the principles of his church. Many ministers have felt that if they defended law and order or argued for saving the schools, before the Sibley Commission in Georgia, they have done their work; and that was it. I would say that that has nothing to do with the unique privilege that society has given them to invoke the moral imperative. They are not invoking it.

The final technique that we saw in Little Rock, and which I think is widespread among ministers, is the "every man a priest" technique. Here, the minister does express his opinion on race to some extent; and then he turns and says, "Well, you know, after all in our church every man is a priest before God, and my opinion really isn't worth any more than yours anyway." So after stating his ideas quite clearly, he would then set it up for the laity to say, "Well, he's crazy anyway, so it doesn't matter what he says." In other words, if you will pardon an analogy from the game of pool, having made a good shot, he takes the "English" off the ball. I am really not a good enough churchman to speak in proper terms, I am afraid.

Who, then, was left in Little Rock to defend principles? The white ministers who publicly defended Christian principle in Little Rock tended to be men who were least encumbered by organizational restriction. They were the ministers who represented numerically small denominations; who had not been long at their posts; who were young and did not serve large and affluent parishes; whose parishes were not engaged in membership drives or building programs or fundraising campaigns. In other words, the freer the minister from organizational constraints, the more likely he was to defend integration publicly. My point is that ministerial behavior in crises is less a matter of courage than it is a matter of pressures for money and members squelching principle. One man, an integrationist, in a prominent church, said, "I've spent seventeen years of my life of my life building up this church, and I am not about to destroy it in this crisis." Another man, a bishop in the Episcopal church, said, "Good Christians, good Episcopalians, can be either segregationist or integrationist, but the main thing is that we all have reconciliation in the church." What he meant was reconciliation without repentance, which I think is really a strange concept of Christianity.

I would like to turn now to the individual level. I believe that the two structural problems—barriers, shall we say, to effective social action—would not be so important were it not for the third thing—the "myth of moderation." If we did not have such an all pervasive myth of moderation among some of the clergy, and particularly among the laity, the first two barriers would not be so detrimental to effective social action. The word "moderate" in the South is certainly the most ambiguous term in the South today. I have even heard Ralph McGill called a moderate, which I think is a great insult to a great liberal. Some racist Klansmen call themselves "moderate," and the Citizens' Councils say they are moderates trying to avoid violence. I do not mean that kind of moderation. I am talking about the upper-middle- or upper-class white man in the South who feels that he is obligated to hold this middle-of-the-road position. He feels that he is being shot at from both sides by two sets of extremists who are really very much alike. On the one side he has the Klan and the Citizens' Council, and they are shooting at him, burning crosses and blowing up buildings. He feels that these people are terrible; and he doesn't like them but what can he do about them. On the other hand, he says, "Now the NAACP, the Southern Regional Council, the Institute at Fisk, these people, they are extremists too and really they are very much like the Citizens' Council." They are different sides of the road, to be sure, but they are not really the same.

We all know these people run our towns; they run the South. It is the moderate, not the racists, who established segregation as an institution, to start with, in the 1880s and 1890s. It is the moderate today who maintains it, not the racist. It was not the racist who prevented successful integration in Little Rock; it was the moderate who did everything he could to make sure that integration, in a real sense, would not come about in the public schools in Little Rock. The moderate abhors violence, but he, in fact, invites it unwittingly by saying that time is the only solution. The moderate is tireless in the belief that the hearts and minds of men are not changed by law and that traditions cannot be changed overnight. He is paternalistic and longs for the "good race relations" of the past. He regrets the current breakdown of interracial communication. Of course, none ever really existed to break down; but he believes somehow this is broken down. This is a great fault of the NAACP. The moderate deeply resents interference into *his* problem—the Negro problem is *his* problem, as he puts it—from the North. He agrees with the racist in feeling that the 1954 Supreme Court decision was not based on legal precedent. And then, most relevant to what we are talking about, the moderate feels the church has no business in racial matters. And so he advocated reconciliation without repentance. The stern Jesus is very conveniently forgotten—or maybe never realized, as a matter of fact.

It is the moderate who gives us our violence, not the bomb throwers. The moderate sets up the situation by which the bomb throwers just fill in the gaps. Let me give you an example outside the Negro field—the Jewish temple desecrations. What did the newspapers say about the temple desecrations? They said, "Well, the hoodlums are sick; they are either juvenile delinquents or they are crazy." I would like to argue the very opposite. Those hoodlums or "sick people," so-called, are reflecting American culture better than we are sitting here at the Fisk Institute. If they are sick, we are sicker. In other words, it was not just a phenomenon of a bunch of kids, out of their heads, painting swastikas on synagogues. In fact, they were accurately reflecting a deep schism in American culture of anti-Semitism, and doing a very good job to it. A moderate would not be caught with a paintbrush in his hand, but he helps set up the situation that leads to the kids' doing the next logical thing. I think you see the same thing in integration. The moderate screams, "If you make us integrate through the federal courts we are going to have violence." He says this long enough and often enough; and he gets it. Then he starts wringing his hands at these awful people throwing bombs. Of course, since 1955 the moderate has been building up the climate for the bomb throwers; and so it is a little hard to be sympathetic when suddenly he gets worried about the bombs.

The hearts and minds of men *are* changed by law. This is one of the best principles established in social science study of race relations today. If the hearts and minds of men were not changed by law, we would still be on our hands and knees in Western Europe. Laws do change attitudes and behavior, and you know it in your own behavior. They usually do this by changing behavior first, whereupon the attitudes follow. The great fallacy here, which the segregationist repeats, is that you always have to change a man's mind before you change his behavior. Psychology oversold this view a generation or so ago. We now know better, but we are having trouble contradicting ourselves. In race relations typically, and particularly in the South, you change behavior first. It is much easier to do that; and then attitudes change. I am sure white attitudes toward integrated lunch counters in Nashville have already changed, if we had some good measure of it. But they did not change before you had them integrated. They have changed *because* you had them integrated.

The most pertinent research example I can think of is in Charlottesville, Virginia. Two years ago in the middle of their interracial crisis a very fine sociologist from Columbia did a study there. The study showed that 20 percent of the white population in Charlottesville was integrationist. That percentage is high because of the University of Virginia—and Mr. Jefferson, I should hope. Forty-five percent, roughly, were adamant segregationists. and the remaining 35 percent were in the middle—ambivalent one way or another. He did another study just a few months ago—after Charlottesville had, in fact, integrated for over a year. Now 30 rather than 20 percent of Charlottesville's white community are pro-integration. The segregationists group had dwindled to 20 percent and the ambivalent group had increased to 50 percent. You can see what is happening. Some of the segregationists have become ambivalent and some of the ambivalent have become integrationist. The change has come about because their community has had integration, and people are reflecting the change in the community in their attitudes. Well, in other words, hearts and minds of men are changed.

The moderate talks as if the South is still very poor and in the late nineteenth century and that you are trying to change race relations in the situation which obtained immediately after the Civil War. In fact, most of the South's traditions have already changed. Really, the only strong nineteenth-century vestige left in southern culture is segregation; and it was late nineteenth century at that. The integrationist movement has asked not that tradition be changed overnight—they have changed already—but that only one segment of the culture catch up with the rest of the cultural lag.

Today, Negro leaders are chosen by Negroes by virtue of what they do within the Negro community. So the moderate finds these people strange and militant, and they are difficult to get along with if what you expect are handpicked "Uncle Toms." They are not.

It would be very flattering for those of us in the social sciences to think that seven research studies changed the course of history, because of one footnote in the 1954 May 17 decision—one footnote that mentioned seven references. Indeed, no one before ever thought social science changed anything, including social science. Now, we do not really think it changed this decision either. Flattering though it is, we modestly withdraw from the field and say that it was the court itself completely. Let me give you reasons for this. The 1896 *Plessy v. Ferguson* "separate but equal decision," so dear to the hearts of our segregationist friends, was just as socially scientific as the 1954 decision. It included all of the social terms of its times—terms like "racial instincts" and "natural affinity." As you know, the court cases built up from 1910 steadily with only a couple of reversals. Negroes kept winning civil rights suits. This trend started in 1910; and if you like to be a flag-waving Confederate you can point out that what changed in 1910 was that a southern man became chief justice—Chief Justice White, who was a former private in the Confederate Army. Now, in addition, there was a precedent for 1954 which was not cited, unfortunately, in the decision. In 1873, twenty-three years before *Plessy v. Ferguson*, there was a decision—*Washington, Alexandria and Georgetown Railroad v. Catherine Brown*—which ruled that separate railroad cars were inherently unequal and discriminatory. In other words, the 1896 Supreme Court was itself a glaring reversal of legal precedent.

There are many things on the front of religious leadership in race which certainly portend rather encouraging things in the future. The sit-ins, of course, are the classic case, particularly since it comes from Christian leadership in the Negro community. Now we have native white southerners joining in the protest; and this begins to take it off the racial conflict basis—black man against white man—and put it on the more realistic basis of integrationist versus segregationist. Most of the white students I have had a chance to interview, who joined the sit-ins, were motivated by religious reasons.

I think also important is the fact that the white ministerial support of these sit-ins has been greater than for any other such protest in the history of the church. The lofty announcements are fine; but I am talking about the local effects. In almost all of the cities in North Carolina, for instance, the ministerial organizations came up with very strong statements in support of the sit-ins. Also, many denominations are showing a renewed interest in their internal problems. Now there is one segregationist argument which I accept in full; and that is the churches have no right to speak about secular integration as long as their own institutions remain so tightly segregated. And so I think that internal inspection by Christians of their own denominations is rather long overdue. And I believe that this is going on now.

There are two things that I would summarize. We very much need a rebalancing Protestantism. I am not arguing that the church be totally principled and forget all considerations of money and members. What we have set up, for the most part, are big businesses—churches of 5,000 members. A minister with a Chamber of Commerce sign hanging over his desk is not rare now in the ministry. This is the sort of thing I think we have to start worrying about. We must inject some principle and idealism into this huge organizational plant we have set up in the name of Christianity.

Secondly, we can do now with much less moderation. I think we could get along handsomely without any of it. I would like to end with the words of an ardent segregationist sect minister in Little Rock who summarized the whole thing. He said, "You know this is an old old church here that I preach in. Been a Baptist church for over a hundred years, sir, in the Little Rock area. A hundred years ago the pastor of this church would get up in the pulpit and deliver some of the best defenses of slavery you have ever heard or could imagine." He said, "Today, if I got up in that pulpit and delivered those brilliant defenses of slavery, they would laugh me out of the church." He added, "This is what worries me. Today, in that same pulpit I am getting up delivering some of the most brilliant defenses of segregation you have ever heard. What bothers me is, if anybody a hundred years from now in that same pulpit got up and tried to deliver my brilliant defenses of segregation, they will laugh him out of the pulpit."

§21 John W. Deschner

John W. Deschner was born October 23, 1923, in Stillwater, Minnesota. He married literary critic Margareta Neovius, and the two raised sons Martin, Paul, and Thomas. Deschner received a B.A. from the University of Texas in 1944, a B.D. from Yale University in 1947, and thirteen years later received his D.Th. from the University of Basel in Switzerland. His dissertation director was Karl Barth. Deschner was a professor at Perkins School of Theology at Southern Methodist University from 1956 to his retirement in 1991. He died July 28, 2000. Deschner's associations, publications, and honors are too numerous to recount, but one informal honor conveys his students' affection for him: his nickname was "God the Son," as part of the trinity of top-shelf theologians, including Albert Outler (Father) and Schubert Ogden (Spirit) at Perkins School.

In this July 1960 address to the World Student Christian Federation in Strasbourg, France, his lecture is one of numerous components of a teaching conference. He initially admits the formulaic nature of such lectures, whose components include analysis of a crisis, why Christianity transcends the crisis, and a concluding challenge to students to answer the problems posed by their contemporaries. In this case, says Deschner, the formula does not suffice, because Christianity is not clearly transcendent in this case, and students are suspicious of Christian paths of the crisis. He uses his local experience (University Park, Texas) to explain that when black leaders approached students to discourage sit-ins in favor of informal arrangements to improve race relations, students preferred an active role in creating an "I-Thou" relationship between the races, where white students understand reflexively their own suffering because of how African Americans are mistreated. He then embarks on an analysis of the contemporary student in three contexts: church, world, and vocation. The experience of church in local congregations is humiliating for young people. Deschner encourages students to embrace suffering as a sign that personal dissatisfaction is proof of a living hope to change the church for the better. The experience of world connotes common experiences of violence (and hopefully nonviolence)—a result of the need for action when language becomes obsolete; security, for which Christian discipline is an excellent outlet; and integrity, which demands that students share the passion and suffering of Christ. The lecture concludes with an exhortation to embrace a vocation that shares Christ's suffering while looking to the church for understanding, acknowledgment, and support of one's compassionate mission.

Christian Students and the Challenge of Our Times

July 1960
Strasbourg, France

In a sense, it is presumptuous of me to address you on the theme of this speech. You are Christian students, and you know for yourselves the challenge of your times. So I would ask you not to think of this as a teaching address, but as a series of questions to help you face for yourselves the challenge of our times. In a way this address has a very humble function in this program: after twenty addresses on the theological consensus, and on the threshold of eight more about the secular world, I want to be sure that the delegates are really present, that it is the real man and woman who is listening to all this!

Now, in order to do that I have to depart from a well-established SCM tradition about this address. This is usually a very challenging address, either at the beginning or at the end of a conference. It normally has three points: the first point analyzes our times, preferably as a crisis. The second point shows why the Christian understanding transcends the crisis, and remains fundamentally undisturbed by it. The third point then challenges Christian students to answer the problems of their contemporaries.

I depart from this outline partly for the practical reason that both you and I are no longer so sure that our Christian understanding transcends the crisis of our times. Or rather, we are learning to see that Christ is not above but within the crises of our times, making them real crises of decision for or against himself. We can no longer simply challenge Christian students to give the so-called Christian answer to modern man.

But there is another reason why I cannot simply challenge you to learn to give the Christian answer to your times. I wonder if the whole attempt to understand, to formulate, at least to conceptualize the Christian's relation to the crisis is not viewed with suspicion by contemporary students, believers as well as unbelievers. There is something in this generation which profoundly suspects a system. Have you heard the famous war novel by my fellow countryman, *The Naked and the Dead*, by Norman Mailer? It is a bitter story of the fighting on a muddy, hot, unimportant island in the Pacific. The essential conflict, however, is not that between the opposing troops, but the conflict between the American troops and their own general. All their hatred is saved for him. Why? Because he is the one man on this island to whom the whole bitter mess makes sense, and these men feel in their bones that there is no relation between the senselessness of their existence and his knowledge of its meaning. There is something of that in contemporary students. And that doesn't necessarily mean that they are less responsible than their parents; they may be more responsible, in fact. For they are preoccupied with the question of action and inaction, decision and indecision. One of our delegates said the other day, "I am not against the study of basic principles, but our basic problem is the problem of action." You know the *power* of meaninglessness in a way quite new for modern history. They know that men suffer in seemingly meaningless ways, but their hope is not so much to illumine that suffering, as to help to bear it. I believe that the contemporary Christian student is not nearly so much concerned with apologetics as his father was; but he may be more concerned with compassion. He is not nearly so concerned to understand the mission of the church, as he is to discern, almost by intuition, his own role in it. (And he is ready for it to be a costly role.) He is prepared, far more than we have realized, to act when it is not understandable to prudent men why this student must act, especially when he can act in the name of what is personal and human.

The sit-in lunch counter demonstrations in my country offer a good example. Recently, some of the important Negro leaders of the southern city where I live came to our theological students to explain why we should *not* make any sit-in demonstrations at the moment. Secret negotiations were underway between Negro and white leaders, they told us, which promised real improvement for the Negro's situation. I trust those leaders, for they have already produced social change in our city. They understand strategy; they know how to be effective. But our young Negro students were full of deep questions about precisely this prudence and strategy and waiting. They are eager to go downtown and sit in at white lunch counters, and they are ready to suffer abuse, to be arrested, imprisoned, tried, fined—as some delegates to this conference have been. Why? Not simply to effect social change, but to bring about a basic human, I-Thou encounter between Negro and white, an encounter which segregation denies them. A Negro student explained quite simply, "We didn't only want to open up a lunch counter; we wanted to let people know we are human." She was ready to suffer in order to awaken me, a white man, to the fact that I am suffering until she is free to be a human being.

If it is correct that Christian students of this generation are not deeply interested in questions of the theological, rational strategy of missions, then this conference faces a peculiar problem. For we are met here to transmit to a new generation an ecumenical consensus about the unity and mission of the church. But you question not only the content of the consensus, but the relevance of beginning with consensus. This is not due to any hostility to the fathers (by whom I mean here anyone over thirty!): I suspect that you are quite ready to acknowledge the consensus as a monument to the father's achievement. Your problem lies in *beginning* where the father's ended. In a way, a consensus offers you too much, and at the same time not more than a consensus. You are also asking for our obedience, for our example, for honesty about our temptations and failures, for an insight into our way of judging, our sense of proportion; you would like to see a demonstration of real ecumenical style. But you are pleading for the freedom to discover your own consensus at the end of your own day. I, for one, hope that you will take that freedom and use it well. The task of the two generations is one, but there is a real distance between the generations, and for your own sake you must respect it. No one but you, yourselves, can understand the vocation which God has of this generation. And if you hear it well, you will astonish the churches with your demands upon them for backing and support.

I would like to use my remaining time, now, to invite you to look at this contemporary student, which you are, in three contexts: in the church, in the world, and in your vocation. And my purpose in all three respects is to ask you to reflect upon what the great themes, slogans, ideas of this conference mean for yourself. And I can only ask questions. You must decide the answers—you must decide the content of this address—for yourself.

This conference has spoken a great deal about the missionary church, which must have open windows and doors, so its members may go out into the world, and so the nonbeliever may find his way into the church. If I am correct, however, the problem for most of you is not to be persuaded of this, but rather to see how a life of witness in the world can have any real base in the actual life of the local congregation, as we know it. Am I wrong in thinking that many delegates need to be persuaded not only to go out of the church, but also to go in? In fact, for some, this acceptance of membership in a local congregation has all the feeling of a mission to a strange country. And added to it is a humiliation—a humiliation of accepting personal responsibility for this congregation in the eyes of your contemporaries in the university. I am aware that for many the local congregation is a much more promising and happy reality than I have described, yet I suspect that even in those cases you will understand what I mean when I say: membership in the local congregation adds a dimension not only of grace, fellowship, encouragement, but also an element of humiliation to the life of witness in the world. I could give many examples. Not long ago in South America I heard ex-SCM members speaking about a terrible loneliness in the somewhat conservative evangelical congregations: they felt that their problems of secular vocation had no place there, and they frankly longed at times to return to the fellowship of the SCM. Charles Long has written of the same problem in Asia, and examples could be given in great number from America and Europe as well. The German SCM, where things often go deeper than elsewhere, even speaks of helping new converts "to become strong enough to be sent into the churches!" To say it quite bluntly, although the church is home base for the mission, more than a few Christian students do not feel at home in the local congregation.

And yet the most significant thing about the student's attitude toward the church today is not his disappointment and humiliation with church life, but his almost unshakable willingness to hope better things for it, and to accept identification with it. You must say whether that statement is factually correct. If it is true, it is a significant fact, because this willingness to be in the church, though dissatisfied, is one of the essential signs that God intends to bring about the renewal of his church. We don't usually think of the personal cost of the renewal of the church, but it is there, and each one of you will be called to pay it. There is such a thing as an ecumenical suffering; it is one of the most important fruits of the ecumenical movement and should be of this conference also. We often wonder how to take back to our local situations the fruit of a conference such as this. So we take notes, and collect documents, and plan reports. But God has a much simpler way to make this conference locally relevant: he simply makes us dissatisfied, he opens our eyes to the wretchedness of the church, and sends us home to let that suffering become the seed ground for the renewal of the church. Do not, therefore, waste the restlessness, the humiliation, the suffering which you feel over your congregation and your SCM (and the Federation!) as a result of this conference: it is not yours alone; it is God's precious gift, and he intends for it to bear fruit in and for the church. Do you think you are alone in your suffering about the church? No: there is another whose passion has endured far longer than ours, and who invites us into his passion, his redemptive passion for the congregation.

This readiness to be faithful to your vision of the church's reality, and to bear the personal cost of this vision in responsible church membership, is the concrete personal meaning of much that has been said from this platform about the church. In a word, this conference ought to mean six hundred *tougher* church members, who are ready to be misunderstood, who are ready to think and act resolutely as churchmen, who are ready to love and exercise patience and self-control and kindness, and above all, who acknowledge their need for the means of grace and use them.

I may have erred here and there in this description of how the Christian student feels the challenge of his church, today, but I am pretty sure of this: the mission of today's student begins with a clarification of his faithful membership in the church.

I cannot make here another analysis of the character of the world in which we live. Others will do that. I wish, rather, to examine with you how this student generation feels or experiences its world, and what the concrete meaning of Christian faith may be for the Christian student who shares with his non-Christian brother a common experience of these reactions. And I would like to characterize this reaction in a threefold way. It seems that this generation, facing its world, has a characteristic fascination with violence, security, and integrity.

Their fascination with *violence* has been noted by many. It is both the result and the impulse of a revolutionary era. Françoise Florentin has reminded us of the necessity for violence to break up the frozen patterns of tradition—especially in language—which no longer have authentic meaning. Students feel that necessity even when they don't understand it. They are ready to lose themselves in action, partly as a protest, partly as a passionate search for identity and meaning. Much of this love of violence expresses itself pointlessly or even *destructively* in the love of motion and speed, the use of stimulants and narcotics, in chaotic personal relationships, in meaningless acts of personal and social rebellion. But the same basic attitude, the same protest and search, can express itself in more ordered and *purposive* ways, in courageous violence, such as one finds in revolutionary action. Even the nonviolent revolutions of our time have their root in this generation's sense for the immediate, and its readiness to respond, to *commit itself*, to throw its existence into the balance. You yourself represent and know recent examples in South Korea, Japan, Turkey, the American South, to name only a few. Some try to see in this fascination with action and even violence a sickness of students. I do not think so; or rather, if there is sickness, it is a sickness of a world so dehumanized and organized that one cannot think or speak clearly in it anymore; words and concepts are too unwieldy and brittle: one can only act. Students today—and Christian students among them—are ready for *decisive action*, for costly commitment, before all the understandings have been clarified. That is how their world is affecting them, and there is something good in it, for Christ's mission is a costly mission; he asks men to leave everything and follow him; and their readiness to respond to the missionary call may be hindered only by our weak courage in presenting it.

At the opposite pole is there concern for *security*. When everything is changing, and must change, there is no longer any firm context for growth, and young people need a context for growth. And so we witness all about us the *attempt to find structures* within which there are clearly defined roles which one can learn, which, so to speak, define who one is. We hear about the revival of student corporations in continental universities, or about the organization man in America. One of the most striking examples in my country is the increase in marriage of quite young people—sometimes boys and girls in high school—seeking in the mutual roles of husband and wife the structure within which growth can occur. One of the tragedies of this security of the structures is the paralyzing inner contradiction it creates between the need to act and the need for structures. There is something deeper in this impulse here than a mere failure of nerve before the modern world. For many young people are seeking *an inner security* which they can carry with them in the struggles of this world, a security which is not bound to an organization. One senses it in their hunger for an ordered style of life in a disordered age, for an inner discipline which can give shape and effectiveness to decision. Negro student demonstration leaders in one southern city met daily at 6:00 a.m. for discussion, not simply because they needed to make plans, but also because the discipline of rising early and meeting together seemed appropriate to their world of courageous action. I think there is something deeply right and significant about this *hunger for discipline*. Bonhoeffer, you remember, also agreed: the need for a secret Christian discipline precisely at the point where Christianity becomes most worldly. Students today, I believe, want that discipline and are ready to pay the price for it. That is how their world is affecting them and there is something good in it, for Christ comes to them with the offer of an inner order which clarifies, and does not hinder, courageous action.

The most attractive characteristic of the contemporary student's response to the world is his passion for *integrity*, honesty. He is determined to be himself. He has an intense dislike for what is artificial. At my university, this artificial student, who lets himself be defined by his organization, and takes his official title seriously, has a special name: he is called a "pseudo." In the modern American novel he is called the "phony": and that means someone who not only likes to play roles, but who likes to watch himself playing them. Or you could express it this way: the phony likes to watch himself be something; the honest man does things. This generation has little patience with "phonies." Its passion for integrity goes deep. It may well be that this is merely an aspect of the contemporary student's search for his true *identity* among all the roles he must play. But that is a very serious search, and one for which he is ready to make *sacrifices*, if only he may be assured of his integrity in doing so, if only he may believe that the one making the sacrifice is truly himself. He does not require great slogans or ideals, but only to see what is true and necessary behind the façade. There is almost an audible longing for an authentic, costly service. One sometimes wonders if the missionary movement doesn't hinder Christ's work by asking far too little of students. They are ready for poverty, for obedience, yes, even in some case, for celibacy, if they can only sense that this costly decision and discipline is honest, represents true selfhood. And here we approach *a very critical point* as the gospel understands it. For there is a temptation today to believe that the real man is the one who hurts. Sacrifice hurts. Therefore, sacrifice represents a way of finding the real man. But the real man, in the light of the gospel, is a mystery. He is known by God alone and to us only by the eye of faith. Who am I, asked Bonhoeffer, and answered, I am the one thou lovest. The modern student's search for integrity cannot be answered simply in his readiness to sacrifice, nor in his flight into violent action, nor in his clinging to artificial roles. He will begin to find his identity when he is led to face the most disturbing of all questions: who does God confront *me* as one who suffers? Why does he insist on beginning his relationship with *me* as the crucified? True identity begins at the point where Christ's passion confronts human astonishment—my astonishment. And the joy for which that student searches lies in learning to acknowledge and share the fellowship of Christ's passion.

That is enough, perhaps, to indicate that students today experience the world in a characteristic way. It evokes from them a fascination with violence, security, and honesty. But by God's grace students may also experience this world as a sphere of courageous decision, as the demand for inner discipline, and the theater of God's search for man's integrity.

We must not try to describe the vocation of the student who is *this* church member, who experiences the world in *this* way. In other days, the vocation to costly discipleship has been clearly received in particular forms. I doubt whether this generation understands its Christian vocation in such clear detail. Or, rather, it may be possible to describe the vocation itself more clearly, precisely because we cannot be so explicit about its external forms. I wish to make three remarks about it:

It is a vocation to fellow-suffering with Christ (I almost wish I could use a good old word, "compassion" to signify that my vocation is to offer a co-passion, a "compassion" alongside Christ's passion.) A vocation to compassion means a life identified with God's passion for this world. Here I am glad to acknowledge what D. Bonhoeffer has taught us about the unavoidable relation between *witness, suffering, and Christian joy*. This modern world, he says, will have nothing to do with a religious Christianity any longer. By a religious Christianity he meant two things: on the one hand, a metaphysical Christianity, which is all ideas about God's otherness, and which calls upon God only when human possibilities are exhausted. On the other hand, a religious Christianity is a Christianity of inwardness, which is all concerned about the inner state of the soul, its sin, and its individual salvation. But, said Bonhoeffer, the modern world may find itself interested in a nonreligious Christianity. What could he mean? For fifteen years theologians have tried to unravel his notion. But it is not a matter of the right words at all. It is for Bonhoeffer a matter of acts. Bonhoeffer sees what D. T. Niles was explaining yesterday morning: that God is at the center of this world, loving his children wherever they are, and patiently bearing the cost of their continued existence until they freely turn to him. T. S. Eliot looked out over the rooftops of London, and sensed, as he put it, "some infinitely tender, infinitely suffering thing." That is what Bonhoeffer sensed, and he longed for Christians who would go and join God in his suffering there, and find there the joy of authentic life. A nonreligious interpretation of Christianity is, in a word, a life of compassion—a sharing in the sufferings of God in this world, for this world.

But again, one could characterize the Christian vocation in our day—and especially its worldliness—in this way: *we have a vocation to accept as our own our brother's distance from the church.* It is easy to romanticize the demand to be in the world. It is not being in the world as such which is important, but being beside our brother in the world. That is our place; that is where the conversation with him arises. I wish here only to plead that this conversation should not turn to Christ and his church lightly or cheaply. Out of love for both the brother and Jesus Christ, it must be a conversation in which we make our own the brother's distance from the church. I do not mean that we refuse to speak to him of Christ and the church, but rather that we may learn to speak with more modesty about them, refusing the cliché that violated the distance he feels from these realities. The conversation of witness can be an intense human conversation precisely because Christ is really there in the world with you. You do not have to bring him into the situation with an abstraction, or a bit of theology. It has taken time for me to learn that God does not always witness through conversations as clear as those he has with his friend. (These are gifts of the spirit!) Often we have little to say; we are sometimes perplexed about how to speak; or we find ourselves often just being silent. But those can be signs of true witness as well as eloquence. We often witness best to the power of Christ when it is clear that we, for our part, don't quite have the conversation under our own control.

But we can be faithful to the brother, and that means standing beside him, and accepting as our own his distance from the church.

My final characterization of the vocation of this student generation corresponds to the second. *It belongs to our vocation to seek from the churches understanding, acknowledgment, and support of this form of the mission.* This does not mean asking the churches to confine themselves to the kind of mission this generation finds most characteristic of its vocation. The church's mission is manifold, and includes much of tradition which this generation will gratefully receive and continue. But God has created a new situation in our hearts, and he intends it to bear fruit for the renewal of the church. If our ecumenical suffering is genuine, if our sense of vocation into the world is true, then for Christ's own sake, let us *ask something new of the churches.*

I have neither the time nor the skill to tell you what this new thing might be. It ought to be our task here to think it out—not how church structures can be changed, for that is a complicated technical matter—but the main principles for which we should ask of the church's understanding, acknowledgment, support, and possibly some adaptation of their structure. I can only give a few indications of what you must already sense. Our generation feels a need for a more *humble* missionary institution, especially in its ecclesiastical and cultural claims, and in its claims when raising money. Our generation feels a need for a mission institution whose ecumenical obedience and political alertness will eliminate for the inquirer the widespread obstacles of Christian divisiveness and Christian irrelevance. We ask for a mission institution in which every trace of *racial discrimination* and segregation is eliminated. Above all—and this sums up our pleas—we ask for *congregations* where the living word of God is clearly preached and the sacraments are rightly administered, so that Christian witness may point to the church without hesitation and say to the brother, "There you will experience the life of Christ."

And we ask this, not as irresponsible children who want all things at once, but as Christians who have heard the vocation of God, and are quietly and resolutely determined to be the church of which we speak.

My time is up. The main point of my speech is very simple. This generation deeply longs that its ecumenical suffering and its passion for the secular could be made fruitful for Christ and his church. We ask the missionary institution and the congregations for help that this may be so.

We see a cross set up here in the auditorium of a modern technical university. And across this cross falls the dove of God—his own Holy Spirit—pointing our devotion to the place where this cross is anchored in the heart of this world's technical life. We are witnesses of that: that here in this secular place is God's own holy of holies. But have you noticed that the more we contemplate this revelation, the more the descending dove takes the form of the Pentecostal flame of witness, a flame which shows us that self-same cross of Christ's passion to be our own cross of compassion with him. The dove descending—the Pentecostal flame: the cross of Christ's passion anchored in the world—our vocation of compassion. "All this is from God, who through Christ reconciled us to himself, and gave us the ministry of reconciliation" (II Corinthians 5:18) "that his joy might be in us, and that our joy might be full" (John 15:11).

§22 Lillian Smith

Lillian Eugenia Smith was born on December 12, 1897, in Jasper, Florida. She was the eighth of ten children born to the family of a prominent business and civic leader. As a young girl she had her first confusing and emotionally devastating confrontation with race. Her parents had agreed to adopt a young white girl who had been discovered living with local blacks in "Colored Town." The young Lillian immediately took to her new best friend, Janie. But three weeks later it was discovered that Janie was in fact black and would have to go back to "Colored Town." Despite Lillian's vehement protestations, and unanswered questions, Janie was quickly returned to the "shack" on the other side of town. In 1915, when her father lost his turpentine mills, the Smiths repaired to their summer home in Clayton, Georgia. Ms. Smith attended Piedmont College and studied her first love, music, at the Peabody Conservatory. Between 1922 and 1925 she taught, under Methodist auspices, at a school for girls in Huzhou, China. In 1925, as her father's health was failing, she ran Laurel Falls Camp for Girls, a cloistered and progressive haven where girls could learn poetry, dance, and drama and discuss taboo subjects such as race, gender relations, segregation, and sex.

Upon her father's death in 1930, she continued to run the camp while also caring for her ailing mother. She and a camp counselor, Paula Snelling, began publishing a literary quarterly titled *Psuedopodia* in 1936. The liberal forum became the *North Georgia Review* (1937) and later, the *South Today* (1942). Lillian ended the quarterly in 1945 to concentrate on her own writing. Her best-selling novel, *Strange Fruit*, was published in 1944 after rejection by seven different publishers; it would sell more than three million copies and be translated into fifteen languages. Her autobiographical *Killers of the Dream* (1949) was simply ignored until people could better understand it in the 1960s. By 1953 Ms. Smith was already well along in her battle with cancer, which would take her on September 28, 1966, shortly after she had voiced her discontent with the civil rights movement's takeover by people who had abandoned nonviolence. She is buried adjacent to a chimney from the gymnasium at Laurel Falls. Her papers are housed in Special Collections at the University of Florida and at the University of Georgia. However, many of her private papers related to her long relationship with Paula Snelling have been destroyed to protect their privacy.

Smith's bona fides with the young activists of the movement are attested to by her invitation to speak at this Student Nonviolent Coordinating Committee conference. Barely six months old, the fledgling group of college activists formalized its organizational structure at this conference; it would soon change the dynamic of the civil rights movement as it put boots (and overalls) on the ground throughout the Deep South. In her address, delivered just weeks before the 1960 presidential election in which a virulent anti-Catholicism surfaced, Smith employs a childhood story to great rhetorical effect. The South was still trying to buy its way into the future with useless currency. Instead of national security, the South would have the nation focus on the dangers of interracial marriage, thus throwing into relief just how low (and dangerous) southern politics had devolved. Smith warns her young charges that the devil hadn't infected only the souls of old white southern men; he was also eager to claim movement hearts and minds with the allure of publicity and money. Christ, too, had been tempted; and since this was a most Judeo-Christian movement, temptations would indeed come, Smith warns.

§◦℘

Are We Still Buying a New World with Old Confederate Bills?
October 16, 1960
Atlanta, Georgia

I am glad to see old friends again; and proud to speak to this group of students. Why am I proud? Because it is good to see courage showing itself in our South: good to see the young running risks for important things; good to see thousands of students choosing the hard way, for that is the only way our South can be freed from its ancient fears and tyrannies. I regret that there are so few southern white students, as yet, working side by side with you; I am sorry they have not yet realized that segregation is their enemy also; that it harms their minds and souls as much as it does yours; that it blocks their freedom and their future as severely as it does yours. When they do see they will not be afraid to do their share; they too have courage; it is vision they do not, as yet, possess.

It is this future, yours and theirs, this new world in the making that I want to talk about. What is it? Where is it coming from? Who is creating it? Who is paying for it? What kind of currency are we using in this great transaction?

Let's begin to answer these questions by taking a look, first, at our South, and ourselves:

Ever since I remember, southern politicians have been trying to put over a Big Deal: they have been trying to buy a new life for the people, a new world, with old Confederate bills. And they don't seem to know why it can't be done. They do not, even now, understand why the old Confederate bills they flash around are not real currency. They have not learned a bitter lesson I learned, when I was six years old.

Let me tell you that story: We children found an old trunk in the attic; we opened it and to our delighted astonishment saw it was chock-full of money; paper money, piles of it. We felt rich; richer than the Rockefeller children or any children. We knew we could now buy anything we wanted. So we stuffed a basket full of the bills and raced down to the drugstore. We marched in, my brother and I—aged eight and six—and asked for five pounds of candy. "We have lots of money," we said. "We're coming every day and buying five pounds of candy." Then we showed the man our basket of bills. There they were: hundreds of Confederate bills. He looked at the basket, picked up a bill, dropped it, shook his head, then he said a devastating thing, "That money," he said, "is not worth a penny."

My brother did not give in. He said, "We have a whole trunk full at home. How about that? I can run and bring you another basketful." It is hard for an eight-year-old—and some grown people—to realize that a lot of nothing is worth no more than a little of nothing.

But the man in the drugstore knew. He said, "Son, if you had a roomful it wouldn't be worth a cent. That money won't buy anything." I was easy with tears in those days, and I let them come. The sound of my heartbreak filled the drugstore. It was too much for the manager. He scooped me up some candy and filled our hands and then told us to go home and burn that money. He said, "Don't keep it around; it will mix you up; get you all mixed up about everything."

I let out a new howl. "I thought money was *always* money," I said.

"Money is not money, sister, unless it is based on something real. This is old Confederate money and there is no Confederacy. See? It has no value because there's *nothing back of it.*"

That was the day my education began. But our southern politicians? Well, they weren't there that day and they have not yet learned this basic lesson. They are still trying to buy a future for the South, and for our country, with currency that is worthless: with ideas that have no validity, opinions that are not based on facts, values that are not human and earthsize. They keep flashing the old bills around, and they still believe they'll get their bargain.

But how can they believe this? How can intelligent men, in this tumultuous, changing decade of the sixties, tell our people that we must hold on to segregation, we must cling to old spurious fears, we must cling to archaic defenses? How can they solemnly declare, in this age of nuclear weapons, that the greatest danger facing the South and this nation is the danger that a few white people and a few Negroes may possibly marry each other?

How can any man in his senses say these things—when he can turn on TV and see for himself how Khrushchev works. How can he believe this is a white man's world when all he has to do to learn the score is count the Afro-Asian votes in the United Nations? Surely he knows, surely every American knows, today, that these votes can be and will be the deciding factor in any world issue. How then can our politicians say that intermarriage is our number one concern? It is our great hazard! Or is our number one hazard the fact that the Communist powers may win the admiration and allegiance of these new nations while we are still clinging to a past gone forever, still using moral and intellectual currency that has no value in this present world?

Is it segregation that we want or is it national security? Is it segregation or is it a desire to keep the earth safe from nuclear war?

Ask the southern politician and he does not answer. He keeps on doggedly, stubbornly trying to buy a seat in the legislature or a seat in Congress by telling the voters he will pay for it by seeing that they have plenty of segregation; plenty of Confederate money.

And people listen to this nonsense. Presidents of banks listen; heads of industry, ministers, storekeepers, and ordinary people. They listen because, like my little brother and me, they want something for nothing.

It is an old human trait, and a few of us are free from it. You read in the paper, did you not, about the slick operator who came to Georgia this past month offering to businessmen and farmers a machine that makes money by duplication. It worked like this: He made up a mysterious fluid, took out a ten-dollar bill, swished it around in the fluid, and pulled out four ten-dollar bills. And some well-to-do farmers and businessmen fell for this old trick. One gentleman who had just cleared $18,000 from his peanut crop put the whole sum into these machines that can "make money by duplication."

We say, how can people be so stupid? But all we have to do is look around us. We know the South has fallen for such trickery year in and year out; and watching Mr. Nixon work, it seems to me the Republicans and quite a few Democrats are falling for the same old sleight-of-hand tricks: the juggling of spurious fears with spurious hopes and spurious accusations and calling the mixture "a new life for our people."

Let's come closer to home: let's look at the Baptists and Methodists and other denominations, who are spreading bigoted talk against the Catholics. Once more, clutching at a spurious danger to keep from looking at the real dangers confronting us. Here are preachers arousing hate and fear against Catholics when they should be leading their congregations to the asking of important questions such as: How can we make brotherhood work? How can we create warm, Christian understanding relations between people? How can we lift away the barriers that are smothering the human spirit? Here are preachers appealing not to the conscience of their congregations but to their irrational dreads! Seducing them into playacting: for it is playacting to pretend to fight a battle that was won by Martin Luther three hundred years ago. It is silly, childish, and dangerous to pretend that the pope, who doesn't even own a popgun, is our great national enemy! It must delight Mr. Khrushchev to see how easy it is to confuse some of the American people. While he is here, he who is so adept at creating confusion, he may learn a few new tricks from us.

My father was an astute man who liked to use old-fashioned phrases. Were he alive today he would say all this is the work of the devil. And I think I rather agree. The devil did not die at the end of medievalism. He appears in every age; he gives himself a fresh new image, but he always appears. We speak of evil today; it is intellectually fashionable and philosophically wise to do so; we often use Dr. Paul Tillich's phrases, and Martin Buber's, and Karl Jaspers', but the word *devil* is hard to match: it has so much life and energy in it and is, I think, a better symbol of what we are talking about.

The devil always appears when something important is going on. He comes to get his share, as that great theologian Denis de Rougemont reminds us. He appears at critical moments to confuse our minds; he delights in persuading us to fear false dangers and fight false battles. He must be hilarious over the ease with which he has persuaded many Protestant preachers and their congregations to fight the already won battles of the Reformation instead of concentrating on the real conflicts of the 1960s. He must delight in the fog of hate and fear that is whirling through minds, driving even some good Democrats to vote for Mr. Nixon because they think he is more "Christian" than is Mr. Kennedy, and will protect us, also, from the pope. It is funny but it is a matter for tears, not laughter.

The devil knows that if you want to destroy a man, all you need do is fill him with false hopes and false fears. These will blind him to his true direction, and he will inevitably turn away from the future and destroy himself and those close to him.

It is as true of a nation: fill its people with false hopes and false fears, and they will do the rest; they will go straight to their appointment with death; and they will drag all nations friendly to them down into the maelstrom of their moral and mental confusion.

The false fear of "the Catholic menace"; the false fear of "intermarriage of the races," the false fear that compassionate concern for people's needs is a giant step toward socialism: these fears are looming up like monstrous ghosts, today, blinding us to the magnificent opportunities we Americans have to help bring the whole world to a higher plateau of free, creative human endeavor; blinding us to our role as the world's good neighbor, a good neighbor not a fellow conspirator; a neighbor concerned for all children in the world, concerned for the human being's right to grow and learn and create.

The evil within the human heart is a chilling thing to contemplate. And it is in every one of us. Dormant hates, dormant greed, dormant lust for power, restless foolish fears, the desire to get something for nothing, the willingness to cheat, to betray great causes for small ambitions; the irresponsible temptation to arouse men's anxiety so as to profit from their panic.

These things we see in politicians; these things you, as members of the Negro race, see in white folks. Do you also see how the devil gets his share of your life? Do you see how he stirs your false fears and false hopes and exploits your hurts and humiliations, making you choose wrong leaders, vote for the wrong party, sometimes, to take your revenge?

Do you think the leaders of the young African nations are listening to the devil's whispers as he tempts them to use their color, their black skins, to build for themselves political power—just as the white man did in the eighteenth and nineteenth and early twentieth centuries? Just as our southern demagogues still try to do? Are some of them turning to Khrushchev because of their deep hurts? Are they even now making wrong choices as to the friends who will really help them? Is the devil telling them, "The white race sinned in a big way; why don't you now sin in an equally big way? It's equality you want, isn't it? OK. If you want equality then you have an equal right to sin, don't you? To discriminate, to exploit and build power and take revenge?" I don't doubt for a moment that the leaders of the new nations are being whispered to by the devil and his earthly henchmen, even in their sleep and dreams. Why not? Are they different from the rest of us? I doubt it. Are they different from Christ, who was also tempted?

But let's come closer to home. Let's look at this truly important nonviolent movement of the students: this historic movement. A movement that has as its immediate goal a small, vivid, heart-clutching aim: to open lunch counters in stores so that Negro women and their children—and others, too, of course—while shopping can have a place to sit down and eat. But the sit-in movement is much more: it has great moral goals and uses moral methods. Its vocabulary lifts the heart: nonviolence . . . love . . . truth . . . compassion . . . reconciliation. Words that the young and the brave take seriously enough to go to jail for.

It is, and I say this reverently, God's movement: it is a flowering of the Judaic-Christian ethic; it is built on the sanctity of the person, on the dignity of man, on the spiritual power of love, on the light of reason; it is grounded on a certitude that there is a divine center in each one of us; it is based on faith in the redemptive power of sacrifice.

What better place than this for the devil's hang-out? The plain bad people do the devil's work for him. But when there's work to do among good folks the devil does it himself. This is where he exhibits his stupendous versatility and talent.

How is he working or about to work in the nonviolent movement? In his usual way: by whispering it is possible to get something for nothing. He has already done rather a good job on some of the college presidents. The Devil was ready for them. He whispered, "Remember the money; take care of those funds for the college and let the students take care of civil rights. You'd better fire a few of them, you know; don't be caught collaborating with them; if you're caught, you may not get that money. And money is money," says the Devil. He's been working on the businessmen too. "Too much of this will hurt you financially," he whispers. "You get along fine with white folks, but these kids—they're too young to know how to lick 'em up. Oh sure, put up bond for the boys and girls, get 'em out of jail, it's not respectable to stay in jail; but tell' em enough's enough. Tell 'em to take it easy now."

But this isn't enough for the Devil. He is jealous of goodness and decency, jealous of a young, clean conscience, jealous of any man or woman, girl or boy, who holds his integrity sacred. So he impudently walks around the campuses where the movement was born. What doing? I think you know. Whispering things like this: "You've done a fine job, but it's time now you got something out of it for yourself. Get your name in the paper; build yourself into a leader; make a big deal out of all this publicity."

And then he shrewdly goes to the heart of the matter: to the ones who are working to coordinate the movement and who are doing it at great personal sacrifice. He may not have whispered to them yet, but if he hasn't already, he will. Make no mistake about it. He'll tell them, "You folks need money. Can't grow without money. So take it when it is offered you, even though it has a few dirty strings tied to it. After all, money is money you know."

How will you students answer these whispers? Will you say, "Is money always money, or is it sometimes Confederate bills? Or other currency of no value to us? Is this a big deal for the organization or is it a betrayal of a great cause for thirty pieces of silver? Am I helping to win civil rights for the people, or am I losing my own soul?"

How those questions are answered will determine the future of the non-violent sit-in movement. It is up to you. You alone, each one of you, in the quietness of your heart, must answer. What happens in the South during the next decade depends on how our people respond to the diabolical temptations to sell out big causes for little ones. What happens to our country depends on our skill in separating false fears from rational ones, false dangers from the real ones confronting the whole world. What happens will depend on whether we choose to live in a past full of ghosts or in a future full of hard jobs and great opportunities.

I say these hard things to you because I respect and admire you. I have a feeling of awe as I consider the bravery and spirit of self-sacrifice that many of you have shown the whole world this past year. I want your movement to succeed: I want it to reach high and attain that quality of spiritual excellence which is necessary if it is to transform our region into a better place for Negro and white to live and if it is to do its part in transforming the whole world. I believe it has magnificent possibilities: I want only to suggest some of the dangers that may betray you, and beg you to take care. Do this: try to recognize the Devil when he comes around you; don't be betrayed by his new image.

You have an important work ahead of you, and it is yours to do: only yours. We who are older cannot do it.

For the River Jordan is a chilly place. Full of whirlpools and quicksand. Only the young and the brave can cross it and still have strength for their new jobs. But you must do it if you are to bring not only your race but all our people to the Promised Land, the new world the youth of the entire earth must make together.

We of the older generation cannot go on that great journey with you. We cannot help build the new frontier. But there is something we can do: we can make of our lives, our knowledge, our experiences, our wisdom, and our hopes and faith and insight a *bridge*, a strong sure bridge, over which you can cross into the new unmade world. Perhaps in this way we who are older can help keep you out of the quicksands and the worst whirlpools. Perhaps by our firm support, our unwavering belief in you we can give you that extra lift you are going to need. I hope so. And now let me say, God bless you.

1961

1961

§23 O. Merrill Boggs

Rev. O. Merrill Boggs was born on May 31, 1920, in Lima, Ohio. In 1941 he married. The Boggses raised two children, David and Carol Ann. Rev. Boggs attended Bluffton College, receiving a B.A. in sociology in 1952. He received a master's degree at Lexington Theological Seminary in Kentucky in 1957. His first pastorate was Bluffton-Beaver Dam Parish of the Christian Church of Ohio, from 1948 to 1952. His second pastorate at College Hill Christian Church in Cincinnati lasted from 1952 to 1965. From 1965 to 1975, he served as associate director and executive director of the Cincinnati Industrial Mission, where he led over 4,000 industrial managers in seminars geared toward opening management jobs to African Americans. The next eight years he was invited by the City of Peoria to run federally funded employment and training programs for the disadvantaged. During this period he married Margaurette Woll, who passed away in 2003, leaving Boggs a surviving stepson, Mark Woll. He retired in 1984. At the age of ninety-one he attends weekly dances with his fiancée, Gloria Patmore.

This sermon of February 12, 1961, at College Hill Christian Church in Cincinnati, Ohio, was entitled "This Time of Testing." The audience included all seven men who made up the board of elders for the church. The sermon is organized into four related Aristotelian points, but pulls into this standard format sensitively arranged information from settings both global and local. Fairly wide-ranging is a quote from the dean of Yale Divinity School, Liston Pope. More international yet is his observation that the United Nations struggles with race relations as well. This sermon occurs just two months shy of UN resolutions 1597 and 1598, which decried apartheid conditions in South Africa. Before connecting South African events to local events, he momentarily defuses the guilt of the moment with humor. He reminds the audience that Noah, not God, cursed Ham, and that Noah was hungover at the time he uttered the curse. But eventually Rev. Boggs ties events to the local. He looks in the mirror, and asks his congregation to perform the same task. He asks his fellow Disciples of Christ why African Americans from College Hill do not want to join the congregation. Results of this self-examination were immediate. The elders convened right after the service to approve unanimously a list of local African American families Rev. Boggs had invited to visit the church on a weekly basis, and by year's end, a few were appointed deacons.

This Time of Testing
February 12, 1961
Cincinnati, Ohio

> Even now the axe is laid to the root of the trees; every tree therefore that does not bear good fruit is cut down and thrown into the fire.
>
> Matthew 3:10

As noted by the front and back pages of our bulletin for this morning, the churches throughout our nation are focusing their attention today on the problem of race relations. There was a time, not long ago, when this subject didn't raise much interest among the rank and file of church members, but that is no longer true. Most people, of course, are still trying to avoid the subject, hoping that if they ignore it, it will go away like a bad dream. But it refuses to be ignored, and beneath our apparent indifference we all know that the relations between the races has become the most vital issue of our time.

The United Nations General Assembly has recently adjourned after the stormiest session of its history. The United Nations itself has never been so close to self-destruction. And the main issue? The relations between the races stirred up and used to be sure by the rivalries between the great power blocs, but centrally important nevertheless. The world of nations is reaping the harvest of suspicion and resentment that has been maturing for three centuries.

Nor is this problem confined to the international scene. Increasingly, race relations has become one of the major problems within our own nation. The problem, of course, is not new. What is new is that the American Negro, like his African cousin, has begun to feel and act like our pioneer forefathers who risked their fortunes and their lives that we might have a land where *all* men are free and equal. As Martin Luther King, pastor of the Dexter Avenue Baptist Church in Montgomery, Alabama, has said, "A revolutionary change has taken place in the Negro's conception of his own nature and destiny. Once he thought of himself as an inferior and patiently accepted injustice and exploitation. Those days are gone!"

Yes, my friends, those days are gone! And they are gone because of a social revolution which our forefathers began in 1775, a revolution which is only now coming to its full fruition. And because this is a revolution founded on and growing out of the revolutionary gospel of Jesus Christ, who called all men to live together as brothers, then we who claim to be his disciples have a special responsibility for directing that revolution to its divinely intended conclusion. So, this morning I suggest we consider not what the government, or unions, or industry, or other secular organizations are doing about the problems of race relations—though what they are doing is important—but rather that we should consider the peculiar contribution possible for the church. The most usual approaches to racial questions in America have been political or sociological in nature. This has been true even in our churches, whose pronouncements on such questions have generally sounded like watered-down sociological documents inspired by some degree of moral concern.

By the same token, the announced reasons for concern have often been prudential in character: that is to say, it has been argued that we must give greater equality to minority racial groups to prevent them from becoming disillusioned about Christianity, or to preserve democracy, or to enlist the energies and loyalties of colored peoples in the struggle against Communism, or to protect America's reputation in other parts of the world.

Similarly, the proposed solutions to race questions, including those advanced by churchmen, have generally been nontheological in character: educate public opinion; pass a law and then enforce it; desegregate schools, public facilities, and residential neighborhoods; and protect the constitutional rights of individuals regardless of race.

Now all of these are excellent proposals, and we feel frustrated that we make so little progress toward their realization. We meet in our state and national world gatherings and reaffirm and reaffirm, but still the local churches largely confirm the old ways in their practice. There was a conference in Washington, D.C., a few years ago on the subject of public hygiene. After the deliberation had proceeded for a day or two, one delegate rose to remark, "The fundamental problem is that too many people here are talking hy-giene and practicing low-giene."

The world urges us to "practice what we preach," which is a very worthy but worldly admonition, since it assumes that our problem is simply that of closing the gap between creed and deed. Like St. Paul our difficulty is lack of willpower; that which we would we do not. But is not our problem, the problem of those who confess the name of Christ and gather in his church, a far more profound one? As Dr. Liston Pope, Dean of Yale Divinity School, to whom I owe so much for my understanding of this subject, so insight-fully puts it, "Is [our problem] not that of discerning who we are, we who are sometimes called 'the people of God,' and of discovering the obedience required if we are to be followers of Christ?" And, my friends, if we do not deserve the name of Christ, as a denomination or local church or individual church member, let us confess it! For in the very confession, if it is penitent rather than apologetic, we may be shown the way toward being more loyal to our Lord.

All thoughtful churchmen must be grateful to the social scientists for the pioneer work they have done on racial patterns; they have exposed ineq-uities and iniquities of which we had been too largely unaware. And as American Christians we desire to preserve our democracy and to defend our nation against external threats and to improve its reputation in the world. But these motives, important as they are, can hardly be primary among us; do not even the publicans [say] the same?

Christians must "march to the music of a different drummer." And even if we march, as is likely to happen in a civilization deeply informed by Christian influences whose sources it does not know—even if we march alongside those who hear only the drums of a changing world, moving toward the same social goals to which they are committed, we shall march under different orders, and with a passion that once sent the first Christians into arenas of death and ultimately to the heart of a tormented empire.

Christians, and especially Protestants, naturally turn to the Bible as their charter and constitution. But here we find no clear teaching about "race" in the modern sense of the term—that is, about race as a biologi-cal phenomenon that divides human beings physically into clearly distinct groups. The peoples of the Bible were obviously aware of group differences; there are innumerable references to nations, tribes, and tongues. Physical differences were often noted, but in themselves were seldom if ever the basis for discrimination.

The method most often employed to support either segregation or integration on biblical grounds is, of course, that of quoting or misquoting verses out of context. For example, those who believe that the Bible teaches the racial inferiority of the Negro often lean heavily on the "curse" placed on the son of Ham by his grandfather, Noah (who incidentally had just risen from a naked and drunken stupor)—"slave of slaves shall he be to his brothers." By strange feats of genealogy it is assumed that Ham was the forebear of the Africans; by stranger leaps in exposition, it comes to be assumed that it was God who cursed the descendants of Ham. The text clearly indicates that Noah pronounced the curse, not God, and also permits the inference that he had a hangover at the time.

On the other side of the argument is the perennial appeal to the well-known verse from the Book of Acts: "[God] hath made of one blood all nations of men for to dwell on all the face of the earth." This verse unquestionably proclaims the unity of mankind through God's creation, but the term "blood" is not to be understood in a racial sense. It signifies the principle and unity of life through God's creative act. The Revised Standard Version omits the term entirely. In any event, honesty would require that one should go on to include the remainder of the verse, which is often used by supporters of segregation: "having determined allotted periods and the boundaries of their habitation."

Many other examples of the effort to read racial ideas back into the Bible might be given. But "one little world shall fell" them, and that is that the very notion of "race," as it is commonly understood at the present time, is a modern idea, no more than three or four centuries old at the most.

The Bible contains incomparable teaching about human relations, of course, and race relations are only a particular (and probably temporary) aspect of human relations. Scriptural teaching is therefore by no means irrelevant to our modern race problems. For there in the Bible we learn that God created (and creates) all men in his own image. There we read, in the story of the Fall, that man in his pride rebels against this Creator, sets himself up as the judge of what is good, and fractures the unity of creation. Cain raises his hand against his brother, Abel, and Esau seeks to betray his brother, Jacob. At Babel man fractures the unity of creation again, again because in his own cunning he seeks to scale the ramparts of heaven, and he is reduced to a confusion of tongues. So, we are taught in the Scriptures, observes Liston Pope, "that human diversity, except between sexes, follows on the sin and fall of man, not from God's creation, except as God gave man the freedom and other conditions under which this could happen. By immediate inference, racial distinction and discrimination are man's fault, not God's design."

Through all the cosmic drama of biblical history there runs a mighty theme which rises at last to unbearable climax to show us what manner of people we are. God condescends to choose a people as his own, and to make with them a covenant to be their God.

There are no racial implications in this doctrine of the Chosen People: foreigners who become part of them are to be included in God's care, and "many nations" will emerge from those chosen. Marriage with foreign women is forbidden, but only lest defection from Israel's God result. What we would call racial intermarriage does not appear to be either prohibited or advocated as such in the Bible. Nor does the choice by God of a particular people give to them any privilege over other nations, in the long run, except that of having knowledge of the one true God. Indeed, Israel learns with difficulty in time that she must by her own suffering bring the other nations also to salvation.

Jesus of Nazareth comes as the fulfillment of the mission given to Israel. The central message of the gospel, later made even more specific by the eloquence of St. Paul, is that Jesus Christ, through his life on earth, his death for all men, and his resurrection as the hope of all men, has brought reconciliation between man and God and between man and man. Those who accept him as their Lord live in a new dimension in which love and unity reign, though still tainted by sin. This unity is not only spiritual; it pervades life in all its relationships and it seeks even to remake society.

Out of faith in the life, death, and resurrection of Jesus Christ came a new community composed of many peoples—men "from every nation under heaven" (fifteen are named in Acts 2) were present at Pentecost, generally considered to have been the beginning of the larger Christian community, the birthday of the church. Each was speaking his own tongue, but in a common bond of unity in Christ.

Through many tribulations this community swept out across the world, gathering up Greek and Jew, slave and free man, barbarian, Scythian, Roman, Egyptian, Asian, European, American, African. For nearly eighteen centuries the church knew little ethnic discrimination within its life. Not until white men began to overrun the world did this new division among men by races come to pass; not until the nineteenth century did elaborate justifications of it begin to appear, and these originated entirely outside the churches. At times in certain churches, still a small minority, found for the most part in the United States and the Union of South Africa, these pagan theories have largely supplanted the ancient Christian doctrines, and have perverted the life of the churches themselves, so that they use these theories to interpret even the Bible.

In this long perspective, embracing the centuries from the day of Creation to our own day of judgment, *who are we?* We say that we are the people of God, the new Israel, God's elect, a new chosen race. Are we? Were we, would we tolerate "the dividing wall of hostility" whose destruction was proclaimed by St. Paul 1,900 years ago? Can a church still call itself a church when it shows a partiality not shown by God?

Perhaps our greatest need, if we are once again to be the people of God, is that of knowing who God's people are, of recapturing a sense of God's church as it has been revealed in the Scriptures and through many centuries. In those terms, many of our churches may not deserve the name. They are social clubs maintained by the pride and prejudice of man. They are voluntary groups setting their own standards of membership, not descendants of the church that came from Pentecost, and ultimately from a cross.

It has been said—and rightly so—that "eleven o'clock on Sunday morning is the most segregated hour in the week." I am happy to say that on a district, state, and national level our brotherhood of Christian churches is almost completely integrated, and that such is true of the various councils of churches. But at the local level this same inclusiveness of the different races is sadly lacking. And it is at the level of the local church and community, where people must live and work and worship face-to-face, day after day, that the crucial test will come. At this level, the churches have lagged behind the Supreme Court as the conscience of the people on questions of race, and they have fallen far behind trade unions, factories, schools, department stores, athletic gatherings, and most other major areas of human association as far as achievement of integration in their own life is concerned. Instead of being out ahead of the slow-moving secular majorities, the church is too often trailing along behind. As Dr. Carlyle Marney, Southern Baptist minister from Charlotte, North Carolina, said at the ministers' breakfast at the Louisville assembly of our International Convention last October, the church is rarely out on the scrimmage line of life but wants to rush in after the touchdown and make the extra point!

We must face up to the fact that we have failed to establish brotherhood in the world because we have not yet succeeded in establishing it within our own country. And we have not succeeded in making brotherhood a reality in our own nation because we have failed to make it a reality within the church itself. We have failed to be the *church!*, the church as founded by Jesus Christ, inviting and welcoming into its fellowship all who would accept Christ as their Lord and Savior, regardless of race or color or nationality.

Now it's true, of course, that we don't explicitly bar Negroes from membership in our congregation. And the elders of this church, and, I believe, most of our congregation, are fully aware that if a Negro should come forward in this sanctuary and present himself for membership we would have no alternative but to accept him. But why doesn't this happen? Certainly not because we have no Negroes in College Hill, for we have. I suggest it is primarily because they are afraid that they would not be welcome. And so I suggest that we let them know that they *are* welcome! It isn't enough just to sit back on the sidelines and wait. Jesus commanded those who would be his disciples to *go out into the world* and make disciples of all who would confess him Lord.

Now, my friends, I realize that this is not an easy step for us to take, not even for me who was born and reared in the North. It isn't *easy*, but if we are to be the Church of Jesus Christ, if we are to follow him and not ourselves, it is *necessary*! Christian behavior has nothing to do with what we *want* to do, or are *ready* to do, or what does not violate the local mores. Christian behavior has only to do with the uncompromising demands of Almighty God as revealed through the life and teaching of Jesus Christ.

As Carlyle Marney put it to us ministers at Louisville, "The commitment, call, and claim on us in our time do not come from the Communist party . . . or the Supreme Court . . . or the Constitution, or the NAACP, or any one of (the 'thousand-and-one') chartered do-good orders in America. Our charter, claim, and call come from Jesus as the Christ." And that call is to create the "Blessed Community," a new fellowship that is based not on kinship of race or class, but on kinship "in Christ" in whom there is neither Jew nor Greek, slave nor free, white nor black, for all are one. Will you do it, not because it is easy, for it isn't, but because it is God's will?

§24 William B. Selah

Reverend William Bryan Selah was born February 17, 1896, in Sedalia, Missouri. His mother died five weeks after giving birth to twins. Bill Selah was raised by a Mrs. Selah and her daughter Miss Selah, the nurse who assisted the birth and looked after his mother until her death. While the Selahs moved to Kansas City, Missouri, Bill's twin sister, Almeda, was raised in Parsons, Kansas, by a Mr. and Mrs. Jacobs. Initially, Bill intended to study law and pursued that study for a year at Kansas City School of Law. But while attending Central Methodist Church, Selah came under the influence of Rev. Edwin Dubose, who encouraged him to undertake a liberal, rational approach to religion. Selah received his B.A. at Central Methodist College in Fayette, Missouri, in 1921. On September 12, 1922, he married Naomi May Willis in Independence, Missouri, and the couple would have three children. From 1922 to 1924, Selah pursued advanced training at Yale Divinity School. Central College conferred on W. B. Selah an honorary doctor of divinity degree in 1934. Selah's clerical career began with his trial ordination with the Southwest Missouri Conference in 1921. He was ordained as a deacon in 1922, and as an elder in 1924. His full connection with the conference came in 1926. Selah held pastorates in Paris (1921–1923), Clinton (1924–1927), Fayette (1927–1932), and Central Methodist Church (Kansas City, 1932–1937), all Missouri congregations. He pastored St. John's Methodist Church in Memphis, Tennessee (1937–1941), and St. Luke's Methodist Church in Oklahoma City (1941–1945). From 1945 to 1963, Dr. Selah was senior minister at Galloway Memorial Methodist Church in Jackson, Mississippi, the state's largest and most influential Methodist church. During his tenure there, Selah took a moderate position on integration, but in 1961 when his church board passed a resolution to turn away blacks who came to worship, Selah vowed to resign if that day ever came. On June 9, 1963, five African Americans, including Jackson's Medgar Evers, were stopped outside his congregation when they tried to join the service. They crossed the street instead, where a Catholic church welcomed them. When associate minister Jerry Furr advised Selah of what had happened, Selah cut the service short and resigned that very day. "I know in conscience there can be no color bar in a Christian church," Selah stated upon resignation. Evers would be murdered three days later. Selah quickly left the state of Mississippi and took a position as vice president of his alma mater Central Methodist College, retiring a year later. Furr departed for Nevada. Galloway Memorial lost nearly half its membership in the wake of Selah's departure. Selah's successor, Dr. W. J. Cunningham, took the exact same stance. Those loyal to Selah's ideals started a new church, Christ Methodist, which eclipsed Galloway's stature and is still the most influential Methodist congregation in the state. Dr. Selah died in Huntsville, Alabama, on May 14, 1985, after twenty years of service and activism in the Monte Sano United Methodist Church in Huntsville, Alabama. His papers are housed at Millsaps College and the University of Mississippi.

Selah's November 11, 1961, sermon to Galloway parishioners focuses on the requirements of brotherhood. He begins with two assertions: God is the father of all humans; and all humans are our brothers. From these assumptions, he explains, we see that a single person may not approach God individually in prayer unless that individual is right with the brotherhood. Dr. Selah was famous for staking out analytical space for moderate stances, and this sermon is no exception. He outlines his position on how he would regard the Freedom Riders if they tried to attend the church. He does not specifically say, "Yankee go home," but that is the gist. While he sees no solution to barriers to brotherhood in civil disobedience, he also narrowly condemns the "color bar." There is no sin in wanting to be with one's own people, but absolute prohibitions of black visitors whose intent is to worship God are unacceptable in Christian circles. He ends the sermon with an elaborate pastiche of what Christian brotherhood looks like: Protestants, Catholics, and Jews must join hands against extremists such as Klansmen and Communists.

ৎৡ৵

Brotherhood
November 11, 1961
Galloway United Methodist Church, Jackson, Mississippi

Jesus said, "One is your Father [sic] and you are all brothers." According to Jesus, all men belong to the family of God and are therefore brothers. The doctrine of the Fatherhood of God and the brotherhood of man is fundamental in Christ's teaching. We cannot be right with God until we are right with our brothers; and all men are our brothers.

Prayer is a method of tuning in with God. But Jesus makes it clear that we cannot reach God in prayer if we have wronged a brother. He said to the worshipers of his day, "If when you bring your gift to the altar, you remember that your brother has taught against you; go first and be reconciled with your brother and then come and offer your gift." Coleridge caught the spirit of Christian prayer when he said:

He prayeth best who loveth best
    All things both great and small;
For the dear God who loveth us,
    He made and loveth all.

Jesus taught us when we pray to say "Our Father"—not my Father. Do I have a right to ask God to bless me or do something for me that I am not willing that he should do for every human being?

Jesus makes it clear that we will be judged not by our theological opinions but by the way we treat men, not by our creeds but by our deeds. Jesus identifies himself with every man, and says, "Inasmuch as ye did it unto the least of these my brethren ye did it unto me." God is concerned with the way we treat his other children.

Now, in the light of this central teaching of Christianity that God cares how we treat other people, let us look for a moment at our race relationships.

For sixteen years I have preached from this pulpit the law of Christian love. This law means that we must seek for all men, black and white, the same justice, the same rights, and the same opportunities to find the abundant life that we seek for ourselves. Nothing less than this is Christian love. To discriminate against a man because of his color is contrary to the will of God. Forced segregation is wrong. We should treat men not on the basis of color but on the basis of conduct.

At a meeting of the official board of this church in June 1961, the question was discussed about how to handle the Freedom Riders if they came to the church. During the discussion I made a statement and asked that it be made a matter of public record. Here is the essence of that statement.

Only in an atmosphere of goodwill can we hope to reach a peaceful solution of the race problem. I would say to the Freedom Riders that their coming here had not increased interracial goodwill or helped in the solution of the race problem. My advice to them would be to go home and let the southern people, black and white, solve this problem by orderly and constitutional means.

Let me nail down this Christian principle—there can be no color bar in a Christian church. It is not sinful for white people to prefer to worship with white people or for colored people to prefer to worship with colored people. The sin comes when a church seeks to erect a color bar before the cross of Christ. As Christians, we cannot say to anyone, "You cannot come into the house of God." But we can raise the question, Do you come to demonstrate or to worship? There can be no color bar to keep sincere worshippers out.

Neither the General Conference, nor the Annual Conference, nor the Council of Bishops, nor the preacher, nor the official board of the local church can put up a color bar in the church. That matter is determined by the nature of Christianity. The house of God is a house of prayer for all people—black and white.

There is nothing in the regulations of the church to bar colored people from membership. When a person seeks membership, he is not asked about the color of his skin. He is asked about his faith in God as revealed in Christ, and he is asked to promise to support and to attend the church. Salvation is not by color but by faith.

Since, as a matter of Christian principle, colored people cannot be barred either from worshipping here or from membership, what would I do in the present tense situation if a colored person applied for membership? I would have to tell him that he would feel more comfortable with his own people and that it was his duty to join a Negro church and help it.

What should a white church do in a community that contains only a few Negro families, not enough to support a church of their own? The white people would invite the Negro people to come in with them.

Negroes are not apt to seek membership in white churches. The Negro preachers in Jackson tell me that their people do not want to intermingle with the whites but that they do resent the color bars. As someone has said, "Take the dare out of it and ninety percent of the problem is solved." There can be no color bar in a Christian institution. Racial bigotry is a denial of Christian brotherhood.

Religious bigotry is a denial of brotherhood. I do not minimize the differences between Catholicism and Protestantism. I respect Roman Catholics and honor their right to hold and propagate their faith. But I could not be a Catholic. I do not believe that the pope is infallible even when he speaks ex cathedra on matters of religion and morals. No man is infallible. No institution is infallible. Only God is infallible. I do not believe that public money should go to the support of Catholic schools or the schools of any denomination. I disagree with the Catholic interpretation of the sacrament of the Lord's Supper. I dislike the Catholic attitude that it is the only true church, the only authorized agent of Christ on earth. I do not believe that the Catholic Church or any church has a monopoly on truth. The truth of God—and all truth is of God—belongs to any man who finds and follows it. I believe in the separation of church and state and in religious liberty.

I do not minimize the difference between these churches. But I think that in a world where every spiritual interpretation of life is denied by the Communists and other materialists we would be wise to stress the things we have in common. After all, the things we hold in common are more fundamental than the things that divide us. Let us look at some of the things we have in common. We worship the same God. "One is your Father and ye are all brethren." "What doth the Lord require of thee but to do justly, to love mercy and work humbly." "I perceive that God is no respecter of persons; but in every nation he that feareth Him, and worketh righteousness is acceptable with him." These things are taught in all the churches.

Jesus Christ is Savior and Lord. He is "the Christ, the Son of the living God." In him God has revealed his purpose and his love. Catholics and Protestants agree on that. Our Jewish friends revere Jesus as a great teacher and prophet but not as the Son of God.

Man is a child of God. "Now are we sons of God." The dignity and worth of human personality in the sight of God is a proposition held by Jews and Christians alike. Good religion stands before every social order with one pointed question: What are you doing to God's children?

The moral law, woven by the Eternal into the fabric of life long before it was given verbal expression, is recognized as the will of God by both Jews and Christians. "Thou shalt not steal, thou shalt not commit adultery, etc., thou shalt love thy neighbor as thyself. Do unto others as ye would that others do unto you." All these rules for living are expressions of that great moral order in which we live and they are accepted as such by Jews and Catholics and Protestants.

Like the islands of the sea, which display many surface differences but basically are united in the floor of the ocean, so the churches have their surface differences, but basically they are united in reverence for God and human personality and in acknowledgment of His moral law.

In 1787 the Constitutional Convention, composed of representatives from the thirteen colonies, met in Philadelphia to form "a more perfect union." At one time in the proceedings it seemed that, due to colonial jealousies, the convention would fail. At this point Benjamin Franklin reminded the delegates that the predatory powers of Europe stood ready and eager to seize them, colony by colony. "Gentlemen," he said, "we must hang together or we will hang separately." It was good advice and fortunately for us it was heeded.

Today, the churches—Jewish, Catholic, Protestant—are engaged in a life and death struggle with Communism. We had better hang together or we will hang separately. If the Communists win, our churches will be turned into museums, our leaders liquidated, and our children will be educated as atheists. The philosophy of Communism and the philosophy of Christianity are forever opposed. Communism denies God; Christianity affirms him. Communism says that man is a puppet of the state; Christianity says that man is a child of God. Communism claims that man's freedom and rights come from the state. The state gives and the state can take away. Christianity claims that "all men are endowed" not by the state but "by their creator with certain inalienable rights among which are life, liberty and the pursuit of happiness." The state does not confer these rights; neither can it take them away.

The methods used by the Communists to further their cause are diametrically opposed to the methods Christians may employ. (By their methods ye shall know them.) Falsehood and fraud, violence and intimidation—these are the methods of Communism. Reason and persuasion, goodwill and truth—these are the only methods Christians may use. Because Communism and Christianity are incompatible in philosophy and in method of operation, every great church has publicly declared itself opposed to Communism.

Now, in view of the Communist threat, the churches—Jewish, Catholic, Protestant—would better hang together or they will hang separately. We cannot afford the luxury of unholy contention and bigotry. Bigotry weakens a nation by dividing it into contentious groups. It sets sect against sect and thus plays into the hands of the men in the Kremlin. They certainly will rejoice if Catholics and Protestants and Jews are at each others' throats.

Brotherhood strengthens a nation. It teaches a man to say to his neighbor who belongs to a different church, I don't agree with your theology but I will defend your right to hold it. I find your form of worship uncongenial, but I will defend your right to worship God as you see fit. We serve the same God. We pray for the coming of the reign of righteousness on earth. We hold to the same moral standards. So let us have done with pettiness and bickering. Let us stand shoulder to shoulder against the forces of paganism and bigotry, and work together to make America strong, remembering that strife among us causes the Communist to rejoice while cooperation among us fills them with dismay.

But do I hear you say that you are out to beat the Catholics? But how will you do it? You cannot do it by the methods of bigotry, slander, vilification, hate, persecution. In 1924 I lived in Clinton, Missouri. Out of the darkness came the Ku Klux Klan, claiming to be 100 percent American. "They trusted in themselves that they were righteous and despised others" who sought to live in love and charity with all their neighbors. They gathered in pastures at night and sang hymns around a fiery cross. The saddest spectacle under the stars is a group of men singing Christian songs around a cross while they engender hatred. One day I met the Catholic priest and said to him, "Father, the Klan is going to put you out of business." He grinned at me and replied, "Don't worry about me. Before the Klan came I had difficulty getting my people to church and getting them to support the program. Now they all come and the treasury is full." The Klan's bigotry did not stop those Catholics; it only caused them to rally to the support of their church.

Do you want to see Protestantism triumphant? The only decent and effective way to do it is to make Protestantism strong; to give the world a better interpretation of the meaning of religion; to display a finer form of loyalty and reverence; to do more for the widow and the orphan; to live a more Christ-like life; to be more brotherly. In the long run bigotry fails; love wins.

But, someone says, Catholics are narrow and bigoted. But it is not fair to say that all Catholics are narrow. Officially, I suppose, the Catholic Church does not recognize our churches as churches, and that attitude smacks of bigotry. But it will do no good to fight bigotry with bigotry. We have been told that we must fight fire with fire, bigotry with bigotry. Must we? When we fight fire with fire the only result is a bigger conflagration. When we meet bigotry with bigotry the result is the crucifixion of Christian love and a weakening of the nation. One thing is certain—bigotry does not pay. It curdles the milk of human kindness. It destroys the goodwill without which a good community spirit is impossible. It blinds men to the glory of God and the beauty of brotherhood. It robs the bigot himself of peace; for prejudice and the peace of God cannot dwell together in the same heart. And what is more, in the present struggle for the survival of spiritual values, it plays into the hands of the dictators.

Bigotry is a threat to freedom. We teach our children to repeat the Pledge of Allegiance. "I pledge allegiance to the flag—with liberty and justice for all." "For all"—that means for black and white, Jew and Gentile, for those who agree with us and those who do not. Only as we grant freedom to those who disagree with us can we hope to preserve our own freedom. When we seek by harassment or intimidation to silence our opponents, we imperil our own liberty. Moreover, men who have faith in their own news are not afraid of opposition. They know that when truth and falsehood are given a fair field, truth will finally prevail because God is with it.

> Truth crushed to earth will rise again,
>   The eternal years of God are hers;
> But error, wounded, writhes in pain
>   And dies among her worshipers.

Even the bigot must be allowed to speak his mind. He may win a temporary following, but sooner or later men will turn away from him in disgust and disillusionment. For most men want the truth, and they will not be content forever with falsehood. They know that only the truth can make them free.

Recently some bigot bombed a Jewish synagogue. Do we not realize that when that Jewish church was blasted your church and mine were threatened? For the blind hate that strikes one church would destroy every organization dedicated to justice and brotherhood.

A mob lynched a man. It does not matter whether he was black or white. That mob did more than kill a man; it struck at the foundation of law and order. It struck at every man's liberty; for there can be no liberty apart from obedience to law. As Thomas Jefferson said, "Obedience to law is liberty." That mob was the incarnation of bigotry.

Bigotry weakens our nation by dividing it into hostile groups. It sets race against race, church against church, section against section. This makes it easier for the Communists to do their diabolical work.

Brotherhood strengthens our nation. It creates an atmosphere in which men who differ in color and creed can work together to make America great.

America! America! God shed His grace on thee,
And crown thy good with brotherhood
From sea to shining sea.

1962

1962

§25 William Sloane Coffin Jr.

William Sloane Coffin Jr. was born on June 1, 1924, in New York City to a prominent manufacturing and ministerial family. Attending both private and public schools and following the death of his father in 1933, Coffin aspired to be a concert pianist. After graduating from Phillips Academy in 1942, and a year matriculating at Yale University, Sloane joined the Army and rose to the rank of captain by the time of his discharge in 1947. Upon completing his Yale degree in 1949, Coffin joined the CIA, where he worked in counter-Soviet espionage during the Korean War. Back in the United States, Coffin completed a bachelor of divinity degree at Yale in 1956; two years later he was hired by his alma mater as chaplain, a position he would hold for seventeen years, and from which the nation would come to know this activist member of the clergy. Influenced by theologian Reinhold Niebuhr, Coffin's public civil rights activism dates to an arrest in May 1961: as a participant in the Freedom Rides, an effort to integrate interstate transportation facilities in the Deep South, Coffin was arrested in Montgomery, Alabama. More than two years later, Coffin was instrumental in recruiting white Yale undergraduates to participate in the Mississippi Freedom Vote, a three-week campaign to stage a parallel "mock" election in which the state's disenfranchised blacks were encouraged to vote. The enormous success of that campaign—80,000 black Mississippians cast ballots—encouraged leaders in the Council of Federated Organizations (COFO) to stage Mississippi's Freedom Summer seven months later; the Freedom Vote also engendered creation of the Mississippi Freedom Democratic Party (MFDP). After leaving

Yale in 1975, Coffin became senior pastor at the iconic Riverside Church in Manhattan, where he continued his public campaigns against militarism, poverty, and church-sponsored homophobia. Never long out of the crucible of social justice campaigns, Coffin died at his home in Strafford, Vermont, on April 12, 2006. He is survived by his third wife, Randy Wilson Coffin, and two children. His papers are housed at Yale University.

Coffin's radio address examines four subjects: the dignity of man, the locus of prejudice, the church's attitude toward violence, and the role of the minister. Man's dignity is premised on the fact that God doesn't employ a "graded scale of worth," and per Paul's teaching, though many we are also one in the Body of Christ. As such, Coffin redefines common classifications such that "Negroes aren't even Negroes"—at least not in God's eyes. Borrowing from psychology and philosophy, Coffin argues that we are born with a self that can love and hate, but fundamentally sees itself at the center of the world. Only a "disturbing voice" typified in the teachings of Christ can combat the prejudices of self. But that voice will also "invite violence," and much as Christ's voice led to his crucifixion, proponents of nonviolence will also have to sacrifice to call attention to racial injustices. Employing antithesis throughout his address, Coffin at one point states, "For peace, . . . is never the absence of tension but the presence of justice." Martin Luther King Jr. would use almost the identical wording in his canonical 1963 "Letter from Birmingham Jail." Finally, Coffin urges his fellow clergy to embrace the prophetic role—even when it is often at loggerheads with the more quotidian priestly.

❧

The Prophetic Role
January 14, 1962
New Haven, Connecticut

The press has a universal and very strong predilection toward the sensational rather than the valuable. Therefore, I think we can be compassionate if occasionally our own newspaper seems to stress something controversial, rather than something which is perhaps less controversial, but worthy of discussion. I'm sure, in short, that no one is here tonight because any people might be controversial, but because the question is important and hopefully the discussion will be valuable. I do hope this will not mean that we will be anything less than frank; that would be very unfortunate. But I, for one, will try, although I don't always succeed, to heed the very wise advice given me, and a great many other people, by Dean Inge when he said, "Personalize your sympathies, depersonalize your antipathies." Now, I've lined out for myself what I'm afraid is much too tall an order, and I run the risk of being a little superficial, only touching on the high points of the various areas I'm going to have to cover in the thirty or so minutes which have been allotted to me. I want to say a word, first, about what the church means by "the dignity of man"; then a word about the locus of prejudice, and then a word about the church and its attitude toward the various structures of society and toward violence, and finally, if I may, just a word about the dilemma of every minister.

Now in the mouths of cynical politicians, those more interested in the vote than the voter, "dignity of man" is a hackneyed phrase, maudlin, senti-mental—sentimentality being that emotion which does not arise out of the truth, but which is poured on top. It is far more moving when it is used by humanists like Kreutsch or Erich Fromm, or any of the southern school of agrarians, people who are quite properly concerned with the dehumanizing consequences of totalitarianism and a mass technical civilization, conse-quences which are depicted in that trend in modern art which first distorted the human image, then broke it up, and then caused it to disappear alto-gether. But humanism, if it is atheistically motivated, always has a difficult time defining what it means by the "dignity of man." Camus, for instance, says man's love for man can be born of other things than an arithmetic com-putation of interests or a theoretical confidence in human nature. But he inevitably has a hard time defining just what these other things are.

At this particular point, I think, the Christian church is a little bit better off. What does it mean, then, by the "dignity of man"? Part of what is meant is, to me at least, beautifully symbolized in that famous picture of Michel-angelo on the Sistine Chapel ceiling, the picture of the Creation when God, you remember, comes down surrounded by cherubim, seraphim, and these marvelous swirling robes of glory and extends a finger to Adam lying there with an expectant look in his eye, but still lifeless until the finger of God touches him. Now here it is symbolized that the "dignity of man" is conferred upon man by God; bestowed upon man by God. Man does not achieve it; he receives it as a gift. When the church talks about man being made in the image of God, the glory belongs to God and only reflectively to man. It has been said that from a Christian point of view the value of man is analogous to the value of a piece of paper on which a precious signature has been written. In short, it is a fundamental, theological presupposition of the Christian church that it is not because we have value that we are loved by God, but because we are loved by God that we have value. This is the hardest presupposition for any of us ever to accept. It means we never have to prove ourselves, only express ourselves. But this means, as regards race relations, that there can be no graded scale of worth. Men cannot be said, for instance, to have value because of his self-awareness. This would put the mystic, in the eyes of God, ahead of the dullards. It cannot be said that man's worth derives from his rational capacities as much as intellectuals would like to believe so, because this would put an intellectual, again in the eyes of God, ahead of a worker. One cannot say that even knowledge of good and evil constitutes the worth of man because this would put a pathological liar outside the ken of God's love.

All these qualities are essential for a complete person, but in none of them, nor in all of them, does the value of man reside. I think the ministry of Jesus indicates that He was primarily concerned to discover the image of God, no matter how torn or how distorted or how faded the image, in every derelict, whore, prodigal, or profligate with whom he came in contact. There's a very nice story, I think, illustrating this point. In the sixteenth century an impoverished beggar was brought to an operating table of some doctors in Italy. And the doctors said in the Latin they were sure he would not understand, *Faciamus experimentum in anima vile* (Let's experiment on this vile fellow). And the beggar, who was actually an impoverished student later to become the world-renowned scholar Marc Antoine Muret, quite properly, from a Christian point of view, replied from the marble slab, *Animam vilem appalas pro qua Christus non dedignatus mort est* (You call vile one for whom Christ did not disdain to die). If Christ then died for all men indiscriminately, to discriminate against any man in terms of value is not only, in humanistic terms, an offense to the human spirit, but from a religious point of view it is blasphemy in the face of God.

Now let's take a closer look at this word "equality" when we say that all men are "equal," because the church is not, as the law, interested in equality of rights or equality of opportunity, but rather in equality of people. And the original sense of the word, if my scholarship is right at this point, equality didn't mean sameness, but it meant oneness. St. Paul has put this to the Christian church in his classic phrase, "For just as the body is one and has many members and all the members of the body, though many a one, so we though many, are one." In fact, I think it can be said that our very oneness in God from a Christian point of view allows for all these dissimilarities of individuals, because when all hearts are one, nothing else has to be one. So the second point that I'd like to stress under the category of the "dignity of man" is that from a Christian point of view, God is not only Father of Man but father of each man, again as depicted in the picture of Michelangelo. Man is never, then, from a Christian point of view a holiday statistic when he dies or, more specifically, Negroes are never a labor commodity, or a housing problem, or a category of crime, illiteracy, or immorality. In fact, Negroes aren't even Negroes. For each Negro, as each white, each red, or each yellow, is absolutely unprecedented, irrepeatable, and irreplaceable. Now then, to sum up this presupposition: if God loves, as seen in the life of Christ, all men indiscriminately and each man as if he were all men, and if, as Christians, we are followers of Christ, then a perfectly impossible requirement has been laid upon all of us. Christianity has not been tried and failed; it has very rarely ever been tried. For as Christians we're not required just to be just. Justice can make Negro and white sit in the same place in the same bus, but it cannot make them want to be together. As Christians, it is not enough for us to be tolerant—because tolerance is really controlled antagonism—it's an armistice, not a peace. As Christians we are called upon to love, with the same type of love that God has shown for each man in the life of Christ. Very simply put, it means that we are asked to recognize that the brotherhood of man, in fact, exists. If you want to talk about reality, living realistically, you have to talk about the brotherhood of man as an actual fact. We as Christians are not called upon to create the brotherhood of man, only to recognize it. And in as much as in us lies, to find, show it forth, in our lives.

Now, if this is the essential truth about human relationships, let us turn briefly to the existential truth. Men obviously do not live as brothers, even though in fact, in reality, they are brothers, and particularly when they belong to different races. Now the question of prejudice, I'm sure you know, and I would just like to have you know that I know, is a very complicated one. And I'm aware of the fact that I'm now about to oversimplify, but I think it can be said that there are ultimately two basic schools of thought regarding prejudice. One of them has received a rather classic expression in the song, "You've got to be taught to hate and fear / you've got to be taught from year to year / you have to have it drummed in your tender little ears / you've got to be carefully taught." Now, according to this school of thought, prejudice is not natural; it is artificial. It is not cohesive, but adhesive to the human personality. As Kyle Hazelden says, and I would like to say that I'm very much indebted to him for a great many of my own remarks tonight, according to this school of thought, "Prejudice is a stain on the garments of personality which a man acquires when he brushes up against the social order." Prejudice from this point of view is not a cause but a result, which in turn becomes a cause, and thereby a self-perpetuating system is set up. Carey McWilliams says, "Race relations are not based on prejudice. Prejudice is a by-product of race relations as influenced by other factors." By other factors he may mean economic factors: the invention of our great New Haven inventor, Eli Whitney. Or he may mean historical factors, the War between the States, in which, as Lillian Smith says, the moral arguments of the North were oh so right and the motives of the North were oh so selfish. That could be called, perhaps, a psychological reason. And there is a psychological explanation of this same point of view. Once you degrade somebody, the sense of guilt makes it imperative to justify the entire procedure. So the only defense left is to hate the object. We also have to, in all candor, and with great shame, put in religious reasons. For very early in the game, particularly in the southern church, manners and morals got hopelessly confused, and the manners, which debase the Negro, won out over the morals, which should have elevated him. Religion is, as Marx says, very often the "opiate of the people"—there's no question about it.

Now, while much can be said from this point of view and, as I said, I have oversimplified it, nevertheless from a Christian point of view it is based on a faulty presupposition: namely, that a man is essentially a social thing, a sort of nothingness which is nurtured by society into a somethingness and can be explained essentially by social facts. Now from a Christian point of view this presupposition is wrong. And not only from a Christian point of view but also I think it would be fair to say from a Nietzschean point of view, and certainly from a Freudian point of view, because from the point of view of these people man is born with a self that has a capacity to love and a proclivity to hate. Children are not born prejudiced in a racial sense, but are born hostile with a sort of undifferentiated hostility which society then gives form and substance to. In other words, from a Christian point of view, society does provide the ground, the soil, in which the seed can germinate and grow. But the seed is already within the person. Therefore, Christians cannot charge the evil of prejudice to corrupt society. Prejudice is most fundamental[ly] an expression of man's inherent, his constitutional self-centeredness. I think there's an excellent statement of this in the beginning of Toynbee's book *An Historian's View of Religion*, when he says that every living creature is striving to make itself into the center of the universe, and in the act is entering into rivalry with every other living creature. Self-centeredness is thus a necessity of life but this necessity is also a sin. Self-centeredness is also an intellectual error, because no living creature is in truth the center of the universe, and it is also a moral error, because no living creature has a right to act as if he were the center of the universe.

Now if this is the case, then the church, if it is to get to the heart of the matter whether in terms of the requirement placed on every Christian or in terms of the obstacles, which prevent every Christian from fulfilling the requirements, must get to the heart of every man. The primary concern of the church is not with social structures, nor with political parties, or any other type of social or economic or political organization; its primary concern is with the heart of every man. Now, of course, to speak to the heart of every man it needs a voice, and because the "pretender" is seated so firmly on the throne in the heart, it needs a disturbing voice. The Bible makes this very clear. Mark Twain once was asked, "Do you believe everything in the Bible?" And he said, "Certainly not, but it's the things that I do understand that are hardest of all." In terms of the Old Testament, Moses didn't wait around for Pharaoh's hard heart to soften; he went down to Pharaoh and he said, "Let my people go!" And Amos wasn't shy about leaving Israel and going up into Judah and prophesying there. Jonah went all the way to Nineveh in order to say, "Thus, saith the Lord." And in the New Testament, this sentimental picture of the gentleman from Galilee, Hofmann's Christ, for instance, is one of the worst distortions of Christianity that exists. The voice of Jesus clearly illustrated this classic statement, "God must afflict the comfortable in order to comfort the afflicted."

Although there was an unending wellspring of love behind his voice, this love in no way blunted the truth of what he said. And what he said, of course, was so disturbing that he was crucified. The cross simply foreshadows the ease with which piety and religiosity, the church and the state, have always tried to cope with a disturbing God. In another context, we might also discuss the way rationalism and cynicism try and cope with a disturbing God in much the same way. However, I do think it's right to go on to point out that Jesus did not direct his voice exclusively to the heart of every man, but challenged the unjust people who were governing the society in which he lived—both the perpetrators and the victims of injustice—which, of course, was why he was crucified. If he hadn't bothered with people in high places, they would have left him alone. I think in this case, he was simply being consistent. I think we can ask ourselves, is it not contradictory for a Christian to show compassion to a Negro as an individual without at the same time being concerned with the structures of society which makes him an object of compassion?

Here, let me just read a brief statement again from Kyle Hazelden, who is dealing with the situation particularly in the South: "The social system becomes as amoral, insensitive, and non-rational about human welfare as was the coming of the atomic bomb. Being indifferent to human values, it yet provides the ground for ignorant and prejudiced judges. It crowds the Negro into shack and ghetto and rebukes him for being unclean. It deprives him of the instruments of elemental hygiene and counts his vulnerability to tuberculosis as evidence of his inferiority. It hinders his access to the polls and offers a scarcity of registered Negro voters as evidence of political indifference. It builds on the soul of the suppressed Negro intolerable pressures of bitterness and rebellion and indicts him as exceptionally criminal. It obstructs the training of his mind and offers tests and surveys to prove that he is not the intellectual equal of the white man. It prohibits Negro children from municipal parks, playgrounds, swimming pools, libraries, and tennis courts, and complains that Negro children are always getting into trouble. It holds the Negro to menial jobs, prevents his being upgraded, pays him unequal wages for equal work, and condemns him as lazy, listless, and lacking in ambition. Thus the social system itself becomes the soil and climate in which racial prejudice has wild and luxurious growth, and drops at the end of each season a rich yield of seeds for the next crop of racial discrimination."

Here we see the enormous amount of truth in that first account of prejudice, which sees prejudice as a result, rather than as a cause. This leads me to the conclusion that while it is true that you cannot legislate morality, you can legislate conditions which are more conducive to morality. It is precisely because we are so prone to evil that we need the support of a good legal, political, and economic structure. I think Paul Tillich has probably put this in a most succinct way when he says, "Since the law cannot be wholly internalized in the conscience of imperfect man, conscience must be internalized into law." The law then does play a moral role, and, as such, the church must be concerned with it. And, as Hazelden points out, the procedure, of course, is to elevate the people to the level of the law, rather than lower the law to the level of the people. It is better to have laws which exceed the generosities of the people than to legalize by omission injustices which violate the rights and dignities of man. Here, of course, I've been talking about the higher role of law. Some of you may feel that it's too Calvinistic in its optimism, for Calvin was very optimistic about the moral possibilities of law. Perhaps we could at least agree on a more basic, lower role of law: the law is not around to make bad men good, but to make innocent men safe. It is not to create morality, but to prevent immorality. As Martin Luther King says, "You can't make them love us, but you can stop them from lynching us." Now if you do try to prevent them from lynching Negroes, if you try to prevent men from segregating buses and parks and libraries and theaters and all the other public utilities, you are, of course, going to disturb the peace. Let's put it more strongly—you're going to invite, I don't say incite, I say invite, violence.

Here I would say that we Yankees are really lacking in compassion if we don't understand why it is that this type of violence takes place in the South. And if I can share what has been a wonderful experience for me I would suggest that for this type of understanding you read Lillian Smith's *Killers of the Dream*. Here she talks about the mesh of feeling and memory, which is called loyalty to a southerner. "We know guilt without understanding it, and there is no tie that binds men closer to the past and each other than that. Our umbilical cord is now being cut, and we southerners had identified with a long sorrowful past on such deep levels of love and guilt and hate that we did not know how to break old bonds without pulling our whole lives down. Change is the evil word. A shrill clanking that makes us know too well our servitude. Change means leaving one's memory, one's sins, one's ambivalent pleasures at the room where one was born." There are so many things which just prevent the moderate from being able to see his way straight. And, of course, it has to be remembered that for the bigoted, the really bigoted person, prejudice is like alcohol to the alcoholic. It is no longer a problem; it is a solution. And he's not going to listen to any man who tries to take the whole solution of his life away from him. It is naïve to say that you can educate men out of this when their lives are not motivated by love of the truth, but by hate of the truth. Therefore, I come back to the point that if you do prevent them from segregating, you are going to disturb the peace.

Now what does the church have to say about this? I think if you look at the life of Jesus, you have to recognize that he was perhaps the chief disturber of the peace. For peace, from a Christian point of view, is never the absence of tension but the presence of justice. And as outlined earlier, Christian love always lies beyond, and not on this side of justice. Now to disturb the peace, no matter how phony or immoral the peace may be, will, of course, have bad consequences. One of the first consequences is that the races are going to be separated. I think what we see today is the old separate but equal concept giving away to an equal but separate concept. Never before in most places in the country, but particularly in the South, have the races been more separate. Now it is a Christian responsibility to minimize those losses, and there are certain policies which seem to represent more responsibility on the part of Christians. I would suggest that the nonviolent fighters are fighting not men, but fighting a past that has denied them freedom and responsibility. They're fighting it in such a way that the aftermath will be at least less evil than as if they had espoused open violence. Personally, I think that it's quite in keeping with the life of Christ to offer one's self up—if not directly to be crucified—as a sort of sacrifice in order to call people's attention to this type of injustice. (Don't forget the fifty-seven stitches in the face of old Farmer, the first man who was beaten up in Montgomery). I think it is exactly why Socrates took the cup, why Nathan Hale said, "Yes, you can shoot me," and why Jesus went to the cross. I think if we're going to take seriously the responsibilities of a Christian we have to be quite impressed with the seriousness with which these people work out the most responsible course of action in the given situation.

Now my time is up. Let me just close now with a word on the dilemma of a minister. Traditionally, every minister is given two roles: classically they are called the priestly and the prophetic role. The priestly role is to administer the sacraments, to baptize, to bury, to heal when possible, to counsel people in all types of situations. The prophetic role is the role of the disturber of the peace; to bring the minister himself, to bring the congregation, to bring the entire Christian church, to bring the entire social order under some type of judgment. It is a very necessary role for the church to perform. It is precisely because of its understanding of this role that the Soviet Union will not allow the Christian church its full play in Russia because Communists understand much better than we Christians do, very often, that the cross is higher than the flag. Now you can appreciate that if one plays a prophetic role it's going to mitigate against his priestly role. There are going to be those who will hate him, not only disagree with him, but violently hate him, perhaps for good reasons and perhaps, also, for bad reasons. Every minister, therefore, finds himself in the difficult situation where he tries to balance in some responsible way his priestly responsibilities and his prophetic ones. I think that the church by and large in our country has been remiss in its prophetic role. And it was precisely when the voice of the church was silent and withdrawn that Jim Crowism established itself in this country. Therefore, if we are to err today perhaps we should err on the compensatory side, on the side of the prophetic role. And personally I think that it is very, very dangerous philosophy or theology to try to improve on Jesus. We cannot forget that it was his prophetic role that ended his priestly role at the age of thirty-three.

As ministers we have to try and be responsive. For we cannot forget whom our model is, and we cannot forget that the requirements of Christian love are fantastically difficult. They must not be in any way distorted or perverted for some type of substitute, sentimental understanding of love. Our job is to try to make sure that the finger of God finally does reach the finger of outstretched man and that man comes alive only through that particular touch. As St. Paul said, "Even though I have all knowledge and all faith so that I can move mountains, if I have not love, I have nothing."

§26 Adam Daniel Beittel

Dr. Adam Daniel Beittel was born on December 19, 1898, in Lancaster, Pennsylvania. The youngest of five children, Beittel's parents, Jeanne Chesser and William Henry Beittel, owned a dry goods store and their children worked there growing up. Young Beittel was nicknamed "Spib" by his Lancaster classmates, and what he lacked in physical stature, he more than made up for in intellect. Mathematically and musically inclined, Spib was also an esteemed debater and orator in the Red and Black Literary Society. After graduating as his high school valedictorian, Beittel headed west to Findlay College in west-central Ohio, where he studied religion. Upon completing his studies in 1922, Beittel pursued a master's degree at racially progressive Oberlin College. He married Ruth Stoner Fox in 1924, and the couple would have two children. After Oberlin, he earned a bachelor's and a doctoral degree in divinity from the University of Chicago. His dissertation, completed in 1929, focused on the rise of the Virgin Birth tradition. Instead of immediately pursuing a career in academia, Beittel was ordained by the United Church of Christ. His first congregation took him to the frontier, to Big Timber, Montana; he later served a church in Nashville after expressing his racially progressive views to his Spring Grove (today, Richmond), Indiana, congregants. Beittel began his academic career at Earlham College, a Quaker school in Indiana. He then moved south to Guilford College, where he served as dean and taught sociology. From 1945 to 1952, Beittel was president of Talladega College in Alabama, an historically black college founded with financial aid from the American Missionary Association in 1867. Beittel was forced out for his "ambiguous attitude" on the question of racial segregation; in other words, Beittel was not a believer in the racial status quo in Alabama. After an eight-year stint as dean of the chapel at Beloit College in Wisconsin, Beittel was named president of Tougaloo Southern Christian College in 1960. The Jackson, Mississippi-based historically black college quickly became central to the student movement then sweeping the state, and Dr. A. D. Beittel was right in the middle of it. Rather than discouraging Tougaloo students from participating, and unlike most of his HBCU president colleagues, Beittel actively supported their efforts at desegregating Mississippi's public facilities. His outspokenness and support for his students cost him his job four years later when he was forced out by Tougaloo's trustees—an action facilitated by the State Sovereignty Commission, who actively spied on the college and its progressive president. After leaving Tougaloo, Beittel served as director of the Mississippi program for the American Friends Service Committee, and he also was the chairman of the board of directors of the Child Development Group of Mississippi, who administered the state's Head Start program. Beittel eventually retired to northern California, where he died on July 26, 1988, just sixteen days before the death of his wife of nearly sixty-four years. Their two boys survived them.

In this address at the College of the Bible (today Lexington Theological Seminary), Beittel seeks to inform the gathering sponsored by the Disciples of Christ of the myriad problems faced by integration-seeking Mississippians. First, and in Jackson, whites and blacks cannot even share interracial news; the Hederman brothers see to it that blacks and whites remain estranged from each other. Similarly, William Simmons, head of the local White Citizens' Council, is not interested in truth, but in promulgating white supremacy. But the crux of Beittel's critique of interracial relations in Mississippi focuses on economics; that is, with the White Citizens' Council carefully monitoring race relations, economic pressure would be brought to bear on anyone getting out of his or her "place." Whether it is a potential tax on Tougaloo's property and assets, or the employment of the son of a member of the Mississippi Council on Human Relations, economic terrorism mitigated most civil rights work—even among the churches. Beittel does not hold back in his criticism of Catholics, Protestants, and Jews: they have been "deaf, dumb, and blind." Though he does not mention his name, Beittel singles out Jackson rabbi Perry Nussbaum. Though Nussbaum held a fine interdenominational luncheon, no blacks were invited to attend; his congregants simply wouldn't allow it for fear of retaliation. Beittel closes by suggesting that white Protestant ministers must lead in Mississippi, but that is not likely given the realities of white congregations mired in white supremacy and a culture of segregation.

⤜⤛

Race Relations in Mississippi
July 20, 1962
Lexington, Kentucky

I want to commend the College of the Bible for getting up this kind of consultation regarding a very real and important problem in this area of our country. I was in a conference called by the Commission on Civil Rights in Washington in May 1962. There were about a hundred important people there invited from over the country. It was opened by a brief address by the attorney general of the United States, who said, "The problem that we are dealing with is one of the most important international problems that the United States faces today. I just came back from a trip around the world, and almost every place I would stop the question of civil rights for American minorities was inevitably brought up. What you are dealing with here is not only a regional or national problem; it is a very important international problem."

One of the things that a meeting of this kind seems to offer to us and the thing which we miss so much in Mississippi is the opportunity for communication. In the city of Jackson at the present time, we have two daily newspapers, one morning, one evening, both owned by the same people who also own one of the two TV channels. The attitude of the editorial staff of these papers is not one designed to produce news about what is going on in Mississippi. Anything good about the Negroes in the Jackson area goes on the Negro page and is sent only to Negroes. Therefore, it is not known by the white community. It is exceedingly difficult to get factual information in this controversial area before most of the citizens of Jackson and many of the citizens of Mississippi. They get a very distorted picture.

I interviewed the president of the Citizens' Council of Jackson a few weeks ago. I had never met him before. I went to see him primarily because he had made a speech, and in this speech he had made some very serious misstatements concerning the Mississippi Council on Human Relations, which we have recently reorganized in the state of Mississippi. I found out that the paper had not distorted what he said because he had made the misstatements which were quoted in the newspaper. I said, "Well, these statements are not true." He said, "I don't think I shall necessarily believe that they're not true because you say they are not true." I said, "I would agree, I wouldn't expect you to. But I would expect you to be interested in the truth." But he showed no interest in that whatsoever. The point is that he said was useful for his purpose and he was perfectly willing to let it stand as it was because the truth might not be so useful. The point of view is that they know the answers, they proceed to [avoid] the answers, and they do not care to discuss the facts that may lie behind them.

I was born and reared in Pennsylvania. Most of the last thirty years I have been living in Tennessee, North Carolina, Alabama, and now Mississippi. Tougaloo Southern Christian College, which I have the privilege of representing, was founded by the American Missionary Association in 1869. The American Missionary Association at the close of the Civil War established literally hundreds of schools. Southern Christian Institute was founded by the Disciples in 1875, and it eventually developed a junior college. This junior college of the Southern Christian Institute and Tougaloo College were merged to form Tougaloo Southern Christian College in 1954.

Tougaloo has stood and does stand for a belief in integration in a highly segregated society. Segregation essentially is a way of behavior, the purpose of which is to maintain white supremacy. Segregation must be distinguished from the voluntary separation of a group. Segregation is enforced on one group by another in attempt to make a belief in the superiority of one group and the inferiority of another appear rational.

Two years ago we were persuaded to come back to Mississippi because we were told that things were about to happen there. And they have happened.

I think perhaps one of the most outstanding of these was the sit-in in the library by many of our students. We are an educational institution. We do not plan sit-ins. This sit-in was planned by our students without the guidance of the president or the dean of the college. At the time I was in Atlanta attending a meeting of the board of directors of the United Negro College Fund. I received a telephone call in the early afternoon saying, "Nine of your students are in jail." They went to jail because they visited the library and were told to leave and they did not leave. So they were arrested.

When I got back that night, I learned about the details, and in the morning I went to the jail to visit our students. The students came up for trial in a couple of days and were convicted of breach of the peace and given a sentence, a jail sentence and a fine. It was appealed, they put up bonds, and the nine were released. This was in March 1961. The present status of the case is the same. They are still out on bail. Their cases have never come up on appeal.

I think it was important because the general attitude of the state of Mississippi was, "Negroes in Mississippi are satisfied. They prefer segregation.

They like it this way." When some of the students sat in the library, it was evident that they did not prefer segregation. This was breaking the pattern that Mississippi Negroes were supposed to follow.

One after the other a whole series of events took place that same summer (1961). A great many Freedom Riders came to Jackson. The college for the most part did not have students or faculty who were involved in the Freedom Rides, but a good many of these Freedom Riders came to the campus. When an interracial group of people comes to Jackson and wants a place to sit down, they are very apt to come to Tougaloo. This is what they and a great many Freedom Riders did before they went to jail, and after they were released they visited us at Tougaloo.

In July 1961 a very distinguished group of religious leaders from all over the country came to Tougaloo. I received a telephone call from Dr. Charles S. McCoy of the Pacific School of Religion saying, "We are very much concerned about the number of people who have been going to jail in Jackson, the Freedom Riders. We think the church should be concerned about this matter. We have a group of religious leaders from over the country who would like to have a one-day conference in the Jackson area. May we meet at Tougaloo?" I said, "Of course you may meet at Tougaloo," and they came. It was a rather distinguished group of people—the dean of the Union Theological Seminary in New York was in the group, there were Jews, Roman Catholics, and Quakers, but for the most part they were Protestants. Some of them were preachers, but not all. They had a one-day conference, and at the close about half of the group made an appointment with the attorney general in Washington and went to the airport and took a plane to Washington. When the other half of the group went to the airport to get a cup of coffee, they went to jail.

I suppose we got more adverse criticism at the college in August 1961, when, after our summer school had closed, about two hundred Freedom Riders were brought back for arraignment on one day, Negro and white. The group wanted to stay together. About a hundred of them were accommodated on the Tougaloo campus. This was regarded as being extremely seditious, and we met a certain amount of opposition. All we did was to provide a place where the mixed group could spend a few hours together.

Then in September the Episcopal prayer pilgrimage came, twenty-eight Episcopal ministers who started out from New Orleans to their national gathering in Detroit. They were particularly concerned about laying the burden of this matter on the church. They spent a day at Tougaloo at a conference, a very devout group of men. There were two Episcopal ministers who came down from Birmingham, not because they were interested in the prayer pilgrimage but they were very much afraid the prayer pilgrimage would come to Birmingham. They were very well received by the group, and they did have a very interesting discussion with them. Later, fifteen of these Episcopal ministers went to jail, because they went to the bus station. These Episcopal pastors sent two men into the bus station to sit and read magazines, just to see what would happen. They saw fifteen men come in, all wearing clerical collars. They started down toward the restaurant in the bus station, but before they got there they were asked what they wanted. They said they wanted to get some food before they took a bus, and they were ordered immediately to get out. They did not get out, so they were arrested.

I was very much interested in the two men who saw all this. They came back immediately to the campus and reported to the rest of the group; they were, in our modern terms, "shook up." They said that it was difficult for them to realize that this could happen in the United States of America. For them to see fifteen of their brethren of the cloth rounded up by the police and put into the paddy wagon and taken to jail because they wanted a cup of coffee seemed to be something that they could not quite believe could happen in our country.

A little later in the fall of 1961, four of our students were arrested for attempting to picket the Negro fair. We have two fairs in Jackson. We have a white fair that lasts a week, and then what is left of it lasts over about three days the following week for Negroes. Well, these students, four of our very best, made some posters advising Negroes not to attend the Negro fair. As they neared the fairgrounds, the policemen apparently knew why they were coming. They had their posters under their arms, they weren't on display, but as soon as they got out of the car the posters were confiscated by the policemen. Then the students began to advise people not to go to the fair. Only a few minutes elapsed before the four of them were rounded up and taken to jail. They were not charged with breach of peace as hundreds of Freedom Riders had been charged; they were charged with obstruction of pedestrian traffic. It turned out to be a more serious offense than breach of peace because the fines and the jail sentences were greater.

I have been somewhat disillusioned with the manner in which the federal court operates in the state of Mississippi. In July 1961, I was in a federal court in Jackson on an injunction proceeding which had been asked for against the people who operated all the terminals in the city. This included the attorney general of the state and all the authorities who really had to do with promoting and promulgating and implementing segregation. There was a three-man panel of federal judges. The presiding judge was from Atlanta; the two other judges were from Mississippi. They met and immediately the state asked for a continuance of the case. They said the one man in the attorney general's department who usually prosecutes cases of this kind or defends the state if this case was brought against the state was ill. Therefore, they needed a continuance of this case. The NAACP attorney, Mrs. Motley, said she saw no reason for a continuance of the case; so the matter had to be decided by the panel of judges. The judges asked for an intermission. They went out and said they would be gone about five minutes. They came back after thirty minutes, and the presiding judge made a surprising statement. He said, "An injunction proceeding, Ladies and Gentlemen, is brought because there seems to be, on the part of the people who bring the injunction proceeding, an emergency. However, this is a little different from an ordinary case. When I sue a man for ten thousand dollars, if it is not tried now, it is tried later and I get interest on my money and I do not lose anything. An injunction is presumably to relieve an abuse; for this reason you do not postpone an injunction proceeding very easily." Besides that he said, "The attorney general's office had thirty days to prepare the case, which is longer than is usually granted an injunction proceeding, and so from my standpoint," said the presiding judge from Atlanta, "I see no reason for granting the state's request to postpone this case until a later time." But said he, "The case will be postponed." He said, "We are a panel of three, I have already expressed my opinion but I have been outvoted by the two Mississippi judges."

Very often I am asked whether the college has suffered a great deal of harassment because we have been accused of harboring Freedom Riders and welcoming to our campus interracial groups. We do have a completely integrated faculty. We have had some white students this year. The board of trustees has gone on record that we believe that integration should happen in Negro schools as well as in white schools. Have we suffered a great deal of harassment on this account?

I think surprisingly enough we haven't. I am not quite sure why. There have been certain subtle kinds of harassment but not nearly as much as one might expect. Even though we got a lot of publicity on TV and newspapers at the time that our students conducted a sit-in at the library, and were tried, there were no direct, outward, open acts of harassment that gave us serious trouble.

We have had some mistreatment by deputy sheriffs. We get along a little better with the city policemen than we do with the deputy sheriffs. They arrested one of our students last fall and abused him before they took him to jail and abused him after he was in jail, beat him up quite a little, with no provocation whatever. His parents, who lived in Jackson, paid a fine to get him out of jail in the morning. When I tried to find out from both the sheriff's office and the justice of the peace what the fine was paid for, nobody knew. All I know is that he was required to pay forty-five dollars to get out of jail.

I called those students in and got the whole story in a day or two. I suggested that if one were willing we would write this story up, and get it just as accurate as possible, then he could swear to it and we could turn it over to the local advisory committee of the Civil Rights Commission. That is the kind of thing they wanted to send to Washington to the Civil Rights Commission. He said, "I think that would be a good idea. I will be glad to cooperate." So I got the data from him and organized it for an affidavit and then called him back. I said, "Now I want you to go over this with me to be sure that this is exactly right. Then if it is accurate, we will have it written up in final form and you can make an affidavit to it and we will send it in to the advisory committee of the Civil Rights Commission." He said, "I think we had better not do this." I said, "Why not?" "Well," He said, "My mother works for the public schools in Jackson. Also, the father of one of the other boys that was in the car is employed by Jackson State College, and I think we had better not do it." Well, this is just an illustration of the kind of thing that happens all the time. Economic pressure is tremendously powerful.

This kind of pressure is resorted to very easily in Mississippi. A few months ago, a leading Episcopal rector in town, a very fine person, was criticized because he had permitted his church to be used for an interracial meeting. It was simply a downtown central place where different racial groups could meet together for a purely religious purpose. As the man in charge of the church, he should have been careful to see that this kind of meeting was not held there. He succeeded in winning that battle, and he is still there. But how long he will be there I do not know. This came out in a conversation I had with this rector in my office not long ago. He said that because of his wife he is not at all sure that he wants to stay on in Jackson and be under this pressure all the time.

Recently, we reorganized the Mississippi Council of Human Relations. The council had been in existence for a number of years before I went to Mississippi. Affiliated with the Southern Regional Council in Atlanta, it is an organization where people who want to improve conditions join together to talk and see what can be done.

The day before the reorganization, the Citizens' Council sent out a letter, including mimeographed copies of letters and of the enclosures in my letter. I will read you only their letter, dated May 2, 1962, "Special Memorandum to all members of Jackson Citizens' Council. This memorandum is to advise you of an important development concerning race relations in the Jackson area. Please note the enclosed photostatic copies, concerning the supposed reorganization of the Mississippi Council of Human Relations and the policies of this integrated group. You will note that several members of the planning committee are Jackson residents. As you may recall, the old Mississippi Council on Human Relations was thoroughly discredited during public hearings of the Louisiana joint legislative committee in Baton Rouge during March 1957. Undisputed testimony on three of these meetings showed 'Subversion and racial unrest' and disclosed that the Mississippi Council on Human Relations was affiliated with the notorious Southern Regional Council, which was financed by the Ford Fund for the Republic. Once the truth became known, the Mississippi Council on Human Relations dropped out of sight. Now as the enclosures show, an attempt is being made to reorganize it on the same basis, still connected with the Southern Regional Council. Obviously such a group would do nothing to improve race relations in Mississippi. It could serve only to create undesirable racial frictions since its primary purpose would be the undermining of our peacefully segregated social structure." Now here is the threat: "We are confident that members of the Jackson Citizens' Council will know how to deal with this threat to our community." It was signed by the president of the Mississippi Citizens' Council.

We went ahead with the meeting, but the intimidation worked. It had been agreed that a local, semiretired Methodist businessman in Jackson who was very much concerned about race relations as far as religion is concerned would be the chairman of the reorganized Mississippi Council. He just could not make any sense out of supporting segregation and have it fit in with what he believes Christianity means. We would have three vice-chairmen, one of whom was to be Bishop Brunini, who is the Catholic bishop in the area. One was to be Rabbi Mantinband, a Jewish rabbi from Hattiesburg. The third was to be a Negro college president from the northern part of the state. We had a regional distribution, a racial distribution, and a religious distribution.

Out of these four people, three of them have been intimidated to such an extent that they could not accept office in the organization. Mr. Hearn, the chairman, very reluctantly said, "Well, there has been such pressure brought on my son, who operates a filling station and automobile repair shop in Jackson, that he is scared to death that his business will simply be boycotted and he will be put out of business if I serve as chairman of this group." Rabbi Mantinband, who had been working with this kind of thing for years in Alabama before he came to Mississippi and had gotten by somehow with his congregation, had such pressure brought on his congregation that he said, "I will have to refuse to take office. I am just as much interested as ever and I want to continue showing my goodwill, but I cannot be your vice president." And this is true also of the Catholic bishop.

I say this kind of intimidation does work. If they carry out the threat that a member of the legislature made some months ago, it will work in the college, too. He threatened that when the legislature met this last year, he was going to present a bill removing us from any exemption from tax on real estate. We have five hundred acres of land, which is pretty good land, and we have several million dollars worth of buildings. If they put taxes on that the same as they tax profit-making business, we would have to close. We could not afford to pay the tax. But we pay plenty of taxes anyway in Mississippi. We have to pay sales tax on everything the college buys, and that amounts to a pretty big sum in a year. We do not pay real estate tax on our property.

In spite of all this and in spite of the attempts of the activities like this Jackson Citizens' Council, social changes are coming about in Mississippi. I mentioned that the segregation signs had been removed in the terminals—bus terminals, railroad terminals, and the air terminals. This is not saying that we are integrated, because we have a way in Mississippi of getting around the law in any way we can. They have solved the problem of the restaurant in the airport according to Harry Golden's vertical method. They have taken out all the chairs and tables so you can stand up now. A colored friend and I could go in together and get a cup of coffee and stand up at the counter. But no place to sit down.

We have had a lot of trouble in the past with buses in Jackson. The drivers of buses have insisted on Negroes going to the rear of the bus. I heard this story the other day: A Negro woman came into the bus and sat down just across from a white man. The white man did not get excited, but the bus driver did. He came back to the Negro woman and said, "Will you please move to the back of the bus?" She said, "I am perfectly satisfied with the seat I have." And she stayed. He became rather indignant, and as soon as he came to the next policeman he stopped his bus. He said to the policeman, "Will you please arrest this woman?" The policeman looked around and said, "I don't see any sign in your bus that says anybody has to sit in any particular place. I do not have any authority to arrest her." So the bus driver has to eat crow and start the bus with the woman sitting at the same spot and the white man sitting at the same spot. Now this is new in Jackson, Mississippi.

I have been very much interested in watching the developments in Jackson. They built a new stadium, and it was used first last fall. It was built by the city with city funds. When the first football games were held last fall, there were no Negroes admitted. Even though Negro taxes helped build it. But what I am interested in watching is, this thing will not pay unless you have postseason games, and to have postseason games you will have increasing trouble finding anybody to play with who may not have a Negro on the team.

Where has the church stood in the midst of all this controversy which I have outlined for you? On the side of the angels? Too often, I am afraid, the church has been deaf, dumb, and blind. It is not directly allied with the forces of reaction. When you were speaking about the churches opening their doors to human beings as human beings, I couldn't help think, I must admit, of a church in Jackson. One of our faculty members in Jackson was on the official board of the church. He was serving on the board of ushers not so long ago, and I asked him what he would do if a well-dressed Negro couple came to the door of the church. He said, "We are given written instructions. Our written instructions are that if a Negro person or couple came to the church, we would immediately meet them before they got inside and very politely say to them, 'We will provide you transportation to a Negro church in Jackson. We are sure you made a mistake by coming here.' So I said, "Suppose they said they did not make a mistake. After all, this church is air-conditioned, and we prefer an air-conditioned church. Besides it is a rather attractive church and we would like to hear this minister preach." "Well," he said, "we would still have to say it. We have official instructions what we shall do if a Negro comes, even though he is a member of our denomination and even though he may be a minister, he is to be taken over to the Negro church."

Well, too often this has been the attitude of the local church. I have talked with a good many of the leading ministers of Jackson. I suppose the most common attitude of these men is, "What we are doing is not right. This is not the way it ought to be done. This is not the Christian solution to this problem. But if I were to say on Sunday morning what I believe about this problem, I would be looking for a new job on Monday." Of course, I feel like saying, "Well, maybe you ought to be looking for a new job for the glory of God," but they don't see it that way.

This is not true of only one denomination. A half dozen denominations with good men; men who are concerned; men who wish they were able to speak out; but who say "under the circumstances in which we live here I cannot." The Jewish rabbi, the Catholic bishop, and the Protestant ministers are united in this.

I have been trying to find a place for the meeting of the next Mississippi Council on Human Relations. We should ask them again on the campus, but we feel, as the executive committee felt, that it would be much better if we could meet in a downtown church. One of the men on the executive committee was to interview the Methodists, and he talked with one of the leading Methodist ministers in town. "Well," he said, "I wish it were possible for you to meet in our church, but I just do not believe it is possible at the present time." My job was to talk to the Catholic bishop and the rabbi. They both said the same thing.

The rabbi had a very interesting institute at his synagogue last winter, one of these institutes which are set up primarily for Christian ministers to interpret Judaism to them. We had a really capable psychologist there. He gave two very interesting lectures. A discussion was followed with a luncheon. It was a well set-up affair. The rabbi asked for criticism. So I accepted his invitation. I told him I thought the speeches were good, the fellowship was good, even the meal was good. Also I thought it was a very fine thing to have this kind of gathering where we could meet together and discuss and talk together representing a variety of denominations. But I asked him, "Do you think anything would have happened if you had invited, maybe, three of four of the leading Negro ministers of this town who would have gotten a good deal out of this? After all, it's your synagogue, it does not belong to the Citizens' Council, it does not belong to the mayor of Jackson. Do you think anything would have happened if you had done that?" He did not even write me a letter; he called me up. He said, "I appreciate very much what you said about the meeting we had here, about the speaker, fellowship, and all that, but when it comes to inviting Negro ministers, I suppose the millennium will come some day but we are not there yet."

Now that puts it off a little bit. He is a fine person, he is a very intelligent man, and his own attitude is very good, but he does not think his congregation would stand it. It is also pretty bad if you cannot meet together as human beings in this city of Lexington. I am quite concerned that on the local level it is very difficult to have the church speak up. As a matter of fact, at one time the First Christian Church of Jackson spoke out. Their official board passed with one dissenting vote a resolution condemning Tougaloo

Southern Christian College because we had permitted Freedom Riders to come and spend some time on the campus. Some of you may have read the article in the *Saturday Evening Post* "Are Southern Ministers Failing the South?" which appeared over a year ago. The man who wrote the article was a southerner who believed that we should be hearing a prophetic voice of Christian religion from the pulpit.

I was at a meeting at a Catholic bishop's home a few months ago. He invited in a group of seventeen or eighteen men for dinner. There were two businessmen from Jackson, neither of whom are Catholic, there was the Jewish rabbi, and there was a faculty member from my campus. Also, there must have been about ten Catholic priests from various parts of the state of Mississippi, a couple of them colored, the rest white. In the course of our conversation we talked about what could be done to try to get some progress along this line in Jackson. One young priest said, "About the only group of people that I can think of in Jackson who ought to be able to speak out and be heard would be a group of Protestant ministers. We Catholics are too few; there is not enough of us to really make a dent in the community. I could name you a dozen leading Protestant ministers in this town; if they would get together and formulate a statement of what they believed this community ought to be doing in this matter, I think the community would pay attention to it." I think he was right.

There was not anybody in that meeting who thought the Protestant ministers would do it. I am a Christian minister, too, but I do not face the problem of holding a congregation together with a good many Citizens' Council members at the present time in Jackson. This is the problem faced by some of the Christian ministers. But if this problem is going to be solved with the leadership of organizations like the NAACP and CORE and the other nonviolent groups and the Christian church is going to follow along somewhere in the rear, then when the history of this period is written it will *not* be written with a very good story about the Christian church.

§27 Andrew Young

Andrew Jackson Young Jr. was born in New Orleans, March 12, 1932. He grew up in a middle-class family, the son of a black dentist (his namesake) and a Creole woman (Daisy Fuller) whose light-complected family members had the option of passe blanc (passing as white). After studying his freshman year at Dillard University, Young transferred to Howard University, where he earned a B.S. in biology in 1951. Though he contemplated dentistry, he decided on a religious vocation. In 1954 he married Jean Childs, with whom he eventually had three daughters. In 1955 he earned a bachelor of divinity from Hartford Theological Seminary. While at Hartford, he was a youth organizer for the Connecticut Council of Churches. With his seminary training complete, he pastored Bethany Congregation in Thomasville, Georgia. In 1957 he joined the executive staff at the National Council of Churches in New York, and in 1961 he joined the Citizenship School Program at the Southern Christian Leadership Conference (SCLC) in Atlanta. In 1964 he became the SCLC's executive director. In 1970 he resigned from SCLC to run for office. He won the party nomination for a congressional seat that year, and in 1972 became the first African American representative from Georgia since the radical Republican era. He was reelected in 1974 and 1976. In 1977 President Jimmy Carter appointed him as the first African American U.S. ambassador to the United Nations. In 1981 Young was elected mayor of Atlanta and was reelected in 1985. While he was mayor, the Democratic National Committee held its annual meeting in Atlanta, and following his second term, he was instrumental in bringing the Olympic games to Atlanta. In the 1990s, 2000s, and 2010s he has been a stalwart philanthropist for his own and many other foundations while occasionally considering further service in elected office.

This July 1962 speech in Lexington, Kentucky, is an account of his work with the SCLC's Citizenship School Program. He begins with a brief resume of his hometown, education, and SCLC function. His talk, however, avoids the banal secular functions of the citizenship school to focus on the contemporary historical import of the Holy Spirit. The initial contemporary problem, he argues, is cast well by James Reston: we are led by nineteenth-century men within eighteenth-century institutions to solve twentieth-century problems. Adenauer, Eisenhower, De Gaulle, and Khruschev are from an obsolete era. The result is systemic breakdown in Albany, Georgia, nationalism and revolution throughout the world, poverty, dehumanization, and conflict. Our solution is not old ideas, and our solution is not an integration of the current status quo of gray flannel suits, split-levels, and Metrecal (a diet drink). Rather, the solution lies in the Christian idea of incarnation, God's active presence in social history. God comes into history through human participation in his image and obedience. The result is we become children of God. This concept has a particular history especially amenable to Rev. Young's analysis. The concept of "children of God" was first coined by stoics—Greek slaves who schooled Rome's wealthy citizens. Young points out that being a child of God may seem routine to the privileged (to wit, the Brahmans of our society), but being a child of God is a radical new birth for the downtrodden. They remain servants, of course, as the beloved community is not about freedom and material gain, but they receive discernment (the ability to do what God wants), courage, and a radical new sense of preparation for the way of the cross. He offers an anecdote of marchers carrying towels and bars of soap in case the night brought with it a trip to jail. This rebirth gives us hope in a third race of people with the tools to cope with twentieth-century problems.

ৡৡ

The Church and Citizenship Education of the Negro in the South

July 1962
Lexington, Kentucky

I was born in New Orleans. I went to Howard University to do my undergraduate work and then to Hartford Seminary. I served a little town and country parish down in south Georgia for about three years. This was a Congregational Christian church. From there I went to work with the National Council of Churches as associate director of their department of youth work and stayed there for almost four years.

I have been down in Atlanta now for just about a year in a program that is really a joint project between the United Church of Christ and the Southern Christian Leadership Conference. This is a citizenship education program which attempts to train local community leaders to go back and involve their neighbors in citizenship classes. The program is supported by a grant from the Field Foundation at a training center in McIntosh, Georgia. I am the administrator of that foundation grant. The foundation asks us to teach them to go back and teach others.

What I am about to say to you now is not the kind of talk that we do for the foundation. It is rather more or less a Christian interpretation of what we are trying to do. As far as the foundation is concerned, I think we have to concern ourselves primarily with methods, with the content of citizenship education—that is, with some kind of secular curriculum. I do not really have much faith in this secular curriculum, and I think we just go through the motions of this curriculum in order that the Holy Spirit might have a context in which to work. I think it is the latter section of my job—the context in which I think we see the Holy Spirit working—that I want to talk with you about, "The Church and Citizenship Education of the Negro in the South."

One of the most interesting little expressions that I have heard in a long time I heard from Mr. James Reston of the *New York Times*, as he spoke to a group of students visiting in his office while analyzing the world's problems. He said, "One of the things that is wrong with the world is that we have a lot of nineteenth-century men working in eighteenth-century institutions trying to deal with twentieth-century problems." If you think that through a little bit, you will realize that basically most of the patterns of thought in which we are involved are nineteenth-century thought problems. In a very real sense, we are nineteenth-century men. At that time Adenauer, Eisenhower, De Gaulle, and Khrushchev were the world leaders—all men who really in effect were nineteenth-century men.

I think the situation is changing a little bit, but it is not changing sufficiently so that the general climate that we live in is really and truly of the twentieth century. I think one of the nineteenth-century myths that clings with us is this old notion of the inevitability of progress and the fact that things will automatically get better. This is still very much a part of the American tradition. Another myth is that reason reigns supreme—that if we just think things out and take our time and gradually understand what's going on, we can rationally come to grips with anything and solve the problems of the world. Third in this series of myths is the belief that human nature is basically good and that life is basically pleasurable and should be pleasurable. Now these are some of the things that influence—perhaps not the cutting edge of American society—but certainly the rank and file of middle-class American life and certainly the life in most of our churches.

One eighteenth-century institution is the church itself, which is basically the village church of the eighteenth century. Our flight to the suburbs is, I think, an attempt to create an eighteenth-century island that will keep out all of the foreign influence of the twentieth century. We hope that will allow us to still have the nice, comfortable family church about which we remember hearing our grandparents talk. The family itself, as most of us think about it, is thought of in eighteenth-century terms. We think that the family is a stable, compact, and secure unit which can care for the upbringing of the young—as it could, certainly, in rural society. Government exists to preserve order with a maximum of liberty, and this was certainly the case with the institutions of the government which began to take shape in the eighteenth century.

In looking at our twentieth-century situation, we can see that many of these things are no longer practical. One of our problems down in Albany, Georgia, is the fact that government is no longer able to cope with the present situation. All of the laws on the books in the southern states were put there after the Civil War by a South that was angry at northern intervention and by a South that sought to legally preserve the system of segregation and transform physical slavery into a psychological and emotional slavery that would keep the Negro inferior. So when people say why we don't go through the courts—why is it necessary for this kind of mass demonstration—they forget that there is no legal precedent in the South, with the exception of the Fourteenth Amendment, that is, in any way, geared to assure basic rights for its Negro citizens today.

When we look at some of the twentieth-century problems such as nationalism and revolutions that are going on around the world, we realize that many of these movements are related to the rising aspirations of the colored races. When you think of the poverty that is on the face of the earth, when you think of the fact that people no longer think of themselves as under a stigma because they have certain colors in their complexions, when you think of the science and technological revolution that has created a mass society and has also dehumanized human relations, when you think of the problems of the world such as achieving peace and brotherhood, these nineteenth-century myths and eighteenth-century institutions are far from being prepared to cope with this kind of a world.

Instead of just thinking in terms of what we are teaching the southern Negro, I think we have to see that this is a problem of the whole church. The Church must engage in the preparation for all her sons to come on into this twentieth century as responsible sons of God. Citizenship training for the Negro in the South cannot be interpreted as merely bringing up their so-called "cultural level," shall we say, to the level of that of the white community. Too often this is what is implied. It is illustrated in a little incident that occurred just the other day in Albany. We had finally gotten one of the policemen to come inside when he was supposedly guarding the house to keep us from being bombed. We invited him in for a glass of ice tea. We said, "Come on in, we believe in integration in this house," and his answer was, "Oh, I wouldn't mind integration if everybody was like you." Implied in this is that when Negroes get a certain cultural level, when they develop certain skills, when they become somebody, then we will accept them and live with them.

I say that the whole meaning of government as existing by the consent of those being governed and for the purpose of securing their basic rights and liberty is denied by this kind of condition under which a Negro can be a full citizen. I don't think there are any limitations to prevent a person from becoming a full, participating member of a democracy. Basic to democracy is the fact that this is a God-given right. If Negroes have no more to hope for than equality with the white man, then they might as well give up. A recent article in *Playboy* expressed this idea by saying this may only mean integration into oblivion. Negro writers across the South and North are saying now, "Who wants to integrate a sinking ship?"

There certainly is something basically wrong with our society, and we should avoid all temptations to say that the summum bonum of life, or the whole meaning of life, is that which is experienced and lived in middle-class America. We tell our people in our citizenship classes all the time that we are not working for the freedom to sin as white men have sinned, that life must hold more for us than a gray flannel suit and split-level families taking Metrecal.

When you go back to the spiritual foundation of all of this and when you ask, what do you mean by citizenship education, then I go back to the Incarnation. I think that as God came into history through the life and death and events surrounding Jesus Christ, he is also present in the events of contemporary history. If men are created in his image and thrown into a harsh and often brutal arena of history, their lives are shaped in his presence and they are accepted as they are and offered the challenge of loving obedience. I think God knows the kind of world into which he calls us. He accepts us in that world as we are, and the Bible reminds us continually that it is while we are yet sinners that God calls us to be partners. We become fellow heirs with Christ, breaking down the dividing wall of hostility between man and man and man and God, and sharing literally in the fulfillment of creation.

If we take this message of the Incarnation seriously—if we really see that man is called into fellowship with God to share in the purposes of God—then life has a different dimension from that of some of the nineteenth-century notions that are characteristically American. When a man becomes aware of this and realizes that he is a child of God, then something happens to him. It doesn't mean very much for citizens in the majority group—the Brahmans of our society—to be told that they are children of God because, in a sense, they already feel that they are children of God. In fact, they have been taught that their parents were gods! They are brought up to become gods and to worship those things around which their own lives center. But when you say this to a person who has been downtrodden, who has been cast aside, and who has been continually brainwashed from birth, you have said something quite revolutionary.

I think we often underestimate the extent to which we are brainwashed. When we first moved to New York, our first baby, our little daughter, who had been born in Georgia, was two years old. She had never had any unpleasant racial experiences in Georgia, mostly because segregation was so complete. But we were one of the first Negro families in suburban New York, living in an integrated community. It wasn't long before she came home and asked, "Mommy, I'm not black and nasty, am I?" There was nothing like this ever said at home, but somewhere in this community she had already become aware that being colored was something of a disadvantage. In a very interesting little book called *Prejudice and Your Child* by Kenneth Bancroft Clark of City College, in New York, we discovered a series of little tests to determine the extent of color awareness and self-hatred in a child. So we began to work with some of these little tests with our children. It was amazing to see the amount of hostility and self-hatred that already had crept into the life of a child that was not yet three years old. One of the little illustrations is that you give a child a tree to color, then a banana, then an apple, and then a little girl. Of course, the little girl could color the tree green and the banana yellow and the apple red. But when she got to the little girl, instead of holding the crayon in her fingers as she had on the others, she grabbed a purple crayon in her fist and vigorously marked all over the page. You get the sense here that the color identity even in a child is very much in question.

I think our little daughter had a much better early background than most American Negroes. But when you tell a child down in the Delta of Mississippi that he is created in the image of God and that God has called him into fellowship and God wants him to serve as an obedient servant, you have offered him more hope than he ever imagined. There are no techniques or methods for developing this kind of new citizen we are talking about. It certainly is a gift of grace. It comes as we respond in faith to the challenge and opportunity of life as we are reborn as servants of the new society—this beloved community that we talk so much about.

There are no methods, there are no techniques for this kind of life. So Negroes have been guilty of the most surprising kinds of behavior when they are under the influences of this kind of spirit. One such person is living down in Cleveland, Mississippi. She is a young girl [Diane Nash] that was the leader in the Nashville sit-in movement. Then she became a member of the Freedom Ride coordinating committee. She married a young fellow who happens to be a field representative on our staff of the Southern Christian Leadership Conference. She is now expecting a baby in the little town of Cleveland, Mississippi.

In the course of her work with the Freedom Rides, she coordinated some of the Freedom Ride activities into Jackson. She also was guilty of going around spreading this gospel of equality and sonship among some of the young people in Jackson, Mississippi. As a result of their hearing this gospel, this good news, that you are a child of God, they wanted to act like it. So she taught them that they should love their enemies and that non-violently they should offer themselves in the presence of their enemies to remind their enemies that they are their equals. When these young people went to the Greyhound bus station there in Jackson, of course, you know what happened to them. They were arrested on a breach of the peace charge, but she was charged with contributing to the delinquency of a minor. She was faced with the possibility of spending at least two years in prison as a result of such a charge. At the time she was pregnant.

Her case was called last May. Her natural reaction might have been to leave the state and just never live in Mississippi anymore. This is what everybody, including her lawyers, expected her to do. When I called her husband about this, he said, "Well, I wonder what we can do." He said, "I don't see how we can escape this opportunity." He said, "It seems this is something we have been led into. It's kind of like Abraham taking Isaac up on the mountain to sacrifice him. He didn't know the Lord would provide a ram in the bulrushes, but he had to go ahead on faith and the Lord did provide." And he added, "I guess we just have to go ahead on faith. I don't see the Lord ordering us to leave Mississippi." So with this kind of radical Christian background that grew out of an experience of the fact that they were truly sons of God, she presented herself before the court and had the audacity to sit on the wrong side of the courtroom which was reserved for whites, and they gave her ten days in the county prison. They didn't give her the two years; they postponed her case indefinitely.

But when you feel that you are a child of God, the Incarnation is a reality in your life. When you have been deprived of some of this "God-awareness," you cannot just hear it and talk about it; you have to begin to live it. So this is what you see happening.

Now by contrast, this is not what is traditionally experienced in the American church in its majority expression. A French youth worker, when he came over here and was asked to characterize the American church, said, "The American church seems to me to be like people who have been given a very great mansion and a beautiful piece of property and it's theirs, so they set up institutions to praise the fact that they have it. They set up other institutions to study all about it. All the people in America can tell you all about this very wonderful gift, but none of them have ever dared to live there." I think that when an underprivileged people have received such a wonderful thing they do dare to live there.

This, I think, is the basis of Christian citizenship training in our society now. The nonviolent movements are becoming schools for the new American, because here people learn that life is not basically good. They know the evil of men, and yet they learn also that life involves the necessity of suffering for what is right. They can have no illusions about the way in which the world actually exists. This is not a suffering that is imposed upon them; it is a creative and voluntary suffering.

It is quite a moving thing to see people take this kind of suffering upon themselves. In fact, it is hard to sit still and not be caught in it yourself. While these people down in Albany were talking about going to jail, they walk around the streets with their towels across their shoulders. They know that at any time during the day or night a mass meeting may be called, and this they assume is the time when a nonviolent demonstration will take place. Consequently, they have their towels with them so that when they go to jail they already have the towel and bar of soap in their pockets. This kind of voluntary suffering seems almost neurotic. Yet the genuineness and seriousness of it leads you to see that here is a new creature.

Here is a person who has received the gift of sonship, and if we read our Bibles correctly we know that if we once begin to act as if we are children of God and followers of Christ, sooner or later we run into some crosses. Not only is the Incarnation a source of our citizenship training or education or commitment, but the inevitable cross which follows such an understanding of the Incarnation becomes a time when people really learn the power of love as a moral force capable of overcoming the evils of the world. This actual living in the world under the influence of the Incarnation and the suffering such living brings seems to be creating the new creature. Here they find the rebirth that they have so long sought.

They receive along with this what the World Council of Churches talks about all the time as "the gift of discernment." In a very real sense, the job of directing a nonviolent movement is one of understanding what God wants you to do. It is far different from the usual daily routine in America, and I find myself doing a whole lot more praying these days. The value of intercessory prayer, which in seminary or in the traditional parish life or in

National Council of Churches committee meetings seems quite irrelevant and unnecessary, becomes a real part of your everyday existence. You know that you and those in jail cannot make it without this constant intercession on their behalf. This creates a spiritual climate which is like that of the early church and along with it this gift of discernment.

A very interesting experience occurred last Friday night and Saturday. We were all living together in the home of the doctor that is the president of the Albany movement. The people were somewhat outraged because Dr. King would not lead them in a mass demonstration that night. The talk going all through the Negro community was that Martin Luther King was going "chicken." The people were ready to go to jail, and jail going had been an effective way of expressing their discontent with this system of segregation. This had been the way that they had been able to discover their sonship and realize it in some sense. They were now—because they had gone to jail back in December—they were now able to hold their heads up and act like men. No longer were they persons who "laugh when they're not tickled and scratch when they don't itch, and shuffle"; they had dramatically refuted all the old stereotypes about the Negro. This had been cast off now because of an experience that they had in jail. Jail to them was the way of answering all of their grievances, and so they were anxious to go to jail. Some of us of less depth were ready to go with them. When Dr. King was not quite so sure, and when he avoided every question from us about why not, and seemed to resent our pressuring him, we began to wonder about him ourselves.

There was involved here, as we discovered later on the next day, an awareness of the fact that here were people who were committed to jail going but who as yet did not fully understand the whole idea of nonviolence. Here were people that were probably going for the wrong reasons also. Consequently, putting off the public demonstration until some kind of training and some kind of purification of the motives involved was achieved on the part of the people was certainly something that was a product of this gift of discernment. I think that when Dr. King finally came around to talking in religious terms he said, "You know you just cannot irresponsibly send a thousand people off to fill up the jails of the South. This might mean long periods of illness, it might mean poor food, [and] it might mean the wreckage of the families involved. You cannot take this kind of decision upon yourself until you do feel as though there is some spiritual urging in this direction."

I think that this gift of discernment which the church seemed to have in its periods of activity is something that is growing out of this new experience that we have of being willing to face up to the cross. We are coming to have more understanding of the nature and purpose of God as a result of living in his world and working to break down some of the barriers of hostility that exist in this world. We as Christians know, even though this is as far as we have gotten so far, that following crucifixion there is resurrection. I think it is with this faith in mind that you are able to plunge your community into temporary chaos. You realize, as did Jeremiah, that it is necessary to break down and to pluck up in order to build and to plant. It is our Christian conviction that God raises up from the dead not only men but also perhaps social orders. When you see these persons who have had this experience becoming new creatures, your faith is encouraged and increased. You get some of the feeling of what Paul Tillich might have been talking about in *The Courage to Be*. As a result of being persons, as a result of suffering voluntarily as God's children, you find a new creature with a new courage being born. This first-class citizenship then equals world-changing citizenship. And you have something completely different from the status quo kind of Christianity that many of us have been used to.

This is the answer to some of the problems that we have experienced as a result of being segregated. Certainly, it upsets us that the level of morality is so low in the Negro community, that the crime rate is so high, and that there is so much serious alcoholism. But those of us who have preached and tried to be a pastor to Negro congregations realize the futility of stating a verbal gospel. We realize that the verbal gospel has not the power to change. But plunging into the Christian life, the living gospel active in the world, does change the world.

You find a man in the Negro community who is called "boy" all week long and who is intimidated by the fact that he is colored. Perhaps he has an I.Q. of 125 or 130 and yet is forced to work only as a porter. He pushes a broom all week and takes orders from some young snip that is not nearly as intelligent nor works as hard and yet who gets twice as much money. Under this kind of system, it is no wonder that on weekends he seeks a bottle. It is no wonder that he is sexually excessive, because the only place that he can successfully affirm his manhood is in the sex act itself. So when you see all of these crimes that are associated with race, you have to think that these are probably not racial crimes. Rather, these are crimes which are brought on by a system which is basically unjust and which so corrupts people on both sides of the system that a certain amount of misery and poverty and hardship is the only logical result.

But once people have been caught up in what it means to be a new creature, once people have become aware of God as their Father and have made a decision to voluntarily share with him in the fulfillment of this society and this world, you find a kind of Christian citizenship is being born which we have seen too few times in the church's history. We saw it in the early church. We saw it in the Reformation. We saw it in some of the Christians who sparked the abolitionist movement. We saw it in the beginnings of the foreign missionary enterprises. We see it now again in some of these students in the nonviolent movements for racial justice.

Now this is not a racism, for it is not just Negroes who are experiencing this kind of a rebirth in this day and age. Not all Negroes are heroes, and not all whites bourgeois. If Fisk University is any indication, the only two faculty members who took part in the demonstrations and went to jail happened to be white. None of the Negro faculty members sufficiently identified with this kind of radical movement to become a part of it. But somehow we have a collection of those who choose to become involved.

We see in a sense a new reformation that is coming into being in the Negro church. Sunday morning is perhaps no longer the hour in which the real church meets. The social community of those like-minded, the intimate fellowship meets on Sunday morning at eleven o'clock, but the real church that comes together to take upon itself the responsibility of changing the world meets on Monday night. It is an interdenominational fellowship. It is the mass meeting where the people from all the churches come together to find out what the sufferings of the last week were and what the marching orders of the next will be. This is the company of the committed that is gathering to hear their missionary orders. They have no institutions to preserve except as these court costs get a little high and they have to raise a certain amount of money to take care of that. But these are the people of God in our time, we think.

In a sense, when we talk about the citizenship training for Negroes in the South, we hope nevertheless that out of this experience there might be born a new American that is more truly the third race that the church started out to be in the beginning. We hope that as a result of this kind of suffering and resurrection together in local communities, breaking down the walls of hostility there, that we might be beginning to create a people both white and black, that have decided that they are going to commit themselves to live a continued life of radical obedience.

Perhaps from this group we might have a citizen that is trained to cope with the problems of the twentieth century throughout the world. This is because they have found in this testing ground of the American South and of the border states an experience of Jesus Christ which is both historic and relevant in the present and that will continue to lead them in the future. Those who choose Freedom Rides, those who choose sit-ins, those who choose jail-ins might some day be choosing some new form of radical Christian obedience that might result in another experience of the redemptive community actually redeeming those of us that are not so committed.

§28 John David Maguire

Dr. John David Maguire was born on August 7, 1932, in Montgomery, Alabama. He and Lillian married on August 29, 1953, and raised three daughters, Anne King Turner, Catherine, and Mary. Dr. Maguire received his B.A. from Washington and Lee University in 1953. He earned a bachelor of divinity in 1956 and a Ph.D. in 1960, both at Yale University, where he became close with chaplain William Sloane Coffin. Shortly after earning his doctorate, he was jailed in Montgomery, Alabama, for his part as a Freedom Rider. In addition to his two Fulbright Scholarships (Scotland 1953, Germany 1965), he served as associate provost at Wesleyan University (1960–1970), president of SUNY and Old Westbury (1970–1981), and president of Claremont University Center and Graduate School (1981–1998), and he is currently senior fellow at Claremont's Institute for Democratic Renewal, an organization dedicated to social and racial justice. Dr. Maguire is also the founding chair of the board for the Martin Luther King Jr. Center for Nonviolent Social Change.

In this sermon of September 27, 1962, in Birmingham, Alabama, he reminds the African American audience that he grew up a minister's son in Birmingham, though those in the audience could not attend that church, and John Maguire did not attend theirs. He then sets out a simple address with three components: the problem with the church, Jesus' solution, and what now is left to be done. The problem is segregation, whose theological source is the division of the divine commission as if loving God were different than loving one's neighbor. The solution is Christian unity as quoted from chapter 4 of Luke. Before turning to a practical solution, Dr. Maguire poisons the well ironically: taverns seem to be able to integrate more easily than congregations. His solution is first, to recognize fellow creatures, humans, and brothers in whichever order is possible; second, to build on our differences rather than deny them; and third, to recognize that this issue is urgent, and cannot be put off any longer. As if he does not believe his exhortations were strong enough, he returns to observe, "[God] will elect and infuse another institution where there can be exchanged love." Mercifully, he does not refer explicitly to the tavern again. To further impress upon the audience the severity of the situation, he concludes with the image of a shrinking turtle.

౷౿

The Church in Race Relations
September 27, 1962
Birmingham, Alabama

Tonight is a homecoming for me. Although I was jailed for "freedom riding" in Montgomery, the city of my birth, Birmingham was the place where I grew up. But as a boy I knew none of you personally, despite the fact that we acknowledged the same Lord, who, [it] says in Scripture, "is our peace, having made us both one and broken down the wall of hostility." My father was a minister here in Birmingham, but you couldn't come to our church, and I didn't come to yours, despite our common worship of the One whom, says St. Paul, "there is neither slave nor free, male nor female, Jew nor Greek, but all are one."

Things have not changed much in the years since I lived here. Before I indicate the gospel vision of how things were *meant to be* in the Church, and how we can *move toward* realizing that vision, I should review the sad, shabby current situation in the Church.

Every denomination in America, even those we think most socially conservative, now has a few showcase churches where there exists token integration. The vast majority, however, tied to local prejudice and custom, reflect the discrimination omnipresent in the land. Change in the churches has been only token. Indeed, the difference in the treatment of racial and religious minorities in various regions of our country is largely a matter of degree. And as a Negro friend told me, "It hurts wherever it is encountered, in Rochester or Roanoke, Middletown, Montgomery, Binghamton, or Birmingham." Eleven o'clock on Sunday morning *is* the nation's most segregated hour, and the church the most segregated of all human institutions.

We have been "educated" to understand the reasons for this situation, but they are not justified. First, in both Negro and white churches there is the prevailing notion that they are only for those "like us," our club. Ministers, often directly dependent on the church for their livelihood, know that efforts at integration will disturb their members and cause trouble. And frankly, they hate trouble more than they do injustice and their failure to be

God's true community. A wise man once said, "All churches are either circles, closed little rings for only those of like kind, adding up to nothing. Or,
they are crosses, reaching from height to depth and infinitely reaching out to
all men in every direction." Too many churches, Negro and white, are circles.

A second reason for the failure of American churches to embrace the
full human community, white and Negro, is our yielding to the chasm which
separates us in every other aspect of life. Having committed psychological
secession from the real world, the white church member is insulated from
the stream of things and hardly realizes the scope, the intensity, the power
of the worldwide revolution for human rights now going on. He goes on
worshiping his white "God" who presides over a segregated heaven. The
Negro church member, on the other hand, pressing for his rights at point
after point in society, rejoices in one institution to which he can return
and be refreshed with people like him and not have to be on guard. Separated from each other, suspicious of each other, we shall worship together in
church only when we can ride together in busses, study in the same schools,
and vote in the same booths. That is why the *total* civil rights movement is
so important, for while the church can and should *lead*, it also *reflects* the
shape of things.

But the third reason we have failed to be God's church is really theological. For a long time, we've misconceived the gospel itself. We have separated
"souls" from "bodies," and understood our ministry as the saving of those
souls. We have divided the one great commandment of Jesus in two:

> Thou shalt love the Lord thy God with all thy heart, with all thy soul,
> and with all thy mind: *and* Thou shalt love thy neighbor as thyself. (Matt.
> 22:37-39)

Having separated the parts, we put them in sequence, suggesting that the
first is what God really requires—the completion of a transaction solely
between the soul and him; and then, as a second stage, almost an after-
thought—the now saved soul may turn to his neighbor. Save men's souls,
then attack discrimination.

But the gospel, once divided, keeps on splitting. Love gets separated
from justice. Those so sure of their soul salvation slow down in concern for
their brothers. Men are fooled into thinking they can "get right with God"
without getting right with each other. The cross gets ripped apart. We carry
around the vertical beam—God's redeeming word to individuals that they
are forgiven—while forgetting the horizontal thrust—that there is no love
without justice, no faith without obedience, no salvation that is not social.

Only when you have both the horizontal *and* the vertical thrusts have you the life-redeeming Cross.

Clubby, segregated, gospel-distorting churches. That, sadly, is the situation with most white churches in America and many Negro ones as well.

This sickening situation is only highlighted when you turn to the Scripture and see Jesus' vision of what his church was meant to be. He declared his dream the first day he preached in his own hometown:

> And he came to Nazareth, where he had been brought up; and he went to the synagogue, as his custom was, on the Sabbath day. And he stood up and read; and there was given to him the book of the prophet Isaiah. He opened the book and found the place where it was written, "The Spirit of the Lord is upon me, because he has anointed me to preach good news to the poor. He has sent me to proclaim release to the captive and recovering of sight to the blind, to set at liberty those who are oppressed, to proclaim the acceptable year of the Lord." And he closed the book, and gave it back to the attendant, and sat down. . . . Then he said, "Today this scripture has been fulfilled in your hearing." (Luke 4:16-21)

Notice, first, that Jesus says, "This is *now* fulfilled." How surprisingly literal Jesus is. He declares, "People are in captivity. I am their freedom." "People are blind: I *am* the restoration of their sight." "I am the liberty for the oppressed." We cannot escape the indivisible social character of his proclamation. Oppression, bondage, and blindness are being suffered by a mass of men. They are actual, physical conditions. They cannot be spiritualized away. Jesus *is* the gospel. He is God's declaration in person. There is no *soul* salvation without *social* redemption.

The second element is Jesus' conviction that all men are literally one, created by one Lord and sons of one Father. This fact forever shatters the major misconception today—that some men (the whites) can set the timetable for the freedom of others. It exposes the churchly heresy—that men can presume favor from the Heavenly Father while refusing kinship with some of his sons, their brothers. It puts the drive toward integrating our churches in the proper context. For, when once aroused, we *do* open our doors, we are not granting a right which *we* bestow or a privilege which *we* give. We are simply reoffering an invitation already issued by God himself. We are only reconfirming this fact that men are one. "I *am* the liberty for those who are oppressed." The ancient lawgiver Solon was asked when perfect justice would come to Athens. His answer reflects this sense of human solidarity: "When those who have not themselves suffered injustice are as indignant as those who have."

Jesus' vision also had a third element. He saw that since the world constantly split justice and love, his church must be the place where they are united. It must never retreat from the world, providing a haven for those who resist change, having to be dragged, kicking and screaming, into the twentieth century. It must never lag *behind* the state, which is of course what most churches have done. While labor unions, political parties, and the Supreme Court have denounced segregation in certain areas of our common life, the churches still nail to their crosses the sign "For our kind only." Indeed, the Supreme Court seems poised to rule that proprietors of no establishment serving the public may forcibly keep folk out. A few months ago, Justice Douglas declared:

> One can close the doors of his home to anyone he desires. But one who operates an enterprise under license from the people enjoys a privilege that derives from the people (and so must serve them).

How ironical the prospect of the town's taverns being forced toward fellowship while churches lag behind. In Jesus' vision, the church was to lead, not lag. America now needs *some* institution, not only to desegregate but genuinely to integrate—to show the rest of society how an integrated society flourishes. Not only our legal efforts up to now but most of our personal associations have moved only to the stage of desegregation. But desegregation, after all, is a matter of external relations, the apparent elimination of covert discrimination in the public order. Integration is a much deeper reality, having to do with home and hearth and the eradication of those deep-seated prejudices within the heart. The world now needs some institution where integration, not just desegregation, flourishes, where friendships, loyalties, and social exchanges are experienced, in order to have a model, a guide. That is the call of the church, to become such an institution, where integration is genuinely practiced.

Jesus' vision, then, was of an institution where salvation was social, where men acknowledged their oneness, where justice and love were united. He called it "the leaven in the loaf," "the remnant redeeming the larger society."

What a tremendous gap between Jesus' vision and the sickening situation in the churches today. How can we possibly move from where we are to a point where that holy vision becomes actual?

We must, first, cease perpetuating broken fellowship. As we open our doors we do not have to *create* a community from nothing, but cooperate with making concrete the full human community already created by Christ. We are bringing to light a hidden fact. So long as it is submerged, part of us is buried. Whites are not, therefore, doing something *for* the minorities. Negroes are not being unnaturally charitable. We are doing it for our own sakes, for the salvaging of our own humanity. We are, in short, engaged together in the common reclamation of our souls. We are seeking to make manifest our salvation. But be it known that this mending of broken fellowship is terribly hard when a group is fighting for its rights. It is so difficult to avoid "us" against "them" thinking. A tension develops in the understanding of the church itself when it serves as a launching pad for demonstrations and actions to achieve minority group rights. The church rings with songs and slogans of "attack," "assault," and "victory." "Them" becomes the object of the attack. Yet the church was conceived as an open community, embracing all. Fidelity to Jesus' vision thus requires the abandonment of "us" against "them" thinking, however difficult that is. We must let our spirits be led along the path noted by a recent writer:

> I was out walking one day and in the distance I saw an animal. I came up closer and saw it was a man. I came up closer still and saw it was my brother.

Second, if we are to move from our present segregated churches to realize Jesus' vision for his church, we are going to have to cease denying our differences and begin building on them.

When we become concerned about race relations, we often try, as a quick cure, to deny our actual differences. We urge men to act as though there were not differences of background, economic status, skin color. Indeed, in enthusiasm for our new vision of God as the Father of all men, we declare that he sees no differences, that he is color-blind, and that we ought to follow suit.

But that is cheap grace, a misleading manner of speech, for it suggests God's commitment to a deficiency for the sake of pretending a sameness among men. Men are different. God knows it, and so do we. And we can never restore a lasting fellowship by pretending it isn't so. Rather we must realize as real that unity in diversity, breaking through to a situation where we can acknowledge our differences and yet find them no barrier, where we can rejoice in our diversities, recognizing that they build up rich fellowship, not block it. This way, the Negro need not become a middle-class white before he is "acceptable" in the fellowship, and the white need not feel he must deny that fact in order to have warm, human exchange with Negroes.

Finally, we must discover the urgency of now. The problem of prejudice is an urgent problem *now*. It is not a southern problem or a northern problem but an omnipresent human problem, everywhere. Aristotle the Greek, whom otherwise we revere, made in his lifetime two shocking pronouncements. Holding two stones, one large, one small, he declared by deduction that, dropped from a great height, the larger and heavier one would hit first.

Nearly a millennium elapsed before the young Italian Galileo demonstrated that gravity does not discriminate between big rocks and little ones: they fall at the same rate of speed.

In "social science," Aristotle declared that some men—the Greeks—were born to rule, and that others—the Chinese and the people north of Greece—were barbarians, born to be ruled.

A few centuries later, a young Jew, our Lord, demonstrated the foolishness and futility of the pretensions to inherent superiority, or inherent inferiority. He claimed the holders of this view to be in bondage, to be blind. He said "No" to the inference that because men are different, some are better. They *are* one, here and now, but now, as then, men deny it. *Now* is the time for all those who love the Lord to repeat his message now and live that conviction in their lives.

If we fail to be the church, like Christ's cross reaching out to all men in every direction, then we are finished. "The Spirit bloweth where it listeth." God will move on. He will elect and infuse another institution where there can be exchanged love.

The hypocrisy of the Christian mission abroad will be revealed, and the irrelevance of the church to real life will be exposed—irrelevance already deeply suspected by growing numbers of men.

Most seriously, we shall lose our souls. The unpardonable sin, thought the poet Milton, was when a man—like Lucifer—so repeatedly says, "Evil, be thou my good," so persistently lives a lie, that he loses the power to tell the difference. America's segregated churches are near that point. Having denied our oneness in Christ and having used our religious language to justify our separation, we now stand in peril.

Our hope and our calling is speak [sic] a new word on the oneness of man and to follow that word with action. Only "the Word become flesh" can save. Only as we *act out* the gospel can it be heard, and now is the time. St. Augustine spoke to us all:

Those that sit at rest while others take pains are tender turtles and buy their quiet with disgrace.

§29 Hodding Carter Jr.

William Hodding Carter Jr. was born on February 3, 1907, in Hammond, Louisiana. A precocious and gifted child, Carter graduated as high school valedictorian at the age of sixteen. As a young boy Carter accidentally came across the body of a lynched black man in the woods; that image, and what it represented, stayed with him for the rest of his life. Unlike many of his Deep South contemporaries, Carter went north for his college education, first to Bowdoin College in Maine, where he graduated in 1927, and a year later he did graduate work in journalism at Columbia University in New York City. He returned south to New Orleans in 1929 to take a reporting job with the *New Orleans Item-Tribune*; later he worked for the United Press and the Associated Press. During this latter job in Jackson, Carter was fired for insubordination. He married Betty Werlein in 1931 and the coupled moved back to Hammond, where they started their own newspaper, the *Daily Courier*. Carter cut his editorial teeth at the *Courier* by criticizing the notorious Louisiana demagogue Huey Long. His principled and well-written stands earned him national attention—and some national writing assignments. In 1936 the young couple moved to the Mississippi Delta town of Greenville and, with help from the famed local writer William Alexander Percy, founded the *Delta Star*. Two years later the young couple bought out Greenville's competing newspaper, and their enterprise became the *Delta Democrat-Times*. After World War II, during which Carter served in the Office of War Information and wrote for *Yank* and *Stars and Stripes*, the thirty-nine-year-old won a Pulitzer Prize for editorial writing regarding the United States' treatment of Nisei, Japanese American men who had fought for the United States. As the 1950s unfolded in Mississippi, Carter was one of the very few progressive white newspaper voices; his editorial writing on the Emmett Till case, in particular, earned national attention. In 1960 Carter handed over editorial duties of the paper to his son, Hodding Carter III, while he headed south and west to be writer-in-residence at Tulane University. The nationally recognized writer and publisher died on April 4, 1972, survived by his wife and son. His papers are housed at Mississippi State University.

Less than two weeks after James Meredith integrated the University of Mississippi, and still suffering from the remnants of tear gas, Carter delivered

this fascinating meditation on his home state. His address qual parts history, religion, sociology, and psychology, Carter attempts to limn for his
northern and well-educated interlocutors just how Mississippi became the
nation's most notorious state. It functions rhetorically more as apology and
less as indictment—though Carter is not timid in his criticism, especially
of then-governor Ross Barnett. Seven interrelated factors in particular had
shaped the white Mississippian mindset: blacks functioned as "whipping
boys" for the state's maladies; the state's best educated were rapidly leaving; Protestant religious fundamentalists viewed blacks as eternal hewers
of wood and drawers of water, and thus educated ministers were at the
mercy of staunchly racist congregations; Mississippi whites preferred stump
spellbinders and local folklore over facts and reason; conservatism was intimately related to a long history with agriculture and the superiority complex
it engendered; and finally, the state had no nonsectarian private colleges
where freedom of thought and expression might be nurtured. Carter closes
on a note of optimism as the events at Ole Miss and the nation's reaction
to the *Brown* decision revealed a still indivisible nation where racial justice
was likely to prevail.

ᬛᬛ

The Why of Mississippi

October 11, 1962
University of New Hampshire, Durham, New Hampshire

Mr. Chase, members of the faculty of the university, students, and friends.
I must make a number of apologies or explanations in advance. The first is
that this is the second time I have ever read a talk. I don't know whether the
results are going to be happy or not. In connection with that, my secretary
gave me the wrong copy, and I have a faint version of what I have written,
and I may have trouble somewhat in reading it, especially as I am about to
undergo an eye operation arising out of a long-time-ago war injury to it, but
I will do my best in that respect.

The second apology has to do with my voice. You will notice it will probably get very gravelly now and then. I went to two doctors in New Orleans
before coming here. They were not quite sure of the cause until we realized
that over the past eight days the wind had been blowing from north to south
in our area, bringing the remnants of the fumes of tear gas that blanketed
the University of Mississippi some little while ago.

My third apology has to do with a nervousness which I think you will find understandable. In the last nine months I have made three appearances in New England on matters related to our problems. The first was last December at Brown University. From what I said, or rather didn't say—I don't believe as a newspaperman in saying that I was misquoted, but I was—but at any rate some of my fellow Mississippians burned me in effigy. It was a lovely effigy, I'm told. It was more than life-size, which means a pretty big effigy. The second of these talks was made at a Harvard Law School forum, and the result there was that a whole pile of my newspapers, which had been consigned to a nearby town, were taken out of the bus station and burned. Mississippians like to play with matches, and the papers were burned on the main street of that town.

Last summer—we spend our summers in Maine—I talked to the Maine Bankers Association at Poland Spring. They weren't too original in Mississippi that time—they just burned me in effigy again. A week ago another southern editor said a kind word or two about me on a television program, and I have a cross burned on my lawn. That's the first time that has happened, but again, fire and matches. Now what is going to happen after this one, I don't know.

The things I say, and I am saying things which are critical, I think on considerable thought I am trying to balance through explanation or through the other side of the coin. I can understand the feeling of southerners in having antipathy for those who say only the bad and don't counterbalance it with the good, and there is much good to be said about us too, and this I am going to try to do in the paper. So if my fellow newspapermen are here, I just say, "Have a heart. It's still too warm in Mississippi for large fires."

It was with a heavy heart that I asked the University of New Hampshire for permission to change the subject of my talk. I had intended to evaluate Andrew Johnson against the contemporary southern and national background. Instead I now propose to speak of the tragedy which has befallen my state and our nation and of what I think are the explanations therefore.

But first I cannot help but comment briefly and extemporaneously on Andrew Johnson, who succeeded the martyred Lincoln as president and whose behavior as a courageous, patriotic American and as a beleaguered chief executive has not received the recognition he deserves. I say that I am speaking extemporaneously as I did not bring with me the previously prepared paper on Andrew Johnson. I am writing a book about him, and it is one of the reasons I wanted to talk about him. I think he has been grossly underestimated. He was in the American ideal, the American saga: the poor boy, the bound-boy apprenticed out, a virtual slave as a child, almost illiterate until manhood and marriage, an humble tailor who became successively state legislator, governor, congressman, U.S. senator, vice president of the U.S. as a Democrat during the war, a loyal Union Democrat, and lastly, because of the murder of Lincoln, president of the United States. He had the tragic distinction of being the only president to face impeachment trial. He was not found guilty by one vote. We of Bowdoin are proud that one vote was cast unexpectedly by the senator from Maine, who was a Bowdoin man.

But to me Andrew Johnson represents a militant moderation. As a young man he fought bitterly and successfully with everything he had for the government by the entrenched and the aristocratic leaders of middle and west Tennessee. He was removed from Carolina as a very young man to Tennessee, from where he went to Washington. He was ahead of his time in a number of respects in visionary legislation. He was, for my money, the most courageous of American presidents, the only one ever, of American governors first, to serve as a wartime governor in a territory and a state (his own state of Tennessee) where at least 60 percent and possibly more of the people prayed for his death. Nightly he faced them down. He remained loyal throughout the war, the only southern senator to stay in the Senate. All the others left and went with the Confederacy. Andrew Johnson alone stayed to face the hatred, the contempt, the threats upon his life, and all else you might expect in such parlous times, in such tense times as these.

He ran, as you may know, for the vice presidency on Lincoln's Union ticket. It was not called the Republican ticket for very good reasons during the war. He ran as a Union Democrat with a Republican running mate, Abraham Lincoln, and of course they were elected and tragically soon thereafter Abraham Lincoln was assassinated. Andrew Johnson replaced him as president and there he faced a different kind of venom, hatred, destructiveness, lack of forgiveness—this time on the part of what was called the radical Republican block in Congress, which was bent on further punishing the defeated South and grinding them almost literally into the earth. He faced up to those people in whose hearts there was no spirit of conciliation or forgiveness. For his pains, as I said, he was almost destroyed politically. He won out, he defended the South, he effected a pattern of readmission or regaining of citizenship that was equitable and fair, and did much to heal wounds, and he lived to see his policies triumph. After his term of president was over, he did not seek to succeed himself. He went to Tennessee and returned again to Congress and lived out a long life representing Tennessee there.

I repeat, he is a great American who is sorely needed today in the South and in the nation. Again I say, a militant kind of conciliator, a man who tried to oppose the extremes both in his own region and the extremes in the nation and in the party and in the region which he had espoused, the North, the Union. I wish I could give two papers: one about him, a man who has been too greatly neglected, as well as the paper I am giving.

I am a southerner by ancestry, by birth, by residence, and by inclination. I am not ashamed of being a Deep Southerner or a Mississippian. I love the state in which I have lived for twenty-six years and where I intend to live out my life—Deo volente, as a great aunt used to say—for more reasons than simply to prove that I can.

Mississippi is a good state, plagued with a problem almost as old as man himself, that of how to establish communication and equality and fellow-ship among people of different races and cultures. Behind our billboards it is a beautiful state. Not the least aspect of that beauty is the epochal resto-ration to new and diversified usefulness of land abused for a century and a half. Even amid the dreadful turmoil there do exist amity and affection and even respect among individual members of the two races. Despite the headlines, the record of two million Mississippians as a law-abiding people is one of the best statistically in the nation, and this comes from the F.B.I. report. Our divorce rate is almost the lowest, which is important if the fam-ily unit is important. Ours is the not often broken serenity of the small town and the countryside, which many, among them myself, prefer to the noise of vast marketplaces. There are still Americans who would rather hunt ducks than seek out a new restaurant or a nightspot. Derided for our educational lags, Mississippi has produced a quantitatively and qualitatively dispropor-tionate number of American writers; and I know from experience that it is impossible to visit any sizable city in the United States without meeting Mississippians who have attained the success and respect which they might also have found at home, and who talk lovingly of the places of their birth and rearing.

This love of the homeplace and of state is not readily comprehended by the newer American, the mobile American, or the anonymous American of the metropolis. But it is a strong thread in the American warp and woof; and one that should not be torn at or mocked. Pride in past and identifica-tion with place are valuable national assets.

White Mississippians who are heartsick over what is happening in our state will still bet on Mississippi. One reason has to do with courage, however misdirected. I hold no brief for Governor Ross Barnett. In fact, I hold him in utmost contempt. But whatever the motivations, it takes guts of a kind to stand up to the United States of America. It takes guts for my young fellow townsman, State Representative Joe Wroten, to tell the other 102 of his fellow Mississippi legislators just what kind of idiots they are making of themselves. There were two men—this boy was the more vocal of the two—two men in the entire legislature who warned of the consequences and denounced the governor for his leadership toward chaos. This boy was one of them.

It takes guts for another Mississippian, James Meredith, whose skin is black, to risk his life hour by hour to prove something to his nation, to his people and his critics, and to himself.

And Mississippi is blessed with the conviction of its best white leadership and its citizenry at large, regardless of political differences or social dilemmas or stubborn obstructionism, that we are going places. In the quarter century of my residence there, Mississippi has been transformed about beyond recognition. The transformation is far from complete; but its continuance is certain, for we have the raw materials and the human materials upon which hope and certainty rest. In agricultural and industrial development we are catching up. This is something that has a special meaning in this time of crisis and condemnation. The gyrations of a governor may obscure this truth, but they cannot destroy it. And in the process of catching up, my fellow Mississippians will discover that their present fears will prove to be groundless.

When Governor Ernest Vandiver of Georgia suggested in September that it was time for Mississippi to decide whether she was one of the fifty states, and behave accordingly, he put his finger on a singular characteristic. For almost one hundred years many Mississippians and most Mississippi politicians have refused, at least publicly, to acknowledge four facts. The first unacknowledged fact is that our state was and is bound by the successive implications of the War between the States. The second is the validity of Supreme Court decisions that many Mississippians find distasteful. The third is national will. The fourth is the American concept that enforced second-rate citizenship is alien to the democratic dream.

In this reluctance to accept or adjust to a national pattern, Mississippi has not been alone among the southern states. Her uniqueness lies in the persistence, the belligerence, the continuity, and the massiveness of her resistance. Accordingly, considerable numbers of her citizens see no inconsistency in accepting from the federal government, on the one hand, a variety of benefits, which in sum total considerably exceed the aggregate amount which they pay in taxes to that government; and on the other, in defying the central authority almost to the point of sedition and by whatever means are at hand. Our governor has repeatedly shown his contempt for the federal, executive, and judicial branches. Our legislature has almost hysterically derided federal statutes and judicial decisions and orders. Again and again, that legislature has vociferously shown its scorn for the men in the White House and on the federal bench. The end result has been military intervention, violence, and death, as any intelligent Mississippian foresaw.

There are two general keys to the behavior which has brought a variety of reactions in much of the rest of the nation: bewilderment, anger, frustration, pity, concern, and in some quarters even admiration. One is the presence of the Negro in the highest national ratio to whites and at the lowest national educational, social, and moral levels (for reasons which are popularly though not properly ascribed to color). The second is the extraordinarily low caliber of so many of Mississippi's professional politicians. There are other, more proximate reasons, which we will examine later.

Mississippi would probably not be conformist even were her Negro population no larger than that of North Dakota or New Hampshire. Mississippians behave differently in several respects—and certainly not always with harmful results—from most of their American compatriots. Ours is the only state to retain a cynically disregarded prohibition law. Incidentally we collect a state tax on this illegally dispensed liquor and wink an official eye at our delightful Gulf Coast, whose tourist trade requires openly operated bars and cocktail lounges and liquor stores. Mississippi forbids jury service to women along with mental incompetents and convicted wrongdoers. Mississippi, together with two other states, retains the poll tax both as a requisite for voting and as an article of faith and defiance. In 1960 a plurality of Mississippi voters cast their ballots for independent, unpledged presidential electors without even knowing for whom these electors would vote. (It turned out that Senator Harry Byrd of Virginia was the lucky man.) White Mississippians pride themselves on their independence, yet demand group conformity to an extent not exceeded and seldom equaled anywhere in the country. Many Mississippians still spend considerable spare time cussing out Yankees, but go to their local polling booths, whenever the opportunity presents itself, to vote overwhelmingly for bond issues to build industrial plants for migrating Yankee industry. Mississippi has produced a William Faulkner, an Elvis Presley, a Leontyne Price.

How do people get that way, you ask? I will try now to answer with other than the two general reasons which I first stated.

A helpless, perpetual whipping boy is a happily advantageous item in the demagogue's stock in trade. Mississippi's population is still nearly 45 percentNegro; the Negroes' voting strength is the smallest both proportionately and absolute numbers anywhere in the nation. As far as I can ascertain, out of some 900,000 Negroes in Mississippi, less than 10,000 vote. I am proud to say that almost half of those vote in our own county—one of two in eighty-two counties where the Negro is not interfered with in exercising that right.

For effective political achievement this Negro vote may be said to be nonexistent. Most white Mississippians intend to keep the political scene that way whatever opinions the federal government may have on the subject. And so the temptation to raise the racial specter, to tell warningly, "Nigger, nigger, look out for the nigger" during a political campaign, is so strong as to be, for most Mississippi politicians, irresistible. An enfranchised Negro population would considerably change not only the present political tactics but the political climate. But it is likely that before the Mississippi Negro votes in politically potent numbers, migration will have reduced his overall numbers to the point where he cannot be used as a sure-fire bogeyman.

A second explanation—and these are not necessarily in order of importance—lies in the sad annual exodus of a majority of the better-educated young Mississippians of both races. Mostly they seek economic opportunities lacking at home. It has been estimated variously that from 50 percent to 70 percent of Mississippi college graduates leave the state annually. The highest proportion of those who remain are either agricultural college graduates or law school graduates; and, to the latter, politics beckons as the readiest road to recognition. The domination of a state legislature by political lawyers is not an unmixed blessing.

Next, the religious factor.

Mississippi churchgoers, a good majority of the population, belong for the most part to the evangelical Protestant sects. Probably most of them are fundamentalists, believing sincerely in the inferences in the Old Testament that the Negro is and will remain an inferior hewer of wood and drawer of water. Moreover, except in the minority of churches which have some sort of hierarchical discipline, the dissenting, educated ministers are at the mercy of congregations which permit no such communistic doctrine as that of man's equality.

A fourth explanation is that Mississippi is essentially a frontier state with the frontier preference for the freewheeling stump spellbinder against the reasonable moderate expositor; and for the comforting delusions of folklore against the realities of historical truth. It is not so much that Mississippi cherishes its memories of Civil War heroism and privation and indignities as that its people know so little about that war whose evocation is still important to our politicians. It is one thing to extol the very real heroism during the siege of Vicksburg, for instance, and the military genius of General Nathan Bedford Forrest. It is another thing to point to the strong Union sentiment in Mississippi before and during and after the war. And one has only to attend a University of Mississippi football game or a major political rally to discover that the strains of "Dixie" and the unfurling of a Confederate flag bring far louder cheers than do the sight or sound of "The Star Spangled Banner."

Again, political charlatanism aside, most political philosophers who live in Mississippi believe in a strict interpretation of the Constitution of the United States, and especially in the provisions which reserve to the several states all powers not expressly delegated to the federal government. Whatever else Governor Barnett may believe—and one of his beliefs is that his present conduct will win him election to the United States Senate—I am certain that he holds sincerely to the doctrine of states' rights under which he is manipulating.

A sixth explanation is that Mississippi, last of the states to emerge from an archaic, one-sidedly single-crop agricultural economy, reflects profoundly the conservatism inherent in such an economy. Her prophets and leaders are mostly patriarchal old men or younger men with the conservative ideas of the older. Neither category admires or encourages new ideas or intellectual debate. As corollary to the agricultural heritage, Mississippi has been cursed historically with the poverty which blights that heritage. She has been handicapped also by an almost complete restriction of white-Negro relationships to that of white employer and uneducated or little-educated, unskilled or semiskilled Negro worker who demonstrably is still culturally inferior. It is not a contact designed to win white willingness to grant political rights to the Negro. This is especially true in the great plantation areas of Mississippi, notably in the Yazoo-Mississippi Delta where I live, and where, until recent years, the planter was unchallenged as political leader and as extralegal arbiter of all disputes within the limits of his broad acres. There is no white inclination in such areas, where the Negro-white ratio is still roughly two and one-half to one, to permit political control by a majority under an unrestricted franchise. Whatever the morality of such a position, its motivations are, I think, understandable.

Again, political dishonesty and opportunism flourish at every level in every state, as anyone living near Boston knows. In such a state as Mississippi, where white domination is the principal point of agreement among the white citizenry, and where factionalism is generally substituted for issues in a one-party, "courthouse crowd" political system, the chance for effective political or social stirrings are scant indeed.

And lastly, there is another factor, relatively minor but cumulatively significant. Higher education in Mississippi is almost entirely in the hands of the state. To a lesser extent it is in the hands of the church-related institution. The nonsectarian, privately endowed college literally does not exist in Mississippi. This can result in a general indifference to, if not an actual threat to, academic freedom in respect to the intellectual exchange between provocative teacher and inquiring student.

To me, one of the healthiest things, if it can be described as healthy, to come out of the tragedy at Ole Miss has been that a number of the professors of that institution, acting in concert as members of their own professional organization (the American Association of University Professors), have come out strongly against the prefatory events and the political interferences that marked the rioting and what has come after. It is a sound and good, if overdue, result.

And now for some more immediate causes for what has been happening in my state in recent months and days, and specifically on the campus of the University of Mississippi.

I have said that the caliber of Mississippi's politicians is, in general, poor. Perhaps the most striking proof is our Governor Barnett, whose almost unbelievable defiance of federal authority and of the orders of the United States Circuit Court of Appeals led directly to the rioting which claimed two lives on the university campus, caused injury to hundreds and much senseless destruction. The man is an ambitious demagogue who sees in his present course an opportunity for political advancement. Mississippi governors cannot succeed themselves. Governor Barnett has his eye on the seat in the United States Senate now occupied by an honorable conservative, Senator John Stennis. I am thankful that the senatorial campaign is another two years away. If a vote were taken today, Barnett would most probably be elected.

But the governor of Mississippi is not alone to be blamed. Churchmen, most of our newspapers, our more moderate and wiser politicians, and our educators alike have abdicated. They refused to try to assume open leadership at any time during the months in which any perceptive citizen of Mississippi was becoming increasingly aware that the behavior of Barnett and the state legislature could have only one, inevitable result.

Also, a succession of national administration, prior to the present one, contributed, however unwittingly, to disaster. Except for the example of Little Rock, Mississippians have had no reason since Reconstruction to doubt that they could not handle their racial affairs however they wanted without any meaningful interference from the federal government. This belief has been strengthened in recent years—and even in the more distant past—by the virtual abdication of the Congress in matters relating to the implementation of constitutional guarantees to all Americans. The federal courts, and now the executive branch of our government, have sought to fill the vacuum. It is not a happy fact to contemplate.

And lastly, the South has been able to declare, in bitter truth, that those who say that racial discrimination is a southern phenomenon alone are hypocrites or liars or fools. There is no city or state in all our nation in which the Negro is treated economically and politically, as a first-class citizen. Mississippi and the South know this; and the knowledge may well have helped strengthen the spirit of lawless resistance.

Now, for the consequences.

The saddest and most divisive legacy of this collision between Mississippi and the federal government clash is, in a word, hatred. New scars are crisscrossing old ones. The hatred of most white Mississippians for the Kennedy administration, for the federal bayonet, and for the Negro and the nonconforming white Mississippian is a terrible and grievous thing to see and sense and experience. It will not last forever, but it will last a long, long time.

I might inject a short personal note here. I have been publishing newspapers in Louisiana and Mississippi for thirty years, and from time to time we have been up against some pretty hard characters, and we have had to face some rather unpleasant events, criticism, and the like. This business of being burned in effigy is nothing. They burn football coaches in effigy—or anybody they feel like. That doesn't worry anyone. But when people, supposedly sane, civilized people, will spend evening after evening calling—as has happened to my family and myself ever since the riots—calling, and no matter either a man or woman answered, shouting the foulest kind of obscenities (and not all the people doing the calling were men), who do this night after night with their obscenities coupled with threats, and then they hang up without even giving you a chance to cuss back, I have never run into this extent before. It is slowing down, I believe. I hope it is quieting.

We are having a reaction on the part of clergymen and the like and the businessmen in our communities in Mississippi which is heartening and hopeful. But, let me say again, I have never felt that the temper of my people was as high or as hot, that they were as hate-filled, as now.

I can understand it, that what happened to us was historical and certainly none of us like to see federal bayonets on the campus of our college and in our state. But as men in my own town have said, when we defy the law we get what we deserve and we deserve what we get.

The pitting of American against American, of soldier against lawless civilian, of Negro against white, of—if only in an emotional sense—of a state against the nation, gives ammunition to our enemies, and, to all Americans who love their country, a sick and hollow feeling in the stomach and in the mind.

Not the least of the consequences will be an almost certain strengthening of the states' rights third-party movement. Though it will be most successful in the Deep South, and especially in Mississippi, Alabama, South Carolina, and possibly Louisiana, it will not be restricted to these bastions of resistance. And though I do not predict that such a movement can throw or will throw the election of our next president into Congress, this could happen, especially if the next election turns out to be as close as was that of 1960.

Nor do I have to emphasize to you here, whose love of academic freedom and of your university is strong, what has happened to a fine institution of which we Mississippians have long been proud. The University of Mississippi has suffered a cruel and undeserved blow. There were but a minority of students who took part in the rioting, but even fifty, or even twenty, would be too many. The troublemakers were mostly hoodlums, crackpots, racists from outside. As for the faculty, a few may believe Governor Barnett was right in his resistance; but I know of none personally. Yet the university which they serve as teachers or administrators may yet experience severe disciplinary action on the part of the Southern Association of College and Secondary Schools and even the ultimate catastrophe of temporary closure.

But not all the present or ultimate results are negative or destructive or dangerous to our political and social order. We can be comforted and reassured by these evident truths:

1. General Edwin Walker, who personally led the insurrectionists on the Ole Miss campus, has been exposed once and for all for what he is: a seditious psychopath.

2. Through the public statements of their governors and other leaders, and through the lawful conduct of their citizens, a one-sided majority of the once solid southern states has shown that, no matter how distasteful are the race-related decisions of the U.S. Supreme Court, it knows that ours is one nation indivisible and that acceptance of judicial decisions is a vital pillar which supports the nation.
3. It is not likely that any state will again attempt to invoke the fantastic doctrine of interposition, under which an individual state can seek to nullify or disregard the nation's law or the nation itself.
4. The people of our country, North and South, may have been shocked into the realization that we must reassert our profound belief that there is more that unites us than are issues which divide us; and that never again must it become necessary to employ the armed might of the nation to put down civil insurrection in any state for any reason.

Let me restate, in conclusion, something I said at the beginning. I love Mississippi. I know that most of my fellow Mississippians are basically loyal citizens of the United States. I know also that they are angry, bewildered, frustrated at this turning point in the history of our state and the South. The condemnation of the nation will not bring them to their senses or to their knees. The understanding of the nation is needful in this time of painful and epochal transition. And it would be well if every citizen of the United States, looking at Mississippi with pity or scorn or outrage, were to say to himself, "There but for the grace of God go I."

§30 Alex D. Dickson Jr.

Bishop Alex D. Dickson was born on New Africa Plantation in Alligator, Mississippi, on September 9, 1926. He earned a B.B.A. from the University of Mississippi in 1949, an M.Div. (1958) and D.Div. (1984) from the University of the South, and an M.Ed. (1970) from Mississippi College. He married Charnelle Perkins in 1948. They had three sons, Alex (deceased), Charles (of Sylva, N.C.), and John (of Memphis). Right Rev. Dickson was ordained as an Episcopal deacon and priest in 1958. He served as a parish priest in Mississippi from 1958 to 1968. He assumed increasing responsibilities, and was consecrated bishop of West Tennessee in 1983, where he served until his retirement in 1994. Following Charnelle's passing, he married Jane Carver. He currently serves as bishop in residence at St. Michael's Church (S.C.), while also assisting a mission church in Cashiers (N.C.) during summers. His papers reside with him at St. Michael's.

In this sermon of October 14, 1962, Rev. Dickson directly addresses his parishioners at St. Columb's in Jackson, Mississippi. James Meredith had integrated Ole Miss two weeks earlier. The ensuing chaos had resulted in the deaths of international journalist Paul Guihard and jukebox repairman Ray Gunter. Some 20,000 members of various armed services including military police, army engineers, border patrols, nationalized Mississippi guardsmen, and others defended the peace with tear gas to halt the mob's advance with rocks, lead pipes, firearms, and concrete rubble with wire handles. Hundreds were injured. Episcopal priests Duncan M. Gray Jr. and Wofford K. Smith were on campus trying to reconcile the angry crowds. Gray was a former Ole Miss chaplain who served as rector for St. Peter's Church in Oxford, Mississippi, while Smith was the campus chaplain at the time of the melee. Both priests were attempting to mediate and actively disarm vigilantes wishing to prevent integration via force. Rev. Dickson rose to St. Columb's pulpit to defend the controversial action of his fellow clergy. He begins the sermon by categorizing the varying opinions toward the conduct of Gray and Smith—some agree with their words and support them with prayers; some disagree with their words, but support their right to say and do these things, and support them in prayer; some resent all the priests say and do, and feel the place for the priest is the pulpit or sick room; some feel the priest has no right to speak out in the field of politics and social relations. The focal point of Dickson's message is this final category: whether the clergy have appropriate authority to speak and act in the chaotic, controversial world. His response begins with the words of ordination for a priest "in the church of God," not just the Episcopal Church. This responsibility incurs duties in the entire area assigned, not just the church building proper. Second, he argues that baptism unites the individual to the body of Christ. If the rest of the body of Christ was on campus, the priests had to be on campus, too. Third, ordination vows refer to the duty faithfully to dispense the Word and sacraments, the Word being the person of Jesus Christ as recorded in Scriptures. Fourth, Rev. Dickson reminds the congregation that he was born and raised in Mississippi, and also had misgivings about overcentralization of governmental power in this case. He reminds the congregation that regardless of whether the secular legal battles are settled, law and order are divinely approved. Fifth, returning to the life of Jesus Christ, Rev. Dickson points out that while the image of priests in a melee may embarrass some, Jesus was criticized for spending time among publicans and sinners. These priests were about their business dispensing the Word of God. In conclusion, he offers a third way between integration and segregation: congregating in a rational manner to make more reasonable choices about living in a responsible community.

ço⊸ç

The Right to a Free Pulpit
October 14, 1962
St. Columb's Episcopal Church, Jackson, Mississippi

Throughout the recent tragic happenings at the University of Mississippi, the rector of St. Peter's, Oxford, and the Episcopal chaplain at the university have been in the news frequently. From the news stories and interviews we know that our priests in Oxford have been right in the middle of things, trying to offer Christian leadership in the midst of chaos and destruction. At the real risk of life and limb and personal position, these two men were among the handful of people who were on the scene of battle trying to persuade everyone to stop the rioting and return to a state of law and order. They served as mediators in truce talks; they interposed themselves between the crowds and rabble-rousing individuals who were stirring the people into a frenzy; finally, they actually removed rocks and bottles from the hands of rioters. And, in the week following the riots, they joined with all of the Oxford clergymen in calling for a day of repentance.

I'm sure that many of you have mixed feelings about the work of our two fearless and devoted priests in this area. I'm sure that some of you agree with all that they have said and done, and you have supported them with your prayers. I'm sure that others of you have disagreed with some things they have said, but you support their right to say them, and you support their efforts to bring about the restoration of law and order. And, of course, I'm sure that some of you resent all that they have said and done, and feel that the place for a parson is in the pulpit and the sick room. Some even feel that a priest has no right to speak out in the field of politics and social relations.

It is this question that I wish to address this morning—the right to a free pulpit, and the right to minister to people where they are each day of the week, not just in church for one hour on Sunday morning.

When a priest is ordained in the Episcopal Church, these words are used: "*Receive the Holy Ghost for the Office and Work of a Priest in the Church of God*, now committed unto thee by the Imposition of our hands. Whose sins thou dost forgive, they are forgiven; and whose sins thou dost retain, they are retained. And *be thou a faithful Dispenser of the Word of God* and of his holy Sacraments; in the Name of the Father, and of the Son, and of the Holy Ghost."

There are two sections that I particularly want to call to your attention to these words of ordination. "*Receive the Holy Ghost for the Office and Work of a Priest in the Church of God.*" Notice that the man is ordained as "a Priest in the Church of God," not as a priest in the Episcopal Church. And, as such, he has a pastoral responsibility toward all the people in the area to which he is assigned, not just the Episcopalians.

And another thing, we believe that when you are baptized, you are made a living member of the Body of Christ, the Church. Thereafter, wherever you go, you go as the church, whether you want to or not; whatever you do, you do as the church. Whether you bring glory, or condemnation, you do so as the church, as the Body of Christ. Through individual baptized Christians the church went to the campus; the church caused a riot; the church threw rocks, and bricks, and broken glass, and threw acid, and fired shotguns. The church, through individual baptized Christians, also fired tear gas, and ordered troops, and made arrest.

And, so you see, because the church was already at the campus, it was absolutely necessary that the priests of the Church of God be there, too. Be there to seek to bring peace and order and sanity; be there to minister to the wounded; be there to call the church to repentance.

The second part of the words of ordination that I call to your attention is "*And be thou a faithful Dispenser of the Word of God, and of His holy Sacraments; in the Name of the Father, and of the Son, and of the Holy Ghost.*" The priest is ordered by the church to be a faithful dispenser of the Word of God. Now, that doesn't just mean preaching about the Bible. It means that, but it means much more. First of all, the Word of God here is capitalized. The Word of God is the Person, Jesus Christ. In the beginning of the Gospel according to St. John, we read, "In the beginning was the Word, and the Word was with God, and the Word was God. . . . And the Word was made flesh and dwelt among us, full of grace and truth."

Therefore, to be a faithful dispenser of the Word of God, the priest must do more than just tell Bible stories. He must preach Jesus Christ, and him crucified. And if he is going to preach Jesus Christ, then he must preach him as he is recorded in the Holy Scriptures. In the Scripture, we learn that Jesus was to be found not just in the synagogue on the Sabbath, but out in the world where people were living, and fighting, and sinning and dying. He was found cleansing the temple, criticizing the religious and political leaders, and condemning their hypocrisy; He was found feeding the hungry, healing the sick, giving sight to the blind, and hearing to the deaf; and, finally, he was found dying on the cross, convicted by a mob that had been worked into a frenzy by self-concerned religious and political leaders.

It is this Word of God that the priest is ordered to be faithful in dispensing. Ordered to relate this Word of God to that which people are doing and saying. Ordered to bring the judgment of God, as well as his redemption, to bear on every situation.

It is for this reason that I make my plea this morning that the Church of God continue to give its priesthood the freedom of the pulpit, and the freedom of ministry it must have, if it is going to be faithful in dispensing the Word of God.

I make my plea, because the climate in Mississippi for the past eight years has not been one conducive to freedom. The official dogma of massive resistance to desegregation has been laid down, and anyone who dares to question the wisdom of this dogma is subject to intense social, economic, and physical reprisal. No one, absolutely no one, must question publicly the accepted solution.

Now, I am a Mississippian. I'm not an outsider. I speak with a natural southern accent. I was born in Alligator, and I have lived in Moorehead, Cleveland, Greenwood, Rolling Fork, and now Jackson. I went to high school in Cleveland, Mississippi. I went to college at Ole Miss; and I did my theological study at the University of the South. I, too, love Mississippi, and I want to spend the rest of my life serving the Church of God in Mississippi. I have lived and worked with Negroes all my life, and I am quite aware how complex this racial problem has become in this, my beloved state. And I deplore the use of force in trying to solve this problem. I am also quite concerned over the overcentralization of the government resulting in the great loss of individual freedom. But in trying to preserve these liberties, we are coming dangerously close to destroying them ourselves.

The world would have us think that there are only two solutions to this racial conflict. There must be either total segregation, or total integration. But I declare unto you that there is a third way—the way of congregation.

To congregate means to gather; and if the people of God will gather together and seek God's answer to this problem through worship, and study and fellowship; if we, as the people of God, will earnestly seek a positive solution, rather than negative resistance; if we will talk about this and bring God into the conversation; then the Word of God can be effectively ministered to the faithful.

The question of whether a decision handed down by the Supreme Court is the "law of the land" may yet be undecided. This is a question for lawyers and judges to decide. And it is true that all laws do not have the divine imprimatur; but it is certain that a decision for law and order does have divine approval. And each living member of the Church of God is called upon to make this decision.

In conclusion, let me say this—you may have been embarrassed as Episcopalians by the presence of our priests on the campus at Ole Miss in the midst of rioting and destruction—the Pharisees and scribes criticized our Lord for working among publicans and sinners; and you may disagree with what they said from the pulpit (which, by the way, was only partially quoted in our Jackson papers), but a prayerful reading of the words of ordination will declare unto you that they were about their business as priests seeking to be faithful dispensers of the Word of God.

1963

1963

§31 Roy C. Clark

Dr. Roy C. Clark was born on July 24, 1920, in Mobile, Alabama. He earned a B.A. degree from Millsaps College in Jackson, Mississippi, in 1941; three years later he was awarded a B.D. (divinity) degree from Yale University. He married Esther Maddox in 1945, and the couple had two daughters. Clark served five different Methodist churches in Mississippi from 1944 to 1963, including parishes in Pascagoula, Wesson, Centerville, Forest, and Jackson. Upon leaving the state amid major demonstrations in downtown Jackson in August, Clark next served a congregation in Memphis, and four years later, in 1967, he pastored West End Church in Nashville, Tennessee. Clark was elected to the episcopacy of the United Methodist Church in 1980 and served the Columbia, South Carolina, Episcopal Area until his retirement in 1988. After his wife Esther passed in 1991, Clark married Marion Salisbury. Still an active and vibrant presence at ninety-one years of age, Clark presently serves as bishop in residence at his former parish in Nashville.

Unless his listener was paying close attention to this message, the subject of race and racial justice is hardly present in Roy Clark's January message to his Methodist parishioners. The subject comes up for a brief mention only halfway through the address. But what Clark does emphasize with great conviction, logical exposition, and not infrequent repetition is this: the church—his church—simply must be willing to foster a climate of free expression, a climate that, in turn, must not be met with intimidation or reprisals. Presently Clark argues that Christian segregationists are being heard without negative consequences; the same cannot be said for Christian integrationists. Clark bolsters his case not with America's sacred founding texts but with the pronouncements of Christ and with the writings of Paul. Not one to back away from a fight, Clark likens his adversaries to Judas, the Sanhedrin, Pilate, and then the mob—all complicit in the execution of Christ. Clark closes his address by dropping another bomb on his congregants: those who profess to be Christians and who claim to know with certainty God's will regarding the integration question simply are not Christians. And they will be judged accordingly.

Eight months after he delivered this bold message, and by mutual consent, Dr. Clark left his pulpit at Capitol Street Methodist. In a recent interview, Clark admitted that ten years of his preaching on the subject had engendered a hostility that no amount of Christian forbearance could endure.

❧❧

Coming to Grips with the Real Issue
January 13, 1963
Capitol Street Methodist Church, Jackson, Mississippi

When the ruling council of elders and scribes charged Peter and the apostles with disobedience, saying, "We strictly charged you not to teach in this name (of Jesus Christ), yet here you have filled Jerusalem with your teaching," they replied, "We must obey God rather than men."

Peter's answer expresses the Christian principle of life. A Christian is one who seeks to know and to obey the will of God as it is made known in Jesus Christ. A sincere Christian knows that he must obey God not men, nor man-directed ways of life, nor his own desires and wishes, nor anything else but God's will.

A sincere Christian knows that obeying God involves all of life. He recognized the inspired truth in Paul's appeal to the Colossian Christians: "Whatever you do, in word or deed, do everything in the name of the Lord Jesus Christ." I remember saying in a sermon in 1955 that "a Christian is not one who does some special things; rather, he is one who does everything in a special way." He obeys God rather than men in all of life.

We Protestants emphasize another principle of Christian living which we believe to be a basic New Testament principle—namely, that obedience to God is a personal, individual responsibility which cannot be transferred to anyone or anything else. This individual responsibility is illustrated by

Martin Luther in his historic stand before the Diet of Worms. When told to recant—i.e., take back some of his writings and renounce some of his convictions, he said, "Unless I be shown"—not unless the church tells him but unless he, personally, be shown—"by Scripture"—i.e., by the source book of our knowledge of God in Christ—"and reason"—the best insight of which he was capable after inquiry and thought—"I cannot do otherwise. God help me, here I stand."

It is each man's terrible responsibility and wonderful freedom to find God's will for his own life. The church bears its witness to the truth in Christ, but it does not decide for him. He does this for himself. Others may enlighten him by their thinking, but he makes up his own mind. He cannot transfer this terrible responsibility to others by majority vote or by crowd pressure. Even if all the world goes one way, but the Christian man feels that God wants something else, he must obey God not men. He cannot transfer his personal responsibility to obey God to custom, or tradition, or an institution, or to anything else.

The Christian principle—we must obey God rather than men—added to the Protestant principle—each individual is personally responsible before God—demands that every man be given the freedom of Christian conviction and its expression. If God is my king then I must be free to obey my king. The church and state must grant the right of Christian conscience and its expression to every man. We must be free to worship and serve God according to the direction of our Christian conscience.

Recently some fellow ministers and I shared in formulating a statement setting forth this Christian doctrine of individual responsibility and freedom. I would like to read it to you.

> In the light of recent events we affirm the Protestant heritage of freedom of Christian conscience and its expression.
>
> We uphold the layman in his full freedom to follow the honest dictates of his Christian conscience without prejudice or reprisal against him.
>
> We uphold the preacher in his full freedom to express his Christian convictions without prejudice or reprisal against him.
>
> We call upon both preacher and layman to exercise this freedom with charity toward those who disagree and with a sense of responsibility for the church and society.
>
> We remind both preacher and layman that "we must all appear before the judgment seat of Christ, so that each one may receive good or evil, according to what he has done in the body."

> We encourage full and free expression of Christian convictions by ministers and laymen with mutual respect for one another.

Now, obviously, freedom of Christian conviction and its expression is a vital current issue in our church and our state. It has always been an issue in the life of the church and has come to the fore with special urgency in periods of great change. Now is our time in Christian history to deal with this issue in our own church and state.

The issue of freedom of Christian conviction and its expression has been highlighted—but not created, of course—by a statement of conviction issued recently by twenty-eight ministers. Following the appearance of their statement most, if not all, of the twenty-eight ministers received criticism in their local churches and beyond. Two of them, to the best of my knowledge at this hour, have been deprived of the privilege of continuing to minister to their congregations, at least for the time being, and possibly permanently. The continued status of several others was, and may likely still be, in question as efforts were made in official boards to have them censored or removed. A number of the ministers and their families have been under heavy harassment by telephone and otherwise. Threats of physical violence forced in some instances a change of residence for varying lengths of time. One of the ministers suffered damage to his automobile, although in fairness it should be said that in all likelihood this destructive act was not committed by a member of his church, and it is questionable that it was even committed by a member of the community in which he lived.

Now all of this came in reaction to the publication in a church paper and then in the press of a statement of Christian conscience by a group of ministers who were described in these terms by a state newspaper: "These ministers are all native Mississippians, all dedicated to their church work in the state. They are not 'outsiders,' integrationists or Communists. They're merely Mississippi ministers who feel called upon to make their position clear during a time of strife, turmoil and bitterness—much of which could hardly be condoned by the savior of the Christian faith, Jesus Christ."

Their statement of conscientious conviction condemned no one and demanded agreement of no one but did set forth certain basic convictions commonly held among them, most of which when interpreted in their own way could be agreed to by a great number of Mississippi Methodists. A state editor said of this statement, "The statement of the ministers does not bear the earmarks of irresponsibility; on the contrary it seems to have been a sensible one to those individuals who read it carefully."

Well, whether or not this is your judgment of the statement, it does express convictions, most if not all of which I have expressed in one form or another many times in this pulpit. A number of persons have said to me that this is a statement with which they could agree provided, of course, they could interpret it in their way.

In the light of the reaction to this statement, it seems clear that the main issue in our church and state is no longer segregation or desegregation. The main issue is this: Do ministers and laymen have the right to freely discuss the merits or demerits of segregation and related subjects without reprisal or intimidation? Do we have the freedom of Christian conscience and its expression?

Before you give your final answer to that, please follow me a bit further in my thinking. It is important to remember that there is a distinction between the expression of conscientious disagreement and reprisal against the person with whom we disagree. There is a difference between public and private debate and the effort to deprive another of his livelihood, tranquility, or reputation because of this debate. Put in terms of the local church, there is a difference between a minister and Sunday school teacher disagreeing with an open and honest debate between them, and the effort on the part of the minister to deprive the Sunday school teacher of his right to teach because they disagree. I think you see the distinction I am making. Plainly put, each Christian has the right to follow his Christian conscience and to work for his Christian convictions in proper ways. This right, however, does not include for Christian people the right of reprisal or intimidation toward those who disagree with us.

In saying that the main issue before us today is not segregation or desegregation, I am not saying that that issue is unimportant. It is important, obviously. A majority of the people of the Methodist churches of Mississippi prefer at this time to maintain segregation. We know this without voting on it. Let me point out something else—namely, that under the constitution of the Methodist Church, the churches of Mississippi cannot be desegregated until a two-thirds majority of our people want that to take place. In the Methodist Church we have "states' rights," if you please. No one, to my knowledge, has attempted to and no one can bring about the desegregation of Mississippi Methodist churches until two-thirds of you who make up the church want it. So I say that in the light of the majority opinion of Methodists and the light of the constitutional procedures involved, the most urgent issue before us is not segregation or desegregation; it is rather whether or not Mississippi ministers and laymen have the freedom to openly disagree, if they so desire, with the majority about segregation and related matters without unfair reprisal against them.

I have talked and listened to a number of laymen in the last week. A majority of those to whom I have talked tell me they think they can sincerely follow the light they now have in Christ—i.e., obey God—and support segregation. That is their privilege. I have been saying to such laymen this week the same thing George Fox said to William Penn. Where Fox, the pacifist, said to Penn, the soldier, "Wear the sword as long as the Lord will let you," I have been saying to laymen, "Support segregation as long as the Lord will let you." But the most pressing moral issue before us is, do I and others like me, who sincerely believe by our light from Christ that justice and love require modification in the segregated way of life, have the same right to believe as we do and to express this belief and to work for it in appropriate ways without prejudice or reprisal against ourselves or our families?

Let me be specific: This week a local newspaper published a letter from a young minister of the Mississippi Conference. He supported segregation and most of the other things many Mississippians apparently support now. To the best of my knowledge, after publicly stating his position, he has received no threatening phone calls. He and his family have not been harassed. His official board has not met in secret session to determine his fate. No violence has been committed against his property. Now the issue I raise—I think it is a moral issue—is do those of us who differ with this young man have the same right to express in similar ways our viewpoints with the same freedom from molestation?

In defense of the consequences which some of the twenty-eight have encountered, it is sometimes said, and has been said to me two or three times this week, laymen and ministers have freedom to express their convictions provided they are willing to take the consequences. There is one great element of truth in this contention. Jesus called it "counting the cost." Surely in the use of his freedom every man should consider the consequences and be prepared to take them. That is a good doctrine for the man who is using his freedom, but what about the man who brings on the consequences?

Without attempting to be dramatic, I ask you to look at our Lord. He went to Jerusalem with his eyes wide open. He did not have to go. He exercised his freedom. He knew what was waiting for him. He got it. He took it like a man. But, now, does this mean that Judas, who helped the consequences come, is without moral responsibility? Or that the Sanhedrin, which charged our Lord falsely with intentions he never had in order to inflame the mob and force Pilate's hand, is without moral responsibility? Does this freedom to act with consequence mean cynical Pilate is without moral responsibility for his part in bringing the consequences? Does it mark as right the confused emotions of individuals who had become a mob and shouted for the release of a notorious criminal while calling for the blood of the Prince of Peace?

You see, it is one thing to say that when a man uses his freedom he ought to be willing to take the consequences, but it is another thing when you are one who is helping to give the consequences. Today in Cuba, in Hungary, in Moscow a man is also free to say there what he wishes if he is willing to face the consequences. I do not believe—and I am absolutely sincere in this—there is a person in a Methodist church who, when he really thinks about it, wants to create the sort of climate here in which you are free to speak provided you are willing to go to a Mississippi equivalent of Siberia.

I think we can all agree that we are in deep trouble when men fear to speak their minds on serious matters of public and moral concern because of what will happen to them. I believe we are too deeply committed to our Lord, who said, "Blessed are the merciful for they shall obtain mercy" to further that kind of condition. Should we be tempted, let us ponder the words of our Lord and of St. Paul:

> You have heard that it was said "you shall love your neighbor and hate your enemy." But I say to you, Love your enemies (or those you think are your enemies—sometimes your enemies turn out to be your true friends) and pray for those who persecute you (or whom you think persecute you). (Matthew 5:7, 43, 44)

> Repay no one evil for evil, but take thought for what is noble in the sight of all. (Romans 12:17)

> Brethren, if a man is overtaken in a trespass, you who are spiritual should restore him in the spirit of gentleness. Look to yourself, lest you too be tempted. (Galatians 6:1)

> But the fruit of the Spirit is love, joy, peace, patience, kindness, goodness, faithfulness, gentleness, self-control; against such there is no law. (Galatians 5:22)

I ask your attention to one further thought, and then I come to a conclusion. Each of us should remember that an essential part of obeying God is to always be open to more light about God's will. Earlier I defined a

Christian as one who is honestly and sincerely seeking to know and follow the will of God as it is made known in Jesus Christ. I want to follow that definition of a Christian with these three statements:

In my judgment a person can support segregation and be a Christian *if* he is *honestly* seeking to know and to follow the light God has given us in the life and teachings of Jesus Christ. A person can support desegregation and be a Christian *if* he is *honestly* seeking to know and follow the light God has given us in the life and teachings of Jesus Christ.

But, now, I am going to make the kind of statement I do not remember having made in nine and a half years of preaching here. I do not believe I have ever said before that a person cannot be a Christian if he does so and so, but I am going to risk that kind of statement this morning. In my judgment neither person referred to above—i.e., the one who supports segregation or supports desegregation—can be a Christian if he decides he has all the light there is on the subject and is not open to new and more light. Even less could he afford to try to keep others from expressing the light of their Christian conscience. A Christian will not say to God about any moral issue, "I have the final answer; there is nothing more I need to learn about your will."

In the statement of the twenty-eight ministers the phrase "unalterably opposed" was used. I would not have signed a statement with that word in it. I do not believe it was meant in its literal sense. I do not believe the Christian person ever says, "My mind is made up. It will not be altered under any circumstances. This is it." When Martin Luther defended the great principles of evangelical faith, he never said, "I have the final truth." He said rather, "Unless I am shown by Scripture and reason, here I stand." The door was left open to further light. So it must always be left open by sincere Christians.

How can we receive more light? Only by making the church the fellowship in which the light of Christ as each man sees it is fully and freely shared. How can this be if we are not free to express and discuss our convictions even—and especially—when we disagree. We in the church must keep open the right to free discussion of our Christian viewpoints with charity for those who disagree in order to enable God to bring the new insights each one of us needs no matter what his opinion about any subject this morning.

I conclude by asking three things of you:

One, I ask you to respect the Christian conscience of the other man. I ask this of people on both sides of the segregation issue. Too quickly we jump to malign the character of someone else with whom we disagree. Let us give every man the credit for being sincere in his Christian conscience. Let us not accuse him of being the dupe of somebody else. Let us respect the integrity of each other's conscience. I do not know all the influences that shaped my conscience on racial justice—I probably got some of my concern from my father, and he probably got his from his father, who, as a Methodist layman with great love for his Lord, had a deep sense of concern for the feelings of all men, including Negroes. I could tell you a story this morning of the protest he made in his time against something he thought was unjust. I want the integrity of my conscience, nurtured in three generations of Christian devotion, respected, and I will respect yours as well.

Secondly, let us *exercise our* freedom of Christian conviction with charity toward those who disagree. Let us expect that we shall have the right to express our viewpoint without prejudice against us. Let us grant the same right to others. Let us never ask for ourselves what we are not willing to give to others.

Third, let us all remember that this is no inconsequential business we are in. It has to do with the solemn duty to obey God rather than men. Charles Wesley states the responsibility of each one of us. Let us carefully consider his words:

"A charge to keep I have, A God to glorify.
　　A never-dying soul to save, And fit it for the sky.
To serve the present age, My calling to fulfill;
　　O may it all my powers engage To do my Master's will!
Arm me with jealous care, As in Thy sight to live,
　　And, oh, Thy servant, Lord, prepare A strict account to give.
Help me to watch and pray, And on Thyself rely,
　　Assured, if I my trust betray, I shall for ever die."

Let us pray.

O Lord God, let us always obey the command of our Lord, "Whatsoever ye would that men should do to you, do ye also unto them." Amen.

§32 Sargent Shriver

Robert Sargent Shriver Jr. was born November 9, 1915, in Westminster, Maryland. Activism was a long family tradition dating at least as early as 1776 at Maryland's founding, continuing with Shriver's mother, Hilda, a women's suffrage activist. Shriver attended Canterbury Prep school before earning bachelor's (1938) and law (1941) degrees at Yale University, where he also edited the *Yale Daily News*. The Shrivers hailed from the oft-disputed Electoral Palatinate. Perhaps out of this sense of historical complexity, Shriver was initially critical of U.S. involvement in World War II, though he enlisted in the Navy after taking the bar exam in 1941. He received a purple heart for shrapnel wounds sustained at Guadalcanal. At the end of the war, Shriver worked for Joseph P. Kennedy Sr., and in 1953 married his daughter, Eunice. They raised five children, including Maria, a journalist and former first lady of California. Shriver's administrative roles in several administrations are too numerous to detail, but a few stand out, including his founding directorship of the Peace Corps during the Kennedy administration, vice presidential nomination as running mate to George McGovern in 1968, and ambassadorship to France (1968–1970). The Clinton administration awarded him the Presidential Medal of Freedom, the highest civilian honor in the United States. He died on January 18, 2011. Many of his papers can be found at the John F. Kennedy Presidential Library and the Maryland Historical Society.

In his speech of January 14, 1963, "America, Race, and the World," Shriver addresses an ecumenical audience at the National Conference on Religion and Race, cosponsored by the National Council of Churches, the Synagogue Council of America, and the National Catholic Welfare Conference. They gather to commemorate the one-hundredth anniversary of the Emancipation Proclamation. Shriver, then the director of the Peace Corps, begins with an anecdote about America's loss of conscience from African American author James Baldwin. His stated purpose in this speech is to awaken that conscience. He calls religious leaders to action even in the face of persecution, citing the activism of American clergy during the pre–Civil War era. He calls clergy to take the same stance during the 1960s racial struggles. Shriver challenges churches to specific action: "I wonder, furthermore, why each minister, rabbi, and priest does not map a specific program for his congregation—a program which will produce concrete gains over the next twelve months." He suggests action such as doubling the number of African American families in congregations, training African American lay leaders to participate fully in congregational affairs, and asking members to volunteer 10 percent of their time to help. Distinguishing between the role of government and the role of religion, Shriver calls on clergy to "help us to see what is our task, inspire us with the faith that God is above us and with us and that *he* will help us. *We* will do what is right. Stir our consciences."

ڡ‌ﻌ

Religion and Race
January 14, 1963
Chicago, Illinois

In a powerful and moving essay the Negro author James Baldwin has described an incident which happened to him only a few miles from here at Chicago's O'Hare Airport. He and two Negro friends—all well over thirty—were refused service in the airport lounge on the pretense they were too young. After a long, noisy altercation, and after calling the manager, they were finally served. During the entire affair not one of the many white people said a word to help. When it was all over one of the Negroes, a Korean War veteran, turned to the young white man beside him and said, "You know, that fight was your fight too." The young man turned to him, saying, "I lost my conscience a long time ago," and turned and walked out.

The purpose of this meeting is to reawaken that conscience—to direct the immense power of religion to shaping the conduct and thoughts of men toward their brother in a manner consistent with the compassion and love on which our spiritual tradition rests.

In so doing you follow in a great tradition. From the time of the ancient Hebrew prophet and the dispersal of the money changers, men of God have taught us that social problems are moral problems on a huge scale, that a religion which would struggle to remove oppression from the world of men would not be able to create the world of the spirit. This tradition, one which is also deeply imbedded in our own country's history, was never more evident than in the years preceding the proclamation of the emancipation whose centenary we celebrate now. At that time men of God, men of all faiths, men of the North, and men of the South took to pulpit, to press, and to public squares to demand an end to the moral evil of slavery.

Many religious leaders who followed this path suffered for it. Many were condemned by their congregations and deprived of their position. Churches were burned and physical violence was often the reward of those who spoke freely. But their efforts were a significant force in ending slavery and reshaping our society. And by their acts they not only restored dignity and hope to millions of Americans—they immeasurably elevated and strengthened the churches which they served.

Today, a century later, we are given the same great opportunity. Today again the problem of racial wrongs and racial hatred is the central moral problem of our republic. Today again hostility and misunderstanding, and even violence, awaits the man who attempts to translate the meaning of God's love into the acts and thoughts of man. Today again the hope for happiness of millions of Negro Americans can be profoundly affected by your efforts. And today again religion has one of the rare historical opportunities to renew its own purpose, enhance the dignity of its social role, and strengthen its institutions and its heritage by pitting itself against vast and powerful social forces which deny the role of God in the affairs of man. It is, of course, difficult for me to speak of these matters to this audience of scholars and teachers, men of great learning and men who have shaped the religious institutions of today's America.

I am not a theologian.

I am not an "expert" in race relations.

My only credentials in speaking to you are my experience here in Chicago with the Interracial Council, my work with the Peace Corps, and a layman's strong faith in making faith personally meaningful in a disturbing world.

As an official of the government I am encouraged by a meeting like this. Justice for men is a common objective of religion and government and the exclusive domain of neither.

I hope the traditional American regard for the separation of church and state will never be interpreted as an excuse for either to preempt—or ignore— the vigorous pursuit of human dignity and freedom which are the legitimate concerns of both church and state.

But laws and government are at best coarse and inefficient instruments for remolding social institutions or illuminating the dark places of the human heart. They can deal only with the broadest and most obvious problems: guarding against segregation in schools but not against the thousands of incidents of discrimination and hatred which give the lie to what is learned in the schoolroom. They can carry sweeping mandates, but the process of their enforcement is so ponderous that it takes the entire energies of the nation to secure entrance of a single Negro into an unwilling white university while thousands more are without hope of entering.

They can call for the highest standards of moral conduct, but those standards are only tortuously and imperceptibly imposed upon a community which does not accept them, verifying the dictate of Walter Rauschenbush that "laws do not create moral conviction, they merely recognize and enforce them."

For even though law can compel and even educate, in the last analysis, the rule of law depends upon a legal order which embodies the convictions, decisions, and judgments of the men it governs.

If we recognize that laws alone are inadequate, that legislatures and presidents cannot impose moral convictions, then we must look to those institutions whose task it is to teach moral values, to restate eternal principles in terms of today's conflicts, and to conform the daily conduct of men to the guide values of justice, of love, and of compassion. Preeminent among those institutions is religion and the church.

Henry Ward Beecher once wrote, "That man is not a shepherd of his flocks who fails to teach the flock how to apply moral trust to every phase of ordinary practical duty." This is one of the great lessons of the history of religion. It is a lesson of Scriptures and traditions. And it is also a lesson taught by Abraham, Moses, and Christ.

I find it alarming, therefore, when the government looks to religious community for its share of the task and encounters, too often, a bland philosophy of laissez-faire.

As a layman, for example, I wonder why I can go to church fifty-two times a year and not hear one sermon on the practical problems of race relations? I wonder why a conference like this does not lead to a continuing exchange of views and ideas and to a coordination of efforts to solve specific problems throughout the year. I wonder, furthermore, why each minister, rabbi, and priest does not map a specific program for his congregation—a program which will produce concrete gains over the next twelve months. Such a program could do many things.

It could bring to an end segregation in those churches and church schools where it exists.

It could include a pledge to double the number of Negro families in the congregation where Negroes now attend.

It could include the establishment of interracial councils where none exists.

It could introduce Negroes to every social and community event which the church sponsors or participates in.

It could train lay Negro teachers and leaders to participate fully in congregational affairs.

If such a program intended finally to bury religious laissez-faire in racial problems where instituted, it would encourage each member of the congregation to pledge a tithe of his time to removing racial barriers at work, at play, and at worship.

I wonder why an appeal requesting every church member to give a tithe of his time has not been made already. Just a few Sundays ago a Catholic weekly newspaper, the *Sunday Visitor*, the whole front page was devoted to this subject of tithing, but the discussion was focused primarily on the financial aspect of tithing. George Romney, the new Republican governor of Michigan, impressed me with his recent statement acknowledging quite openly that he was accustomed to giving a tithe of his income to the Mormon Church. But isn't it easier to give a tithe of your money than to give a tithe of your time? Isn't the time when you give yourself more important than the money?

Let me be more specific. The Peace Corps has shown what Americans will do when they are challenged by a high purpose. They respond enthusiastically no matter what the personal cost.

Thousands of them volunteered to serve even in the days when the skeptics and cynics were ridiculing the Peace Corps as "a children's crusade," "a beatniks' boondoggle," and a "Kiddy Korps."

They deliberately chose a hard—and to some an unpopular—course because first, it is voluntary; second, it demands their utmost; third, it is worthwhile.

These volunteers have already written the moral to a story that is still being told. That moral: "A nation cannot require too much of its citizens if the cause is right."

Do our churches expect too little of their members in solving race problems?

Suppose 5,000 congregations in America were to set up volunteer groups to combat racial prejudice and eliminate racial tensions in 5,000 religious precincts throughout America. And suppose 5,000 were to become 10,000 or 20,000?

In thousands of communities religiously inspired volunteers would be inviting Negro families to personal social functions.

They would be organizing and joining interracial councils, securing entrance of Negroes into previously all-white neighborhoods, insuring enforcement of constitutional rights to equal opportunity, and improving living conditions in segregated neighborhoods.

A profound new force would be at work in America, emanating from the deepest wells of religious inspiration and reaching for the noblest summits of human experience. That combination would be invincible.

There will be those who scoff at so pointed an effort by organized religion to deal with the major social disorder.

Some will cry "busybodies," but they will not be the first. When a group of English bishops tried to mediate the bitter British coal strike of 1926, Prime Minister Baldwin retorted by asking how they would like it if he referred the revision of the Athanasian Creed to the Iron and Steel Federation.

Some critics will want to ignore the church's word on the thesis that it is irrelevant—like the corporation president who said, "Of course, segregation is wrong from the Christian point of view. Let's not discuss it from that point of view."

Still others will argue, "So what? Go ahead. You won't [do] any good but you won't do any harm either."

Few people read much history—as William Temple reminded us—otherwise they would know that history abounds with dramatic examples of the impact made by the spirit of religion upon the life of mankind.

The abolition of the slave trade, for example, was carried through by Wilberforce and his friends in the inspiration of their Christian faith. Other faiths can point to similar accomplishments.

More recently, efforts by churches and synagogues have illustrated what can be accomplished. After his school system was desegregated, one Kentucky superintendent said, "I believe ministers and lay church leaders made the greatest contribution in getting the general public to accept desegregation."

You may be familiar with the inspiring experience in St. Louis. The six-hundred-member Church Federation set aside a Sunday for thanksgiving prayer for public school desegregation. It challenged pastors and members to take an open stand for integration. The cardinal called in a general letter for all Catholic pastors to influence their hundreds of thousands of parishioners to cooperate. The Rabbinical Association urged all citizens to work and pray for its success.

On the other end, we know what can happen when religious leadership is absent. Remember Clinton, Tennessee? Ugly violence flared there when desegregation was attempted. It took 650 National Guardsmen and thirty-nine state highway troopers led by a burly 290-pound commander to restore order after days of tension.

When a special report was written to analyze what had happened in Clinton, this significant sentence appeared: "Churches were not utilized to any extent in Clinton, Tennessee."

During the crisis a Baptist minister escorted Negro students through the howling crowds. He was beaten by the mob, but his courage was unshaken. What might have happened at Clinton had the religious community rallied to support him?

One man is not enough.

There must be others.

I said earlier there is no reliable justice without the machinery of justice: the government. But the machinery of justice cannot be effective without men and women who have the will and character to make it work.

There is where we come again to religion. What is it that produces men and women with the will and character to make the machinery of justice work if it is not religious faith?

The maxim is true that politics is the art of the possible. The constant challenge we face in politics is to enlarge the area of the possible—"to lengthen the stakes," in biblical language.

But to do that requires that men change their objective. But they can't change their objective unless they change their prejudices, and that requires changes in men's attitudes, and that requires changes in men's minds, and that requires changes in men's hearts—that the human heart is the business of religion.

So I ask, "Is there any way of creating a social order of justice if religion does not do its work in the minds and hearts of men?

I don't think so.

Is there any way of winning racial equality if religion does not permeate its adherents with its urgent sense of personal responsibility for the injustice of our present system?

I cannot stress this too much. We believe the success of the Peace Corps is due to the fact that thousands of Americans are willing to take personal responsibility for bringing peace to the world.

They have seen their task and have set forth to do it.

In race relations there is a strong tendency to blame "society" for our errors. We pass the blame on to anyone of a number of impersonal causes—environment, education, etc. Shakespeare was right: "This is the excellent sophistry of the world, that when we are sick in fortune, often in surfeit of our own behavior, we make guilty of all disasters the sun, the moon, and the stars, as if we are fools, by heavenly compulsion, knaves, thieves and teachers by spherical predominance." But he was also right when he went on to say, "The fault, dear Brutus, is not in our stars, but in ourselves." It is the province of religion to instill a sense of personal responsibility into mankind: "If you want to cleanse the stream" so the old proverb goes—"get at the source." The attitudes and concepts, the prejudice and hate which pollute the stream of political life—government can deal with their symptoms; religion must deal with their source. I think that this is what the Presbyterian General Assembly had in mind a hundred years ago when it declared, "The sphere of the church is wider and more searching than the sphere of the magistrate." Religion reaches into the sanctuary of human experience, where attitudes are formed.

We can agree government has its business, religion has its.

The important thing is to get on with the job. We have tried in the Peace Corps to try to deal positively with the problem. For example, we set out deliberately to recruit as many Negroes and representatives of other minority groups as possible for jobs in every echelon. We knew Negroes would not ordinarily seek out these jobs, so we decided to seek them out. Today 7.4 percent of our higher echelon positions are filled by Negroes. Other government agencies employ .8 percent Negroes in similar grades. Twenty-four percent of our other positions are filled by Negroes. The figure for other agencies is 5.5 percent.

We made another breakthrough. In the beginning we were told that the Peace Corps would never get invited to the Muslim countries because our policies require that our volunteers be recruited without discrimination, that they be assigned without discrimination, and that they be received without discrimination.

I remember one senator's comment in particular: "You'll never be in the Arab Republic!"

The truth of the matter is the Peace Corps is operating in *three* Muslim countries. Some of our volunteers are Jewish, and I am proud to report that every one of them has been well received by their Muslim hosts.

When I told this to Golda Meir, foreign minister of Israel, she found it almost impossible to believe that Jewish volunteers had received a hospitable welcome from Muslim hosts.

We sent a Chinese American doctor to Ghana. When he rose to speak to his students they could not believe he was from the United States—"that place across the sea where no colored man can go to school." They thought he was a Chinese Communist.

In Nepal we sent four volunteers to teach in a small college. Three of them were visited one night by a young Marxist student who had studied in Peking and who had already won a scholarship to Lumumba University in Moscow. This student had also just been elected to a place on the important "panchayat" council which runs the city government.

He came to rib the volunteers about discrimination in America. "Just a minute," they interrupted him, "we will let Carl Jorgenson talk about that." And they called for a fourth volunteer who was studying in his room. Carl Jorgenson walked in, a tall young Negro, a top graduate of Harvard, the son of a leader of the NAACP in Washington. "Sure, let's talk about it," he said. And they did. The young Marxist—stunned that America would let a Negro in the Peace Corps, that a Negro could graduate from Harvard, that he would be living with three white Americans—has come back time and time again to discuss America with the volunteers.

In the first days of the Peace Corps we were told that Protestant volunteers would never be accepted in the villages of Latin America. We heard that the campesinos had been told that if they talked to a Peace Corps volunteer their souls would be in danger of hell.

The truth, ladies and gentlemen, is that we have volunteers all over Latin America—many of them Protestant young men and women—and there has not yet been one incident of discrimination.

I might add that the first two volunteers killed in service died in a plane crash in Colombia with thirty-two Colombians. One was a Jewish boy from Chicago. The other was a young Baptist from Missouri. They died in a Catholic country. *El Tiempe*, the principal newspaper of Bogota, editorialized, "They were the first to fulfill the Rite of Blood which united them (with Colombians) in an indissoluble tie . . . their blood . . . [has] fallen with those of our fellow countrymen. The sacrifice of blood is truly consummated. Two races were forged together in this dramatic accident. That this be not in vain is the ardent hope of millions of human beings."

There is only one real explanation of our success in the field of race relations. We made a deliberate effort to change old patterns. If I have any justification to speak to this august body, it is to encourage you to make a conscious deliberate assault on racial barriers. From our experience in the Peace Corps I know those barriers are vulnerable.

Let me close with a pledge and a request.

We in government will continue our efforts. We will move with all the instruments at our command to achieve justice among men. That is our pledge to you. My request is simply this: help us. If there is to be a social order allowing the fullest possible development of individual personality, if there is to be the widest and deepest fellowship among men of different races, we need what Maritain has called democracy of the person. You can bring it about.

Help us to see what is our task, inspire us with the faith that God is above us and with us and that He will help us. We will do what is right. Stir our consciences. Strengthen our wills. Inspire and challenge us to take our principles into the toughest walks of life and make them work.

§33 Joachim Prinz

Dr. Joachim Prinz was born into a well-to-do merchant family in Burkhardts-dorf, Upper Silesia, on May 10, 1902. Young Prinz was very close to his mother, but his conservative father did not approve of his aspirations to be a rabbinical student. He studied at the University of Berlin and the University of Breslau, and earned a Ph.D. in philosophy, with a minor in art history from the University of Giessen in 1924. He married his first wife, Lucie Horovitz, and was ordained a rabbi at the Jewish Theological Seminary in Breslau in 1925. Tragically, Lucie died in 1931 shortly after giving birth to their first child, who was named in her honor. Prinz married Hilde Gold-schmidt in 1932, and together they had four children, including a daughter they adopted, Jo Seelmann, whose family had been killed at Auschwitz.

Prinz served as a rabbi in Berlin for twelve years and quickly became one of the most sought-after rabbis in Germany. Frequently did he speak out eloquently and forcefully against Nazism, and frequently was he harassed and/or arrested for his views. He actively encouraged Jews to leave Germany ahead of the persecution he saw coming. Prinz was ordered to leave Germany by the Nazis in 1937 for his criticism of the regime. He and his family emigrated to the United States at the invitation of Rabbi Stephen Wise, and they eventually settled in Newark, New Jersey. He was named rabbi of Temple B'nai Abraham in 1939 and served its congregants for thirty-eight years until his retirement in 1977. Prinz became deeply involved with political and social matters. He served as president of the American Jewish Congress and served two terms as chairman of the Conference of Presidents of Major American Jewish Organizations. Prinz was also one of the ten founding chairmen of the 1963 March on Washington. After his retirement in 1977, Prinz continued to preach on High Holy Days. He died on September 30, 1988. His papers are housed at the American Jewish Archives in Cincinnati, Ohio.

Rabbi Prinz delivered his brief remarks at the March on Washington just before the final speaker of the afternoon, Dr. Martin Luther King, whose resounding "I Have a Dream" speech quickly became the dominant memory and message of that signature event. Overshadowed were speakers such as John Lewis, Fred Shuttlesworth, Eugene Carson Blake, and Mathew Ahmann, to say nothing of the "tribute" to the women of the movement. Also forgotten in the echo of King's eloquence is that the impetus behind the march came out of the successes in Birmingham, ongoing protests in Cambridge, Maryland, Albany, Georgia, Danville, Virginia, and Jackson, Mississippi. King and other movement leaders leveraged these events and the national support they had engendered to force President Kennedy to act, which he finally did on June 11, 1963, by committing his administration to widespread and meaningful civil rights legislation. The NAACP's Medgar Evers was murdered just hours after Kennedy's announcement.

Prinz's address functions rhetorically to enact his message; that is, Prinz notes, "The most urgent, the most disgraceful, the most shameful and the most tragic problem is silence." Recalling days thirty years earlier when he often heard a defeaning silence amid the persecution of Jews, Prinz calls on his audience to be vocal advocates for racial justice—in a word, to speak out against an oppression antithetical to America's ideals. Prinz's act of speaking out against silence enacts the very speech he avows, thus embodying his argument.

৩৵৶

A Nation of Silent Onlookers

August 28, 1963
March on Washington, Washington, D.C.

I speak to you as an American Jew. As Americans we share the profound concern of millions of people about the shame and disgrace of inequality and injustice, which make a mockery of the great American idea.

As Jews we bring to this great demonstration, in which thousands of us proudly participate, a twofold experience—one of the spirit and one of our history.

In the realm of the spirit, our fathers taught us thousands of years ago that when God created man, he created him as everybody's neighbor. "Neighbor" is not a geographic term. It is a moral concept. It means our collective responsibility for this preservation of man's dignity and integrity.

From our Jewish historic experience of three and a half thousand years we say: our ancient history began with slavery and the yearning for freedom. During the Middle Ages my people lived for a thousand years in the ghettos of Europe. Our modern history begins with a proclamation of emancipation.

It is for these reasons that it is not merely sympathy and compassion for the black people of America that motivates us. It is above all and beyond all such sympathies and emotions a sense of complete identification and solidarity born of our own painful historic experience.

When I was the rabbi of the Jewish community in Berlin under the Hitler regime, I learned many things. The most important thing that I learned under those tragic circumstances was that bigotry and hatred are not the most urgent problem. The most urgent, the most disgraceful, the most shameful, and the most tragic problem is silence.

A great people which had created a great civilization had become a nation of silent onlookers. They remained silent in the face of hate, in the face of brutality, and in the face of mass murder.

America must not become a nation of onlookers. America must not remain silent. Not merely black America, but all of America. It must speak up and act, from the president down to the humblest of us, and not for the sake of the Negro, not for the sake of the black community, but for the sake of the image, the dream, the idea, and the aspiration of America itself.

Our children, yours and mine, in every school across the land, every morning pledge allegiance to the flag of the United States and to the republic for which it stands, and then they, the children, speak fervently and innocently of this land as the land of "liberty and justice for all."

The time, I believe, has come to work together—for it is not enough to hope together, and it is not enough to pray together—to work together that the children's oath, pronounced every morning from Maine to California, from North to South, that this oath will become a glorious, unshakeable reality in a morally renewed and united America.

§34 Milton L. Grafman

Rabbi Milton Louis Grafman was born on April 21, 1907, in Washington, D.C. His cantor father, Reuben, was instrumental in introducing his son to the Hebrew language and the Torah. After graduating from high school in Pittsburgh, Pennsylvania, Grafman matriculated at the University of Pittsburgh and the University of Cincinnati, where he earned his bachelor's degree in 1926. Five years later he married Ida Weinstein, and the couple would have two children. He studied for the rabbinate at Hebrew Union College and was ordained in 1933. For eight years he served Temple Adath Israel in Lexington, Kentucky, then moved south to become senior rabbi at Birmingham, Alabama's Temple Emanu-El in December 1941. During a trip to Europe in 1938, Grafman was horrified to see how the Nazis treated German Jews. The memory of that trip stayed with him long after his return; it also informed his staunchly Zionist views following the war. While Grafman is infamously remembered for the events in Birmingham in 1963, he was no stranger to racial controversy. In February 1956 the University of Mississippi had cancelled an appearance by Rev. Alvin Kershaw following revelations that the minister would donate some of his recent game show winnings to the NAACP. That decision prompted Grafman to cancel a scheduled visit to Ole Miss, as the rabbi could not abide the egregious restrictions on freedom of expression. Grafman's principled stand was met with a steady stream of hate mail back home in Birmingham.

Grafman is remembered far less for his progressive stands on racial inequality than he is for being one of eight clergy addressed in Martin Luther King Jr.'s "Letter from Birmingham Jail." Now a canonical state paper, King's letter took as its point of departure a letter published in two Birmingham newspapers on April 13, 1963, by the eight locals. The ministers' joint missive called for an end to demonstrations, and it excoriated "outsiders" for inflaming the situation; too, their use of the phrase "law and order" connoted for many the racial status quo—in a word, continued segregation. For the remainder of his long life Grafman would receive hate mail for his perceived obstructionist role in the Birmingham crisis. Grafman retired from Temple Emanu-El in 1975 after thirty-four years of service. So admired and beloved was he by his fellow clergy that Grafman was selected to head the Birmingham Ministerial Association in 1974; he was the first rabbi to hold this post. Grafman died on May 28, 1995. His papers are housed at the Birmingham Public Library, and several speeches are held by the American Jewish Archives.

The following two addresses are the Friday evening Kaddish (a memo-rial for the dead) and the Rosh Hashanah morning sermon, which occured-just days after the murders of Carol Robertson, Denise McNair, Addie May Collins, and Cynthia Wesley. Rabbi Grafman pours out his soul to his Birmingham congregants. His grief and his anger are directed at the "nice people" of the city, as well as the "liberals" in his own synagogue. They hadn't been willing to take a public stand against the city's injustices—unlike their rabbi. The "lonely road" Grafman has walked, and continues to walk, should trouble his listeners, whose "guts" and courage await open expres-sion in places like the local newspaper. That exhortation seems to cause Grafman to veer into the personal—again—and to reveal his pain caused by Dr. King's letter. Grafman closes his anguished sermon by calling on his congregants to write checks—for the continued safety of the synagogue and for the rebuilding of the Sixteenth Street Baptist Church.

၄ၜၑ

Sick at Heart: Kaddish for Bombing Victims
September 18, 1963
Kaddish for Bombing Victims

Let us bow our heads in silence. Memory of Carol Robertson, Denise McNair, Addie Mae Collins, Cynthia Wesley, James Robinson, Virgil Ware, brutally murdered, wantonly killed, insanely slain, whose death we mourn, whose families we would comfort, the shame of whose murder we would and we must have our city atone. Memory of all our own loved ones, who departed from among us. These departed who we now remem-ber have entered into the peace of life eternal, may they still live on earth in the acts of goodness they performed, and in the hearts of those who cher-ish their memory. May the beauty of their life abide among us as a loving benediction.

Y'hei shlama raba min-sh'maya v'chayim aleinu
v'al-kol-yisrael, v'im'ru: "amen."

Oseh shalom bimromav, hu ya'aseh shalom aleinu
v'al kol-yisrael, v'imru: "amen."

[Translation: May there be abundant peace from heaven, and life, for us and for all Israel; and say, Amen.

May the father of peace send peace to all who mourn and comfort all the bereaved from among us. Amen.]

[Choir]

Father, to thee we look in all our sorrow,
thou art the fountain whence our healing flows;
dark though the night, joy cometh with the morrow;
safely they rest who on thy love repose.

September 19, 1963
Rosh Hashanah Morning Service, Birmingham, Alabama

Friends, it's with a great deal of fear and trepidation that I stand before you at this moment and begin to speak to you at this moment in our service when the rabbi is supposed to bring some message of hope and inspiration, or help carry you not really through the day but through the year to come.

I have been a rabbi for thirty years. I started conducting services on the High Holidays four years before that. Thirty-four years is a long time. I began my public speaking experience at age eight when I engaged in the debate—resolve that Washington was the greater American than Lincoln—at age eight before a little club I belonged to called the Paul Revere Club. It never worries me to stand up before a congregation. I have no fear of public speaking. Audiences and congregations do not terrify me. Sizes mean nothing to me. I love my Saturday morning service, where only a handful are in attendance, and I speak to them from my heart, week in and week out, just as sincerely as I can to the multitudes that [are] assembled here or at any other time. It isn't a trepidation that stems from appearing before a vast congregation, because this morning I am going to do something I haven't done in thirty-four years as a student and rabbi.

It has always been my conviction that every rabbi owes his best to his congregation when they come to hear him. His best may not be good enough for them, but at least it should be the best that he was capable of that week. And it should be the result of two things as many of you have heard me say—of perspiration and inspiration. And when there is inspiration, in my opinion, it must be 95 percent perspiration and preparation and the 5 percent inspiration will come.

I feel a sense of trepidation because for the first time in all my years as student and rabbi, I stand before a High Holiday congregation unprepared.

I have gotten up before my congregation on a Friday night or a Saturday morning, and have done what I think every man who is honest must do. And I have said to my congregation I'm going to speak to you extemporaneously, off the cuff as it were, I was sick this week; or the pressures were so great that I didn't have time to think. So I want you to know before I begin to speak that I haven't prepared. Those occasions have been rare, that I have been honest enough with the congregation to tell them so before I began to speak. During the summer months when informally I teach rather than preach, of course there is no outline, but I am preaching and teaching out of the accumulated reservoir of years of study and absorption in my faith, but never have I done this. And there are several reasons for it. There are several reasons for it.

Very frankly, this has been a horrible summer! This has been a horrible year! These are troublous times. Very frankly, I hardly knew the Rosh Hashanah was about to begin tomorrow night. There has been no time for thinking and preparation and outline. There was no opportunity to make certain that I would stay within the respectable twenty minutes.

There are things that are upon my heart that I want to say to you. There are many things that I have been accumulating for thirty years as a rabbi and twenty-three years almost in this congregation which I may not say this morning, but which I hope and pray God if he gives me the years so that I can retire with full strength and vigor, that I may share with you some of these thoughts that have accumulated over the years that I have been your rabbi.

The calculated risk that I am doing today, because I don't know what's going to come out of my mouth; I don't know how long it is going to take; I don't know how you are going to receive it. But there [are] certain things that have to be said, and I'm going to say them. It will not be the first time that I took a calculated risk.

I'm just as sick at heart as you are about what's happened in our city. I have been sick about it for years. Anybody with a shred of humanity in him could not have been but horrified by what happened Saturday or Sunday.

And I'm sick at heart for a lot of other reasons. I'm sick at heart because of the attitude not of the people who either by direction or indirection were responsible for the death of those children. Not for the people that by direction or indirection are responsible for the horrible image that this city of ours has throughout the country, and this Jewish community has throughout the country!

And I'm sick at heart because of what the so-called *nice* people, not only in the city of Birmingham, but in Temple Emanu-El—the liberals in Temple Emanu-El, the people that sneer at everything that happens in this city, who point the finger at everyone beginning with the rabbi, who ought to put the blame upon everyone but themselves. I am sick at heart [about] their attitude also. I am sick and tired of finger-pointing. I am weary of reasons and rationalizations. And I am weary of people congregating in their homes and their places of business over their coffee, wherever they may be, I am weary of people calling me on the telephone and asking me what are you doing? What is the temple doing? What is the Jewish community doing? I am tired of liberals and reactionaries coming into my study, and wanting to know what's going on.

If I have the time, I might try to tell you what your rabbi's been doing. I answer to my conscience. You'll have to answer to yours. I want you to know as your rabbi, and for eight years as the rabbi of the Temple Adath Israel in Lexington, Kentucky, I have never been unmindful of two things. I have never been unmindful of my responsibility to God, and the obligation that that belief in God places upon me in my relationship to my fellow man. And I have also never been unmindful of the fact that as your rabbi I cannot speak for you.

My name may go on a thousand documents or statements. I cannot commit you; we have no hierarchy, thank God, in the Jewish religion. I cannot speak as a bishop, though I speak along with bishops. I am no pope, no rabbi is a pope. The Union of American Hebrew Congregations in the Central Conference of American Rabbis can speak for nobody as far as the individual few is concerned. And I have always been mindful of that.

I have been mindful also that I owe you something. I have always been mindful that I owe you a responsibility. That I must think of your welfare. I must think of your security. I must bear in mind that nothing I say or do will in any way bring shame or disgrace or, God forbid, destruction to you as a congregation, to this Jewish community, and to this beautiful house of God.

I travel a lonely road, friends; that is why it is difficult to talk. You know it's awful lonely to be a rabbi, at least this kind of rabbi. I took my ordination very seriously. I did not have to be a rabbi. I could have been a successful businessman, a very successful businessman. I could have been a tremendous lawyer. I know it; that is what I intended to be originally.

I chose to be a rabbi. I chose to serve my people. I chose to dedicate myself to my God and to my people, and I tried to serve them, I've tried to serve them. I have tried to serve them in as good and as fine, decent, ethical, moral, upright manner. This is one of the reasons why when I received letters from members of my congregation that are snide and I receive letters from colleagues, when a man who is connected with the Union of American Hebrew Congregations has the audacity to call me on the eve of Rosh Hashanah to indicate to me what he thinks my moral duty is. When he knows nothing about what I have been doing as far as what has been transpiring in this community. I am only human and I don't like it. And I resent it!

I resent a lot of things. I resent liberals who are liberals for political reasons. I resent liberals who have political aspirations, who have something economic to gain. Just as I resent reactionaries and conservatives for the same reason. All this—I said I have not thought out what I was going to say yet. And it's a lonely road I travel because you see, as a rabbi, no matter how close you may think you are to me, in the final analysis I am still an outsider. Rabbis come and rabbis go. Blood is thicker than water. Business partners and men who have business relationships are much thicker than the relationship with the rabbi. Professional man, the rabbi is nice to have around when you need him, nice to have him do the dirty work for you. It's a lonely road that you travel. You don't know when the people that you knocked yourself out for within six hours are going to try to destroy you. It's a lonely road that you travel.

And I travel a lonely road in this whole racial situation. I travel a lonely road because I want justice and I want equality for the Negro, but I also want fairness, equalit, and decency for the white man. I want this problem to be worked out not in the basis of politics. I want it not to be worked out in the faces of who can shout the loudest to get the votes. I don't want it worked out on the basis of whether the American Jewish Community and the Anti-defamation League or the Union of American Hebrew Congregations and American Jewish powers gets credit for having shouted the loudest. This is what we have been subject to. This is why we have been stymied in many respects.

What I am trying to do, friends, is this—that regardless of what you read on television, see on television, regardless of what you read in the paper, even the attorney general this morning, I heard him on television, indicated that there was at least some little reservoir of goodwill here, that was an effort being made. He was wrong when he said the religious forces were not trying to do anything. For two years, there have been religious leaders, including myself, who have been trying to develop a rapport with the Negro religious leadership in this community. And have been having a difficult time. And the difficulty has been because they no less than we have been stymied because though the aims may be the same between themselves and Martin Luther King and Mr. Farmer and anybody else, they do not agree, the leadership in the main with whom I come in contact, with the methodology.

And I tell you all this by way of saying that for days there have been about twenty of us that have been meeting—colored and white—and since this terrible thing happened, and I pleaded with them particularly. I said to them if Birmingham has anything to repent of, to atone for, let it be the white community of Birmingham that makes the atonement. Let us not have fundraising throughout the country to rebuild that church, to pay for the funeral expenses. You can't repay these people for the loss of their children, but whatever we can do to help them, hospital expenses, but let us do it! Let the white people of Birmingham do it! Let it not be a Roman circus! Stop holding us up to shame and contume [sic] throughout the world.

There are these decent people in the city of Birmingham, there are decent white people. Everybody is not a Connor. Everybody is not a Wallace. There are just as many decent Christian white people in this community as there are Jews; there are more of them because there are more Christians in this community.

I'll tell you what the problem is. The problem is very simply that all you nice people, and I'm talking about the members of my congregation, because when I meet with these colored ministers, I feel I've got to try to explain at least the Protestant ministers to them, and I say look I don't have this problem. I get up in front of my congregation; I have done it many times. So you don't like what I'm going to say. The congregation is not going to split in half. You might get twenty people split up, but not in half. And they don't like what I have to say, I don't have to worry about getting another position even at my age, but these men do have a problem.

They are part of a Methodist conference or an Episcopal conference. They are part of a diocese in a Baptist church; there is individual autonomy in the churches, but once a man has his black mark against him, he is through in the South. And many of these men can't speak up because they are hamstrung about this situation.

I'm not going to talk about it—I'm going to talk about you. I'm going to talk about those of you [who] particularly keep talking about what ought to be done. What have you done? You know how the image of this city is created? It isn't created by Wallace; and it isn't created by Connor or by Hanes. It is created by those letters to the editor in the newspaper.

I want to know how many Jews sitting in this room have written a letter to the editor of the *Birmingham Post-Herald* or the *News*. What's the matter, haven't you got the guts to do it? You afraid you might have harassing calls; I've had them since 1955 because I referred to the governor two months ago as bellicose and signed a statement to the effect that everyone including him has to obey laws until they are changed and court decisions until they are reversed. My life was actually threatened, though no one knows about it, and for three—two and one half months—my home [was] under surveillance. It is a calculated risk. It is a calculated risk what I'm saying from this pulpit right now.

Every measure of security has been taken for your safety. Every measure and a great cost incidentally financially. And in fact a sacrifice on the part of many of our own members. But stop being liberals in your parlors, and in your offices. I know of only two men in this community—one's a member of my congregation sitting in here right now, and the other is a not a member of my congregation. And if you don't like the word "guts" from the pulpit, it's the only word that can be used. Who have had the guts, the guts, to challenge Connor and Wallace and segregation and the whole problem of integration and everything else? I'm not going to mention any names. But you know about whom I am talking, and you know that I am telling the truth.

I'm here to say that if you want [to] change this, you are going to have to start standing up and being counted. If you tell me you have got children—I remember a number of years ago where a United States senator was arrested because he walked into the door of a church and an attorney said to me, "I would give everything to defend that man, but I've got a wife and two children"—this attitude that had prevailed in this town, and it still prevails.

Sure you are sitting ducks because you are Jews, but so am I. But when the question came up as to whether my name should be appended to these statements that went out last January, that went out last April, that went out yesterday, the reason my name was on them was because somebody thought perhaps my name shouldn't be on it. It is a calculated risk. Are you willing to take the risk? Are you willing to be harassed? Are you willing to be threatened?

Now until you are, then you are going to have to permit this city to be turned over to the people that write the *Birmingham News* and say that Wallace is the greatest thing that ever happened to this country; that Art Hanes has to be put back into office; that the city council plan of reform has to be overturned. This is the first thing. This is the first thing.

I was once criticized for using this expression, and maybe it has no place in the pulpit, but I'm talking to you from the heart, and I told you I didn't prepare. You are either going to put up or you're going to have to shut up. You are either going to have to put up or you are going to have to stop talking and acting like liberals. You are going to have to stop being horrified at what happens. We are only 3,900 Jewish men, women, and children. I [am] conscious of this fact. I'm not asking you to go out and lead a crusade. But in heaven's sake, can't you do at least what I have done and joining with other Christians? I admit that I wouldn't have signed my name to these statements alone, but with Bishop Murray, Bishop Durick, and with Bishop Carpenter, and Bishop Harmon, I felt that I was protecting you and there was a measure of security for myself. And you have got to talk to your Christian friends; this is the first thing.

Next thing I want to say is this; let's stop talking about being liberals if we don't mean it. Where were you yesterday afternoon at 3:30? I'll tell you where I was. I was at the Sixth Avenue Baptist Church—Negro. I was at that funeral. I'm no hero. Anybody knows I'm no hero, I'm no martyr. I don't want to get killed, I don't want to have this temple bombed, and I don't want my home bombed. And I don't want to be knocked off gangster style. I was warned by a law enforcement official not to go there. I was told and several of us knew that there was a calculated risk that this thing could be turned into [a] political orgy instead of a funeral.

Certain things did go according to the way we wanted them to go. We met in Carpenter House, some twenty of us. Would you like to know who they are?

Bishop Carpenter; Bishop Durick; Bishop Harmon; Bishop Murchison (who is a Negro); Bishop Charles Goldman (Negro); Bishop Murray; Rabbi Grafman; I. T. Beale; Thomas Edgar (these are Methodist whites); Rev. McMurray (a Negro); Earl Stallings of the Baptist Church; Rev. J. A. Well (Negro); Howard Gregg, president [of] Daniel Payne College; John Porter of the Sixth Avenue Baptist Church; Father Allen; Bishop Durick; and Dr. Pitts, president of Miles College.

There were a lot of things that we decided we wanted to do. It was my suggestion that all of us at that moment walk over to the *Birmingham News* and talk to Mr. Vincent Townson and tell him what we, we twenty, wanted done; and then to go to the mayor and the city council. But we were there for four hours at Carpenter House, and there was a limit to what we could do yesterday.

And much of this happened, has come out of that meeting. And we determined that this people had us stand up; we determined that we would go and meet at Our Lady of Fatima Church—not to be part of a procession. We did not want to go to be on television. We didn't want to make heroes of ourselves. Four children, four children had been brutally killed. All we wanted to do was to go there and express our grief and our sorrow to show these Negro families that we felt the depth of their sorrow—we shared it. All we wanted to do was to say to the Negro community, you are not alone. There are white people. This was all. And we were going to casually walk over there.

What happened of course was we suddenly found ourselves in a procession. When I walked up those steps to that church, I never knew that there were that many—I sold cameras by the way and photographic material in order to work my way through college—I thought I knew all about cameras. I didn't know there were so many cameras—television, still, or otherwise—in the whole United States of America. I didn't see myself, but I was told on the Huntley-Brinkley program that there I was walking right next to Carlton Blake of the Presbyterian Church. This was not why I went. This is not why Bishop Murray and Bishop Carpenter went. And this is the part that I want to say to you that I am sick about: I am sick about making a Roman circus out of every episode that happens. Of whipping up hatred throughout the country when we are trying to whip up love in this country and we need your help.

May I say that I have over here if I had the time, I would like to read—which I'm not going to take—letters that I have received from out of the country. These are from people who read Martin Luther King's letter from a Birmingham jail, he sent in answer to myself and eight other clergymen, a beautiful literary document, but a vicious one. He did us an injustice.

The things that hurt us that when an organization like the Anti-defamation League that is supposed to be devoted to protecting Jews publishes this thing and lets a rabbi be damned throughout the world. This is something else that kind of makes you sick. But all we said in January when we appealed to the white population for law and order, we didn't get a pat on the back. And the few pats—we didn't want them—but when we did, we got some snide comments in the very same letters. Though when we appealed to the Negro community for law and order and felt with the president and the attorney general that those demonstrations in April were unwise and untimely and [a] new administration locally should be given an opportunity, we were in a power vacuum when we wrote that letter.

I wish you could read these letters that have come to me from Jews who said they are ashamed to be Jewish because I am a rabbi. I got one in the mail this morning on Rosh Hashanah, a greeting. What I'm trying to say this morning is this, and to those of you who are liberals, I want to say that I am opposed to whipping up hatred against the Negro, but for people who are for the Negro, they must stop whipping up hatred against white people and against those of us for trying to help.

All I want to say to you this morning is this: You have got to do something, friends. You have got to stand up and be counted. That is all there is to it. Now there is one thing you can do, and I am a little disappointed. I don't know whether it will work or not. I was one of four clergymen that was horrified that when the mayor asked for [a] reward fund of $50,000 maybe he shouldn't have mentioned a figure. I thought that there would be an outpouring the next day.

When our board met and this congregation decided to put up $1,000 after someone suggested $600, $500, a member of our board said there are 630 members in our congregation. If [he's right], figure it out, gave $2, underwrote $2, it would have been $1,200 right there. And after weeks, a measly $17,000.

John Buchanan did a tremendous job. I only helped on the periphery. But it has gone up to $75,000. We are going to go up to $100,000, we can, and then I have liberals say to me what good will this do?

Well, the attorney general today reiterated the fact that when there is a dynamiting, there is no evidence. We know this. There are no fingerprints, no clues. The Birmingham police is working night and day, the FBI will get credit, but I can tell you that Birmingham police and the sheriff locally are dedicated to solving these bombings that are taking place. The FBI will get the credit, but they [are] dedicated and they are helping the FBI. They are determined to catch these people.

One of the ways you can get them to talk, I was a chaplain at the Narcotics Farm in Lexington for narcotic addicts. We had a whole separate wing for informers. How do you suppose they catch all of those narcotics? Man runs out of money, and so he informs on somebody in order to get money for narcotics. It ain't nice. Maybe it's not the nice thing, but these are murderers that are abroad. Now if somebody will talk for $25,000 or $50,000 or $100,000, let's put up the money. Let's put up the money because these people have got to be caught. We know from whom, we think we know from whom this stems.

And let me say, these people are primarily anti-Semitic, and this is where you have got a stake. Because let me tell you, if they get away with this, nobody's going to be safe and the first ones that will not be safe will be the members of the Jewish community. Now the next thing, and you lag way behind on this, I can tell you, the next thing let me say is that week after week back there you want to pick them up when you go out, sign them and send them in to reward City Hall if you are willing to underwrite help, underwrite this reward fund. I want the white people, Bishop Carpenter, Bishop Murray, we want the white people to rebuild this church. We want Birmingham to make atonement. And we are trying to see that people don't go off in fifty different directions.

There has been a fund set up, it's called, I have it, I wrote it down, I think it is called the Sixteenth Avenue Baptist Church Memorial Fund. I'll get it here in a minute; it's someplace around here. You can read it in the newspaper. Is that it, the Sixteenth Street Baptist Memorial Fund?

I tell you what I would like to see you do. You know, in our meeting Tuesday, I suggested that the newspapers do like they do with the Good Fellow's Fund, like the *Birmingham News* did a tremendous job on the surplus food problem and they simply asked for money. They published the names. Ninety-seven thousand dollars rolled in, but we are going to need more than $97,000. One of the Negro ministers, president of Daniel Payne College, said no. He said let's not put anybody on the spot. He said even the money is not important. I would rather have less money, but more people. I would rather that we could say 100,000 people in the city of Birmingham contributed, $200,000 contributed, a dollar apiece rather than say fifty men contributed $200,000; and I had to agree with him, because I think this is part of the purging process.

And what I would like you to do is this. I would like really not to put you on the spot, but I would like you to be able to feel what my congregation is going to do. You think about it and pray over it. We are going to have to find out how much insurance is covered. Not going to be any deal like what happened like with the A. D. King home where the insurance was paid and then money was raised, nothing like this. We are going to know how much insurance is covered on that church, probably have to be almost completely rebuilt. We are going to find out how much it is going to cost to rebuild that church and we are going to rebuild it better than it was, but we don't want to do it with money from Chicago and New York and San Francisco. White money from Birmingham, Christian, Protestant, Catholic, Jewish money.

And may I suggest to you that you think this over, write a generous check to the Sixteenth Street Baptist Fund. You can send it to me. I would like to be able to say that every member of my congregation—I'm not interested in the amount, I won't even look at the amount—I just want to be able to know that there were this many people from Temple Emanu-El that made a contribution. I'll see that it is turned over to the First National Bank or to the Birmingham Trust National Bank.

And if there is a Jew in this congregation, a Jew in this community, whose heart does not move him, if for no other reason than sympathy, let alone the pride of rectifying an injustice, then I feel that this whole service has been in vain. Now one of the things that worries me about my congregation is, very frankly, we all want everything. We all want everything nice and good, but we want somebody else to do it. We want somebody else to pay for it, don't we?

Let me say this to you, friends. You came here and it was safe and secure here. This place has been under total security guard since five o'clock Sunday. It is going to remain this way until at least September 30, when we hope by that time there are going to be developments [that] will make this unnecessary. I want you to know this is going to cost this congregation $2,000, including the voluntary help. Costing $2,000 so that you could come here on Rosh Hashanah, Yom Kippur, your kids can come and you don't have to worry.

I wonder, I wonder how many people in this congregation here are going to sit down tomorrow and write a letter to Mr. Bernard Feld, president of this congregation, and say, "Dear Mr. Feld, I appreciate the efforts that the board of directors have made to make certain that we could come to our temple safely and secur[ely]." I wonder how many of you are going to send a check in that letter to cover that $2,000.

This isn't the way I like to talk on Rosh Hashanah. I told you, I have never done this before. These are terrible times. And it's time to stand up and be counted. It is time to do things. It is time to pay the price, whether it is in personal safety and security or whether it is in money. The question is are you ready to pay the price, because if you are not, God help this city. This city isn't dead yet, not by a long shot. It's almost dead.

You and decent Christians in this community can revive this city. Dr. J. L. Ware, Dr. Pitts, said to me just the other day, and I said to them, you know, I'm glad I'm in the South than the North. I was raised in the north. It is going to be horrible up there. I said some day we are going to work out an accommodation and it's going to be a far superior accommodation than anything north of the Mason-Dixon Line, and both of them said, you are so right. Once we get to understand each other, this is going to be the greatest area in the country. You have got a stake and a share in that area in this city. You could make it possible.

Please forgive me for having spoken to you maybe in a rambling manner, maybe in an illogical manner, too long, but I warned you when I started, I was unprepared. I simply want to talk to you about what was on my heart. And the Talmud said that words that leave the heart enter the heart. I hope that the words that have come from my heart have entered yours. I hope that the prayers of our magnificent liturgy, which tell the same story and which came from the heart of our great sages and seers over the centuries, have entered yours. And I know that you join in the prayer that perhaps this Rosh Hashanah will usher in a new era and a new day—for us, for our city, our state, our country, and for all mankind. Amen.

§35 James Baldwin, Reinhold Niebuhr, and Thomas Kilgore

James Baldwin was born August 2, 1924, in Harlem, to a family struggling with poverty, disease, and abuse. He attended DeWitt Clinton High School, where he served as literary editor to the school newspaper. He attended the New School as well. As a youth he became a Pentecostal minister before abandoning religion. As a young adult he made the decision to expatriate to Paris, which spoke to his feelings about racial and sexual preference biases. His literary corpus is too elaborate to detail briefly, but many regard his fiction in superlative terms. Occasionally Baldwin returned to the United States, often to participate in civil rights protests such as the 1963 Freedom Day in Selma, Alabama. He died as viscerally as he lived, in Saint-Paul-de-Vence, of stomach cancer late in 1987.

Thomas Kilgore Jr. was born in Woodruff, South Carolina, in 1913 to a family which would eventually have twelve children, of which he was the sixth. He graduated from Morehouse College in 1935, and received his degree in divinity from Union Theological Seminary, where he studied under the direction of Reinhold Niebuhr. He pastored Friendship Baptist Church, in Harlem, for sixteen years, finishing the last twenty-two years of his career as pastor of Second Baptist Church in Los Angeles. His dedication to civil rights was lifelong, whether the venue was voter registration drives or university-community relations. He died in February 1984. His papers are housed at the University of Southern California Regional History Collection.

Karl Paul Reinhold Niebuhr was born June 21, 1892, in Wright City, Missouri, to a family of German-speaking German Evangelicals whose former denomination of Prussian Church Union is now part of the United Church of Christ. He attended Elmhurst College, where he graduated in 1910. He then attended Eden Seminary and Yale Divinity School, where he received a bachelor of divinity in 1914 and a master of arts in 1915. He abandoned formal training while at Yale for a pastoral appointment, but eventually returned to academia on the faculty of Union Theological Seminary. Reinhold, his brother H. Richard, and sister Hulda were prominent intellectuals. In 1931 Reinhold married Ursula Compton, who attended graduate school at Union Theological Seminary, and served on the faculty of Barnard College. He retired in 1960, and died on June 1, 1971. His papers can be found primarily at the Library of Congress and Union Theological Seminary.

This dialogue comes courtesy of the Protestant Council's production *The Meaning of the Birmingham Tragedy*, which aired September 22, 1963, one week after the Sixteenth Street Baptist Church bombing, which killed four girls during children's week Sunday school activities. Dr. Kilgore moderates the dialogue between Niebuhr and Baldwin. Dr. Niebuhr's interactions are notable in several ways. First, he had survived a series of strokes beginning in 1952, which rendered him unable to participate in civil rights marches the way he would have preferred. Yet his intellect and speaking capacities remained with him to an impressive extent. He also clearly revels in the privilege of dialogue with his former student and the eccentric Baldwin, delivering an ironic punch line for which all three pause to laugh. Baldwin's participation requires repeated exposures to appreciate fully: his voice is a relentless staccato of consonants, as if he were composing at a manual typewriter keyboard missing its ink ribbon; his vowels mutate to partially Parisian pronunciations; and his anger reflects proportionately the gravity of the senseless bombing a week earlier, replete with ironic epithets used commonly at the time which now are uncomfortable to repeat out loud. If there were an Olympics for antiheroes of the winter solstice, the Baldwinian boycott of birthday presents for the baby Jesus would earn the bronze, edged out for silver by the Seussian Grinch, and for gold by the Dickensian Scrooge.

ᢍᢍ

The Face of Christ

Aired on September 22, 1963
New York, New York

UNKNOWN: The Sixteenth Street Church in Birmingham was bombed last Sunday. Four children, Denise McNair, Addie Mae Collins, Carol Robertson, and Cynthia Wesley, were murdered. Later two others, Virgil Ware and Johnny Robinson, were shot and killed. In remembrance of these latest martyrs in the long list of those who have died in the cause of justice and freedom, this program is dedicated: *The Meaning of the Birmingham Tragedy.* Does the missing face of Christ on this stained glass window which survived the bombing suggest a meaning? James Baldwin, noted author, and Dr. Reinhold Niebuhr, well-renowned theologian, will give their views. In presenting this special program, the Protestant Council insists that your view, your sense of responsibility, is the really important factor in making sure that the Birmingham children have not died in vain. And now your host, Dr. Thomas Kilgore Jr., minister of the Friendship Baptist Church and New York director for the Southern Christian Leadership Conference.

KILGORE: Mr. Baldwin, does this faceless picture suggest to you a meaning of the Birmingham tragedy?

BALDWIN: It suggests to me several meanings. If I were gonna be cynical this morning, I would say that the absence of the face is something of an achievement, since we've been victimized all along by an alabaster Christ. And it suggests much more seriously something else. And to me it sums up the crisis that we've been living through. If Christ has no face, then perhaps it is time that we who in one way or another invented and are responsible for our deities give him a new face, give him a new consciousness, and make the whole ideal, the whole hope of Christian love, a reality. And as far as I can tell, it has never really been a reality in the two thousand years since his assassination.

KILGORE: Dr. Niebuhr, what does this picture say to you?

NIEBUHR: Well, I would agree with Mr. Baldwin on this. I think that on the whole, this moral crisis that we've lived in, as far as the church is concerned, represents a failure in the church, particularly the Protestant Church. Catholicism, that's another problem, and it hasn't been failing in the racial situation as Protestantism has. As far as the church is concerned, I think we have to admit first of all that we have miserably failed to give the

Christian message a real content, a real face, the face of Christ. I think I'd be a little hesitant to say love because I think one of the failings of the Protestant churches is that we say love when we're dealing with group relations, but we think of justice. The Negro doesn't love the white man collectively, or the white man the Negro, collectively. The thing is, the pope was more right than we Protestants were in his encyclical, the late pope, in *Mater et Magistra*. Love is a motive but justice is the instrument. We've got to realize in Protestant Christianity that there is such a thing as a motive of love with justice as the instrument of this love, and justice means respect for the other person across racial boundaries. We haven't comprehended the real mystery of group prejudice.

KILGORE: Now I should say the church, we recognize it in our country, there are many facets, many various groups. Would you say that there's any group or segment of the American Christian church that has faced up to this problem any more definitely than others?

NIEBUHR: Well, of course, this is a revolution, and the Negro church has been significant. Well, you're a member of the Southern Christian Leadership Conference. The Negro church has been the leadership of this movement, one of the many leaderships, because the Negro has also secular as well as Christian movements. The white churches failed. The Negro church has rerealized itself in this crisis. I should say that, from my standpoint, Martin Luther King is one of the great Americans of our day. He has related nonviolence to resistance. People ask me, since I am such a strong anti-pacifist how I can have this admiration for a pacifist? Well, I have a simple answer to that, and that is that King's doctrine of nonviolent resistance is not pacifism. Pacifism of really the classic kind is when you are concerned about your own purity, and not responsibility, and the great ethical divide is between the people who want to be pure and those who want to be responsible, and I think King has noticed this difference.

KILGORE: Mr. Baldwin, would you like to speak to that?

BALDWIN: That's quite a, it's a very loaded subject. But I do think, you know, there is a great paradox occurring in this country now. What you say about the Negro church, for example, is I think entirely true, and Martin has used the Negro church, really, as a kind of tool, not only to liberate, you know, Negroes, but to liberate the entire country. On the basis of the evidence, and maybe I've overstated it a little bit, but as far as one can tell, the only people in the country at the moment who believe either in Christianity or in the country are the most despised minority in it. Negroes have done, with a really incredible and agonized restraint, more, it seems to me, in this decade to force Americans to begin to reassess themselves than has been done since I was born. It's ironical, I've got to say, that the people who were slaves here, the most beaten and despised people here, and for so long, should be at this moment, and I mean this, absolutely the only hope this country has. It doesn't have any other. None of the descendants of Europe seem to be able to do, or have taken on themselves to do what Negroes are now trying to do, and this is not a chauvinistic or racial argument. It probably has something to do with the nature of life itself, which forces you in the extreme to discover what you really live by, whereas most Americans have been for so long so safe and so sleepy that they don't any longer have any real sense of what they live by. I think they really think it may be Coca-Cola.

NIEBUHR: Mr. Baldwin, I quite agree with that. And I think that history throws a light on it. We were in a revolutionary situation and all through history it was the despised minority, the proletarians, the peasants, the poor, who recaptured the heights and depths of faith, and the country itself choked in its own fat as we are inclined to choke in our own fat. The only question I would raise about it is whether there is not a leaven in the other classes that would correspond to the light of truth in the despised minority. This is a revolution, and look at the history of revolution. You find that in every revolution, of the middle class for the sake of justice against the aristocracy, of the industrial workers against the middle class, there are always some heroic spirits, or let us say, honest spirits, who cooperated with the revolutionists. The revolutionists challenge the whole, what they call in English, "the establishment," but some of the members of the other classes also cooperated with the revolutionists, and I think that's the significant thing in our present revolutionary situation. You say the Negro is the only genuine proletarian thing, socially. In my opinion he is a revolutionist, he's got to be the revolutionist, he's got to recapture many of our revolutionary traditions and Christian traditions and moral traditions. Nevertheless, we can't be quiet, and I think you're not, if I've read you correctly, and I've read almost everything that you've written, you're not throwing out the white man as white man.

BALDWIN: No, no, no. I don't mean to say that. But I do mean to say this, that the bulk of the white Protestant majority in this country has exhibited a really staggering level of irresponsibility, an immoral washing of the hands, you know, and really because segregation means among other things that they do not know what goes on in my kitchen. You know? I don't mean to say the white people are villains or devils or anything like that.

NIEBUHR: But they're irresponsible

BALDWIN: What?

NIEBUHR: They're irresponsible, you say.

BALDWIN: Yeah. Morally irresponsible.

NIEBUHR: Yeah.

BALDWIN: Criminally responsible.

NIEBUHR: Yeah.

BALDWIN: Because this is their country, too. There is no one, what I'm trying to say is that, for example, I don't suppose that everyone in Birmingham, all the white people in Birmingham are monstrous people, but they are mainly silent people, you know, and that is a crime in itself. That's what I mean.

KILGORE: Mr. Baldwin, this leads me to another question. Eugene Patterson, the editor of the *Atlanta Constitution*, writing last Monday, mentioned the fact that there was a collective guilt in connection with the bombing of this church and the killing of these girls, and also said that in some way we have got to appeal to the "Good South," meaning that there are these people who are willing if appealed to. Now how are we gonna do that?

BALDWIN: Well, I think it's a little misstated. It's not the Good South one's got to appeal to. In fact, there's no one to appeal to. What one's got to do is very much harder than that. One's got to undo the work which was begun during the time of the Reconstruction. The Good South, like the Good Nation, is trapped by the nature of the political representatives it throws up. The South is still ruled, essentially ruled, which means that Washington is controlled by the rural interest, and it is a southern oligarchy, and under the circumstances what you have is Senator Eastland holding such terrifying power. And this is something, this is not something the South did. It is something the country did. There is no single acre of American soil where a Negro can be considered or is a free man. One doesn't appeal. One changes a situation. New York is as segregated a city as any city in Alabama. And so is Boston. And so is Chicago. And so is Philadelphia. And so is Detroit. It is something the country has done for more than one hundred years, not only to Negroes, but to itself.

NIEBUHR: What you are saying is that you are transferring collective guilt, I think correctly, to collective responsibility.

BALDWIN: That's right.

NIEBUHR: And you're saying that there are infinite gradations of responsibility, and all forms of silence is itself a responsibility. I think one could well compare the situation of the so-called Good Americans to the German situation in the Nazi period. Who were the anti-Nazis? Well, during the occupation after the war, one of our political officers said we had all these questionnaires and they told us what we should have known in the first place, and that was that there were only 5 percent clear Nazis, only 2 percent clear anti-Nazis, and the other ones were . . .

BALDWIN: Uncommitted.

NIEBUHR: Uncommitted in various stages of lack of commitment.

KILGORE: Mr. Baldwin, you said we've got to undo what's been done over a period of a hundred or more years. This means assigning responsibility, then. Whose responsibility is it? Is it the Negro's responsibility? Is it the federal government's responsibility? Who starts this undoing?

BALDWIN: We, the people, do. We, whoever cares about this country, begin it. And what we have to do, it seems to me, really, is let the government know that it is responsible to us, and what we have to know is that we are responsible for it. We have no right. We have no right to allow ourselves to be represented by, let us say, a Barry Goldwater or by a Senator Eastland. We have no right to fantastic abdication of political responsibility, which is a hallmark of all America today. This is where we begin. We put pressure on Washington to change our situation. We put pressure on Washington to do something about the phenomenon called urban renewal, which means moving Negroes out. That is all it ever means. For example, this is done with federal money. Okay? For example, you make school boards understand that you do not integrate a school by putting kids in buses and driving them to Queens. You integrate a school by integrating a neighborhood. In order to integrate a neighborhood, you attack the real estate interest and the banks. For example, you know it is a crime in this country now, a kind of moral crime, to suggest that there is something wrong with the economic structure. But in fact there is something wrong with the economic structure, since in any case it is unable to create full employment. Now I know that the unemployment rate among Negroes is twice as what it is among whites. But numerically speaking more white people are out of jobs than Negroes. And the economy as it is presently constructed can do nothing about this at all. No, I'm not asking for a ticket to Moscow or Peking. No. I'm not. I am not, ladies and gentlemen, a Communist. But it is time for us to look very hard at the facts of our life.

NIEBUHR: But that gets us way beyond the racial issue. That comes down to very complex economic issues.

BALDWIN: Indeed. Well, what is called a racial issue never is a racial issue as it turns out anyway. Because what is called a racial issue here is simply the fact that I am visibly the descendant of slaves. I was in the beginning in this country, and I still am, a source of cheap labor. And the pathological rationalizations Americans have used to defend themselves against this fact [have] much created our present dilemma. I never believed I was happy down on the levee. I never said I was a happy, shiftless, watermelon-eating darkie. The country did. And what is much worse, the country believed it and still does. They thought I was happy in my place. I never was happy in my place. And the nature of the crisis we are going through is that all of a sudden Americans are forced to realize not only that I am not happy in it, but I'm not going to stay in it.

NIEBUHR: Mr. Baldwin, aren't you saying that the racial prejudices aggravated the class situation, the class structure of American society?

BALDWIN: No, I'm not saying that. Racial prejudice, as far as that goes, is endemic, as far as I can tell, to human life. Everybody hates everybody. You know, Greeks hate Turks, for example; you know I could go on and on. All throughout Europe, there used to be tribal warfare. I'm not interested in that so much as I'm interested in the fact that in this country, for which we are responsible, it's not the prejudice which menaces us, it's the power given to the most base elements of the American citizenry. I don't care, you know, if Senator Eastland or Barry Goldwater don't like me. I don't want them to like me. I do care that they have the power to keep me out of a home, out of a job, and to put my child under the needle. I care about that. I don't care what they think or what they feel. I care about their power. And I accuse the American republic of having created the vacuum which gives them their power, which is going to destroy this country.

KILGORE: Dr. Niebuhr, can we shift to another concept? You have spent years as a theological professor and dealing with problems of the church. What is the church in America able to do, at this point, in correcting these massive evils?

NIEBUHR: Well, I'm afraid that I must agree with Mr. Baldwin that in the past the Protestant church in particular and to some degree the Catholic Church, but only to some degree, has been irrelevant to the problem of collective justice, whether it's racial or economic. I think one of the great heresies of Protestantism is the individualistic heresy. It can't deal with collective problems—the relationship of classes to each other, the differentiation of responsibility, and so forth. We always sentimentalize love. That's why when we talk about the love of Christ, I say we must recognize that love is the motive, but justice is the instrument. And I'm afraid that Protestantism faces a real crisis in its own life, and that is, on the one hand, to guard the significance of the person, the individual, and to preach love in interpersonal relationship[s], family relations, and so forth, and guide people in the way of love; and on the other hand, to transmute love into justice in recognition of the respect for the other person, integrity, and honesty. And this we have failed at, I think.

KILGORE: Mr. Baldwin, recently you have talked about the possibility of a boycott by Negroes across the country as a type of leverage to bring this country to understand the gravity of this problem. Would you tell us something about that?

BALDWIN: Well, what I—we—demand is that the country, the country, the people that make up this country, not allow the massacre of the innocents to simply pass unnoticed. It's much worse than passing unavenged, to pass unnoticed. We call ourselves a Christian nation, and Christmas in this country, as in other countries, but we are responsible for this one, is mainly like the church, if I may say so—a tremendous commercial endeavor, a tremendous commercial enterprise. Well, I don't think that we have the right to celebrate Christmas this year, and if it is not a Christian nation, it is certainly a commercial nation. If all the people of the country, black and white, who would like to have the country back again, who would like to begin again to honor the ideals we say we do, I think we should not buy anything for Christmas, not a nail file, not a toothbrush. At least when you can't reach a man's conscience you can reach his pocketbook. I think that once you tell those children there will be no Santa Claus this year because your brothers and sisters, I mean it doesn't matter what color you are, your cocitizens were murdered in Sunday school, and until the country deals with this fact, we will not have a Christmas. I think this is very important. I really urge everyone who is listening to me now, to buy nothing for Christmas and furthermore, to try to find out what national companies operate in Birmingham, and boycott every single one of them, and that would include General Motors.

KILGORE: Dr. Niebuhr, what is your reaction?

NIEBUHR: Mr. Reston, in this morning's *New York Times*, talks about the power structure in Birmingham, and I thought this significant. He gave all the national companies that were in the power structure of Birmingham and said in effect there is a horrible lack of communication between the white man and the Negro in Birmingham. These people, if they wanted to, could easily bridge this gap, because these are national companies, and it's not only Earl Blake and ex-secretary Royal—

BALDWIN: Are you talking about that peculiar commissioner who presently is down in Birmingham?

NIEBUHR: Yeah, I am.

BALDWIN: To investigate what?

NIEBUHR: To investigate how to establish communications—

BALDWIN: It's an insult!

NIEBUHR: Yeah.

BALDWIN: It's an insult!

NIEBUHR: But, I really, coming back to this thing, I think that one of the ironic things about Mr. Baldwin's proposal is that this might also save Christmas. . .

[Collective laughter from all three.]

NIEBUHR: . . . Because Christmas, beginning just after Thanksgiving day, you have this horrible canned music in every department store . . .

BALDWIN: Let's replace it with Ray Charles.

NIEBUHR: . . .which displays the commercialization of the Christmas holy day in a terrible way.

KILGORE: I'd like to raise one other question, and it has to do with this. Many are saying, and I saw a picket line the other day in front of the United Nations, in which one of the signs said, "Arm the Negro," and many people are saying that maybe as this violence increases, it has to be reacted against by counterviolence. What do you think about that?

BALDWIN: I'll tell you what I think. I think several things about it. First of all, before I go any further, I am very struck by the fact that the only time in my only experience, and I'm nearly forty years old, and I never read this in the history books so far, the only time that nonviolence has been admired is when Negroes practice it. The history of England, the history of France, the history of this country, is the history of nothing but violence and bloodshed. And we are it. We are proud of it. If you doubt me, you look at television tonight. We love it. What is the question of a Negro with a gun, you know? It suddenly becomes a moral question for the very first and only time, and suddenly you find a whole nation, this is what this nation has done for the last decade, nearly, admiring Martin Luther King, admiring all those children on those barricades, admiring their discipline and their heroism, and doing nothing whatever to help them.

NIEBUHR: I have a little different approach to this. I say we are in a period of revolution, and revolution means violence, but this revolution is taking place in the context of a legal system which doesn't practice violence. Now I would've said—

BALDWIN: *It depends where you are in that system.*

NIEBUHR: But the Negro has violence practiced against him.

BALDWIN: By the legal system.

NIEBUHR: By the legal system. Now this is a paradoxical situation, but I wouldn't say that the answer is violence for the Negro. I honor the principle of nonviolence, not for purely moral reasons, because Mr. Baldwin says and is quite right, we honor the Revolutionary War, the Civil War, and so forth, but because it is pragmatically the only way that a minority group can deal with a majority group.

KILGORE: Thank you, gentlemen, and on behalf of the Protestant Council, I want to thank our guests this morning, Dr. Reinhold Niebuhr and Mr. James Baldwin. And now, what can you do? What can you do to show your feeling toward this tragic incident? This evening at three o'clock at Foley Square a meeting is being held at which all of the city is invited and again at six o'clock this evening at the Salem Methodist Church on Seventh Avenue and 129th Street. This is one way that you can show your interest in this great tragedy. Thank you.

§36 John Beecher

John Henry Newman Beecher was born on January 22, 1904, in New York City, a direct descendant of Harriet Beecher Stowe. When Beecher was three his father, an executive with U.S. Steel, moved the family to Birmingham, Alabama. Beecher's later labor activism was directly related to his youth working in the local mills. A peripatetic scholar his entire life, Beecher attended the University of Notre Dame, Virginia Military Institute, Cornell, Middlebury College, and the University of Alabama. He went on to complete a master's degree in English at the University of Wisconsin. Beecher pursued doctoral studies at the University of North Carolina in sociology, working with Howard Odum on his ambitious book project, *Southern Regions of the United States.* In 1926 he married Virginia St. Clair Donovan, and their union would result in four children. Beecher would wed three more times. As the Great Depression deepened in the 1930s, Beecher worked throughout the South with the federal government's Emergency Relief Administration. During the war, and as a commissioned officer, Beecher voluntarily served on the SS *Booker T. Washington*, an integrated troop transport ship. After the war Beecher took a job teaching sociology at San Francisco State University, but his tenure there was short-lived when he refused to sign the Levering loyalty oath. Instead Beecher wrote poetry, tended to his printing business, and ranched. Beecher spent the sixties as a traveling poet-in-residence and as an increasingly well-renowned journalist and poet. His writing reached a broad audience of academics and laypeople through outlets such as *Ramparts,* the *San Francisco Chronicle,* the *New York Times,* and *The Nation.* Beecher was eventually reinstated to his teaching post in San Francisco after the California Supreme Court overturned the Levering Act. Beecher died on May 11, 1980. His papers are housed at Duke University and are widely available on microfilm.

Beecher spares nary a word of vituperation on his hometown before his California audience. Speaking at a memorial rally two weeks after four girls were killed in a Birmingham church bombing, Beecher offers a highly personal narrative of coming of age in the "Magic City." His work as a writer stems directly from working in the city's steel mills, where black laborers were daily demeaned. White citizens of the city experienced a geographical oasis with bountiful material gifts; its black citizens experienced a geography of total despair—social, political, economic, and educational. That complex was "diabolically organized against the Negro" in Birmingham by a police force and a public safety commissioner (Bull Connor) run exclusively by the Klan. Beecher is haunted by the murder of a Catholic priest, Father Coyle, by a "Christian" Klansman who was cheered, and acquitted, for his actions. Moreover, for a city that claims to be the "most Christian in the nation" with its 680 churches, the evil of segregation and white supremacy continues unabated, unaffected even by the vicissitudes of time. But Beecher does see hope on the horizon for his hometown, if the federal government and the movement's allies work together to eradicate the evil virus.

❧❧

Their Blood Cries Out

September 29, 1963
Community Rally, San Jose, California

As a boy growing up in Birmingham, I was what was then called a "booster," filled with fierce pride in my hometown. When I was off at school or camp, I would do battle with any boy who spoke ill of it, especially if he came from Atlanta. I thought Birmingham would inevitably become the greatest city in the South, and one of the greatest in the nation. I dreamed of the day when its name would be on the lips of the world. That day has come at last, but how different it is from what I then imagined. My city is now universally known in every land of every continent on earth as a symbol of violence and oppression rather than of liberty and opportunity for all. Once called "the Magic City" because of its spectacular growth and illimitable industrial potential, Birmingham is now referred to as a struggling, dying city—indeed, as a city already dead. Perhaps it would be better if it actually were defunct, and the ground salted whereon it stood. But unfortunately the city lives after its fashion, plague-stricken, a menace to the whole nation of which it is inextricably a part. Through the atrocities which have become synonymous with Birmingham, the terror under which its quarter-million Negroes are prostrated, America is exposed throughout the world as a whited sepulcher full of corruption. Even our friends and allies turn away their eyes in disgust. We stand revealed as hypocrites who violate within our own borders, in areas subject to our laws and Constitution, the very principles which we preach to others. We who cannot protect our own citizens in the peaceable exercise of their legal rights, in the sanctity of their homes and places of worship, have the effrontery to pose as liberators of mankind. Whom do we deceive but ourselves?

For more than twenty years I have been exiled from Birmingham, the city of my youth and early manhood, as the poet Dante was from his native Florence. This exile was forced on me because I was known to subscribe to the dangerous doctrine that all men are created equal, and because I had worked as a newspaper editor, public servant, and poet to create the conditions of human equality in Birmingham. I was not formally excommunicated with bell, book, and candle from the ranks of true believers in white supremacy forever. Nor was I banished by decree of the Podestàs. It was simply made impossible for me to earn a living and support my family there any longer. That is how it is done. Get out or starve. So I got out.

Let me tell you about Birmingham. It is a city blessed by nature as are few cities anywhere. It lies in a long Appalachian valley flanked by a mountain of iron ore. A few miles distant from the iron deposit is a rich coal field. Underneath the valley floor is an abundance of limestone. It used to be generally believed that Birmingham was destined to become the greatest center of heavy industry in the world because nowhere else were found together the three needful ingredients for the manufacture of steel—iron ore, coal, and limestone.

For its white residents, Birmingham is a far more attractive city than its northern counterparts, Pittsburgh, Youngstown, and Gary. Lovely suburban districts spread over the surrounding mountains. There are many superb golf courses which I used to play, miles of bridle paths through the woodland ways, nearby rivers, and huge artificial lakes for recreation and boating. But the quarter-million Negroes who constitute a third of the metropolitan area's population are crowded into some of the most sordid ghettos in the nation, mile after dreary mile of squared shacks resembling the location for the natives surrounding Johannesburg and Durban in the Union of South Africa. Not only are Birmingham's Negroes forced to live under subhuman conditions in these horrible slums, but their economic horizons are severely hemmed in as well. No Negro can be a professional or white-collar worker except in an all-Negro enterprise, of which there are extremely few in this center of heavy industry requiring tremendous capital investment. The same great corporations which in Pittsburgh, Youngstown, and Gary allow Negroes to rise as high in the hierarchy of labor as their skills and native abilities permit, in Birmingham, go along with prevailing patterns of economic injustice and restrict all Negroes, no matter how capable, to the most common labor and the nasty or mind-killing jobs no white man will take.

Forty-three years ago this month, I went to work on the open hearth in the Ensley plant of the United States Steel Corporation in Birmingham. I was sixteen years old, working for experience before going off to college. At that time I had ambitions of becoming a metallurgical engineer rather than a poet. I observed everything with youthful keenness and avidity. I noted that all the good jobs were reserved for white men, and only the undesirable ones for Negroes. I discovered, however, that human excellence and potential skill were by no means the monopoly of the Caucasians, but that the Negroes also were liberally endowed with abilities which they were given absolutely no opportunity to exercise. My first writing sprang spontaneously out of this recognition, and dealt passionately with the injustice done to the black man in the steel mill where I worked.

That, as I said, was forty-three years ago. Since then we have had President Harding's "normalcy"; President Coolidge's prosperity; President Hoover's boom and bust; President Roosevelt's New Deal, accompanied by the organization of industrial labor into unions solemnly committed to the principles of equality; World War II; the Korean War, in which many more Negroes served; the immense postwar expansion of the economy during the administrations of Presidents Truman and Eisenhower; and now, President Kennedy's New Frontier, but the Negro is just where he was in the Birmingham steel mills forty-three years ago. Indeed his position has actually deteriorated because mechanization and automation in the steel industry have abolished many of the lowliest shovel-and-wheelbarrow jobs which were formerly allocated to him. Not one step has the Negro been able to advance against the walls of discrimination which hedges him on every side.

This most fundamental evil of merciless economic discrimination against the Negro is compounded by many others—political, social, educational. They all form a complex which must be attacked as a whole if justice is ever to be done. The dispatching of a couple of presidentially appointed mediators into the city, no matter how well intentioned they and the president who sent them may be, can be nothing more than a deceptive maneuver; a stalling for time. But time runs out. The evil strikes deep into the national fabric and does not die out, but spreads with frightening speed.

This is not just a matter of a fanatical, dictatorial Dixie demagogue and his stormtroopers with their Confederate flag front license plates. It goes beyond the mob of insurrectionaries who stomped the Freedom Riders, castrated Negroes at random, and most recently shot dead a thirteen-year-old Negro boy who was innocently riding the handlebars of his brother's bicycle—this last abomination being perpetrated appropriately enough by a couple of Eagle Scouts returning from a segregationist rally on a motorbike. Not ignorant rednecks, but "model youths," the flower of Birmingham's clear-eyed, God-fearing Boy Scouts! No, the evil transcends all of this. It transcends even the terrorism of the bombers, which has culminated with the blasting of the Sixteenth Street Baptist Church and the hideous murders of the four little girls who we commemorate here today. The evil goes to the very roots of a social system deliberately and diabolically organized against the Negro, one which rules Birmingham and much of the South with a rod of steel, and which spreads its sinister influence over the entire country.

What is it that we in our naïveté expect? That the so-called authorities in Birmingham will put a stop to the terror they themselves have called into being for the express purpose of crushing the movement of Negro liberation? Permit me to reminisce for a few moments. In my childhood, the city was under the absolute control of the hooded order, the Ku Klux Klan, which not only rode out on most nights to flog women and perform other such acts of anonymous heroism, but operated a potent political machine. Without Klan endorsement, you could not be a dogcatcher or on the garbage wagons in Birmingham. The police force was Klan to a man. Not a single Catholic, Jew, or Negro was permitted to serve on it. Down to this very day, a metropolis one-third Negro has not a single black policeman.

In 1937, this Ku Klux Klan police force came under the control of Birmingham's infamous public safety commissioner, "Bull" Connor, the same man who in 1963 broke up the peaceable demonstration of thousands of Negro schoolchildren with police dogs and fire hoses, a display of wanton ferocity which astonished and sickened the entire world. But this public spectacle of sadism simply revealed the true face of the secret terror which has long afflicted the Negroes of Birmingham, as well as such whites as have cared to challenge the power structure in any way.

For close to a generation, "Bull" Connor shaped a police force inherited from the Ku Klux Klan into a well-nigh perfect instrument for the suppression not of crime but of liberty. Antilabor outrages perpetrated by the Birmingham cops were among the most shameful in the nation. But of course the primary objective of "Bull's" police was to keep the Negro down. Any Negro they picked up, whether innocent or guilty of paltry misdemeanor or more serious offense, was worked over on general principles, so that all Negroes lived—and live today—in permanent fear of and contempt for the brutal guardians of law and order. Police terror and torture—this has been the immemorial method of Birmingham's rulers to oppress the Negro population, and to prevent their ever exercising the rights guaranteed to them by the United States Constitution itself. In Birmingham, the Constitution is null and void. It has always been a dead letter. Just words, words, words, of no more force and effect than the Sermon on the Mount in a city of 680 churches which likes to boast that it is the most Christian in the nation.

Lest you get the erroneous idea that it is only the Negro population which is oppressed by the power structure of Birmingham, permit me to reminisce again about the Klan era. At that period, Catholics suffered grievously from police brutality and sordid frame-ups. So far as I know this story has never been adequately reported. No Catholic could work for the city or county, or teach in the public schools. Klan strong-arm committees made the rounds of the business houses, threatening their proprietors with physical harm and boycott if they did not discharge some clerk, secretary, or salesperson who was known to be a Catholic. In all too many cases the frightened employers complied and purged their Catholic workers. At this same period, Alabama sent to the United States Senate a ranting bigot by the name of Cotton Tom Heflin whose sole stock in trade was anti-Catholic hate-peddling. According to Cotton Tom in an oration I recall which packed Birmingham's huge Municipal Auditorium, the pope of Rome was preparing to sail his vast navy up the Potomac to seize the Capitol at Washington.

As the crowning crime in this anti-Catholic persecution, in 1921, Father James E. Coyle, the saintly pastor of St. Paul's, a downtown Catholic church, which is now the procathedral, was murdered by a Klan minister of the gospel. The sanctimonious fiend coolly walked up on the rectory porch and emptied his pistol into Father Coyle, who was sitting there reading his breviary. The crime was committed in full view of numerous passersby on a busy downtown street in the middle of the afternoon, right next door to the county courthouse and the Birmingham jail, so renowned in song. There was no question of the facts. But was Father Coyle's psalm-intoning assassin brought to justice and hanged in the courtyard of that handy calaboose? He was not! On the contrary, he was triumphantly acquitted by a jury of his despicable peers, Klansman all. While the self-styled "good people" of that day kept mum as little mice, Father Coyle's murderer was acclaimed as a public hero.

Between the Birmingham of that day and the city of today, what difference can we detect? Now as then, the "good white people," the blessed moderates, with a single honorable exception—attorney Charles Morgan—play the ignoble role of the three monkeys, seeing no evil, hearing no evil, and keeping their cowardly mouths shut. They too have been terrorized into silence and ignoble acquiescence by the monstrous conspiracy of religious bigotry, master racism, and bomb-throwing violence. Now as then, they ask in small, querulous voices only to be left alone to work out their community problems undisturbed by what they term outside interference. What they have in mind of course is the sweeping of the whole malodorous mess under the rug.

Who can doubt that the police of Birmingham are actually covering up for the bombers of the Sixteenth Street Baptist Church? Perhaps these little forays into homicide are simply off-duty recreation for some members of the force. Fifty bombings of Negro homes and churches and every one unsolved. Suppose these had been bombings of white homes and churches by Negroes? Assuredly the police would have collared the criminals within a few hours—and if they hadn't been able to lay hands on the right ones, any Negroes would have been made to serve. You may be very certain that the police would have rounded them up by the hundreds, and framed as many as would be required to still the howls for Negro blood which would have gone up on every side. This very police force is the same which a few years ago was exposed before the whole world as working hand in glove with the burglars of Birmingham in breaking and entering and plundering the homes of the citizenry. Can anyone expect this thoroughly corrupt instrument to be of any service at all in the present crisis, or to fill any purpose except the one for which it was created—namely, to perpetuate institutionalized injustice?

We hear raised today the spurious cry of "state's rights" in support of the discrimination and segregation, as a century ago it was raised in defense of human slavery. No sensible person can quarrel with the principle that local problems are in general best dealt with on the local level by local authorities, within the general context of the federal Constitution. But when in an American city and state the Constitution is degraded to a mere scrap of paper, its solemn guarantees set at naught by a lawless governor, a gangster police, and a conspiracy of terrorists—with the tacit support of the pillars of the community, Birmingham's "Big Mules"—that the federal power is imperiled and must intervene if it is to survive. No compromise is possible under the present circumstances. Either the principle of "equal justice under law" applies to every part of the Union, or it will soon apply to none.

The whole people of the United States is concerned in this dreadful matter. Once again we must pledge our lives, our fortunes, and our sacred honor to a renewal of the battle against tyranny first joined in 1776. At whatever cost, we will make good from North to South and shore to shore the fundamental tenet of the Declaration of Independence that all men are created equal. We will embody this in working human relations everywhere within our borders. We will at long last implement the explicit guarantees of equal rights contained in the Constitution. If this entails the use of troops and the establishment of direct federal rule in Birmingham and other sections of the South currently in revolt, so be it. Certain it is that men like Governor Wallace hold office solely by virtue of the fact that the vast majority of their Negro constituents are barred from the polls by force and fraud. We chide Fidel Castro for not holding elections in Cuba. Why, there hasn't been an honest election in Alabama or Mississippi, South Carolina, Georgia, or Louisiana within the lifetime of any person seated in this hall! How long must we twentieth-century Americans endure an anachronistic perversion of democratic representative government as thoroughly dishonest as the rotten borough system which throttled England in the early nineteenth century? Listen to this description of that system, from the pages of the *Encyclopedia Britannica*. The boroughs "were strongholds of corrupt and bigoted obscurantism in the midst of a country transformed by industrial development and alive with new political, economic, and social movements." Is not this a perfect analogy to the Alabama of George Wallace and the Mississippi of Ross Barnett? The whole nation suffers by virtue of the excessive influence of congressmen and senators from the rotten boroughs of the South, men who every day betray the principles on which the nation was founded, men whose oaths to support and defend the Constitution are, in the Shakespearean phrase, "as false as dicers' oaths."

It is not as if we had no potential allies in the South. The Negro liberation movement in that region has come of age. If given the unstinting federal support it warrants, and undergirded with the economic resources of the friends of democracy in the rest of the country, it will win even greater victories than it has already achieved through nonviolent protest and legal actions. By cooperating with the Negro's fight for freedom, we can deal effectively with the virus of bigotry and racism at its prime source in the South, with some hope of containing it before it spreads into areas now relatively uninfected by it. We have no choice but to engage this evil and choke the life out of it. The alternative is to see this country engulfed by a tide of hatred and terrorism in which the worst excesses of the Secret Army Organization in Algeria will be rivaled and perhaps even surpassed in savage barbarity.

[Beecher concludes by reading three poems.]

§37 Slater King

Slater Hunter King was born on October 18, 1927, to Margaret Allegra Slater King and Clennon Washington King, one of the most prominent black families in Albany, Georgia. The elder King left his family home in the Florida Panhandle town of Two Egg, headed on foot for Booker T. Washington's Tuskegee Institute, 180 miles away. Washington's entrepreneurial ethic never left C. W. King as he opened restaurants, businesses, and a newspaper in southwestern Georgia. He was also a cofounder of the Albany chapter of the NAACP. Slater and his siblings inherited their father's unflinching commitment to black capital formation and racial uplift. After graduating from Fisk University with a degree in economics, Slater moved back to Albany and entered the real estate and insurance businesses. In 1948 he married Valencia Laverne Benham, and the couple had two sons. They later divorced and he married Marion Townsend in 1956. In the fall of 1961, two Student Nonviolent Coordinating Committee (SNCC) workers, Cordell Reagon and Charles Sherrod (his wife, Shirley Sherrod, would make national news in 2010), came to Albany in hopes of organizing a movement. They were given the name of C. W. King as a vital community contact. A movement quickly developed in November 1961, and Slater King became vice president and later president of the Albany movement. His organizing earned him many arrests, including his first on December 17, 1961, which catalyzed much of Albany's black community. The following year his wife was beaten by police officers outside of a Camilla, Georgia, jail, leading to a miscarriage just months later. As protest activity waxed and waned in Albany, Slater King's commitment never wavered, and in September 1963 he declared his candidacy for mayor, the first black man ever to do so in Albany. While he received more than 2,500 votes, he lost the Democratic primary to James V. Davis, who garnered 7,220 votes. Making King's defeat more bitter and perplexing was the fact that his vote total represented less than half of registered black voters in the area. King understood, though, that his candidacy was highly rhetorical; he later remarked that he wanted to free black minds from the belief that a black man should not run for elected office. Slater King's life was cut tragically short on March 7, 1969, when his car hydroplaned off of Route 55 in Dawson, Georgia and collided with another vehicle. He was survived by his wife and four children. His papers are housed at Fisk University.

The men and women of the Albany movement have yet to receive their rhetorical due. Dr. William Anderson, Rev. Samuel Wells, and Bernice Johnson Reagon, among many others, helped lead an impassioned movement, and yet we know nothing of their rhetorical leadership. So, too, with Slater King. Here in a brief stump speech delivered to his neighbors in Albany, we see something of his oratorical talents. King calls for a white-black partnership in which both sides talk openly and honestly with each other in a spirit of Christian love. The present "Berlin Wall" in Albany is a direct result of miscommunication between the races. Whites simply cannot rely on their black maids to provide an accurate gauge of local black sentiment; the master/servant relationship won't permit it. Similarly, the local newspaper features only negative news about Albany's blacks, thus distorting the white mind. Christian whites must risk being labeled "nigger lover" if indeed a rebirth of interracial community is to occur. King also makes an implicit critique of black men, given his rhetorical emphasis on black women's earning power, their work ethic, and the lack of oversight of, and accountability for, black children. Without overtly saying so, King urges black men to take more responsibility—for their wives, for their children, and for their community.

A Rebirth of Albany

September 1963
Albany, Georgia

Good evening, ladies and gentlemen:

I always feel that when we are at home with our loved ones gathered around, that it is a *sacred* place, and often strangers are not allowed in sacred places.

I am a stranger to *many* of you, and I am very grateful to you for allowing me to enter the sanctity of your homes. My name is Slater King, a candidate for mayor in the city of Albany. I was *born* in Albany, graduated from a local high school, then attended Fisk University—graduated after four years with a B.A. degree, and I have done further study in insurance and accounting. I am presently in business as a partner in the firm of King and King, which is engaged in real estate brokerage and casualty insurance.

I chose to run as mayor of the city because we have momentous problems affecting the city, which *urgently* demand *dynamic* leadership that is *willing* to go forth to face these problems *squarely, without evasions or hesitations.* In *many* cities across the South, we have seen a dynamic type of *white* leadership come forth, but so far, in Albany, this leadership *has not* come forth. We need leadership that will be able to stand between the colored and white communities and attempt to chart the course that will lead toward *greater* freedom and security for *both*.

But presently, I have been impressed that the local political leadership wishes to continue the *master and servant relationship* in Albany, between the two races, when it *should be* one of *partnership.*

The present political administration has *even refused* to grant such a *minor and simple* request as the forming of a biracial committee to begin working on the solutions to many of the problems between the two communities. It is *certain* that in *no city* can 30 percent of the population be ignored and given *absolutely no* representation or voice and expect to have *anything* other than chaos and confusion.

In the meantime, cities all around us that have *never* had the record for being as progressive as Albany have lately grown economically—at a *much faster* pace than Albany. One Valdostan made a comment in the Valdosta daily paper that "We will never have the trouble Albany has, because we will *always* sit down with *all* of our citizens to attempt to work out our differences." To me, this is a Christian and *only* way to do it.

Another reason I am running for mayor is that I *love* this city *and* its people, and I have *great faith* in their ability to resolve their differences *if ever they know the facts.*

In Russia, they say that there is an Iron Curtain between them and the countries of the west, and in Germany, there is the Berlin Wall, but I *must say* that here in Albany, *we have the people wall* between colored and white communities. You *never know the real* situation as it exists in the colored community, and *we never know the real* situation as it exists in the white community. Therefore, often you have *two* hostile communities, both staring *ignorantly* at one another.

To begin with, about the *only* contact that most whites have with Negroes is with their maids, and often we will hear whites make the statement, "My maid says she is perfectly satisfied with things as they are." The maids are *not* going to tell you the *truth*, because most Negroes are in the habit of telling whites what they want to hear. If a maid is asked, "Are you satisfied?" she is usually *always* going to say, "Yes, ma'am," because she knows that is what is expected of her. But I wonder, really, *how could* most of us *expect* her to be satisfied when about the *only* mode of employment open to Negro women in Albany is as maids, and the pay for the same ranges from ten to twenty dollars per week, with the *majority* of them receiving fifteen dollars.

Too often the maid is the *sole* support of the Negro family and how, *in many cases*, she manages to pay a minimum of rent of $8.50 a week for a one-bedroom apartment, buy groceries, pay for medical care, clothes, and utilities, I *do not know*. But, of course, we know that the majority of the Negro community lacks even the *bare necessities*. We *must* be aware, too, that the bare essentials are *necessary for the making of good citizens*, and at the moment, we are not making these bare necessities available for a large portion of Albany citizenry. Many Negro children *burned to death* in fires last year, here in Albany, because domestics and colored maids went to the white house to take care of white children and had no one to look after their own babies and small children, who were often left alone to attend themselves.

In my opinion, our only daily newspaper *slants the news* and, except on *rare* occasions, *no other news* is reported about Negroes except that which is bad; it is spotlighted on the front page. *Unemployment among Negroes is 70 percent higher than among* whites here in Albany, and because of automation, these figures will grow.

There is *not one* Negro policeman in our city when even much smaller southern towns that have not been so *"progressive"* as Albany do have Negro policemen.

There is *not one* Negro fireman, *not one* Negro clerk in the Water Department, although Negroes pay *over one million* dollars annually for utilities here in Albany.

In fact, in *most* of the city's employment, Negroes are hired *only* as janitors or maids, although Negroes pay a *heavier* percentage of tax—by ratio to their wealth.

In many of the Negro sections, not too far from the heart of town, outdoor privies still exist as a menace to the health of the total community.

The residents of the Lincoln Heights subdivision here have requested of the city *for the past thirteen years* that they furnish paving and sewers, to be paid for by the residents of their subdivision. The city has seen fit to pave and add sewerage to *no less* than fifteen subdivisions since this time. But each time that the Lincoln Heights subdivision asks again, there is *always* some excuse—such as "lack of money" or some other flimsy excuse.

There are over two thousand Negro juvenile delinquents who walk the streets of Albany each day; they know they will not be reprimanded, because we do not have *even one Negro male* truant officer.

These are just a *few* of the momentous problems that face us. These problems were created by the *whole community* and they are going to have to be solved by the whole community, but the attitude of our present politicians is to act as though *no* problems exist between races of the community at this time.

I want to see this great city that has stood out as a beacon of hope to boys and girls from many surrounding counties continue to stand out as a beacon of hope to people in other counties and communities.

I have great faith in the whites who live in Albany:

That they will rise up and let their voices be heard.

That they will cry out for mediation and for us to sit down together to work out our differences.

That they will demand that emotionalism and name-calling has no place in our city government.

We *must* begin to be more *honest* with ourselves. I think of how all of us call ourselves Christians. We say we believe in God, and one of the first requisites of a true Christian is that he practices *love toward all*, and yet, to many whites, the worst name that they can be called is a nigger lover. The name is used by many whites to frighten other whites who might attempt to work toward better relations between whites and blacks.

I only state this to show how we have been *dishonest* with ourselves and until we show *some love, care, or concern for one another*, our community will only steadily move towards the brink of destruction.

There are Negroes who will say that the white man is not to be trusted and that no Negro should have faith in him. They say, "Let us have nothing to do with them." *I cannot agree* with this attitude because we have *always* seen that there have been whites who have been our friends. But because of the growing tensions and the seeming inability of many whites to take a stand, there are growing feelings of bitterness among Negroes.

We are working *hard* to *avoid* this, but *only* if we have the cooperation of other *Christian* whites can we help to *stop the growing seeds of bitterness.*

I see a vision of a rebirth of Albany, a rebirth that will make it more dynamic and powerful than anything that we have seen heretofore.

It is with regret that I see that hate abounds in our city, and yet I see a chance of bringing love. In our city, there is great misunderstanding, and yet there can be understanding. There is presently confusion, and yet there can be clarity and peace. There are many who still stand in fear and insecurity, and I would like to be an instrument to help bring security. There is great unemployment, and I would like to work to help open new avenues of employment. I *truly* want to see Albany live up to the great city that it has a promise of becoming. I *cannot*, by myself, do these things. Many of them often lie *outside* of the purview of the mayor's office.

But with the *love of God* in each of our hearts and working together in a spirit of brotherhood and cooperation, we can, together, make our dreams become a reality.

In closing, what I am asking of you may be very painful, but I am asking that as you go into the voting booth, alone with only your conscience and God that you vote not for black or white man, but vote *only* for that man whom you feel will work, filled with the spirit of God, for the peace of *all* Albany, and will help to push our great city onward to prosperity for all.

§38 William Harrison Pipes

William Harrison Pipes was born on January 3, 1912, to sharecropping parents in Inverness, Mississippi, centered in the cotton-rich Delta region of the state. Despite his humble beginnings in "the most southern place on earth," Pipes was determined to get an education. He worked his way through Tuskegee High School and Institute, graduating with a B.S. degree in 1935. At Atlanta University, Pipes secured his M.A. degree in 1937, and did a thesis on the speechmaking of Booker T. Washington. Six years later Pipes earned his doctorate in speech at the University of Michigan; in so doing, he became the first black Ph.D. in the burgeoning field of speech and speech communication. For his dissertation Pipes examined the speaking styles of what he termed "old-time Negro preaching," a style of preaching that catered to rural blacks in Macon County, Georgia—and to many uneducated blacks all over the Deep South. His pathbreaking study, published in 1945 in the *Quarterly Journal of Speech*, and later as a book in 1951, highlighted the relationship between poor, rural blacks and reli-gious speechmaking, which aimed only at weekly emotional catharsis and not social uplift. After completing his degrees, Pipes became president of Alcorn A&M College (later Alcorn State University), where one of his stu-dents was Medgar Evers. Pipes left Lorman, Mississippi, to become dean of English and Speech at Philander Smith College in Little Rock, Arkansas, a position he held for seven years. As a former president and dean, Pipes entered Michigan State University as a forty-five-year-old "rookie," when he took an assistant professor position in 1957. He quickly ascended the ranks there and in 1968 became the first black professor to reach the rank of full professor. He retired from academia in 1976, and passed away five years later at the age of sixty-nine in 1981. He was survived by his wife, Anna H. Russell Pipes, and three children, one of whom, Harriette Pipes McAdoo, became a distinguished professor at Michigan State.

In this address before his fellow YMCA members in Lansing, Pipes invokes a question that would find deep cultural resonance thirty-five years later: "What would Jesus do?" That question holds the key not only to then contemporary race relations in the North and South but also perhaps more importantly for Pipes, to the worldwide struggle between democracy and Communism. If Americans would invoke the question, and act on the ostensibly unproblematic answer, Cold War victory was ensured. But if, by 1978, Americans had not surrendered their religious hypocrisy, democracy was likely doomed since Communists would continue to exploit the prob-lematic cleavage between Americans' words and deeds.

ዿ዆

What Would Jesus Do?
November 8, 1963
YMCA "Men and Religion Luncheon," Lansing, Michigan

[*Author's Note:* To me, the murder of Mississippi civil rights worker Medgar Evers (my former student) was horrifying. When I heard the radio news that morning, I sat down and wept; I have never been quite the same again. (For the first time, I got out into the streets with other sign-carrying protesters—even marched in Washington, August 28.) Perhaps this was the death gasp of my "Uncle Tom" thinking and acting. And what outraged me most in all of this is the historical lethargy of the American churches.]

Mr. Chairman, friends:

President Hannah of Michigan State University, the chairman of the United States Civil Rights Commission, said recently, "The most important problem facing the United States . . . is race conflict." Now, the very fact that I, a Negro whose grandfather was a Mississippi slave—the very fact that I stand here this morning talking with you as a member and steward of the Central Methodist Church, and as a professor of one of America's great universities, seems to indicate that in this country—and certainly in Michigan—we are moving in the direction of better racial understanding. But then there is Birmingham, Alabama; and Jackson, Mississippi—where Medgar Evers, my former student, was murdered by a shot in the back—and I assure you that his murder will *not* be punished to the full extent of the law.

I say to you today with all sincerity that the hour is very late in this matter of better American racial relationships (despite progress made) if the *free world* is to win out over the *world of Communism*. And let me say here that it is regrettable that better racial relationships in the United States have not come as a result of our laws, our beliefs, our religious principles. But America has always had *time* for things to improve—"with all deliberate speed" was the way the Supreme Court looked at the elimination of segregated education. From a legal or religious point of view, this is a ridiculous way of ending injustice. Imagine telling a man to stop beating his wife "with all deliberate speed." But America, I say, has always had plenty of time to get around to racial justice at home—until now.

Dr. John H. Furbay (noted writer, traveler, and expert on world affairs) said in Lansing recently, "By 1978 (just fifteen years from now) the issues splitting the world today will be decisively settled. It will either be a *Communist world* or one reflecting beliefs of *Western democracies*." The Russian and American sputniks and cosmonauts now circle the earth looking for information about outer space; within fifteen years they'll have the necessary information about outer space, and they could be up there looking for targets. The real outcome of this struggle between Communism and democracy will be determined not by what happens way out there in outer space (or by behind-the-scenes maneuvering in foreign countries) but by what happens *close down here* in the *hearts of men*. The outcome depends upon which way the uncommitted areas of the world will go—whether to the side of Communism or to the side of the democracies. The war is really under way; and if these *undecided countries* were to be won over to Communism right now, democracy would lose. *These uncommitted areas* of the world, particularly, are India, Africa, and Southeast Asia. (And it is worthy of note that most of these people are nonwhites.)

Now, here is the heart of democracy's struggle. In our Declaration of Independence (to use American democracy as an example), in our Constitution, in our religions, we *proclaim* the brotherhood of man and the human dignity of the human race; we *proclaim* that "all men are created equal" with certain basic rights. But these are *proclamations*; these are *mere words*. Communists point out to *the uncommitted areas of the world* not just our *words*, but our *deeds*. They point to Little Rock, Arkansas; they point to the Birmingham, Alabama, church-bombing murder of little children; they point to Mississippi's Medgar Evers—murdered because he struggled for the freedom and brotherhood guaranteed and promised by our Constitution and religion. But the Communists, in pointing out to the uncommitted areas of the world that the American *says* one thing but *does* another, play up such matters—in the South and in the North. And perhaps a most telling blow used by godless Russia upon the uncommitted areas of the world is our *church*. Here, at least, in God's church, one would expect to find *in deed* the brotherhood of man being practiced. In a country where (according to a recent Census Bureau report) "96 percent of the people subscribe to some form of religion"—in such a country one would *expect* the United States churches to take the lead in the matter of racial integration in the schools, for example. (And, incidentally, in the matter of American slavery, with the exception of the Quakers, no religious group as a whole took the lead in destroying this institution.) In the current Negro revolt against segregation and discrimination in voting, employment, hearings, etc., the church as a whole is strangely silent. What have the churches done in Little Rock, Birmingham, and Mississippi? The courts, not the churches, have taken the lead. Why, in Louisiana, Catholics there asked the pope to remove a bishop who integrated the parish schools in the state, in keeping with the law. *Indeed, it is said that the eleven o'clock hour on Sunday morning is America's most segregated hour!* It is a sad commentary on our religion. And it's good proof for the Communists of our hypocrisy. (In my own Methodist Church, as you know, we have—even here in Michigan—a segregated central jurisdiction.)

You may very well ask, "But what are we to do to eliminate the hypocrisy, to save the world for democracy during the next years?" For a Christian, the answer is simple.

In making any decision on a racial matter, let's ask ourselves in all sincerity, *"What would Jesus do?"* And therein, I believe, is to be found a solution to America's (and to democracy's) dilemma of *proclaiming* the brotherhood of man while *practicing* something else. In every decision of a racial nature, if we could get every American professing religion to ask himself—and to act accordingly—"What would Jesus do?" we would soon have this thing licked. In education, in housing; in anything. "What would Jesus do?" Let's look at two recent situations in which this principle might have been used.

You probably read the news story of the white American lieutenant stationed in Germany. When his new captain—a Negro—reported to take command of the group, the captain saluted the men and proceeded to shake hands with each of the officers in his group. The white lieutenant, who was from San Antonio, Texas, saluted but refused to shake hands with a Negro. The matter almost became another "Ole Miss" situation; but here is my point. Regardless of the lieutenant's rights not to shake hands—regardless of his Texas bringing up—if as a Christian he could have asked himself sincerely at the time the Negro captain's hand was extended, "What would Jesus do in this situation?" I believe the white lieutenant would have shaken the Negro captain's hand. And there would have been one less incident for the Communists to use to convince the uncommitted areas of the world that American democracy is a fraud; that her religion is hypocrisy.

Now, this acting Christ-like and *being* a Christian can apply to the discriminated (the victim) as well as to the man who discriminates. Just one personal example: Negroes resent being called "George." All Negro bellhops, shoeshine boys, and the like are called "George" by many whites. Negroes resent the term, because it suggests inferiority. Dr. Thurman, a professor in my department at MSU, addresses me as "George," despite the fact that I've told him I resent it. But here is my chance to practice what I'm preaching. When this man calls me "George," I should ask myself, "How would Christ react? What would Jesus do?" Thus, a basis of mental nonviolence in the Negro revolt.

I believe, then, that herein rests an answer to the question "What are we to do to eliminate this hypocrisy in order to save the world for democracy during the next fifteen years?" In matters of racial relations, let's all of us act on the basis of what we sincerely believe Jesus would do.

In this manner we *could* strike at the *heart* of the struggle between democracy and Communism. Both Russia and the United States are certain to conquer outer space—but what about this thing close to us here, the hearts of men? And therein rests the challenge to the American church. And this is a most serious challenge. Just look at the success in the spread of Communism. In less than fifty years Communism can boast of as many converts as Christianity, although Christianity has been *proclaimed* for more than 1,900 years. Now, does this mean that Christianity has failed? No, indeed. The fact is that Christianity has never really been tried. A Communist is a Communist through and through; he *practices* what he *preaches*. But what is a *Christian*? In his actions, many a *Christian* certainly is not *Christ-like*.

Today's demand to end second-class citizenship is a worldwide struggle between democracy and Communism. We must somehow show men and women everywhere that, in this space-age struggle for the minds of men, there must be *in deed* as well as in word *human dignity for every member of the human race*. Millions still suffer in India under the old religious caste system; South Africa has triple segregation—whites, blacks, and colored. Ours, then, must become a worldwide crusade of *brotherhood*. In churches, in "Y" meetings like this—everywhere—we must help spread the urgency of first-class citizenship for *all of our peoples*.

Now, it would be thoughtless and ungrateful for me not to mention the great progress which we in this country have already made in racial matters. And some ministers and church members *have* been active; I marched with them recently in Detroit and in Washington. Suffice it to say that as a Negro I know of no other country I would prefer to the United States to live in—whether in my former homes of Mississippi and Little Rock, Arkansas, or in Lansing, Michigan. Progress is being made on the race relations front. But are we moving fast enough to win over the *uncommitted areas of the world*? Fifteen years for deciding between Communism and democracy can be a very short time indeed—much shorter than the one hundred years the Negro has prayed and fought for the freedom promised him in the Declaration of Independence and the Thirteenth, Fourteenth, and Fifteenth Amendments to the United States Constitution. I firmly believe that a great "shot in the arm" to democracy can come from the church if *Christians*, for example, would simply become more Christ-like; if in every decision of a racial nature, we would ask ourselves sincerely, "What would Jesus do?"

1964

1964

§39 Vincent Harding

Dr. Vincent Gordon Harding was born on July 25, 1931, and was raised by his mother in the West Indian section of New York City. During his youth, Harding attended the Victory Tabernacle Church in Harlem, where he was moved by sermons on peaceful activism. The ideas seemed to stick with young Harding: after two years serving as a draftee in the United States Army he was left "deeply disturbed" by his experiences and explored conscientious objector status. After receiving his bachelor's degree in history from City College of New York and a master's degree in journalism from Columbia University, he pursued a second master's and later a Ph.D. in history at the University of Chicago. During his matriculation, Harding discovered the writings of the early Anabaptists; their self-sacrificing love and acceptance of death resonated deeply with him. Harding also encountered the cultural descendants of the Anabaptist movement—Mennonites—at Woodlawn Mennonite Church in Chicago. In that congregation was schoolteacher and social worker Rosemarie Freeney, a graduate of Goshen College, a Mennonite college. The two would later marry and she would be a stable source of encouragement and support. Woodlawn's congregants asked Harding to serve as associate pastor in 1958, making it one of the few racially integrated Mennonite houses of worship. Later that year, Harding and four others traveled throughout the South, studying race relations and drawing comparisons between southern segregation and northern separation. During this trip Harding met with Martin Luther King Jr. in Atlanta.

King, who was recovering from a near fatal attack, invited Harding to come south and work for the movement.

Three years later, in 1961, the recently married Hardings moved to Atlanta, starting a Mennonite voluntary service unit—Mennonite House—which Harding described as "a combination residence for an interracial team of local Movement participants and social service volunteers . . . and a base of operations for our own ministry of reconciliation." During their four-year ministry in Atlanta, the Hardings were deeply involved in the movement, working with the Southern Christian Leadership Conference, the Student Nonviolent Coordinating Committee, and the Congress of Racial Equality. Vincent traveled, gave speeches, demonstrated, and negotiated with community leaders. Harding became the primary voice for the civil rights movement within the Mennonite Church. He challenged church leaders to hold true to the best of Mennonite ideals: egalitarianism, pacifism, discipleship, and integrity. To Harding, the Mennonite Church and the civil rights movement, with a shared focus on nonviolence, conversed directly with one another. But Harding was also a controversial figure as he attempted to mediate the two cultures. In his attempt to twin the orthodoxies of Mennonite culture with the goals of the movement, Harding discovered that even within the walls of Mennonite churches, views on integration were ambivalent.

In 1964, at a conference on Mennonites and race in Atlanta, Georgia, Harding, the only African American Mennonite who spoke, delivered a vivid, haunting speech, a speech seared with pain. It would be one of the last addresses Harding gave to the Mennonite community, as he was exasperated by the hypocrisy within the church. He wondered how Mennonites could profess "nonconformity" with the world while standing silently by, conforming to racial inequality in mainstream culture. Soon after, a weary and disappointed Vincent Harding asked for and received a six-month leave of absence from the Mennonite Church. A year later Harding was offered a teaching position at Spellman College. He quietly withdrew from the Mennonite world, and never went back. However, his Mennonite values would influence his actions throughout his life.

Following Dr. King's assassination in 1968, Coretta Scott King asked Harding to help found the Martin Luther King Jr. Documentation Project and the Memorial Center, including the Institute of the Black World, a center for research and advocacy. The center provided intellectual and ideological guidance for the new academic field of black studies. Harding became its first director. Harding was later the senior academic consultant for the acclaimed civil rights documentary series *Eyes on the Prize*, he authored several books, and he continued to be involved with social justice movements around the world, using the Veterans of Hope Project, founded in 1997, to document the struggles of people working toward freedom and democracy. Harding currently resides in Denver, Colorado, serving as chairperson of the Veterans of Hope Project and professor emeritus at the Iliff School of Theology, where Harding taught as professor of religion and social transformation from 1981 to 2004. He was the first African American on faculty.

Even though Harding was disillusioned with the Mennonite community's sluggish action, his speech is still sprinkled with the inclusive "we" and "us." He challenges the Mennonite Church to take up its cross, rediscover its voice, and act. Harding admonishes the church for its delayed entrance into the civil rights movement, but proclaims that "action without knowledge is highly irresponsible." And knowledge Harding offers. "Decade of Crisis" expounds upon the centuries-long wrestling match between oppressed and oppressor that led up to the civil rights movement. To understand the current decade—the 1960s—one must understand the countless decades of humiliation, scarcity, and denied human rights. Harding narrates the decades, weaving together history and emotion to emphasize the importance of his words. In the present he describes how the fight for freedom is long from over, emphasizing how something as simple and lawful as voting, riding a bus, or attending school is fraught with danger. Harding's speech offers a stinging rebuke, but it also asks a question, a question that repeats itself long after the page is gone, an afterimage deep within the mind— "When will it be too late for us? When shall we discover God at work in the midst of this crisis, calling his church to judgment, to repentance, to renewal? When will it be too late for us?"

Decade of Crisis
February 25, 1964
Atlanta, Georgia

When Eugene Carson Blake, stated clerk of the United Presbyterian Church, went to Baltimore last year to stand on the receiving end of segregation and fire hoses and jail, he went to stand by those who were oppressed, to walk with them, to demonstrate with them the hurt and humiliation and hope they felt. As he joined the demonstration line with fellow ministers he said to those who had already borne the heat of many battles, he said—"We come late, but we come."

In a certain elementary—very elementary—sense, these words apply to us. Like Blake, we too are those followers of the Christ who have long trailed off at a great distance as he walked among his oppressed brothers. Like Blake, we Mennonites come late, very late. For the decade that has changed the course of this nation's history is now almost past, and we must surely be repentant children when we come as Christians at so late a date to examine with some care the crisis through which our nation has been passing. While others are acting, we are only now investigating, but investigate we must, for action without knowledge is highly irresponsible.

We call this a decade of crisis, and so it is. Few other spans of years could be called more crucial and decisive than the period that began on May 17, 1954, when Chief Justice Warren spoke for the Supreme Court the words of their unanimous decision regarding segregation in public schools. How shall we view it, though? How understand these years of trial and opportunity, years of testing and fear and great pain?

There is no hope for understanding this decade if we see it as though it stood alone in history, as though it were some strange, unexplained aberration on the American scene. For it is certainly not that. The decade that now closes is intimately tied to every decade that this nation has known, and it presents itself as a true, frightening witness to the fact that nations, like individuals, do reap what they sow.

This decade of crisis must be seen as inextricably bound to the decade that began with the year 1619. The decade that saw men and women ripped from their homes and families and stuffed on ships like cattle and brought to this land to be our slaves. We must see those children of God in chains to understand this decade. We must see the thousands who leaped into the shark-filled oceans rather than become slaves. We must see the thousands more who starved themselves to death on board ship in protest against the life prepared for them. And we must see therefore the deep vein of protest that has been present in the Negro since the day he was first raped from his home. We must catch, too, the deep companion vein of guilt that has run deeply, though unexpressed, through the lives of his captors and owners. To understand this decade we cannot afford to miss the many things that began in that decade. The accommodation and deceit on the part of the Negro that made survival possible. The inner death that made holding men as slaves a Christian act. To understand this moment, these other moments must be placed in sharp relief, moments when we—you and I—began that deep poisoning of the springs of true relationships, and set out on that path that would take black men and white men down long and bitter rehearsals of hell.

To understand this decade is impossible without a proper view of the decades that followed that fearful beginning. Decades of unpaid labor, decades of lies and cheating by oppressed and oppressor, decades of hatred suppressed and sometimes transferred, decades of rape approved by society, decades of convenient adultery, decades of the destruction of black families though the tap of an auctioneer's gavel—these are the decades we must see. The years, the tens and ten times ten years when men and women were treated as property, when education was denied, when humanity was denied, when God was therefore denied. Decades of deep scars to a million spirits. Decades when the church, by and large, either stood by silently or blessed it all with its cursed blessings.

Who dares see 1964 without the vision of an earlier century—the last one—when the Christian churches stood by and said slavery was not a religious issue but a political issue? For when they repeated that blasphemy decade after decade they and others came to believe it, and for a political problem so deeply entrenched politicians know of only one answer—war. And because the issue—in spite of what the churches said—*was* religious and spiritual and moral, war really solved very little, and the decade following the holocaust brought hope and bitterness, reconstruction and reaction, and when it was done the Negro was caught in a slavery almost as great—some say greater—as that he had left. Now he was a wage slave—tenant farmer, sharecropper, with no possessions of his own, soon to have the recently gained franchise wrenched from his hand, soon to be deserted by the reformers of the North when political power became more important than mere black men. Meanwhile, of course, the churches stood by and said they had to preach the gospel and could not worry about such things in a decade of despair.

The context for our time is also the decade of the 1890s, when the Supreme Court announced that the doctrine of separate but equal was the law of the land. The context of our time are the following decades that saw that doctrine enforced through intimidation, lynching, castration, and deep degradation. But these were also decades of growing impatience. Decade of the founding of the National Association for the Advancement of Colored People. Decade of World War I when Negro servicemen saw the rest of the world for the first time, and fought for democracy in segregated units. These were decades of migration when Negroes moved into the cities, north and south. These were decades of an upsurge of lynchings, decades of depression, decades when Negroes learned to put their confidence in the federal government because a man named Roosevelt there seemed to care about them.

To see and know these things and many more is to know how this decade now passing first came into being. It was, of course, immediately preceded by a decade of war and recovery and more subtle kinds of war. The decade that preceded this one began with a strange sight, the sight of Negroes in uniforms being pushed out of service clubs and USOs. It began with the sight of Negro soldiers and servicewomen discriminated against in the service and abused in a thousand major and minor ways outside the camps, while they wore the uniform of supposed honor. It was a decade that began with the sight of Negro soldiers guarding German prisoners of war on a train and having to sit by hungry while Germans ate in the Jim Crow dining cars, because the Germans were white and the guards were only Negroes. Men do not easily forget such things.

Nor do they forget 1946 in Columbia, Tennessee, when police and state troopers invaded the Negro section, looted its stores, and broke into its homes, beating women and children, riddling two men with bullets, placing scores of others in jail. Somehow that year stands out in their minds, for it was in that year on July 16 that the following sign appeared on the doors of Negro churches in Fitzgerald, Georgia. "The first Nigger who votes in Georgia will be a dead Nigger." And they remember how the next day a young Negro World War II veteran went to vote. And they remember how, three days later, he was dragged from his home and shot by four white men. There another sign went up on the church doors: "The first Nigger to vote will never vote again."

Such memories are mentioned here not because they were unusual, but because they were repeated scores of times in communities throughout the South in the decade before the court decision—the time that some men speak of as peaceful and harmonious, the time they refer to as a time of good race relations. Others feel those descriptions are hard to take, for they neglect the central facts. Such descriptions forget the long nights of humiliation that come when a man is driving or riding a bus with no place to eat or drink or find physical relief. It forgets the segregation that a man could never explain to his son. Descriptions of peace and harmony neglect the scores of persons who died because a hospital would not take them in on account of their race. These were part of the decade that preceded the court order. But there was more. In 1949 a handful of Negro cotton and tobacco farmers in Clarendon County, South Carolina, decided to sign a petition asking that their children's school be made equal with the white school—for separate was never equal in those years. Their petition came four years after the NAACP had decided to launch an all-out attack on school segregation, so eventually their case was joined together with cases from Washington, D.C., from Topeka, Kansas, and elsewhere in a suit that asked for the outlawing of all segregated public school education. The beginning was in Clarendon County, in the context of a score of decades of fear and humiliations, of hope and discrimination, of death and long dyings, a context which cannot be ignored if we would understand the origins of our present moment.

The first arguments on the case had come in 1952; then it was reargued in 1953, with the battery of NAACP lawyers facing some of the best legal minds the southern states could muster. By now the case had come to be known as *Brown v. Topeka*, and as the year 1954 began it was generally believed that the court would announce its decision before the close of the spring term. On Monday, May 17, Justice Earl Warren read the unanimous decision of the tribunal. At its heart were these words: "To separate children from those of similar age and qualifications solely because of their race generates a feeling of inferiority as to their status . . . that may affect their hearts and minds in a way unlikely ever to be undone." So the announcement came: "Separate educational facilities are inherently unequal." According to the words of the decision segregated public facilities were both illegal and immoral. (And yet many of us continued and still continue to send our children without a word of protest or repentance.)

Here was the sign for which many persons had been waiting. For almost a century since Emancipation the Negroes had had to labor under the burden of segregation with little sense of help from any side. They had looked to the unions, to Congress, even to the churches and had found little or no help. Now the Supreme Court of the land had declared itself on their side. The law of the land was indeed to be the law of liberty and justice for all. This was a new day of justice. An irreversible movement had begun.

It was soon clear, though, that nothing would be handed out on a platter. The way of equal justice would be long and hard in this land of the free. Shortly after the decision Senator Eastland of Mississippi spoke the sentiments of many persons when he said quite simply, "The South will not obey." And in his native county of Sunflower a group of men gathered on July 11, 1954, to form the first White Citizens' Council. The opposition, a strong, hard, determined opposition, was beginning to form. And as men watched the lines emerging they saw no reason to notice the twenty-five year-old minister, who, just before the court decision, preached his first sermon as pastor of historic Dexter Avenue Baptist Church in Montgomery, Ala-bama. His name was Martin Luther King Jr.

There were more than enough signs that the court decision had crystal-lized the opposition. Many white persons were deeply afraid. For decades the initiative had been in their hands. They had given "their" Negroes what they thought they needed. They had made all the decisions for the commu-nity. They had been taught and lived by the maxim that segregation (of cer-tain kinds) was not only the southern way of life, but God's own ordained way. Now all this was being challenged. Therefore they fought back with increasing ferocity, bringing to the surface feelings long smoothed over by both black and white. They were assisted by the court's failure to set a defi-nite deadline for total desegregation.

It was because of this opposition that the first Negro students in the border states who tried to take the court decision seriously were turned back and sometimes physically rebuffed. It was this new and growing sense of crisis that helped to explain the ambush shooting in May 1955 of the first Negro to register since Reconstruction in Belzoni, Mississippi. It helped, too, perhaps, to explain how in 1955 a fourteen-year-old Negro boy visit-ing from Chicago named Emmett Till could be charged with whistling at a white Mississippi woman, dragged from bed near midnight, and later be found dead in the Tallahatchie River with a seventy-five-pound weight around his neck. The "niggers" had to be kept in their place.

Sensing this kind of opposition, the Supreme Court came forward in May 1955 with an enabling order which indicated that public school inte-gration was to be achieved with "all deliberate speed." It had become clear that with a few exceptions the communities of the South did not intend to act without prodding, and this was meant to be a serious prod. Immediately, the NAACP followed up the new court order by filing desegregation suits in more than forty communities; and the Southern resistance grew. Therefore, in the fall when Negro children tried again to enroll on a desegregated basis, in almost every case they were turned away.

Shortly before the end of 1955 a new, unpredicted element broke into the situation. In Montgomery, Alabama, buses had been segregated ever since they first appeared. There was a white section and a Negro section in the back of it. If the white section filled up, the Negroes were compelled to get up and give their seats to new white passengers. On Thursday afternoon, December 1, Mrs. Rosa Parks, a seamstress, was on her way home from a tiring day of work. She was sitting near the front of the Negro section, and both sections had filled up when she was ordered by the driver to get up and give her seat to a white man. This was nothing new, but Mrs. Parks was tired; tired physically, and tired of such humiliation; and she decided to keep her seat. She was placed under arrest, and a new departure for the decade began. After a day of consultations some of the Negro leaders of Montgomery decided that Mrs. Parks' arrest should be the occasion for an act that had been long overdue on their part. They would stop riding buses on which human beings were treated in such a manner. At first they thought they would try it for a day, but it seemed fitting to them that they should continue until the bus company changed its policies. They chose as their spokesman the young, Atlanta-born minister who had joined their community just the year before—Martin Luther King. And out of his background of Gandhian philosophy and Christian training he began to articulate their cause.

At meeting after meeting he told the Negro people and the world that "Our concern is not to put the bus company out of business, but to put justice in business." He sought to convince the people that they had a responsibility to refuse to cooperate with the evil of the segregated bus. "He who passively accepts evil," King said, "is as much involved in it as he who helps to perpetrate it. He who accepts evil without protesting against it is really cooperating with it." So, he began the long walk, the walk of men and women determined to be free. Nor was it entirely coincidental that such a walk began in the same year that twenty-nine Asian and African nations met in Bandung, Indonesia, to declare their own determination toward freedom. Indeed it was fitting that both the new departure of the American revolution and the new, united voice of the one-time colonial people should come together, for the decade of crisis in America is intrinsically a part of that crisis known throughout the world—the crisis of encounter when the oppressed finally discover themselves and then meet their oppressors, and demand to be set free. So the movement of truth is one.

There are no such moments without great danger and the possibility of deep suffering, though. And on January 30, 1955, Martin King discovered this when word came to him that his house had been bombed. His first thought was of his wife and child. He had left them there. He rushed home to find them unharmed; but gathered in front of the badly damaged house was a growing crowd of Negroes, angry and resentful that this should have been done to their leader. The danger of a clash between them and the policemen seemed imminent so King went back out to speak to them. He said, "If you have weapons, take them home; if you don't have them, please do not seek to get them. We cannot solve this problem through retaliatory violence. We must meet violence with nonviolence. Remember the words of Jesus: 'He who lives by the sword will perish by the sword.'" He urged them to leave peacefully and said, "We must love our white brothers no matter what they do to us. We must make them know we love them. Jesus still cries out, 'Love your enemies; bless them that curse you, pray for them that despitefully use you!' This is what we must live by. We must meet hate with love. Remember," he said as he ended, "if I am stopped this movement will not stop, because God is with the movement. Go home with this . . . radiant assurance."

In those words Martin King articulated the deepest and highest insights of the nonviolent movement and set the tone for a decade. Without an understanding of this complex man and his accomplishments through the people of Montgomery, the decade is misunderstood. They placed their indelible stamp on it. The mothers and fathers and grandparents who with the young walked for a year, organized car pools, and held fast rather than cooperate with evil—this is, to a large degree, their decade. And their spirit was best caught by the old lady who was offered a ride on the way home from work, and who refused after a four-mile walk, saying, "My feets is tired, but my soul is rested."

On November 13 of that year the Supreme Court upheld a lower court decision that segregation on state and local buses was unconstitutional. On December 20, the court order reached Montgomery, and men and women who chose to were able to ride in dignity. But they knew the battle had just begun, for in the very year that they walked to and from work, a young Negro woman named Autherine Lucy tried to walk into their state-supported university, only to be met by mobs and stones and finally expulsion. The way was still long.

Strangely enough, 1957 began in somewhat the same way as the previous year, with the frightening roar of dynamite in Montgomery. The opposition did not intend to be silent about the victory on the buses, and this time the home and church of Ralph Abernathy, three other Negro churches, and the home of the lone white ministerial supporter in Montgomery were all bombed. But the focus of events was now moving from this embattled city to Washington, D.C. There the Senate was engaged in debate of the first civil rights bill to come before it since Reconstruction days. After a southern filibuster that lasted 125 hours with only one brief interruption, the bill was passed in both the Senate and the House. Dealing primarily with the right of Negroes to vote in the South, it gave the attorney general power to seek court orders against local officials who tried to keep Negroes from voting. Then, somewhat belatedly, the legislative branch of the government entered into the decade of crisis.

Nevertheless, the center of the nation's attention was still on the terror that had grown out of the 1954 and 1955 school decisions. For throughout the South, especially in Tennessee, Arkansas, Kentucky, and North Carolina, there were sharp reactions when September came again. In Birmingham Fred Shuttlesworth, Negro leader there, was beaten with fists and tire chains when he attempted to enroll his children in an all-white school. In Nashville, mobs gathered at most of the newly desegregated schools and one of them was bombed. In Charlotte, North Carolina, the lone young Negro pioneer had to listen to shouts of "Go back to Africa, you burr head," and he had to dodge spit and erasers. In Sturgis, Kentucky, Negro children were escorted into school by armed soldiers. In Clinton, Tennessee, John Kasper the racist was active, and was believed to be involved in the bombing of a Negro residential area. This was the reaction of the middle South to children going to school. They were not marching, not picketing, not sitting-in; just going to school, and the reception was bombs and mobs and troops. And just often enough to keep hope alive there were a few courageous white persons who walked by their side.

However, the most indelible symbol of this resistance to justice was found in the name of Little Rock. It was ironic that Little Rock should have been the place, for it was there almost a century before that the first free schools in Arkansas were organized—by a group of Negro citizens. However, in 1957, a governor, likely catering to the fears of some of his most pathetic supporters, sought to defy the government of the United States. Striking out against the Little Rock School Board's plan for token desegregation, Orval Faubus sent his State Guards to prevent nine Negro students from entering Central High School. Nine lonely students—facing troops and a mob because they wanted a better education. Finally, after too much delay and too much silence, the president of the United States felt he was left with no other choice than to counter force with force. (And those who don't believe in armed force must ask where they were in the time when preparations of a different kind were needed.) Paratroops came to Little Rock in September 1957, and stayed well into the next spring, offering what seemed to be the only guarantee that nine children could go to school. But after the children got inside the battle was not over. The sly kicks in the hall were there. The sharp punches to the jaw were there. The innumerable bowls of soup spilled on their back were there. But even this was not without hope, for in the midst of the hatred and fear, one girl was heard to say, "I got integrated today. That was the first time I'd ever gone to school with a Negro, and it didn't hurt a bit."

There was much hurting to come, though, not only for Little Rock, but for the entire nation; for as the new year began its character became clear—another year of bombings and violence directed against the Supreme Court ruling. There was a difference, though. In 1958 the bombs were no longer directed against the Negro community alone. They exploded in the lives of all who dared to speak for justice and brotherhood; and one of the most instructive facts about that year was the fact that apart from desegregated schools, Negro residences, and Negro churches, the primary targets were Jewish synagogues. Jewish synagogues—not white, Protestant, evangelical churches. The Jews were bombed because some of them dared to speak up for justice. They spoke up in the words of the Virginia rabbi who said publicly that explosive year, "A Jew who remains silent in the face of prejudice leveled at another of God's children is traitorous to the basic principle of Judaism. I will not be intimidated. I will not betray my heritage." So the synagogues were bombed while Protestants remained safe and silent. Though segregation was illegal, the Protestants of the South were silent. Though it was sinful and immoral, we were silent, and preached instead about alcohol and tithing.

In the middle of that difficult summer Orval Faubus acted again and closed down all four high schools in Little Rock. With such capriciousness the lives of thousands of young persons were attacked. Some went to private institutions, but most had no schooling at all. Anything was better than integration.

Though the main patterns of the decade seemed to be repeating themselves, close observers may have caught two new departures in 1958. Following the lead of the 1957 Civil Rights Act, the NAACP announced an intensive voter registration campaign for the South. Here was another area in which the federal government had finally declared itself, and the civil rights organization was quick to respond, for they knew that a great deal could be different when a group of voteless people achieved the vote. Steadily, voting became an increasingly attractive arena of action for the protest organizations.

Something else entered the scene before the year was over. Almost unnoticed in Wichita, Kansas, and Oklahoma City, groups of Negro and white young persons offered in 1958 the intimations of a relatively new strategy in their struggle against injustice. They went into lunch counters and remained seated until they were either served or arrested. There were important successes in those two cities, but no one could have possibly guessed how effective this means of protest would soon become.

Not only was it too soon for anyone to recognize such possibilities, but it was also evident that most concerned persons were still caught up with the battle for equality in education, and in 1959 the first crack came in Virginia's celebrated wall of "massive resistance" to desegregation. In February, Arlington and Norfolk became the first cities in the state to capitulate. But in the same state another county (Prince Edward) closed all of its schools rather than desegregate. Such actions were like a thousand slaps in the face to many Negroes. They were additional ways of saying, "We don't want you. You're not good enough. We must quarantine you because there's something wrong." More and more as Negro young people looked at this response to a Supreme Court ruling they wondered whether or not there was a more effective way in which they might bring about a desegregated atmosphere in their own lifetime. They grew more impatient with such rebuffs and delays. Some grew more bitter, especially when they read in midyear accounts which said that there had been at least five hundred bombings, beatings, and killings since the second Supreme Court ruling of 1955. The road was going to be hard, not only in the South but in the North as well. And some suggestions of the hard northern road was given that year when a group of Negro parents boycotted a school in their Harlem ghetto, complaining of discriminatory educational policies. So it appeared more and more that the South was everywhere, and crisis was on every hand, if a man only looked.

Even those who were very dim of sight and hard of hearing could not avoid the sudden illumination and the great announcement that came on February 1, 1960, out of Greensboro, North Carolina. There a group of four Negro students from North Carolina A&T College simply decided they had had enough. Again and again they had gone into five- and ten-cent stores and bought goods, and then tried to push out of their minds the humiliating fact that they could not sit down at the lunch counter as all other human customers. On that chilly day, though, they sat down, and in effect, they said politely, "We have come to be served, we have come to be human, what will you do?" They found themselves in jail, but before long a new spirit had captured the Negro college campuses. In two months, sit-ins, as they were called, had spread to sixty-five southern and border cities. Before the year was over more than two hundred cities were called to a moment of truth. The students were saying, "We are tired of the lies you tell concerning how satisfied we are. We are not satisfied. We are tired of accommodating and making believe everything is just fine. We will accommodate to nothing less than humanity. Too long have you passed us by without really looking, like scenery on the street. Well, the time has come for that to stop. You must see us as we are. We are native southerners, not outsiders. We have come to say that time is running out. One hundred years after emancipation is too long to wait for freedom. We are not satisfied. We want all of the rights and responsibilities of American citizens. We will not be patient. Hear this now!" And their message grated against the ears of Negroes and whites alike, against the tender ears of all supporters of the status quo—or as some put it, the "status crow."

In Montgomery and Baton Rouge the message was the same. In Nashville and Knoxville, the students came and sat. In Atlanta and Durham, they marched and sang and sat and went to jail singing. And one boy wrote to his mother, "Don't worry, Mom. Going to jail for this is not like going for killing or stealing or being drunk. This is a good jail going. This is going to jail so that we can all be free." Throughout the South that spirit spread, from campus to campus, among the children of the cotton fields and river towns. They were reaching maturity through pain. Swimming-in, standing-in, wading-in, kneeling-in. They wanted to be in, outsiders no more, strangers no more, fellow citizens now. They were met with closed doors, with tear gas, with fire hoses, with their own inner weaknesses, but they continued.

During Easter vacation that year, the students gathered together. Most had not known each other before, so they came to meet, to exchange stories and songs and strategies. They came and connected together to go on with the struggle. And before 1960 had ended several thousands of them had been arrested, and more than two hundred had been expelled from college. Here was the new spirit, going often beyond NAACP and SCLC and all others. These became the vanguard of the social revolution, and they were well-spoken for when one of their group said that Easter, "The greatest progress of the American Negro in the future will not be made in Congress or in the Supreme Court—it will come in the jails."

(With such spirit among them one is tempted to ask again: is it accidental that in the year of the Negro student renaissance in America there occurred in South Africa one of the largest marches ever held against apartheid, as 30,000 blacks demonstrated in Johannesburg near the end of March? Is it accidental, or is there a spirit of freedom abroad in the world, a spirit that will not be suppressed? And if it is the spirit of freedom, is it not akin to the Spirit of God?)

Hardly had the nation begun to catch its breath from the sit-ins when early in 1961 the Congress of Racial Equality announced that it would send an interracial company of travelers through the South to test compliance with the Supreme Court and Interstate Commerce Commission rulings on desegregated travel facilities. While men wondered what would happen to these Freedom Riders, a young Air Force veteran in Mississippi applied for admission to the best university in his native state. He was turned down, and as a result, James Meredith filed a suit for admission in a federal district court. No one knew how long it would take, but they knew that Mississippi had vowed "Never," and they wondered how similar Meredith's experience would be to the two Negro students from Atlanta, Georgia, who had entered their state university that year and had been met by a riot and suspension. But the courts had eventually ordered the university to readmit Charlayne Hunter and Hamilton Holmes, and another breach in the walls of segregation was made by brave young persons.

Bravery of the highest order was required for the twelve CORE-sponsored travelers who boarded a South-bound bus in Washington, D.C., on May 4, 1961. Indeed, they could not imagine what they would meet before the term "Freedom Rider" was etched into the memory of a nation and a world. All went well until Alabama. Negroes and whites had traveled and rested and eaten together all the way. But near Anniston, Alabama, their bus was waylaid and burned; and on Mother's Day in Birmingham they were brutally beaten by a waiting mob—with the police amazingly absent. After Birmingham a new group took up the ride and went on to Montgomery, where mobs and beatings again met them as they tried to use the waiting room and restaurant facilities together. Four hundred federal marshals came to protect them. But they meant to keep on to the next destination—Jackson, Mississippi. Under the convoy of two battalions of National Guardsmen, twenty-two cars filled with Alabama Highway Patrolmen, three Army reconnaissance planes, and one helicopter—with such an entourage the busload of twelve "true believers" was escorted to the Mississippi state line. In Jackson, they met not a mob, but jail, and were joined in time by some three hundred other persons who were determined that America should one day be free. The ride ended in Jackson late in the spring of 1961, stalled by Mississippi justice, and some cases are still pending, but the story did not stop. For a few days later, on May 29, Attorney General Kennedy, obviously moved by the Freedom Riders, requested the ICC to send down a definitive ruling on desegregation of all the interstate travel facilities. This came in September, to be effective November 1, but even there the story, instead of ending, takes on a new beginning, like so many of the stories of this decade, as if they were formed and moved by a power other than their own.

When the new ICC ruling came to Albany, Georgia, in November 1961 it found fertile ground. The Negroes of the city had been granted no meaningful action on their grievances by their elected officials, though they had legally petitioned against racial discrimination for a long time. Therefore when a group of students tested the Albany railroad station's compliance with the desegregation law, and were arrested, the community was ready to respond. Protest marches and prayer vigils were held on behalf of the arrested students. In turn each group of demonstrators was arrested. By the time local leaders asked Martin Luther King Jr. to come to Albany, almost four hundred persons had been jailed, and Dr. King led another three hundred citizens in marches protesting the city's enforcement of an illegal and immoral system. By the middle of December more than seven hundred persons were in jail, most of them for the first time in their lives. As a result they learned something about voluntarily suffering for a cause—taking up a cross. And though their specific gains were intangible, a new spirit grasped the community, and men and women throughout the South were inspired by Albany's contribution to the decade of crisis, a contribution of courage. In Savannah, Georgia, a widespread boycott of downtown stores became the Negroes' sharp and dangerous response to segregation, a response forced out of them by the failure of the "good" people of the city to act against injustice. Meanwhile, other means of protest continued, each with its own cost; for instance, when Negro tenant farmers in western Tennessee dared attempt to vote for the first time since Reconstruction, many were evicted from their homes—leading to the building of a tent city that still stands.

Somehow, though, there was a growing awareness that the problems of the Negro tenant farmers were not entirely a matter of political oppression. Many machines were now available to do their jobs, and they were more and more expendable. This was a growing problem throughout the nation for Negroes and whites, and being lowest on many lists, Negroes found it especially difficult to see a solution as 1962 began. The problem of underemployment helped draw the crisis out of the exclusive domain of the South, and as more and more conflicts arose over schools, housing, and employment in the North, it was increasingly clear that the crisis was nationwide. The crisis really unvalued the future of the Negro in America, and therefore it was ultimately the crisis of the future of America. Nothing demonstrated this more clearly than those days in September when one young Negro man, James Meredith, held the attention of the nation and the world. By September 10, 1962, Supreme Court Justice Hugo Black (of Alabama!) had ruled that Meredith should be admitted to the university of his native state without delay. Unfortunately, the Kennedy brothers under-estimated the determination of Mississippi to remain out of the Union, and tried to bargain too long. After a number of thwarted attempts, Meredith finally came on campus on Sunday, September 30, but that night a riot broke loose, due to federal and state negligence and miscalculation. As a result, two men lost their lives as federal troops finally came to insure James Meredith a place in his university. The troops were there because the problem was not Meredith's, it was not the Negroes', it was not Mississippi's, it was America's, a crisis beyond compare.

This was the highlight, but many other events marked the seriousness of the moment. In this year, Albany, Georgia, became a password again as Negro citizens were joined by scores of white friends from the North in their protest against the harshly resistant segregated life of the city. Elsewhere, the young students moved away from an emphasis on sit-ins to voter registration, and they decided to tackle some of the most difficult areas of the Deep South. For they remembered what had happened to a man in Fitzgerald, Georgia, "the first Negro to vote." Taking their lives in their hands (some placed them in God's hands) they moved into the areas of deepest fear and antagonism, believing the good news of freedom was needed in such places. So they went to Selma, Alabama; Americus, Georgia; Greenwood, Mississippi—living and sometimes dying simply to make it possible for a man to vote in a free country. The churches where they met were blown up and burned. The houses where they slept were raked with bullets, but they worked on, sometimes praying, often singing, "We shall overcome some day," singing, "The Lord will see us through. . . ."

When 1963 began President Kennedy was told, "Race is the crisis of our nation. Civil rights must be given first priority in your State of the Union message and on your legislative agenda." He did not believe it then. He said there were other things more important—like a tax cut. Many persons agreed with him. There was still time to work out matters on the racial issue, they thought. They knew there would probably be more demonstrations, though, and when 1963 began a few persons thought they knew where the newest expression of the American crisis would come. Few suspected Birmingham—reputedly the most segregated city in the world. But there it came. After seven years of brave, often reckless work by Fred Shuttlesworth, Martin L. King was called to that city to lead a nonviolent struggle against the evil of segregation. On Good Friday morning, King and his friend Ralph Abernathy prepared to go to jail. As they waited for these leaders, some of the Negro people of Birmingham sat in a church that day and heard a minister say, "If you really love Bull Connor [the symbol of Birmingham's system of segregation] you'll leave this church, march out on the street, and go to jail—go to free Bull Connor from this system of segregation that's killing him and us." Thus the significance of the day and the significance of the moment were not lost. For a group of persons were being called upon to put love into painful, redemptive action, following King and Abernathy, who sensed they were following their own Master. Thus as Abernathy prepared to leave the church, he said, "I'm going out now, out to jail; yes, some people call it Birmingham Jail, but I call it Calvary."

So he marched and hundreds marched with him on Good Friday, 1963. Through one long, difficult month they marched. Thus was the battle waged. Men and women and children with songs and hopes faced policemen with dogs and guns and fire hoses. The jails began to be filled. When it seemed clear that thousands more were ready to join the thousands who had gone to jail for their freedom, negotiations began, and a truce was called, but Birmingham became another mark of the American crisis.

Then, after Birmingham and Danville and Nashville and Cambridge and a score of other places, the Kennedys were ready to declare a "moral crisis" and ask for a civil rights bill. But it would be too late for the rights of some persons. It would be too late for the former postman William Moore, walking the roads of Alabama to his death. It would be too late for Medgar Evers in front of his house in Jackson. It would be too late for four little girls in church in Birmingham. Perhaps in a sense it was too late even for John F. Kennedy in a car in Dallas. Too late was the crisis discovered. And in spite of a march of 250,000 persons, and the death of a precious few, 1964 began with the impression that for many men and women in America the crisis had not yet been discovered. When will it be too late for us? When shall we discover God at work in the midst of this crisis, calling his church to judgment, to repentance to renewal? When will it be too late for us?

§40 Mathew Ahmann

Mathew H. Ahmann was born on September 10, 1931, in St. Cloud, Minnesota. While few recognize his name, Ahmann helped organize three of the signature events of the American civil rights movement. He earned a bachelor's degree from St. John's University in Collegeville, Minnesota, in 1952 and later had graduate training in sociology at the University of Chicago. He married Margaret Cunningham on September 18, 1954. Three years later, in an important step for his lifelong career, he became the field representative for the Chicago Catholic Interracial Council and subsequently the assistant and acting director of that organization. In 1960, at the age of twenty-nine, he became the founding director of the National Catholic Conference for Interracial Justice, an organization that united local Catholic interracial councils across the nation. In that capacity Ahmann served as the executive secretary of the important National Conference on Religion and Race, a four-day conference in Chicago that brought together leading religious figures from across the country to address the racial crisis—and the Protestant, Catholic, and Jewish responses to it. Eight months later, Ahmann helped organize the March on Washington, speaking on the same dais as Martin Luther King Jr. And in 1965, Ahmann organized priests, nuns, and the Catholic laity to march from Selma to Montgomery. He left the NCCIJ in 1969 to become executive director of the Commission on Church and Society for the Archdiocese of San Antonio. Later he served as associate director of government relations of Catholic Charities USA. Ahmann died on December 31, 2001, and is survived by his wife, six children, and thirteen grandchildren.

Delivered at the Minnesota Conference on Religion and Race, and heavily reflective of his organizing efforts in 1963, Ahmann's address is a call to action to the white church—particularly its laymen, whom he openly excoriates. He candidly disparages the lack of effort from white religious communities in aiding in civil rights initiatives and urges his audience to "redouble our effort, use the power that is ours to effect change." Ahmann posits the need for programs that facilitate "bonds of friendship" between whites and minorities to foster a sense of urgency in white congregations so that they may be more prone to push their resources and effectiveness to their outermost boundaries to effect change. Ahmann's address is primarily a "list of needed commitments" that extends past the civil rights movement to include the mistreatment of American Indians as well. Throughout the address, Ahmann appeals to the conscience of white congregations and argues that to fail to fight on behalf of their minority counterparts to the fullest extent of their resources would indeed be a "God-damned thing." His memorable closing features the cadences of August 28, 1963.

❧

Race: Challenge to Religion
February 27, 1964
Minnesota Conference on Religion and Race
Minneapolis, Minnesota

Racial events of 1963, some blessed, some evil, unpredicted, and unforeseen in 1962, disrupted the programs of religious and secular civil rights organizations. But these events—Birmingham, and the March on Washington on the national scene, and countless demonstrations on the local scene—deeply affected the role of the religious communities of our country in race relations.

The "racial crisis" forced the conscience of millions of Americans, leaders and followers, to confront the issue of racial injustice, and provided unprecedented opportunity for attitude and social change. A good part of this openness to change still exists, though a resistance on the part of the white people of our country has manifest[ed] itself. Here, I fear, religious groups who should have provided interpretation to their white constituencies were not ready to take advantage of the change.

It is difficult to unravel and differentiate the effects of the National Conference on Religion and Race, and Birmingham, and the march, but it is clear that the interreligious spirit and approach developed from the January meeting helped gear countless local religious communities to a more adequate response to the crisis of 1963.

Yet, despite significant initiatives taken by many national religious denominations, and despite significant initiatives in many cities around the country—within denominational life, and cooperative across religious lines—understanding of the nature of the racial crisis still escapes the religious community. As a result, religious efforts to secure interracial justice generally follow the Negro initiative, rather than appear side by side or integrated with it. The one exception, and all of us can thank God for that, has been the forceful role of the Negro ministry.

While significant new trends of constructive social change for racial integration have begun in our religious communities this past year, there are still few signs of voluntary efforts by that portion of the religious population of our cities which are white to secure extensive desegregation or meet the legitimate grievances of the Negro community.

Given the social history and organization of our religious communities, the response to the racial crisis is sadly not likely to change drastically, though the present accelerated trend will continue. Our theology, however, and our claim to inspiration by God, make more radical demands and place no limit on the role of religion. A breakthrough to assuming initiative, along with Negro leadership, is possible but not likely. And generally the problem is the layman. Though clerical leaders have not exhausted their teaching, by and large, in many communities, it is the layman who is behind and hampering the response of the institution.

The more reasonable expectation is a role on the part of predominantly white religious groups to gradually take larger and more significant steps in meeting the just demands and needs of Negroes by desegregation, providing leadership in that creative mediation of conflict which will produce advances to interracial justice, and by the increased use of the moral force of religious leadership to pressure concessions from the white community of the country.

However, we hope, pray, and must work for a more radical response on the part of ourselves and our religious groups. We must work for an effective joining of the demand for justice now, and for those efforts so necessary to demonstrate to our constituencies the need to practice all the dictums of our faith. The toleration of racism within our religious communities is blasphemous, a denial of our God and our relationship with him, and a "God-damned thing."

What are we doing here this evening? This is the time of the freedom revolution. Why did we bother to come together? It's pretty late for a conference. If you look around the room, we are a pretty white group. There are no poor joining in our comradeship and in our discussions.

There is only worth in coming together for these discussions if it means we are going to redouble our effort, use the power that is ours to effect change—change in the hearts of people, including ourselves, and changes in the nature of our cities and the segregation patterns foisted upon our people. We have within our denominations the bulk of the people of our cities and states. We must admit we have not yet done our job. Our members are the decision makers, the men and women who control our resources. Except for the shabby treatment too frequently afforded American Indians, Minnesota does not have the ghettos and the violent conflict of other locales. I am a native of Minnesota. I know that our ghettos are not as large, but our discrimination is as apparent. Our job and housing discrimination is as rank. Our social discrimination is as abominable.

We religious people feel too comfortable with our expanded role in race relations. We don't adequately realize the suffering of those subject to discrimination, be they Negro or American Indian. We don't adequately realize the nature of the crisis. We feel what we do is adequate, but we don't do anywhere near all we can. Our programs in race relations—that problem we call the most severe social and moral problem of our county—our programs in race relations are still avocations. We frequently stay off the streets because we are polite, then afraid when deep within us we know that our presence on the streets may make the difference. We say that only the polite Negro, our social equal, can live in our neighborhoods, and face the insidious danger that we will increase our discrimination on social and economic grounds. Is such discrimination any more moral?

Candidly, the Conference on Religion and Race, despite its benefits, has not moved this country. It was Birmingham and Dr. Martin Luther King. It has been Negroes who have produced the change—change within us, within our religious groups, within our government, and in the whole climate of the country. We should repent, yes, for the sins of our past, and true, we should be glad for our accomplishments, especially our new gains. But we must realize how far we have to go and admit that we can and must do much more to forge the community of love our country so badly needs. If the problems raised by the relationship of white people to American Indians and to Negroes cannot be successfully resolved within a short period of time in Minnesota, how much hope is there for Chicago or New York, or Birmingham or Jackson?

The greatest benefit of 1963 has been the growth of the vital spirit and sense in the Negro community, which says we are not afraid—no longer are we afraid to make major sacrifices even to lose our lives to bring freedom to our people. The freedom revolution can transform our institutions, our very lives, and we must be part of it.

But remember the Harris *Newsweek* polls. These indicate where we are: 85 percent of the white people of this country think Negroes laugh a lot; 76 percent of the white people of our country think that Negroes have less ambition than whites; 71 percent of white people think that Negroes smell different; 50 percent of white people think that Negroes have less native intelligence; 86 percent of white people think that Negroes in the United States are inferior to white people.

Only 34 percent of the white people of our country think that the Negro revolt is supported by the rank and file of Negroes. On the other hand, 78 percent of Negroes say integrated housing is desirable; 91 percent of Negroes say the Negro revolt is supported by the rank and file of Negroes; 74 percent of whites say that Negroes are moving too fast. Only 8 percent of the Negroes think that Negroes are moving too fast.

James Baldwin says, "Actually, I don't want to marry your daughter. I just want to get you off my back."

The increased pace of the Negro revolt in 1963 and the obvious conflict between Negro and white values exposed in the two *Newsweek* opinion polls indicate continued racial conflict in 1964. The place of breakout of conflict because of these opposing sets of values concerning racial justice is not easy to predict. Nor is it possible to tell in advance which events will be contagious and escalate into affairs moving the conscience of the Nation.

Stiffening white resistance to Negro and white demands for social progress, public pressure techniques may dampen the conflict in some areas, but may quicken it in others, until public authority has to step in to maintain law and order.

It is clear, however, that demands for interracial justice "now" require substantial concessions toward racial integration on the part of the white community.

The opportunities for progress made possible by the stirring of the white conscience resulting from the Negro revolt can best be capitalized on by religious groups. Coupled with Negro pressure, organized religion is the one force which has a possibility of shaping the national consensus necessary to give us a truly integrated society.

To realize the possibility before them, religious groups have to boldly step up the institutional efforts to convert their own adherents, and to use the moral forces they represent. This stepping-up process has begun in the Protestant, and the Jewish, and the Catholic communities.

What's happened since January 1963, or since Birmingham, in the world of religion? Some seventy conferences on religion and race have been held in various parts of the country, and many have launched ongoing interreligious race programs involving top religious and lay leadership. I've just come from the Toledo Conference on Religion and Race to meet with you in Minnesota. Last spring at an unusual board meeting of the National Council of Churches, described by some as a religious experience, the council's commission on religion and race was formed and given a mandate to get involved in the Negro revolt. National Council of Church staff, frequently on loan from many denominations, are deeply involved in the racial crisis in many parts of our country, and have taken significant initiative in a host of projects. At its convention in Des Moines, Iowa, last summer, the United Presbyterian

Church formed its own commission on religion and race with a budget of $500,000. At the same convention, Presbyterians who felt the official church body would not move rapidly enough formed the Presbyterian Interracial Council to prod that body on. Work has been going on within the various Lutheran bodies also: I can call to mind especially the work of the National Lutheran Council, and the work of the Missouri Synod's Lutheran Human Relations Association. Similar stepped-up efforts in race relations have been launched by the American Baptist Convention, the National Council of the Protestant Episcopal Church, and many other Protestant denominations.

In the Jewish community, teams of rabbis have been formed by several conferences of rabbis to be available on call to assist the Negro community in various parts of the country. The main secular Jewish agencies, the American Jewish Committee, the American Jewish Congress, have employed staff full-time in race relations for the first time. Though long deeply involved in civil rights, these agencies have begun to make use of their resources in a manner similar to the programs of the major civil rights organizations. Also in the Jewish community a new program has been launched by the Social Action Commission of the Union of American Hebrew Congregations and the Central Conference of American Rabbis. Under auspices of this commission, Reformed Jewish congregations the country over are going through an educational process in the adoption of an individual and congregational statement of practical power in race relations.

In the Roman Catholic community over forty new pastoral letters have been issued by bishops around the country within the past twelve months, many of them announcing new programs and the commitment of more Catholic resources to the civil rights battle. Those of us who are Roman Catholics have witnessed the marvelous freedom the nun has as she has begun to take her place alongside of others protesting racial discrimination.

And finally thousands of white Christians and Jews joined in the great and dignified tribute to American democracy, the August 28 March on Washington.

Religion has begun to make practical commitments. What does that mean in our local cities and towns across the nation?

First of all, stepped-up denominational educational efforts are urgently needed; straight-from-the-shoulder preaching of the word of God so that the individual conscience cannot escape the decision that must be made. Urgently needed is an expansion of programs to build human contacts across racial lines to develop the bonds of friendship between Negroes and whites and American Indians. In some cases the Friendship House home visit technique might be used, even though initially it is quite artificial. Negroes and whites and American Indian must step up their work on common civic problems. It is urgent, too, that continued use be made of the public hearing of grievances in keeping with the great American tradition of protest. The Christian churches have an urgent problem before them in dealing with separate white and Negro church tradition. The relationship between the white and the Negro ministry is not much better than the relationship between white and Negro people at large. With the exception of the specific Negro denominations, the major religious denominations of Protestantism and the Roman Catholic Church are considered by the Negro community to be white churches.

Efforts must be made by our religious groups to watch our urban renewal projects like hawks to see that they are used to benefit all of the people of our cities and to see that relocation made necessary by them is used to expand freedom in the housing market. The challenge must be offered to the attempt of the real estate profession to disclaim responsibility for racial segregation in housing. The country over, real estate boards are deeply involved in efforts to repeal those fair housing laws which have been adopted while stating that neighborhood housing patterns are the responsibility only of the property owner. The National Real Estate Board has even drawn up a property owner bill of rights. We must confront our real estate leaders with a religious witness, and demonstrate effectively to them that the ownership of property carries with it social responsibility, and that by no means does any man have the moral right to discriminate in the sale or rental of his property, on the basis of race, or religion. We must launch vigorous efforts to enable Negro people to move freely throughout our communities, if necessary even locating mortgage financing and by protecting the minority group family when he chooses to move into an all-white area.

Now is the time for the religious institutions of our country to use their building, contract, and purchasing power to help bring an end to discrimination in the employment field. Now is the time for religious leaders to sit down with the important employer members of their congregations to discuss with them what can be done to launch new employment programs for members of our minority groups.

We hear repeatedly the request for a resolution of our racial problems around the bargaining table. That bargaining table is only meaningful if the white people with the power and willingness to make commitments sit around it too. Very simply, predominantly white religious groups can make or break the civil rights revolution in this country. For we can deliver—if we so choose—the power to that bargaining table.

There are three other major concerns before us where religious influence must be felt. A good civil rights bill is now going on the agenda of our U.S. Senate. It's acknowledged in many quarters of this country that its relatively smooth passage through the House has been due to the resurgence of interest in racial justice on the part of religious groups. Now religious groups have to work to break the filibuster and to see that the civil rights bill retains its public accommodations and fair employment provisions. Attention on our part should be directed not only to the Senate, but also to the White House. We can afford no crippling compromises on the part of the civil rights bill of 1963.

But even if the Senate ratifies the treaty God long ago made with man, our race relations problems will not be solved. Our country is filled with thirty-eight million poverty-stricken people. We need a job for every man. Coupled with the cry for "freedom now" is the claim that a job for every man is a just demand. Whitney Young of the National Urban League has called for a U.S. Marshall Plan. We need an unprecedented national effort to improve the economy and the availability of jobs, which will reduce the hostility and conflict produced by the frustration of unemployment, competition for jobs, and lack of job advancement. Progress for full racial justice can best be made in a full economy when all Americans can be gainfully employed at the highest level of their ability. Private and religious resources should be used, too, to eliminate the heritage of poverty and disability inflicted upon members of our minority groups. One religious worker in the civil rights field has properly suggested that we consider mortgaging our debt-free religious institutions to meet the real needs of the poor of today.

Finally, I could not leave the list of needed commitments on our part— the list of concrete and practical programs in which we must engage—without a more direct observation of our responsibility to deal fairly with American Indians. Discrimination is rank in the towns around reservations, and a transition between the reservation and the city is fraught with insecurity. How is it that a great people such as ours could dispossess those who originally roamed our land, whose land it was, and then turn our callused backs away? More effective federal programs to insure the rights of Negroes are surely needed, but in a state such as Minnesota, all of us bear keen personal responsibility.

Let me return to the freedom movement. In the past year we have been witness to a growing movement which can truthfully be called a nonviolent revolution. Negro citizens want their rights—the same rights the average white man has now. And they want human respect and fraternity now. The nonviolent freedom revolution will touch every part of our lives. New, up-and-coming Negro leadership is through waiting and is pushing at the seam of our ghettos. The goals of the racial revolution are shared deeply in every strata of the Negro community. Rights will be granted or our country will be in trouble. The summer of 1963 will be but a candle to the summer of 1964.

This revolution can radically strengthen the spirit of our country and our dedication to democracy. It can save our country from mediocrity. It can, as well, help reform the roots of our religious commitment. It is a two-part revolution. It is a revolution of conscience—a moral revolution as well as a practical revolution. Religious relevance to man is at test. What man can live through a Birmingham and not be forced to decide whether he is on the side of right or wrong? What man looking at the six thousand white pickets circling Chicago's city hall not too long ago cannot recognize racism within their chants against freedom in the housing market? The demands of our Negro citizens are just demands. The religious white man must agree.

The winds of the racial revolution have begun to blow on the reeds of conscience. Now you and I have to decide whether our religious commitment is merely superficial religiosity, or whether we agree with God. Now we have to decide that Negro claims are just.

Now is the time for you and I to go to work.

Now is the time for practical programs.

Now is the time for straight-from-the-shoulder preaching of the meaning of God's relationship with man.

Now is the time for the massive resources of organized religion to flow into the civil rights struggle.

Now is the time to give our energy and ourselves humbly in sacrifice as Negroes and some whites have been doing.

With Dr. Martin Luther King we have a dream of an America where all men can move freely—where the essential rights of all are recognized.

We have a dream of an America of justice.

We have a dream of an America where brother loves brother.

We seek forgiveness for the sins of the past—for our support of prejudice, for what we have done or not done to maintain the status quo.

We dedicate ourselves to a program of action.

We dedicate ourselves to an ongoing interreligious conference on religion and race.

We bear the responsibilities for the Harlems of the whole country.

The racial problem has long been a dilemma of conscience—but it is that no more. We feel a righteous anger. And, as never before, we have the opportunity to seize the initiative to make this a country of brothers living side by side in freedom. We all can agree with the American Catholic bishops who have said, "Discrimination based on race or color cannot be reconciled with the truth that God has created all men with equal rights and dignity." Christians will agree with the 1963 statement of the General Assembly of the National Council of Churches that "At the point of race, the Christian church must now profess or deny Christ. No imperative requires more immediate obedience than the new commandment which He gave to His church, 'that you love one another'—the clear demand for obedience to Christ in race relations leaves no alternative."

With Rabbi Abraham Heschel we weep and ask, "Religion and race, how can the two be uttered together?"

Let me close by reference to a dream reported by William Stringfellow, a prophetic Episcopalian layman:

"On one of those steaming, stinking, stifling nights that each summer brings to Harlem tenements, I had a dream:

"I was walking in Harlem on 125th Street in broad daylight. I seemed to be the only white man in sight. The passerby stared at me balefully. Then two Negroes stopped me and asked for a light. When I searched my pockets for a match, one of them sank a knife into my belly. I fell. I bled. After a while, I died.

"I woke quickly. I felt my stomach. There wasn't any blood. I smoked a cigarette and thought about the dream:

"The assault in the dream seemed unprovoked and vicious. The death in the dream seemed useless and, therefore, all the more expensive. The victim in the dream seemed innocent of offense to those who murdered him. Except for the fact that the victim was a white man. The victim was murdered by a black man because he was a white man. The murder was retribution. The motive was revenge.

"No white man is innocent. I am not innocent. Then I cried."

As we set to work—don't offer an ideal—offer yourself.

§41 Stephen Gill Spottswood

Stephen Gill Spottswood was born on July 18, 1897, the only child of Mary Elizabeth Gray Spottswood and Abraham Lincoln Spottswood. Reared in a religious home in Boston, where he graduated from high school, Spottswood attended Albright College in Reading, Pennsylvania. After graduating from Albright in 1917, he earned his bachelors of theology degree from Gordon Divinity School in Boston in 1919. That same year he married Viola Estelle Booker, and the couple would have five children. Five years later he graduated with his Ph.D. from Yale Divinity School. Spottswood served AME Zion churches in Maine, Connecticut, North Carolina, Indiana, and New York before coming to John Wesley National AME Zion Church in Washington, D.C., in 1936. After serving as head minister at John Wesley for sixteen years, Spottswood was appointed as bishop; in that role, which he held until his retirement in 1972, he supervised more than three hundred churches in a dozen states. Actively involved in the NAACP since 1919, Spottswood was eventually elected president of the Washington, D.C., branch. In 1955 he was elected to the NAACP's board of directors, and six years later he became board chairman. Following the death of his first wife, Spottswood remarried, to Mattie Johnson Elliott in 1969. Spottswood would serve as chairman of the NAACP until his death on December 1, 1974. His papers are housed at the Amistad Research Center at Tulane University and at the Library of Congress.

In this moving tribute to the NAACP's Mississippi field secretary, Medgar Evers, Spottswood commemorates the fallen martyr on the one-year anniversary of his murder. On June 11, 1963, and just hours before Evers would be murdered in his own driveway, President John F. Kennedy made an address to the nation in which he announced his commitment to major civil rights legislation. That announcement would culminate in the Civil Rights Act of 1964, which President Lyndon Johnson would sign into law on July 2, 1964. Spottswood skillfully connects Evers' commitment to civil rights and his martyrdom with that legislation. And while the act won't usher in that "perfect state" of which Spottswood speaks, Evers' "life-blood" will be a vital part of the nation's future; such laws will ensure that he "yet speaketh."

❧

He Being Dead Yet Speaketh

June 12, 1964

Jackson, Mississippi

One year ago today, on the eve of the Michigan Conference, asleep in the parsonage—home of our son, the Reverend Stephen Paul Spottswood, I was awakened by a voice trembling with emotion, saying, "Dad, wake up, I have bad news for you. *They* shot and killed Medgar Evers last night." I jumped out of bed, crying, "O God, O God!" and fell to my knees where I wept in prayer.

Medgar Evers was like my son—a spiritual son of the fight for freedom. He began to work as NAACP field secretary for Mississippi at about the same time I came to this state as bishop of the African Methodist Episcopal Zion Church. I had watched him grow as a most effective freedom fighter, highly efficient, tireless in the expenditure of energy, uncompromising with the enemy, fearless, brave, and true! And he had also developed as a superb orator, whose spoken word was as solid as his consistent conduct of program. His last radio-television message will remain a classic in the annals of democracy's advance in this state, most resistant to desegregation and the fulfillment of the Constitution for all the citizens, white and black, alike.

I saw him in all sections of the state, organizing, planning, speaking, from Hernando County to the Gulf. I saw him standing boldly in Meridian, fearlessly in Biloxi, and with astute courage in Sunflower, Quitman, and Panola Counties. I saw him in Clarksdale and Greenwood, in Jackson, in Sardis, in Laurel, in Hattiesburg, in Pascagoula, and always he was working for God and freedom. Often in danger and constantly threatened, he could not be intimidated or retarded. He marched steadfastly to his duty until the final fatal night rang down the curtain on his role in the drama of freedom.

One year ago today! After nine years of brilliant leadership in the field of civil rights here in his native Mississippi, the outstanding field secretary for the National Association for the Advancement of Colored People, Medgar Wiley Evers, was shot to death by an assassin, at the end of a weary day, as he stepped from his automobile in front of his home.

He was the leader around which freedom's fight in the Magnolia State had been built. His voice rallied the forces in the fight for freedom, after the Reverend George Lee had been killed on his county courthouse steps; after Gus Courts had been shot in his place of business; after Emmett Till had been lynched in tortuous murder.

When the Interstate Commerce Commission outlawed segregation in public transportation, Medgar Evers sat up front in the buses although beaten, arrested, and threatened, showing the characteristic courage of the man he was. When test cases were needed to desegregate Jackson's public schools, like Abraham, he offered his own son upon the altar of the public good, by seeking his admission to and suing for his admission to a public school previously enrolling white children only.

This past year has been one of heartbreak for his family and heartache for all of us who called him friend. But it has also been a year of regirding for the battle against entrenched intolerance and resistance to the law of the land as handed down by the Supreme Court of the United States. We have been given an immense thrust forward in the fight to freedom by the slaying of Medgar Evers.

All through the years men have been martyrs to freedom. 1963 was a year of great martyrdom. First, William Moore, on a solitary walk to Alabama and to death. Last, the thirty-fifth president of the United States on a Dallas street. The depth of this martyrdom was pointed up by the six children (four while in Sunday School) killed in Birmingham in one day.

However, the real symbol of this dying-for-freedom's sake is shown by the death of Medgar Evers. He was in the midst of activity for freedom. He represented the best of leadership. He was calm, confident, and courageous. He carried his load without complaining. Uncompromising, he pushed ahead. He, himself, represented the highest standards of American citizenship. He had a fine mind, possessed good training, and, above all, he had character!

Medgar Evers epitomized service, out of love. He loved his country, he loved his native Mississippi, and he loved his family. He fought for freedom, driven by the great love of his heart! He finally gave up his life, and the master-teacher declared:

> Greater love hath no man than this
> That a man lay down his life
> For his friends.

However, the death of this valiant NAACP leader has stimulated *freedom's crusade* to a far larger degree than any anticipated incident could have furnished stimulation.

Spurred by the January 1963 Conference on Religion and Race, the churches planned greater involvement in the civil rights struggle, but following Mr. Evers' assassination the churches no longer hesitated. Heretofore, they had passed many resolutions supporting basic civil rights and had given token support to the movement.

But after the assassin killed Mr. Evers, the involvement of the churches was complete, total, and self-sacrificing, and today we can say with humble pride, "The church is marching!"

Of the quarter-million Americans who marched in Washington last August, fully forty thousand were white Americans, and of this number thirty thousand were churchmen.

All our civil rights leaders, from President Lyndon Baines Johnson, emphasize that the responsibility for basic civil rights is a moral responsibility. The force that won us the great cloture victory in the Senate Wednesday (June 9, 1964, 71–29) was a spiritual force, and it was brought into being by the repeated emphasis that civil rights is our moral responsibility.

When this battle is won—and it will be won—despite the deterrents—wholesale arrests, cold fire hoses in the winter, and electric cattle prods the year around; the beatings, the cross burnings and the killings—when this battle is won, it will be a spiritual victory and the church, thank God, will have been the vanguard of that victory!

Freedom's crusade indicates that since the passing of Mr. Evers, one hundred thousand youth, white and black, have joined the nonviolent action forces for freedom. Great involvement on the part of adults across the country has already been noted. Persons numbering in the millions joined the NAACP and other organizations in the freedom movement after Mr. Evers died.

More dollars than we ever dreamed of came our way in the latter half of 1963. More friends have stood up and been counted. More newspaper editorials favoring our cause and more magazine articles supporting civil rights than ever before have been written in the twelve months we note today.

Personnel for this crusade is no problem, except the problem of numbers. People, especially young people, from many ethnic backgrounds, representing largely the three major faiths of this country but from all the major religions of the world, are on tiptoe, anxious to serve, willing to die for civil rights! They come in large numbers, by the hundred, by the thousand, by the ten thousand, reiterating Isaiah's great, volunteering speech, "Here am I . . . Send me!"

This crusade has a *great unifying quality*. Freedom is the one thing all men of goodwill, regardless of philosophical or religious background, may unite upon. Back in 1963 the Pro Deo movement of the Roman Catholic

Church gave a dinner in New York City, honoring Cardinal Bea, who is the Vatican Council authority and leader for the ecumenical movement. Most major religions of the world had speakers on the program. Mr. Grace, prominent Catholic layman, spoke for his church. Henry P. Van Dusen spoke for the Protestants. Rabbi Heschel represented Judaism. Secretary-General U Thant of the United Nations represented Buddhism. The then president of the United Nations Assembly said a piece for Mohammedism, and down the line they went.

When it became my turn to speak, I told the story of the NAACP—how we had started back in 1909 with white and Negro Americans, with many religious and philosophical backgrounds, all united on the principle of freedom, as well as mentioning that the NAACP and the freedom movement are like that today. Then I pointed out that it was freedom that each speaker had emphasized as the paramount theme of his religion. Human rights, each one declared, was the cornerstone of his faith. To use a trite phrase of today's vernacular, I am glad to say, "This is *true!*"

As never before, we are united today in the fight for freedom. Two million Americans, white and black, are actively engaged in this nonviolent aggression to make the Constitution come alive for all our citizens. We black Americans, twenty million strong, are united for freedom. Whether he is found on city street or rural road, farmer, teacher, factory employee, clerical and professional, you will find this black American united, determined, and unafraid on the issue of the hour—full freedom for all mankind—in Mississippi or Michigan; in America or Africa; all over the world.

The blood of Medgar Evers is in the civil rights bill which the Senate will pass in a few days. When passed, although far-reaching, no great miracle will have taken place. We shall have to continue the fight, city by city, county by county, to enforce the provisions of the bill. But, at long last, our law will have caught up to our courts.

The blood of all the martyrs of 1963 will be in the bill: William Moore, four little Sunday School girls in Birmingham, and two innocent boys not remotely connected with the freedom movement, and the battered skull of John Fitzgerald Kennedy, who wrote his own *Profile in Courage* by going into Dallas two weeks after Adlai Stevenson, United States ambassador in the United Nations, had been attacked in this same city.

But Medgar Evers' lifeblood will be in the civil rights bill more than all the others because he served freedom's cause here where resistance to democracy is hardest and fiercest! He eloquently and logically proclaimed the provisions of the United States Constitution and Bill of Rights for full citizenship of all Americans in Mississippi and everywhere in our beloved country. He could have worked in other parts of the country for the NAACP. He was qualified to fill many a role in the drama of professional or indus-trial life, but he chose the path of freedom; he chose his native state in which to serve; he lay down his life on the altar of freedom, and tonight we declare his spirit stalks the corridors of the United States Senate as seventy-nine out of one hundred solons of our Congress voted for cloture June 10. A seventy-nine per centum victory for civil rights—an impressive, "Willie Mays" batting average of .790!

The fruit of his life is in his family as represented in the moving, poignant speech of Myrlie Evers here tonight, of her children, of her great heroic self.

The fruit of his life will find itself here in the full freedom of all people. First of all, like the mantle of Elijah falling upon Elisha, Medgar Evers' mantle has fallen upon his brother, Charles, who leads the fight for free-dom in their native Mississippi. Indomitable leadership like that of fearless, aggressive State Conference president Dr. Aaron Henry is *the fruit of his life.* The youth heritors of Medgar Evers' life are fully represented by the active, aggressive, and intelligent leadership of your Robert Moses and John-nie Frazier. These personalities are but representative of the hundreds and thousands of freedom fighters, who carry on the battle for human dignity and equality under the Constitution here in Mississippi.

The fruit of his life will be fulfilled in the day when brotherhood will abound in this and all the fifty states of the Union; when the basic rights of equal opportunity in every area of living, housing, employment, education, voting, office holding, public accommodation, public recreation facilities, public worship are given to black and white Americans alike, without any type of discrimination.

The fruit of his life was fulfilled today in the Senate when the Stennis Amendment to the civil rights bill (a sinister suggestion of the possibilities of police state denial of every human right to our persecuted minority, like reprehensible apartheid enforcement laws of South Africa) was defeated by an overwhelming majority, 72 to 21.

In the book of Hebrews, commenting on the witness of Abel, after his death, the author declares, "God testifying of his gifts: and by it *he being dead yet speaketh."*

Medgar Evers speaks tonight as the most meaningful civil rights bill is on the threshold of passage in the Congress of the United States.

Medgar Evers speaks tonight as millions of freedom fighters around the world—in America, Africa, Malaysia, and Asia—draw a phalanx of close ranks.

Medgar Evers will speak when the day dawns that full freedom will be given to all Americans—when Americans, regardless of color, may live in peace, prosperity, and popularity, in integrated communities; when education will be classified by intelligence quotient and not by complexion; when employment and in job training and apprenticeship will be open to all; when black citizens shall register and vote without restraint, without fear, and disenfranchisement will be forgotten in the full swing of universal-participating suffrage.

In that day, when true democracy will flow like a river through all the states, from Maine to Hawaii and from Alaska to Florida—in that day when brotherhood will be the heartbeat of humanity and we shall dwell in a perfect state where "every citizen is a sovereign but no one cares to wear a crown"—in that day when men of every complexion, every culture, every heritage, every history shall be blended into the brotherhood of man, under the fatherhood of God, Medgar Evers shall not have died in vain. He, who gave his life for freedom, shall not have died without fulfillment. In that day, we shall say, "He being dead, yet speaketh!"

§42 Leon A. Jick

Leon A. Jick was born October 4, 1924, in St. Louis to a Zionist family. He attended Washington University in St. Louis, but halted studies in 1941 to join the Army Air Corps, then resumed studies to earn a bachelor's degree in 1947. Following college, he worked in the office of Habonim, a labor Zionist youth movement. His initial intent was to travel to Palestine, but he could not obtain a visa. Instead he embarked to Marseilles, France to work with displaced people in postwar Europe. In 1948, when Israel became a nation-state, Jick observed aliyah, emigration to Israel, where he co-founded the Kibbutz Gesher Haziv in Western Galilee. He also taught English at Bet Berl Institute in Kfar Saba. Upon returning to the United States, he attended Hebrew Union College, where he was ordained. He then became an assistant rabbi in Boston. In 1957, he became rabbi at the Free Synagogue of Westchester, New York, where he served in that capacity until 1966. From 1966 to 1990, Jick joined the faculty of Brandeis University, where he served as professor, department chair, and dean. During the early years of his academic career, he also advanced in his doctoral studies, earning a Ph.D. from Columbia University in 1973. In addition to his energetic production in ancient Near Eastern studies, he was founding president of the Association of Jewish Studies. His teaching penchant was to help students understand the cause of the Holocaust. He was also a political activist for environmental and civil rights' concerns, and was jailed with fifteen other rabbis in St. Augustine, Florida, for their participation in a march with Dr. Martin Luther King Jr. Jick was also a family man, devoted to Millicent (née Fink), their four sons, and their grandchildren. He died in May 2005, and his papers reside at Brandeis University.

In this June 25, 1964, speech Jick reports recent events and reflects on them with fellow activists. What is the end of jailings and resistance, he ponders? Murder and mayhem are the answer. The victims of the killing are law and justice. After this pronouncement, he attempts to answer the question so frequently posed to him: "Why get involved? It's not your business to interfere." This question was asked first by murderous Cain: "Am I my brother's keeper?" He mentions a case in the Bronx where heinous crimes occurred while citizens irresponsibly drew their shades. He appeals to the authority of the Torah, love and care for one's brother. He also appeals to the secular ideals of life, liberty, and the pursuit of happiness before fusing the two ideals with his belief that God extended these rights to all mankind. From there he turns to his motives for answering Martin Luther King's call to march with the just and courageous. He reads a Yiddish poem from 1943 Poland which implores, "It burns brothers," as a plea to take responsibility for threats to the community at large. Throughout the sermon Rabbi Jick makes use of poetic redundance, a venerable ancient Near Eastern tradition, repeating the phrases "not my business," and "nobody knows." He refers to the Psalmist and then to the Sermon on the Mount before returning to fragments of his experiences in jail. His final words exhort congregants (especially those from his home base, Mount Vernon, New York) to let the black community know it is not alone, approach elected officials, provide material means for the movement, and side with God.

Which Side Are You On?

June 25, 1964
Mt. Vernon, New York

We live in times when events move very swiftly. Very often evil seems to stride with seven league boots. Since my return from St. Augustine, so many dreadful things have come to pass that recent experience seem[s] almost too distant to bear repetition from this pulpit. At the same time subsequent events have sharpened and emphasized the reasons why sixteen rabbis went to St. Augustine. Perhaps it is most important than ever to discuss these reasons, not simply to recall what was, but to understand what continues to develop and what it means to us.

Let us begin at the end. Let us open with the conclusion. The end is: murder and mayhem are abroad in our land! In the land of the free and the home of the brave, hooligans, sadists, and savages roam the streets and freely work violence without restraint. They have no fear because those who wear badges and uniforms, the policemen and the sheriffs, are their men.

It is not only citizens who are imperiled. It is not only individuals who are abused and victimized. Law itself has been slain. Justice has been murdered in broad daylight, in civilized America.

At such a time, men and women not too different from ourselves, seated comfortably in the air-conditioned ease of bar mitzvah parties and wedding receptions, have said to me in these last days, "It isn't your business. Outsiders shouldn't interfere." Those who say this raise a more serious question than perhaps they themselves understand. They raise what may be the most important question we are called upon to answer these days. Those who say, "It isn't your business and you shouldn't interfere"—and they are many—are raising the question, what is my business? This is the first question for us to consider. Not the question of Negro-white relationships, not civil rights, but the question, what is my business? How far does my concern extend? For whom am I responsible?

This is a very old question, as a matter of fact—it is a question which is asked as far back as the days of the Bible. The Bible asks it in these words: "Am I my brother's keeper?"

The answers which men give to this question differ greatly. There are those among us who stood by recently as a young woman was raped in the Bronx. There are others who drew their shades when a woman was murdered beneath their window in Queens. These people were saying, "Nothing outside my skin concerns me. Nothing outside the four walls of my house is my business." That is what some say.

If we believe in God, if we believe in the words of the Torah (the Torah which teaches, "Thou shalt not stand idly by the blood of thy brother"; the Torah which teaches, "Thou shalt not hate thy brother in thy heart but thou shalt love thy neighbor as thyself"), if we believe in America and its ideals (if we believe that all men are created with inalienable rights to life—not to speak of liberty and the pursuit of happiness), if these are more than mere words, more than sham and hypocritical talk, then our concern must extend beyond the walls of our house, beyond our block—beyond our town. Surely our concern must extend to all the corners of our land. Ultimately if we believe in God, this concern must extend to all mankind.

Now then, if terror and violence and the murder of justice in my country—if the destruction of law and order in my America is not my business, then whose business is it? What is my business—if this is not my business?

When a victim of injustice calls out and cries for help, woe is us, if men and women draw their shades and like the good residents of Queens, like the good Germans, say, "It's not my business." They are calling; the victims of injustice are calling. They called directly and personally to me and to my colleagues. Martin Luther King, in a telegram to the Central Conference of American Rabbis meeting at its annual convention in Atlantic City, called for help and asked men to join with him in a prophetic witness. Who could stand idly by and draw the shades and say, "It's not my business"?

We went to St. Augustine in response to a call to heed and to join in a protest against injustice and lawlessness. Whatever small contribution we may have made, and it is very small, we gained a great deal. It was a rare and unforgettable privilege to join hands with those who work in a just and peaceful cause and who do their work in just and peaceful ways. In St. Augustine we met a group of men whose like one does not find very often—courageous, selfless, long-suffering men, who have nothing to gain but the joy of serving and the satisfaction of accomplishment, who risk their lives every single day, who bear on their bodies countless physical wounds and scars as they strive to achieve the elemental rights which ought to be the birthright of every American and every human being.

As I drove through the streets of St. Augustine seeing and feeling the tension around, a persistent association overflowed my thoughts. The text of a song repeated itself over and over in my mind:

It burns brothers, it burns.
Alas, our poor little town is burning
And you stand and look on thus with folded hands
And you stand and look on, while our town burns.

The poem, dear friends, was not written this year, not about St. Augustine nor by a Negro, not even in the English language. It was written in 1943 by a Jew. The town of which it speaks is in Poland, and the language in which it was written is Yiddish.

In 1943 people, including many of our own people, stood by while towns and their inhabitants burned; they looked on with folded hands and said, "It's not my business." We dare not stand and look with folded hands in 1964 as towns burn, as America burns.

Whatever doubts or hesitations we rabbis may have had about our trip evaporated when we entered the St. Augustine church where the Negro community had assembled. We who were there shall not soon forget the stirring and heartfelt excitement which greeted us—shouts and cheers, hymns and hallelujahs, pulsating and resounding. We shall never forget the words of Hosea Williams of Savannah, Georgia, one of the leaders in this struggle. As we prepared to march through the streets of St. Augustine, he said to the congregation, "We shall march past the old slave market to awaken the sleeping conscience of the people of St. Augustine and America. As we march we shall sing, 'I love everybody—you can't make me doubt it. I love everybody in my heart.' And we shall sing, "Nobody knows the trouble I've seen . . . nobody . . . nobody.' "

At that moment, we knew why we had come, we knew why we could not have stayed away from what was simply a human duty. We knew also how little we really understood of Negro Americans and their ordeal—how little we knew of "the troubles they've seen"—and we were grateful for the experience of sharing just a little with one courageous community in its life and in its struggle.

So we marched quietly, no words spoken, and we sang quietly and we prayed quietly for America, for all men, for the hard-hearted and the persecutors. We were told, we rabbis, that our presence strengthened the morale of the Negro community in St. Augustine. We hope this is true. We know with certainty that they strengthened ours.

On that march, we saw other faces and heard other voices—faces contorted with hate, voices raised in abuse—and we learned what we should have known all the time, that the haters are a minority—little more than a handful. But they are violent and vicious, and they have intimidated the decent people who stand by in silence. It is known and acknowledged in St. Augustine that the local police are Klan-controlled. What semblance of "law and order" can there be under such conditions? Without outside assistance there is no hope for justice for those who seek their rights in St. Augustine and in large portions of the South of America.

We learned later that the state police, who were in town, arrested a local policeman who was found with a lead pipe up his sleeve. This is the nature of police protection in St. Augustine, Florida.

The following morning we rabbis conducted our own prayer service, and we learned something from that too, as we recited the prayers which have become so familiar to us—we thought of those whom we would meet in our congregations when we returned home. We thought of those who would tell us that our action had nothing to do with Judaism, that rabbis ought to stay inside synagogues. That morning when we read the prayers and when we repeated the words "O rock of Israel—redeem those who are oppressed—and deliver those who are persecuted"—when we prayed to God as "Thou who freest the captives" and as we read from the Torah portion of that week, the account of Israel's travail in the desert en route to freedom—the old text and the old experience took on a new meaning for us. We rediscovered our link with our tradition. We rediscovered, too, a renewed trust in Him who is the stay and trust of the righteous and the source of man's striving for freedom. This was confirmed for us by the readings which Dr. King selected from the Bible just before we marched a second time. He read the Twenty-ninth Psalm—"The Lord is my stay and trust—of whom shall I be afraid." From the New Testament he read the words of one of our kinsmen—him whom the Christians call Christ—"Blessed are those who suffer for righteousness sake."

The precise events of this second march may be better known to you than they are to me. You probably witnessed the entire episode on television while I and a number of my colleagues finished reciting the Twenty-third Psalm in a police car on the way to St. Johns County Jail.

What stood out in those few moments of confrontation was the tremendous contrast between gentle and just words and deeds as represented by the protestors and the harsh, frantic, frenetic viciousness of the persecutors. It could not be mistaken, where justice lay, where hope lay, where America's heart and interest lay.

In jail we undertook a fast in protest against the segregation which was imposed upon us and against the fact that the Reverend Fred Shuttlesworth and the Reverend C. T. Vivian, who had been arrested with us, were separated from us. I must tell you that this fast was no great act of virtue. It was easy to fast since we weren't given anything to eat. Our twenty-six hours in jail—sixteen rabbis, one Jewish laymen, and two Christians—were spent in a cell meant for six, without food, without a cup to drink, without the essential elements of hygiene. For those few hours we experienced only a tiny taste of what millions of Negro Americans suffer throughout their lives as their daily fare. If this was the treatment of rabbis, imagine the fate which is meted out to young Negro men and women who commit the heinous crime of standing up for their rights.

While we did not receive food, we did receive visitors. One of those was a local dignitary with a cattle prod in his hand who proceeded to tell us at some length that since he had been a member of a Marine Corps, he didn't mind killing at all. In fact, he almost relished it. He was providing the proper setting in which we might appreciate the experience of being jailed and contemplate just exactly what we risked by our presence. Another visitor, who welcomed us when we arrived in jail, was the head of the local Ku Klux Klan. He is a deputy sheriff in St. Johns County and a real "balabus" in the jail. He was there when we arrived, and he returned later to boast and to taunt us and to say, "You know who I am."

Tell this to those who speak of law and order. Tell this to those who say that demonstrators are breaking the law—and that outsiders should not interfere. Tell them that the chief of the Klan is the boss of the jail, that his henchmen are the police, and that murder is rampant in America. How much longer, dear friends, can America afford to bear the burden of redneck, Klan-inspired bigotry?

We were arraigned the next day before a local judge and released [on] $900 bail for each of us. Our bail was provided for us by [the] Legal Defense Fund of the NAACP.

As we sat outside the judge's chambers, reintegrated again, waiting to be arraigned, I for one felt a sense of terrible remorse. We had come, we had seen, and we had remained for a few hours, made a small gesture, and now we were on our way home back to our loving families and our congregations, leaving behind those who bear the brunt of this trouble. I voiced this feeling to one of our Negro colleagues, Rev. C. T. Vivian, one of the gentlest, warmest human beings it has ever been my pleasure to know. He reassured me, and he also gave me a job to do. First, he said, his people knew that we had come only for a very short time and that our coming had helped. He said it had helped remind an embattled Negro community that they were not altogether isolated and alone. It was important for them to see faces from the outside, white faces, which were friendly, which restored their confidence that there were human beings in this world. It may also be, he said, that we stirred the conscience of some of the local whites. Perhaps the conscience of the wicked was troubled—perhaps the conscience of the righteous gained new strength. This was the reassurance.

And he bestowed a task. The task was to carry the message abroad in our land. The message that the cause is just, that the cause can win and will win—the message that even southern whites in large numbers are ready for a settlement, are ready to abide by the law and order. Those who do violence must be punished. They must be arrested. One swift stroke, one swift move which shows the bigots and the incitors that they are not free from punishment and the whole atmosphere will change. We cannot wait to change men's hearts, but the law can be enforced. The redneck sadists who are responsible for violence and murder are active only so long as they are sure that they are immune from punishment. They are great heroes when they need not to be afraid of recriminations. They are great heroes when the numbers are fifteen to one against nonviolent Negroes and whites who do not fight back. But let the law be enforced—let law act, not against those who seek to implement it but against those who seek to destroy it—and lawlessness and murder will come to an end.

We have a share in bringing about that transformation. Do not be deterred by those who say that it is not our business. Do not be deterred by those who say that intervention will "make things worse"—worse for whom?

We must not be deterred by those who point to acts of violence by Negroes and say, "You see what Negroes did on the subways in New York?" Let the guilty in New York be punished, not men and women in St. Augustine. Let more police be hired when there are crimes. We do not punish innocent men and women for the crimes of a few. This is only a pretext to avoid doing what must be done. It is a poor pretext because even this violence in the North will not ease until there is justice everywhere. The best hope that someday such senseless violence will be eliminated is in doing justice now. Let us not be deterred or thrown off of the track by those who point the finger and say, "The irresponsibility of some Negroes is our excuse for injustice"—it is no excuse.

Let us not be deterred by timidity or apathy, especially not by Jewish timidity, especially not by those who say, "Well, it's alright, but rabbis shouldn't get involved, Jews shouldn't get involved." Let those who fear for the "image of the Jew" in America concern themselves with Jewish slumlords, not with Jewish civil rights workers. This "image" does not frighten me; indeed this is an image which belongs to us.

Let us then not be deterred. We must act whenever and wherever we can. This means that we must write to President Johnson and to Attorney General Kennedy demanding federal protection for all the citizens of America. There is more than enough cause. Americans deserve protection, and if they cannot receive it from the local authorities or the state authorities, let them have it from the federal government. Let federal forces act to protect the rights of the citizens of America; let us write to express our view in this matter.

More than this, let us write too, to Martin Luther King and to his people in St. Augustine and elsewhere, expressing our sympathy and support, our admiration for those who patiently, peacefully, nonviolently pursue the cause of justice and their rights. More than writing, let us contribute of our means to those who lead in the struggle for justice.

Let us finally determine to apply the same principles of justice and the same equality of opportunity to underprivileged Americans everywhere, even in Mount Vernon. We shall undoubtedly in the years ahead differ greatly as to the means through which this program can be put into effect. We shall differ greatly as to what needs to be done and how quickly it can be achieved. But let us recognize that whatever our differences about means, we cannot differ as to goals.

Let us vow that we shall be concerned and shall not rest until the benefits of freedom and opportunity are shared by all Americans whoever they are, wherever they live. A great battle is being waged, a battle in which each of us is being called upon to answer the challenge: which side are you on? Let us be on God's side, for then surely, he will be on ours.

§43 Theo O. Fisher

Dr. Theo O. Fisher was born in Melbourne, Australia. After obtaining a degree from Melbourne College of the Bible, he emigrated to the United States in 1937. He received a B.S.L., B.A., and M.A. from Butler University. Butler awarded him an honorary doctorate in 1954. He was also a student at Mansfield College, Oxford University, in 1965. Fisher married Georgine Cofield in 1940. They had five children together. During World War II, he served as an Air Force chaplain in New Guinea, the Philippines, Japan, and stateside. Disciples of Christ pastorates included Northwood Christian Church, in Indianapolis (1939 to 1964), Monte Vista Christian Church, in Albuquerque, New Mexico (1966 to 1976), and several interim ministries following his retirement. He died in July 2001.

This unflinching sermon of July 26, 1964, was among his final addresses to his Indianapolis congregation after two and a half decades of his pastorate. He begins the sermon by saying his original intent was not to discuss racial justice—simply the golden rule. But national events had necessitated otherwise, as he was on his way to spend a week in Mississippi to minister to young students participating in Freedom Summer. Mickey Schwerner, Andrew Goodman, and James Chaney had disappeared five weeks before this sermon, though no one was certain they were dead. Members of the

Northwood congregation had mixed attitudes on Fisher's imminent departure for Mississippi, including one who drafted an anonymous letter suggesting he stay in Mississippi permanently. He reminds the congregation that he does not want to go to Mississippi, that he would prefer to spend time near a lake in Michigan, and that he would bear the expense using vacation time and his own money. The rest of the sermon discusses his motives for traveling to Mississippi. First, the president of the United States asked him to go. Second, Fisher felt he could not preach one way but live another relative to justice. Third, he felt ministers could help weed out the beatniks and adventurers who could potentially participate in Freedom Summer for the wrong reasons. Fourth, a delegation of some fifty Christian church ministers had decided to participate as well. After a brief digression on his experiences as an army chaplain who ministered to African American troops, he admits finally that guilt might also be a motivating factor. A comic anecdote about living in a cemetery because the neighbors are peaceful precedes the coda of unanimous wisdom on the subject from the secular Solon and the sacred Golden Rule.

◆◆◆

Wearing Another Man's Shoes
July 26, 1964
Indianapolis, Indiana

I would like to express a word of my personal appreciation, and I'm sure your appreciation too, this morning to our choirs, under the direction of Mr. Lamberson, who serve us so beautifully through all the year and so faithfully and particularly in these last summer weeks. They add so much to our worship experience, and I am always very, very grateful for their devotion and the lovely music that they bring us.

I had planned, this morning, to preach on the subject of the Golden Rule, "Do unto others as you would have them do unto you." Put yourself in the other man's shoes, and as a result of the experience develop a heart of understanding and sympathy for him. This had not been planned as a sermon on race relations but rather a sermon on human relations—which can well include race relations and all the relationship of life, whether it be in marriage or in business or in school or wherever we are placed—to have this rule as one of the rules of our life to "do unto others as we would have them do unto us."

Because I plan to go to Mississippi for seven to ten days, a number of people have inquired about this, and I feel I owe it to you to tell you why I'm going. As we know, the whole question of race is a very explosive one. People's emotions, their economics, their whole way of life is touched in one way or another by this question that confronts us all in this time in history. We are in the middle of a revolution that is a worldwide revolution, and we are all involved, whether we realize it or not. We will all be touched by it. We sometimes wish we could turn our backs on it and it would go away, or if we don't look on it, it doesn't exist, but it does exist, and it won't go away, and we have to decide, each one of us, what we're going to do about it.

There have been a variety of responses to the announcement that I was going to Mississippi. There are those who approve and applaud my decision. There are those who are kindly anxious for my safety. There are those who disapprove but recognize my right to go, and there are those who disapprove and are offended, like the anonymous letter writer who suggested it would perhaps be a good idea if I'd stay in Mississippi. Why go at all? Why go to Mississippi? Well, first of all, let me assure you I didn't want to go. Let me assure you that I am not looking forward to going to Mississippi. I would much sooner be going to the lake in Michigan at this time of the year and not go into this situation of crisis. I want to tell you I am going on my own vacation time and will be back to preach the last Sunday in August, and I will pay my own expenses.

I am going because, first of all, I was asked to go. It started with a letter from the president of the United States, who requested that some senior ministers be enlisted to go to Mississippi to minister to hundreds of young, white northern students who have given their summer to teach in freedom schools, and my conscience would not let me say no. I have preached from this pulpit my belief in justice and freedom for all men. I have preached about the "strong" bearing the burdens of the "weak," and I do not want to preach to others things that I am unwilling to do myself. That's one reason I'm going to Mississippi.

"What is the church doing there anyway?" you say. "Isn't it just creating more violence and more trouble?" The church is not going into Mississippi to create tension but to assist in averting violence. Over a thousand white students from the North were expected in Mississippi this summer. They had been recruited by the Council of Federated Organizations to help in a program in Mississippi. Now after this had happened, the church—seeing the increased resistance to social change in our country, the anger and the fear in southern states toward the rumored "invasion" and the growing impatience of Negro leadership with the slowness of progress—realized that this summer would be a time of very serious crisis.

It was crucial that the church do everything possible to see that the right kind of young people went to Mississippi, and so the church, through the National Council of Churches, volunteered to be an agent of assistance and of reconciliation, and the first mission it took was to properly screen these young people to weed out the beatniks and the adventurers and the inadequately trained and the emotionally unstable and to see that the young people who did go were good representatives going for the right motive. They wanted to see that they were intelligently and responsibly related to existing programs designed to meet such massive needs as literacy, training, voter education, voter registration, citizenship education, and community development. The church, through the National Council of Churches, entered into this program in a spirit of reconciliation.

You ask, "What is this program? What is it all about?" Well, there are three phases to the program that are being conducted in Mississippi. First of all, there are freedom schools, and today freedom schools will, for the most part, draw tenth-, eleventh-, and twelfth-grade students from the immediate locale. Each school will have a very high teacher-student ratio so that instruction can be as individual as possible. Curriculum for those schools will cover a wide area: remedial work in reading, math, and basic grammar; seminars in political science and humanit[ies], journalism and creative writing; recreational programs such as dramatics, music appreciation, arts and crafts, athletics, movies; and voter registration fieldwork.

The second phase in this program is the establishment of community centers. The community centers program projects a network of educational and recreational centers across the state. Conceived as a long-range program, the centers will provide a variety of programs geared to serve the basic needs of the Negro communities presently ignored by the state's racist political structure. In addition, a dynamic focus for the development of community organizations will be formed. The educational features of the centers will include: job-training programs for the unskilled and unemployed, literacy and remedial programs for adults and young people, and public health programs such as prenatal and infant care and nutrition. Centers will also provide adult education workshops on such topics as family relations, federal service programs, and home improvement. Each center will provide a well-rounded library to which Negroes, in many communities, have no access at the present time.

The third phase, which causes all the "fire," is voter registration. This program will help Negroes to register and exercise their voting privileges as citizens.

Now, the difficulties for all summer volunteers working together as a team in the midst of a crisis situation is bound to create tension which they hope a qualified minister counselor can help alleviate. This is the reason for inviting ministers to go south. This is the reason why some forty to fifty ministers of the Christian Church are going south, and this is the reason that ministers of the Christian Church are going south, and this is the reason that ministers from most of the denominations will be represented in Mississippi this summer.

The letter inviting me to go has this paragraph in it:

> The need for your response cannot be emphasized too much. We simply must recognize the fact that the racial problem in America can engulf our society in more tragic ways yet if people of goodwill don't take the initiative. This responsibility, we believe, rests even more heavily upon representatives of religious faith. This is one reason, among others, that we appeal to you.

The church has another phase to its program, for it is not only going to Negroes in the colored community, but it is seeking to render a ministry of reconciliation and of understanding on the part of the church and to the white community that is caught up in the tensions of rapidly changing social patterns, to interpret to them this program and what they are trying to do. The situation is sad and difficult. It has been said that the Delta area of the state of Mississippi manifests, in full display, the total complexities of the problem of racial injustice and persistent poverty. It is an area of chronic need, and at the same time pivotal for healing and redemption in all other areas.

The moral mandate that compels Christians anywhere to help all brothers everywhere demands that these needs be met. One of the shocking things in this time has been the apathy of people of goodwill—their indifference, their neglect, their unconcern, their seeming hope that these things will take care of themselves, their seeming indifference to the sorrows that tear the land apart. As a Christian, I feel I must be concerned. And whether you agree with this particular notion or not, this is something I feel I must do.

There is an issue that is beyond all of this, and that is the issue of freedom. Some friends of mine who were going to Florida this summer said, "We have very carefully planned our trip so that we will not go through

Mississippi." I believe Americans should be appalled and horrified that any American should be afraid to travel anywhere in this country or to stand in any state in this free land and claim his rights of freedom of speech and freedom of assembly.

I served as a chaplain for the Air Force in Mississippi, and what's more, I served colored troops in Mississippi. I served as a chaplain in South Carolina, and what's more, I served my troops by choice, some colored troops that others wouldn't serve. It was all right for me as a minister of the gospel to go to Mississippi during the war to serve men who were training to give their lives for their country. I claim the same privilege in days of peace to go anywhere as a Christian in this land to express my faith or to serve the causes of the church. Don't fence me in. Let's not lose the universality of the church. When I became a citizen of the United States, I didn't become a citizen of Indiana. I became a citizen of the United States, and Mississippi is my country. We should be horrified that any citizens of this country should be cowed by brutality or threat of violence and have to live their lives in an atmosphere of fear, afraid to claim or act upon their citizenship rights, and a protest should go up from the throat of every free man.

Jesus identified himself with the weak, with the dispossessed, with the sick, with the troubled, and with the outcast. There were religious snobs who drew back and criticized him for lowering himself by having anything to do with Samaritans or with publicans and sinners. With some people, Jesus was very unpopular because he dared to mix with what they regarded as the lower classes and with publicans and with sinners. We dare not fall into the same sin of religious snobbery that walks by on the other side of the road about its religious duties and is unmoved by a fellow human being in a time of his need for friendship and for help. We are not appointed by God as Christians to form a tight, secure little society for ourselves but to be his agents of reconciliation and to help every man to grow to the full stature of his possibilities as a free son of God.

My going to Mississippi is at least the attempt to say, "I sympathize and believe in the cause of justice and of freedom." Jesus said that the test of our religion is our willingness to serve the needs of mankind, and in serving those needs, we serve Jesus Christ, our Lord—"I was sick and in prison, and you visited me." One of our ministers, in a recent week, wrote an article in The Christian, our church paper, concerning civil wrongs. And there are many civil wrongs, and we need to be just as concerned about the civil wrongs as the civil rights. And I do not stand to uphold violence and lawlessness and mobs and rioting.

The Negro pleads for equal justice, and he must also accept equal justice.

As Mr. Roy Wilkins, the NAACP executive, said, commenting on Negro gangs in New York, "Punks must be treated as punks whether they are colored or white, and there must be equal justice for all. And Negroes who wish to walk in cultured society must become cultured before they claim that privilege. Negroes who want better jobs must become educated for better jobs and not just expect them because they are Negroes. But Negroes must be given every freedom to become better educated, to become cultured, and when equipped for a better job not to be barred from employment just because he is a Negro." The work in Mississippi is an attempt to help Negroes get these freedoms which are guaranteed to them by the laws of this free land.

One time, Jesus set his face to go to Jerusalem, and Peter tried to stand in his way and bar him from going. I wonder what arguments Peter used, whether he said something like this, "Lord, what in the world can you accomplish in a week? You will only destroy the peace of the city and make things worse. You'll stir up the mob. Things are tense down there, and you'll only be involved in trouble. Why don't you come to Lake Galilee with us and forget about it." And Jesus answered his faithful friend by saying, "Get thee behind me, Satan. You are a hindrance to me, for you are not on the side of God but on the side of men."

Let me add a footnote to this sermon. Perhaps I go to Mississippi as a penance, a penance for my own prejudice, a penance for the times when I was silent when I should have spoken out, a penance for the times when I spoke out when I should have kept silent. I want to assure you I don't go feeling like a knight in armor, and I would not have made this public before going if it had of been my choice. I don't go feeling that I have the answers to this problem. I feel very inadequate, and I know my offering of a week is a very inadequate offer, and I know that all of the answers to these tremendous problems that face us as citizens and as Christians are going to be a long time coming, but I believe we'd better be concerned, each one of us, about trying to find the answer. I go, I want you to know, with very deep sympathy for our white brethren who are caught in rapid and disturbing social change. I go with respect for the great host of white southerners who are honestly and diligently seeking to find answers in a spirit of concern.

Ten churches have been burned in recent weeks. A story in one of our papers told how the white citizens of one town were rebuilding the colored church which had been burned to the ground. There are Christian people of concern and goodwill who are seeking answers, and a small percentage of the southern population is responsible for the vicious, cruel beatings and murders and bombings which has cast a shadow across this land. It is time that people of goodwill took over.

I had a letter from our friend Wallace O. Lee, in Florida. He was trying to assure me that he went to church each Sunday, and he told me what the preacher said. And he said that this preacher was telling an incident from his boyhood. He said his father was superintendent of a cemetery, and they moved into a house right in the middle of the cemetery, where they were surrounded by graves. And one day, some of their old friends came to visit them in their new home, and they asked the question which had been asked a hundred times, "How do you like living in a cemetery?" And the man's grandmother, who lived with them, spoke up and said, "We like it fine. Our neighbors are the most peaceful and considerate of any neighbors we've ever had."

We all have to be concerned about being good neighbors, and whether we agree or disagree about what is the right way to go about seeking an answer to our problems, we all have to seek to have the spirit of the Lord Jesus Christ. The trouble about this issue is that our emotions are so deeply stirred that we are so often governed by our emotions and not by our minds or by our hearts. The Christian has to be concerned not only with his emotions, which are important, but he loves the Lord God with his mind and with his heart too. And we are called to be reconciling agents of the Lord Jesus Christ—spirits of goodwill. May this church and this people by their spirits and their concern and their love for one another be such an agency in days of trouble and of need.

Someone once asked Solon how justice could be achieved in Athens. And the great lawgiver replied, "It can be achieved if those people who are not directly affected by a wrong are just as indignant as those who are personally hurt."

"Do unto others as you would have them do unto you."

§44 Arthur Lelyveld

Rabbi Arthur J. Lelyveld was born in New York City on February 6, 1913. After graduating from George Washington High School at the age of fifteen, Lelyveld attended Columbia University, eventually graduating Phi Beta Kappa and serving as editor in chief of the *Columbia Daily Spectator*. After receiving his master's degree in Hebrew letters from Hebrew Union College in Cincinnati, Ohio, Lelyveld served as rabbi of Temple Israel in

Omaha, Nebraska, from 1942 to 1944. A pacifist and conscientious objector during World War II, Lelyveld left Omaha to lead the Zionist Organization of America in New York City. Lelyveld's lifelong commitment to education and religion is reflected in his role as the national director of the B'nai B'rith Hillel Foundation. In 1958 Lelyveld left New York City to become rabbi of Anshe Chesed-Fairmount Temple in the east Cleveland suburb of Beachwood; he served Fairmount until his retirement in 1986. During the 1960s, Lelyveld served on the board of the Cleveland chapter of the NAACP. He and his first wife, Toby Bookholtz, had three sons, including Joseph Lelyveld, who would become executive editor of the *New York Times* and publish a 2005 memoir that cast a spotlight on his often absent parents. Lelyveld and his second wife, Teela Stovsky, had one daughter. Always an educator, Lelyveld was the Bernard Rich Hollander lecturer in Jewish thought at John Carroll University. He died in Beachwood on April 15, 1996, from a brain tumor.

Along with many of his fellow clergy, Lelyveld answered the Council of Federated Organizations' call to bear witness in Mississippi during the summer of 1964. On the morning of July 10, while canvassing for a voter registration drive in Hattiesburg, Lelyveld was badly beaten by two white tire-iron-wielding men. His bloodied face and body were featured the following day on the front page of the *New York Journal–American*; it remains an iconic image of what became known as Freedom Summer. Lelyveld's beating came just nineteen days after the disappearance of civil rights workers James Chaney, Andrew Goodman, and Mickey Schwerner, whose bodies were eventually discovered in an earthen dam outside of Philadelphia, in Neshoba County. A close friend of Goodman's parents, Robert and Carolyn, Lelyveld delivered a short eulogy to a crowd of more than 1,200 mourners. Given the unprecedented publicity of the murders, Lelyveld's words were quoted around the world. With great concision, Rabbi Lelyveld expertly melds Jewish and Christian rhetorical traditions; in so doing, he transcends potential divisions by situating Andrew Goodman in a revered eternal present in which Christian and Jew can each make sense of and honor his sacrifice. Lelyveld is also at pains to specify that the twenty-year-old Goodman knowingly embraced possible martyrdom; his was not a starry-eyed and fleeting freedom high but rather a purposeful and informed commitment to racial justice. Lelyveld's words indeed proved prophetic: to this day, the phrase "Goodman, Schwerner, and Chaney" function as potent shorthand for the innumerable sacrifices of movement participants.

❧❧

Earning the Kingdom in an Hour*

August 9, 1964
New York, New York

My dear Carolyn, dear Bob, Jonathan, David, dear friends of Andrew Goodman and of human freedom:

There are two levels of our grief today; paradoxically, the two are one. First and foremost, inevitably we grieve for a precious individual, for potentialities unfulfilled, for a beloved son, a youth filled with gallant concern for man, for human rights. You have told me, my dear friends, about the rare blend of tenderness and of manliness that marked his unfolding year, of his intellectual curiosity, of his search for meaning, for significance; and nothing we can say here this morning can eradicate your pain or restore your loss.

But the tragedy of Andrew Goodman cannot be separated from the tragedy of mankind. The word which Jewish tradition speaks at moments such as this is the word "May his soul be bound up in the bond of all the living."

And this is how, from now on, we shall see Andrew Goodman—bound up in the bond of all the living—for he, with James Chaney and with Michael Schwerner, has become an eternal evocation for all the host of rare and beautiful young men and women who are carrying forward that struggle to which Andy and his companions gave their lives, who patiently instruct the old and the young in their citizenship rights, who offer fellowship to those who have been dispossessed and who, as they go from door to door and porch to porch, or sit and teach in freedom schools, or follow the labyrinth of Mississippi voter-registration traps, offering kindliness and in self-identification the assurance most needed by any one of us, the assurance to that ennobled and wonderful Negro community of Mississippi, that they are not alone.

Not one of these young people who are walking the streets of Hattiesburg or Camden or Laurel or Gulfport or Greenville, not one of them, and certainly neither Andy nor James nor Michael, would have us in resentment or vindictiveness add to the store of hatred in the world. They pledged themselves in the way of nonviolence. They learned how to receive blows,

---

* The original unpublished manuscript is "Andrew Goodman, 1943-1964: Eulogies Delivered at the Funeral Service of Andrew Goodman, August 9, 1964, at the Meetinghouse of the Society for Ethical Culture, United States: s.n., 1964."

not how to inflict them. They were trained to bear hurts, not to retaliate. Theirs is the way of love and constructive service.

I've heard many, speaking deeply out of the metaphors of Christianity, describe that way of love as the way of the cross; I've heard William String-fellow speak of the destruction, of the inevitable doom that awaits us in this struggle, and expound the view that service inevitably brings sacrifice. "Blessed are they who are persecuted for righteousness' sake."

Andy, like his parents, like his brothers, was a proud and self-accepting Jew. The tradition out of which he came uses different words, but knows as surely and as intimately the fact that martyrdom is an ever-possible crown for genuine conviction.

We speak of those who give their lives that the Divine Presence may be made manifest among men. Our tradition assures us that it is far better to be among the persecuted and the pursued than to be the persecutor or the pursuer. Your response, dear Carolyn and Bob, has been a response in that spirit, a response that the work of redemption must go forward. The workers of the Council of Federated Organizations in Mississippi echo this determination. They provide, in their continuing endeavor, a living and dynamic memorial as they struggle to help a whole people win its way from bondage to freedom.

There are those, the rabbis assure us, who earn the kingdom in an hour, for a life is not judged by its length. Andy, who will be part of all that is swift and loving and brave and beautiful forever, won his kingdom in an hour. To die in a cause so pure is to transcend all life experience. To assume the risks so knowingly and so willingly is to rise above all that is craven, sordid, limiting.

Andrew Goodman assumed the risk of his service in full knowledge of what he was doing, for he wrote, "People must have dignity and identity," and he added, "The road to freedom is uphill and arduous," and so it is; and in continuing devotion and in fellowship with Andrew Goodman we say, "We shall overcome."

May his soul be bound up in the bond of all the living.

Amen.

§45 Cecil Albert Roberts

Dr. Cecil Albert Roberts Jr. was born on October 17, 1931, in Waco, Texas. Upon finishing high school in Fort Worth, Roberts enrolled at Baylor University. At Baylor, Roberts was a popular speaker at campus-wide revivals, and he traveled the state with the Baylor Religious Hour choir, where he met his future wife, Dolores Mae Patterson; they married in 1953, and the nuptials were performed by Charles Wellborn at Waco's Seventh and James Baptist Church. Roberts pursued his bachelor's degree and doctorate in theology at Southwestern Baptist Seminary in Fort Worth. He completed the latter degree in 1959, writing his dissertation on Jonathan Edwards' doctrine of religious experience. While he was matriculating at Southwestern, Roberts was also the head minister at the First Baptist Church of Altus, Oklahoma, which grew significantly—in people and tithes—under Roberts' leadership. His rising star was such that Tallahassee, Florida's First Baptist Church sought out the thirty-year-old to lead their four-thousand-member congregation. Congregants of the church included university faculty, college presidents, and leaders in state government. According to current First Baptist pastor Doug Dortch, Roberts was the preeminent pulpiteer in Southern Baptist life as the sixties began. After beginning at First Baptist on July 29, 1962, he quickly ascended Tallahassee's social hierarchy, serving first as chaplain of Florida State University's football team and also as the chaplain of the Florida state legislature. In 1963 the Tallahassee Junior Chamber of Commerce named Roberts as its Young Man of the Year. The following year the Florida Junior Chamber of Commerce named him as one of its five Men of the Year. Such was Roberts' following in national Baptist circles that he was elected president of the 35,000-member Southern Baptist Pastors' Conference in 1966, presumably to be followed by the presidency of the Southern Baptist Convention the following year. His charmed life, though, came to an abrupt halt on October 22, 1966. That evening, three members of a prominent Tallahassee family were murdered in their home on a quiet cul-de-sac. Although Roberts was exonerated—he was at the FSU home football game that evening—he had been identified as a suspect because Mrs. Sims, one of the victims, had served as First Baptist Church secretary. However, many Tallahasseans believe that Roberts was targeted because of his progressive views on race, and the subsequent integration of First Baptist. Local gossip threw his ministry into disarray. He left Tallahassee on May 1, 1967, for a year of postdoctoral training at Harvard Divinity School with the help of his Southwestern mentor, Dr. John P. Newport. After Harvard, Roberts became assistant professor of philosophy at Stephen F. Austin University, a position he held until 1971, when he moved to Houston and established a religious consulting business. Roberts' life came to a sad and tragic end on November 15, 1978. As he was sleeping alongside of a highway in Houston, his car was struck by a semi; he was killed instantly. Roberts left behind his wife and four children, who survive him, and remember his talents, to the present day.

Without even listening to the audio of this address, we can hear and appreciate the power of Dr. Roberts' finely calibrated narrative skills. In what amounts to an hour-plus story of how he tried to integrate Tallahassee's First Baptist Church in January 1964—and ultimately failed—Roberts skillfully leads his Baptist minister interlocutors to an unlikely climax: influential local blacks forced him to see his ostensible failure as a rousing success. Roberts quotes extensively from his opposition as the debate played out at First Baptist; in so doing his listeners can understand the vicelike ties binding culture and religion in the Deep South. As with any skilled raconteur, Roberts leaves his audience asking for more—most notably, what happened in the wake of the civil war in his own church.

The Christian Ethic and Segregation
August 23, 1964
Glorieta, New Mexico

Thank you, Bill. It is a real privilege to be here and to have this opportunity to speak this morning. They have given me the subject "Segregation and the Christian Ethic." When they asked me to come and speak in relation to this, they asked me mainly to speak in relation to our situation in Tallahassee, Florida. Now that being the case, I probably should have entitled my experience as "The Mistakes of a Moderate." One big mistake I have made in the last couple of years was to think that there was such a thing as a moderate in the South.

Now my trouble basically began when I lied to a pulpit committee and a pulpit committee lied to me. Now I didn't intend to lie, and I didn't even realize I was lying, and I don't think they intended to lie, and I don't think they realized they were lying. You know, I have found that it is a good thing the pulpit committees don't tell the truth, and it is a good thing the preachers don't know the future, because otherwise we might never get anything done. But the day that I got on the plane to fly to Tallahassee to interview and be interviewed by the pulpit committee there, the word "integration" was a word that has been blown to me from some distant wind. I had slept through it in seminary classes, and I had read in the newspapers about Little Rock, Arkansas, and I thought to myself, "Well, it is amazing—I didn't realize it could happen like that in America"; but I figured we could afford to have one town like that in America. The church I was pastor of in Altus, Oklahoma, had a Spanish mission, and they were in our church more than they were in other churches. We had Negroes in practically every Sunday evening service. Our young people wouldn't think about going to the football game on the bus unless their Negro students that they ran around with in school were also on the bus. The valedictorian of our high school in Altus was a Negro and went on and is today a medical student on a scholarship at Harvard University. Our star football player was a Negro. So consequently this wasn't even a matter of consideration. I can remember that I was preaching through the books of the New Testament and preached a sermon on Philemon one time in Altus and applied it to race, and the people just slept through it. They weren't interested enough even to listen!

I went to Tallahassee, and about the only thing that I had been given was a copy of the church policy. The only thing that I can recall about the church policy was that there wasn't anything in there about race, and so I got down there and all the pulpit committee was doing was taking me from one tea to the next tea, and I was meeting a lot of people, but we weren't getting much done, and so I asked if I could meet the deacons, a wonderful group of men. We met on Sunday afternoon, and during the course I just said, "Now you men need to know me; I need to know you. Ask me any questions you would like to ask." Well, they asked me all kinds of questions, and after awhile one of the men said, "What do you think about integration? What are you going to do about it?" I said, "Well, now I believe the pastor ought to pastor a church in relation to the environment where it is and begin with people where they are. However," I said, "I would expect the church to make room for my convictions." Now when I said I would pastor a group of people where they were, that was my lie, but I didn't realize where these people were. I was still thinking about Altus, Oklahoma. And so that day after I had made the statement they were pleased. We all went away happy, because they had interpreted what I said one way; I had interpreted in another way. Frankly, I suppose it all boiled down to the fact that *they never dreamed that I would ever press and I never dreamed that they would ever resist.*

As time went on things changed because I walked out of the committee and it worried me about the question, and I went back to the pulpit committee and I said, "Does your church have any kind of policy regarding the Negro race?" and they said, "No, no policy." Well, now that was their lie. What they meant was, "We do not have anything that is written down on paper," but I was fixing to find out in the next two months that there was a thing that in the law courts in the South that any judge will back up, and that is that when something by custom and usage over a period of time has been in effect it becomes the policy of the church even though it is unwritten, especially when it has a hundred years to back it up and about ten years for people to become emotionally involved in it.

Well, September rolled around a couple of months after I got there, and one evening I was invited to an ushers' meeting with all the new ushers of the church. I went just as innocently as I could, and while they were there they said, "By the way, preacher, I think these men would like to know what your attitude would be if a Negro should come to church, what we should do." So I got up that night and said I have been asked what I would like for you to do—I would just simply like for you to seat them and let it go at that. They would be coming for one of two reasons: they would be coming to test us or they would be coming to worship. Either way it is our responsibility to let them in. No questions about it. And so there were a few rumbles. A couple of men said something, but there were forty men and I felt like a couple of rumbles out of forty was all right. Well, the next week everything began to break loose. Suddenly there was a need for a deacons' meeting to be called. The deacons wanted to know what I said at the ushers' meeting. So we had a deacons' meeting, and I once again said exactly what I had previously said. I would like for them to seat those who came without question. Well, once again there were a couple of rumbles, but the great host of men said, "Do it, but just don't talk about it; just don't say anything about it to the church." Once again they had their tongue in their cheek, because they were giving approval to what I was requesting based on the fact that this was a situation that they were praying would never come to pass.

However, within a matter of weeks it did come to pass. I was told one night after a service that some Negroes who had come to worship in our service had been turned away. It didn't sit well with me. It bothered me a lot, and now we needed another deacons' meeting. We had another deacons' meeting. This time we got down to a little bit clearer position. They said, "The ones who are coming are coming to test us. They are coming for ulterior motives." I said, "How do you know?" They said, "Well, we just know those are the only ones who would come to our church." I said, "All right, let me find out." So we came to a decision that night by a sizable vote that any other Negro should come to our church would be seated and then immediately after the service he be brought to me and let me talk with him. Well, about a week later, Sunday morning I was getting ready to preach. I was in my study, and it was about three minutes until eleven, and a knock on the door, and there stood a man who had been chairman of the deacons, one of the finest men I have ever met in my life, who I loved with all of my heart. He was standing there, and there was a Negro man with him. He said, "Now, preacher, this gentleman came this morning and we didn't see him, and he went inside and sat down and we did just what you told us to do. We went down and got him and told him that you wanted to talk to him. So here he is and you probably want to get his name and address before you send him on his way." Then the deacon left and there I was. Well, it was about a minute and half until the service started, and our eleven o'clock service is on television, so I didn't have a lot of time to waste. I asked the gentleman his name, and I said, "Do you honestly want to worship with us this morning?" He said, "I surely do"; and I said, "Well, let me ask you this. Are you a part of organized group in town?" "No." I said, "Well, now it doesn't really make any difference to me because I am going to take you with me in the door I go in, but it would help me not to look so naïve if I could at least know who you are." "No, I'm just passing through town," he answered. So I said, "Let's go," and I went down to a door very near where I went in and I opened the door and saw a deacon there at the front. I knew exactly what his reaction would be. I went out and I introduced him to this particular gentleman and seated him and continued with the service. Well, that didn't sit well at all, and the thing that multiplied or compounded the problem was that the very next night there was a forced entrance on the state theater, which is right exactly across the street from our church. One hundred and fifty Negroes tried to force their way in so that they could be arrested, and the man who led the group who was the vice president of CORE at the time was the man I had put in the service on Sunday morning, which made it appear that either I was awfully, awfully naïve or that I was in cahoots. Either way it went I was in a situation, but at least this brought us to the position where I was going to have an opportunity to let my church respond in a way I knew it would respond, because immediately a couple of our men I heard had gone to a judge and they were going to sue the church, bring a restraining order against the church that no Negro could enter until the church approved the unwritten policy that it had, because it had a policy even though it was unwritten. Well, I didn't believe that the unwritten policy would hold up. I didn't believe there was anything to it, and I didn't believe really that the majority of our people would go along with it. So we had a Wednesday night meeting, a regular business meeting, to give our people an opportunity to affirm or deny the fact that the church had an unwritten policy. I don't recall what it was, but by a vote of about nine hundred to twenty they heartily approved the fact that the church did have a policy, although it was unwritten, and that they wanted to retain it at that particular time while further study was made on the subject.

But at any rate, after that service on Wednesday night, I no longer had the ideal picture of my church in mind. Although I loved the people and I love them now with all my heart, I realized that I was pastor of a church that was almost 98 percent segregationist in spirit. So I could do but one thing and that was to go back to my knees and pray that the opening would come whereby we could meet this thing on an upper level because the only thing that our people would say, they didn't even want to talk about the Negro, they just wanted to talk about pressure groups, people who with no genuine purpose at all were trying to force their way into our church and that it was un-Christian what they were trying to do and we were not obligated to respond. I couldn't believe that this was the real reason, but I didn't have any other reason that I could honestly stand on with the people because I hadn't known how they felt then.

The church had had an age-old practice there of having an international student day in November. Florida State University has almost 150 international students plus faculty members, and on a given day we always honored them. Every Sunday during the school year I have twenty-five or so people out there whose skins are all different colors. Many of them far darker than the ones that were of most concern to our people, so it wasn't skin pigment that was concerning our people directly. India was always represented in our services. Pakistan and Thailand were always represented in our services. Although the church would have an international student day, this particular year we preceded it with a party for the international students to be held at my home. Mrs. Oeita Bottorff planned the game party, an American party for them. We had about sixty-five or seventy to attend that night, and among all of the rest who came five came from Nigeria and South Africa. Tallahassee is also the home of Florida A&M, one of the finest Negro universities in the country. There are about 2,600 students there. These five particular ones from Nigeria and South Africa came from Florida A&M, but they were international students. They were here for a reason. One was the son of dignitary in his own country. One was the son of a product of Southern Baptist missions in Nigeria. That night we had a wonderful time, and at the end of the evening I invited all of those who were there to be sure and attend the international student day that we would have at our church in several weeks. As those weeks went by and word got around, several of my men began to come to me and say, "Now, preacher, don't embarrass us on this international student day. We can handle anybody from anywhere, any country on the face of the earth, but don't, don't bring anyone from Nigeria. Don't bring anyone from South Africa. We are going to be at the back door and we are going to check them in. Don't embarrass us by letting us have to turn away some of these international students."

Well, I realized now that it wasn't pressure groups, it was the fear of that dominant group that was at their door. You know, this was something that came home to me last year when I had an opportunity to travel with a group in Europe and the Middle East, Russia. *It is easy for everybody on the earth to love anyone except their neighbor.* Jews don't have any trouble loving Americans on the other side of the earth. They just can't love those Arabs right next to them. East Berliners received us heartily; they just didn't like the West Berliners. The Turks received us; they just didn't like those Arabs. All across the earth it is the same. People can love everyone but their neighbor. This was our problem. The fear of the dominant neighbor at the door.

Well, I didn't know exactly what to do. I prayed that God would give me some kind of evidence of what to do. Should I just go ahead and bring these international students in as we had done before? Then I thought, "No, this is a Baptist church." I was there that Wednesday night when we endorsed the policy of the church, and when Baptist churches take another move beyond that, they take it through democratic procedures, so it fell to my responsibility to contact the three who were still in town. Two had left the country. It fell to my responsibility to contract three from Nigeria and South Africa and indicate to them that our church on international student day could welcome anybody from anywhere on the face of the earth except their countries. I can't tell you what went on in my heart when I had to take this message to a person whose reason for being in America was because his father had been led to Christ by Southern Baptist mission efforts, but I told them that this was not a permanent thing, and as I told them that I prayed to God that I was telling the truth.

A couple of weeks after this had to be done ,the WMU invited me to be the speaker for missions week. The first Sunday night I spoke on "We Look at Missions," and on Monday night I spoke on "Missions Look at Us," and on that night I read Dr. Cauthen's statement about what is happening on our mission fields, and I related that which it had been my responsibility to do, which most people in our church did not know. I knew that the moment I was able to tell our people that we had turned away someone from Nigeria, someone whose father had been won to Christ through mission efforts,

100 percent of them were going to line up and say, "We can never afford to let this happen again. Doors must be wide open. We can never take this chance again." I began the process of preparing a recommendation. Christmas holidays were upon us. As soon as everyone returned from the Christmas holidays, I prepared a report, a recommendation, which I gave to our deacons outlining my own part on the matter, my own feeling of what I felt like a church had to do, must do. The deacons responded wonderfully. Thirty-one out of forty-eight endorsed the recommendation to open the doors of our church to all men irrespective of race, creed, color, but I found out something else that I didn't know about a Baptist church. I used to think that the deacons represented the cross section of the church. I used to think anything therefore that carried in the deacons' meeting might get some kind of rebuff on the church floor, but that it would always carry, that it would always proportionately probably go in the church floor as it had gone in the deacons' meeting. But this is not true in the South anymore, because when a lot of these men became deacons no one knew that we were going someday to be in a revolution and have our consciences seared. We have 4,500 members in our church, about 3,000 of them either right there in Tallahassee or right around within driving distance. Hundreds and hundreds of them I had never seen before in two years, but I was going to have an opportunity to see them. The time came on Wednesday night when [the] recommendation of the deacons was going to be taken to our church. Now we had a problem because when the little policy of our church was brought forth it wasn't written to stand the test of a group of lawyers tearing at each other. It was just meant to kind of help Christians who loved each other get along from week to week. So the policy of our church was that any recommendation that was not voted on Wednesday night had to carry by a majority vote in order to push it on to the following Sunday. Now there was no question in my mind what would and would not carry in our Sunday morning service, because you know you can always count on the fact that so many people would have the right attitude about a thing will remain passive in their attempts to exert themselves. A woman who says, "Oh, everybody knows exactly how I feel but I am not going to come and get in any row. Someone hands me a ballot quietly on a Sunday I'll quietly do what I think is right, but I'm not going to come up there in front of everybody and make a nut out of myself." Also we had a lot of college students, many, many college students. But as time came for Wednesday night service to come upon us, one church member began a calling campaign, calling every member of the church. Every resident member received a phone call from the

committee, and the call said, "Come and help us keep things like they have always been." That was all the call said. "Just come and vote as you please, but come and help us keep things like they have always been." This is the member who took up the December issue of the Royal Service and said that it could not be used because Dr. Cauthen mentioned race on the center pages in a special report. This is the member who would not allow prayer cards to be put on the tables that had been issued by our Convention WMU because on one of the days we were requested to pray for South Africa. And this would bring too much of an application to home.

So Wednesday night rolled around. Very seldom does the pastor have an opportunity to have a prayer meeting crowd quite like that, and as I say, I did not know that it was my people, there were so many whom I had never seen. Now you have to understand this. Please let me make this just as clear as I can. I am a pastor of a church, of a group of people, that I love with all my heart, and for the life of me to this very day I could not walk through their midst and divide the spiritually deep Christians from the shallow Christians on the basis of their attitude toward race. I could not do it. We have people who have given their life, their blood, their efforts, their heart, their soul, they have given everything in their own human frailty they know how to give in the name of Jesus Christ for years and year and years, but this matter of the Negro is one thing that represents a blind spot within their thinking, and they don't even know how to explain their feelings about so many of them.

I remember one man who said to me, "Preacher, it wasn't a question of whether I was right or wrong. This one issue represented the first time in my life when I didn't care if I was wrong because being wrong didn't matter. It was that I knew what I was and was not going to do, and I was not going to do a certain thing." So they are people who I love with all my heart. Those that identified themselves as being shallow, immensely shallow regarding this issue have also identified themselves as being shallow in other issues that have come along. But it is a great concern, and it helped me to see the magnitude of what I was up against, when not just a poor hypocritical Christian took a certain position, but when people whom to this day I admire and respect began to take a certain position. This helped me to realize how much growing needed to be done in the mind and hearts, how much fear needed to be dispelled, how much Christian application needed to be made.

Now that night, since the moderator himself was a very, very strong segregationist, we did not know how he was going to handle the meeting, and as we were walking into the auditorium he indicated to me that there would be four who would speak against the issue and four who would speak for it. No preparation had been made as such to speak for it because, you see, we didn't feel like we ought to be talking about the issue. As I said a moment ago, our church policy was that if there was something to be voted on of great dimensions, in order for it to be voted on Sunday morning the procedure had to be voted on Wednesday night. Now, for instance, our deacons had made two recommendations. Number one, they recommended that the doors of our church be opened, and number two, they recommended that this be voted on by our church on Sunday morning, by ballot vote. Now this is the way I was called to this church on Sunday morning, by ballot vote. This is the way we pass our budget on Sunday morning by vote. But you see these votes had never been tested, because basically the policy says that if it is tested the procedure has to be passed by majority on Wednesday night. Now this meant that if the church rejected the deacons, procedure on Wednesday night they in essence rejected the whole issue, and it would never even come to the church. So there was no way for us to get around what had to be done on Wednesday night. Now once again when parliamentary procedure was a little bit put aside because those who came to the platform to speak against the issue did not speak against the procedure, they spoke against the issue itself, although the vote that Wednesday night was against the procedure, but everything was in the balance. Through all of this I was trying to find the Christian ethic of my own. I was trying to find where a person could and could not stand. I was trying to find how far a person could go before he couldn't go any farther. I thought it might be helpful to you to hear some of the things that these [people] said who came to the platform that night speaking against this issue.

Now the first one, I'll just call him number one—I don't think there is any reason for calling their name, although these things were said in a spirit of honesty and love and I don't think there would be any great problem, but I don't think that is necessary. The first man is sixty-five years old. This man [who] came to the platform, with the exception of two churches, had been responsible in the last forty-five years either directly or indirectly as chairman of our missions committee for every other Baptist church in Tallahassee. He has a great missions heart. He came to the platform and mentioned the fact that he had been chairman of the missions committee for years and years, and then this was the pivot around which he put his thinking. He said, "This is a great church, not because of me, not because of you, not because of any of these others, but because of those who preceded us.

They had visions, they had courage. They had determination to see a great church grow in the city of Tallahassee. I was a member of this church when Baptists were looked down upon. We were laughed at but we have come to the place now where I am happy to say that Baptists are looked up to. We are looked on as people who are solid. We are trying to carry the Word of God to lost people, and I am going to vote against this proposal, not that I have anything against anybody. I think this church is making wonderful strides; let's don't do something that will stop it."

Then the next man who came, once again, is a man who was chairman of the deacons when I came, and I must say that I believe to this very day if he was called upon to do so he would lie down and die on my behalf. He is one of the dearest friends I have ever had on this earth. He and his wife and my wife and I along with some others are going to be taking a trip to Europe, I hope, next year. Here's his report. Just the crux of it. He said, "As I served on this race relations committee and counseled with several hundred people I became firmly convinced that the majority of the permanent members of this church do not want members of the Negro race admitted to the services of this church. The first fifty-four people that I counseled with, nine of those people told me flat that if you let the Negroes into this church me and my family are leaving this church. One of those men told me he had been a deacon in this church for twenty-nine years. Another told me he had been a member of this church for thirty years. He had raised his family, his children, had married in this church, but he was leaving the church. Another lady talked with me, a director of a Training Union department. She said to me she wouldn't stay in the church if we admitted Negroes and would leave the church. I'm telling you this because I want you to know that many of the oldest and finest families of our church intend to leave this church if Negroes are admitted. Then, as I served as chairman of ushers and greeters and stood on the front of this church on Sunday morning, I have had many mothers to call me and say they wanted to thank me for the small part I played in keeping the Negroes out of this church so their small children wouldn't have to associate with them. Then I stood on the front of the church, and I had old ladies of this church come by and put their arm around me and say, 'Thank you for not turning the Negroes in this church on me.' In my estimation if you vote to seat the Negro you are just asking for many more battles like we have tonight in our church. The next problem would be church membership, then joining the Sunday school, joining the Training Union, or some Negro lady will bring her baby and want to put the baby in the nursery, and then finally what are we going to do in the social activities of the church? Are we going to take them or are we not going to take them? Ladies and gentle-men, I don't think this church can stand to fight these battles over and over again. I know I can't. I have been in the middle of it, and I will fight this one and want to settle this issue for all, and I come to you tonight asking you to vote against this report that the deacons are bringing to you, and we can come to church Sunday and we can worship the Lord. Our pastor can bring us a good sermon, and we will have settled this issue once and for all. So let's settle it tonight by rejecting this report and the recommendation of our deacons."

The third speaker came and said, "I want to ask you a few questions and as I ask them I want to look for two answers. Can we help the Negro race? Can we help our church? If we would open these doors Sunday, could a Negro sitting there in the church worship, could he sit here better and wor-ship God than he could in his own church? Could his thoughts be of heav-enly things better here than in his own church? How about you sitting next to him and near him? Where will your thoughts be? How about you ladies? We are an outgoing church. We don't meet Sunday and quit normally. Can you ladies honestly, gladly welcome the Negro ladies into your home for prayer meeting, circle meeting? If you do, can your prayer meeting, your circle meeting be the same with them there as they would be if they were not there? I think not. Many times have you men called a friend, a member of your Sunday school class for a cup of coffee for lunch, and at this time you discussed the Sunday school or Training Union project or you discussed something that was coming up, a Sunday school party or something. Can you and will you do this same thing with a Negro member of your class? I think not. I ask you ladies again when your sons or daughters in Training Union want to have a party, can you have them bring in the Negroes? Can you welcome the Negro into your home like you would the others whether Sunday School, prayer meeting, circle meeting visiting a sick person, will you and can you let your wives and daughters go into colored sections of town at night alone to make these visits? I think not. If we cannot do these things as we have been doing with members of our own race or color, we are not operating as we have been. We are not operating as efficiently as we should and as I think God wants us to. If we cannot do these things as well with the Negro there as we can without him, I cannot see letting the Negro in our church is helping either him or our church. He cannot wor-ship here as good as he could in his own church. We have some very good colored churches, very good colored pastors in this town. These churches and people, they need their own members. They can do more good here.

They can win more Christians in their own church than they can in ours, and I can see where little can be gained by them coming to our church. The effectiveness of both our church and theirs is lost. I think if we can help both the colored people and our own selves this is God's will. I think we can only do this by keeping our doors closed to the Negro race because we cannot open them to public membership in our church, and I think we can only serve God best by remaining as we are. I ask you tonight please vote against, vote no on this proposal so that our church can stay together so we can financially, physically, spiritually grow together to obtain what God would have us do."

The fourth man came to the platform and said, "As your budget pledging chairman charged with the financial responsibility of raising $287,000 I oppose this action on economic grounds. Also I oppose the action as president of the Brotherhood of this church representing the men of this church. I oppose the change on the basis of history and on the basis of the desires and the will of the majority of this congregation and the will of God. Now how do you determine God's will in this issue when so many people have such different and diverse opinions? First, you look at the leadership of the church. Is the leadership united in this issue? The answer is that it is not. Many officers, many teachers are completely opposed on social grounds as I am, as well as on economic grounds. Secondly, taking a look at what other Christians say in the line of history, has God blessed this church? The answer is overwhelmingly yes, he has. Has God sent leadership to this church? The answer is yes, he has. Is the leadership of this church always correct? No, it is not. We are but men. We must then look at other circumstances. Look at the political crisis which is right at our doorstep. Look at the revolution going on with the Negro. Can we say God is in the midst of us? Not necessarily. It might be the devil. Is the situation that forces us to open the doors then to the church that had been blessed of God for one hundred years under a policy and procedure and practice where the church has grown from building, to building, has been prospering constantly, and then we say a social circumstance, not a moral, a social circumstance, causes us to change our view. I tell you this is not as I find it in the Word of God. As an officer of this church I urge you not to follow it. Next, economically, we have general agreement that we can raise a budget of $287,000; when the church is in turmoil—just the opposite. We have general agreement that it would be difficult. And in completing let me close by saying I urge you not to change the policy, and I urge you consistent with what I believe to be the practice of this church affirmed by God on the basis of past blessings."

The men who came to speak in behalf of this, I don't think I need to read their statements as closely as that, because I think you pretty well know the spirit in which they came. It wasn't so important what the first man who came up and spoke in behalf of the recommendation said; it was important who he was. City attorney of Tallahassee five years ago, he was the one who wrote the legal terminology to keep the Negro out of the church in Tallahassee. He is the man who told me that he didn't care whether he was right or wrong. Being wrong didn't make any difference. He is the man who came one night to the deacons' meeting five o'clock in the afternoon with his mind made up. He knew what he was going to do, but he made the mistake of praying and he said, "In a spiritual experience God turned me around and said, 'Don't you ever again in all your life hold the view you have been holding.'"

And incidentally, let me share this with you; I hope on Tuesday night at nine o'clock after the major service I hope you will make your way to the church auditorium, where four of our high school kids are going to present a play entitled "Onesimus." I have written this little play and our kids give it. I think the thing that really broke my heart most is that I found that our young people were just as prejudiced as they could be, because all they had ever heard about these things was what they heard over the coffee table at home. First time that we had a vote on this thing they voted against it, and the last time they voted they voted for it, but they weren't voting for it. They were voting for me. They still had all the prejudice down in their hearts, most of them, they just didn't have any direction, but these kids have come a long way. On their choir trip on the way out here the preacher on Sunday night preached on Christianity and race relations, and our kids gave this play afterwards, and it has done something for them. Now the reason I mention it is that after the gentleman that I am talking about had an experience with the Lord and realized how wrong he could be, he was brokenhearted because his own boy, his own boy had almost been lost to the Christian life in general. This particular attitude in his own life concerned him because his teenage boy had more prejudice than he did. Well, his boy plays Onesimus in this play, and I hope you will have an opportunity to see what he does. But he came and gave his testimony to the church.

When I first came to Tallahassee the next man who came made it clear to me that he didn't want this issue discussed anywhere at any time under any circumstances. Once again in one of those numberless deacons' meetings we had on this thing we came to a stop one night and said, "Let's all get on our knees and pray." This man got down on his knees and prayed, and this is the testimony he gave to the church that night. He said, "I got down on my knees and I said, I'm not afraid to pray about this thing. If the preacher thinks I'm afraid to pray he's crazy. I got down on my knees and I started praying but," he said, "I couldn't pray for thinking, because all of a sudden when I shut my eyes and bowed my head I saw myself sitting on the back row of our auditorium, and I turned around and I looked out there on the back steps, and I saw those five Negroes we had turned away from the church the week before, and all of a sudden I turned and I looked up there in the pulpit and the pastor was gone, and in his place was Jesus Christ and the thought ran through my mind, 'What is he going to do? Is he going to turn them away? Or is he going to let them in?'" He said, "Ladies and gentlemen, from that moment forward on my knees there will never again be a question what my response and attitude must be to this circumstance."

A couple of others came, and then we voted. At the end of the vote the proposal was 626 in favor of it, 640 against it, so it was rejected. We returned to our homes, and we were brokenhearted. We didn't know where to go, what to do. It seemed like the whole world had just come to an end in one brief night in the Baptist church. Interestingly enough because of our television people all over the town had been following it—the university, thousands upon thousands of Negroes had been following it via television. I suppose to be pastor of a segregated church I preach to more Negroes than any other pastor in the South. The next day the newspaper at Florida State University carried an editorial caption which read, "God Loses." The first sentence said, "God lost round one Wednesday night and it looks as if the fight is over, at least for the time being," and then a very appropriate story that is very interesting.

The next night a group of people met, a group of those people who wanted this so desperately they didn't realize how much they wanted it. They met on Thursday night thinking in terms of starting a new church. Well, this wasn't at cross currents with what I was thinking because I had been thinking in terms of getting out of there. I didn't know whether I was mad or sick or discouraged or disgusted or afraid or what, but I was some- thing, and I just didn't want to be around there, so that Thursday night, oh a fairly large number met, and the interesting thing is those who wanted this represented over half of our $310,000 total receipts, so when you talk about economic determination they had the economics on their side. They wanted to just move on out. A distinguished professor of the School of Education of Florida State said, "Now preacher, let's go. We can go right on out there to the university school, we can use that auditorium, we've got all of the classrooms we need, and we can just move the whole church staff right on out there; your salaries are the same; let's go. This church has got a $500,000 mortgage against it, and in six months they will be screaming for us to take it off their hands. Let's get out of here."

Well, I wanted to get out, but I didn't want to take that much with me. The more I thought about it, the longer I thought about it, I felt I had a right to leave, but I did not have a right to tear a church in two—especially, as I said a minute ago, it wasn't divided between the good guys and the bad guys. It was divided between people who were afraid, between people who don't understand, between people who haven't given themselves a chance to grow in this area just like they haven't given themselves a chance to grow in some other areas in the Christian life. I hadn't split the church when I found out that some of our leaders took social drinks. I didn't know whether I had a right to split the church when a large number of our people were afraid of this. I told them to pray about it. I said, "Let's don't do anything tonight. Let's pray about it and let's meet again on Saturday night."

In between Thursday night and Saturday night I had to find someone who could tell me what a Christian ethic was in regard to this, who could tell me a place where I could stand and be consistent with what I believed with all my heart. Through the process of these months I had become very close to several of the professors of Florida A&M. They followed us on television, they corresponded with me, they encouraged me, they did this and that and the other. One of them was named Dr. Neyland, professor of history at the Negro university. I called him Saturday morning and said, "Dr. Neyland, would you mind getting me together five or six men so that evening I could just sit down and talk with them. I don't want any of the ones who are a part of the organized effort. I would like as far as possible to get men who are removed from active participation. I would like to get some of your older, your wiser men. I would just like to talk." So he said he would, and at six o'clock that evening I took my assistant and we started out. I carry the names of these men; I shall always remember them. We started out, and we went out into an area of town, went to the home, walked in the door, and there were about six Negro gentlemen sitting around. I don't suppose any of them except Dr. Neyland were under sixty years of age. No, there is one other, Dr. Smith, head of the department of sociology. Every one of them were Ph.Ds. A couple of them had white hair. I walked in and we had coffee together, and they knew so much of what was going on, and yet I needed to fill them in on some of the personal things that had taken place here and there.

I said, "Now, gentlemen, the thing that I want to ask you is how can I now best help the cause of Christ, and what now can I do and should I do in relation to this defeat?" I'll never forget Dr. Anderson sitting on the piano bench. All you could see was the white of his eyes coming out at you. He straightened up and said, "Defeat? Victory! Victory! Why," he said, "son, I have been in Tallahassee for thirty years. I remember the day back there when the Baptist pastors of Tallahassee presented a written document telling how and why biblically God had created the Negro as inferior to the white." He said, "I never thought I would live to see the day when there would be a hundred people in this town who openly and publicly would admit they didn't mind associating with Negroes and," he said, "to think there are six hundred of them in the First Baptist Church of Tallahassee." Then another one immediately spoke up and said, "You mean, Dr. Roberts, you might leave? As long as we have waited for help?" He said, "Now I'll have to apologize, I'm not a man of the cloth. I don't know how God works." He said, "Now it seems to me that probably the way God works with ministers is by leading them to places of need and," he said, "we have a lot of need in Tallahassee. Now," he said, "I suppose the day will come when God will lead you away from here, and it seems to me, what little I know about it, that when that time comes he is going to point out a place somewhere else that has got so much more need that you must go, but to go from need to nothing just when we need you most, I just can't understand this."

Well, I left there that nigh,t and I tell you my heart was filled. I knew I was going to stick around, but I didn't know what good it was going to do. I didn't get home good until my phone started ringing. NBC, CBS, AP, UP were calling saying that they thought I needed to know that there was going to be a forced entrance at First Baptist in reaction the next morning to the vote Wednesday night. One hundred and fifty were going to come and try to force their way in. All major mass media had been alerted, and when they told me I thought to myself, "Well, I wish they wouldn't come, but I don't blame them." I couldn't sleep that night. I just sat up. About one o'clock in the morning I began to have knocks at the front door. I opened the door the first time, and a Negro man handed me a letter. It said, "Dear Rev. Roberts: This letter comes to express our appreciation for your efforts to bring into being a recognition of the worth of all individuals in the congregation of First Baptist Church. We wish to commend the deacon board which brought this recommendation to the membership, but most of all we want to commend those 626 members of the congregation who voted in favor of opening the services to all persons. We believe this perhaps to be the greatest expression of Christian conscience ever displayed in this section of the state. Prior to this vote we had planned a mass demonstration at First Baptist Church in the morning. Because of the encouraging nature of events we decided to postpone the demonstration and await the changing atmosphere which will render unnecessary further demonstrations at First Baptist. With best wishes for greater success and in Christian brotherhood, we remain, sincerely yours." This came from the CORE organization.

About thirty minutes later another knock, and there was another Negro who came from the NAACP. About thirty minutes later there was another knock, and there was another letter saying about the same thing from the Florida State Teachers Association. Soon it was evident that the Negroes were not going to come the next morning because they wanted to help and not hurt.

You know it is a strange thing where I found the Christian ethic. I didn't find it in a seminary; I didn't find it in the extreme efforts of segregationists; I didn't find it in suggestions of those who were favoring the opposite view; but I found it in the Negro himself. I found it sitting there in a room that night with a group of men loved of God and who love God with all their hearts, men who all the time they have been on this earth have never known anything but failure. This was my first defeat. They had never known anything but defeat, but the only thing that kept them going was the fact that each failure had been a little less severe than the one before, and most of all they had a tremendous love for God and Christian patience. Therefore my Christian ethic is this: I am a human being and because I am a human being I am subject to human feelings. Three times a week I have two black arms in my kitchen, and I like them there. Once a week I have black arms mowing my yard, and I like them there. I don't want one of my three daughters to marry a Negro. I like to be with people of certain interests because I am a human being and these are my feelings, but I am also a Christian and my Bible tells me that when two men have the same Father they are brothers. My Bible tells me furthermore that I am to love my neighbor not according to my wants or to my likes, but I am to love my neighbor as I love myself, and therefore my problem, a question that I ask my heart, is not what I want or what I like, but under God, what is right.

What is the next step? Well, the next step was taken about six o'clock in the morning, Thursday morning, after we had the vote on Wednesday night. The wife of one of those four men who spoke against the proposal, herself when she stood up, she stood up and voted against it, and yet like so many others that I saw that night she voted against it with tears streaming down her cheeks. Early before sunrise the following morning she wrote a letter. She said, "For a long time before you came to my church I prayed that God would send a man that was interested in first of all the souls of people. I believe you are. To me this means that if you cannot constantly visit the sick physically, I believe you are spending your time helping those who are spiritually sick, and this is what Christ said we should do, and it means I would have thought less of you as a Christian if you had not taken the stand you took last night on letting those of other races worship with us. Not because I expect my pastor to be perfect, but because I appreciate your standing for what you feel God through his Holy Spirit is leading you for Christ's sake to do. This says to me no matter what others may say or do or think or feel that you are putting souls first. Thank God for that."

One of the other four men who spoke against it is to be chairman of the deacons this year in Tallahassee, because I asked for it. I asked him and knew his attitude, but I asked for him so I could have the privilege this next year of every week getting on my knees with him praying with him as he and I together try to find the difference between what we want and what is right.

1965

1965

§46 Clarence Jordan

Clarence Leonard Jordan (pronounced Jur-dan) was born on July 12, 1912, in Talbotton, Georgia. The seventh of ten children and raised in a progressive Southern Baptist home, as a young boy Jordan remembered awakening to the moans of a black prisoner being tortured in a nearby camp by a white warden; earlier that evening the warden had been present with Jordan at a religious revival. "This started a great conflict in me," recalled Jordan. "I was bitter against God." At the University of Georgia, where he studied agriculture, Jordan was active in the Baptist Student Union, which exposed him to the denomination's liberal tradition. Jordan later dropped out of the campus ROTC officers program and became a committed pacifist involved in the Fellowship of Reconciliation (FOR). Jesus' Sermon on the Mount convinced him that one's enemies must be loved and forgiven, not slaughtered. After graduating from Georgia, Jordan headed north to the Southern Baptist Theological Seminary in Louisville, where he earned both an M.A. and a Ph.D. As part of a scholarship, Jordan taught part-time at historically black Simmons College in Louisville, an experience that forced him to confront the problems of black educational achievement. Jordan angered many of his white Baptist friends and colleagues when he broke bread with local blacks; social equality was simply beyond the pale for many. Jordan married Florence in 1936, and the couple would have four children.

Jordan's life took a fairly dramatic turn in 1941 when he met Baptist missionary and professor Martin England. After extensive conversation and planning, the two committed to the idea of creating an interracial farming cooperative that would emphasize agricultural education and local missions. If rural southern blacks could be trained in better agricultural methods, their lives would improve accordingly. But this cooperative experiment was also infused with the first century church's ideal of communal living, in which material possessions were shared in common. Such a living arrangement could function as God's Kingdom in the here and now—not the bye and bye. In November 1942, Jordan and England purchased 440 acres in Sumter County, Georgia, just outside of Americus. They named their community Koinonia, Greek for fellowship. Perhaps not surprisingly, such a radical experiment in interracial cooperative living in the heart of the Jim Crow South was met with hostility—but not until the mid-1950s, when massive resistance followed in the wake of the *Brown* decision. Koinonia was the target of frequent gunfire, bombings, and arson, especially in 1956, when word got around Americus that Jordan was helping two black students integrate his alma mater. Later, in the early 1960s, when the Student Nonviolent Coordinating Committee attempted to organize in Albany and Americus, Koinonia Farm served as a safe haven for movement activists. Jordan's life was cut short on October 29, 1969, when he suffered a massive heart attack and died at the age of fifty-seven. At his request he was buried in an unmarked grave on the Koinonia grounds. His papers are housed at the University of Georgia. To the present day Koinonia maintains an active and profitable presence in southwestern Georgia.

As a scholar of New Testament Greek, Jordan uses the fifth chapter of the Gospel of Matthew—the famous Sermon on the Mount—as his text before an audience of Mennonite college students. Translated into a distinctly southern vernacular, one for which he would become posthumously famous, Jordan outlines what it truly means to love each other as oneself. It is a love that transcends race and nation to include all of humanity. It is also a love that on Jordan's reading does not seek a motive beyond itself. Instead of using love as a tactic or a strategy, love is but a quiet willingness to reconcile even with an obstreperous fool, as he illustrates with an extended story with a local bigot. In making the claim that Christ does not advocate for putting on demonstrations, however nonviolent and infused with love, Jordan makes an implicit critique of the civil rights movement's dominant rhetorical strategy: to confront hate with nonviolent resistance.

৩৵

Loving Our Enemies
February 8, 1965
Goshen, Indiana

I am particularly grateful for this privilege of being with you, for as we get older, we become more appreciative of contacts with younger people. Someone has said that if you wish to stay young, you should go around with younger people. One might observe also if you wish to die young you may try to keep up with them. It's even getting hard this day in time to keep up with old folks. I heard the story a while back of a girl who came home for spring holidays, and she was anxious to renew fellowship with the community about, and she was out rather late one night and came in thinking she would not disturb her mother, and she almost made it to her bedroom when she stumbled over a chair and woke her mother up. Her mother said, "Is that you, Martie?" "Yes, Mother." "What time is it?" She says, "It's . . . uh . . . uh . . . it's plenty after 12." She said, "Did you lock the door when you came in?" She said, "Yes, Mother, I locked the door." She said, "Well, Martie, go back down and unlock it. Your grandmother hasn't come in yet."

As the basis for our thought this morning, I should like to read a passage from the fifth chapter of Matthew. Now, I shall be translating throughout the week from the Greek Testament, and my translation might not always coincide exactly with the version you may be familiar with. So, please give to me the freedom to translate, bearing in mind that our Lord did not speak King James' English. He spoke Greek. So I shall translate it from the Greek, and maybe you might want to even hear a word or two of the Greek in the words of Jesus himself as he actually said it. Now, it may have a little southern accent, I don't know, but this is the way it begins off in the Greek:

Well, that's enough of that. I'll translate it: "You have heard that it has been said to the old-timers, 'Take an eye for an eye and a tooth for a tooth.' But I want to tell you all never to resist evil with evil. But whoever slaps you on your right cheek, turn to him the other. (I have found it even better if somebody slaps you on the right cheek to turn to him both heels.) And whoever wants to go to court with you and take away your shirt, let him have your undershirt. And whoever makes you go a mile, go with him two. Give to anybody who asks, and don't turn your back on the guy who wants to borrow from you. You have all heard that it was said you should love your neighbor and hate your enemy. But I want to tell you love your enemies, and pray for those who try to do you in, so that you might be sons of your spiritual Father. For he makes his sun to rise upon the wicked and the good, and he lets his rain fall upon the righteous and the unrighteous. For if you love only those who love you, what's your advantage? Don't even beatniks do that? And if you greet only your brothers, what is your distinctive? Don't even uncommitted people do as much? Now *you*, you people must be mature just as your spiritual Father is mature."

Beyond all doubt, man's most vexing problem, from prehistoric time to the present, has not been how to pass a final examination. His most vexing problem has not been how to get a degree, a high-salary job, to marry a beautiful girl, and get a slick car, and live in a swank house in the suburbs. These problems are but trivia in comparison to the problem of learning how to respond maturely to those who oppose us. We have learned how to respond to our friends, but to our enemies—ah, that is the problem. How can we be mature? How can we make a grown-up response to people who want to do us in? To hound us, to beat us, to persecute us? We would expect our Lord to be quite clear in his teachings on the subject, and he was. He begins by going deep back into history and digging up various responses that men have made, and I think all of us will respond in one of four ways with which our Lord dealt. One is the method of unlimited retaliation. Somebody knocks out your eye, you knock them both out. Somebody knocks out your tooth, knock them all out if you can get to him. If somebody kills your dog, you kill his cow. If he kills your cow, you kill his mule. If he kills your mule, you kill him! No limit to the amount of retaliation. Unbridled anger. Unbridled vengeance. Now, mankind seems early to have outgrown this idea, but has lapsed back into it with the invention of the atom bomb. This seems to be the principle which dominates the State Department of most so-called civilized nations. You bomb us, we'll obliterate you. You bomb a little city, we'll annihilate a whole nation. Unlimited, massive retaliation. Now this was so childish, so barbaric, so beastly that it never occurred to our Lord that anyone within his hearing would ever resort to it. He just didn't know twentieth-century man. He picked it up there and said, "But now wait. If somebody knocks out your eye, don't knock both of his out. The old prophet said, Moses said, 'One eye for an eye. One tooth for a tooth.' If he knocks out your eye, don't knock them both out, just knock out one eye. If he knocks out your tooth, don't knock out all of his teeth, just knock out one tooth." This was the first effort at restraint on the strong. Now, he says, "Moses gave you that idea, but it is not enough. Let us move on up to another one. And so the old prophets came along and said, 'Love your neighbor, and hate your enemy.' This was the first glimmerings of limited love. If your neighbor knocks out your tooth, forgive him. But if he's a person of another race or another nation, give him the works." In other words, limit your love to your own little group, your own nation, your own race. This is the rule of limited love. The concept enables man to live together as nations, limiting their love to their own nation, but it does not enable them to live together as a world family. Now this seems to be the place that most of us really are today. We love America, and limit our love to the shores and the boundaries of the United States. I think most of us reflect the idea that's inscribed on an old tombstone in Mississippi. It says, "Here lies John Henry Simpson. In his lifetime he killed ninety-nine Indians, and lived in the blessed hope of making it one hundred, until he fell asleep in the arms of Jesus." Now, Indians don't count. Ninty-nine of them, you can live in "the blessed hope" of getting just one more and round it out in an even hundred, and still fall asleep in the arms of Jesus. But if you had killed just one white man, you'd fall asleep in a noose. You see, it's all right to kill Indians because we don't care about Indians, but you better not kill a white man. So, a nation can drop an atom bomb on brown people, yellow people, and annihilate two whole *cities* of people and we give him the Congressional Medal. If he kills one man in the United States, we give him the electric chair.

Love your neighbor, those of your own race, your own group. Down in Georgia, some kids working in the civil rights movement ran out of gas—it was an integrated group—and they were out in the country and two of the white ones decided they'd go for some gas. So they came to a farmer and asked him if he had some gas. "Yes, sure." And he got them out a gallon of gas and said, "Where's your car?" They said, "'bout a mile up the road." And he said, "Well, get in. I'll take you up there," and they said, "No, we . . . we'll walk." And he said, "Why no, it's too hot. I wouldn't think about letting you walk! Get in!" "No," they said, "Uh, we . . . we'd just rather walk. We need the exercise." "Well," he said, "no, it's too hot. Come on. Get in. I'll take you up there." So very reluctantly, the two white kids got in with this white farmer, and they drove along and drove along and finally, he said, "Where's your car?" They said, "There it is, right over there." So, they stopped and got out and the farmer realized it was some of those integrationists. And he became infuriated! He grabbed his can, put it back in the car, and drove off in a huff. If they had been all white, he would have been a fine southern gentleman, a deacon in the Baptist church, asleep in the arms of Jesus. But now he's dealing with people of a different race, and he can't love *those* people.

Jesus said it is not enough to limit your love to your own nation, to your own race, to your own group. You must respond with love even to those outside of it, respond with love to those who hate you. This concept enables man to live together not as nations, but as the human race. We are not at the stage of history where we will either take this step or perish. For we have learned with consummate skill to destroy mankind. We have learned how to efficiently annihilate the human race. But, somehow or another, we shrink with horror from the prospects not of annihilation but of reconciliation. We will either be reconciled, we shall either love one another, or we shall perish.

Now, Jesus did not advocate nonviolence. He was not advocating passive resistance. He does not say, "If your enemy slaps you on your right check, put on a demonstration protesting your rights to preserve at least the rouge on that particular cheek." He is not commanding us to demand our rights. The only right love has is the right to give itself. Now, this, at times, may be passive. That is, you may do nothing to a man who opposes you. I was at the Sumter County livestock sale sometime back buying some calves that we needed at the farm, and I bought them and was just about getting ready to leave when the town's arch-segregationist came in. Well, I didn't want to have a consultation with him at that moment, and I kind of shrunk down behind everybody else and looked for a mouse-hole but couldn't find one, and finally he came in and looked all around and saw me. He came over and stood about two or three feet in front of me and yelled at the top of his voice—even above the noise of the auctioneer—"[Here's] that ole Jordan fella here, folks: We ain't killed him yet but we can kill 'im now. We got 'im here by himself!" Well, I started looking for even a knothole to get through at that time. I couldn't find one. And then he looked at me and he raised his voice again, he said, "You ain't nothin' but a . . . a . . ." he said. "You ain't nothing but a . . ." Well, he made a positive statement. He made a positive statement that on my mama's side, I had some canine ancestry, let's put it that way. Now, down where I come from, when somebody attributes to you that kind of pedigree, you're supposed to respond. And I felt my fist getting into position to respond. About that time, he used God's name and called me that kind of a . . . named me that kind of pedigree. And then he took a little deeper breath and called me something else, and I noticed that, while he didn't have any teeth, he did have tonsils, and I thought that this would be a nice time to perform a public tonsillectomy. But somehow, God gave me the power to restrain myself, and the little fellow kept on calling me increasingly long names. I didn't know there were that many species around until he called me those. Well, he finally gave up and went outside, and there was a good big old two-hundred-pound farmer sitting next to me, and I noticed every time this fellow would call me by one of those names, this farmer would kind of do like that; and this big old farmer moved over next to me. He said, "You know what?" And I thought he was getting ready to take up where this little fellow had just left off. I said, "What?" He said, "I wanta know how come you didn't hit that little fella?" He said, "You coulda beat the . . . you could . . . you coulda . . . you coulda really whooped him with one arm tied behind your back." I said, "I think that is a correct appraisal of the situation." He said, "Well, how come you didn't hit him?" I said, "My friend, there are two reasons why I didn't hit him. One's purely selfish. If I'd a hit that little segregationist, everybody in this sale barn woulda jumped on me and *mopped up* the floor with me. And I just don't want my wife married to a mop. That's one reason I didn't hit him. But the real reason was I'm tryin' to be a follower of Jesus Christ and he has taught me to love my enemies." I said, "Now, while I must confess, I had the minimum amount of love for this little fellow at the time, at least I did him no harm." And this old fellow said, "Is *that* what it means to be a Christian?" I said, "Friend, that isn't all that it means, but that's a part of it." We sat for awhile talking about being a Christian.

So I might say that it is not enough to just merely not harm your enemies. Somehow or another, we must go beyond that. Love is not merely a weapon. It is not a strategy, and it may or may not work. To do good to those who hate you is such a stupendous folly it can't be expected to work. Love didn't work for Jesus. No man has ever loved as he loved, but it didn't work. He wound up on a cross. And yet it *does* work if your motive is *not* to make it work. Love works in the home. But if you say, "Well, you know it really works to love your wife. If you love her, she'll darn your socks and bake you pie every day." If that is the motive for love, I doubt that your wife will darn your socks or bake you pies. But love does work. I think Abraham Lincoln said it so well one day, old Thaddeus Stevens, a very bitter man from Massachusetts who was in the cabinet—after the war was over, there was much sentiment in the North to just crush the South. Thaddeus Stevens shared this. One day, when Mr. Lincoln was advocating binding up the wounds of the nation, forgiveness, reconciliation, old Thaddeus Stevens pounded the table and said, "Mr. Lincoln! I think enemies ought to be destroyed!" Mr. Lincoln quietly said, "Mr. Stevens, do not I destroy my enemies when I make him my friend?"

In the long run, it is the only way that really does work. For when the cards are all in, and the final chapter of history is written, when time is rolled up as a garment, and God is all and in all—in that final day, it will be the peacemakers, not the warriors, who will be called the sons of God.

§47 Ralph J. Bunche

Dr. Ralph Johnson Bunche was born on August 7, 1903, in Detroit, Michigan. His father, Fred Bunche, was a barber and his mother, Olive (née Johnson) Bunche, was an amateur musician. Olive died in New Mexico from complications related to tuberculosis when Bunche was thirteen. Not long thereafter Fred Bunche remarried, and the child never saw his father again. Bunche's maternal grandmother, Lucy "Nana" Johnson, who had been born into slavery, took him and his two sisters to live in Los Angeles. There Bunche sold newspapers, worked for a carpet-laying firm, did odd jobs, and flourished under the watchful eye of his grandmother. His academic prowess and public speaking ability were evident at a young age. Bunche was the valedictorian of his class at Jefferson High School, where he also debated and competed in football, basketball, baseball, and track. At UCLA he earned an athletic scholarship, worked a janitorial job, played on championship varsity basketball teams, and was active in debate and campus journalism. Bunche graduated summa cum laude and valedictorian of the class of 1927, majoring in international relations. He earned a master's degree in political science from Harvard in 1928. For the next six years, he alternated between teaching at Howard University and working toward a doctorate at Harvard. Bunche married Ruth Ethel Harris in 1930; their union would produce three children. He completed his dissertation on the decolonization in Africa in 1934. Bunche wrote *A World View of Race* in 1936, and he also participated directly in the Carnegie Corporation's well-known survey of the Negro in America, under the direction of the Swedish sociologist Gunnar Myrdal, which resulted in the 1944 publication of Myrdal's seminal book *An American Dilemma*. During research for that book, specifically queries related to interracial sex, Bunche and Myrdal barely escaped an Alabama lynch mob. Bunche worked tirelessly for the federal government and the United Nations. An adviser to the Department of State and to the military on Africa and colonial areas of strategic military importance during World War II, Bunche moved from his first position as an analyst in the Office of Strategic Services to the desk of acting chief of the Division of Dependent Area Affairs in the State Department. From 1947 to 1949 Bunche worked on the confrontation between Arabs and Jews in Palestine as principal secretary of the UN Palestine Commission. On September 17, 1948, Bunche was named acting UN mediator on Palestine. After eleven months of virtually ceaseless negotiating, he secured an armistice between Israel and several Arab countries—an achievement for which he won the NAACP's Spingarn Medal and the 1950 Nobel Peace Prize. Bunche also worked closely with former first lady Eleanor Roosevelt in drafting the UN's Declaration of Human Rights. Bunche would go on to receive more than forty honorary degrees; he also won the Medal of Freedom and the Presidential Medal of Honor. One of the most accomplished men of the twentieth century, Bunche resigned as UN undersecretary-general on October 1, 1971, due to heart disease and diabetes. He died on December 9, 1971. His papers are housed at UCLA, the United Nations, and the Schomburg Center of the New York Public Library.

At the personal invitation of Dr. Martin Luther King Jr., Bunche participated in the historic Selma-to-Montgomery march and spoke at its conclusion on the steps of the state capitol. With momentum from the death of Jimmy Lee Jackson, to its culmination in the Voting Rights Act of 1965, the Selma campaign riveted the nation's attention. Following the televised brutal beatings of "Bloody Sunday," March 7, and the beating, and eventual death, of Rev. James Reeb, activists walked the fifty miles to Montgomery over several days. That the nation's highest-ranking black diplomat spoke at its culmination speaks directly to the march's importance. Not surprisingly, Bunche's brief remarks, while addressed directly to Alabama's governor George Wallace, seek to frame the march in broader terms. This was not an Alabama problem nor even a regional one stoked by "outside agitators"; rather it was "an all-American attack on an all-American problem." While Bunche praises King by name, no doubt leaders of the Student Nonviolent Coordinating Committee (SNCC) chafed at their omission; after all, SNCC's Bernard and Colia Lafayette began organizing Selma in the spring of 1963, long before King and his Southern Christian Leadership Conference got involved. Just hours after Bunche's remarks, Detroit housewife and mother of five Viola Liuzzo was gunned down on Route 80 as she transported civil rights workers between Selma and Montgomery. One of the Klansmen involved in the murder, Gary Thomas Rowe, was a paid FBI informant.

❦

The March on Montgomery
March 25, 1965
Montgomery, Alabama

By God, we are here: little more need be said.

No words could be as eloquent as this magnificent, historic march, which has been made possible by the superlative leadership of Dr. King and his associates.

This morning as we walked together, I said to Dr. King that this must be your greatest triumph in the sense of all the obstacles that had to be overcome; and he agreed that it was.

Incidentally, I have discovered in the course of this march that in addition to being a great leader, Dr. King is quite a walker. In fact he walked with such ease, in a gliding sneaky sort of stride, that I began to wonder whether he was not getting a little help from the Lord. The Lord was certainly not helping my aching legs.

Governor Wallace and some others denounce many of us who are not Alabamians of being "outsiders" and "meddlers," and that includes me.

I stoutly deny this.

I am here as an American; an American with a conscience, a sense of justice, and a deep concern for all of the people and problems of the country. I am here to identify with the just cause of the right of Alabama Negroes to vote as our president himself has said every good American should.

I say to Governor Wallace that no American can ever be an "outsider" anywhere in this country. And, Governor, all these people out here, who have come in a great phalanx, are very great Americans, black and white, the greatest, for they seek to bring unity and maximum strength to this country to the end that it may become, as it can become, white and black together, the greatest society not only of contemporary times but in the entire history of mankind. And lest the governor has forgotten it, Alabama lost its attempt to leave this Union more than a century ago. Apparently, he has forgotten it, for I see the Confederate flag flying up there over the dome of the capitol. I have never spoken before under the shadow of that flag, and I must say that it makes me feel uneasy, even a bit treacherous to do so. That flag should have come down over a century ago.

If Governor Wallace or anyone else doubted that two southern causes have been forever lost—the cause of the Confederacy and the inhuman, un-American attempt to keep Negro citizens suppressed and oppressed—all doubts had to be dissipated when we marched through Confederate Square, not long ago, singing "We Shall Overcome."

What we are doing here is an all-American attack on an all-American problem.

In the UN we have known from the beginning that secure foundations for peace in the world can be built only upon the principles and practices of equal rights and status for all peoples, respect and dignity for all men.

The world, I can assure you, is overwhelmingly with us.

I am sorry that it was necessary for protection to be given to the march by federalizing the Alabama National Guard. But the fact that the government did so was an indication of the firm determination of our government to protect the human rights of all its citizens.

But I have a word of advice for our government if there is a next time: be sure that the federalized troops are not wearing Confederate flags on their jackets.

There's a great old song saying, "There'll be some changes made." Well, our presence here today testifies that some changes have been made in Alabama, and a whole lot more are going to be made and very quickly.

I earnestly salute every one of you for expressing by your presence here the finest in the American tradition; you are in truth the modern-day "minutemen" of the American national conscience. You have written a great new chapter in the heroic history of American freedom.

§48 Stanley Yedwab

Rabbi Stanley Yedwab was born on October 4, 1930, in Brooklyn, New York, to immigrant parents from Poland and Russia. Though his parents were not devout practitioners of their religion, young Stanley eagerly used the occasion of his bar mitzvah to deliver a didactic lecture on Jewish ethics. His lecture was persuasive to the extent that local rabbi Ralph Silverstein invited the teenager to be a junior rabbi in his Brooklyn congregation—an invitation Yedwab eagerly accepted. The origins of his commitment to social justice began early, in the suburbs of New Jersey, when he and his younger brother were frequently harassed by local members of the American German Bund, a Nazi satellite organization in the United States. Yedwab attended Brooklyn College and majored in philosophy and Hebrew; later he matriculated at Hebrew Union College and graduated with an M.A. in Hebrew letters in 1954; simultaneously was he ordained as a rabbi.

The year prior he married Myra Kitowitz, and the couple would have two children. Yedwab headed south and west in 1957, to Lubbock, Texas, where he served a small synagogue as head rabbi. Two years later he came back east to lead Temple Beth Am Shalom in Lakewood, New Jersey; he would retire from this position thirty-eight years later. Yedwab's guiding philosophy came from the Hebrew phrase "tikkum olam," or repairing the world, which quickly became a hallmark of his ministry. With congregants he and his wife participated in the March on Washington. Two years later Yedwab simply had to be in Montgomery on March 25 to witness the culmination of the historic march from Selma. That same day he learned of the death of Viola Liuzzo, who was gunned down on the very road that led marchers to the capital. Rabbi Yedwab's activism extended in many directions: providing a safe haven for Russian Jews and Vietnamese exiles; administering an antipoverty program in Ocean County; and frequent interfaith and interracial religious services. Still spry and repairing his world, Yedwab lives in Seattle, Washington, and ministers occasionally to two congregations in Port Angeles and Walla Walla.

Before an interdenominational and interracial gathering in Lakewood, New Jersey, Rabbi Yedwab eulogizes only the latest martyr in the civil rights movement. Detroit housewife and mother of five Viola Liuzzo had come to Selma because of what she, and millions of others, had seen on March 7—the public beating and humiliation of innocent black marchers on their way to the Alabama state capitol in Montgomery. On March 25, civil rights marchers celebrated upon reaching their destination, and Liuzzo later ferried marchers back to Selma in her 1963 Oldsmobile. On her return trip, she was gunned down as she drove east on Highway 80. Four Klansmen were quickly arrested, one of whom, Gary Thomas Rowe, was an FBI informant. Quickly did the smear campaign against Liuzzo begin: what was a thirty-nine-year-old white mother of five doing in Selma? Why wasn't she protesting racial inequality back in Detroit? And perhaps most insidious, just what was she doing with a nineteen-year-old black man in her car that night? Yedwab does his rhetorical best to recontextualize Liuzzo's sacrifice: it was precisely because she had five children that she was in Selma; she had "five good reasons" for being there. Yedwab presciently notes that Liuzzo would indeed be remembered as helping the nation create a new freedom road; today the National Park Service commemorates much of Highway 80, and the site of Liuzzo's murder remains a poignant and sacred place on that road.

༺∽༻

Memorial Eulogy for Mrs. Viola Liuzzo
April 4, 1965
Mrs. Viola Liuzzo Memorial
Lakewood, New Jersey

I did not know Mrs. Viola Liuzzo. Neither did you, the citizens of Lakewood, know her. Yet I mourn her! You good people have gathered here to mourn her. Indeed America and the whole world have been brutally shocked by her death. Why are we so deeply moved? Why this memorial service to her memory?

Most of us have long recognized that prejudice and segregation are wrong. But *all* of us even in this fine city have grown accustomed to prejudice. We have, so to speak, learned to live with it. If we are Negro we learn to live on the bitter end of prejudice; if white, we learn to live with the callous end.

But suddenly we cannot escape the shocking realization that prejudice kills. No, I don't mean Mrs. Liuzzo alone. The bomb, the bullet, the night rider are not segregation's most dangerous weapons, only its most villainous. Segregation is a wall of indifference and hatred. It boxes people into a prison of prejudice and then it lets them sit and die a little bit at a time. Prejudice is a two-way sword—one side cuts down the hated, the other side mutilates the hater. I know Mrs. Viola Liuzzo will be remembered. For her death taught us how prejudice kills.

Why did she die? Why did she have to die?

It is a desolate road that stretches from Selma to Montgomery, Alabama. Highway 80 is made desolate not only by the swamps it traverses, but even more by the history it encompasses, the events that stand like milestones on its black surface. Blood has stained Route 80; most recently the blood of this brave woman whom we memorialize today. By now, a week after her death, the dark soil of Alabama has already absorbed her blood. But I say that the conscience of the South, the conscience of America will not so easily absorb the guilt of that black moment when mortally wounded by a rifle bullet, her car careened off the road of Highway 80. The significance of this highway is not that a death has occurred on it. Highway death is a commonplace. The significance of this highway is that it leads not only through space but through time.

Through all of its history, blood has stained Route 80. It stretches back into time as a wilderness trail on which the first Negro was hauled into slavery. It symbolized the years of backbreaking toil and aborted slave revolts that led to the Civil War. And then for the next hundred years it was a highway of prejudice, a road to segregated communities. It was here with the lash that the Negro was taught not to respect property but to be property. Not to seek education, but to fear a lashing for acquiring it. Not to know the joy of being the head of a family, but to stand helpless before the lash as his wife was used at the whim of a master, his children sold at the whim of the mistress. Even his religion was given to him not for the sake of his soul but that he might be made more passive in the face of tyranny. But with his creative genius, the Negro people have turned this faith into the greatest moral force in America today. Negroes are willing to face jail, cattle prods, tear gas, police dogs, armed with the belief in love, nonviolence, [and] brotherhood. These shall overcome. Mrs. Liuzzo shared in that faith.

But the tide on Route 80 is beginning to turn. In the words of Martin Luther King, we are on the move now! In that hectic and historic week, the black man and the white man together began to march. To march away from prejudice and hatred. Mrs. Viola Liuzzo was part of that march. The highway of prejudice has become a highway to freedom. The route that Mrs. Liuzzo treaded from Selma to Montgomery is not fifty miles long—it is three hundred years long. We are on the move now.

How terrible that even the road to freedom must be marked by indelible milestones of blood and tragedy. Mrs. Viola Liuzzo will be remembered, for her death is one of the first milestones on a new Route 80. The road to freedom! We did not want her to die, but her death is not in vain. The stupid, vindictive fury of prejudice is digging its own grave with her death.

My eulogy is almost over now. But there is one more thought that I must express because circumstance demands it.

The most famous of all eulogies delivered on the occasion of another assassination begins, "I have come to bury Caesar, not to praise him." On the contrary, I had planned originally only to praise, to honor Mrs. Viola Liuzzo, martyr of Montgomery. Instead I now find it necessary to defend her.

What was she doing there? I have been asked . . . a woman with five children? Why didn't she stay home where she belonged? What guilt must lie on the American conscience that there are some who turn bravery into a reproach. The victim has become the villain, thereby robbing villainy of its sting. Assassination [and] violence are complacently slurred over, and the bravery of a noble woman is considered the cause of her death. The good and the bad mingle, blur, [and] interchange and we live in the grayness of moral vacuum. Mrs. Viola Liuzzo did not want to live in such a world. Surely some of the men in the Boston Tea party had wives and children. History does not condemn them. Or consider the pioneer women who braved the frontier and opened up a new world, risking not only her own life but the lives of her children as well. History does not condemn the pioneer woman—it praises her. Need a pioneer travel in a covered wagon to be recognized as such?

A mother is responsible for her child's environment. Do we really believe that a child's environment begins at the front doorbell and ends at the barbeque pit in the backyard? To me, Mrs. Liuzzo's five children form five good reasons for her participating, five personal stakes in the future. Mrs. Liuzzo had five times the reason to be in Montgomery than any single man or woman. Mrs. Liuzzo felt that it was her duty as a mother to create the kind of world that she would want her children to grow up in. She owed it to her children not to let them be scared by the poisoned blade of prejudice. For her segregation had outlived its uselessness.

Mrs. Viola Liuzzo will be remembered, for her death has taught us our own duty. Here in our own city, our own country, we must learn not to live with segregation, we must throw off the shackles of indifference, the blindness of apathy. Mrs. Viola Liuzzo will be remembered. Our deeds will be her memorial.

§49 Daniel Germann

Daniel Victor Germann was born in Los Angeles on November 9, 1929, the third son of John and Irene Germann. After graduating from Loyola High School, he attended Loyola Marymount University and Los Angeles Junior Seminary before completing his undergraduate studies at Gonzaga University. From 1957 to 1960 he taught English and Latin at Loyola High School. From 1960 to 1964 he studied theology at Alma College in Los Gatos. He was ordained June 12, 1963, by Cardinal Timothy Manning at Blessed Sacrament Church. From 1964 to 1965 he taught theology at Loyola Marymount University. In 1970, Germann received the doctorate of sacred theology from the University of Louvain, writing a thesis on secularization and Vatican II. From 1970 to 2000, he served on the theology faculty at Santa Clara University. He died after a long struggle with Parkinson's disease on July 24, 2007.

In this sermon of June 20, 1965, to a congregation in Bogalusa, Louisiana, Germann addresses a congregation as an outsider from California in the contexts of Bishop Cody's efforts to carry out the integration plan designed by Archbishop Rummel, who had recently passed away after suffering a hard fall. Perhaps more importantly, just eighteen days prior, African American police officer Oneal Moore had been gunned down by white assailants less than a mile from his home. Three important issues stand out in this address. First, Germann addresses congregants with a familiarity and sensitivity that few people would be able to duplicate as a visitor from so far away. He identifies the underlying issue of integration as fear, manifest as suspicion, caution, avoiding others, and frozen inertia. He shares candidly that he experiences the same fear while visiting parishioners he does not know in a setting that is also unknown. Second, he gives people the benefit of the doubt as to their motives and responses. Paralysis due to a state of fear, he explains, is normal, though action is still required of us. Third, he points out that new behaviors are to be expected and have their own persuasive logic. Vatican II had just closed in December, introducing many new practices. Germann observes, "Saying mass this morning, we were saying it for the first time with the altar turned around, facing you," because it helps us worship as a family, face to face. The sermon ends with the exhortation that Christian communion, worship, and example have no place for fear. We are all required to give our lives.

❧❧

What Our Amen Means
June 20, 1965
Bogalusa, Louisiana

In the name of the Father, and the Son, and the Holy Spirit, amen. I think it is an opportune time to comment a little bit on the epistle of today's mass, the letter of Archbishop Cody, and on the devotion of the Sacred Heart. Perhaps I'd better introduce myself, since my face is new, I think, for most of you here in Bogalusa. My name is Father Germann, and I come from way off on the West Coast, Los Angeles. As my accent obviously betrays, I'm not from this beautiful South.

Devotion to the Sacred Heart, as the archbishop has explained to us in this letter, developed in the church to meet a very real need of its time, and this need is a need that we now feel, I think, in a new way. When devotion to the Sacred Heart was introduced, the problem was this: people were afraid of God. Strange as it may seem, they had seen God as a God of hate.

A God to be feared, an angry God; someone before whom you bowed low, but not someone you responded to from love. People were afraid to receive Holy Communion, afraid to even look at the host in which Jesus Christ is present. So in response to this, this devotion developed, in which the visible love of God, Jesus Christ, is recalled to all of us, especially as one who loves us, and thus, the symbol of the heart. This is the idea of this devotion; it recalls that God is love and that Christ is love made visible. The response to such love is to love God and to love others back.

Nowadays, I think, this problem is with us again, but with a little different approach. It seems to me that nowadays the problem is not so much fear of God, but what I keep running into is fear of one another. This, too, is a very un-Christian thing. We have been told that our response to Christ's love is to love God and to love one another, so that if we fear God or are afraid of one another, there's something wrong with this kind of love: we aren't responding to Christ as we should.

Somehow [we have] become identified with this vast community, here in the United States, who is afraid to frequently get to know one another or talk to one another. Students I teach in Los Angeles are afraid to open up and talk to one another, or even communicate with one another. Instead of hearing what people in the early Church said—"Look at these Christians, how they love one another"—it seems that now we hear, "Look at these Christians, how they are afraid of each other."

In talking about fear, I want to stretch this out a little bit if I can, because there are a lot of ways that fear is expressed. If I am afraid of someone, I am suspicious of that person. I am cautious about what I do. I am afraid to step out, for fear of what that person will think about me, say about me, or do to me. I refuse to sit down and talk to people whom I fear or don't know. I imagine all sorts of things about people whom I fear, or do not know. I become frozen, actually into inaction. You've seen someone, you're all familiar with the expression: to be paralyzed in fear. And this is what I think, in varying degrees, is happening. Sometimes, among us Catholics here in the United States, we literally get paralyzed, afraid to act, afraid to do what we know is right, afraid to love because we are caught up in fear. Sometimes this takes on extremes, and the extreme of fear, which was disguised in this morning's epistle, is hate; likewise, a very un-Christian thing, as explained by John, when he says any who hates his brother is a murderer. As you know, no murderer has eternal life abiding within him. He makes it quite clear, and yet we run into this hate.

On the West Coast we run into a strange thing, in which we find Catholics joining such organizations as the John Birch Society with their hates, suspicions, and un-Christian-like attitudes. Here in the South, I've been told that there are some Catholics who are even joining the Ku Klux Klan, a group not only opposed to Negroes, but opposed to and hates Catholics. This I find so puzzling. It seems so contrary to what Archbishop Cody, or to what Jesus Christ is talking about. It seems like we are substituting hate and fear for love and generosity and courage, and this puzzles me. Isn't it true that when we focus this kind of a reaction, that it comes out in many, many ways on the present problem that confronts all of us here in the U.S.—the problem of the relationship between the white and the Negro people? We run into this same problem, that we are afraid, afraid to act, so we confront the situation in terms of caution, fear, suspicion, that we are frozen and unable to step out and say what we think, to say what we really feel. I could say this, I think, of myself, standing up here in the pulpit right now. I would be described as an outsider, I suppose, to you, the citizens of Bogalusa. And so I feel afraid, because I feel I don't know you. And so, I feel that if I talk about civil rights, or if I talk about the Negro people who desperately need the support of their white brothers in Christ, that I would feel afraid of this. Someone may be angry with me, or someone may want to hurt me, or want to say bad things to Father Bordenave about me. And this is such a puzzling thing, because we are Christians, and we are apt to love each other and not to hate and to fear. But for some reason, this happens.

It's a heartening thing to come here and to hear of some of the good things that have been happening—for example, I have heard that despite the great tensions in the town that there is an effort to negotiate, to settle these problems as adults, as responsible people settle these problems. This is something I think we should all attempt to support and encourage.

I heard recently that the archbishop of the diocese went out of his way to visit the widow of Mr. Moore, the fellow who was shot, the deputy. I think that this is a very Christian thing to do; this is what Christ would do. He would visit the widow, He wouldn't ask the widow if she was a Catholic; he wouldn't ask the widow if she was white; he would just visit her. I admire Archbishop Cody very much for this act of love.

I find it heartening to realize that your church here in Bogalusa is integrated, and that Negroes, the pastor told us, are free to sit anywhere they wish. This is something that is good, something that those of us from the West Coast are so heartened to hear about, because you hear all these other stories about the South. This is a good thing, so we can hope that things will continue in this way of understanding and of love.

Soon the schools will be integrated, soon perhaps we will have Negro servers, and Negroes in the choir, so the whole things will be a family, as we are brothers and sisters in Christ.

I must also admit, I think, that coming to Bogalusa, I do experience a city that is somewhat gripped in fear, and this is why I feel strange to speak this way this morning. I have felt the suspicion, I have seen some of the segregation that still exists, I have been puzzled by some of the inaction. I was wondering if it was fear of losing one's job, fear of having someone yell at us, or of beating us up, or of killing us, or what. I don't understand it, and it seems so lacking, a family that falls apart when we don't love one another.

It's all very simple, really, when we listen to this epistle, when we listen to the letter of Archbishop Cody, or when we follow the devotion of the Sacred Heart. It's very simple because all we are saying is this: that Jesus Christ loves us, each of us. He loves us so much that he died for us. He was murdered for us, and he lives inside each one of us, and he says, "Love me back." And we say, "How do we love you back?" And he says, "By loving me and by loving others as I have loved you." The love that he showed for us was an unconditional love. It was a love without stopping; it was a love that said, "I will even lay down my life for my brothers." And this is all he's asking us to do, what he did. And he lives in us to give us the strength to do this. This is Christianity, whether this is expressed in a political, or social, or economic area. This is Christianity; it is always the same, whether this is expressed in a family, it is always expressed the same. God loves us, and we must love him back by loving others. We love him as he has loved us: totally.

Saying mass this morning, we were saying it for the first time with the altar turned around, facing you. The idea of this is so that we can pray together as a family, and worship: you uniting with me, the celebrant, all of us, brothers and sisters in Christ, no matter where we come from, or no matter what the color our skin happens to be. We are brothers united in one Body and one Blood, that of Jesus Christ. And, therefore, at the end of the eucharistic prayer, just before the Our Father, when all of us say, "Amen" together, what we are saying is yes, God the Father, we acknowledge that you have loved us. We acknowledge that everything we have is from you, and we say this "yes" in union with Jesus Christ, in union with one another, all of us as a family. This "yes" means that we will go out and bring this love to others, in very practical and specific ways.

Here in our city and when I move into other places where I will be going, each of us has this responsibility. This is what our "Amen" means. And then we stand and say the Our Father, as brothers and sisters praying to our one Father; then all of us together will receive Holy Communion. And when we receive the Body and Blood of Christ we are more closely united at this banquet in the one body of Christ, each of us again say "Amen," yes, to come to me, Jesus Christ, you who loves me, you who laid down your life for me. Fill me with your life, with your strength, with your courage, help me to love others as you have loved me. I find it difficult, Jesus Christ, to do this, but I am a member of your family and it is a family that is all being filled with your life, and your love, and your courage. Help us all to love one another. In the name of the Father and of the Son and of the Holy Spirit.

§50 Clifford J. Durr

Clifford Judkins Durr was born on March 2, 1899, to John Wesley Durr and Lucy Judkins Durr, a privileged white family in Montgomery, Alabama. His grandfather, John Wesley Durr, was a cotton factor, and his grandfather James Henry Judkins owned a plantation; both were captains in the Confederate Army. Durr was elected president of his class at the University of Alabama, where he graduated in 1919 after serving briefly in the military during World War I. That same year Durr won a Rhodes scholarship to Oxford University in England. He graduated in 1922 with a law degree.

After returning to the states, Durr joined a prominent law firm in Birmingham, Alabama, in 1924. A few years later, Durr found himself without a job when he objected to the firing of a secretary. In 1926 Durr married Birmingham's Virginia Heard Foster; the two of them would make one of the most powerful and committed civil liberties-civil rights duos in American history. Durr's new brother-in-law, Alabama senator and future Supreme Court Justice Hugo Black, asked him to come to Washington, D.C., to serve as legal counsel with the Reconstruction Finance Corporation (RFC), a key organization in President Roosevelt's plans for economic recovery. Durr served as a productive and innovative lawyer for the RFC for seven years. In 1941 Durr was appointed as a commissioner to the Federal Communications Commission, which he served for seven years. While there, Durr focused on protecting public interests rather than advocating for corporate banking or broadcasting interests. He resigned from the FCC in protest of President Truman's Federal Loyalty Oath Order, which he saw as abusive of FCC employee rights. After Durr resigned, he opened a law practice in

Washington, D.C.; he was one of the few lawyers willing to represent federal employees who had lost their jobs as a result of the loyalty oath program. He also represented those who were members of or closely aligned with the Communist Party and those falsely accused of membership. He took many of these cases without charging a fee. In 1951, and after a short stint with the National Farmers Union in Colorado, the Durrs moved back to Alabama because of financial devastation and poor health. Back in Montgomery the Durrs became prominent in the fight for civil rights—and as a direct consequence, polite white society shunned them. In 1954 NAACP president and local black activist E. D. Nixon introduced the Durrs to a talented seamstress looking for work, Rosa Parks. Virginia Durr hired her on the spot, and the two flaunted Jim Crow custom by becoming close friends. History has often overlooked the fact that it was Virginia Durr who helped orchestrate a two-week scholarship for Parks in 1955 to attend the Highlander Folk School in Monteagle, Tennessee, where the demure Parks was trained by the legendary civil rights activist Septima Clark. Four months after her training, Parks refused to get up from her seat on a Montgomery city bus; her training and that act of defiance are not unrelated.

In 1969 the Durrs moved to Clifford's grandfather's farm in Wetumpka. The lifelong Presbyterian died on May 12, 1975, survived by his wife and four daughters. His papers are housed at the Alabama Department of Archives and History in Montgomery, Alabama, just a stone's throw from the National Civil Rights Memorial.

In this fascinating and highly autobiographical address, Clifford Durr offers a timeless critique of the political dangers of timid speech. To make that critique Durr offers up a most unlikely pair of heroes: Adam and Eve; on his account they had the temerity to challenge God by giving up the good life in the Garden for the chance to think for themselves. Their sin amounted to the "highest form of morality." The more modern sinner suffers from a willingness simply to conform to that which happens to be popular; moreover, that conformity often takes the form of an extended public silence—when, in fact, disruptive speech is needed. Durr illustrates by drawing on his experiences in Washington, D.C., and back home in Montgomery, Alabama. In both places, and under very different circumstances—supposed Communist affiliation and the black freedom movement—Durr illustrates how the dangers of seemingly minor expedience imperil the larger society; right is too easily converted to wrong because of the "fear of eviction from the 'Garden of Acceptability.'" Much like everyday Germans in Nazi Germany, white southerners who look the other way or who make excuses for the racist status quo imperil the entire nation. Durr also aims his vitriol squarely at the white Montgomery clergy, who have no trouble defending Tom Coleman, who murdered Episcopal priest Jonathan Daniel and maimed Catholic priest Richard Morrisroe. Perhaps not surprisingly, Durr closes his rhetorically conspicuous address by urging his St. Louis listeners to unabashedly cross-examine the so-called experts, who, after such questioning, might reveal themselves to be less expert than we'd thought.

෨෪෬

The Relevance of Morality
November 3, 1965
Washington University, St. Louis, Missouri

The invitation to be with you today here at Washington University in the city of St. Louis revived in my mind bright memories of childhood. It also unearthed a long buried association of ideas.

When I think of St. Louis, I think of education, and when I think of education, I think of a cow made of butter.

I assure you that the association has no derogatory implications. I am in favor of St. Louis and of education and of cows. In their different ways, all of them are admirable.

Moreover, the origin of this association of ideas can be explained quite simply, without the aid of ink blot tests or psychiatric probing into the dark recesses of my psyche. It lies right out in the open of the consciousness, in the childhood memories I have mentioned.

Three score and more years ago, my grandpa, with the reluctant consent of my mother, brought me out to St. Louis to see the World's Fair of 1904 (or was it 1903?). I can still remember the conclusion of his argument to my mother, which took place within my hearing. It was high time, he said, that she started thinking of my education. Education was important, and it could not be started too soon. Moreover, it was not just a matter of going to school. Children, like grown people, should travel and see what this country of ours was like, and here I was, going on five years old and I had never been any farther away from home than his farm, which was less than twenty miles away. He said that there was nothing more educational than a world's fair, because there, he argued, one could see exhibits gathered from all over the world, and a boy ought to know how people in other countries lived and did things, and not just the people in Montgomery, Alabama, and Elmore County.

I am afraid the vagueness of my present recollection of that visit would be somewhat disappointing to Grandpa, but there is one thing I do remember vividly: that cow made of butter. I am not sure whether she was in the dairy products exhibit or just at the entrance of the livestock exhibit, but there she stood, a life-sized golden cow, made entirely of butter. Her flanks were angular, her belly large, and her udder firm and round, as a good milk cow should be. Her horns were gracefully curved and set evenly on her head, and the brush of her tail was just right. There was even a contented look in her eyes.

I am sure she was a Jersey, because Peggy Lou was a Jersey and she was my favorite of all the cows on Grandpa's farm. But Peggy Lou was only a cow. This butter cow was a thing of beauty, a work of art.

As I stood spellbound by her beauty, a sense of wonder and curiosity began to stir within me. It was quite warm in the building—why didn't she melt? How long would a boy have to churn to get enough butter to make a life-sized butter cow of his own? If she was all mashed up and made into regular pats, how many waffles or buckwheat cakes would she butter?

But, in time, a less pleasant sensation began to take over, a disturbing sense of concern that such a beautiful, golden, life-sized image of a cow could not switch her tail, or chew her cud, or eat grass, or give milk, or have a calf.

I began to feel tired and sleepy from so much walking and standing. I became homesick. I wanted to see Peggy Lou again and her calf. I wanted to watch her eat grass and hear her milk squirt against the sides of the pail at milking time.

Grandpa was right, after all. The St. Louis World's Fair was educational. What more does education have to offer than an awareness of beauty, a sense of awe and wonder and curiosity, and above all, of concern for the realities rather than images? The rest is mere stockpiling of facts and training in techniques and method.

I realize I am here as one speaker in a series on special events and not historical events, but as you know, the past is prologue, so I hope you won't mind if, in order to get a running start for my plunge into the present, I back up into a period even earlier than the St. Louis World's Fair.

Before man was evicted from the Garden of Eden and set loose on his own, he was endowed with the capacity to distinguish right from wrong. However, the making of choices requires effort and the consequences of acting on them are sometimes painful, so ever since that memorable event, Man, with the ever-ready help of his preachers, priests, teachers, and rulers, has been inclined to pretend that right was wrong, or wrong was right, or that he could not tell the difference between them. However, he has never quite succeeded in kidding himself. That is the reason why, I think, that our churches are filled with people seeking peace of mind, justification by faith, salvation by grace, and forgiveness without repentance; and why we have more neuroses and psychoses than ten times our present supply of psychiatrists could possibly deal with, and, I suspect, also the reason why we now seek our very survival in a balance of terrors, when the scientific and technological skills which produce the terrors, could, if applied in full force to the alleviation of man's miseries and want, could soon dispel the justification for the terrors as well as the terrors themselves.

In this, the literary age of the nonhero, I would like to offer a couple of true heroes for your consideration, in the hope that you might consider accepting their behavior as an example, rather than their fate as a warning. I refer to our common ancestors, Adam and Eve.

By accepted standards of success, they "had it made." Wealthy beyond the demands of avarice, whatever they wanted in the way of worldly goods was theirs for the taking. Their social position was secure. They were not just among the First Families, they were the First Family, yet they gave it all up in exchange for the right to know and think things out for themselves, to be themselves and make their own decisions. If they ever whined over the labor and sweat and sorrow that were the consequences of their bargain, it is not on record, and I doubt very much if they were overwhelmed with shame when they discovered that by taking on the responsibilities of maturity, they had been converted from impotent and sterile consumers of fruit, into vital human beings, endowed with the divine power of thought and creativity and the power of procreation with others after their own image.

It is a strange God indeed who would plant the tree of the knowledge of good and evil right in the midst of the Garden of Eden and then forbid the eating of its fruit, and, after creating Man in His own image, seek to frustrate his strivings "to be as gods, knowing good and evil."

Yet the preachers tell us that Adam and Eve committed a terrible sin. Tempted by the devil himself, in the guise of a serpent, and in defiance of higher authority, they bartered away their innocence for knowledge and understanding, a sin so grievous that it penetrated into their very genes and has corrupted the bloodstream of us, their miserable descendants, to this very day.

As I am not a theologian, I shall not attempt to argue the question of whether the sin of Adam lay in his disobedience or in the loss of his innocence. Be that as it may, the present-day version of that sin can be simply defined as follows: "Sin is any want of conformity unto, or transgression of, what has popularly or officially been declared to be so."

So, "believe and be saved" (or at least keep quiet about your disbeliefs). Whether or not this slogan provides the only guidepost to spiritual salvation, it is very practical temporal advice if one wants to avoid eviction from the Garden of the Acceptable and the sweat and sorrow that goes with it.

I suggest, however, for your consideration, that in a time of strife and change and turmoil, such as that in which we are now living, when old, familiar guideposts have been knocked askew and when our scientific and technological powers have developed beyond our developments in the art of human relations, the sin of Adam may well be the highest form of morality. It may well be, also, our best hope of survival. At a time when responsible thought and speech are so desperately needed, silence can be the deadly sin. For silence leaves a moral and intellectual vacuum, into which evil and all kinds of irrational and ugly things can flow, all too often disguised in the habiliments of good.

What I like best about the form of government we call American is that under its Constitution as it now stands, government is not and cannot be completely sovereign. The First Amendment to the Constitution, with its guarantees of freedom of speech, thought, press, and religion, and assembly and petition, says to government in no uncertain tones, "Here is an area which you should not and shall not enter, the area of the human mind and spirit." I cannot go along with the theory that the individual rights guaranteed by that Constitution must be balanced off against the demands of national security, or domestic tranquility, not only because I feel that in such a balancing, the thumbs of the judges will inevitably be weighed on the scales, but also because I believe that these rights are the greatest source of our national strength and hence our security. Free men will be the best defenders of their country, because they have a stake worth defending, and free minds will be the most alert in detecting the dangers that threaten it and in devising methods of defense.

Are the powers of our government really separated into only three divisions, the legislative, the executive, and the judiciary? What about us, the people? Are we not a fourth element in the governmental structure? Can our responsibilities be met by silence or complacent agreement? Is it not a duty as well as a right to dissent when the occasion requires even though the consequences of dissent may not always be pleasant?

If what I shall have to say hereafter, in an effort to illustrate what I have already said, seems a mere personal narrative or an expression of personal opinion, I offer no apologies on that account alone, for how can anyone speak with meaning except about the things he himself has seen and felt and thought? Moreover, I have neither the qualification nor the right to say to you, "Here are the answers." All I can say is, "Here is what I have seen and felt and thought, here is the way it looks to me, and hope that when my experiences and observations are added to or discounted by your own, the end product might make sense.

I have lived in the city of Montgomery, Alabama, during the entire period of the current struggles of the Negroes for equality in citizenship. I shall not attempt to tell you what it is like to be a Negro in Montgomery, Alabama, or anywhere, for I have not had that experience. But sometimes when I try to imagine myself in their position, I find myself marveling at their patience and restraint and their ability to control their bitterness with their sense of humor. I have been concerned with the civil rights of Negroes not because they are Negroes but because they are people and because I fall into that same category, and I know from my years of experience as a lawyer that our legal and constitutional safeguards are not selective and that they must protect everyone, or, in time, they will protect no one. I am disturbed over what we southern whites are doing to the Negroes in our attempt to deny them the rights which the supreme law of our land has long said were theirs, but I am even more disturbed over what we are doing to ourselves, not only economically and politically, but to the integrity of our own hearts and minds.

However, having lived in Washington, D.C., during the rise and peak of the sickness we now call "McCarthyism" (although it started long before the Wisconsin senator's rise to power and, I fear, did not end with his death), I am unable to see what, until fairly recently, at least, has come to be called "the southern problem" in narrowly regional terms, or, for that matter, in terms of "civil rights."

In the South, I have seen American citizens denied the rights which the Constitution says are theirs, because of their color. In Washington, I have seen American citizens denied these rights because of their beliefs and associations, and even their reputed beliefs and associations. In the South, such rights are denied by converting the apparatus of the law into an instrument of lawlessness; in Washington, they were denied by bypassing the law, through the imposition of punishments unknown to the law.

In the South, the justification assigned for the denial of such rights is the protection of "states' rights" and the "southern way of life." In Washington, the justification was the protection of the "American form of government" and the "American way of life." I have represented Negroes and "nigger-lovers" in southern courtrooms, and in Washington I have represented people charged with "unacceptable ideas" in klieg-lighted congressional hearing rooms and behind closed doors of loyalty boards. I can assure you that neither experience is a pleasant one, nor reassuring that American freedom is wholly secure, or American or southern justice wholly just.

I am not sure that physical wounds inflicted by the club or the cattle prod are more cruel than the emotional wounds inflicted in klieg-lighted hearing rooms or behind the closed doors of loyalty boards, or that imprisonment in the city jail a harsher punishment than deprivation of one's reputation and means of livelihood.

In Montgomery, Alabama, I have had to send some of my clients to a physician following their encounters with the protectors of our "southerness." In Washington, I have had to send some of them to psychiatrists following their encounters with the protectors of our "Americanism."

In the South, good, dedicated men have been murdered for doing what they believed to be right. In Washington, good, dedicated men have been driven to suicide for doing what they believed to be right.

In the South, it was all done in the name of our "sacred southern tradition"; in Washington, in the name of our "sacred American tradition."

In Washington as in Montgomery, I have seen expediency become God and protest against wrong, a sin against the Holy Ghost. In Washington, as in Montgomery, I have seen men remain silent when they wanted to say, "These things which are being done are wrong," and I have seen the resulting deterioration of their minds and spirits.

I saw your own chancellor, when a young member of Congress from Massachusetts, stand boldly on the floor of the House of Representatives in Washington and say to Martin Dies of Texas, then chairman of the House Committee on Un-American Activities, "What you are doing is wrong," and I saw him roundly denounced by some of his fellow congressmen who knew that he was right, and who had given Martin Dies the authority, in the name of Congress, to do what they knew was wrong.

In both Washington and Montgomery, I have seen ambitious men confuse loyalty to themselves and their own projects with loyalty to their country, and humble men confuse their ignorance with patriotism and even religious faith.

In Washington and Montgomery, I have seen the developing moral and intellectual vacuum as a result of the silence or of the rationalization of men in positions of power and responsibility, who knew right from wrong but lacked the moral courage to say so.

In the North, East, and West, as well as in the South, I have seen colleges and universities remain silent about things that mattered, even to their own academic integrity; and churches retreat from the Judeo-Christian ethic, which they profess, into dogma and ritual.

My first personal experience with "McCarthyism" occurred some nine years before Senator McCarthy projected himself into fame with his famous Wheeling, West Virginia, speech, in which he charged that the State Department had on its rolls 97 or 107 or 67 (the number being very adjustable) "card-carrying Communists." I was, of course, then aware of the Dies Committee, which had attracted public attention by exposing Shirley Temple, then a moppet of ten years old, as a dangerous "subversive" and vigorously quizzing the director of the WPA Theatre Project about the Communist affiliations of a playwright by the name of Christopher Marlowe, one of whose plays he had directed. The director of the WPA project was forced to admit his negligence in failing to make a thorough ideological check, either on the said Marlowe or on one William Shakespeare, another playwright of the same vintage.

So Congressman Dies' standing as an expert on Americanism was in some disrepute when he wrote to the Federal Communications Commission in the fall of 1941, demanding that it fire, forthwith, a quite able and responsible commission employee by the name of Goodwin Watson, because he was a member of certain "Communist fronts" listed in the congressman's letter. The letter was handed to the press before it was put in the mail. Because I was then a new member of the commission and had no responsibility for employing Dr. Watson, I was asked to investigate the charges.

As Dr. Watson's qualifications, as well as his reputation, had been carefully checked before he was employed, it seemed to me that the logical starting point of my investigation should be the "Communist front" organizations mentioned in the letter. The first one was the "League for Non-participation in Japanese Aggression." The chairman was Henry L. Stimson, then secretary of war, and the vice chairman was a rather distinguished admiral in the Navy. The organization had been set up shortly after the Japanese invasion of China, and its object was to urge an embargo on the sale of scrap iron and oil to Japan, lest it later be used against us, as of course it was.

The next organization, as I recall, was the Council against Intolerance in America. The cochairmen were William Allen White of the *Emporia Gazette*, a colorful Republican small-town newspaper editor, and a Republican senator from New Jersey. On the national board were Alfred E. Smith, former governor of New York and Democratic candidate for president in 1928, William Green of the American Federation of Labor, and Senator Carter Glass of Virginia, then chairman of the Senate Committee on Banking and Currency, and a number of other equally "communistic"-minded gentleman, including quite an array of nationally known religious leaders, Catholic, Protestant, and Jewish.

Upon the completion of my investigation, I reported my findings to my fellow commissioners. The situation was indeed serious. Limiting myself to the organizations listed in the Dies letter and applying the test of membership, I found that just about every member of the cabinet, twelve senators, led by Carter Glass, thirty-six members of the House of Representatives, and five members of the U.S. Supreme Court, led by Chief Justice Hughes, were all "Communists." My list even included a member of the Dies Committee itself who was a "Communist" by these standards, on three counts. The chief justice, I might add, had become somewhat outraged by the denial of the use of Constitution Hall for a concert by Marian Anderson, because she was a Negro. So, his whiskers flying in the breeze, he had joined forces with the "Marian Anderson Concert Committee," which staged a concert for her from the steps of the Lincoln Memorial, where she had an audience exceeding the capacity of Constitution Hall some twenty times over.

At this commission meeting, my innocent eyes were opened to the fact that right and freedom could not be protected by words alone, however eloquent. All agreed that the charges were stupid and that Dr. Watson was performing his duties loyally and capably, but said three of my colleagues in effect, "We have got to consider our relations with Congress—what does one man matter?" "Let's fire him right now." The other four of us, constituting a majority, issued a public statement, analyzing the charges and saying that we could not, consistent with our oaths of office to support and defend the Constitution of the United States, fire a man merely because of the "unacceptability" of his ideas or of the organizations he had joined.

The three dissenters were right in their concern over the effect on our relations with Congress, for the House of Representatives promptly adopted a rider to the FCC appropriation bill, saying, "No part of this appropriation shall be used to pay any compensation to Goodwin Watson."

Interestingly, the most vigorous opposition to the rider came from a "Black Belt" congressman from Selma, Alabama, who not only challenged the rider on the floor as a bill of attainder, an ex post facto law, and a denial of due process and the rights guaranteed by the First Amendment, but called the commission members on the phone to say in effect, "I understand you are worried over your relations with Congress. I just want to say to you that if you fire Goodwin Watson before the United States Supreme Court says you have got to, you are going to have all the trouble with Congress that I can cause you. I don't know this man, and I don't know what he thinks, or care about what he thinks. That is his business and not mine, but I do care about the Constitution of the United States, and when the government of this country starts policing people's thinking, we are heading down the same road as Hitler's Germany."

We took the fight to the U.S. Senate, which rejected the House rider by a unanimous vote, the senators taking pretty much the same position as that of the Black Belt congressman from Selma.

I became publicly identified with the fight in the Senate, and the next thing I knew I was being investigated by the FBI. The FBI report was officially sent to the commission, and I, of course, immediately had a copy routed to my desk. I still have it. It is one of my prized possessions.

Confidential informant T said I was in the "active indices" (which is investigese for mailing list) of some organization which had been reported "by a source believed to be reliable to be Communist infiltrated." Confidential informant T2 and T3 and T4, who were well informed as to the activities of the Communists in the District of Columbia, said they had never even heard of me. Confidential informant T5 and T6, 7, and 8, presumably neighbors, said that so far as they knew I was not rowdy when drunk, did not beat my wife, and they had not seen any conspiratorial activities going on around my house. T9 and 10 and 11 and 12, presumably fellow members of the legal staff of the Reconstruction Finance Corporation, where I had previously worked, said I had carried my fair share of the load in shoring up the financial structure of the country after its collapse during the Depression and they had no reason to think I was about to undermine it again. The investigation so far proving negative, the special agent then turned to the records of the Dies Committee, which showed no information about one Clifford J. Durr but did show that "according to the *Daily Worker*" one Virginia Foster Durr, residing at the same address, had appeared before a committee of Congress and made a statement in opposition to the poll tax as a prerequisite for voting in federal elections. This shocking disclosure was also [reported in] the *Washington Post*, the *Washington Star*, the *New York Times*, and quite a number of other rather solid newspapers, but that was wholly irrelevant, as was the fact that the idea of the bill to abolish the poll tax had originated in the Women's Division of the Democratic National Committee, which was trying to figure out some way of getting southern women to vote when their husbands would not pay their poll tax.

So they had me. Having then been married to this Virginia Foster Durr for over fifteen years, I could hardly deny that I was in "association" with her, and as our last baby was only a few weeks old, I could not have made out a very convincing case if I had tried to argue that the "association" was not "sympathetic."

The next year the House again put a rider on the appropriation bill, this time extending it to other agencies so as to include not only Dr. Watson but also William Dodd, the son of the distinguished southern historian and former ambassador to Germany, and Robert Morse Lovett, retired professor from the University of Chicago, who was then governor of the Virgin Islands. Again the U.S. Senate rejected the rider by a unanimous vote, but this time the House members of the Conference Committee refused to give way. It was in time of war, and the fiscal year was running out, and important agencies of government were about to be left without funds; so after several votes, the Senate finally gave in.

President Roosevelt signed the bill, issuing at the same time a public statement saying that the rider violated the most fundamental provision of the Constitution and that he was signing it only because it would be disastrous to shut down the operations of the agencies involved, in time of war, and because he was sure the rights of the men would be vindicated in the courts. They were, by the U.S. Supreme Court in the very important case of *U.S. v. Lovett, Watson and Dodd*, and we continued with the business of winning the war, with firm confidence in the ability of our American ideas to hold their own.

However, when the armed might of the enemy had been crushed and victory had been won, it was discovered that we were in greater peril than ever. Our American ideas, it seemed, were rather frail and delicate things, after all, and unable to hold their own, and they were under attack, not only from abroad but from sinister, conspiratorial forces right here at home. This time John Rankin of Mississippi became the official guardian of our thoughts. The House Committee on Un-American Activities was made a permanent committee of Congress, and Rankin was named as chairman, to be followed in a very short time by Parnell Thomas of New Jersey. And so we moved from Martin Dies, through Rankin, Thomas, McCarran, and later Eastland of the United States Senate and innumerable committees on un-American activities in the various states, to Joe McCarthy.

I do not think it unfair to say that any resemblance between the American ideas of any of the gentlemen I have just named and those of, let us say, Thomas Jefferson or James Madison or Abraham Lincoln is not even coincidental. It just does not exist.

It is not my purpose here to recount the human destruction brought about by these "Americanists" in the name of "Americanism." I shall not go into the tale of the moral and intellectual devastation left in their wake, in government, in the theater, radio, television, the screen, our schools and universities, and even our churches. But I would like to suggest to you that the danger to this country then lay, as it lies today, not so much in the viciousness or the stupidity of demagogues as in the silence of good men which leaves the rantings of the demagogues unanswered.

There are, of course, good men who do speak out, but all too often not enough of them or not soon enough, so they are ground down early and regarded as no great loss because they brought it on themselves by committing the inexcusable sin of inexpediency.

Isn't there a responsibility of leadership that goes with the position and power of leadership?

In Washington, Dies, Rankin, Thomas, and McCarthy never disturbed me as much as the silence of intelligent men, in high positions who, fearing that their own immaculate linen might be spotted by the mud that the "Americanists" were so recklessly hurling, rationalized their silence: "I have got my own job to do, and I must not destroy my effectiveness by impairing my relations with Congress." Eventually the rationalizations became, "I deplore the methods of McCarthy, but after all he is alerting us to the dangers," thus giving sanction of their prestige and position to the fears that McCarthy was feeding on and shifting the issue from one of basic American values to one of mere techniques and procedure. When McCarthy, in his arrogance, finally took on the United States Army and discovered that he now had an opponent bigger than he was, many of these same men began to speak boldly again: "I have said all along that McCarthy was a scoundrel and a blatherskite." They lied, but they believed their lies because they had to in order to nourish the remnants of their own self-respect.

Within a few years, the same senators who had stood up so magnificently in opposition to the rider barring Goodwin Watson from employment were voting in favor of every appropriation and power that first

Senator McCarran and then later Senator McCarthy asked for. They even abandoned one of their own, Senator Millard Tydings of Maryland, when he had the courage to say that McCarthy was doing evil things to our government and to our country. I do not believe that they were then any more afraid of "Communism" taking us over than they were at the time of the vote against the Goodwin Watson rider, but they were afraid of the public hysteria that McCarthy had been able to build up by reason of their default in leadership. They were afraid to appear *not* to be afraid, lest their own "Americanism" be questioned.

Within five years after President Truman, as a senator, had voted against the Goodwin Watson rider, he issued Executive Order 9835, setting up his own loyalty program, vesting in our national police organization supervisory power over the beliefs and associations of all government employees, regardless of the importance of their jobs, or the relationships of the jobs to national security. The technique of thought control, which we regarded with abhorrence when exercised in Germany or Russia, came into being. Yet, it was all done in the name of protecting our constitutional processes and our American freedom, so it became accepted as a part of our "American way of life" without effective protest.

Certainly the country was not in as great a danger in 1947 as it was in 1942, when our ships were being torpedoed by German submarines just beyond the mouth of the Mississippi River and within sight of the Atlantic City boardwalk. The president himself had characterized the charges of Parnell Thomas, and others of his kind, that the government was dangerously infiltrated by "subversives" as sheer poppycock, which, of course it was. In private conversations he justified the issuance of the order by saying he had to take the play away from Parnell Thomas in order to keep something worse from happening. Yet by the order, he used the power and prestige of the office of the presidency to fan the flames of fear and hatred which Parnell Thomas had kindled.

The Constitution of the United States in 1947 read just as it did in 1942, and the oath to protect it against all enemies, domestic as well as foreign, was as binding on a president as on a senator.

I am well aware of the old saying that a politician cannot become a statesman until he has first been elected, but isn't there somewhere a responsibility for honest political leadership? In a democratic society is honesty with the minds of people less important than honesty with their tax dollars?

The Montgomery part of the story begins on a Monday morning in May of 1954 with the opinion of the United States Supreme Court in the case of

Brown v. The Board of Education, holding that the segregation of schoolchil-dren in the public schools because of their race was unconstitutional, and that the practice would have to be discontinued. In Montgomery, the first response to that opinion was surprisingly moderate. I talked to a number of my fellow Montgomerians who were typically southern in their racial attitudes. The response of many of them was, "Well, we don't like it, but the U.S. Supreme Court has spoken and we will have to live with it, and we can." I talked to a number of fellow members of the bar who said, in effect, "Like it or not, the Supreme Court has only said what the Fourteenth Amendment requires. The separate but equal doctrine of *Plessy v. Ferguson* was a rationalization of the conditions existing at that time, but the Negro had made a lot of headway over the past sixty years, educationally and oth-erwise, and there is no reason to expect him to wait any longer for the rights which the Constitution has guaranteed to him for nearly a century."

However, the good citizens waited in the hope that someone else would take the leadership, and the White Citizens' Councils began to move into the resulting vacuum. At first the editorial pages of our local paper referred to these councils as nothing more than "manicured Ku Klux Klan" and said that we had more than a bellyful of this kind of thing in the 1920s and wanted no more of it. Our senators and our congressmen politely declined invitations to address the councils on the grounds of pressing duties in Washington. Then the tribal tom-toms began to beat: "States' Rights," "The Southern Way of Life," "Domination from Washington," "Rape of the Constitution," "Interposition." In a short time the local newspaper began to change its tune: "We were wrong about the Citizens' Councils. They are not like the Klan at all. They believe in law and order, and, of course, all good southerners believe in segregation." Then began a series of feature articles on police brutality and the denial of civil rights in northern cities. It was titled, "Tell It Not in Askalon." The content was, "Look at the hypocrisy of those damned Yankees who are trying to criticize the way we do things down here."

Within a year our senators and congressmen were joining in the tribal chant, and it became increasingly difficult to distinguish their cries from those of the most extreme of our white supremacists. The lawyers who had said that the U.S. Supreme Court had been constitutionally right were now saying that it was constitutionally wrong; that the court had usurped legisla-tive powers never intended to be given to it by the founding fathers, and the reversal of their opinions was not based upon further legal research. Right began to be converted into wrong by the fear of eviction from the "Garden of Acceptability."

Then came the so-called "bus boycott." At first, letters to the editor said, "We all know that the Negroes have been treated rudely and unfairly on our city busses. They have a just grievance. Let's correct it." But the letters soon stopped. I do not know whether they ceased to be published or ceased to be written. We began to meet our problems with the silence of "nice people" and the slogans of those who were not so nice. The cry became, "outside agitators," "nigger lovers," and "The Second Reconstruction."

The silence became increasingly filled with the slogans, and the rationalizations began: "I know it is wrong, but after all, when the chips are down, I am a southern white man, and I have got to stand up and be counted as a southern white man." "We know our 'good Negroes' were happy with their lot until they were stirred up by all these outsiders. It must be the Communists." Then came the anonymous telephone calls throughout the night, both obscene and threatening to those who had said that Negroes were citizens and should be treated as citizens. "Would you want your daughter to marry a . . . ?" or "It is only one step from the schoolroom to the bedroom," or "You are nothing but a Goddamned nigger-loving Communist and your time is coming."

Then the silencing of preachers who felt impelled to preach an occasional sermon on brotherhood and the forcing out, or outright dismissal, of those who refused to be silenced; the steady retreat from religious principles into dogma; and the growth of the congregations of those who preached powerful sermons about the curse of Ham, or more gentle ones about how the redbirds and the blackbirds did not mate because God had made them different.

Then the bombing of the Negro churches, the high-pressure fire hoses, the dogs and cattle prods, and then deliberately planned murders and the absence of convictions; and now the rationalizations of nice, respectable people: "We deplore violence, but after all they brought it on themselves"; and "Of course we don't condone murder, but if she had just stayed at home and looked after her children like she should have, or if he had only stayed up there and preached the gospel to his own people, instead of coming down here and trying to stir things up, it wouldn't have happened."

As I was preparing my notes for what I am saying to you now, my eye came across the following in an editorial in the morning paper, commending Montgomerians for their restraint at the time of the march from Selma last spring:

"Montgomery remained away when the federalized Selma marchers shagged up Dexter Avenue. Downtown Montgomery was as forsaken as Moscow when Napoleon marched in. It was a disciplined achievement of Montgomery's population, and it had a withering effect. Only the Liuzzo mischance cut across the achievement of restraint."

Only a "*mischance?*" "Restraint?" Is restraint enough? Don't all of us just as citizens, or for that matter as people, have some responsibility for the moral climate which leads to the beatings and the bombings and the killings, and don't we lawyers and teachers and preachers and newspaper editors, who profess a dedication to justice and the pursuit of truth and great religious principles and fairness and responsibility in the presentation of news and ideas, don't we have a particular responsibility for the preservation of the principles which we profess?

Where are we heading when the best we have to offer is "restraint" and rationalization? Lurking underneath the pressures to conform, to be "acceptable" and be regarded by our fellows as a "right-minded" and "God-fearing, patriotic citizens," is the disturbing recollection of the reaction of good, loyal, patriotic Germans to the concentration camps and the gas chambers, who said, "We didn't know it was going on." Or, "What could we have done about it anyway?" And of their rationalizations in the early and mid-1930s when they said, "We deplore the excesses of the Nazis in their treatment of the Jews, but if the Jews had only stayed in their part of town instead of trying to mix with the Nordic community, it wouldn't have happened. They brought it on themselves. And, after all, we are good, patriotic Germans, and the Communists are behind it all."

A few weeks ago, I drove over to the courthouse of an adjoining county to observe the trial of a well-regarded local citizen and part-time deputy sheriff. He had killed a young seminary student with a blast from his shotgun and sent another blast through the back of a Catholic priest, who is still lingering between life and death in a Chicago hospital. The indictment for the first offense was "manslaughter" and for the second offense "assault."

As I listened to the trial, the prosecution's own witness, a domino-playing crony of the defendant, placed "what looked like a knife blade" in the hands of the seminary student, and what "looked like a pistol barrel" in the hands of the priest. Neither of these ephemeral weapons had been seen by anyone until a split second before the shotgun blasts, nor were they ever seen again after the blast, and no one seemed greatly concerned over their origin or their present whereabouts. Having been long aware of the strange way of justice in "bloody Lowndes County," I cannot say that I was shocked by these judicial proceedings, but I was feeling rather sickened when, at a recess of the trial, the minister of one of our more respectable city churches came up and greeted me with a pleasant smile of happy good fellowship on his face. I asked him what had brought him to the Hayneville courthouse, hoping against my fears that he would say, "An idealistic young seminary student and an idealistic young priest have been killed for doing what they thought was right. My presence here is a witness to my hope that enough justice will be done to discourage the killing of other idealistic young people." Instead his reply was, "Well, Bob called me up this morning at breakfast and said we both needed some 'relaxation' so we decided we would come over and watch the trial." He then proceeded to assure me that although he was a northerner, he fully understood and sympathized with the southern position and that nothing made him more indignant than the hypocrisy of the northerners who righteously condemned the happenings in Mississippi and in Selma and in Hayneville, but did little if anything about the happenings in Harlem, or Rochester, or Chicago and Los Angeles.

I could only reply that I was a southerner and bowed to none in my indignation over the hypocrisy of the "damned Yankees" but that the happenings in Mississippi and Selma and Hayneville and Montgomery were our responsibility, as southerners, and we could not justify them by pointing to the happenings in the North and West and East. And that, moreover, I did not like the idea of a "damned Yankee" coming to the South and telling us what fine folks we were because we were no worse than the hypocritical "damned Yankees."

I concede that right and wrong are not always easily distinguishable, but a member of this minister's congregation assured me that they all loved his sermons because "he preached right out of the Bible." It is my recollection that the Bible has something to say very specifically about the rights and wrongs of killing and of bearing false witness.

The "Bob" he mentioned was the minister of an equally respectable but even larger church. At the conclusion of the trial, he pronounced his public benediction upon the defendant, the court, the jury, the trial, and all that went with it. He is also a northerner.

Sometimes I, as a southerner, grow quite annoyed with the "outside agitators," but I find them much easier to take than the "outside tranquilizers" of whom we have quite a few in our Southland. It seems at times as if righteous indignation increases in direct ratio to the distance from the wrongs which provoke it. We, of the Deep South, bow to none in our sense of outrage over the denials of civil liberties in Russia or China or Cuba.

I have mentioned silence and the shouting of slogans as less than adequate methods for dealing with the problems that confront us. There is another danger, to shout, "Let's pass a law," and when the laws are passed, to relax and assume that all is now well. To borrow the words of St. Paul, "We know the law is good if a man use it lawfully," but laws do not enforce themselves, and they do not hold up indefinitely without an undergirding of accepted morality.

Here in the South, we have had a surprising amount of compliance with the Civil Rights Act of 1964 and 1965, and Negroes are being registered to vote in increasing numbers under the pressure of the federal government. It is now beginning to be acceptable to say, "Let's obey the law, because all this violence and disorder is impairing our 'image' as an attractive location for new industry. It is hurting business. It is providing propaganda for the Communists to use against us." However, few if any, unless they are Negroes, are yet willing to say, "Let's obey the law because it is right."

Legislatively, we have just about caught up with where we were eighty years ago. The Thirteenth, Fourteenth, Fifteenth Amendments have all been embedded in the Constitution for nearly a century, and the Civil Rights Act of 1964 is little, if any, advance on the Civil Rights Act of 1875. By the time of the Tilden-Hayes deal of 1876, the moral fervor of the abolitionists was spent, and through economic necessity the Negroes were soon forced back into a form of economic bondage which was only little better than the slavery from which they had been so recently freed. Even then the Fifteenth Amendment to our Constitution was in effect and said quite clearly:

"The right of citizens of the United States to vote shall not be denied or abridged by the United States or by any State on account of race, color, or previous condition of servitude."

Even then public officials, both state and federal, were bound by their oaths of office to support and defend the Constitution. Had they been true to their oaths, there would have been no Civil Rights Acts of 1964 and 1965 because there would have been no occasion for them.

I suppose the Deep South is backward. It is just beginning to catch up with "McCarthyism." For some time now our state sovereignty commissions have been busy converting black into red, and the weapons of McCarthyism are increasingly being used in the battle against civil rights. Disturbingly, much of the ammunition for these weapons is still being manufactured and packaged in Washington, D.C., in the Senate Subcommittee on Internal Security and in the House Committee on Un-American Activities, and very few of the crusading civil libertarians above the Potomac are raising their voices in protest.

So, as I have said, the "southern problem" is not just a problem of the South. Germ warfare is a dangerous business, for the germs of McCarthyism dropped in the South can easily spread back to the North and East and West and re-infect the country, and the war in Vietnam provides a favorable culture for their growth and spread.

Do we prove the wisdom and justice and compassion of our foreign policy by hurling the same old garbage of the McCarthy era at its critics? Is a young man who is called upon to offer his life for his country necessarily "communistically inspired" or a "traitor" or a "coward," just because he wants to be sure that the cause for which he is called upon to offer his life is worth dying for? Does love of country demand that politics stop at the water's edge? When the issues involved may be the survival not only of our country but of civilization, may not a deep love of country inspire a man to say, "Let's hold up a while and take a careful look at things and reason together and be sure we know where we are going before we go too far"?

These are certainly difficult and complex times, and choosing between right and wrong is not easy, but if we duck the choice, it will be made for us without our advice or consent, custom-made or mass-produced and neatly packaged in cellophane, or in the less tidy wrappings of smears and threats and violence.

Is it safe to leave all the decisions to our "experts" on the plea that the issues involved are beyond our puny powers of comprehension? Maybe each of us has more to contribute to the common pot of experience and understanding than we are willing to admit. Maybe by a critical cross-examination of the "experts," we can learn a lot of the things we need to know, including perhaps that the "expert" himself is not as knowledgeable or as understanding as he pretends, or as we believe him to be.

My butter cow was only an image, but nevertheless an image of solid reality. Our words are often images of mere abstractions, and abstractions can be hard to grasp until they are given substance by our own personal experiences and observations and the contributions of our own hearts as well as of our own minds.

Good and evil, we say, are relative. That is often so, but relative to what? Maybe when we ask ourselves what is right and what is wrong, we would be helped in finding the answers if we asked another question, that one posed by the psalmist a long time ago: "What is man?"

All too often the answer comes in terms of a stereotype, the Negro, the southern whites, the redneck or the cracker, the damned Yankee, the Protestant, the Catholic, the Jew, the Western man, the Asiatic man, the liberal, the moderate, the extremist, the right-minded citizen, the Communist-minded do-gooder, crackpot, dupe, or agitator. Sometimes the answer comes in colder terms; a statistic, a unit of consumption, a digit in a population count or a labor force or a pool of unemployed; personnel, or a link in an organizational flowchart; a unit in a military force, a name in a casualty list, or a number in a boastful count of enemy dead.

Maybe the psalmist was in an overly optimistic mood when he gave his answer: "Thou has made him a little lower than the angels." But he is a sometimes ornery and sometimes magnificent member of this damned human race. After all, he is what it is all about.

PERMISSIONS ACKNOWLEDGMENTS

The editors of this anthology and Baylor University Press are grateful to the following people and groups for their kind permission to reprint texts.

Ahmann, Mathew: Courtesy of Margaret Ahmann.

Baldwin, James: Courtesy of James Baldwin Estate and WTTW.

Baumgard, Herbert M.: Courtesy of Herbert M. Baumgard and Jonathan Baumgard.

Beecher, John: Courtesy of Barbara M. Beecher.

Beittel, Adam Daniel: Courtesy of the family of Adam Daniel Beittel.

Bergman, Leo A.: Permission granted by the family of Rabbi Leo A. Bergman, by his sons William H. Bergman and Leo A. Bergman, Jr.

Boggs, O. Merrill: Courtesy of O. Merrill Boggs.

Brown, Aubrey N.: Courtesy of Ele Bigger and the Brown family.

Bunche, Ralph J.: Courtesy of Sidney Rosoff and the Ralph Bunche estate.

Carter, Hodding, Jr.: Courtesy of Hodding Carter III.

Clark, Roy C.: Courtesy of Roy C. Clark.

Coffin, William Sloane, Jr.: Permission granted by the Coffin family and the Sermon Archive Project (www.williamsloanecoffin.org).

Cuninggim, Merrimon: Courtesy of Penny Cuninggim.

De Laine, Joseph A.: Courtesy of Ophelia De Laine Gona and Joseph De Laine.

Deschner, John W.: Courtesy of Martin Deschner.

Dickson, Alex D., Jr.: Courtesy of Alex D. Dickson, Jr.

Diggs, Charles C., Jr.: Courtesy of Darlene Diggs.

Durr, Clifford J.: Courtesy of Virginia Foster Durr.

Fisher, Theo O.: Courtesy of Lisa Fisher-Giombolini.

Germann, Daniel: Courtesy of Bob Germann.

Golden, Harry: Courtesy of Richard Goldhurst. Unpublished speech, University of North Carolina, Charlotte, N.C.

Gordon, Clyde: Courtesy of Paul and David Gordon.

Grafman, Milton L.: Courtesy of Stephen W. Grafman.

Harding, Vincent: Courtesy of Rachel Harding.

Inge, C. O.: Courtesy of J. Faye Inge.

Jick, Leon A.: Courtesy of the family of Leon Jick.

Jordan, Clarence: Courtesy of Amanda Moore and Koinonia Farm.

Kilgore, Thomas: By permission of Jini Kilgore Cockroft and WTTW.

King, Slater: Courtesy of Jonathan King and the King family.

Kling, Simcha: Courtesy of Adina Kling.

Lelyveld, Arthur: Courtesy of Teela Lelyveld.

Maguire, John David: Courtesy of John D. Maguire.

Marshall, Thurgood: Courtesy of Cecilia Suyat Marshall.

Maston, Thomas Buford: Courtesy of Paige Patterson.

McGill, Ralph: Courtesy of Mary Welch and Mary Lynn McGill.

Morgan, Edward P.: Courtesy of Linda Hardberger.

Niebuhr, Reinhold: Courtesy of Elisabeth Sifton and WTTW.

Pettigrew, Thomas F.: Courtesy of Thomas Pettigrew.

Pipes, William Harrison: Courtesy of David McAdoo and the Pipes family.

Prinz, Joachim: Courtesy of Jonathan and Deborah Prinz.

Roberts, Cecil Albert: Courtesy of Dolores P. Roberts.

Rothschild, Jacob M.: Courtesy of Bill Rothschild, Janice Rothschild Blumberg, and Marcia Rothschild.

Selah, William B.: Courtesy of the William B. Selah family.

Shriver, Sargent: Courtesy of the Sargent Shriver family and Sargent Shriver Peace Institute.

Silverman, William B.: Courtesy of Eldon Silverman.

Smith, Lillian: Courtesy of Nancy Smith Fichter and The Lillian E. Smith Foundation, Inc.

Spottswood, Stephen Gill: Courtesy of Stephanie Spottswood and the Stephen Gill Spottswood Papers, Amistad Research Center, New Orleans, La.

Stagg, Paul L.: Courtesy of Brenda Butler.

Steele, Charles Kenzie (C. K.): Courtesy of Darryl and Derek Steele.

Yedwab, Stanley: Courtesy of Stanley Yedwab.

Young, Andrew: Courtesy of Andrew J. Young.

INDEX